CONSCIOUSNESS: NEW PHILOSOPHICAL PERSPECTIVES

CONSCIOUSNESS IN PHILOSOPHICAL PERSPECTIVES

CONSCIOUSNESS

New Philosophical Perspectives

Edited by
QUENTIN SMITH
and
ALEKSANDAR JOKIC

CLARENDON PRESS · OXFORD

OXFORD

UNIVERSITY PRESS

Great Clarendon Street, Oxford OX2 6DP

Oxford University Press is a department of the University of Oxford.
It furthers the University's objective of excellence in research, scholarship,
and education by publishing worldwide in

Oxford New York

Auckland Bangkok Buenos Aires Cape Town Chennai
Dar es Salaam Delhi Hong Kong Istanbul Karachi Kolkata
Kuala Lumpur Madrid Melbourne Mexico City Mumbai Nairobi
São Paulo Shanghai Taipei Tokyo Toronto

Oxford is a registered trade mark of Oxford University Press
in the UK and in certain other countries

Published in the United States
by Oxford University Press Inc., New York

British Library Cataloguing in Publication Data

Data available

Library of Congress Cataloging in Publication Data
Consciousness: new philosophical perspectives/edited by Quentin Smith and Aleksandar Jokic.
p. cm.
Includes index.
1. Consciousness. I. Smith, Quentin, 1952- II. Jokic, Aleksandar.

B808.9 .C667 2002   126–dc21   2002032657

ISBN 0–19–924128–7 (hbk.)
ISBN 0–19–924129–5 (pbk.)

1 3 5 7 9 10 8 6 4 2

Typeset in 10.5/12.5pt Minion
by Kolam Information Services Pvt Ltd., Pondicherry, India
Printed in Great Britain
on acid-free paper by
Biddles Ltd., Guildford & King's Lynn.

PREFACE

This book is a result of a longer project that began, but only began, with a conference on 'The Nature of Consciousness' sponsored by the Center for Philosophical Education (CPE) at Santa Barbara City College, 6–8 November 1998. I first started thinking about organizing a conference on this topic about a year earlier and later one of the speakers I initially invited—my co-editor Quentin Smith—helped with the selection and invitation process that determined the final line-up of speakers. Eight out of the twenty contributors to this book were the speakers at the conference: David Chalmers, Tim Crane, Brian Loar, Shaun Nichols and Stephen Stich, Quentin Smith, Michael Tye, and Robert Van Gulick. The enthusiasm generated by the high quality of the presentations and resulting philosophical discussions convinced Quentin Smith and me to encourage further efforts by this group to develop the ideas about consciousness that emerged from the conference. With a view to publication, the conference papers went through several significant revisions and substantial expansions between late 1998 and early 2002. During this time, the working group enlarged to include twelve additional scholars in the field, namely, Kristin Andrews, Anthony Brueckner and E. Beroukhim, James Fetzer, Joseph Levine, Michael Lockwood, Barry Loewer, William Lycan, Brian McLaughlin, Don Page, David Papineau, and Ernest Sosa. The brunt of the work on expanding this project was done by Quentin Smith, and gradually there emerged the four-part structure that is reflected in the way the book is organized. Consequently, true to the title of this book, we offer to the reader eighteen new essays on consciousness, representing the most recent, original work of the authors, many of whom rank amongst the most well-known contemporary philosophers.

Thanks are due first of all to Dr Steven Humphrey, President of the CPE's Executive Board, who supported the creation and the programmes of the Center in general and the project on consciousness in particular. The road from an idea to its realization is often replete with challenges and in order to be travelled requires persistence and patience; this is a fact the book's contributors know full well, and for this they deserve credit. Although this book is in no way a conference proceedings, and though some contributors are not directly related to or even aware of various CPE projects, it is also true that without CPE this book would not exist. Hence, Smith and I are grateful for the invisible binding role CPE has played in uniting the different efforts that finally led to this book.

A.J.

Portland, Oregon
February 2002

CONTENTS

Part Three
Consciousness and the Brain

Part Four
Quantum Mechanics and Consciousness

LIST OF FIGURES

LIST OF CONTRIBUTORS

Quentin Smith is Professor of Philosophy and Distinguished Faculty Scholar at Western Michigan University. His books include *Language and Time* (1993), *Theism, Atheism, and Big Bang Cosmology* (1993), and *The Felt Meanings of the World* (1986); he has written over a hundred articles, including more than twenty articles on consciousness, intentionality, and the emotions.

Aleksandar Jokic is Professor of Philosophy at Portland State University, and Director of the Center for Philosophical Education in Santa Barbara. He is the author of *Aspects of Scientific Discovery* (1996), and the editor of *War Crimes and Collective Wrongdoing* (2001) and (with Quentin Smith) *Time, Tense, and Reference* (2002).

Kristin Andrews is a Philosophy Professor at York University, specializing in the philosophy of psychology. She received her doctorate from the University of Minnesota and has published in such journals as *Journal of Consciousness Studies* and *Philosophical Psychology.*

Eskandar Alex Beroukhim recently received a JD from the University of California at Davis, and is currently a clerk for the Federal Court in the District of Wyoming.

Anthony Brueckner is Professor of Philosophy, University of California, Santa Barbara, has published numerous articles on such topics as scepticism, transcendental arguments, self-knowledge, and the nature of mental content.

David Chalmers is Professor of Philosophy and Associate Director of the Center for Consciousness Studies at the University of Arizona, and author of *The Conscious Mind* (1996).

Tim Crane is Reader in Philosophy at University College, London, and Director of the Philosophy Programme of the School of Advanced Study in the University of London. He is the author of *The Mechanical Mind* (1995) and *Elements of Mind* (2001), and the editor of *The Contents of Experience* (1992), *Dispositions: A Debate* (1995), and (with Sarah Patterson) *History of the Mind–Body Problem* (2000).

James Fetzer is Distinguished McKnight University Professor at the University of Minnesota, Duluth. He has published more than a hundred articles and reviews and twenty books on the philosophy of science and on the theoretical foundations of computer science, artificial intelligence, and cognitive science.

Joseph Levine is Professor of Philosophy at The Ohio State University. He is the author of *Purple Haze: The Puzzle of Consciousness* (2001).

Brian Loar is Professor of Philosophy at Rutgers University.

Michael Lockwood is a Fellow of Green College, Oxford, and author of *Mind, Brain, and the Quantum* (1989).

Barry Loewer is Professor of Philosophy at Rutgers University.

William G. Lycan is Professor of Philosophy at the University of North Carolina, Chapel Hill. His books include *Consciousness* (1987), *Consciousness and Experience* (1996), and *Real Conditionals* (2001).

Brian P. McLaughlin is Professor of Philosophy at Rutgers University and is the author of numerous articles on the philosophy of mind, metaphysics, and philosophical logic.

Shaun Nichols is Harry Lightsey Associate Professor of Humanities at the College of Charleston. He has published papers in *Philosophy of Science, Cognition, Mind and Language* and *Philosophical Topics*, on topics including moral judgement, altruism, and folk psychology. He is the author (with Stephen Stich) of *Mindreading* (Oxford University Press: forthcoming).

Don Page is a Fellow of the Canadian Institute for Advanced Research Cosmology and Gravity Program and a Professor of Physics at the University of Alberta in Edmonton, Canada. He works mainly in theoretical gravitational physics (general relativity, black hole thermodynamics and information, and quantum cosmology), but he also has interests in the foundations of quantum mechanics, consciousness, and the relationships between science and Christianity.

David Papineau is Professor of Philosophy at King's College, London. His books include *Reality and Representation* (1987), *Philosophical Naturalism* (1993), and *Thinking about Consciousness* (2002).

Ernest Sosa is Romeo Elton Professor of Natural Theology and Professor of Philosophy at Brown University and a regular Distinguished Visiting Professor of Philosophy at Rutgers University. He has published papers on epistemology and metaphysics.

Stephen Stich is Board of Governors Professor of Philosophy and Cognitive Science at Rutgers University. His books include *From Folk Psychology to Cognitive Science* (1983), *The Fragmentation of Reason* (1990), and *Deconstructing the Mind* (1996).

Michael Tye has produced a number of books which include *Ten Problems of Consciousness* (1995) and *Consciousness, Color, and Content* (2000).

Robert Van Gulick is Professor of Philosophy and Director of the Cognitive Science Program at Syracuse University, New York.

Introduction

QUENTIN SMITH

The nature of consciousness has proved as elusive, ambiguous, and questionable as the nature of intentionality, sensory qualities, and mentality. Two extremes of theories of consciousness, from a form of dualism to a form of physicalism, may be identified, one occupied by Brentano's theory and the other by Paul Churchland's theory.

Brentano lies at one extreme: in *Psychology from an Empirical Standpoint* he argues that all mental phenomena are intentional acts and intentional acts are identical with conscious acts (1973: 138). Brentano even holds that irreducible sensory qualia are not only distinct from consciousness but from all mental phenomena; they are *physical* phenomena (ibid. 78–9). Sensed warmth, cold, redness, and even images that appear in the imagination are physical phenomena, not mental phenomena. Note that by 'redness' Brentano does not mean a source of light waves, nor a brain state, but rather the sensed quale that some contemporary representationalists would say is a phenomenal content that represents a source of light rays. Contemporary representationalists or intentionalists often argue that sensory qualia are intentional or have intentionality. For Brentano, they are instead objects of intentional acts; they are not themselves intentional. In inner perception, to use Brentano's terminology, we are conscious of sensory qualia such as redness and warmth, and the 'consciousness of' these qualia is the intentional act that has these qualia for its intentional object. Mental access to physical things, such as mountains, requires *judgements* pertaining to sensory physical phenomena to be intentional objects of other (*judging*) intentional acts. So long as we remember that Brentano used the terms 'consciousness', 'intentionality', 'mental phenomena', and 'physical phenomena' in ways different from contemporary philosophers of mind, we may say that Brentano's equivalences lie at one end of the extreme in the various theories of consciousness. For Brentano, it is the case that *consciousness = intentionality = mentality.*

At the other end of the extreme, we have Paul Churchland's theory in *The Engine of Reason, the Seat of the Soul* (1995: 213–23), which states that consciousness is the neural activity of the intralaminar nucleus of the thalamus. Churchland's theory (which he puts forth as a proposal) implies that what Brentano called 'consciousness', 'intentionality', and 'mentality' do not exist. For Churchland, even the physical phenomena Brentano discussed, the sensory qualia of colours, odours, tastes, etc., do not exist. In so far as these words, 'consciousness', 'mental', 'colours', 'odours' have a verifiable meaning, they refer to arrays of neuronal firings or other configurations of mass-energy. In particular, Churchland (1995: 221) proposes that consciousness is a neural network radiating to and from the intralaminar nucleus, a network that connects this nucleus to all areas of the cerebral cortex. The variations in the level of neural activity are the contents of consciousness (which Churchland does not distinguish from acts of consciousness); conscious activities are non-periodic variations from the steady 40-Hz oscillations in the neural activity of the cortex. Since there are non-representational conscious and mental states, we do not have an equivalence among consciousness, representation ('intentionality') and mentality. Rather, the equivalence is: *consciousness = non-periodic variations in neural activity of the recurrent network radiating to and from the intralaminar nucleus of the thalamus, a network that extends to every area of the cerebral cortex.*

In between Brentano and Churchland are most contemporary philosophers of mind and cognitive scientists. *Consciousness* is often distinguished from *intentionality*, with some intentional states being characterized as unconscious and others as conscious. Here intentionality is not an intentional act in Brentano's sense, but an intentional object in Brentano's sense, specifically, what Brentano calls a physical phenomenon. Brentano's intentional acts do not play a large role in contemporary discussions and intentionality is typically associated with what Brentano would call intentional objects of inner perception. Consciousness is also usually distinguished from *mentality*; mental states or processes can be unconscious, other mental states can be non-intentional, and still other mental states can be both unconscious and non-intentional. This by no means exhausts theories of consciousness. Sometimes consciousness is identified with what is now called phenomenal content (what Brentano called 'physical phenomena'); others identify it with a system S that possesses a higher-order belief that it is in S, or with a system S that has another informational state that monitors S. Still others suggest that there is no such thing as consciousness (Rey 1988: 6) or that 'consciousness might go the way of "caloric fluid" or "vital spirit"' (Patricia Churchland 1988: 277).

A book of original essays on consciousness should reflect this diversity and not specify at the outset what consciousness is, define consciousness, or even delimit the extension or intension of the word 'consciousness'. Rather, the reader should be presented with some of the most recent theories about consciousness (and the variously related notions of intentionality, phenomenal content, mentality, etc.) and learn about this diversity from the authors of the chapters themselves.

Debates about consciousness focus on at least four broad topics, corresponding to the four parts of this book. The first three are intentionality and phenomenal content (Part One), self-consciousness or knowledge of our own and others' mental states (Part Two), and the problem of consciousness and the brain (Part Three). Part Four focuses on a topic that is only recently being discussed by philosophers of mind: the idea that classical mechanics is the wrong mechanics to assume in one's study of consciousness, and that the adoption of quantum mechanics instead will require us to reconceive familiar philosophical views about the *nature* of consciousness. Quantum mechanics can tell us about consciousness and conscious states, and not merely about the subcellular level of the brain or the physical basis that 'gives rise' to consciousness (Part Four).

Part One on 'Intentionality and Phenomenal Content' includes chapters by Tye, Crane, Levine, Loar, and McLaughlin that exhibit the various views that may be taken about intentionalism (sometimes called representationalism) and phenomenal qualities or contents, such as whether phenomenal contents are intentional, accompany intentionality, or are objects of intentional consciousness.

Part Two on 'Knowing Mental States' includes Nichols and Stich's criticism of the Theory Theory and their development of their Monitoring Mechanism Theory of self-consciousness, as well as Andrews's criticism of the *predication/ explanation symmetry assumption* underlying both the Theory Theory and Simulation accounts of how mental states of other people are known. Chalmers's and Sosa's chapters focus on knowledge of our own experiences and both have relevance to debates about foundationalism in epistemology.

Part Three focuses on the debate about the relation of consciousness to the brain. Fetzer develops a semiotic theory of the mind and body that aims to shed light on consciousness and the mind–body problem. Van Gulick focuses on the nature and meaning of the so-called 'explanatory gap'. Papineau addresses a different issue, 'theories of consciousness'; he argues that extant theories of consciousness attempt to answer a pseudo-question. Lycan further develops the materialist's *perspectival* response to the Knowledge Argument, and Brueckner and Beroukhim criticize McGinn's mysterian theory, i.e. that there is a natural property responsible for consciousness to which we are cognitively closed.

Part Four is entitled 'Quantum Mechanics and Consciousness', and is about a new area in the philosophy of mind. Traditionally, philosophers of mind or cognitive scientists have assumed that psychology or neurophysiology are the sciences most relevant to the philosophy of mind. But it is argued by Smith that quantum mechanics is the most relevant science. Although philosophers tend to associate the conjunction of quantum mechanics and consciousness with the popular writings of the physicist Roger Penrose, more rigorous *philosophical* work in this area is actually quite different from the Penrose (and Penrose–Hammeroff) theory. This work is represented here by Lockwood, Page (himself a physicist), Loewer, and Smith. The four chapters in Part Four are designed on the whole to be accessible to philosophers who do not have a mathematical expertise in quantum mechanics.

REFERENCES

BRENTANO, FRANZ (1973), *Psychology from an Empirical Standpoint* (New York: Humanities Press).

CHURCHLAND, PATRICIA S. (1988), *Matter and Consciousness* (Cambridge, Mass.: MIT Press).

CHURCHLAND, PAUL (1995), *The Engine of Reason, the Seat of the Soul* (Cambridge, Mass.: MIT Press).

REY, GEORGE (1988), 'A Question About Consciousness', in H. Otto and J. Tuedio (eds.), *Perspectives on the Mind* (Dordrecht: D. Reidel), 5–24.

Part One

Intentionality and Phenomenal Content

1. Blurry Images, Double Vision, and Other Oddities: New Problems for Representationalism?

MICHAEL TYE

Representationalism is a thesis about the phenomenal character of experiences, about their immediate subjective or felt qualities.[1] The thesis is sometimes stated as a supervenience claim: necessarily, experiences that are alike in their representational contents are alike in their phenomenal character (Lycan 1996a). In its strong form, representationalism is an identity thesis (Dretske 1995; Tye 1995, 2000). It asserts that phenomenal character is one and the same as representational content that meets certain further conditions. Representationalists are sometimes also content-externalists. The combination of representationalism about phenomenal character with externalism about content yields phenomenal externalism (the view that qualia ain't in the head).

Objections to representationalism often take the form of putative counter-examples. One class of these consists of cases in which, it is claimed, experiences have the same representational content but different phenomenal character. Christopher Peacocke (1983) adduces examples of this sort. Another class is made up of problem cases in which allegedly experiences have different representational contents (of the relevant sort) but the same phenomenal character. Ned Block's (1990) Inverted Earth example is of this type. The latter cases only threaten strong representationalism, the former are intended to refute representationalism in both its strong and weaker forms. Counter-examples are also sometimes given in which supposedly experience of one sort or another is present but in which there is no state with representational content. Swampman—the molecule by molecule replica of Donald

---

[1] Philosophers who advocate representationalism include Dretske (1995); Harman (1990); Lycan (1996a); McDowell (1994); Rey (1992); White (1995); and Tye (1995). There are also prominent critics (among them Block (1990, 1996, 1998a, b); McGinn (1991); and Peacocke (1983)). Shoemaker (1994) has a complex, mixed position.

Davidson, formed accidentally by the chemical reaction that occurs in a swamp when a partially submerged log is hit by lightning—is one such counter-example, according to some philosophers. But there are more mundane cases. Consider the exogenous feeling of depression. That, it may seem, has no representational content. Cases of the third sort, depending upon how they are elucidated further, can pose a challenge to either strong or weaker versions of representationalism.

Here I will concentrate almost entirely on visual experience and the question of whether there are any clear counter-examples to the following modality-specific, weak representational thesis:

(R) Necessarily, visual experiences that are alike with respect to their representational contents are alike phenomenally.

This thesis seems to me to have considerable interest in itself; for if it is true, it tells us something important and striking about the metaphysical *basis* of visual phenomenology. And if it is false, then strong representationalism—the thesis that phenomenal character is one and the same as representational content that meets certain further conditions—is automatically false too. At the end of the chapter I shall also make some remarks on two examples that purport to show that (R) cannot be strengthened to cover experiences in different sensory modalities that are alike in their representational contents.

The problem cases upon which I shall focus are all real world ones. So, there is no question about whether the cases *could* occur. Those who think that the inverted spectrum supplies a possible counter-example to (R) will, no doubt, take the view that this attention to the actual is too confining. After all, (R) is a modal thesis. To refute it, we only need a possible exception.

This is true, of course, as far as it goes. However, if the necessity in (R) is metaphysical, then counter-examples must be metaphysically possible. Mere conceptual possibility will not suffice. Whether the inverted spectrum really does provide metaphysically possible cases of visual experiences that are phenomenally inverted and yet representationally identical is open to dispute. Indeed it may be disputed whether such cases are even conceptually possible. I do not want to become embroiled in that dispute here.[2] My aim is more modest: I want to see if there are any clear-cut, actual cases that involve representational identity and phenomenal difference.

I shall have relatively little to say about the original Peacocke (1983) examples. There are now well-known replies to these examples by representationalists (Harman 1990; DeBellis 1991; Tye 1991); and I think that it is fair to say that a good many philosophers are persuaded by these replies. My primary interest is in a range of new problem cases that have surfaced for thesis (R) in

---

[2] The inverted spectrum is discussed in Tye (1995, 1998, and 2000).

the fifteen years since *Sense and Content* was published. The new cases I shall address, though actual, for the most part involve visual oddities of one sort or another: blurry images, after-images, phosphenes, tunnel vision, vision with eyes closed, double vision. What I shall try to show is that none of these cases is convincing. Representationalism remains unconquered!

The chapter is divided into three sections. In the first section, I sketch out how I think of the various different levels of representational content to be found in visual experience. In the second section, I take up counter-examples to (R). The final section briefly addresses two problem cases for an amodal version of (R).

1. Levels of Content in Visual Experience

Vision is exceedingly complex, too complex to operate all in one stage. It begins with information about light intensity and wavelength at the eye, and ends with a rich and many-layered representation of the visible scene. In between, according to current vision theory, there is processing in a number of semi-independent modules. According to the version of the story told by David Marr (1982), a primal sketch is first computed for each eye. This representation, which is derived directly from the retinal image, is two-dimensional. It specifies the locations of lines and bounded regions of various sorts without any representation of depth. The primal sketch supplies the input to a number of different modules, e.g. binocular stereo, structure from motion, colour, that together generate a single overall representation of the surfaces and bounded regions present in the given field of view. This latter representation, which Marr calls the $2\frac{1}{2}$-D *sketch*, is a vital foundation for further higher-level visual processing.

It is now widely accepted in vision theory that there is a representation similar in character to Marr's $2\frac{1}{2}$-D sketch, even though there is substantial disagreement about just how this representation is constructed.[3] The relevant representation is usually taken to have a matrix-like structure, the cells of which are dedicated to particular lines of sight.[4] Within each cell there are symbols for various local features of any surface at that position in the field of view (for example, distance away, orientation, hue, saturation, brightness, texture, whether a discontinuity in depth is present there, degree of solidity,

---

[3] This representation is sometimes supposed to occur in a medium shared with imagery. See here Kosslyn (1994).

[4] The matrix or array cells need not be physically contiguous at all. Instead, like the arrays found inside computers, they can be widely scattered. What is crucially important is that cells representing adjacent regions of the visual field be operated upon by routines that treat those cells as if they were adjacent. See here Tye (1991, 1995).

and so on).[5] Overlaying the matrix are further symbolic representations of edges, ridges, and boundaries.

In some abnormal cases, parts of the structure of the overall representation here—the *grouped, symbol-filled array*, as we might call it (or just the grouped array)—are missing. For example, patients with an impairment known as apperceptive agnosia (in the narrow sense)—an impairment that is typically brought about by damage to the occipital lobes and surrounding regions (typically by carbon monoxide poisoning)—often have roughly normal perception of purely local features in the field of view, for example, colour and brightness of local surface patches. But they are strikingly impaired in the ability to recognize, match, or even copy simple shapes as well as more complicated figures.[6] In general, they have great difficulty in performing any visual tasks that require combining information *across* local regions of the visual field.[7] For example, when shown Fig. 1.1, one patient consistently read it as 7,415.[8] Evidently he was unable to see two parts of a line with a small gap as parts of a single line.[9]

Is the content of the grouped array described above actually part of the content of ordinary visual experience? The example at Fig. 1.2, taken from Rock (1983), may seem to suggest that the answer to this question is 'no'. The figures certainly look different. They continue to look different even if one tilts one's head 45° to the left as one views the right-hand figure, thereby producing exactly the same retinal image as the left-hand figure. Given that the grouped array is a retinotopic representation, its content, when one views

FIG. 1.1. Effect of apperceptive agnosia. The patient read this stimulus as 7415.

[5] The notion of a surface here is to be understood broadly. A flickering flame, for example, has a constantly changing surface in the relevant senses of 'surface'. A cloud has a surface, as does a spray of water. Glowing matter from exploding fireworks has brightly coloured surfaces. There are no immaterial surfaces, however. In the relevant sense, surfaces are always public, physical entities.

[6] Movement of shapes sometimes helps these patients to identify them. See e.g. R. Efron (1968: 159).

[7] They do better at identifying real objects (e.g. toothbrushes, safety pins), than simple shapes. However, their improved performance here is based on *inferences* from clues provided by colour, texture, etc.

[8] The patient made this identification by tracing around the figure with movements of his hand and relying on local continuity. See here T. Landis et al. (1982).

[9] It has been suggested that the visual experiences of these patients are something like those you or I would undergo, were we to don masks with a large number of pin holes in them.

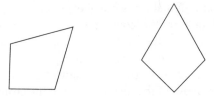

Two identical figures that look different as a function of orientation

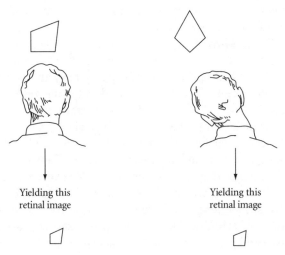

Yielding this   Yielding this
retinal image   retinal image

FIG. 1.2. Effect on perception of orientation of head. The two drawings, although viewed so as
to yield identical retinal images, nevertheless look different to naïve observers.

the right-hand figure, head tilted, is the same as its content, when one
views the left-hand figure, head upright. But phenomenally there is a clear
difference between the two cases.

The phenomenal difference involved in seeing the left-hand figure, head
upright, and seeing the right-hand figure, head tilted, is associated with the
fact that one experiences a quite different overall viewer-relative shape in the
two cases (in the one, the experience is as of an irregular quadrilateral resting
on its side whereas in the other it is as of a regular, upright diamond balanced
on a point). What the example really shows, then, is that there are aspects to
the content of visual experience that are not captured in the grouped array
described above. It does not yet show that the content of the grouped
array does not contribute at all to the content of visual experience.

Consider next just the case in which one shifts one's head 45° to the left as
one looks at the right-hand figure alone (perhaps closing one's eyes as one
does so and reopening them with one's head in the tilted position). I am

strongly inclined to think that one's visual experience does not change in any way. There is a change in the content of the retinotopic grouped array, however. So, it appears that the content of the grouped array is indeed not a component part of the content of the visual experience.

None the less, in seeing the world, we certainly have visual experiences as of surfaces and surface details of the sort specified in the grouped array. How can this be? The answer, I suggest, is that, at the level of visual experience, a representation is constructed and deployed with the same general character as the purely retinotopic grouped array but with a more stable content, reflecting a co-ordinate system whose origin and axes are not fixed relative to the eye alone. In particular, it seems plausible to suppose that while the origin is at the eye, some of the axes (e.g. the up–down axis) are set relative to the body in some way. Given an appropriate co-ordinate system, the content of *this* grouped array will not alter as one tilts one's head while viewing the right-hand figure. It is, I maintain, at this level that an array content may be found that is suitable for inclusion in the content of visual experience.

The grouped array—whatever the details of its origin and axes—does not itself yet represent the viewpoint-independent shapes of any objects visible to the viewer (e.g. whether they are rectangles or circles or cubes or spheres). Nor does it classify seen objects into kinds (e.g. tomato, table, etc.). Patently, however, our visual experiences do both these things. We have experiences as of round coins, as of cylindrical locks, and so on. Representations at these levels are also part and parcel of ordinary visual experience. They form further layers of experiential content.

What about the representation of viewer-relative shapes (and other non-local spatial properties and relations)? As the example from Rock indicates, that too is clearly part of normal visual experience.[10] It is tempting to think that the representation of viewpoint-dependent spatial features does not really form a level distinct from those already differentiated. For it seems plausible to claim that once representations in experience are exactly alike with respect to all local features and their grouping, they must be alike with respect to all viewpoint-dependent spatial features of whole surfaces.

The issue is complex, however. Consider an example taken from Peacocke (1992). Suppose that I am looking straight ahead at Buckingham Palace, and then I look at it again with my face still in the same position but with my body turned 45° to the right. The palace is now experienced as being off to one side from the direction of straight ahead. If the only axis of the relevant grouped array that is set relative to the body rather than the eye is the up–down one, then the content of the grouped array remains constant with the shift in body position. So, there is a change with respect to the representation of a viewer-

---

[10] Indeed a critical part, as we'll see later.

relative spatial property without an accompanying change in the content of the grouped array. Alternatively, if the origin of the grouped array is kept at the eye but *all* its axes are set relative to the body, then the content of the grouped array changes. On the former proposal, a new layer of content needs to be distinguished for some viewer-relative spatial properties. On the latter, an additional layer of content is not clearly necessary.

I hope that it is evident from my remarks so far that the representational content of visual experience is extremely rich. It operates on a number of different levels and it goes far beyond any concepts the creature may have. Consider, for example, the representation of hue at the level of the grouped array. The fact that a patch of surface is represented in my experience as having a certain hue, red_{19}, say, does not demand that I have the concept red_{19}. For I certainly cannot recognize that hue as such when it comes again. I cannot later reliably pick it out from other closely related hues. My ordinary colour judgements, of necessity, abstract away from the myriad of details in my experiences of colour. The reason presumably is that without some constraints on what can be cognitively extracted, there would be information overload.

Likewise, the representation of viewpoint-relative shape properties is naturally taken to be non-conceptual in some cases. Presented with an unusual shape, I will have an experience of that shape, as seen from my viewpoint. But I need have no concept for the presented shape. I need have no ability to recognize that particular viewer-relative shape when I experience it again. Arguably, even the representation of viewpoint-independent shapes is sometimes non-conceptual.[11] But clearly some representation in visual experience is a conceptual matter (e.g. the representation of object types such as car, ball, and telescope).

Some seek to explain the richness of visual experience conceptually by noting that even though the subject often has no appropriate non-indexical concept, he or she is at least aware of the pertinent feature, e.g. red_{19}, as *that* colour or *that* shade or *that* shade of red.[12] This seems to me unsatisfactory. Intuitively, one can have a visual experience without having such general concepts as *colour, shade,* or *shade of red*. Indeed, one can have a visual experience without attending to it or its content at all. Moreover, when one does attend, it seems that the explanation of one's awareness of the relevant feature as *that* feature is, in part, that one is having an experience that represents it. But no such explanation is possible if the content of the experience is already conceptual.

Given the complexity of the content of visual experience, and the number of different channels of information that lie behind its generation, it should not

---

[11] See here Peacocke (1993) for some plausible examples.
[12] See McDowell (1994).

be surprising that in some cases an overall content is produced that is internally inconsistent. An example of this is to be found in the experience one undergoes as one views the 'impossible figure' at Fig. 1.3 (Gregory 1990: 223). One sees each set of stairs as ascending to the next, even though this is impossible. Another example is the waterfall effect, which involves an illusion of movement (originally of a body of water). The most dramatic version of this is obtained by staring at a rotating spiral figure. While rotating, the spiral seems to expand. But after it is stopped, the spiral may seem to contract while none the less also seeming not to get any smaller. Again one experiences an impossibility. In this respect, experience is like belief (Harman 1996).

One further point is perhaps worth making. The term 'experience' can be used in broader and narrower ways. I have assumed in my remarks above that it is correct to say that we have visual experiences as of coins, telescopes, etc. Some may prefer to restrict the term 'experience' to states with non-conceptual content, counting the rest as judgements superimposed upon experience proper. This issue seems to me purely terminological. I am here adopting the broader usage, and I shall assume for the purposes of this chapter that the term 'experience' in (R) is to be understood in a broad way. As for the question of which levels of representational content in experience metaphysically determine its phenomenal character, my own view (Tye 1995) is that the relevant levels are non-conceptual and I shall endeavour to

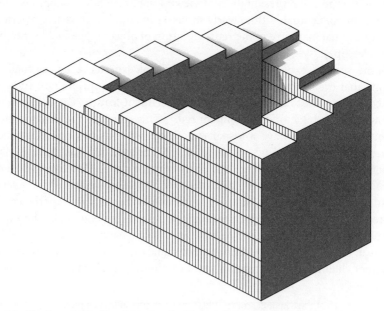

Fig. 1.3. The 'impossible figure'. Reprinted with permission from Gregory (1990).

show that the representationalist can account for the problem cases non-conceptually.

Having filled in the background on the representational content of visual experience, I turn now to a consideration of counter-examples.

2. Replies to Counter-Examples

Case 1: The long, dark tunnel. Suppose that you are located in a very dark tunnel, viewing a brightly lit scene at the end. Ned Block (1993: 183) has claimed that there will be a phenomenal difference in your visual experience if you go from having both eyes open to closing one of them. But, he asserts, the representational content will remain constant: the same objects and properties will be represented.

Reply: This is a variant on one of Peacocke's original cases (as Block acknowledges), and I find it no more compelling than its precursor. It seems to me that if there is a genuine phenomenal difference here at all, it *will* be accompanied by a representational difference. In general, using two eyes increases the size of the visual field slightly and thereby increases representational content: more objects or aspects of the brighly lit scene are represented. Hence the joke by Al Gore that one of the ten best things about being Vice-President is that, from the Vice-President's chair, if you close your left eye, the seal of the podium in the Senate reads, 'President of the United States'. Using two eyes also improves the perception of depth.

Now if the tunnel is sufficiently long and dark, there may well be no difference in the representation of depth. In both cases, all the objects in the scene may appear equally distant. But there may still be a small difference in the representation of the periphery of the far end of the tunnel in the two cases or in where the objects are represented as being, relative to one's eyes in the two cases (they may appear to shift in their relative position a little to the left or right). If the viewing situation is such that there are no changes of this sort, then I simply deny that there is any phenomenal change.

Case 2: The tilted coin. A coin is presented at an oblique angle. The coin occupies an elliptical region of the visual field. This is manifest in the experience. But, according to Peacocke (1993), the coin does not look elliptical. It looks circular. The experience represents the coin as circular. In this respect, it is just like the visual experience of the same coin, held perpendicular to the line of sight. But phenomenally, there is a striking difference.

This case, unlike the others in this section, is not a visual oddity but a commonplace occurrence. It is similar to one of Peacocke's (1983) original cases in which two trees of the same size are viewed, one twice as close as the other. Here, if the situation is normal, the visual experience represents the two trees as being of the same size. They look to the viewer the same size. But the closer tree occupies a larger region in the visual field, and, in this allegedly non-representational respect, it looks different.

Reply: Let me begin with the tree example. Here, I claim, the experience represents the nearer tree as having a facing surface that differs in its view-point-relative size from the facing surface of the further tree, even though it also represents the two trees as having the same viewpoint-independent size. The nearer tree (or its facing surface) is represented as being *larger from here*, while also being represented as being the same objective size as the further tree. There really are two different sorts of feature being represented, then, although they both are concerned with physical objects (or surfaces).

But what exactly is involved in one of two items being larger from here? The obvious answer is that the one item subtends a larger visual angle relative to the eyes of the viewer. In the above case, it seems plausible to suppose that this is encoded in the relevant visual representation via the greater number of filled array cells devoted to regions of the facing surface of the nearer tree.[13]

It is important to realize that the representation of the relational feature of being larger from here is non-conceptual. For a person to undergo an experience that represents one thing as larger relative to his viewing point than another, it suffices that the encoding feature of the array (larger number of filled array cells) suitably track or causally co-vary with the instantiation of the viewpoint-relative relation.[14] The person does not need to have any cognitive grasp of subtended angles.

The key claims I want to make, then, with respect to the tree case are: (1) the nearer tree looks the same objective size as the further tree while also looking larger from the given viewing position. (2) *X* looks *F* to *P* only if *P* undergoes a visual experience with respect to *X* that has a representational content into which *F*-ness enters. (3) Where the sense of 'looks' in (2) is phenomenal, the representation involved is non-conceptual. (4) The relevant non-conceptual, representational relation is a backward-looking tracking relation. Note that, on this account, the perceiver of the two trees is not the subject of any illusion or error: the nearer tree is just as it looks—both larger from here, the viewing position, and the same viewer-independent size as the further tree.

Frank Jackson has suggested to me (in correspondence) a simpler reply to Peacocke's tree example. The two trees look the same objective size, but the nearer tree looks nearer. One's experience thus represents the nearer tree as nearer, and this fact suffices to handle the phenomenal difference in one's

---

[13] For more here, see Tye (1996). For an alternative reply, see Lycan (1996b). This reply is criticized in Tye (1996).

[14] This oversimplifies minimally. For a qualification and a fuller account of non-conceptual representation, see Tye (1995, 1998).

experience of the two trees. I agree with Jackson that the relative distance of objects is typically represented in one's visual experiences, but I question whether this line fully captures the intuitive sense in which it is manifest in one's experience that the nearer tree occupies a larger portion of the visual field. After all, if the conditions were atypical and the relative distance of the two trees were 'lost from one's experience', the nearer tree would still look larger from here (as well as looking objectively larger). And that fact about apparent viewer-relative size remains to be accounted for.

A similar line can be taken with respect to the tilted coin. The coin looks round. It also looks tilted—some parts of its facing surface look nearer than other parts of that surface. The experience thus represents the coin as round, tilted, etc. The coin held perpendicular to the line of sight does not look tilted, however. So, there is an immediate representational difference between the two cases. Furthermore, the tilted coin also looks elliptical from the given viewing position. Here the represented feature is that of having a shape that would be occluded by an ellipse placed in a plane perpendicular to the line of sight. Again the representational is non-conceptual. And again, no illusion is present. The experience is veridical on all levels: the facing surface of the coin really is elliptical from here; the coin really is circular.

Case 3: Blurred vision. If you unfocus your eyes, you can see objects in a blurry way without seeing them as being blurred. Your experience does not represent the objects as blurred. Representationally, it has been claimed, your experience after you unfocus your eyes is the same, in all salient respects, as the experience before. But phenomenally there is a difference.

This case is owed to Paul Boghossian and David Velleman (1989). One rather like it is raised by Ned Block (forthcoming (*b*)). Block asks us to imagine that we are watching a movie screen that fills our whole field of vision. The images on the screen are themselves blurred and look that way. Here Block claims we have clear impressions of blurry images. In the second example, we are reading a programme in the cinema and we then look up at the screen. The images on the screen now may or may not be blurred (as far as we are aware), but we have a blurry impression of them. Block is dubious that the representationalist can capture this difference satisfactorily.

Another everyday example worth mentioning is that of poor eyesight. When I take off my reading-glasses, my vision of nearby things blurs a little. Alternatively, if I stare at a bright light and look away, I have a blurry or fuzzy after-image. Blurriness, it might be claimed, is an aspect of the phenomenal character of my visual experiences in both of these examples that is not fixed by the representational content of the experiences.

Reply: There is indeed *a* difference between the case of seeing objects blurrily and the case of seeing them as blurred. But properly understood, it is no threat to the representationalist's position. When one sees a sharp object *as* blurred, one sees it as having indistinct contours and boundaries. This, we can agree, is not what normally happens when one unfocuses one's eyes or takes off one's glasses. In these cases, one simply loses information. Likewise, when one sees the world through eyes that are half-closed. In seeing blurrily, one undergoes sensory representations that fail to specify just where the boundaries and contours lie. Some information that was present with eyes focused is now missing. In particular, the grouped array contains less definite information about surface depth, orientation, contours, etc.

In the case of squinting, I might add, even though information is lost, one can sometimes come to see something one couldn't see before. For example, when one squints at Fig. 1.4 from a distance, one reduces the amount of information one has about the sharp edges of the blocks. Since representation of the sharp edges interferes with some of the processing that generates representation of large-scale features, the latter actually becomes more efficient during squinting, with the result that one is now able to recognize that the figure is Abraham Lincoln.

To return to blurred vision, in the case of seeing sharp objects as blurred, one's visual experience comments inaccurately on boundaries. It 'says' that the boundaries themselves are fuzzy when they are not. In the cases of seeing blurrily, one's visual experience does not do this. It makes no comment on where exactly the boundaries lie. Here there is no inaccuracy.

There is a further difference between the two cases. When one sees an object or screen image itself as blurred, one brings to bear a conceptual representation of blurriness, a representation that demands that one have a cognitive grasp of what it is for something to have indistinct or fuzzy boundaries. By contrast, in the case of seeing something blurrily, the representation is non-conceptual. A small child with poor eyesight can see things blurrily. It should also be noted that a small child with good eyesight can see blurry things clearly. That too is non-conceptual. A threefold distinction thus emerges: seeing as blurred, seeing blurrily, and seeing clearly something blurred. Only the first of these involves a conceptual representation of blurriness.

The difference, I might add, between seeing a blurred screen image blurrily and seeing that same screen image clearly has to do with the degree of representational indeterminacy in the experience. In seeing the image blurrily, one's experience is less definite about boundaries and surface details than the blurriness in the image warrants. In seeing the same screen image clearly, one's experience accurately captures the image blurriness.

Still, is there really any *phenomenal* difference between seeing blurrily and seeing as blurred or between seeing blurrily a clear thing and seeing clearly a blurred thing? To be sure, there is a difference in higher-order consciousness between realizing that one is seeing blurrily and realizing that one is seeing as blurred, but this is extrinsic and non-phenomenal. There is also normally an

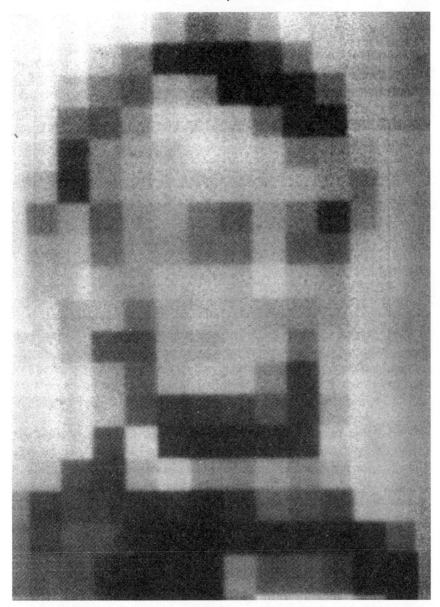

FIG. 1.4. A checkerboard picture devised by Leon D. Harmon. It should be viewed at a distance through half-closed eyes. Reprinted with permission from Harmon (1973).

associated phenomenal difference connected with the presence of character-istic bodily sensations involved in the region of the eyes when one sees blurrily (one's eyes 'feel' different). And seeing as blurred may well be accompanied by a linguistic, auditory image of oneself saying (in one's native tongue) that the relevant thing is blurred. That image, like other images, will have phenomenal features. But leaving these differences aside, is there any inherent phenomenal difference between the two states in typical cases, or between the states of seeing a clear thing blurrily and seeing a blurred thing clearly?

It seems obvious that, in principle, an experimental set-up could be devised that would leave one without any way of telling from the phenomenal character of one's visual experience (*without any additional cues*) whether one had shifted from seeing a sharp screen image through a blur to seeing clearly a suitably blurred version of that same screen image in at least some cases. Still, there does seem to me a purely visual phenomenal difference in some cases too.

Here is an example from Frank Jackson that illustrates the point. Consider a watercolour painting done on wet paper so that the edges of the coloured shapes blur. If I view such a painting with my glasses on, I have a clear impression of a blurry representation. Now consider a watercolour painting done on dry paper with sharp edges to the coloured shapes. Viewing a painting of this sort with my glasses off, I have a blurry impression of a clear representation. Typically, there is a phenomenal difference between the two cases.

Jackson agrees with me that this example presents no problem for representationalism, however. His suggestion (in correspondence) is that with the blurry watercolour, my visual experience represents quite precisely the blurriness of the edges; that is, it represents (a) that the edges definitely fall between spatial regions A and B of the paper and (b) that it is indefinite exactly where between A and B on the paper the edges fall. With the clear watercolour, seen without glasses, my visual experience is silent on the precise locus of the edges; that is, my experience represents that the edges of the coloured shapes definitely fall between A and B while failing to represent exactly where it is between A and B the edges lie.

What about the example of the fuzzy after-image? When one sees an after-image, there is nothing that one sees. The term 'see' here has a phenomenal sense that lacks existential import. It is the sense that is operative when we say that Macbeth saw a dagger. Seeing a blue, circular after-image consists in having a certain kind of visual experience. The experience isn't blue or circular. Rather it is an illusory experience as of something blue and circular (from here), something filmy and hovering in space.[15] The fuzziness of the after-image is most easily accounted for by supposing that it is a straightforward reflection of the representational impoverishment of the relevant visual experience. The experience does not 'say' exactly where the boundaries of the non-existent blue circular thing lie. Again, no difficulty for representationalism.

---

[15] Not everyone accepts that such experiences are always illusory. See the next case.

Case 4: The apparent location of an after-image. A flash bulb goes off. You see a red after-image in front of a photographer's face. You are under no illusion about what you are seeing. You are well aware that the spot you see is an after-image. According to Boghossian and Velleman (1989), you do not see the after-image as actually existing in front of the photographer's face. Rather you see it as a spot that appears there. The after-image *appears to you in* a certain location without *appearing to you to be in* that location. Nothing appears to be in the location in question. The representational content of your experience is (in part) that there is nothing between you and the photographer. Even so, there is a vast difference phenomenologically between this case and that in which you experience the photographer's face without a red after-image in front of it. This difference can only be accounted for, Boghossian and Velleman claim, by reference to a sensory field with intrinsic sensational qualities instantiated in portions of it.

In the case of the colour of the after-image, according to Boghossian and Velleman, the situation is a little different. For here, they maintain, you can see the after-image not just as appearing red but as *being* red. Assuming that your experience is veridical—you see the after-image as an after-image—a further difficulty now arises. What does your experience represent as actually being red? Not any external object (for that would make the experience illusory, which, by hypothesis, say Boghossian and Velleman, it is not). Nor the image itself. On the representationalist view, there is no image in the content of the experience. Once again, it seems that we need to concede that the phenomenology isn't fixed by the representational content. Redness doesn't enter into the content. Rather phenomenal or sensational redness is a feature of a portion of the *sensory* field.

Reply: This conclusion is one we would do well to avoid. For one thing, it smacks of the classical sense-datum theory. For another, colours can certainly be seen as belonging to things in the environment. So, unless in all cases the colours we see are really properties of our visual fields,[16] we face a very puzzling question: how can a portion of a visual field, understood now as a subjective entity, share a property with something objective in the external environment?

Happily, the representationalist need not concern him- or herself with these matters. It seems to me that there is a clear sense in which the basic experiences involved in seeing after-images are *always* illusory. For when one sees an after-image, there is nothing that one thereby sees. As noted earlier, the term 'see' in this context has a phenomenal sense; it is not a success verb. There is also a sense in which some after-image experiences are veridical. For one can indeed see an after-image as an after-image. And in so doing, one makes no mistake,

---

[16] This highly counter-intuitive position is adopted by Boghossian and Velleman (1989). In their view, we mistakenly project colours onto external things.

any more than does the person who hallucinates a pink elephant and who sees the hallucinated elephant as not really existing. The spot one apprehends, like the elephant, is unreal.[17] If the subject of the after-image experience grasps this fact, he can conceptually represent the spot *as* unreal. And that conceptualization can enter into his overall experience, broadly understood. But the fact that some after-image experiences are veridical in the latter sense clearly does not threaten the claim that they are all illusory in the former sense. Once this is admitted, no good reason remains to deny that when one sees a red after-image, redness enters into the content of the experience.

Turning now to the example of apparent location, consider first the case in which one sees a red after-image in front of a much larger background yellow surface without realizing that it is an after-image. Here one undergoes an illusory experience as of something red and filmy, hovering in space in front of something yellow—an experience similar perhaps to that of viewing (in dim lighting) a bloodstain on a transparent sheet of glass, suspended between oneself and a yellow background surface. Now suppose that one realizes that one is having an after-image. One is no longer inclined to believe that there is something red suspended in space before one. None the less, at the *non-conceptual* level, one still undergoes an experience as of something red in front of a yellow background. At this level, one's experience is still phenomenally similar to the veridical experience of the bloodstain. That this is so, if anyone has any doubt, is shown by the fact that even if one is firmly convinced that one is having an after-image, one can be mistaken.[18] But conceptually, things are now different. One now sees the spot one is experiencing as unreal, as not actually being in front of a yellow surface at all.

Accordingly, there is a conflict between the non-conceptual and the conceptual contents of the experience. In the non-conceptual sense, the after-image appears in front of a yellow surface. This is the sense of 'appears' that goes with the non-conceptual, phenomenal sense of 'see'. Even though the spot does not exist, one sees it; and one sees the spot just in case it appears some way. Since one sees what does not exist only if one is subject to an

---

[17] Its status is that of an intentional inexistent, like that of the eternal life some hope for or the golden fleece Jason sought. (In saying this, I do not mean to suggest that we need to quantify over intentional inexistents.)

[18] There is a famous psychological experiment worth mentioning here. It does not involve after-images, but it does bring out how mistakes can be made about whether one is imaging something or actually seeing it (in the success sense of 'see'). In the experiment, subjects in a room with normal lighting were asked to face a screen and to imagine a banana on it. Unknown to the subjects, a projector was set up behind the screen, containing a slide of a banana. Once the subjects reported that they had formed their images, the illumination on the projector was slowly increased so that it eventually cast a picture of a banana on a screen that was clearly visible to any newcomer entering the room. However, none of the subjects ever realized that they were looking at a real picture. Instead, they noticed merely that their 'images' changed in certain ways—for example, orientation—as time passed. For more, see Perky (1910).

illusory experience, appearing at this level is certainly a function of the content of the experience. But it is not dependent upon the concepts one possesses. Although the after-image non-conceptually appears in front of a yellow surface, it does not appear to *be* there. Indeed, it appears *not* to be there. This is the conceptual or epistemic sense of appearing.[19] In general, x appears *to be F* to *P* only if X possesses the concept F (just as P sees x as F only if P possesses the concept F). The after-image experience overall, then, has a content that is necessarily inconsistent. In this respect, it is like experiences of impossible figures (such as Fig. 1.3).

One way to think about this case is to imagine a witness at a trial telling her account of events on some past evening. The judge hears the witness but he has conflicting information from other sources he finds more compelling. So he does not believe her. Indeed, he believes that what she says is false. The subject of the after-image experience in the above example is comparable to the judge here. The former, like the latter, makes a higher-level 'assessment' based on her overall information that is at odds with a lower-level 'report' she has.[20] Both the report and the assessment enter into the after-image experience, broadly understood.[21]

There are many examples of similar non-conceptual/conceptual conflicts in experience. If I find out that I am viewing a *trompe l'œil* painting of a garden of flowers through a window and not a real garden and window as I had supposed, I may come to see what is before my eyes as a clever two-dimensional piece of trickery while still having a visual experience that non-conceptually represents brightly coloured items at varying distances away.[22]

Case 5: Eyes closed towards the sun. This example is again due to Peacocke (1993). Close your eyes and look towards the sun. You will probably experience swirling shapes. But phenomenally, your experience isn't really like visual experiences you undergo of moving shapes in your environment. This case can be viewed as a challenge to the advocate of (R) to say what is different about the representational content of the experience, eyes closed, that determines the different phenomenal character.

---

[19] For more here, see Jackson (1977); Dretske (1995).

[20] One possible relevant piece of information here concerns the way in which the after-image moves with the movement of the eyes.

[21] Of course, the 'report' in the after-image case isn't conceptual. In this important respect, it differs from the report the judge hears from the witness.

[22] In my discussion of case 4, I have spoken as if after-images are one and the same as certain unreal, intentional objects. In the final analysis, I am inclined to reject this unqualified view, since it entails that after-images are not mental entities (any more than are centaurs and unicorns). Another related problem is that the position produces a lack of systematic unity in the treatment of so-called 'phenomenal objects'. For pains, itches, and tickles are surely mental (and necessarily private). On my present view, the term 'after-image' is ambiguous. Sometimes it refers to a visual experience; sometimes it picks out an intentional object. For more on the former usage and the reasons for supposing that after-images are visual experiences, see Tye (1995).

Ned Block (1996) has a similar example. His involves phosphene experiences. Push your eyeballs in for about a minute. You'll experience bright changing colours. But your experience, Block claims, isn't representational.[23] If this is correct, then phenomenally different phosphene experiences have the same representational content, namely none, and (R) is false.

Reply: Representations are typically indeterminate with respect to some aspects of the things they represent. If, for example, I say to you, 'There's a tall man at the door,' my assertion leaves open whether he is wearing a hat, the look on his face, whether he is overweight, and many other features. It simply does not comment on these matters. Likewise, if I draw a picture of the man, I may well leave unspecified how many stripes there are on his shirt, the colour of his cheeks, whether he is wearing a belt. In the case where I experience swirling shapes, there is also representational indeterminacy.

Consider again the earlier example of the tilted coin. Here my experience represents the coin as having certain viewpoint-independent and viewpoint-dependent properties—as being both round and elliptical from here, for example. My experience conceptually classifies it as a public object and as a coin, in particular. When I experience swirling shapes with my eyes closed, my experience is representationally much more impoverished. It does not conceptually represent that there is a public object present. Indeed, there is no representation, conceptual or non-conceptual, of viewpoint-independent properties or of the third spatial dimension. There is representation only in two dimensions and only at the level of the grouped array. Bounded spatial regions are delineated; certain local features are specified, e.g. colour. Thereby certain irregular, viewpoint-dependent, shape features are represented. But the representation goes no further. It makes no further comment.

Of course, on this account, the experience of swirling shapes is inaccurate or illusory. What it 'says' is not the case. There are no items present with the relevant viewer-relative shapes. But this surely is no problem. Given the abnormality of the sensory situation, error is to be expected.

A parallel response can be made to the phosphene case. Again, one's experience is highly indeterminate representationally. But intuitively there is *some* content there. As Harman (1996) notes, the phosphene experience has a phenomenal character rather like those one undergoes when viewing the end of a fireworks show or during the light displays in some rock concerts. The relevant content, then, is plausibly taken to be similar to the non-conceptual content that is present in the latter cases. The main difference is that in the phosphene case, one's experience is illusory. The correctness conditions are not satisfied.

Perhaps it will be said that in both the phosphene case and that of the swirling shapes, one sees the moving expanses as unreal, as not actually being

_____

[23] Or may not be. Block hedges a bit here (see 1996: 35).

in public space at all. So there is representation beyond the level of the grouped array. That seems to me not obvious. What is obvious is that one does not see the expanses as actually being in public space. For that is not how one typically conceives of the expanses in such experiences. But even if one does see the expanses as unreal, there is no pressing difficulty. The experiences now have a conceptual layer of content that is inconsistent with the non-conceptual one, just as in case 4.

The upshot, I suggest, is that there is no immediate difficulty presented by the above examples for representationalism.

Case 6: Double vision. Boghossian and Velleman (1989: 94) have one further case worth mentioning. They say:

If you press the side of one eyeball, you can see this line of type twice without seeing the page as bearing two identical lines of type. Indeed, you cannot even force the resulting experience into representing the existence of two lines, even if you try. Similarly, you can see nearby objects double by focusing on distant objects behind them, and yet you cannot get yourself to see the number of nearby objects as doubling.

The conclusion they draw is that experiences such as these cannot be described correctly in terms of their intentional content alone.

Reply: I am not persuaded. It is certainly the case that when one presses one's eyeball, one has no inclination to think or judge that the number of lines of type has doubled. After all, the duplicate line is fainter than the original, and one knows full well what one is doing. So, in the epistemic or conceptual sense of the term 'appears', it does not appear that the number of lines has doubled. It does not look as if the number of lines has doubled. But phenomenologically there is, of course, a conspicuous change. This, the representationalist can plausibly claim, is because at the level of the grouped array there is a change in representational content. The surface that is identified within the overall experience as the page now has small regions represented as black that were represented as white before (corresponding to those places where one sees the duplicate line).[24]

Where this case differs from that in which one sees two identical lines of type *as* two such lines (leaving aside the issue of faintness) is in a much higher conceptual layer of content. In the latter case, unlike the former, one brings to bear the complex concept *two lines of type* in one's experience. So, once again, there is no representational identity.[25] Likewise for the case of seeing double

---

[24] Of course, I am using the term 'see' here in the phenomenological sense.

[25] Is it possible to see the number of things as doubling while also seeing double? Yes. Suppose one is viewing a movie screen on which the number of images doubles every ten seconds until the screen is full and then the doubling process starts anew. One is aware that this is going on and one sees the number of images as doubling. After a while, one starts to drink alcohol, with the result that one comes to see individual images double. One is now seeing double while also seeing the number of screen images itself as doubling.

and seeing as two *simpliciter*. A small child who cannot count to two and so who cannot see *as* two can still see double.

The fact that seeing double is a representationally distinct state from seeing two things as two, I should note, does not entail that the two states are *inherently* phenomenally different. After all, it is surely the case that an experimental set-up could be produced that adjusted for the faintness usually associated with seeing double and left one unable to say from the phenomenal character of one's visual experience *alone* whether one had shifted from seeing one thing double to seeing two things accurately or vice versa, just as in the earlier example of blurred vision.[26]

Case 7: Sexism, Racism, and Ageism. Most men and nearly all women have non-defective colour vision, as measured by standard colour tests such as those of Ishihara and Farnsworth. But people vary, according to gender, race, and age in their performance in matching experiments. For example, when subjects are shown a screen, one half of which is lit by a mixture of red and green lights and the other by yellow or orange light, and they are asked to adjust the mixture of lights so as to make the two halves of the screen match in colour, they disagree about the location of the match. Where one male subject sees the two sides of the screen as being the same in colour, another female subject may see one side as a little redder or greener. And there are corresponding differences with age and race.

In a recent article, Ned Block (1998a) claims that 'The fact that people match differently gives us reason to suppose that the phenomenal character of an experience of a narrow shade—say a specific Munsell chip—may not be the same for any two persons if they differ in sex, race or age.' There is no difference is the representational content of the shade experiences of the same Munsell chip, however, if the perceivers are normal, according to Block. For if there were, then some shade experiences of normal perceivers would be inaccurate. And that, Block maintains, just isn't plausible: there is no privileged class of *normal* perceivers. To say that the men track the shades accurately and the women do not is sexist. To prefer the young to the old is ageist. To suppose whites get it right and blacks do not is racist. But if there is phenomenal difference without representational difference, then thesis (R) is false.

To see what is wrong with this argument, consider two normal perceivers, Ted and Alice, both of whom are looking at a Munsell chip, M, in ideal viewing circumstances. Let us grant that their colour experiences are veridical. Suppose that there is a mixture of coloured lights, the shade of which Ted

---

[26] Paul Boghossian has commented to me that the case of ambiguous figures presents a further problem for those representationalists who want to claim that phenomenal character is identical with or fixed by non-conceptual representational content. For a discussion of ambiguous figures and a defence of representationalism here, see Tye (1995: 140–1).

exactly matches to the shade of *M* but which Alice distinguishes from it, matching instead the shade of that mixture of lights to a different Munsell chip. Alice, thus, makes a finer discrimination than Ted. This is evidence that there is a phenomenal difference in their experiences of *M*.

It may seem that there is room for another possibility here. For suppose that the mixture of lights is not the same shade as *M* at all, but a distinct shade that Ted cannot distinguish from the shade of the chip whereas Alice can. In this case, it may be suggested, the phenomenal character of their shade experiences of *M* is the same while the phenomenal character of their shade experiences of the mixture of lights is different.

The root problem with this proposal is that phenomenal differences are accessible to appropriately attentive subjects. If the phenomenal character of Ted's shade experience of *M* were different from that of his shade experience of the mixture of lights, then that difference, however small, would be reflected in Ted's judging that *M* and the mixture of lights do not quite match shade-wise. But *ex hypothesi*, Ted judges, on the basis of his experiences, that the two *do* match with respect to shade. So, for Ted, there is no difference in phenomenal character. *M* and the mixture of lights look phenomenally the *same* shade to Ted. On the representationalist view, then, Ted visually represents *M* and the mixture of lights as having the same shade. Since Ted's experience is veridical, it follows that *M* and the mixture of lights have the same shade, contrary to the initial supposition.

The representationalist, thus, should hold that the phenomenal character of Ted's experience of chip *M* is indeed different from that of Alice's experience of *M*. Now *M* looks a certain shade—call that shade '*S*'—to Ted and it also looks a certain shade—call it '*S*''—to Alice. *M* looks the same shade as the mixture of lights to Ted, but the mixture of lights looks a different shade (S') to Alice (that of another chip). If, as the representationalist maintains, phenomenal difference requires representational difference, then the shades Ted and Alice visually represent the chip *M* as having are different. Given that both Ted and Alice have veridical experiences, it follows, on the representationalist view, that the chip is *S and S'*, where *S* is not identical with *S'*. How can this be? How can a single chip (or, for that matter, a single mixture of lights) have multiple shades?

The answer, of course, is that something can have two or more shades so long as at least one of the shades is non-minimal, where a *minimal* shade is one for which there is no *other* shade that is a shade of it. For example, scarlet is a shade of red. Bright scarlet is a shade of scarlet. One and the same entity can be both bright scarlet and scarlet since at least one of these shades is non-minimal. (In fact, both are.)

Consider, then, shades *S* and *S'*. The chip viewed by Ted and Alice can have both shades, since (at least) *S* is non-minimal. *S'* is a shade of *S* that Ted fails to discriminate. Alice picks out S', since she has a more sensitive shade detector than Ted. Her colour vision is attuned to more subtle variations in shade than Ted. Neither has an inaccurate colour experience, however.

Here is a parallel. Suppose that I have scales at home for weighing myself. The scales are calibrated in single units. When I stand on them, they read '162'. In the doctor's office, on the same morning, I am weighed again. His scales are more finely calibrated. They reads '$162\frac{1}{8}$'. On the same scales, a little later, having eaten a snack, I am weighed once more. The reading is now '$162\frac{3}{8}$'. If my home scales still read '162' when I stand on them, then there is a difference in my weight that my home scales fail to register. But that doesn't make them inaccurate. Given their design, they are merely a less sensitive representational device than the scales used by my doctor.

Of course, the reply I have given to Block's argument requires the assumption that things can have shades that *some* normal perceivers fail to discriminate even in ideal circumstances. And some philosophers will reject this assumption. But on an objectivist conception of colour it seems unproblematic. Take another perceptual case, that of depth vision. Obviously, even among normal perceivers, there are subtle differences in the distance of objects that are discriminable only to some of the perceivers. Some normal perceivers have more sensitive (more finely calibrated) depth detectors than others. Likewise in the case of shades of colour.

Block also discusses the case of colour experiences that differ among normal perceivers at a less fine-grained level. Something that looks more red than orange to me may look more orange than red to you; something that I experience as unique green, you may experience as green with a tinge of blue. How can this be, on a representationalist account, if we are both undergoing veridical colour experiences?[27]

The first point to make by way of reply is that there are visual representations both of colours and of (more or less narrow) shades. Since colours comprise or include many shades, in representing something X as having a certain colour, my experience effectively classifies it along with many other things whose colour shades I can discriminate from X. Such classifications will certainly vary somewhat from person to person, and these classifications will be reflected in differences in verbal and non-verbal behaviour in certain situations. Given these differences, there is no difficulty in allowing that a thing can be both more red than orange (for me) and more orange than red (for you). For it suffices that the red (orange) classifications at play in our experiences range over slightly different sets of shades. If a shade in my category of red is in your category of orange, something can look more red

---

[27] The reply given below is one that Block himself acknowledges is available to the representationalist.

than orange to me while looking more orange than red to you. And we can both be right. Likewise for the case of unique green and green tinged with blue.

It is worth stressing that the foregoing talk of visual classifications and categories need not be taken to commit the representationalist to the view that the representation of colours, as opposed to shades, in visual experience always involves the application of colour concepts. To be sure, the classifications typically elicit conceptual responses. But it is open to the representationalist to argue that just as it is possible for a visual experience to represent something as having a certain fine-grained shade without the subject of the experience applying a concept to that shade, so too is it possible for the case of colour. If the visual system is set up so that experiences 'track' colours in the appropriate conditions, they can thereby represent the colours, whether or not the subjects extract that information and use it in their beliefs.

3. Cross-Modal Cases

In this section, I discuss two cases that involve different sensory modalities. These cases purport to refute the following thesis:

(R′) Necessarily, perceptual experiences that are alike with respect to their representational contents are alike phenomenally.

Once again, I shall argue, the representationalist has plausible replies.

The first example is owed to Block (1995). It compares having a visual experience as of something overhead versus having an auditory experience as of something overhead. Block claims that this example shows that there are phenomenal differences that are not representational. Supposedly, there is *no* common phenomenal quality to these experiences, even though they overlap representationally.

In Tye (1995), I pointed out that it isn't obviously true that there is no phenomenal overlap. What is obviously true is that the look and the sound phenomenally differ. In his original discussion, Block (ibid. s. 4.2) says that, in the case he has in mind, one only catches a glimpse so that 'the (phenomenal) difference cannot be ascribed to further representational differences'. So understood, the case is a putative counter-example to (R′).

However, even if one has only a glimpse, there will inevitably be other features represented in the one experience that are not represented in the other. For example, in the case of the auditory experience, one is bound to have some impression of how loud the sound is. One will also normally have some visual impression of the thing's colour and viewer-relative size (whether or not one notices these features, i.e. whether or not one conceptually represents them in one's experience). And those won't be represented in the auditory experience.

Block (1996) now claims that in his original example he had in mind peripheral vision of movement in which there is no representation of colour, size, or shape. The content is just that something is moving over there. But he now concedes that in the auditory experience, there will inevitably be representation of how loud the sound is. He remarks:

That does not ruin the point. It just makes it harder to see. Imagine the experience of hearing something and seeing it in your peripheral vison. It is true that you experience the sound as having a certain loudness, but can't we abstract away from that, concentrating on the perceived location? And isn't there an obvious difference between the auditory experience *as of that location* and the visual experience *as of that location*? (ibid. 38)

His conclusion is that representationally identical experiences in different sensory modalities can differ phenomenally.

I find myself quite perplexed by these remarks. How are we meant to abstract away from the loudness of the sound and focus on the perceived location in the auditory case? After all, as Block grants, we have no auditory experiences that are not as of sounds. Nor can we even imagine having any such experiences (at least I can't). So, it seems to me, we do not have the faintest idea what such experiences are supposed to be like. Perhaps what Block means us to do is to mentally block out the sound in the auditory experience. But now it seems to me not at all obvious that the experience that remains accessible to us is any different phenomenally from the visual one of movement alone (assuming we also mentally block off any further information in the visual experience about the background colours, shapes, etc.).

The second example is one of seeing a round shape and feeling that shape by running one's fingers over it.[28] Suppose that in both cases, one has an experience as of a round shape. Still, the one is a haptic experience and the other a visual experience. Phenomenologically, there is a large difference between the two—a difference (according to some) that (R′) cannot account for.

One obvious immediate reply the representationalist can make is that in seeing the shape, one has an experience as of colour. But colour isn't represented in the content of the haptic experience. Conversely, temperature is represented in the haptic experience, but not in the visual one (or at least not to the same extent). Likewise, there is much more detailed representation of degree of solidity in the haptic experience. Another representational difference pertains to the location of the shape. In vision, the shape is automatically represented as having a certain two-dimensional location relative to the eyes. It is also normally represented as being at a certain distance from the body. In

---

[28] This case was raised at the 1995 SOFIA conference in Cancun, the proceedings of which are published in the volume, *Philosophical Issues*, 7, containing Block, Harman, and Tye (1996). It has also come up several times in conversation.

the haptic case, however, shape is represented via more basic touch and pressure representations of contours derived from sensors in the skin. Here the shape is represented as belonging to a surface with which one is in bodily contact. Moreover (and relatedly) in the haptic experience, there is no representation of the shape's two-dimensional location relative to the eyes. Finally, and very importantly, in the visual case there is representation not only of viewer-independent shape but also of viewer-relative shape (e.g. being elliptical from here). The latter property, of course, is not represented in the haptic experience.

Perhaps it will be replied again that we can abstract away from *all* these differences and focus on the representation of shape itself. Having done so, we will still be left with an obvious phenomenal difference between the visual experience as of a round shape and the haptic experience as of that shape. I can only say again that this seems to me not in the least obvious. Indeed it is hard to make sense of the idea that via such a process of mental abstraction we are left with any distinctively visual or haptic experiences to focus on at all.

That completes my survey of problem cases. The onus now rests with opponents of representationalism to find other, more compelling counter-examples. Given the richness of the content of perceptual experience, I am very doubtful that such counter-examples will be forthcoming either to (R) or to (R′).[29]

REFERENCES

BLOCK, N. (1990), 'Inverted Earth', in J. Tomberlin (ed.), *Philosophical Perspectives*, 4 (Northridge, Calif.: Ridgeview).

—— (1993), Review of D. Dennett, *Consciousness Explained*, *The Journal of Philosophy*, 90: 181–93.

—— (1995), 'On A Confusion about a Function of Consciousness', *Behavioral and Brain Sciences*, 18: 227–47.

—— (1996), 'Mental Paint and Mental Latex', in E. Villenueva (ed.), *Philosophical Issues*, 7 (Northridge, Calif.: Ridgeview).

—— (1998a), 'Is Experience Just Representing?' *Philosophy and Phenomenological Research*, 58: 663–70.

—— (1998b), 'Sexism, Racism, Ageism and the Nature of Consciousness', in *The Philosophy of Sydney Shoemaker*, Philosophical Topics, 26 (1–2).

BOGHOSSIAN, P., and VELLEMAN, D. (1989), 'Colour as a Secondary Quality', *Mind*, 98: 81–103.

[29] Earlier versions of this paper formed the basis for talks at King's College London, the University of Michigan, the University of Mexico, the University of Missouri, and a conference on minds and machines in Palermo, Sicily. I would like to thank John Dilworth and Mark Sainsbury for helpful discussion, and Sydney Shoemaker for a useful comment.

DeBellis, M. (1991), 'The Representational Content of Musical Experience', *Philosophy and Phenomenological Research*, 51: 303–24.

Dretske, F. (1995), *Naturalizing the Mind* (Cambridge, Mass.: MIT Press).

Efron, R. (1968), 'What is Perception?' *Boston Studies in Philosophy of Science*, 4: 159.

Gregory, R. (1990), *Eye and Brain* (London: Weidenfeld & Nicolson).

Harman, G. (1990), 'The Intrinsic Quality of Experience', in J. Tomberlin (ed.), *Philosophical Perspectives*, 4 (Northridge, Calif.: Ridgeview).

—— (1996), 'Qualia and Colour Concepts', in E. Villenueva (ed.), *Philosophical Issues*, 7 (Northridge, Calif.: Ridgeview).

Harmon, Leon D. (1973), 'The Recognition of Faces', *Scientific American* (November), 75.

Jackson, F. (1977), *Perception* (Cambridge: Cambridge University Press).

Kosslyn, S. (1994), *Image and Brain* (Cambridge, Mass.: Harvard University Press).

Landis, T., Graves, R., Benson, F., and Hebben, N. (1982), 'Visual Recognition through Kinaesthetic Mediation', *Psychological Medicine*, 12: 515–31.

Lycan, W. (1996a), *Consciousness and Experience* (Cambridge, Mass.: MIT Press).

—— (1996b), 'Layered Perceptual Representation', in E. Villeneuva (ed.), *Philosophical Issues*, 7 (Northridge, Calif.: Ridgeview).

McDowell, J. (1994), 'The Content of Perceptual Experience', *Philosophical Quarterly*, 46–65.

McGinn, C. (1991), *The Problem of Consciousness* (Oxford: Blackwell).

Marr, D. (1982), *Vision* (San Francisco: W. H. Freeman).

Peacocke, C. (1983), *Sense and Content* (Oxford: Oxford University Press).

—— (1992), 'Scenarios, Concepts, and Perception', in T. Crane (ed.), *The Contents of Experience: Essays on Perception* (Cambridge: Cambridge University Press) 105–35.

—— (1993), 'Review of M. Tye, *The Imagery Debate*', *Philosophy of Science*, 675–7.

Perky, C. (1910), 'An Experimental Study of the Imagination', *American Journal of Psychology*, 21: 422–52.

Rey, G. (1992), 'Sensational Sentences', in M. Davies and G. Humphreys (eds.), *Consciousness: Psychological and Philosophical Essays* (Oxford: Blackwell).

Rock, I. (1983), *The Logic of Perception* (Cambridge, Mass.: MIT Press).

Shoemaker, S. (1994), 'Phenomenal Character', *Nous*, 28: 21–38.

Tye, M. (1991), *The Imagery Debate* (Cambridge, Mass.: MIT Press).

—— (1995), *Ten Problems of Consciousness* (Cambridge, Mass.: MIT Press).

—— (1996), 'Perceptual Experience is a Many-Layered Thing', in E. Villeneuva (ed.), *Philosophical Issues*, 7 (Northridge, Calif.: Ridgeview).

—— (1998), 'Response to Discussants', *Philosophy and Phenomenological Research*, 58: 679–87.

—— (2000), *Consciousness, Colour, and Content* (Cambridge, Mass.: MIT Press).

White, S. (1995), 'Colour and the Narrow Contents of Experience', *Philosophical Topics*, 23.

2. The Intentional Structure of Consciousness

TIM CRANE

1. The Intentional and the Qualitative

Newcomers to the philosophy of mind are sometimes resistant to the idea that pain is a mental state. If asked to defend their view, they might say something like this: pain is a physical state, it is a state of the body. One feels a pain in one's leg to be in the leg, not in the mind. After all, sometimes people distinguish pain which is 'all in the mind' from a genuine pain, sometimes because the second is 'physical' while the first is not. And we also distinguish mental pain (which is normally understood as some kind of emotional distress) from the physical pain one feels in one's body. So what can be meant by saying that pain is a mental state?

Of course, a little reflection shows that this naïve view is mistaken. Pain is a state of consciousness, or an event in consciousness, and whether or not all states of mind are conscious, it is indisputable that only minds, or states of mind, are conscious.[1] But does the naïve view tell us anything about the concept of pain, or the concept of mind? I think it does. I shall give reasons for thinking that consciousness is a form of intentionality, the mind's 'direction upon its objects'. I shall claim that the consciousness involved in bodily sensations such as pain results from the mind's direction upon the part or region of the body where the sensation is felt to be. Given this, it is less suprising that the naïve view of pain says what it does: the apparent

The paper that forms the basis of this chapter has been presented in various forms in a number of places: at the Oxford Philosophical Society, the Cambridge Moral Sciences Club, the 1998 conference on consciousness at Santa Barbara City College, the 1999 meeting of the Australasian Association of Philosophy in Melbourne, and at the Universities of Bristol, Lund, Otago, Sheffield, Uppsala, and Vercelli. For helpful comments and discussion, I thank David Chalmers, Katalin Farkas, Chris Hill, Paul Horwich, Brian Loar, Mike Martin, Adam Morton, Greg McCulloch, Lucy O'Brien, Kim Sterelny, Helen Steward, Michael Tye, and Jerry Valberg. The paper was completed with the help of a grant from the AHRB Research Leave Scheme.

[1] Putting to one side the sort of panpsychism discussed by Thomas Nagel ('Panpsychism' in his *Mortal Questions* (Cambridge: Cambridge University Press, 1979)) and aired as a possibility by David Chalmers, in *The Conscious Mind* (Oxford: Oxford University Press, 1996), at e.g. 293–301.

'physicality' of pain is a consequence of confusing the object of the intentional state—the part of the body in which the pain is felt—with the state of being in pain. The naïve view therefore provides a kind of indirect evidence for what I call *intentionalism*: the view that all mental states are intentional.

Intentionalism is a controversial doctrine, and conscious bodily sensations are often thought to be obvious counter-examples to the view.[2] It is often said that such sensations are 'qualitative' in nature, and qualitative mental states are not intentional. This is the doctrine I call *non-intentionalism* about sensations. Thus David Rosenthal:

> There are two broad categories of mental property. Mental states such as thoughts and desires, often called propositional attitudes, have content that can be described by 'that' clauses. For example, one can have a thought, or desire, that it will rain. These states are said to have intentional properties, or intentionality. Sensations, such as pains and sense impressions, lack intentional content, and have instead qualitative properties of various sorts.[3]

Here intentional properties are described as those with a propositional content and qualitative properties are those properties that are characteristic of sensations. Propositional content is what is ascribed in a 'that'-clause, and is normally assessable as true or false. Now no one should deny that some states of mind have propositional content, and others do not. But the question is whether this distinction is what is being rejected by intentionalists. This depends on whether Rosenthal is right to equate a phenomenon's *being intentional* with its *having propositional content*. If he is right, then intentionalism should be understood as the thesis that all mental states are propositional attitudes: since all intentional states are propositional attitudes and all mental states are intentional. Intentionalism of this form is alluded to in the last sentence of this quotation from Alvin Goldman:

> Philosophers commonly divide mental states into two sorts: those that have and those that lack propositional content. The former are *propositional attitudes*, and the latter *sensations*, *qualia* or the like. Propositional attitudes are recognised by the sentences used to ascribe them, the telltale sign being an embedded 'that'-clause . . . In addition to propositional attitudes, the class of mental states includes sensations like pains, itchy feelings, and perceptual experiences, all of which are said to have qualitative character. However, some theorists hold that even these mental states have propos-

---

[2] The other cases of mental states that are thought to be obvious counter-examples to intentionalism are certain kinds of emotions and moods. I discuss these briefly in 'Intentionality as the Mark of the Mental', in A. O'Hear (ed.), *Current Issues in the Philosophy of Mind* (Cambridge: Cambridge University Press, 1998), s. 3. For a different kind of view, see also Michael Tye, *Ten Problems of Consciousness* (Cambridge, Mass.: MIT Press, 1995), ch. 4.

[3] David Rosenthal, 'Identity Theories', in S. Guttenplan (ed.), *A Companion to the Philosophy of Mind* (Oxford: Blackwell, 1994), 349.

itional content; and a few theorists try to explain away qualitative character in terms of propositional content.[4]

The views Goldman mentions at the end of this quotation are initially implausible. The first credits sensations such as 'itchy feelings' with propositional content; but what is the propositional content supposed to be? When we say things of the form 'X hopes that p', 'X desires that p' and so on, we know what sort of thing it makes sense to put in the place of 'p'—but what are we supposed to put in the place of 'p' in 'X itchy-feels that p', or 'X feels itchily that p'? The second view Goldman mentions 'explains away' the qualitative character of sensations—presumably by showing that such character is illusory. But the qualitative character of sensations is normally introduced in terms of *how the sensation feels*; and what merit can there be in a conception of sensation that says that how a sensation feels is an illusion, something to be explained away? If intentionalism were saying this sort of thing, then it would be of little interest.

My view is that what is at fault here is not intentionalism as such, but the initial distinction between two kinds of mental state. We can immediately see that something is wrong when Goldman and Rosenthal classify perceptual experiences (or sense impressions) as among the states with qualitative character. The reason for doing this is presumably because there is (as Nagel put it) *something it is like* to see, hear, smell, or touch something, just as there is something it is like to have a sensation.[5] But it has long been recognized that perceptual experiences also have propositional content: one sees that the bus is coming, smells that someone is cooking goulash, or hears that the glass broke. So it seems as though perceptual experiences are propositional attitudes that also have qualitative character.

One could respond that all this means is that the distinction between qualitative states and propositional attitudes is not exclusive: some qualitative states can have propositional content. But what exactly is it for a state to be qualitative? What independent grip do we have of the idea of the qualitative, other than in terms of the contrast with propositional content? We can say that perceptions and sensations feel a certain way, to be sure; but it does not take much reflection to realize that the way a perception 'feels' is different from the way a bodily sensation feels; we can talk about how it feels to see red, so long as we do not think of this in terms of a certain 'feel' of redness (say) around one's eyes.[6] So whatever qualitative features are, we should not think of them as being the same in perception as in sensation. The most we can say

---

[4] Alvin I. Goldman, *Epistemology and Cognition* (Cambridge, Mass.: MIT Press, 1986), 14.
[5] Nagel, 'What is it Like to be a Bat?' in *Mortal Questions*.
[6] It is of course important to distinguish between the sense in which a perception 'feels' like something and the sense in which a bodily sensation 'feels' like something. But it would be a mere terminological stipulation to insist on these grounds that perceptions do not 'feel' like

at this stage is that qualitative states of mind are conscious states of mind, and consciousness comes in many forms. But if we say this, then it seems that not just perception, but many other propositional attitudes can have qualitative features, since many propositional attitudes can be conscious. I can consciously realize that now is the time to book the table for the restaurant: there is something it is like for this to suddenly come into my mind. So if the qualitative is just the conscious, then there are many propositional attitudes that are qualitative. And the fact that some propositional attitudes are not conscious just means that we have to distinguish between conscious mental states and non-conscious ones.

In effect, there are two options. The first is that a state of mind is 'qualitative' when it has qualities that are like those of sensation. In this sense, perceptions are not qualitative states. So the category of the qualitative is a subcategory of the conscious. One might be happy with this way of talking, so long as one had a satisfactory way of describing *non*-qualitative conscious states. The second option is to say that a state of mind is qualitative when it is conscious. In this case, perceptions are qualitative, but then so are many other propositional attitudes. One might be happy with this latter way of using the term 'qualitative', but then the distinction being made is essentially that between the conscious and the non-conscious.

It is therefore misleading (at best) to say that the fundamental distinction between states of mind is between qualitative states and propositional attitudes. For depending on how one understands 'qualitative', either qualitative states form a subcategory of conscious states, or 'qualitative' just means the same as *conscious*. Either way, the more natural and fundamental distinction seems to be between the conscious and the non-conscious. And if this is the fundamental distinction between states of mind, then intentionalism does not seem to be such an obviously absurd view: for an intentionalist is then saying that all mental states are intentional, and that some are conscious and some are not. Intentionalism is then not denying consciousness (i.e. the 'qualitative' in the broad sense) or explaining it away; it simply accepts consciousness as a fact, just as non-intentionalism does.

However, there remains a question about what intentionalism should say about the 'qualitative' in the narrower sense (i.e. sensations). For as noted above, it does not seem right, on the face of it, to say that itches and pains are propositional attitudes in anything like the way beliefs are. So how can there be an intentionalist account of sensation? I want to address this problem by first breaking the connection between intentional states and propositional

anything, or that no sense can be made of talk of 'visual sensations': here I disagree with G. McCulloch, 'The Very Idea of the Phenomenological', *Proceedings of the Aristotelian Society*, 93 (1992), 39–57, at 51–2.

attitudes and proposing a somewhat different understanding of intentionality (s. 2). I will then go on to argue that bodily sensations should be thought of as intentional states on this understanding (s. 3). However, the fact that bodily sensations are intentional states does not rule out their having (narrowly) qualitative properties (qualia) in *addition* to their intentional character. One could hold that all mental states are intentional, but that some have non-intentional qualia. This is the view I call 'weak intentionalism'. I discuss this view in s. 4, and reject it. Weak intentionalism is contrasted with strong intentionalism, which says that all mental states have only intentional mental properties. Two types of strong intentionalism are distinguished in s. 5, and I argue for the type that I call the 'perceptual theory'. But before doing anything else, I need to say something about the idea of intentionality.

2. The Idea of Intentionality

I understand intentionality in a traditional way, as the mind's direction or directedness upon its objects. When a state of mind is about something—say, as a belief that *my doctor smokes* is about my doctor—I shall say that the state of mind has an object. (Of course, intentionalism is the view that all mental states have objects; but one should not build this into the definition of intentionality.) An intentional state is a state which has, in J. J. Valberg's phrase, 'a need for an object'.[7] Although one cannot adequately understand what the state is without knowing what its object or objects are, there is none the less a distinction between a state and its objects.[8] The objects of intentional states are sometimes called 'intentional objects', and I will follow this usage. But I do not mean by this that the predicate 'x is an intentional object' is true of a special class of objects having a certain nature. There is no such special class of objects; no one could write a treatise on intentional objects as one might write a treatise on abstract objects, mental objects, or physical objects. For there is nothing interesting or substantial that all intentional objects have in common. Intentional objects are just whatever one's intentional states are directed on. My thought about my doctor is directed on my doctor, on smoking, and on the fact that he smokes: intentional objects can be ordinary objects, properties, events, or states of affairs (so 'object' here

[7] J. J. Valberg, *The Puzzle of Experience* (Oxford: Clarendon Press, 1992), 151 n. 10. See G. E. M. Anscombe, 'The Intentionality of Sensation: A Grammatical Feature', in R. J. Butler (ed.), *Analytical Philosophy*, ser. 2 (Oxford: Basil Blackwell, 1965); and Tim Crane, 'Intentionality', in E. Craig (ed.), *Encyclopedia of Philosophy* (London: Routledge, 1998).

[8] Cf. John Searle: 'It is characteristic of Intentional states, as I use the notion, that there is a distinction between the state and what the state is directed at or about or of', in *Intentionality* (Cambridge: Cambridge University Press, 1983), 2.

does not mean *particular*). One state of mind might also have many intentional objects. And, notoriously, some intentional objects do not exist.

This last fact is one of the most puzzling and much-discussed features of intentionality. But there is not space to say much about it here.[9] All I shall mean by the phrase 'intentional object' is: that at which one's mind is directed. If a state of mind has an object, if is *directed on* an object, then it is intentional. This means that there is an answer to the question, 'On what is your mind directed?' (The question is more natural in specific cases: 'What are you thinking about?' 'What are you afraid of?' 'What do you want?') Sometimes the answer to this question is a word or phrase that picks out nothing: 'Pegasus', 'phlogiston', 'the fountain of youth' all have no reference, but can be answers to the question (e.g.) 'What are you thinking about?' By 'directedness', then, I mean that feature of states of mind in virtue of which they have intentional objects. And by 'some intentional objects do not exist' I mean that some answers to the question, 'on what is your state of mind directed?' have no referents, they refer to nothing.

Directedness is the first essential feature of intentional states. The second is what I call (following Searle) *aspectual shape*.[10] This is the idea that when something is presented to a subject (in thought, perception, desire, and so on) it is always presented under a certain aspect, or in a certain way. There is no such thing as simply thinking about an object, as opposed to thinking about it (say) as *a present from one's mother*, or as *one's most precious possession*. This is what Searle means by 'aspectual shape'. The term is useful, because it is not yet tied to a particular theory or account of intentionality and related phenomena, as some terms are (e.g. Frege's *Sinn* or *sense*). Aspectual shape, like directedness, is something that any theory needs to explain, not a theoretical posit.

An intentional state, then, has an intentional object—this is directedness—and the object is presented under certain aspects and not under others—this is aspectual shape. (I say 'object' for convenience, but bear in mind that an intentional state can have more than one intentional object.) When we say what the object of an intentional state is, we have to pick a certain way of saying it, and this way of talking about the intentional object gives or expresses the *intentional content* of the intentional state. The content of two states can differ even when their objects do not: you and I can be thinking about the same person, but you think of him as Cicero and I think of him as Tully. Our thoughts have the same objects but different contents. In general, we can say that a state's having an intentional content is a matter of its having an intentional object with a certain aspectual shape.

---

[9] I discuss it at greater length in *Elements of Mind* (Oxford University Press, 2001), ch. 1.

[10] John R. Searle, *The Rediscovery of the Mind* (Cambridge, Mass.: MIT Press, 1992), 155.

Non-existent intentional objects mean that we cannot rest with this neat formulation, since we need to understand how something non-existent can be present in a state of mind. This is not the main topic of this paper. But one thing is plain: non-existent intentional objects are not a special kind of object, any more than existent intentional objects are. And since (at least according to the orthdox view, which I accept) there are no non-existent objects, it follows that not every intentional state is a *relation* to an intentional object: for relations must relate what exists. However, this is consistent with saying that all intentional states are relations to intentional contents. For whether or not every state has an existing intentional object, every intentional state must have an intentional content: one cannot think without thinking something, perceive without perceiving something, and want without wanting something. The 'something' here is *what is wanted, what is thought, what is perceived*: this is the intentional content. The content is what one would put into words, if one were to have the words into which to put it.[11] And therefore the content of a state is part of what individuates that state: that is, what distinguishes it from all other states. The other thing that distinguishes an intentional state from all others is whether it is a belief, or a desire, or hope or whatever. Again following Searle, I call this aspect of the state—the relation that relates the subject to the content—the 'intentional mode'.[12]

Every intentional state, then, consists of an intentional content related to the subject by an intentional mode. The structure of intentionality is therefore relational, and may be displayed as follows:

Subject—Intentional mode—Intentional content

Since this is a relation, there are two dimensions of variation in any intentional state of a subject: one may be presented with the same content under various modes (as, for instance, when one can believe or hope the same proposition) and one can be presented with different contents under the same mode (two perceptual states, for example, can have different contents, but under the same mode). To fix any intentional state of a given subject requires that two things therefore be fixed: mode and content.

Much of this fairly abstract description of intentionality should be uncontroversial.[13] But notice that introducing intentionality in this way does not require any particular account of what the modes in question are, and it does not require any particular conception of content (except that it accommodate the phenomenon of aspectual shape). One could, for example, accept the

---

[11] I borrow this way of putting things from an unpublished paper by J. J. Valberg.

[12] Searle, *Intentionality*, ch. 1. I follow Searle in the terminology, but not in some other things: for instance, he denies that intentional states are relations to their contents.

[13] For an example of someone who accepts these points, see Tye, *Ten Problems of Consciousness*, 94–6.

general picture yet hold that the only intentional modes are the propositional attitudes as normally conceived (e.g. belief and desire). Or one could accept a wider class of intentional modes. Similarly, one could accept the general picture yet hold that the only content is propositional content, content that can be said to be true or false. Or one could accept a wider conception of content, and say that some content is propositional and some is not.

But nothing in the very idea of intentionality compels us to choose one way or the other. Other considerations are needed to settle these issues. So, in particular, nothing in the idea of intentionality as outlined above compels us to say that content must be propositional. In fact, I believe that not all content is propositional. A state of mind has propositional content when the content of the state is evaluable as true or false.[14] But many intentional states have, on the face of it, non-truth-evaluable contents. The emotions of love and hate, for example, are directed at particular objects; fear and pity are often the same; desire is often naturally construed as having a non-propositional content; and then there is the phenomenon of *thinking about an object*, which is not always explicable in propositional terms. Some of these examples are controversial, but I will not enter the controversy in this chapter. All I need for the time being is to open up the possibility of non-propositional content, since once this possibility is opened up, then the equation (found in the quotations from Rosenthal and Goldman above) between intentional states and propositional attitudes is not forced upon us. And once this is accepted, then the fact that sensations are not obviously propositional attitudes is not a refutation of intentionalism.

So much for intentionality; but what are non-intentional states supposed to be? Well, if the above definition of intentionality is accepted, then a supposedly non-intentional state or property is one which is mental, (probably) conscious, but has no intentional structure: it is not directed on anything, it has no intentional object, no aspectual shape, and no distinction can be made between anything like *mode* and anything like *content*. The term 'qualia' has been used for such properties, and I will follow this usage. It is also possible to use the term 'qualia' for the 'qualitative' in the broad sense (= the conscious) mentioned in s. 1; but to avoid confusion I will here use the term for qualitative properties in the narrow sense. I will use the term 'phenomenal' for qualitative in the broader sense (after all, the English *phenomenon* derives from the Greek for *appearance*[15]). So the phenomenal character of experience is its conscious character, and an account of the phenomenal character of experience is an account of what it is like to have

---

[14] Ignoring here for simplicity the issue of truth-value gaps.

[15] And as McCulloch aptly points out, one earlier English dictionary definition of the term 'phenomenon' is 'the object of a person's perception; what the senses or mind notice'; 'The very idea of the phenomenological', p. 39.

that experience. In this terminology, then, it is not tautological to say that one can give an account of phenomenal character in terms of qualia. And it is not contradictory to say that one can give an account of phenomenal character in terms of intentionality.[16] These are both substantial theses.

Qualia are either mental states or properties of mental states. For example, one could call the mental state of having a toothache a *quale*, or one could call the particular naggingness of the toothache the *quale*. Intentionalism must reject qualia in the first sense—obviously, since intentionalism is the view that all mental states are intentional. But it need not reject qualia in the second sense. A version of intentionalism—*weak intentionalism*—maintains that all mental states have some intentionality, but that some of these states have qualia-properties. The experience of a toothache, for instance, has intentionality (it is tooth-directed) but on top of this it may have specific qualia that account for its particular feeling. A stronger form of intentionalism says that no mental state has any non-intentional mental properties. In s. 4, I shall argue for strong intentionalism, and against weak intentionalism. But first I must put non-intentionalism to one side.

3. Intentionalism and Non-Intentionalism about Sensation

The quotation from Rosenthal in s. 1 expresses a straightforward non-intentionalist view: there are two kinds of mental states, propositional attitudes and qualia. As noted in s. 1, the view ought to classify sense perception as a kind of hybrid, having both propositional content and qualia. And we also saw that the view should not equate the qualitative with the conscious, since there are conscious mental states (e.g. conscious thoughts) which have no qualia in the sense just defined (s. 2). The consciousness involved in these non-qualitative states must be explained in some other way—for instance, in terms of the states' being the objects of higher-order states (this is the 'Higher-Order Thought' or HOT theory of conscious thought).[17]

---

[16] It should be obvious that I am talking throughout about what Ned Block calls 'phenomenal consciousness': see Ned Block, 'On a Confusion about a Function of Consciousness', *Behavioral and Brain Sciences*, 18 (1995), 227–47; repr. in Ned Block, Owen Flanagan, and Güven Güzeldere (eds.), *The Nature of Consciousness* (Cambridge, Mass.: MIT Press, 1997).

[17] For HOT theories of consciousness, see David Rosenthal, 'Two Concepts of Consciousness', *Philosophical Studies*, 49 (1986), 329–59; D. H. Mellor, 'Conscious Belief', *Proceedings of the Aristotelian Society*, 78 (1977–8), 87–101; Peter Carruthers, 'Brute Experience', *Journal of Philosophy*, 86 (1988), 435–51. Sometimes HOT theories are put forward as theories of all conscious states, not just conscious thoughts. This has the consequence that a sensation is not conscious unless it is the object of a higher-order thought. Also, sometimes consciousness is explained in terms of the *availability* to higher-order thought, while in other cases it is explained in terms of an actual episode or act of thinking. I find all these views implausible, but I do not have space to discuss them here.

So on this non-intentionalist view, there are conscious propositional attitudes that have qualia (e.g. perceptions) and there are conscious propositional
attitudes that have no qualia (e.g. conscious thoughts). If this is granted, then
it has been granted that there can be states of mind that are purely intentional,
which lack qualia, and yet are conscious states. But the existence of conscious
states that are intentional does not trouble non-intentionalism, of course; the
view would only be refuted if there were no qualia. So an intentionalist must
examine the supposed cases of qualia, and show either that they do not exist
or that they have been mistakenly classified as non-intentional. Here the chief
examples, as we saw in s. 1, are bodily sensations. How should an intentionalist argue that bodily sensations are intentional?

There are a number of ways to proceed here, some of which will be
discussed below. (For instance, Michael Tye has argued that pains represent
damage to the body.[18]) But it seems to me that the strongest case for the
intentionality of bodily sensation comes from a correct understanding of their
felt location. It is essential to bodily sensation, as we normally experience it,
that it is felt to have a location in the body.[19] The phenomenological facts are
as follows. Pains and other sensations are felt to be located in parts of the
body. To attend to a sensation is to attend to the (apparent) part or region of
the body where the sensation is felt to be. The location of a bodily sensation
need not be felt to be precise; and it can involve the whole body. A feeling of
nausea can overwhelm the middle of one's whole body, and a feeling
of physical exhaustion can pervade one's whole body. The point is not that
a sensation must be felt to occupy a non-vague relatively circumscribed
location, but that it is is felt to be somewhere within one's body. The necessity
of this would explain why we find it so hard to make sense of the idea of a
sensation of one's own which has a location (say) 10 inches outside one's left
shoulder. Phantom limbs are not such cases: what subjects feel in a phantom
limb pain is not that they have a pain at some distance from the point at
which the limb was severed; rather, thay feel that their body extends further
than it actually does.[20]

That bodily sensation has an apparent location may be uncontroversial;
that its location is *felt* may be less so. The non-intentionalist view mentioned
above might say that the felt location really involves two things: a sensation (a

---

[18] Tye, *Ten Problems of Consciousness*, ch. 4. Tye's view is discussed in s. 2.5.

[19] I mean to describe normal experience; of course there are many interesting borderline
cases (e.g. referred pain; and so-called 'deep pain', apparently unlocatable by the subject) and
many pathological cases that are hard to describe adequately. The extent to which we find these
cases unintelligible tracks the extent to which they depart from the normal case of localizable
sensation.

[20] I am deeply indebted here to M. G. F. Martin, 'Bodily Awareness: A Sense of Ownership', in
J. Bermúdez, N. Eilan, and A. Marcel (eds.), *The Body and the Self* (Cambridge, Mass.: MIT Press,
1995). See also D. M. Armstrong, *Bodily Sensations* (London: Routledge & Kegan Paul, 1962).

quale) and a belief that the sensation is located in a certain part of the body. On this view, the location of a sensation is not part of the feeling of a sensation; rather it is a result of a *belief* about where the sensation is.

But this view cannot be right. Belief is a state of mind that is revisable on the basis of other beliefs and evidence. When rational subjects come to have a reason that tells decisively against a belief, then they revise the belief. So if the apparent location of a sensation is explained by a belief about its location, one would expect the belief to be revised when a subject comes to have a reason to think that the sensation does not have that location. But this is not so. Someone who becomes convinced by the physicalist arguments for identifying sensations with brain states will come to believe that sensations are really located in the brain. But having this belief does not change the apparent location of the sensation in the body. Moreover, this person is not irrational—i.e. does not have a contradictory belief—when they claim that a sensation is in the brain but it seems to be in the leg. Feeling a sensation to be located at a certain place is not the same as believing that one has a sensation located at that place.

If we accept that a sensation is felt to be located at a certain point, then I claim we should accept that sensation-states have intentionality. But why? John Searle has claimed that we should not let our ways of talking mislead us here:

The 'of' of 'conscious of' is not always the 'of' of intentionality. If I am conscious of a knock on the door, my conscious state is intentional, because it makes reference to something beyond itself, the knock on the door. If I am conscious of a pain, the pain is not intentional, because it does not represent anything beyond itself.[21]

But 'I am conscious of a pain' can mean at least three things. First, if being conscious of a pain means that one is aware of being in a pain-state, then it is a higher-order awareness of another mental state, and is as intentional as any other higher-order mental state (its content may be: *I am in pain*). Second, if being conscious of a pain is being aware of a pain-object, then the analogy with a knock on the door holds: the state can be as intentional as being conscious of a knock at the door. For the fact that the pain-object (if there is such a thing) is not itself intentional is no more relevant to the intentionality of the awareness of the pain-object than the non-intentional nature of the knock is relevant to the intentionality of the consciousness of the knock. And finally, being conscious of a pain may simply mean *being in pain*, which is in its nature a conscious state. But the intentionality of this is precisely what is at issue. So how should the question be settled?[22]

---

[21] Searle, *The Rediscovery of the Mind*, 84.

[22] Curiously, in a footnote to the above discussion, Searle qualifies his denial of the intentionality of pains: 'The sense of body location does have intentionality, because it refers to a

In s. 2 I outlined the two essential features of intentionality: directedness and aspectual shape. These features generate what I call the relational structure of intentionality: intentional states involve presentations of intentional objects with aspectual shape. The presentation of an object with an aspectual shape is what I call an intentional content. Subjects are related to intentional contents (e.g. propositions) by intentional modes (e.g. belief). The nature of an intentional state is given by giving its intentional mode and its content.

What are the intentional object, the mode, and the content in the case of bodily sensation? Take the example of a pain in one's ankle. The first thing to note is that this is a form of awareness; and it is not a 'mere' awareness, or 'bare awareness'. It is an awareness *of* one's ankle. It is for this reason that I say, *pace* Searle, that the ankle is the object of the state. Being in this state of pain is a matter of the ankle being presented to one in a certain way. In general, the intentional object of a state S is what is given in an answer to the question, 'what is your mind directed on when in S?'. For example, the correct answer to the question 'What is your belief directed on?' gives the intentional object of your belief. (Though a more idiomatic way of posing the question is to ask, 'What is your belief about?') Now pains are not naturally said to be 'about' things; instead of asking 'What is your pain about?' we ask 'What hurts?' or 'Where does it hurt?', and I am claiming that the answer gives the intentional object of a pain: my leg, my arm, etc. That there is a relational structure here is shown by the fact that there is a distinction between the subject of the experience and the object or region that hurts; that there is an intentional object is shown by the fact that the subject's mind is directed on that object. And as with other intentional objects, there are cases where the intentional object of a sensation does not exist; for example, in phantom limb cases.

The intentional object of the pain—the ankle—is presented to the mind in a certain way. One's ankle is a part of one's foot, it is made up of bones and muscle, but it may not be presented as such in the state of pain. One may have a pain in one's liver, but not have any idea that the liver is where the pain is— one could have a pain that one can only identify as being 'over here' without even knowing that one has a liver. Thus bodily sensations exhibit aspectual shape: their objects are presented in certain ways, to the exclusion of other ways. And the content of a sensation-state is a matter of its object being presented in a certain way. This content need not be propositional.

A full account of this phenomenon would have to probe more deeply into the relationship between the experience of one's body in sensation, in kinaesthesia and proprioception, and the awareness of one's body as a unique and

portion of the body. This aspect of pains is intentional, because it has conditions of satisfaction. In the case of a phantom limb, for example, one can be mistaken, and the possibility of a mistake is at least a good clue that the phenomenon is intentional.' *The Rediscovery of the Mind*, 251 n. 1.

unified object of one's bodily awareness. The account would also have to link bodily awareness with one's sense of one's body in agency. I am not able to give such an account here; but I mark the need for further investigation.

This is all I shall say for the time being about the directedness and aspectual shape of bodily sensations. What about the concept of an intentional mode—how does this apply to sensations? This is a question on which different intentionalist theories differ, so we must leave it until we come to discuss these theories in s. 5. Here I believe I have argued for three things: first, that even non-intentionalists must accept the coherence of purely intentional conscious states; second, that all bodily sensations involve a felt bodily location; and third, that this can be understood as a form of intentionality, as that idea was introduced in s. 2.

4. Weak Intentionalism

Suppose the foregoing points are accepted. And suppose, for the sake of argument, that intentionalist accounts of other mental phenomena, such as moods and so-called 'undirected' emotions, are accepted. (I shall not discuss these phenomena in this chapter.) Then even if one accepted all this, one could still accept that certain mental states have qualia, in addition to their intentional properties. This is the view I call 'weak intentionalism'.

Weak intentionalism says that all mental states are intentional, but that some have non-intentional conscious properties: qualia. The weak intentionalist holds that qualia are higher-order properties of states of mind. And since states are normally understood as instances of properties, qualia are properties of properties. Another way to express weak intentionalism is to say that the intentional nature of certain conscious states does not exhaust their conscious or phenomenal character; two experiences could share their intentional nature and differ in their phenomenal character. Yet another way to express the view is: not every phenomenal or conscious difference in states of mind is an intentional (or a representational) difference. One could be a weak intentionalist about all mental states, or one could apply the view only to particular kinds of mental states: one could say, for instance, that all perceptual experiences have intentional content, and that they also have qualia, but this is not true of beliefs.

Weak intentionalism about perceptual experience is a popular view; it has been defended by Block, Loar, Peacocke, and Shoemaker among others.[23] The

---

[23] See Ned Block, 'Inverted Earth', in Block, Flanagan, and Güzeldere (eds.), *The Nature of Consciousness*; Brian Loar, 'Transparent Experience and the Availability of Qualia' (this volume); Christopher Peacocke, *Sense and Content* (Oxford: Oxford University Press, 1983), ch. 1; Sydney Shoemaker, 'Qualities and Qualia: What's in the Mind?' *Philosophy and Phenomenological Research*, 50 (1990), 109–31.

view is normally defended by describing ways in which the phenomenal character of an experience can change even if the representational content does not (e.g. the inverted spectrum) or cases where the phenomenal character remains the same across changes in representational content (e.g. Block's 'inverted earth'). I do not find these arguments convincing in the case of visual experience; my sympathies are with those who defend a strong intentionalist conception of visual experience by drawing attention to the phenomenon that has come to be known as the 'transparency' of experience.[24] Here my concern is with bodily sensation, since I am taking bodily sensations as one of the main sources of resistance to an intentionalist theory of mind, regardless of what happens to theories of perception. But I will talk for convenience about 'weak intentionalism' as if it were a view about all mental states. (Conceivably someone could agree with me about sensation but none the less hold that some mental states are 'pure' qualia; such a person should understand my term 'weak intentionalism' as meaning 'weak intentionalism about sensation'.)

Since there are not many existing weak intentionalist accounts of sensation, I shall describe a weak intentionalist view of sensation drawing on the weak intentionalist views of perceptual experience just mentioned. On this view, having a pain is an intentional state, for the reasons given in s. 3: it is an awareness of something happening in a part or region of your body. That part or region is the intentional object of the state. But this is not the whole story about the consciousness involved in pain. For there are also qualia that are characteristic of the feeling of pain. Thus, the conscious nature of the sensation-experience is determined by two things: the part of the body the experience presents as its object, and the qualia. We can illustrate this by considering two pains, one in the right ankle and one in the left, which are felt to be in different places and yet in some sense feel the same. The sense in which they feel the same is given by the qualia that the pain-states share. The sense in which they feel different is given by their intentional objects. (I assume here that the location of the sensation is part of how the sensation-state feels, for the reasons given in s. 3.) The view therefore locates the consciousness involved in bodily sensations in two places: in the relation to the body part, and in the intrinsic non-intentional qualia.

What are these non-intentional qualia properties of? The natural answer is that they are apparent properties of the part of the body that hurts. But if we

---

[24] See Gilbert Harman, 'The Intrinsic Quality of Experience', in J. Tomberlin (ed.), *Philosophical Perspectives*, 4 (Northridge, Calif.: Ridgeview, 1990); Michael Tye, 'Visual Qualia and Visual Content', in Tim Crane (ed.), *The Contents of Experience* (Cambridge: Cambridge University Press, 1992). Loar (this volume) argues for the unusual position that the existence of qualia is compatible with the facts about transparency. For an illuminating general discussion of transparency, see M. G. F. Martin, 'The Transparency of Experience', forthcoming.

are to maintain the parallel with the weak intentionalist theory of perception, this cannot be the right answer. In the case of perception, colour-qualia are supposed to be properties of states of mind, not properties of the coloured objects (physical objects do not have qualia, on the normal understanding of qualia). So pain-qualia, construed on the same model, are also properties of mental states: the naggingness of a toothache is a property of the tooth-ache, while the toothache itself is a (partly intentional) state of a conscious subject. A non-intentionalist, by contrast, holds that certain conscious mental states (call them 'pure qualia') have no intentionality at all. So if it is to distinguish itself from non-intentionalism, weak intentionalism must deny that there can be pure qualia: qualia cannot be instantiated *except* as proper-ties of properties: i.e. intentional state types. If qualia were properties of body parts, then they would not be properties of properties. But they must be properties *of properties*, because otherwise there could be instantiations of pure qualia.

I will assume then that according to weak intentionalism, the qualia involved in pain are properties of the intentional state of being in pain, just as putative colour qualia are properties of the perceptual experiences of seeing objects. And I will assume that these properties are instantiated only when the intentional state is instantiated. (If one thought that 'zombies' in David Chalmers's sense were impossible, then one might add 'when and' to the 'only when'.) But is this thesis plausible?

The difficulty with the theory is phenomenological: it derives from the unclarity of what it is to be 'aware of an intrinsic property of a state of mind'. Certainly being aware of a pain in my ankle is not like being aware of a knock at the door. The pain in my ankle seems to be a part of me, and it seems to be the *ankle* which is hurting me. It is not as if I am aware of the location of my ankle, and (in addition to this) I feel that *my being so aware* has a quale. To make sense of this, we have to make sense of the possibility of separating out, in thought, the quale from the intentional awareness. But this requires we can make real sense of pure qualia; and this is denied by the theory. The inten-tionality and the phenomenal character of the pain just do not seem to be separable in this way.

The essence of the objection is this: in a state of pain (in the ankle, say) there do not seem to be two things going on—the intentional awareness of the ankle, and the awareness of the pain-quale. Rather, the awareness of the ankle seems to be *ipso facto* awareness of its hurting. The hurting seems to be in the ankle. How the ankle feels seems to be a property of the ankle. It does not seem to be an intrinsic property of the intentional awareness of the ankle.[25] In

---

[25] This is a point well made by Tye, 'A Representational Theory of Pains and their Phenom-enal nature' in Block, Flanagan, and Güzeldere (eds.), *The Nature of Consciousness*, 333.

this respect, the objection parallels the transparency objection to visual qualia: colours seem to be properties of objects, not intrinsic properties of experiences.

Of course, the idea that colour-qualia are properties of states of mind arises in part from a metaphysical resistance to the idea that things such as surfaces of inanimate objects can have certain sorts of properties.[26] The inverted spectrum shows (allegedly) that the qualitative nature of colours is in the mind, and we might want to say an analogous thing about pain-qualia: the qualia of pain can hardly be in the parts of the body where they are felt to be. But whatever the merits of this resistance, the theory is none the less supposed to save the appearances, the phenomena: for what is the point of a theory of consciousness that puts the phenomena in the wrong place? I propose that we put this theory to one side and see if the other intentionalist alternatives are preferable. Do strong intentionalist theories do any better?

5. Strong Intentionalist Theories of Sensation: Representationalism

These theories say that the conscious character of a sensation consists purely in that state's intentional features. There are three ways this can be understood. It can be understood as locating the conscious character of a mental state in features of the *intentional content* of the state; differences in conscious character must be differences in content. Second, the theory could locate the conscious character of a mental state in features of the *intentional mode*—the subject's relation to that content. And third, differences in content can consist in some combination of differences in content and differences in mode. This threefold distinction is just a result of the fact (outlined in s. 2) that intentional states can differ in their modes, their contents, or both.

Tye has recently advanced a theory of the first sort; this is his *representationalism*.[27] Tye claims that pain (for example) is a representation of damage to the body, or disturbance in the body. The conscious state is a representation of a certain state of affairs, and its phenomenal character is explained in terms of the state of affairs represented. The theory's treatment of pain, however, is not very convincing. It seems clear that there are many varieties of pain, not all of which the suffering subject would be aware of as representing *damage* to the body. Tye responds to this objection that the subject need not possess the concept of damage to the body in order to be in

---

[26] For a hypothesis about how qualia came to be thought of as properties of states of mind, see my 'The Origins of Qualia', in Tim Crane and Sarah Patterson (eds.), *History of the Mind–Body Problem* (London: Routledge, 2000), ss. 4–5.

[27] Tye, *Ten Problems of Consciousness*, chs. 3–7.

pain: the representational content of pain is non-conceptual content. This may be so; but it seems to me that appealing to non-conceptual content puts the explanation of how pain seems beyond the facts that are open to mere phenomenological reflection; it builds in a complexity to the content of pain which, although it may be part of the content of unconscious representations in the subject's brain, is not part of what is *given to* the subject in cases of pain. This brings to the surface a problem with Tye's use of the notion of non-conceptual content, which I shall now explain.

The notion of non-conceptual content has been used in two ways. One way it has been used is to describe the phenomenologically available content of a person's conscious experience: for example, one might be aware of many different colours within one's present visual experience, without having concepts for all these determinate shades of colour. Some describe this as a case where the colours are represented by the non-conceptual content of the experience (or better: they are represented in a non-conceptual state of mind).[28] The other use of the idea of non-conceptual content is in connection with the content of informational states of the brain—say, states of the visual system. Here the idea is that a psychologist might attribute a representation to a state of the brain that has a complex, articulated content, without there being any requirement that the subject whose brain it is can have thoughts with this content. The first notion of non-conceptual content is phenomenological, the second belongs to 'subpersonal' theories of mental processing.[29]

As noted above, Tye considers the objection that someone who feels a pain need not be aware that there is damage occuring in their body, since 'such a proposal is too complicated to fit the phenomenology of pain experiences'. He responds that 'to feel a pain, one need not have the resources to conceptualise what the pain represents'.[30] The content of pain is non-conceptual. Which notion of non-conceptual content is Tye using? This presents a dilemma. If he is using the subpersonal notion of non-conceptual content, then the problem is that there is no requirement that the subpersonal states need enter the subject's awareness at all. So the feature Tye appealed to in order to explain the consciousness of pain (representational content) is now being articulated in terms that deny the need for awareness at all. Tye has explained consciousness in terms of the idea of non-conceptual representational content, an idea that (it is agreed on all sides) has no essential connection to consciousness.[31] Tye's

[28] See Gareth Evans, *The Varieties of Reference* (Oxford: Oxford University Press, 1982), 229. For the distinction between non-conceptual content and non-conceptual states, see Tim Crane, 'Non-conceptual Content', in E. J. Craig (ed.), *Encyclopedia of Philosophy*.

[29] For an excellent discussion of this issue, see Martin Davies, 'Externalism and Experience' in Block, Flanagan, and Güzeldere (eds.), *The Nature of Consciousness*, 309–11.

[30] Tye, 'A Representational Theory of Pains and their Phenomenal Character', ibid. 333.

[31] Here I am indebted to discussions with Fiona McPherson.

opponent can accept that there is non-conceptual subpersonal representation of damage to the body, while still consistently holding that there are qualia that are responsible for the conscious phenomenal character of the state.

On the other hand, if Tye is appealing to the phenomenological notion of non-conceptual content, then he does need to say that the features represented enter into the subject's awareness. In the case of visual experience, the colours manifest themselves to the subject's awareness; one can be aware of things for which one has no concepts. So the subject must, contrary to what Tye says, be aware of tissue damage. Certainly, I am not saying that the subject has to think that there is tissue damage; this needs the concept of tissue damage. But the subject must be aware of it, on Tye's view, in the non-conceptual way. The original objection was not that one *could* not be aware of such things in a non-conceptual way, but that the characterization of the content seemed too complex to characterize the experience of pain.

My diagnosis of the difficulty here is that Tye is appealing to the subpersonal conception of non-conceptual content when responding to the objection that the subject need not be aware of damage, but appealing to the phenomenological conception when using the notion of non-conceptual content to explain consciousness. The latter conception is what he needs. But then he needs to say more about why we should regard the subjects as being (non-conceptually) aware of damage to their bodies. I think the trouble is that Tye has no resources except those of the idea of representation. To see how we might make progress if we used more resources, we should consider the other strong intentionalist alternative.

6. Strong Intentionalist Theories of Bodily Sensation: The Perceptual Theory

Tye's theory locates differences in the phenomenal or conscious character of a sensation in the representational content of the state alone; hence the complexity of the content. The alternative strong intentionalist view says that the phenomenal character of a state is fixed not just by the content, but by the content and the intentional mode. This is the third view I mentioned at the beginning of the previous section, and it is the view I want to defend. (The second view, that the phenomenal character of the state of mind is fixed purely by the mode, has little to be said for it: obviously, any plausible intentionalist view must allow that the intentional object and content contribute to phenomenal character.)

I call this theory the 'perceptual theory', since it treats bodily sensation as a form of perception, the perception of things going on in one's body. (The view derives from D. M. Armstrong.[32]) Consider first a strong intentionalist theory of perception, and what it would say about the phenomenal character of (say) visual experience. The phenomenal character of a visual experience of an aeroplane flying overhead is given by giving its content—the aeroplane, its shape and size, and so on—and by giving the experience's intentional mode: seeing. The phenomenal difference between seeing an aeroplane overhead and hearing one is partly a matter of the content—*what* is experienced—but also a matter of the mode of apprehending this content, the intentional mode in Searle's sense. Certain properties of objects (e.g. colours) can be apprehended only in certain modes, so cannot figure in the content of certain modes (one cannot smell colours). But others are not mode-specific: thus, for example, the difference between seeing shapes and feeling them is partly a matter of the intentional mode in question. According to a strong intentionalist theory of perception, the phenomenal character of a perception is fixed by two things: mode and content.

I say the same thing about bodily sensations. The consciousness involved in bodily sensations is a result of two things: the intentional content of the sensation, and the intentional mode. Consider a pain in one's ankle. I said that the ankle is the intentional object of the pain-state. Like the intentional objects of many outer perceptions (e.g. aeroplanes) the ankle need not itself be a conscious entity. In perception and in sensation, consciousness need not reside in the intentional objects of awareness in order for the state of awareness to be conscious. Fred Dretske puts this point well:

Just as a visual experience of a tree is an awareness of a nonconscious object (the tree) pain is an awareness of a nonconscious bodily condition (an injured, strained or diseased part) . . . pains, tickles and itches stand to physical states of the body (they are experiences of these physical states) the way olfactory, visual and auditory experiences stand to physical states of the environment. In all cases, the experiences are conscious, yes, but not because we are conscious of them, but because they make us conscious of the relevant states of our bodies.[33]

However, we are interested not just in objects of awareness, but in these objects as they are *apprehended under various aspects*—that is, in intentional content. The intentional content of a pain might be something like this: *my ankle hurts*. (This makes the content propositional for simplicity; but remember that I am not committed to all content being propositional.) But we have not fully specified the phenomenal character of this state until we have said in which intentional mode it is presented. Compare: we have not fully specified

[32] See D. M. Armstrong, *Bodily Sensations*; and his *A Materialist Theory of the Mind* (London: Routledge & Kegan Paul, 1968), ch. 14.

[33] Fred Dretske, *Naturalizing the Mind* (Cambridge: Mass.: MIT Press, 1995), 102–3.

the phenomenal character of a perception of an aeroplane overhead until we have said whether the aeroplane is seen or heard.

What is the nature of the mode, in the case of pain? At the very least, it must be that the ankle is *felt*: the content is the content of a feeling, one must feel that one's ankle hurts. Pressing the analogy with perception, we can say that pain is a kind of feeling, just as seeing is a kind of perceiving. There are of course many other kinds of bodily feeling: each of these ways in which one can feel one's body are the intentional modes which have parts of the body as their intentional objects.[34] We can capture the spirit of this view by saying that there is a way in which English misleads when we say that Vladimir has a pain in his ankle, as if the pain were a kind of object he had in his ankle. Rather we might say that Vladimir *pains* his ankle, where *paining* is a relation between the ankle and Vladimir. (This is not suggested as a piece of semantic analysis, but rather as an attempt to make the view vivid. But it is worth pointing out that not all languages talk of pains as if they were objects.)

This presents pain as a kind of relation between oneself and one's body. Given the problems with treating intentionality as a relation to existent intentional objects (s. 2), this cannot be quite right; but we will return to this problem shortly. For there is a more immediate problem with the suggestion: how can it accommodate the fact, which we raised as a problem for weak intentionalism, that pain seems to be *in* the part of the body, that it seems to be a property of the body? When we attend to our pains, as I said in s. 3, we attend to the part of the body in which we feel the pain. This is analogous to the so-called 'transparency' of visual experience: if we want to attend to our visual experiences, what we normally do is to inspect the objects of the experience. (In a slogan: introspection is inspection.) The fact that there is this analogy is good for my perceptual theory; but the fact that attending to the pain is attending to the part that hurts does not seem to be so good. For haven't I said that pain is a way of being aware of one's ankle, and therefore something more like a relation and not a property?

In fact, there is not a problem here, and the transparency analogy does hold up. The way to understand the transparency of sensation is to understand the special nature of the concepts that we apply when we talk and think about our pains. The content of a pain in one's ankle might naturally be put into words as 'my ankle hurts'. On the face of it, this sentence seems to be saying that there is a property of hurting that my ankle has. But on reflection, it is clear that the concept of *hurting* is covertly relational. Something cannot hurt

---

[34] It might be objected, as it was to me by Jerry Levinson, that this proliferates modes unnecessarily. However, the same kind of objection could be raised against a theory that explained differences in consciousness in terms of differences in qualia: there would be very many distinct qualia properties postulated. It is not clear why this should be a problem for either view.

unless it hurts someone; in fact, a part of one's own body cannot hurt unless it hurts *oneself*. We can make no real sense of the idea that a part of one's own body might hurt, without its hurting oneself. Hurting is therefore not just a matter of a part of one's body having an intrinsic property, but rather a matter of that body part and its properties apparently affecting oneself. So what one is attributing to one's ankle when one says that it hurts is something that has what I called in s. 2 a 'relational structure': the content of the sensation is that one's ankle hurts, the object of the sensation is the ankle (apprehended *as* one's ankle) and the mode is the hurting. This relies on the idea that the part of one's body that hurts is *doing something* to oneself, that there is something about the body part that is responsible for one's feeling in this way. Peacocke has plausibly claimed that this is part of the concept of pain: 'To have the concept of pain is to have the concept of a state which allows its possessor to discriminate those (nonpsychological) properties whose possession by a part of his body makes that part hurt him.'[35] This expresses two of the important phenomenological claims about pain for which I have been trying to argue in this section so far: first, that hurting is a matter of a part of the body hurting the subject. This is why I call it an intentional mode. Second, pain presents body parts in a way that the subject can (normally) discriminate them: normal sensations allow the subject to locate the pain, however roughly.

This is close to, but importantly different from, Tye's view that pain represents damage to a part of the body. It differs in two ways, one specific to the claims about pain, the other more general and theoretical. I claimed that damage need not enter into the content of the pain-experience; all that need enter into the content is the part of the body (with a certain aspectual shape) that is hurting. The perceptual theory can agree with Tye that damage to one's body can be represented by a pain experience in the sense that (e.g.) the stimulation of the retina is represented by a visual experience. But this is non-conceptual representation in the subpersonal sense, and this is not our subject here. These disagreements with Tye relate to his specific claims about pain. The more general theoretical difference is that for Tye, differences in conscious states are wholly explained in terms of the representational content of the state. In the case of bodily sensation, the intentional mode is the same in different states: it is *representing*. A pain represents damage, a tickle represents a mild disturbance, orgasm is a 'sensory representation of certain physical changes in the genital region'—and so on.[36] The perceptual view, by

---

[35] Christopher Peacocke, 'Consciousness and Other Minds', *Proceedings of the Aristotelian Society*, Suppl vol. 48 (1984), 115. I am indebted in this paragraph to Peacocke's discussion of the concepts of pain and hurting, though I do not mean to imply that Peacocke holds a perceptual theory of sensation in my sense of the term.

[36] For these views, see Tye, *Ten Problems of Consciousness*, 113, 117, 118.

contrast, does not locate the conscious differences solely in differences in what is represented, but also in the different modes in which one is related to what is represented.

The experience of pain is 'transparent' because to pay attention to a pain is to pay attention to the place that hurts. But one cannot pay attention to the place that hurts without paying attention to the hurting, and the hurting, I have claimed, is the *way* the body part or location is (so to speak) forcing itself into one's consciousness. Therefore, in being aware that one's ankle hurts, one is aware that it is hurting oneself. This is why I say that according to the perceptual theory, the phenomenal character of the pain is given by two things: the content of the experience and the intentional mode.

What is novel about this view is that it locates the phenomenal character of the state partly in the intentional mode. It might be objected that I am simply assuming the phenomenal, stipulating it into existence by my claim that some intentional modes are conscious and some are not. This objection is confused. Of course I am assuming that some mental states have phenomenal character and some do not. But so do those who talk in terms of qualia. Rather than assuming that certain intentional states are by their nature conscious, they assume that there are certain non-intentional properties that are by their nature conscious. If I assume consciousness, so do my opponents. But we have no alternative, since there are no prospects for anything like a *definition* of consciousness in other terms. (Whether this worries you depends on your attitude to physicalism; some remarks on this in s. 7.)

Finally, I need to return to the question of how, on this view, one can have a pain in one's ankle even if one does not have an ankle. The account of the relational structure of intentionality described in s. 2 makes intentionality a relation, not to an actually existing object, but to an intentional content. One part of the point of the idea of content is to express or capture the aspect under which the object of the intentional state is presented; the other part is to distinguish different states in the same mode. And these can be distinguished even when the intentional object does not exist. This is why we cannot say in general that intentional states are relations to intentional objects. As noted in s. 3, phantom limbs show that someone can feel a pain in a part of their body even when this part does not exist. So an intentionalist cannot say that pain is a relation to a body part. Rather, pain is a relation to an intentional content, where the intentional content is the way things seem to the subject. It seems to the subject that they have a limb, and this is compatible with them knowing that the limb does not exist.

It could be said that pain is always a relation to the intentional object, but the intentional object is the *cause* of the pain in the body or brain. But this would break the connection between the idea of an intentional object and the phenomenology, the idea of how things seem to the subject. What the perceptual theory is trying to capture is how things seem. The cause of the sensation in the body may be another matter.

So it can be true, then, that someone can feel a pain in their foot even when they have no foot. And this is compatible with its being appropriate to tell someone 'it's not your foot that hurts, there's no such thing; it's an effect of the amputation'. Compare: it could be true that someone thinks that fate is against them, and this is compatible with its being appropriate to tell them 'it's not fate, there's no such thing; it's just bad luck'. The cases are, in the relevant respects, parallel.

7. Conclusion

I have argued for the perceptual theory of the kind of consciousness involved in sensation in a somewhat indirect way. My general aim, as I said in s. 1, is to dispute the simple division of states of mind into intentional states and qualitative states: this is the essence of the division assumed by non-intentionalism. The best case for this division is often claimed to be the case of bodily sensation. But, I argued, bodily sensations do exhibit the marks of intentionality, specifically in the felt location of sensation. The question then is whether such states of mind also have non-intentional properties (qualia). Weak intentionalism says they do. I claimed that this view is unstable, tending to collapse back into non-intentionalism. If we want to maintain an intentionalist position, then we should adopt strong intentionalism. Having set the rival view (representationalism) to one side, we end up with the perceptual theory. It turns out that, from a phenomenological point of view, this theory is not as strange as it might first seem.

At the beginning of this chapter I asked whether there is anything we can learn from the (admittedly false) naïve view that pain is not a mental state. If an intentional theory of bodily sensation is correct, then we can see why it is so natural to think of pain as a physical state: since it is essential to pain that it feels to be in one's body. But none the less, it is a mental state, because it involves the characteristic mark of the mental: the intentional directedness of the mind upon an object. As Armstrong puts it:

This account of the location of pain enables us to resolve a troublesome dilemma. Consider the following two statements: 'The pain is in my hand' and 'The pain is in my mind'. Ordinary usage makes us want to assent to the first, while a moment's philosophical reflection makes us want to assent to the second. Yet they seem to be in conflict with each other. But once we see that the location of the pain in the hand is an intentional location... it is clear that the two statements are perfectly compatible.[37]

[37] Armstrong, *A Materialist Theory of the Mind*, 316.

This seems to me exactly right, apart from the suggestion that an 'intentional location' is a kind of location, or way of being located. An intentional location is, in this case, simply the felt location of sensation. It is this essential feature of bodily sensation that nourishes an intentional conception of sensation, and therefore the intentionalist conception of the mind.

The perceptual theory of bodily sensation is supposed to be a phenomeno-logical theory, a systematic account or a general description of what it is like to have a certain kind of experience. As such, it does not solve some of the problems that some accounts of consciousness address. The theory is silent on the explanatory gap, it leaves the knowledge argument where it is, and it says nothing about how there can be a physicalist reduction of consciousness. But these are not the only questions about consciousness. There is also another traditional philosophical project: that of 'understanding how different types or aspects of consciousness feature in the fundamental notions of mentality, agency and personhood', as Tyler Burge puts it. Burge continues, 'such understanding will be deepened when it is liberated from ideological and programmatic preoccupations with materialism and functionalism that have dominated the revival of philosophical interest in consciousness'.[38] The view defended in this chapter is put forward as part of an attempt at such an understanding.

[38] Tyler Burge, 'Two Kinds of Consciousness' in Block, Flanagan, and Güzeldere (eds.), *The Nature of Consciousness*, 433.

3. Experience and Representation

JOSEPH LEVINE

1. Qualia, or phenomenal properties of experience, pose a deep and persistent problem for Materialism. Consider the particular throbbing character of a pain in one's toe after stubbing it, or the way a gleaming red fire engine looks in the sunlight. In both cases there is a strong intuition that we are enjoying experiences—conscious, mental states—which can be typed by their qualitative character: the throbbing of the pain or the reddish character of the visual experience. In this sense the qualitative character of an experience, a quale, is a property of the experience. The question then immediately arises: what sort of property is this?

In particular, we might begin by wondering whether qualia, if they are properties of experiences, are intrinsic properties of those experiences. At first blush they seem to be. But if we accept this we have a problem. Assuming we are materialists, and assuming that it is our brains that house our experiences, all properties of experiences must be properties of the brain, or of states of the brain. If we claim that qualia are intrinsic properties of experiences, then they must be intrinsic properties of brain states. But which ones? Well, presumably, the best candidates are those that are coinstantiated with qualia. That is, one has to find out through probing the brain which of its neurophysiological properties are instantiated when one is having a throbbing pain in the toe, or a visual sensation of bright red, and then identify these qualia with their neurophysiological correlates. To have a throbbing pain in the toe is just to have these neurons fire in this way.

Once put this starkly the problem is evident. While many philosophers resist this sort of identity theory because they believe in the possibility of multiple realization—the idea that creatures quite different in their physical constitution could share qualitative experiences—it seems to me that the implausibility of the view goes deeper than that. There is something just utterly arbitrary about the idea that these neurons firing in this way should constitute a toe-throbbing, and these others a reddish visual experience. In fact, it is precisely because of the arbitrary and unmotivated character of the identification of the quale with its neurophysiological correlate that multiple realization itself seems so plausible in the first place.

As soon as one thinks about what really is significant about these particular neurons firing in this particular way it becomes clear that it isn't anything about their intrinsic properties. Rather, their significance derives from their location in a system of neurons, and the significance of their firing as they do derives from the relations that hold between their firing that way and other neurons firing as they do, and ultimately to the way all the neural firings connect to stimuli and responses. After all, what else could it be? Thus the natural way to understand the connection between the neurophysiological properties and the mental properties is just as those who point to multiple realization would have it: the neurophysiological properties *realize* the qualia. On this view, then, qualia are role-properties; roles that are implemented in us by our brain states.

The view that qualia are roles overcomes the problem of the apparently arbitrary connection between an experience's qualitative character and its neurophysiological correlate, since the relation between a role and its imple-menter is far from arbitrary. The problem on this side of the coin is that it is very hard to see how qualia can be identified with role-properties. There is a clear intrinsic 'feel' to them, and thought experiments involving qualia inversions give expression to this deep intuition. After all, what is supposed to be the role with which I identify the throbbing character of my pain in the toe when I stub it? Certainly it is associated with various dispositions, such as the disposition to hop around holding the toe, to swear loudly, not to pay attention to other matters, etc. Also, it is clearly a property I am disposed to instantiate when my toe is stubbed, and certainly it maintains various dispositional relations to other mental states I am prone to occupy. Nevertheless, it is a long way from the obvious claim that throbbing pains-in-the-toe bring in their trail all sorts of dispositions to the claim that they just are a particular bundle of dispositions. As I say, there is too strong an intrinsic 'feel' to them for such a claim to command intuitive assent.

I am not going to argue further against the role view of qualia, since this is not my target here. I bring it up mainly to motivate another view, one that's called 'intentionalism', or 'representationalism'. On this view, qualia are not to be identified either with functional roles or with their internal, neurophysio-logical implementers. Rather, qualia are the intentional contents of sensory states. The qualitative character of a sensation is the property that sensation represents its intentional object as having. On this view, then, the sorts of dispositions mentioned above with which a throbbing pain-in-the-toe is normally associated turn out to be, as one would have thought, only contin-gently related to the sensation itself. On the other hand, the connection between the sensation's qualitative character and its neurophysiological implementation is also contingent, since presumably intentional content is possessed only contingently by the representational vehicles bearing that content.

There are of course many versions of intentionalism, and different ways to categorize them. For my purposes the following two divisions are significant: between wide and narrow, and between external and internal. Wide intentionalism is the doctrine that qualitative character is to be identified with wide intentional content, whatever that turns out to be. Obviously, then, narrow intentionalism is the doctrine that it is narrow content with which we identify qualitative character. For the most part I will only be concerned with wide intentionalism, but I will have something to say about the narrow version. Most adherents of wide intentionalism are also externalists, in the sense that the wide contents they attribute to qualitative experiences are the relevant physical properties of the distal objects of perception. But it is possible to be a wide intentionalist and also an internalist, as will be discussed below. Until further notice, however, read 'intentionalism' in what follows as wide externalist intentionalism.[1]

Now intentionalism, of course, does not vindicate the intuition that qualia are intrinsic properties of experiences. Depending on how one interprets the thesis, they are either relational properties of experiences or intrinsic properties of external objects. So, suppose my mental state, R, is the visual experience I'm having while looking at a red fire engine. On one way of understanding the intentionalist thesis, the qualitative character of R is identical to R's representing the redness of the fire engine. Thus it is a property of R all right, but not an intrinsic one, since representing what it represents is not an intrinsic property of a symbol. On another way of understanding the intentionalist thesis, however, the qualitative character of the experience just is the redness of the fire engine. If, for argument's sake, we allow that redness is itself an intrinsic property of the fire engine, then the qualitative character of the experience turns out to be intrinsic after all; however, it also turns out not really to be a property of the experience.[2] Either way, then, the intentionalist is committed to some deviation from the intuitive starting

---

[1] Defenders of wide externalist intentionalism include Dretske (1995), Lycan (1996), and Tye (1995, 1998). Rey (1996, 1998) defends narrow intentionalism. I'm not sure if anyone defends wide internalist intentionalism, but Byrne (2001) presents it as an option, as will be discussed below.

[2] Does anyone actually hold this version of the view? That's a good question. The philosopher whose presentation of representationalism comes closest to expressing it this way is Dretske; he really does seem to want qualia to be properties of objects, not of our mental states. On the other hand, in discussion he has admitted that it's hard to reconcile this version of the view with phenomena such as hallucinations. He doesn't want to say that there's no qualitative character if it turns out there's no object. At any rate, the difference between the two versions will not matter for what follows.

point. Nevertheless, the fact that an apparently intrinsic property is involved—the redness of the fire engine—does seem to allow the intentionalist to accommodate intuition to an important extent.

There are two other significant virtues of intentionalism. First, it unifies our conception of the mind. Many philosophers follow Brentano in identifying intentionality as the 'mark of the mental'. Yet it is a standard feature of most discussions of the mind–body problem to say that there are two fundamental phenomena that define mentality: intentionality and consciousness. It would obviously be more satisfying, and lead to a more thorough understanding of the mind, if it could be shown that consciousness is in some way reducible to intentionality. Identifying qualia with the intentional contents of sensory states would clearly go a long way towards realizing that hoped-for reduction.

Second, there is independent reason to think that qualitative character and intentional content are not totally separable. As Charles Siewert (1998) has argued convincingly, in at least many cases it is hard to make sense out of the idea that two states could share qualitative character yet differ in their intentional contents.[3] For instance, consider what it's like to perceive a rectangular shape. Could it be just like what that's like, and yet one is representing the shape as circular? That seems almost impossible to conceive. Well, if qualitative character, what it's like, were just a matter of what one's visual experience was representing, then we would have a straightforward explanation for why such a situation was inconceivable.

Despite its virtues, I think intentionalism, at least in its wide externalist form, is untenable. In s. 2 I will show why. In the course of doing so I will discuss in some detail a recent defence of the doctrine by Michael Tye. In s. 3 I will take up again some of the reasons for thinking some version of intentionalism must be right, and see if any version can escape the argument of s. 2 and also meet certain other plausible constraints.

2. Though intentionalism is not subject to certain problems with inversion scenarios that plague functionalism, there are still some thought experiments, and some involving inversions, that undermine the view's plausibility. Intentionalism can escape the inversion objections that involve switching internal roles, since qualitative character, on this view, is independent of a state's internal causal role (at least to a large extent). But so long as we can coherently imagine switching external roles, as it were, intentionalism will conflict with intuition. So, for instance, take Ned Block's (1990) example, 'Inverted Earth'. On Inverted Earth all the colours are inverted with respect to colours on

---

[3] Siewert goes much further and claims that for any phenomenally conscious state it is impossible for another state to share its phenomenal character but differ with respect to what it represents. I discuss his view in Levine (2001b).

Earth. We are then asked to imagine that a traveller from Earth, call her Janet, with inverting lenses implanted in her eyes, goes to Inverted Earth to live. To Janet, given the two inversions that cancel each other out, everything would look normal. Yet, the argument goes, since her internal states would co-vary with the complements of the colours with which they co-varied on Earth, their intentional contents would eventually change. On the intentionalist view, then, Janet's qualia should change too; but this seems absurd, since she notices no change in her qualia.

One serious problem with the example lies in its reliance on the claim that the intentional contents of Janet's visual experiences would shift as a result of her sojourn on Inverted Earth. Of course one can make a case that the contents would shift after enough time, but then again one can also make a case that they wouldn't. In particular, one might appeal to the evolutionary history of Janet's perceptual mechanisms, maintaining that the contents of her visual qualia are fixed by the properties with which they co-varied in the conditions under which they were selected. Thus the intentionalist can escape the consequence that Janet's qualia have changed without her knowledge.

The underlying intuition that Block's example is meant to express is that how things seem to us—what it's like for us—cannot be a matter of how things are outside us. This is not to deny that how things are outside us can cause things to seem a certain way; obviously it's normally because I am exposed to light of a certain sort that I seem to see something red. Rather, the point is that how it is with me experientially cannot be *constituted* by how things are outside my mind. (I say 'my mind' here to allow for the possibility that, for all I know, the core realizers of my mental states might extend beyond my body. I doubt it, but that's an empirical question.)

We can avoid the escape hatch in Block's example by imagining that Inverted Earth is also like Twin Earth. It contains molecule-for-molecule duplicates of ourselves, except for one difference. Our twins evolved with inverting lenses. Thus when Twin-Joe looks at a fire engine, which on Inverted Twin Earth is green, his brain states will be identical to mine when I look at a fire engine, which on Earth is red. In this case it is hard to see how to avoid the consequence that Twin-Joe's visual state has the content that the fire engine is green while mine has the content that the fire engine is red. The intentionalist then has to say that, despite our internal similarity, our experiences have quite different qualitative character.

The problem with this version of the example, however, is that the intentionalist is quite willing to endorse the claim that the twins are having experiences of different qualitative character. According to the intentionalist, just as we are willing to attribute propositional attitudes with different contents to two molecularly identical twins in the original Twin Earth case, so too should we be willing to attribute sensory experiences with different qualia to the twins in the Inverted Twin Earth case. Why, they ask, should we treat the cases differently?[4]

In a recent discussion of this issue Michael Tye (1998), a defender of intentionalism, notes that the standard reply to the intrasubjective version of the Inverted Earth argument, one he himself gave in Tye (1995), isn't adequate. Remember that the intentionalist reply to Block's original case was to say that the intentional contents of Janet's visual experiences wouldn't change as a result of her sojourn on Inverted Earth because intentional content is fixed by reference to the environment in which the relevant perceptual mechanisms are selected. The problem with this reply is that it doesn't deal with the case of Swampman moving to Inverted Earth.

Swampman, as you may remember, is Davidson's (1987) creature who spontaneously coalesces out of swamp gas into a molecular duplicate of a normal man. It certainly seems that such a creature would have qualitative experiences of a determinate type—it would have reddish experiences when looking at a red fire engine—yet, since it/he was not the product of selection, on the view we just presented it appears his visual states would lack intentional content. But if there's no intentional content then there's no qualitative content, and that contradicts our initial assumption.

Initially one might try adopting a split theory: let selectional environment determine content for those creatures having a selectional history and let synchronic causal co-variation determine content for those without such a history. This way Swampman gets to have qualitative experiences. However, we then have a problem with Swampman when he travels to Inverted Earth. We can now run Block's original argument on Swampman and we can't say in reply that the intentional contents of his visual states don't change as a result of the move. So now what?

Before turning to the solution Tye proposes, I want to pause to consider more closely the basis of the strong intuitions that drive the objections to (the externalist version of) intentionalism. As I've argued elsewhere (Levine 1998), I think the matter ultimately comes down to the question of self-knowledge. The problem of self-knowledge can be put this way. I know what it's like for me right now as I visually experience the world around me. In particular, I know what it's like for me to see colours. However, if intentionalism is correct, and if the intentional contents of my colour experiences are identified with the surface properties of distal objects, then it seems I couldn't really know how it is with me without knowing about these surface properties. But this seems absurd. Looking back at Block's Inverted Earth argument, we can see a similar appeal to self-knowledge at work. Why, after all, is it supposed to

---

[4] Dretske (1995) explicitly makes the argument that a consistent externalist about propositional attitude content should endorse externalism about qualitative character.

be so absurd to think that Janet's qualia have changed without her noticing? Well, because what it's like for her is precisely the sort of thing to which she has privileged access. A radical change of visual qualia is something she would know about.

As soon as we bring up the question of self-knowledge, however, the intentionalist can reply as follows. According to widely accepted theories of the contents of thoughts and beliefs, these contents are (at least partly) determined by the natures of the external objects with which we causally interact. The point of Twin Earth is to demonstrate that I and Twin-Joe have thoughts with different contents—with different truth conditions—when we think about our respective samples of the local colourless, odourless liquid. Now some have indeed objected that on this theory of content we cannot account for our apparent ability to know the contents of our own thoughts— to know, as one might put it, what we are thinking. The point is this: if one isn't bothered by this consequence for thought, then why does it matter so much for qualia? Don't we have as much good reason to believe that we know what we're thinking as we have to believe that we know what it's like for us to see red?[5]

There is of course an extensive literature on the topic of externalism and self-knowledge. For present purposes, I want to focus on one line of argument in particular, owed to Burge (1988), to the effect that there is no conflict between an externalist theory of content and self-knowledge. Though he doesn't present it this way, I think Tye's response to Block's Inverted Earth argument can best be seen as an application of the Burgean strategy.

Actually, one can run the Burgean argument two ways.[6] The first goes like this: all states of knowledge, including introspective knowledge, are them-selves propositional attitude states. As such, they have canonical linguistic expressions. (If one adheres to a 'language of thought' model, then they are literally embodied in functional relations to linguistic tokens.) So, in a typical instance of introspecting one's own thought, say about water, we would have two thoughts: first, the thought 'there's some water in the glass in front of me', and second, the thought 'I'm now thinking about the water in the glass in front of me', or something of that sort. The second thought expresses my state of self-knowledge, and it counts as knowledge just in case it is true and also meets whatever reliability and justification conditions are required for knowledge. What's crucial, however, is that since the expression of my self-knowledge uses the very same term 'water' as is used by the thought that is the object of that knowledge, there is no problem from externalist considerations. After all, when introspecting about my water thoughts I don't think about

---

[5] Again, Dretske (1995) makes just this argument.
[6] See Gertler (2001) for an interesting discussion of the various ways of interpreting the Burgean strategy.

H_2O and XYZ, at least not under those descriptions, but about water. Whatever 'water' refers to in the object thought, it also refers to in the meta-thought, the expression of self-knowledge.

On the second interpretation, which is arguably closer to what Burge had in mind, the relation between the object thought and the introspective thought about it is much closer than identity of vocabulary. Rather, the idea is that the introspective thought actually embeds the object thought—the latter, as a token entity (state, event, or whatever) actually constitutes a proper part of the former. When I'm aware of thinking about water there are not two tokens of my representation of water—one in the original thought and the other in the introspective awareness of the original—but rather there is one thought about water and some sort of demonstrative attention mechanism trained on it. That is, I use the very thought token to represent itself as the object of my awareness of it. On this view, where there is only one token of 'water' involved in my awareness of myself as thinking about water, there is even less room for slippage, and thus even less room for externalist worries to undermine self-knowledge.

Let us apply this model now to the case of qualia. I'm looking at a red fire engine, and thus having a reddish visual sensation. I'm also currently aware of the reddish character of my visual sensation. The worry is that if intentionalism is correct and my visual sensation's being reddish depends on its representing red, a particular property of the surfaces of physical objects, then I won't be able, from the inside, to know the qualitative character of my experience. The reply then is to invoke either the embedding relation or the same vocabulary relation. My awareness of what it's like for me now as I gaze upon the red fire engine is itself a representational state, and its content is determined in precisely the same way as the content of the original visual experience is. So either it directly includes the original experience as a proper part, or it is expressed by the very same concepts/representations. Either way, whatever determines the intentional content of the experience will determine the intentional content of the introspective awareness. Hence, there is no room for doubt about what I'm experiencing.

Let us return now to Inverted Earth. Remember, the original Inverted Earth argument had Janet travelling from Earth to Inverted Earth and then remaining there for the rest of her life. Block claimed that by virtue of her long sojourn on Inverted Earth the intentional contents of her visual states would change to reflect the nomological dependencies in her new environment. The example is supposed to be an embarrassment to the intentionalist because it would entail a change of qualia without her noticing. We then noted that the intentionalist need not accept Block's claim about the switch in content in the first place. However, as Tye argues, this reply doesn't cover the case of Swampman.

But now Tye argues, why not just say that indeed the qualia have changed, and so have the contents of Janet's introspective judgements? When she now judges that she is having an experience of a reddish sort, that represents what used to be represented by her judgement that she was having an experience of a greenish sort. But she doesn't notice any change, one might argue. She doesn't form an introspective judgement to the effect that her qualia have changed. Well, the intentionalist argues, that's because she misremembers. Block of course stipulates in his example that Janet suffers from no failure of memory. But depending on how one takes the stipulation, it's either question-begging or insufficient to block the reply. If what he means by a failure of memory is some internal malfunction of the mechanisms responsible for preserving information, then indeed he can stipulate that no such malfunction occurs in Janet. Yet there is still a way for her to misremember. If her current states, due to changes in her environment, no longer represent what they used to, then when she purportedly remembers now what it was like to see a fire engine back on Earth, she is mistaken. It's not through any fault with her memory mechanisms, but it's a mistake none the less. To rule out this sort of mistake as well, of course, begs the question against the intentionalist.[7]

To be clear about what's being proposed here, let's imagine Janet's situation as vividly as possible. Here she is now on Inverted Earth, looking at a green fire engine, which, because of her inverting lenses, is causing her visual system to respond with the same state (characterized neurophysiologically) as it did when she looked at a red fire engine on Earth, without the lenses. She is now asked whether fire engines look the same to her now as they did when she was a child. She then forms an image of a fire engine she remembers seeing as a child—let's say it was a memorable incident. So, she has before her mind a current visual impression and this memory image, and she finds them relatively indiscernible (up to differences in shade, etc.). It sure seems as if she's making a judgement about the intrinsic properties of the two experiences. Can the intentionalist resist that characterization of the situation?

What the intentionalist has to say—what Tye, for one, does say—is that the memory image is wrong. That's not the way the fire engine looked to Janet as a child. Given that the memory image now represents the fire engine as green, and when she originally saw the fire engine she correctly perceived it as red, her memory is mistaken. Of course, as Tye argues, it still is the case that this image is an image *of* the original fire engine, but nevertheless it, as it were, misdescribes it. The moral of the story is clear. If phenomenal changes track

---

[7] Block considers this reply in Block (1996), and accuses the respondent of begging the question by assuming representationalism. Tye, however, argues persuasively that it is Block who is begging the question.

intentional changes, then they do so all the way up the chain of introspective awareness.

So, does this reply work? We started out with a strong conviction that it made no sense to attribute a radical change in Janet's qualia without her awareness. But now, under the pressure of the Burgean strategy, as applied by Tye to this case, we see that what it is to notice a change is itself a cognitive state with an intentional content that is subject to the same changes to which the qualia themselves are allegedly subject. Thus our initial conviction is suspect.

In fact, I think there are two cases that we can still press against the intentionalist that cannot be accounted for by the Burge/Tye strategy. First of all, let's reconsider Swampman. According to Tye, we can avoid the counterintuitive consequence that Swampman fails to have any qualitative experiences so long as we adopt a synchronic co-variation account of content. Swampman's problem is that he has no history—no selectional history, in particular. But so long as his perceptual states currently maintain lawful relations with distal properties he can count as having experiences.

But now consider not Swampman, but Swampbrain-in-a-vat. That is, imagine that a brain molecularly identical to my brain coalesces out of swamp gas inside a vat. What do we say about the contents of those of its brain states that correspond to my perceptual states? Since it has no sense organs we can't appeal to the synchronic lawful relations between these brain states and the distal properties of objects. In fact, depending on how we decide to hook it up, we can imagine that these states could co-vary with any number of different distal properties. Now, when we think about a normal human brain in a vat we can solve the problem of content by appeal to selectional history. Swampbrain, however, has neither selectional history nor currently maintained co-variation relations. Thus, it seems, Tye and other intentionalists have to say that Swampbrain lacks experiences.

Is this such a problem? After all, Swampbrain is a pretty outlandish case, so it may seem as if biting the bullet and maintaining that he/it lacks experiences isn't really so bad. In fact, it seems pretty clear that this is the position that Dretske takes. However, there are good reasons for not biting this bullet, and, what's more, it's clear from Tye's remarks that he in particular doesn't want to take this option. Remember that what motivated his new response to the Inverted Earth problem was precisely his refusal to deny Swampman experiences. The very same considerations, it seems, would militate against denying Swampbrain experiences as well.

But leaving aside questions of consistency, there is a very strong argument for granting qualitative experience to Swampbrain. As I sit here typing at my computer, looking out at the room full of furniture, feeling the air around me, hearing various sounds, I know in some sense that it is possible this is all an illusion. That is, after describing the case of Swampbrain, I realize that, for all I know, I am Swampbrain. I'm not claiming I don't know I'm really in a room, typing on a computer. I'm quite happy to acknowledge that claims to knowledge do not need to rule out all possibilities. My point is only that there is a robust sense in which this possibility is not something I can rule out. On the other hand, if someone were to suggest that it doesn't even appear to me as it does, I'm not even having visual and auditory experiences, I couldn't take that possibility seriously at all. There does seem to me to be a significant, and undeniable asymmetry between the two sorts of possibility, and it's one that can't be accommodated by the (externalist) intentionalist who is willing to go intentional all the way up.[8]

There's another way to put the same point, and in this way it connects quite directly with a discussion by McLaughlin and Tye (1998) of the conflict between externalism and self-knowledge with respect to belief. If externalism is right about qualitative character, and if I can know I am having a qualitative experience merely by having it, or, if you like, in an a priori manner, then it seems I can know a priori that I'm not a Swampbrain. But whatever your favourite theory is about how I can defeat the sceptic, it had better not attribute to me a priori knowledge that I'm not a brain in a vat.

Now it's interesting to note how McLaughlin and Tye respond to the corresponding challenge about belief, for it seems to me that it conflicts with what Tye wants to say about experience. So, suppose one argues thus: I can know a priori that I have a concept of water. My concept of water is an atomic natural kind concept, and therefore I couldn't have it were no water to exist. Therefore, I can know a priori that water exists. But obviously I can't know a priori that water exists, hence the existence of water can't be a necessary condition for my having an atomic natural kind concept of water.

McLaughlin and Tye's reply to this argument is long and involved, but for our purposes the crucial part is what they say about the epistemic position of Toscar, Oscar's molecular twin on Dry Earth, where there isn't in fact any water, though Toscar is under the illusion that there is. They say, 'It is consistent with [externalism] . . . that Toscar has a concept that has exactly the same (narrow) conceptual role as Oscar's concept of water' (1998: 306). What's crucial here is the claim that though Toscar's concept must be different from Oscar's, he still has a concept and it shares a crucial element with Oscar's, namely narrow content. It seems to me that if we adopt the same line in response to the possibility that I'm Swampbrain, we should say this: I can know, from inside, a priori, that I'm having an experience, which

---

[8] It's pretty clear that Dretske is willing to allow that I can't know, 'from the inside', that I'm really having experiences. This point came out fairly clearly in a recent presentation by Dretske at Notre Dame University (February, 2001), though there he was talking about thought, not experience.

includes what it's like for me. On this basis alone, I can no more rule out the possibility that I'm Swampbrain than can Toscar rule out that he's on Dry Earth. Of course there is some way of categorizing the experience such that if I'm Swampbrain I'm having an experience of one sort and if I'm who I think I am I'm having an experience of another sort, and this has to do with the (wide) representational content of the experience. But either way, there's something I have a priori, or privileged, access to, and that's what it's like for me. *That* aspect of my experience can't depend on what's out there.

One problem, then, for the Burge–Tye defence against the self-knowledge objection to intentionalism revolves around the case of Swampbrain. In this case the issue is one of the presence or absence of qualitative character. But there is another, perhaps more serious, problem that stems from the possibility of 'Frege cases' for qualia. That is, it seems possible that there could be creatures who standardly respond to a certain distal stimulus with different perceptual experiences, and only through empirical investigation come to learn that their phenomenally different perceptual states are tracking the same distal property.

Before describing such a case, let me explain why I think this possibility really undermines the (wide externalist) intentionalist position. In any case of representation, there are three components in play: the representation itself, the thing (or property) represented, and a mode of presentation. On some views of direct reference the mode of presentation turns out to be quite thin; perhaps in some sense it reduces to the representation itself, together with some causal relation between the representation and what's represented. Still, we can distinguish these three roles in the representational situation.

What's at issue between the intentionalist and the internalist about qualia is where to locate qualitative, or phenomenal character. Is it what's represented, or is it the mode of representation, or perhaps even the representation itself? (Either of the latter two options is consistent with an internalist view, so let's just collapse them into the mode of presentation option.) Here's where the 'Frege test' comes into play. Can the subject fail to determine a genuine case of identity without suffering a failure of her cognitive mechanisms? If so, then we're dealing with what's represented, not the mode of presentation. But if not, then we're dealing with the mode of presentation.

Notice how it works with Venus and water. Can I simultaneously think of Venus in two different ways and not realize that I'm thinking of the same thing? Of course I can. Can I think of water in two different ways and not realize I'm thinking of the same thing? Again, of course I can. Water, the intentional content of my 'water'-thoughts and of my 'H$_2$O'-thoughts, is not graspable by me in a way that shields me from mistakes of this sort, even if my internal cognitive mechanisms are functioning perfectly. Obviously the same can be said of my cognitive grasp of Venus.

Suppose, on the other hand, someone were to claim that I could simultaneously entertain two thoughts involving the same concept, or term, such as
'water', or involving the same mode of presentation of water, and yet not
realize—what's more, be unable to realize from the resources available from
within my mind—that they are the same. I don't want to claim that there isn't
some way of so describing the situation that it makes sense, but I'm not sure
what it would be. My bet is it would involve some bizarre malfunction of my
cognitive mechanisms. For after all, what individuates a representation, or its
mode of presentation, if not the subject's ability to discern identity or
difference? I can be fooled by accidents of interaction with the environment
into thinking the Morning Star is distinct from the Evening Star, but I can't be
wrong in the same way that my 'Morning Star'-thoughts are distinct from my
'Evening Star'-thoughts.

Now let's bring this to bear on the case of qualia. If colour qualia are modes
of presentation of colours, then it makes perfect sense that there could be
circumstances in which I simultaneously entertain two distinct representations of the same colour, involving distinct phenomenal properties, and not
realize that it is the same colour—i.e. the same property of the surfaces of
external objects. For example, suppose some creatures had eyes on the sides of
their heads, like fish, so their visual fields did not overlap. Suppose further
that the lenses of the two eyes were colour-inverted with respect to each other.
We can also imagine that the creatures have their heads fixed in one position,
so they never look at the same objects with both eyes. On this scenario, they
could be simultaneously looking at two surfaces with the very same reflectance properties, but not know it. What's more, after painstaking scientific
research, they might come to discover this is the case. They might exclaim:
'Wow! What looks green to this eye is really the same colour as what looks red
to that eye!'

However, if we identify the phenomenal characters of the experiences with
what's represented, then we have to say that in this case the two phenomenal
characters would be identical, though the creatures judge them to be different.
Note, I'm not relying on any heavy-duty doctrine of privileged access that
takes mistakes about one's own experiences to be logically impossible. Perhaps there can be such mistakes. What I'm insisting, however, is that when
everything inside is working as it's supposed to and I judge, after due reflection and attention, that I'm having experiences of two distinct types, then it's
an odd view, to say the least, that claims I would be wrong about this. Of
course if qualia are the modes of presentation of the colours, not the colours
themselves, then this all makes sense.

What's crucial about the Frege test is that it deals with type-distinct but
simultaneous mental states. The Burge–Tye reply that attributes the same
contents to introspective state and to object state works when what's at issue is

the identity of a single state, or a comparison involving memory. But how can it help when I judge of two simultaneous presentations that they are distinct? Am I mistaken or not? The intentionalist about qualia has to say that my introspective judgement that these are experiences of distinct types is mistaken. I don't really see any way around that.[9]

3. If what I've argued so far is correct, then it seems as if the intentionalist programme, at least in the form it's usually professed, is in conflict with self-knowledge of qualia. However, I mentioned above that there is a positive argument for intentionalism, one that seems to pull our intuitions strongly in its direction. I borrow this argument from Byrne (2001), though I've simplified it somewhat.

The idea is that if intentionalism is correct, then it is impossible for there to be a difference in qualitative content without a difference in intentional content. The anti-intentionalist, on the other hand, claims that it is possible for different qualia to have the same intentional contents. So, consider this case: I am looking at a red fire engine during the temporal interval t to t_1. From t until t', a point in between t and t_1, my experience has a reddish qualitative character. At t' the qualitative character changes from reddish to greenish, and remains so until I look away at t_1. Let us imagine that I am attending to my visual experience and clearly notice the change. It seems clear that corresponding to the change in qualia is a change in intentional content. That is, what seems to be happening, from what I can tell visually, is that the fire engine has changed colour. Of course I may have good reason to doubt that this really happened, and so I might not believe it changed colour. It might be that someone shone a coloured light on it, or that I've suffered a malfunction in my visual system. Whatever I happen to *think* about what's happened, however, it's clear that it will *appear* to me as if the fire engine has changed colour; and it's how things *appear*, not what I *think*, that counts as the intentional content of my visual state.

Of course the anti-intentionalist can admit this much but still maintain that intersubjectively it is possible for two qualitatively different states to have the same intentional content. This is indeed what the Inverted Twin Earth scenario seems to involve. Byrne, however, argues that if intrasubjectively it's true that there's no qualitative difference without an intentional difference, then it holds

---

[9] Tye himself makes the point that his form of reply to the Inverted Earth case doesn't work for simultaneous presentations, though he doesn't envision this sort of counter-example. In replying to Block's accusation of question-begging, he says: 'Of course the above response commits the strong representationalist to supposing that there can be large changes in the phenomenal character of experiences that are inaccessible from the first-person perspective.... In my view, the core intuition here is only that within a single context, a single external setting, no unnoticeable changes in the phenomenal character can occur' (Tye 1998: 471). Of course he's talking here about changes in a single context, which is not precisely what's going on in my 'fish-head' case; but the same reasoning applies.

for the intersubjective case as well. He reasons thus: suppose it were possible for two subjects to undergo experiences of different phenomenal types but with the same intentional content. Just imagine a third subject who undergoes both these phenomenally different experiences, but with the same contents. Yet this is just the intrasubjective case we agreed was not possible.

Now I think one can object to Byrne's extension of the intrasubjective case to the intersubjective one on various grounds, though, for reasons I'll make clear presently, I'm not inclined to. One might argue: visual qualia are the modes of presentation of visually detected properties such as colour. So within a subject a distinction in modes of presentation will indicate a distinction in what's presented, while the same distinction between subjects need not indicate a difference in what's presented. Different subjects can instantiate different mappings from mode of presentation to what's presented. All that matters, for perception to work properly, is that within a subject there be no ambiguity.

Despite the availability of this response, as I said above, I'm not inclined to avail myself of it. To see why, consider again my case of the inverted-fish-head, which I used to show the applicability of the Frege test to the relation between qualia and colours. According to my argument, in this case it makes sense to say that the two eyes are representing the same external colours via distinct modes of presentation which the creatures involved can discover empirically. But of course this is precisely the sort of case Byrne has in mind when constructing his argument that intersubjective difference in qualia entails a difference in intentional content.[10] What's going on, then? How can the very same case be used both as support for and a counter-example to intentionalism?

There is in fact a curious intuitive tension present in the fish-head case. On the one hand, it certainly seems to make sense to say that unbeknownst to the subject the two visual experiences are about the same objective colour—a surface reflectance property. This appears to cut against intentionalism. Yet, in line with Byrne's argument, it also seems right to say that in some important sense the two experiences are representing the world differently to the subject. The two objectively red surfaces—each seen through a different eye—appear to have different properties to the subject. As we might say, space appears differently filled in on the two sides of the head. This of course seems very much like a difference in intentional content. Can we reconcile these two intuitions?

It's important to note of course that there is nothing like a contradiction here. One can quite consistently maintain that the fish-head case is a counter-example to the position that colour qualia are reducible to (or supervenient on) the representation of objective, physical colours, and also maintain that nevertheless colour qualia are supervenient on intentional contents. Byrne himself is quite careful to separate the general position of

---

[10] In fact he explicitly employs a fish-head type case to make his point.

intentionalism from the particular externalist version that identifies the relevant intentional contents with physical properties of distal stimuli. Still, if, contrary to most intentionalists about qualia, we opt not to identify the relevant contents with physical properties of distal stimuli, then how do we characterize the intentional contents in question?

Of course one might just refuse to take the problem seriously in the first place and insist instead that we treat qualia strictly as modes of presentation, not as what's presented. This, after all, was supposedly the lesson of the fish-head argument. The idea was that since type-distinct qualia can coherently pick out the same distal property, we have reason to identify the qualitative character of a visual experience with the mode of presentation of the object of the experience. If one wants to count this as a version of intentionalism one can: this would be narrow intentionalism, described above.

Having just argued against an externalist version of intentionalism, I readily agree that qualitative character seems to be determined by what is internal to the mind, and so to that extent am friendly to the idea that it is identifiable with narrow content. However, identifying qualitative character with narrow content doesn't really address the argument above. To the extent that one finds it compelling that the two visual fields of the fish-head present different appearances, in the sense of different ways the world appears, this must mean something more than differences in mode of presentation. That is, it seems to involve a difference in the way things are represented as being, not merely a difference in the representations of the way things are. Differences in narrow content are of the second sort, not the first. So again, how can we characterize the intentional content—wide, not narrow—of visual experiences in such a way as to accommodate both the intuition that qualitative character supervenes on it and also that qualitative character supervenes on what is internal to the mind?

One possibility, one that Byrne explicitly mentions, is to treat qualia as representations of sense data. That is, the green and red that apparently fill the two regions of the visual field on each side of the fish-head are indeed distinct properties, just not the physical properties of the surfaces perceived, but mental properties of a mental visual field. Similarly, when experiencing a bodily sensation such as a pain in one's toe, the qualitative character of the pain does reduce to a representation, but the property represented—the painfulness—is itself an irreducibly mental property. Notice how on this view the Frege test does not intrude, since presumably the same mental property cannot appear under distinct modes so that we can't determine from the first-person point of view that it is the same property. It is precisely supposed to be of the nature of a mental property of a mental object, like the redness of a sense datum, that its identity is transparent to the mind. Indeed, its identity is arguably constituted by how it appears.

There are at least two good reasons for avoiding this route, however. First of all, one wants to avoid the metaphysical extravagance of positing sense data if at all possible. But suppose one didn't share this aversion to dualist metaphysics, or suppose one sought to cash out the metaphysics of sense data in materialist terms somehow, it would still go against the spirit of intentionalism about qualia to identify mental properties/objects with what's represented in perception. For most adherents of intentionalism, the principal motivation behind it is the hope of showing that all mentality is a matter of intentionality, of vindicating Brentano's dictum that intentionality is the mark of the mental. If we now introduce a new unreduced mental property/object to serve as the intentional content (unreduced, that is, to intentional content itself), then we have merely relocated the non-intentional mental from the realm of qualia to what it is that qualia represent.

Whether or not one has a stake in reducing the mental to the purely intentional—whether or not, therefore, the second reason for avoiding sense data just mentioned is a compelling one, the first reason is quite sufficient. The metaphysics of sense data is to be avoided if possible. Another option then is to adopt an error theory. Perception presents the world as possessing properties it doesn't have. Which properties? Well, properties such as those sense data would have if they existed. On this view we get much of the benefit of positing sense data, but without the metaphysical baggage and, for those moved by this consideration, without undermining the identification of the mental with the intentional.[11]

I see two problems with the error theory. First, it seems implausible to attribute systematic error to our perceptual systems. There is no malfunction involved, so what basis is there for attributing contents to our perceptual states that are necessarily non-veridical? But, of course, if there are strong enough pressures from other quarters this consideration can be overcome. The second, and more serious, reason for opposing the error theory is this. We were pushed to consider adopting any version of intentionalism by noting how differences in qualitative character seemed to entail differences in how things appear, and therefore differences in intentional content. But if we now adopt an error theory, so that these intentional contents are necessarily empty of reference, then we might well wonder what happened to the qualia? Something, after all, really does appear to be reddish. If it's the distal object, fine. If it's a sense datum, well OK. If it's neither, but we resist the claim that qualitative character supervenes on intentional content, then we can say that the qualitative reddishness is an intrinsic property of the experience, while its

---

[11] Byrne (2001) briefly mentions a position like this, but then moves on. Though Rey defends narrow intentionalism, he also combines it with eliminativism, and the resulting, fairly complicated position could be seen as similar to the idea presented here.

intentional content is the objective redness of the distal object. But if we reject this too, then there is literally nothing that is reddish, and this seems very hard to swallow.[12]

So what it seems we need is a theory that meets the following desiderata. The properties we are acquainted with in experience are really properties of something; they are not cognitive illusions. These properties of experience are representational; they involve presenting the world to us as being some particular way. The representational contents are not, however, either straightforward physical properties of distal objects, or special mental properties of peculiarly mental objects, such as sense data. Is there a theory that meets these constraints?

I can think of only one, and, if I understand him correctly, it's the one defended by Shoemaker (1996). The phenomenal characters of perceptual states do supervene on their intentional contents, but what they represent are, in the first instance, dispositional properties of distal objects. Which disposition? The disposition to cause certain qualitative experiences in us. So, for instance, when I see a red fire engine, the reddishness is presented as a property of the fire engine, but the property really is its disposition to cause me to have a certain, well, reddish experience. There appears to be a whiff of circularity here, but in fact it's quite kosher.

What's nice about this view is the way it handles the fish-head case. In that case, remember, the very same physical property, say a spectral reflectance, caused a reddish sensation in one eye and a greenish one in the other. Since the two eyes evolved that way, there seemed no reason to attribute error to either one. So if the intentional contents of colour experiences are the spectral reflectances of distal objects, we either have to say that qualia do not supervene on intentional contents or that the qualia would be the same for both eyes. But since the subjects distinguished between the experiences caused by what they saw through the two eyes, it seemed we had to say that qualia did not supervene on intentional contents.

On the view on offer now, though, we can have our cake and eat it. The disposition to cause an experience of one type through the right eye is a different property from the disposition to cause an experience of another type through the left eye. These are distinct properties, but not incompatible ones, so the very same objects, with the very same surface reflectances, can have both properties simultaneously. Now above I said that these dispositions are what the perceptual states represent in the 'first instance', but we can add that by representing these dispositions they also represent the categorical grounds of the dispositions in the objects; that is, the surface reflectances themselves.

---

[12] Though of course eliminativists such as Rey (1996) and Dennett (1991) would endorse this consequence. In Levine (2001a) I address eliminativism in some detail.

In this extended sense of what the two experiences resulting from the two eyes of the fish-head represent, they represent the same thing. So in one sense the greenish and reddish experiences have the same content—they track the same surface spectral reflectance—and in another they have different contents, since they attribute different dispositions to the two surfaces.

It's important to emphasize that on the view just outlined, while we can maintain that qualitative character supervenes on intentional content, we do not get the sort of reduction of the qualitative to the intentional that motivates most intentionalists. We get supervenience because it turns out that there's no difference in qualia without a difference in intentional content. But we do not get the reduction, because the intentional contents themselves involve attributing dispositions that are defined in terms of qualia. Intentionalism of this sort does not bring us any closer to a solution to the mind–body problem.

4. In this chapter I have explored the relation between the qualitative character of experience and its intentional content. Most philosophers who defend a version of intentionalism—the doctrine that qualitative character supervenes on intentional content—do so as a way of reducing the problem of qualia to the problem of intentionality. For that reason, they tend to adopt an externalist version of the doctrine, on which the intentional contents on which qualia supervene attribute physical properties to distal objects. I have argued that this version of intentionalism is untenable.

On the other hand, I have admitted that the idea that qualia supervene on intentional contents—when divorced from its externalist interpretation—does have virtue. After surveying various other versions of the doctrine, I argued that the most plausible one is the one defended by Shoemaker (1996), on which the relevant intentional contents attribute dispositional properties to distal objects, but where the dispositions in question essentially involve qualia.[13] This view satisfies various plausibility constraints on a theory of the relation between qualia and intentional contents, but it does not serve the reductive function for which most philosophers of mind hoped to employ intentionalism. So much the worse for reduction.

REFERENCES

BLOCK, N. (1990), 'Inverted Earth', in J. Tomberlin (ed.), *Philosophical Perspectives, 4: Action Theory and Philosophy of Mind* (Atascadero, Calif.: Ridgeview), 53–80.

[13] Needless to say there are subtleties involving Shoemaker's presentation of his view that I glossed over here, so it may not be strictly correct to call what I've presented his position. Also, when it comes to the question of reduction, of course Shoemaker himself does believe that qualia are reducible, but to functional roles and their realizers, not intentional contents. For more on this, see Shoemaker (1984) and Levine (1988).

BLOCK, N. (1996), 'Mental Paint and Mental Latex', in E. Villanueva (ed.), *Philosophical Issues*, 7 (Atascadero, Calif.: Ridgeview).

BURGE, T. (1988), 'Individualism and Self-Knowledge', *Journal of Philosophy*, 85.

BYRNE, A. (2001), 'Intentionalism Defended', *Philosophical Review*, 110/2.

DAVIDSON, D. (1987), 'Knowing One's Own Mind', *APA Proceedings and Addresses*, 60: 441–58.

DENNETT, D. C. (1991), *Consciousness Explained* (Boston: Little, Brown).

DRETSKE, F. (1995), *Naturalizing the Mind* (Cambridge, Mass.: MIT Press).

GERTLER, B. (2001), 'The Mechanics of Self-Knowledge', *Philosophical Topics*, 28: 125–46.

LEVINE, J. (1988), 'Absent and Inverted Qualia Revisited', *Mind & Language*, 3/4: 271–87.

—— (1998), 'Philosophy as Massage: Seeking Cognitive Relief for Conscious Tension', *Philosophical Topics*, 26/1–2: 159–78.

—— (2001a), *Purple Haze: The Puzzle of Consciousness* (New York: Oxford University Press).

—— (2001b), 'Phenomenal Consciousness and the First-Person', commentary on Siewert (1998), *PSYCHE*, 7/10: April 2001.

LYCAN, W. G. (1996), *Consciousness and Experience* (Cambridge, Mass.: MIT Press).

McLAUGHLIN, B., and TYE, M. (1998), 'Externalism, Twin Earth, and Self-Knowledge', in C. Macdonald, B. Smith, and C. Wright (eds.), *Knowing Our Own Minds* (Oxford: Oxford University Press).

REY, G. (1996), *Contemporary Philosophy of Mind: A Contentiously Classical Approach* (Oxford: Blackwell).

—— (1998), 'A Narrow Representationalist Account of Qualitative Experience', in J. Tomberlin (ed.), *Philosophical Perspectives, 12: Language, Mind, and Ontology* (Oxford: Blackwell), 435–57.

SHOEMAKER, S. (1984), *Identity, Cause, and Mind* (Cambridge: Cambridge University Press).

—— (1996), *The First-Person Perspective and Other Essays* (Cambridge and New York: Cambridge University Press).

SIEWERT, C. (1998), *The Significance of Consciousness* (Princeton, NJ: Princeton University Press).

TYE, M. (1995), *Ten Problems of Consciousness: A Representational Theory of the Phenomenal Mind* (Cambridge, Mass.: MIT Press).

—— (1998), 'Inverted Earth, Swampman, and Representationism', in J. Tomberlin (ed.), *Philosophical Perspectives, 12: Language, Mind, and Ontology* (Oxford: Blackwell), 459–77.

4. Transparent Experience and the Availability of Qualia

Two strong intuitions about visual experience seem to conflict radically. One is that visual experiences have discernible qualitative features, often called *qualia*. They are aspects of what it is like to have particular visual experiences, subjective or felt aspects of experiences. They present themselves as intrinsic and non-relational properties of visual experience, and they come in great detail. Almost all qualiphiles think of qualia as introspectable. The competing intuition is that visual experience is *transparent*: when you attend to a visual experience as it is going on, you will notice its objects, i.e. the things you see or apparently see, including their apparent properties and relations, and you will notice your (diaphanous) visual relation to those external objects and properties;[1] and, representationists say, that is all.

I endorse the idea that normal visual experience is transparent, both object-transparent and property-transparent. But I want also to say that there are visual qualia, and that we can directly discern them. This pairing of views is not usual, but I hope it will become plausible. Not to be too paradoxical at the outset, I can say that the resolution will be that we can have two perspectives on our own experiences: in one mode of attention, visual experience is phenomenally transparent, while in another visual qualia are discernible.

1. The Standard View of Qualia

I take the standard view to be this: normal visual experiences of the surface property of being *red*, which may be a primary or secondary quality, have a distinct intrinsic and introspectable property that we may call 'red*'. This property is the subjective feel of those visual experiences, what it is like to have them. Red* is a paradigm visual quale; and according to most proponents of qualia we can discern it by reflecting on our experience, and thereby be aware

---

[1] Confusingly, these properties are also called 'qualia' by some philosophers (e.g. Dretske, Lycan). But here the term is reserved for qualitative features of experience itself.

of it *as* a purely qualitative property of experience and not a property of the ordinary objects of experience. A similar intuition, though not so initially obvious, reveals shape qualia: while angularity is a feature of things out there in space, angularity* and its countless forms are visual qualia.

According to the standard view qualia are not in themselves, not intrinsically, representational or intentional. A way of putting this is to say they are aspects of sensation and not, all on their own at least, perceptual properties; you have to add something to qualia to make them into perceptual properties. Like paint on canvas, qualia are individuated, on this view, independently of their representational or referential properties, and—again like paint—individuated independently even of their purporting to represent, independently of their having intentional properties even in Brentano's sense. We can say that what the standard view defends are *raw* qualia. The standard view seems to me implausible, and I will propose an alternative.

2. Against Qualia

Qualia are not universally loved. They have been seen by many physicalists as a reactionary woolly-minded doctrine that would impede a fully naturalistic account of the mental. Others find them undesirable because of their contribution to Cartesian internalism, which is supposed to lead to bad things— scepticism, or disconnection from the world. These naturalist and anti-internalist complaints about qualia are of course rather different; but qualia-opponents of both sorts might well endorse the same remedy.

The project of getting rid of qualia has to some appeared to require philosophical work. You must argue carefully that the idea of qualia is a mistake: perhaps the idea of qualia is initially seductive but turns out on investigation to be incoherent (cf. 'the' private language argument.) Quite a few philosophers have recently suggested, however, that getting rid of qualia takes virtually no work at all: when you get right down to it and have a good look, qualia don't even seem to be there.

Philosophers who point out that visual experience is transparent, in the above sense, typically regard this as incompatible with the reality of qualia. Those incompatibilists have been called 'representationists' and 'intentionalists'; they hold that the phenomenology of a visual state can deliver *only* how the visual experience represents external things as being. (Cf. Harman 1990; Tye 1995; Dretske 1996; Lycan 1996.) The position to be rebutted then is this, that however scrupulously you attend to your normal visual experience, you will not discern anything like visual qualia; all you will notice is that your visual experience presents certain (apparent) objects and their (apparent) properties. I note that my current visual state presents that desk and that piece of paper, their colours, shapes, and spatial relations. I can attend to nothing else in my experience than my visual relation to some apparently perceived space, its occupants, and their properties, including sometimes exotic, merely intentional, objects. Whoever claims to be able to spot qualia is making things up, or (as Austin reportedly jested about Ayer's claim to be aware of sense data) lying through his teeth.[2] My argument will be that this incompatibilist view is not correct. There is the phenomenon of transparency, but it is compatible with there being visual qualia as well.

3. Some Inconclusive Points on the Side of Qualia

I should say what would count as success in a defence of qualia. I take it to be a conceptual matter; and I would be happy simply to show that qualia make sense, that they are conceivable, and that we apparently know how to discern them in experience. It would also be nice to be able to refute philosophical arguments to the effect that qualia are illusory; and I do think it is possible to answer the standard such arguments. But in this chapter my objective is simply that qualia should make prima-facie sense, and, more specifically, that this can be defended against representationist representations to the contrary.

Some have appealed to the conceivability of inverted spectra in defence of visual qualia on the standard view of them. I imagine that you see a cucumber as having the colour that I think of as 'red'. Does the conceivability of inverted spectra give us qualia? The issue is phenomenological. And what I imagine when I think of you and me as seeing the cucumber's colour differently in fact invites a representationist interpretation, i.e. that what I imagine is that you and I see the cucumber as having different features.[3] That is about apparent properties of objects and not about qualia in our present sense, not about aspects of visual sensation.

Sydney Shoemaker has proposed an elegant defence of qualia that respects the representationist interpretation of the inverted-spectrum intuition. We imagine different people seeing a certain object as having different—as it were personal—colour properties. For Shoemaker (1994) our conception of qualia in the standard sense *derives* from the conceivability of different personal colour properties. Those properties are secondary qualities, dispositions to cause qualia. We perceive those properties as non-dispositional, rather in the way we perceive heaviness as a non-dispositional property of objects, even

---

[2] I owe this anecdote to Laurent Stern.

[3] If the proponent of qualia has an independent argument for the conceivability of qualia, then of course he will also have a direct account of inverted spectra. The point here is that inverted spectra on their own are not a compelling argument for qualia.

though on conceptual reflection it is clear that it is dispositional. Those personal secondary qualities are what we imagine as inverted. We do not discern qualia themselves directly: they are inferred from their making sense of that attractive construal of inverted spectra.

Shoemaker is right in holding that the conceivability of inverted spectra does not entail introspectable qualia. But his defence of qualia abandons what seems to me essential to qualia, that they are phenomenally introspectable. My concept of a quale is the concept of a property that *presents itself as* a non-relational feature of experience. This is not stipulation. I do not know what to make of the idea of a phenomenal quality that cannot be directly attended to. I have no grip on how to conceive such a property, for a quale is *a way it is like* to be in a certain state. (Some find it intelligible that a certain conscious quale might be instanced unconsciously. Even if this makes sense, one's understanding of such a property would be by way of its conscious accessibility. One would think: *that* could occur unconsciously—where 'that' is a concept that presents a property *via* how it is consciously experienced.[4])

Let us return to the issue of whether visual qualia might present themselves as non-intentional, raw qualitative features of visual sensations. It has been suggested that there are clear examples of raw visual qualia at least in marginal visual experiences. Ned Block once proposed phosphenes, which appear when you press fingers against your closed eyelids. And I have been told that recent equipment used for optical diagnosis can splinter and isolate features of visual experience in such a way that a person is inclined to count them as purely sensational, undirected, non-intentional features. That was my informant's inclination,[5] and I am not sceptical of the report. As for phosphenes, I do not myself experience those features as non-intentional: to me they appear to present luminous happenings in strange spaces. But the main point is that it is unclear that our central concern is affected by such examples. What might the discernibility of exotic raw qualia imply about normal visual experience? Clearly not that we can directly discern raw visual qualia in the ordinary case. They might lend weight to Shoemaker's proposal: the occurrence of isolated raw visual qualia might suggest that similar raw qualia are hidden components of normal visual experience. But even then it would give us merely a generic conception of certain properties hidden in ordinary visual experience without specific conceptions of them. It is not clear that this either

---

[4] Another worry about Shoemaker's account of qualia is that there seems to be a difference between heaviness and personal colour properties. In the former case, we have a direct awareness of a qualitative state; we can conceive of what it is like to pick up something heavy. But according to Shoemaker we do not have a direct awareness of colour qualia. In the former case there is a *reason* to identify the property of heaviness with a disposition to produce in one a certain qualitative state, and there is no similar direct reason to identify personal colour properties with dispositions to cause colour qualia.

[5] Thanks to Professor William Craig.

makes sense or would explain the point of asserting the reality of qualia if it did. The simplest and surest way to make sense of qualia is to give them a form whereby they are discernible in all their specificity.

Here is an example of Christopher Peacocke's (1983), offered in defence of qualia. You see two trees along a road that stretches away from you, one tree 100 and the other 200 yards away. The trees appear the same size. But 'the nearer tree occupies more of your visual field than the more distant tree'. (I should say that this way of putting things may suggest sense data rather than qualia.) Peacocke takes this to indicate that there is more to notice in visual experience than its objects, and in particular that one notices aspects of the visual experience itself. Now I am inclined to say he is right about this; one does seem here to notice aspects of *how* the visual experience represents its objects. But it is not obvious that the example shows this on its own. Quite reasonable representationist replies have been made by Hill (in terms of appearances) and by Lycan (peculiar intentional objects)[6], and as against them I find Peacocke's phenomenon an inconclusive argument for qualia. I am pessimistic about defending qualia by trying to defeat representationists at their game. Perhaps no visual phenomenon will all on its own block a determined representationist interpretation.[7] It would be nice to have a way of discerning qualia that makes representationist construals irrelevant.

4. Phenomenal Sameness

According to the representationist, the complex property of an ordinary visual experience that exhausts its phenomenal character consists in the subject's visual relation to certain apparent external objects and their apparent properties and relations. But a veridical visual experience and a visual hallucination can have exactly the same phenomenal character, on an intuitive understanding of the latter. Can the representationist accommodate this phenomenal sameness?

The representationist might say that there really is no sameness here, that there is no introspectable property or even apparent property that the veridical and hallucinatory experiences have in common. There is, I think, an intuitive point behind this, and I will return to it at the end. But there is also a strong and compelling intuition that two such experiences are not merely indistinguishable but also share a positive phenomenal property; and one question is whether representationism can properly describe that property.

---

[6] Hill (1991: 197–9); Lycan (1996: 89 ff.).
[7] Visual blur is a case in point. It seems reasonable to say that a blurred viewing of a scene might be visually equivalent to a clear view of a scene that is in itself 'blurry'.

5. Three Accounts of Hallucinations without Qualia

(a) *Merely Intentional Objects.* Some representationists, for instance Gilbert Harman (1990), construe the phenomenal similarity of a veridical and a hallucinatory experience by invoking 'intentional objects'. What the two experiences have in common are intentional objects to which they ascribe the same properties and relations. The hallucination has what I will call a merely intentional object—it is merely an object of experience with no existence of its own; perhaps it's a Meinong object. I do not deny that the notion of a merely intentional object is phenomenologically apt, or that 'hallucinations have intentional objects' can be a helpful manner of speaking or convey something intuitive. The question is whether there is an inclusive notion of *having an intentional object* that can be understood literally and that accounts for phenomenal sameness by virtue of its applying univocally to both veridical experiences and hallucinations. It would have to invoke a single relation that holds between visual experiences and both ordinary objects of vision and merely intentional objects. It may be tempting to think there is such a relation. Ordinary reflective phenomenology can seem to deliver a relation of 'presenting', instanced by both <this visual state, the tennis ball> and <that visual state, the merely intentional object>. Think of it demonstratively: 'this (diaphanous) presenting-relation holds between visual states and both ordinary objects and merely-intentional objects'.

But, however intuitive the idea, it is I am sure illusory. For consider this. Had the veridical visual experience and the tennis ball not stood in a certain externally determined causal relation—a certain *optical* relation—the experience would not have been *of* that ball. And then the intuitive 'diaphanous' relation would not have held between experience and that tennis ball. But whatever that causal relation is, we can be sure it has no merely intentional objects in its range. And if there is no common relation, we can hardly thereby have explained what phenomenal *sameness* consists in. A common-sense view of the hallucination is that there is nothing there at all, that a visual experience that lacks a real object has no object of any sort. Phenomenal sameness must then be independent of relations to objects both ordinary and abstract.[8]

---

[8] Further possibilities come to mind: (a) There are two relations in the veridical case that extensionally coincide—one causal and other more ethereal, whose range includes both ordinary and Meinong objects. Believe it if you can. (b) As in (a) but where the additional relation is 'deflationary'. It will be a struggle to say how such a deflationary reference relation can have both ordinary and abstract objects in its range (given that the states in its domain are all visual experiences). Moreover, as is well known, deflationary reference relations are not counterfactually sensitive in the right way. (c) There is a relation that somehow supervenes *both*

(b) *Property-complexes.* A more attractive explanation of phenomenal sameness is this: a visual experience, hallucinatory or veridical, represents a complex of external properties and relations instantiated in certain patterns. These properties are ordinary shapes, colours, spatial relations, and the like. That is what a veridical visual experience and its hallucinatory counterpart have in common: they represent the same property-complex. Perhaps this is what some mean by the *intentional content* of a visual perception. (A related idea is that the visual experience has the sense or character of a definite description which contains a self-referring indexical, etc.)

The objection to the property-placing account of phenomenal sameness is this: as we will see, we apparently have no difficulty conceiving of phenomenal sameness across *property-shifts* and even of, as it were, *property-hallucinations.* This I will argue below. If that is so, in what would phenomenal sameness then consist? Not in represented external properties and relations. Non-qualitative resources here could well appear to run out, if my later points about property representation are correct.

(c) *Appearances.* A natural proposal is that what the two experiences have in common is that making true a certain single proposition of the form *it appears that p.* But suppose *p* stands for a Russellian proposition, containing properties, relations, connectives, quantifiers. The appearance presumably has to be anchored in the properties and relations that the visual experience actually represents. And then the proposal seems equivalent to the property-complex analysis. It might be said that appearances express *Fregean* propositions or senses. But what are they? Suppose they are non-psychological entities, 'conditions' that the world may or may not satisfy. It is not easy to understand this unless Fregean propositions entail relations to externally constituted properties. But then if we can argue (as I propose to) that all such relations to external properties can shift even though phenomenal sameness is held constant, Fregean senses will not help. On the other hand, if one means by 'Fregean senses'—in an unhistorical use sometimes encountered—certain psychological factors, then we need to know more. A natural way to think of such factors is as involving in part the very experiential factors that the representationist denies. I doubt that the appearance proposal can get very far.

---

on that optical relation and on some relation that holds between visual experiences and mere intentional objects. This is a tall order. Producing the two subvenient relations (the ordinary causal one, and some relation to abstract objects) will not, it seems to me, *explain* phenomenal sameness. If the supervenient relation is to help, it would have to explain phenomenal sameness intuitively, even if the two subvenient relations do not do so. (Keep in mind that it is essential to the transparency thesis that the veridical experience should not have *both* a real intentional object and a Meinong object.) I do not think such a supervenient relation can be made sense of.

6. How to Spot Qualia

What should we look for? The question concerns normal full-blown visual experiences. As regards them, I cannot make phenomenal sense of visual qualia that leave everything 'intentional' behind. I can make sense of features of experience occurring in the absence of any or all of their normal references, whether external objects, properties, or relations. But this does not mean that we can abstract qualia from the various *ways* in which ordinary visual experiences *purport-to-represent* external objects, properties, and relations. The central idea will be that visual qualia are intrinsically 'directed'. They are qualitative features of experience that present themselves on reflection as purporting-to-refer; but they are conceivable quite independently of all referential properties, including their representing basic spatial properties. I will try to make sense of this phenomenologically. The technique of qualia spotting is fairly simple. One attends to or imagines a visual experience, and conceives of it as lacking some or all of its actual references, whether objects, properties, or relations, and then attends to what phenomenally remains.

7. Object-Directedness

Imagine a psychology experiment in which you are visually presented first with a lemon and then an indistinguishable lemon-hallucination. Not only can you not distinguish these experiences, but you perhaps have a strong inclination to think they exactly resemble each other in a certain visually detailed way. A way of putting this is representational: the two experiences present the real lemon and a merely intentional object as exactly similar, and that is what makes the experiences indistinguishable.

At the same time, one has a good sense of reality, and so wants to hold that the merely intentional lemon is nothing at all, and so not something that can resemble something else. This is reflected in how one engages the two experiences. To begin with, one adopts the perspective of *transparent reflection*. This is the perspective on visual experiences that initially supports representationism. From this perspective, if you have full information and a lively sense of reality, you will think different things about the two experiences. Of the veridical experience you will think 'that lemon is real', and of the hallucination 'that isn't real; there's no such thing as that'. The similarity does not consist in the two experiences' objects, and yet they share something object-wise. One cannot find this shared property from the perspective of transparent reflection, given what one knows of the facts.

At this point, you can take a less engaged perspective and abstract from the real object of the veridical experience. The two experiences 'purport-to-refer'—call this their *object-directedness.* Judging that a hallucination has the property of object-directedness is identical with judging that it has-a-merely-intentional-object, where the latter is existentially non-committal. It is what survives when one takes a sceptical view of the merely-intentional object—'that is nothing; there is no such object as that'. That object-directedness is a non-relational feature that the hallucination shares with the veridical lemon sighting. And given this feature's intimate connection with the inclination to posit merely intentional objects, as well as with our ordinary transparent experience of real objects, it seems appropriate to call this common phenomenal property 'intentional'. This way of attending to experience—discerning directedness—I will call the perspective of *oblique* reflection, the oblique perspective. We abstract from the objects of experience, and attend to *how* the two visual experiences *present* their apparent objects.

Consider judging 'this experience is *of* that merely intentional lemon-like object'. Even though this is about a visual experience one believes to be hallucinatory, it is in its way a transparent reflective judgement. But it takes little to change that transparent perspective to an oblique perspective, in fact two steps: (1) One judges that *that* merely intentional object is nothing—there is no such relation as the apparently transparent relation between this experience and that merely intentional object. (2) One then understands that the experience has the property of *its being exactly like this*—and here the phenomenology is the same, or almost the same given loss of innocence. The property of purporting-to-refer is now understood as a non-relational property of the visual experience with virtually the same phenomenology as the seemingly understood property of the experience's standing in the transparent relation to a merely intentional object. Discard the latter, retain the reflective phenomenology as much as you can, and you have an oblique take on the experience's object-directedness.

It is not as though there is one instance of directedness for each visual experience. Any normal experience is multiply directed, to various large and small would-be particulars, parts and empty spaces. So each such experience has an indefinite number of directed features—those that incline one to say 'that ball', 'that sharp edge', and so on.

The directedness of a visual experience supports a strong disposition to refer demonstratively. But that is not what directedness consists in; for directedness has an occurrent phenomenology, one that makes the idea of merely intentional objects so compelling. If I am in the grip of a hallucination, it hardly does justice to the experience to note that I am disposed to assert 'that lemon is yellow'.

One may be tempted to suppose that *demonstrative concepts* play a role. The object-directedness of a hallucination could suggest the involvement of a concept of the form 'that object', dressed in visual clothes. This could seem to explain how a visual experience can be phenomenally 'directed' without a real object or an intentional object. But that idea goes beyond what I find in the phenomenology of visual experience. My use of 'phenomenal directedness' is not intended to entail the involvement of concepts. I take the interface of perceptual organization and proper conceptualization to be a theoretical and not a phenomenological matter. It may emerge that the phenomenology of visual experience is built on a partially conceptual foundation. But the idea of intentional qualia or phenomenal directedness is intended to be neutral.

In what then does our concept of directedness consist? We cannot define it, for it is a phenomenological concept. We have a feel for what seeing a lemon shares with an indistinguishable hallucination. We can reflect on the two experiences in imagination and discern what they have in common. The proponent of intentional qualia rejects the ontology of merely intentional objects, which are in any case useless in explaining phenomenal sameness. We discern a non-relational phenomenal quality of visual experience that captures that aspect of experience which makes it tempting to take merely intentional objects seriously. From this oblique perspective we step back, withdrawing from the object-involvement of transparent reflection. The non-relational intentional phenomenal quality is found in both veridical and hallucinatory cases. We can identify similar object-directedness throughout all normal visual experiences and in hallucinations phenomenally identical to them. We thereby grasp the general concept of object-directedness. Such higher-order phenomenological concepts are, I want to say, recognitional concepts, type-demonstratives that pick out repeatable phenomena, in this case, intentional features of experience.

8. Colour-Directedness

Visual experience is transparent not only to objects but also to properties and relations—colours, shapes, relations of size, etc. If you attend to two indistinguishable visual experiences of a red thing, it is natural to judge that they present the same colour property. That is a standard representationist intuition, and it seems right. The point to be made is that we can also take a different perspective on colour experience, one that discloses a phenomenal sameness in two experiences that the representationist should regard as representing different properties. From this perspective what the two experiences have in common is a certain phenomenal 'property-directedness', which is a qualitative intentional feature of experiences, independent of their actual property references. Property-directedness comes in a vast variety of qualitative flavours and modes. We will consider two broad categories of such phenomenal qualities of experience, in the present section qualities of colour experience, and, in the following, qualities of shape experience.

Representationists deny that surface colours are identical with dispositions to cause qualia, for they deny that there are introspectable qualia. On their view, colours may be intrinsic properties of surfaces or perhaps dispositions to produce in us something other than qualia. Suppose, with some representationists, that 'red' designates a physical surface property that is quale-independent, and that certain visual experiences transparently represent red, that surface property. The qualiphile holds that this is compatible with the conceivability of colour-qualia. To see this, we consider a simplified version of Ned Block's Inverted Earth, which is a Twin-Earth case for colour experiences (Block 1990). We can conceive of an Inverted-Earthian's having visual experiences that are phenomenally the same as our experiences of red even though her 'red' refers to a surface property other than red. The *reduction* of redness to physical surface properties is beside the point. For the point stands even if we suppose that surface colours are irreducible non-relational properties of surfaces over and above their basic physical properties. What the Inverted Earth thought experiment requires is that we can conceive that those colour properties systematically differ on Earth and Inverted Earth, even though our and our twins' visual experiences are phenomenally the same. I take it that we can conceive of God's arranging that.

Block takes Inverted Earth to be an argument for the conceivability of colour qualia—and so it is, I think. But I do not see it as giving us a grip on raw colour qualia. What is true is that we can conceive colour-related qualitative features of visual experience that are independent of the surface properties of objects, whatever they may be. Those features of experience, however, are best regarded (not as raw qualia but) as property-directed qualia.

I reflect on the two experiences, one as it occurs and the other in imagination, with full knowledge of the external facts. As regards my own experience I judge that it represents its object as red. And I imagine that my twin's experience on Inverted Earth does not represent its object as being red. At the same time, I consistently imagine the two experiences as phenomenally the same. How shall we conceive what they have in common? Two representationist conceptions of the common property come to mind.

(a) Consider Shoemaker-properties again, in this case shared secondary qualities of the objects of the two experiences. Shoemaker preserves the phenomenology by taking such properties to present themselves as categorial properties, that being corrected when we think about them analytically. What makes adopting this proposal interesting in the present context is that it counts what the two experiences have in common as a shared property of its objects. As we saw above, however, that requires hidden raw qualia, and they are difficult to conceive.

(b) It may seem that merely intentional objects crop up not only in hallucinations, but also in the phenomenal sameness of the colour experiences we are imagining. Perhaps what the two visual experiences have in common is a merely intentional 'object', of a sort corresponding to properties rather than particulars. That intentional object—that would-be colour—presents itself as a property of surfaces. Can we make sense of this idea? Such quasi-colour-properties would be abstract objects that are unanchored in real resemblance. We may suppose that it is *as if* there were such merely intentional objects; but it is another thing to endorse them. I take our topic to be what the two experiences actually have in common and not what it is *as if* they have in common. Rather than endorse such merely intentional objects, it is better to regard what the two experiences have in common as having a hope of psychological reality, a property of conscious experience that is a candidate for being a real resemblance. If raw qualia were phenomenologically available they would qualify; they are in a general way the sort of thing we are pursuing.

In the case of the lemon hallucination, I proposed trading 'having a merely intentional object' for the non-relational 'being object-directed'. So with colour qualia. I suggest that what the two colour experiences have in common is a property-directedness with a certain qualitative character. This qualitative state can in different contexts present what are in fact different surface properties, perhaps even different objective colours. And it can occur even in the absence of an object, in a sort of colour hallucination (cf. s. 9).

Phenomenal-directedness is phenomenologically closely related to having merely intentional property objects. If there could be such entities as merely intentional colour-objects, an experience with such an intentional object and an experience with the corresponding object-directedness would be phenomenally indistinguishable. Still these are different ideas. If one conceives a visual experience as having a colour-like merely intentional object, one's reflection on that experience is in its way from a transparent perspective. The state of affairs to which one attends is a would-be relation between the experience and a pseudo-property. One could then judge: 'there is no such entity as that merely-intentional-property, and yet this experience and the experience of my twin are still *like that*.' One may regard the two experiences as sharing a property-directed quale, a way of presenting surface colours. That is how it goes for any sort of phenomenal intentionality. One may get a grip on it by attending as if to a merely-intentional object, judging that there is no such entity there, and then noting that one can conceive of a non-relational phenomenal quality of the experience thus: it is 'like that', it has that directed colour quale. These locutions should be understood with the phenomenon in mind; they are not technical terms, but stand for how one conceives the experience when one rejects the reality of the would-be colour-property. Again, I say that we conceive of that intentional feature from an 'oblique' perspective because the feature is non-relational—one reflects on the experience's intentional and phenomenal features and not on its objects; and one is from that perspective not immersed in the experience in the manner of transparent reflection.

A certain question about the relation of colour-qualia and the visual experience of shapes naturally arises at this point. In reflecting on one's colour experience one normally will also be visually presented with shapes; and so far we have not considered how we might reflect on shape experiences 'obliquely'. In our thought experiment about Inverted Earth, we will apparently have to engage in a bi-perspectival frame of reflection, attending transparently to our shared visual experience's relation to shapes and attending obliquely to the shared colour experience. How might we conceive that?

Consider the following simple limiting case, in which shape plays a vanishingly small role. Imagine looking at a uniformly coloured wall that fills your field of vision, and also imagine your twin's having a phenomenally indistinguishable experience, in the presence of a wall with a different surface property. Conceive the two experiences as sharing a merely intentional quasi-colour-property. This apparently captures the shared phenomenal colour-quality of the two experiences from a transparent perspective. Then imagine judging 'there is no such thing as that "property" ', and also judging that 'the two experiences are phenomenally indistinguishable colour-wise'. In conceiving what it is like to have each of the two experiences, conceive of it non-relationally: *it is like this.* Now on the face of it what they have in common is a property-directed qualitative state. As we suggested above, this colour*-property-directedness is just that non-relational feature of the experience which replaces the intuition of a shared merely-intentional quasi-colour-property. When one then regards the two experiences as presenting the wall in the same way, one abstracts from a conception of them as experiences *of* a certain colour-related property.

When one reflects on a more complex and normal visual experience of shapes, the imaginative project becomes more demanding, attending obliquely to colour-experience and transparently to the experience of shapes. This may in the abstract seem to require two modes of attention that do not harmonize. But perhaps this formula will help: the two visual experiences represent a given shape; they moreover present that shape in a certain colour-wise way, which we can conceive obliquely, as if noting the mediation of a colour filter—although this is not a perfect analogy. If we shift back and forth determinedly, the two properties of the experience—one relational and the other not—phenomenally coincide. But next on the agenda we have a more radical thought experiment, which should eliminate the strain of co-ordinating different reflective perspectives on colour and shape aspects of experience.

9. Isolated Brains

Consider how visual experiences represent spatial properties. Can we hold a visual experience constant and vary the properties that spatial* phenomenal features pick out? We require a more radical imaginative possibility than Inverted Earth. The banal but useful thought experiment involves an isolated brain, a phenomenal duplicate of oneself isolated from past and present ordinary contacts with our world. I will be content if you grant at least a superficial coherence to the thought that my isolated twin-in-a-vat has visual experiences exactly like mine. It seems to me that this is fully coherent, and, more directly to the present point, that such an isolated brain's experiences would not refer to, represent, spatial properties and relations. About reference I am inclined to be completely externalist. The isolated brain does not stand in the right relations to spatial properties for his perceptual states to refer to them. In fact I do not think we are forced to suppose that the spatial* features of the isolated brain's visual experience pick out any properties or relations whatever. If that is right the isolated brain is subject to what, from the outside, may be conceived as a radical property hallucination.

We hold something qualitative constant as we imaginatively shift or remove spatial references, i.e. the rich phenomenal qualities of visual experience. Shape-presenting* qualia might stand for properties other than shapes, or no properties at all. Those phenomenal qualities have a sort of directedness, like colour qualia; they are intrinsically intentional. As I conceive the isolated brain's mental life, it is—even if devoid of reference—as intuitively replete with intentionality as my own. Suppose its visual states fail to refer not only to spatial properties and relations but to any properties or relations. As in the familiar case of object-hallucination, speaking of merely intentional objects here conveys something intuitive, where by 'objects' we mean ersatz spatial properties and relations. But again, taking those intentional objects seriously seems unrealistic; however intuitive they may be, they are just manners of speaking. Better to conceive the spatial* features of the isolated brain's visual experiences as having property-directedness and (for spatial* features that in ordinary vision represent relations such as betweenness) relation-directedness.

How then do we conceive these complex features? We again note that merely intentional objects are inessential to the phenomenology: we make sense of the isolated brain's spatial* experience's being phenomenally the same as ours when we judge that there are no such entities as those merely intentional property and relation-like objects. We can think: an isolated brain could have an experience *just like this*, with this spatial* intentional phenomenal quality, that intentional quality... We have to keep in mind that our reflective recognitional conceptions of these qualities are formed at varying degrees of specificity and generality. We are able to conceive many rather different spatial* features of visual experience as all being curvy* qualia, and many more as all being spatial* qualia. These pattern recognitional abilities have complex interrelations, up, down, and sideways, and we don't know how we do it. That is how a quality space is, a brute psychological phenomenon. For the isolated brain and his normal twin, what it is like to have their experiences is the same; the intentionalized qualia of their visual experiences are the same. We may judge: 'this experience could be *just like this* even if it were not an experience of those particular objects and did not present its particular objects as having those properties, including those spatial properties. *This* is what the experience of my isolated twin would be like.' Again, this perspective on visual experience is from what I am calling the oblique perspective. The non-relational features one holds constant from this perspective deserve to be called *both* intentional and qualia.

10. Qualia: Inferred or Presented?

The question arises whether intentional qualia depend more on theory than on phenomenology, a possibility that could undercut the idea that such states present themselves as features of experience. The thought may go like this.

> The idea of intentional qualia depends on our denying that the visual states of isolated brains represent spatial properties and relations. That denial depends on *theory*, namely, radical externalism about reference. But then intentional qualia are creatures of theory. And if so, how can we conceive them phenomenologically?[9]

The idea perhaps is this: a philosopher who does *not* hold an externalist theory of reference could not think he discerns these intentionalized qualia in his visual experience. As an internalist about reference, he holds that the references of his visual states—*colour properties, shapes, spatial relations*—cannot shift across environments. His account of phenomenal sameness then would presumably be the property-complex account. Now this philosopher is going to have to say, I think, that my account of the phenomenology is just mistaken. He will perhaps understand why I *think* I can discern intentional qualia, certain non-relational features of experience. But he will count this as

---

[9] Thanks to Barry Smith, and to Scott Sturgeon, for raising versions of this question.

an illusion, stemming from my accepting externalism about reference and then—to secure consistency—inventing exotic intentional qualia to play the role of being whatever it is that I imagine as constant across the supposed shifts in reference. The fact is that there are no such shifts of reference, he says, and, once we acknowledge this, those exotic properties will disappear.

Now suppose one adopts agnosticism about reference-externalism. One will think that *something* phenomenologically available can be held constant through the various environments, including the isolated brain's environment. If we are neutral about externalism we are agnostic about the *nature* of that factor. If we accept externalism about perceptual reference, we will perhaps regard those features of experience as intentional qualia. And if we accept internalism about the property-references of, say, spatial features of experience, we will presumably construe those features as intentional property complexes, in the sense of 5(*b*).

The challenge posed by the opening question can be met. Theory does have a bearing, it is true. But theory does not create the phenomenology. From a neutral position there is a certain phenomenology of perceptual experience. What is missing from the neutral position is a conception of the nature of what is thereby presented. If one's intuitions are externalist, one should regard the factor that is held constant across the various environments as a non-relational phenomenal feature of experience. And if one shares my scepticism about the availability of raw qualia, and finds the idea of phenomenal intentionality coherent, one should regard the factor that is held constant as consisting in intentional qualia.

The objection we began with proposed that, because of the essential role of externalism about reference, intentional qualia are theoretical features of experience and cannot be discerned directly. We now see what is wrong and what is right in that. Those features are discerned directly, in all their detail, regardless of what theory we accept. What adopting an externalist theory of reference engenders (putting aside the previous paragraph) is an understanding of what those features are, that is, intentional qualia.

11. Intentional Qualia and Concepts

On the present conception, intentional qualia are not (merely) features of visual sensation, whatever that might mean. We might call them 'percepts', not in a theoretical sense, but simply as labelling what is phenomenally available. And the idea does not exclude the possibility that, in some theoretical sense of 'concept', intentional qualia involve concepts. Indeed I have been told that thinking of intentional qualia as 'conceptualized qualia' makes the idea of directedness clearer. But it is easy to be pulled in the opposite direction. For there is also the thought that percepts are inputs to certain concepts, those concepts being constituted by 'subsuming' percepts, whatever that might come to. In fact I find this idea quite attractive.

As a piece of phenomenology, intentional qualia may help to explain why some find the idea of the narrow content of thoughts plausible. Narrow content must somehow be intuitively intentional. Narrow intentionality cannot be truth-conditions; for they presuppose reference to properties, which is a matter of externally determined relations. (Even if truth-conditions are 'characters' or the like, they presuppose property-references.) So the idea of thoughts having narrow contents may appear to make sense because (1) intentional qualia are phenomenologically real, (2) they are partially constitutive of perception-based concepts; and (3) concepts that are not directly perceptual are intentional via conceptual connections (Loar 2003).

12. Three Frames of Mind: Transparent and Oblique Perspectives

(*a*) *Unreflective transparency.* This is how ordinary in-the-world unselfconscious experience is. One sees the object directly, phenomenologically speaking, i.e. one doesn't see the object by attending to the visual experience, as one might see the man by seeing the coat. But we can step back and judge that this ordinary transparency is the upshot of—as we might say—*exercising* or *undergoing* visual percepts. When I unreflectively see a tennis ball, I undergo a corresponding percept. By undergoing that percept I have not thereby attended to it.

The following two frames of mind are the main point; they involve different ways of framing attention to a visual experience. I assume that attention involves something like concepts. The difference between the two frames of mind stems from the concepts employed in the two ways of attending.

(*b*) *Transparent reflection.* This is the reflective posture that the representationist regards as the only one possible. One reflects on a visual experience, and notes that it stands in a diaphanous visual relation to a certain external state of affairs that consists in the instantiation of external properties and relations. One exercises perceptual concepts (which we may think of as incorporating visual percepts), attending to external objects and their properties and relations, as well as to one's visual relation to those objects and properties, and not attending to the experience's non-relational phenomenal features.

So we understand reflective transparency not only as a matter of attending to an experience and its transparent visual relation to its objects, but also as involving certain visual perceptual concepts. These perceptual concepts are intimately connected with visual percepts, by virtue of the latter's being as it were embedded—filling the empty slot—in the former, concepts of the form *that object, that colour,* and *that shape.* The first is what we can call a singular perceptual demonstrative concept. The latter two we can call visual recognitional concepts, or recognitional 'type-demonstratives' (Loar 1991).

The structure of a simple reflectively transparent attention may then be represented like this:

> [*Attention: concept of this visual experience* + *concept 'is of'* + *visual demonstrative concept ('that object', 'that property').*]

NB: The concepts mentioned following 'attention' are *complements* of the attitude of attending: they are the concepts employed in the attending and not the *objects* of that attending.

(*c*) *Oblique reflection.* There is another manner of framing attention to a visual experience. It is the upshot e.g. of the holding-constant-while-imaginatively-shifting-references routine, in which one's attention is turned reflectively on what is held constant.

> [*Attention: concept of this visual experience* + *concept 'has'* + *recognitional concept of a certain qualitative perceptual property*] namely the perceptual property that this experience has in common with those that are phenomenally exactly similar, including those of the isolated brain. (Again the terms in italics pick out complements of attention and not its objects.)

It appears to me evident that we are capable of this way of attending to a visual experience. Discerning qualia is one of the two ways of framing attention to one's visual experience; it is compatible with what we've been calling the transparency of experience. The latter is not the only option, but is simply what you find when you adopt that attitude (of reflective transparency) which is the dominant untutored manner of reflecting on one's visual experience. The argument of this chapter has been that the less obvious attitude of oblique reflection, and the intentionalized qualia thereby noted, are also fully available.

13. Final Observations

We have characterized phenomenal sameness as it arises from the oblique perspective. Many philosophers though have seemed to take it for granted that phenomenal sameness is found from (what I have been calling) the transparent perspective, the perspective from which one attends to the objects of visual experiences whether they be real or apparent. But this 'transparent' account of phenomenal sameness requires objects that are hard to take seriously. These are of two sorts, what I've been calling merely intentional objects, and sense data. A prevalent assumption of the sense-data tradition required abandoning ordinary transparency in the veridical case; but that is phenomenologically unpersuasive, for phenomenal transparency in the veridical case is difficult to deny. The substitution of merely intentional objects avoids that implausibility, but still posits strange objects to account for hallucinations; but such objects offend against common sense, which says there is nothing there at all. It is an illusion that phenomenal sameness of veridical and hallucinatory experiences can be discerned from the transparent perspective; in the case of a hallucination one should simply judge that there is nothing there. If that is so phenomenal sameness can be intelligibly discerned only from the oblique perspective; and it consists in resemblance in intentional qualia.

If a philosopher agrees about merely intentional objects and sense data, and yet cannot find in his experience what I call oblique reflection and intentional qualia, he will have to say that veridical and hallucinatory experiences have nothing in common that can be pointed to in experience. Two experiences would be indistinguishable from the first-person perspective even though one experience presents an actual state of affairs and the other presents nothing at all. In denying that there is a positive phenomenal sameness here, this is related to 'disjunctivism' (cf. Snowdon 1981; McDowell 1986). If it is right, and all that is available is the transparent perspective, it would be reasonable to treat the two experiences quite differently.[10] But the sense of positive phenomenal sameness is compelling, will not go away, and begs for a coherent rendition. That is provided by the idea of intentional qualia, and the oblique perspective that reveals them.

Should the reality of intentional qualia raise fears of our being isolated from the world? Scepticism itself is the product of epistemological views, and the right way with it is to attack them. There is no point in eviscerating the mind to fix epistemologists' mistakes. As for our sense of connection to the world, it is the upshot of a bit of phenomenology, that is, the transparent perspective on experience. Is this sense of connection compromised by the availability of the oblique perspective? That is a nice complex question. Worries about the divergence of the lived world and science's world arise, in part, from the availability of a phenomenal realm that has its own integrity.

[10] But suppose the opaque perspective were not available. Then perhaps a coherent conception of isolated brains would not be available. And in that case the reason given in the text for rejecting the property-complex account of phenomenal sameness would not be available. Ned Block has suggested to me that McDowell's disjunctive view seems to overlook the view that what the two experiences have in common is that they represent the same property complex. It might be replied that property complexes are not particular states of affairs, and that the disjunctive view can be taken to deny merely that hallucinations involve relations to phenomenally available states of affairs.

Whether such worries can be assuaged is still an open question. But it is rather implausible to answer it by denying the availability of phenomenal sameness.[11]

REFERENCES

BLOCK, N. (1990), 'Inverted Earth', *Philosophical Perspectives*, 4: 53–79.

DRETSKE, F. (1996), 'Phenomenal Externalism', *Philosophical Issues*, 7: 143–58.

HARMAN, G. (1990), 'The Intrinsic Quality of Experience', *Philosophical Perspectives*, 4: 31–52.

HILL, C. (1991), *Sensations* (Cambridge: Cambridge University Press).

LOAR, B. (1991), 'Personal References', in E. Villanueva (ed.), *Information, Semantics and Epistemology* (Oxford: Blackwell).

—— (2003), 'Phenomenal Intentionality as the Basis of Mental Content', in M. Hahn and B. Ramsberg (eds.), *Reflections and Replies* (Cambridge, Mass.: MIT Press).

LYCAN, W. (1996), 'Layered Perceptual Representation', *Philosophical Issues*, 7: 81–100.

MCDOWELL, J. (1986), 'Singular Thought and the Extent of Inner Space', in P. Pettit and J. McDowell (eds.), *Subject, Thought, and Context* (Oxford: Oxford University Press).

PEACOCKE, C. (1983), *Sense and Content* (Oxford: Oxford University Press).

SHOEMAKER, S. (1994), 'Self-Knowledge and "Inner Sense". Lecture III: The Phenomenal Character of Experience', *Philosophy and Phenomenological Research*, 54/2.

TYE, M. (1995), *Ten Problems of Consciousness* (Cambridge, Mass.: MIT Press).

[11] Thanks to Ned Block, Michael Martin, Nenad Miscevic, and Gabriel Segal for very useful remarks on earlier drafts.

5. Colour, Consciousness, and Colour Consciousness

For those of us blessed with sight, colours have been manifest in the scenes before our eyes ever since such scenes first came into focus. Familiarity has not bred understanding, however. The nature of these old acquaintances remains a matter of dispute. The dispute is intimately tied to 'the hard problem' of visual consciousness—the problem of determining the nature of visual consciousness.

1. Revelation

We seek to know the nature of colour. There is a venerable philosophical tradition that tells us that, as in the quest for the Holy Grail and other folk tales of quests, we already possess what we seek, for those of us blessed with sight have been acquainted with the nature of colour since our first experience of it. Bertrand Russell (1912: 47) placed himself squarely in this tradition with the words:

The particular shade of colour that I am seeing ... may have many things to be said about it ... But such statements, though they make me know truths about the colour, do not make me know the colour itself better than I did before: so far as concerns knowledge of the colour itself, as opposed to knowledge of truths about it, I know the colour perfectly and completely when I see it and no further knowledge of it itself is even theoretically possible.

More recently, Galen Strawson (1989: 224) has remarked in a similar vein:

Colour words are words for properties which are of such a kind that their whole and essential nature as properties can be and is fully revealed in sensory-quality experience given only the qualitative character that that experience has.

Mark Johnston (1992) has aptly labelled the doctrine expressed in these passages 'Revelation'.[1] The doctrine is that the nature of a colour is revealed to us in our visual experience of it. Thus, to know the nature of colours, we need only consult our visual experiences.

If our eyes can be trusted, colours pervade physical surfaces, fill volumes of air and liquid, and are manifest at light sources. There is much that we've learned about light and how it interacts with matter. We've investigated how the chemical properties of surfaces and volumes made up of various materials dispose them to interact with light; how rods and cones respond to light; how electrochemical impulses are propagated along the optic nerve to the visual centres of the brain, and resulting patterns of neural activity therein. From an information-theoretic perspective, we've investigated how the visual system might process information about the scenes before our eyes; how, for instance, neural nets might compute the spectral reflectance distributions of the surfaces in such scenes from the spectral power distributions of the radiant fluxes stimulating our retinas. While there is much that we still don't know, we've learned an enormous amount; and research in vision science is moving apace. It is a consequence of the doctrine of Revelation, however, that all we've learned and, indeed, all we can ever hope to learn by scientific investigation will contribute not one whit to our knowledge of the nature of colours themselves. For Revelation entails that there is nothing more that we can learn about the nature of our old acquaintances than what visual experience teaches us. While scientific investigation can uncover the underlying causal conditions for seeing such things as the redness of the surface of a ripe tomato, the greenness of a traffic light, the yellowness of a volume of beer, and the blueness of an expanse of sky, such investigation will reveal nothing about the nature of these colour qualities themselves. As concerns knowledge of them, experience is not merely the best teacher; it is the only teacher.

2. Colours *v.* What It's Like to See Them

Strawson tells us that the nature of a colour will be revealed in our experience of it, 'given only the qualitative character that that experience has'. By 'the qualitative character of an experience', he means what it is like for a subject of the experience to have the experience. I'll use the equivalent description 'the phenomenal character of an experience'.

In considering Revelation, it is important to note that colours are one thing, the phenomenal characters of colour experiences, another. Red, for

---

[1] J. Campbell (1994), who embraces this doctrine, calls it 'transparency'. I reserve the term 'transparency' for a different doctrine to be discussed below.

instance, is not what it's like to see red. Redness is a property of surfaces and volumes and, thereby, of the objects and materials of which they are surfaces and volumes. What it's like to see red is an aspect of visual experiences of red; it is a property of such experiences.[2] The doctrine of Revelation for colours should be distinguished from the doctrine of Revelation for what it's like to see colours—the doctrine that the nature of the phenomenal character of a colour experience is revealed to us when we have the experience. It's one question whether Revelation is true for what it's like to see colours, it's another whether Revelation is true for colours themselves.

Whatever intuitive appeal the doctrine of Revelation for colours enjoys is, I believe, due to two factors: our recognition that knowledge of what it's like to see a colour figures centrally in our understanding of what the colour itself as such is, and the powerful intuitive appeal of the doctrine of Revelation for what it's like to see colours. In due course, I'll offer an account of colour that will reflect the fact that knowledge of what it's like to see a colour figures centrally in our understanding of the colour. The account will be compatible with the doctrine of Revelation for what it's like to see colours, so it will be open to a proponent of that doctrine to embrace the account. The doctrine of Revelation for colours is not, however, entailed by the doctrine of Revelation for what it's like to see colours and the fact that knowledge of what it's like to see a colour figures centrally in our understanding of it. And I'll reject Revelation for colours. I'll argue, on empirical grounds, that if there are colours, they are ways things might be that involve the interaction or potential interaction of matter and electromagnetic radiation, even though that isn't revealed in our colour experience.

The powerful intuitive appeal of the doctrine of Revelation for what it's like to see colours—for the phenomenal characters of colour experiences—seems to me undeniable. Still I believe it too is mistaken, for I think that the phenomenal characters of our experiences are neuroscientific properties, even though that isn't revealed to us when we have the experiences. I won't attempt to argue that here, however. Nor will I assume it.

In ss. 3–13 of this chapter, I will offer an account of colour and examine the issue of colour realism. In ss. 15–17 I'll draw on the results of that examination to argue that the leading intentionalist (or representationalist) approaches to the hard problem of visual consciousness are committed to an untenable view of colour. Finally, in s. 18, I'll try to articulate the intuitive considerations behind the doctrine of Revelation for the phenomenal characters of experiences and say why I think they don't entail it, and why

---

[2] I use 'what it is like to see red' and 'visual experiences of red' as short for, respectively, 'what it is like to see something red' and 'visual experiences of something red'.

one can accept those intuitive considerations while maintaining that the phenomenal characters of colour experiences are neuroscientific properties.

3. A Functional Analysis of Colour

> When we say we perceive colours in objects, it is really just the same as though we said that we perceive in objects something as to whose nature we are ignorant, but which produces in us a very manifest and obvious sensation, called the sensation of colour.
>
> Descartes (1954: 195)

> That idea which we have called the appearance of colour, suggests the conception and belief of some unknown quality, in the body which occasions the idea; and it is to this quality, and not to the idea, that we give the name colour. The various colours, although in their nature equally unknown, are easily distinguished when we think or speak of them, by being associated with the ideas which they excite . . . When we think or speak of any particular colour, however simple the notion may seem to be, which is presented to the imagination, it is really in some sort compounded. It involves an unknown cause, and a known effect. The name of colour belongs indeed to the cause only, and not to the effect. But as the cause is unknown, we can form no distinct conception of it, but by its relation to the known effect.
>
> Reid, *Inquiry Into the Human Mind*, in Stewart (1822: 205)

For simplicity of exposition, I'll frame my basic proposal for a specific colour, redness. But my account is intended to hold for all colours, chromatic and achromatic (white, black, and shades of grey).[3] Here, then, is my basic proposal (refinements will come later):

Basic Proposal. Redness is that property which disposes its bearers to look red to standard visual perceivers in standard conditions of visual observation and which must (as a matter of nomological necessity) be had by everything so disposed.

Redness is a visual property in that it plays a certain role *vis-à-vis* visual consciousness: namely, the role of being the property that disposes its bearers to look red to standard visual perceivers in standard conditions of visual

---

[3] It is also intended to hold for visual properties such as highlighting, glaring, glowing, gleaming, glinting, glistening, glittering, and the like. Moreover, it can be extended to sensory qualities in the aural, gustatory, olfactory, and tactual modalities—to qualities such as the loudness, pitch, and timbre of sounds, the sweetness, saltiness, sourness, and bitterness of tastes, the putridness of odours, the roughness of tangible surfaces, etc. The account can thus be generalized as an account of sensory qualities.

observation and that (nomologically) must be common to everything so disposed. (Hereafter, I will drop '(nomologically) must' and speak simply of the property common to everything so disposed, where 'everything' is to be understood to range over only nomologically possible things.) Call this role 'the redness-role'. According to the basic proposal, then, redness is just that property, whatever it is, that occupies the redness-role. The proposal is intended as a functional or topic-neutral analysis of the concept of redness. The role-description 'that property which...' is intended not only to fix the referent of the concept, but also to express a condition that is necessary and sufficient for satisfying it.[4] Thus, if the proposal is correct, then all that it takes for a property to be redness is just for it to fill the redness-role; filling the role is necessary and sufficient for a property to be redness; for being redness just consists in filling that role. Thus, being red just consists in having a property that fills the role.[5]

4. Our Functional Analysis v. Dispositionalism

It is a consequence of our functional analysis that redness is not the disposition to look red to standard perceivers in standard circumstances, but rather a basis of the disposition: a property that endows something with the disposition.[6] On the dispositional analysis of colour, something is red if and only if it is disposed to look red to standard perceivers in standard circumstances.[7] Our analysis

---

[4] Kripke (1980: 140 n.) once suggested that we could use a related description to fix the reference of colour terms: 'The reference of "yellowness" is fixed by the description "that (manifest) property of objects which causes them, under normal circumstances, to be seen as yellow (i.e., to be sensed by certain visual impressions)".'

[5] This analysis owes a deep debt to 'the Australian materialist' literature on colour: Smart (1961, 1963); Armstrong (1969); K. Campbell (1969, 1993); Jackson and Pargetter (1987); Maund (1995); and Jackson (1996, 1998). These philosophers disagree among themselves about colour. (For example, Campbell and Maund are colour irrealists, while all the others are colour realists.) As will be apparent to those familiar with this literature, I disagree with each of these philosophers on central points about colour. But my analysis falls squarely within this tradition, a tradition that, as I see it, is anticipated in Reid and (though less straightforwardly) in Descartes. My basic proposal appears in McLaughlin (forthcoming a, b); and the basic proposal, minus the second conjunct, appeared in McLaughlin (1999); that earlier proposal of mine is defended in Cohen (2000); see also Cohen (2001).

[6] A disposition can be a basis for another disposition, for possession of one disposition can endow something with another. Perhaps every disposition must ultimately have a categorical (i.e., non-dispositional) basis, but I can leave that open here. Thus, I am not denying that colours are dispositions, only that they are dispositions to look coloured. Frank Jackson (1998) seems to hold that the bases of dispositions must be categorical and that colours are not dispositions to look coloured, but rather bases for such dispositions. However, he also takes properties such as having a triple of integrated reflectances to be plausible candidates for the colours. Such properties are straightforwardly light-dispositions.

[7] Dispositional analyses of colour go back at least to John Locke (1690/1975), but a related idea can be found in, for example, Aristotle's *De Anima*, III, ii, 426a, and in *Metaphysics*, IV. v. 1010b. Locke is sometimes interpreted as holding that dispositionalism captures our common

agrees with the dispositional analysis in one direction: if something is red, then it is disposed to look red to standard perceivers in standard circumstances. But our analysis offers a different explanation of why this is so from the one the dispositional analysis offers. According to the dispositional analysis, the claim is true because redness = the disposition to look red (to standard perceivers in standard circumstances). According to our functional analysis, it's true for a different reason: red things will be disposed to look red because they have the property of redness, which so disposes them. In implying the falsity of the claim that redness is the disposition to look red, our functional analysis is, I believe, faithful to our common conception of redness, for it is part of that conception that redness disposes its bearers to look red. The disposition to look red doesn't do that. Nor does the second-order property of being a basis for the disposition. Only a basis for the disposition does.

The dispositional analysis implies that if something is disposed to look red (to standard perceivers in standard circumstances), then it is red. So, according to it, if there are things that are so disposed, then there are red things. Our analysis doesn't have that implication. Indeed our analysis fails to have that implication even when conjoined with the assumption that the disposition in question has bases. For, on our analysis, being a basis for the disposition to look red doesn't suffice for being redness; to be redness, a property must be a basis common to all things so disposed. Of course, if everything so disposed has a basis that so disposes it, then, if there are disjunctive properties,[8] there will be a property shared by everything so disposed, namely, the disjunction of all the bases. But from the fact that each disjunct disposes its bearers to look red it does not follow that the disjunctive property does; the disjunctive property may very well fail to be a basis for the disposition, even though each disjunct is. So, even if the disposition to look red has bases and there are disjunctive properties, that would not settle whether anything is really red, as opposed to merely being disposed to so look.

To be red, something must have the property of redness. Redness exists if and only if there is an occupant of the redness-role.[9] Whether anything is red

conception of colour; thus see Bennett (1965). But see Mackie (1976) for an interpretation of Locke according to which Locke offered a dispositional conception of colour as a replacement for our common conception of colour, a conception to which he thought nothing in fact answers. In recent years, dispositional analyses can be found in, among other places, McGinn (1983); Peacocke (1984); McDowell (1985); Wiggins (1987); and Johnston (1992). In Johnston (1992), it is acknowledged that the dispositional conception of colour diverges from our common conception, a conception to which Johnston thinks, ever so strictly speaking, nothing in fact answers.

[8] It is controversial whether there are disjunctive properties in a metaphysical (and so non-pleonastic sense) of 'properties'; see Armstrong (1979). I'm using 'properties' in a metaphysical sense.

[9] 'Redness' here expresses the concept of redness, a concept that purports to denote a certain property. The question is whether it succeeds in denoting a property. On our analysis, it will so

thus depends on whether there is an occupant of that role. That's an empirical question that isn't settled by the fact that there are things disposed to look red to standard perceivers in standard circumstances. For there to be an occupant of the redness-role, first, the disposition to look red to standard perceivers in standard circumstances must have bases and, second, there must be a basis that is common to everything so disposed. If the second condition fails to be met, then while our experiences of red purport to present a single property, they fail to do so. Unless both conditions are met, the visual experiences of red had by standard perceivers in standard circumstances will fail to 'track' any property of the things disposed to produce those experiences in them in such circumstances (save, trivially, that of being so disposed and properties entailed by that property).[10]

If our basic proposal is correct as it stands, then should there fail to be occupants of the colour-roles (the redness-role, the blueness-role, etc.), colour irrealism would be true: nothing would be coloured. Visible objects are disposed to look coloured to us and such dispositions are activated when we see them.[11] If nothing is coloured, then projectivism is true: our colour experiences are in systematic error since they purport to present properties of things in the scenes before our eyes that nothing actually has.[12]

Whether colour realism or colour projectivism is true is an issue that I shall not attempt to resolve here. The reason is that its resolution turns, in part, on empirical issues that remain unsettled. However, in due course, I will sketch what I think is the most promising line of defence of colour realism.

5. Will the Circle Be Unbroken?

A disposition to look red is always a disposition to look red to a certain sort of visual perceiver in certain circumstances of visual observation. It is well known

succeed if and only if there is some property that answers to its descriptive content. (On a pleonastic notion of property, there is a property of F-ness if and only if there is a concept of F. As I said, I'm using 'property' in a metaphysical, not in a pleonastic sense.)

[10] Two unrelated points of clarification: first, while I speak of tracking here, I am not appealing to Robert Nozick's (1980) would-be counterfactual analysis of tracking. Second, by 'property entailment', I mean the possession of one property metaphysically necessitating the possession of another (so that there is no possible world in which something has the one, but not the other).

[11] In a very broad sense of colour, we can't (directly) see an object unless it looks some colour to us.

[12] Projectivism goes back at least to Galileo and Descartes, and related ideas can be found as far back as Democritus. In recent years, defences of projectivism can be found in the philosophical literature in, among other places, Campbell (1969, 1993); Mackie (1976); Hardin (1988/1993, 1990); Boghossian and Velleman (1989, 1991); Baldwin (1992); and Maund (1995). Defences can be found in the psychological literature in, among many other places, Cosmides and Tooby (1995), and Kuehni (1997). For a defence of the view that colour irrealism is incoherent, see Stroud (2000).

that how something looks in colour can vary with variations in the visual perceiver (such as the kinds of pigments in the observer's cones, the state of adaptation of the cones, conditions of the perceiver's visual cortex, and so on) and with variations in the environmental circumstances of visual observation (the kind of incident light, the surround of the thing observed, the distance and angle of the thing observed, conditions of the intervening medium, and so on). Since our functional analysis, like the dispositional one, appeals to the notions of a standard visual perceiver and standard circumstances of visual observation, it invites the questions: What kind of visual perceiver is standard? What kind of circumstance of visual observation is standard?

In reply to these questions, one might say that the kind of visual perceiver that is standard is the kind to whom things that were a certain colour, C, would look C in standard circumstances of visual observation, and that the kind of circumstance of visual observation that is standard is the kind in which things that were C would look C to standard visual perceivers. This reply amounts to a functional or topic-neutral analysis of the notions of a standard visual perceiver and standard circumstances of visual observation. While such an analysis is compatible with the truth of our claim that redness is the property that occupies the redness-role, it is unavailable to us since we intend this claim as a functional analysis of the concept of redness. Our basic proposal appeals to the notions of a standard perceiver and standard circumstance in saying what redness is, and, so, the reply in question would take us in a circle. According to our analysis, being redness just consists in occupying the redness-role, a role specified in terms of the notions in question. So, if our analysis is correct, then it can't be the case that being a standard visual perceiver just consists in being a visual perceiver to whom red things would be disposed to look red in standard conditions of visual observation; similarly for being a standard circumstance of visual observation. Since we propose to identify what property (if any) redness is by appeal to the notions of a standard perceiver and standard circumstances, we need to indicate how to identify standard perceivers and circumstances, at least in principle, without identifying redness or having to determine whether anything is red. There is, of course, a Euthyphro question here: Is what makes an experience an experience of red the relationship it bears to redness, or is what makes a property redness the relationship it bearers to experiences of red? If our functional analysis is correct, the answer is the latter. (Our functional analysis shares this consequence with dispositionalism.)

Our common conception of colour seems to involve notions of a normal visual perceiver and normal circumstances of visual observation. We thus speak of 'colour blindness', an abnormality in colour vision, and count visual perceivers suffering from it as undergoing colour illusions in some normal circumstances. And normal perceivers are said to undergo colour illusions in some circumstances of visual observation; we thus count the wall as white, despite the fact that it looks pink to a normal perceiver when bathed in red light.[13] In reply to the questions at issue, let us, just as a first pass, appeal to our actual ordinary standards of normality, those we in fact tacitly invoke in everyday discourse. Our actual everyday notions of a normal perceiver and normal circumstances are of course considerably vague, and hence considerably semantically indeterminate: borderline cases of standard perceivers and standard circumstances abound. But we can recognize clear-cut cases of each. Our actual everyday standards are, I believe, somewhat arbitrary, to some extent a matter of tacit convention rather than standards that were once somehow discovered.[14] It may even be that the standards can vary somewhat with conversational context.[15] Still appeal to these notions will serve to fix our ideas. Thus, for the time being, refinements will come later, let us mean by 'standard visual perceivers' visual perceivers of the kind that count as normal by our actual ordinary standards, and by 'standard circumstances of visual observation', circumstances of the kind that count as normal by our actual ordinary standards. This first-pass reply doesn't result in circularity since we can, in principle, determine whether a type of perceiver or observational circumstance counts as normal in this sense without determining whether anything is red or what property (if any) redness in fact is. Moreover, in due course, I'll revise this first-pass proposal in a way that removes any concern whatsoever about circularity.

Are there circularity worries as concerns 'looks red'? From the fact that something looks red, it does not follow that the something in question is red; indeed it does not even follow that there are (were or will be) any red things. Still there would be a circularity worry if something looks red to a subject only if an experience of the subject bears a relationship to the property redness.

---

[13] Here, as in our functional analysis, I use 'looks' in the phenomenal sense. To someone in the know, a white wall in red light will, of course, not look as if it is pink; it will look as if it is white in red light; similarly, it won't look to be pink, it will look to be white in red light. (This fact reflects one of the things sometimes meant by 'colour constancy'.) Still even to such a perceiver, assuming that she is normal, the white wall will look pink in the phenomenal sense of 'looks'. 'Looks' is used epistemically, rather than phenomenally, in 'looks as if' and 'looks to be' locutions. One difference between the phenomenal and epistemic uses of 'looks' is that while something can look as if it is F (or look to be F) only to a subject that has the concept of F, something can look F—in the phenomenal sense—to a subject that lacks the concept of F. For instance, something can (phenomenally) look right-angled to a subject that lacks the concept of a right angle. Moreover, there is a vast number of specific shades of colour such that something can (phenomenally) look that shade of colour to us, even though we lack a concept of it (see Raffman 1995). The *locus classicus* for discussion of the phenomenal, epistemic, and comparative ('looks like a(n)', e.g. looks like a cat), uses of 'looks' is Chisholm (1957); but see also Jackson (1977), who coined the term 'phenomenal use of "looks"'.

[14] See Hardin (1988/93).

[15] See Chisholm (1957). For present purposes, it won't matter if that is so; we can take the conversational parameters to be fixed.

The fact that something looks red to a subject does not, however, entail that the subject has an experience that bears a relationship to redness, for it doesn't even entail that redness exists. (Something can look demon-possessed, even though there is actually no such property as being demon-possessed.) It is one question whether redness exists; it's another whether anything ever looks red to us, whether we ever have visual experiences of something red.[16] If our functional analysis is correct, then redness exists if and only if some property actually plays the redness-role. That there is such a property doesn't follow from the fact that some things look red to us. Furthermore, as we'll see in the next section, there is a sense in which it is possible for something to have the property of redness and yet not be disposed to look red.

Still a circularity worry of sorts can be seen to arise when we address such questions as this: What is it for something to look red? A natural response is that it is for the something in question to look the way red things would look in colour to standard perceivers in standard circumstances. This natural response does not imply that there actually are (were or will be) any red things, or even that redness exists. We can say what would be the case were someone demon-possessed, even though there is no such property as being demon-possessed. But consider that the natural response to the question what it is for something to look blue is this: it's for it to look the way blue things would look in colour to standard perceivers in standard circumstances. And there are parallel responses to the parallel questions concerning every other way that something might look in colour. How, then, do we understand the different claims made by the responses in question?[17]

It is, of course, not well understood how we understand any claims at all. Understanding is not well understood. But it seems fair to say that, for those of us blessed with normal sight, our knowledge of the phenomenal characters of our colour experiences contributes to our understanding of the claims in question.[18] We know what it's like for something to look red to us and what

[16] Some philosophers would use 'visual experiences as of something red' in this sentence, rather than 'visual experiences of something red'. For they maintain that one can have a visual experience of X only if X exists (obtains, occurs, etc.), but that one can have a visual experience as of X, even if X doesn't exist (obtain, occur, etc.). I see no need for this 'as of' locution. Even though there are no ghosts, it seems to me true that some people are afraid of ghosts; and even though there is no heaven, it seems to me that some people are desirous of entry into heaven. Similarly, it seems to me that one can have a visual experience of X, even if X doesn't exist (obtain, occurs, etc.). Someone suffering from delirium tremens might have a visual hallucination of a pink elephant in the middle of the room, and so have a visual experience of a pink elephant in the middle of the room, even though there is no pink elephant in the middle of the room. But those to whom things don't seem that way can read my 'visual experience of something red' as 'visual experience as of something red'.

[17] I owe this way of spelling out the circularity worry to D. Lewis (1997).

[18] D. Lewis (1997) offers a different answer to the circularity worry, one that I could also accept.

it's like for something to look blue to us, and know that what it's like for us for something to look red to us is different from what it's like for us for something to look blue to us. This knowledge contributes to our understanding of the claims about what it is for something to look red and what it is for something to look blue. Moreover, in so far as this knowledge so contributes, it contributes to our understanding of what redness itself as such is and what blueness itself as such is, for it contributes to our understanding of the redness-role and the blueness-role. This contribution to understanding is one that the congenitally blind are missing, and for this reason, among others, they lack full possession of colour concepts.[19]

6. Might Redness Not Have Been Redness?

Suppose that some property, Φ, fills the redness-role. Then, according to our functional analysis, Φ is redness. But if there is in fact such a property, Φ, it might not have filled the role. Had some of the laws of nature been different from what they in fact are, it would not have disposed its bearers to look red to standard perceivers in standard circumstances, or there would have been another property that also disposes the things that have it to look red to standard perceivers in standard circumstances that is sometimes possessed without Φ being possessed.[20] Either way Φ would not have played the redness-role. Does it follow, then, that redness might not have been redness?

It is of course nonsense to say that something might not have been identical with itself. Still the property that plays the redness-role might not have; and so, in a sense, redness might not have been redness. Descriptions admit of scope distinctions. The description 'the property that plays the redness-role' takes narrow scope in: 'It might be the case that the property that plays the redness-role is not the property that plays the redness-role.'[21] And this claim

[19] They can of course possess colour concepts, even though they can't be in full possession of them. Helen Keller, for instance, had colour concepts. For a debate over the extent to which the blind can possess vision-related concepts, see Magee and Milligan 1995, a fascinating correspondence between a sighted philosopher, Bryan Magee, and a blind philosopher, Martin Milligan, who lost his eyes to cancer at the age of 18 months.

[20] Two unrelated points: First, on the understanding of 'standard visual perceivers' and 'standard conditions of visual observation' suggested as a first pass in the previous section, one or both of these alternatives will hold, provided that at least some of the laws of nature required for a property to play the redness-role are not included in what count as standard circumstances and/or standard perceivers by our actual ordinary criteria. Second, I assume here, not uncontroversially (see Shoemaker 1998), that properties do not have their causal powers essentially. I should note, however, that my views about colour could be recast in a way that makes them compatible with the view that properties have their powers essentially. Nothing essential to my view of colour turns on this issue.

[21] Its scope is narrow because both occurrences of it are within the scope of 'it might be the case that'.

is necessarily false. The fact that the description is sometimes used with narrow scope explains why there is a sense in which redness could not have failed to play the redness-role. The description takes wide scope in: 'The property that plays the redness-role is such that it might not have been the property that plays the redness-role.' And this claim is true. The fact that the description is sometimes used with wide scope explains why there is a sense in which redness could have failed to play the redness-role. This scope distinction thus explains why there is a sense in which redness might not have been redness, and a sense in which redness could not have failed to be redness.

We can achieve further illumination here by appealing to the distinction between rigid and non-rigid descriptions.[22] The descriptions 'the property that actually plays the redness-role' and 'the property that in fact plays the redness-role' are rigid: they pick out the same property in every possible world in which they pick out anything. In contrast, the description 'the property that plays the redness-role' is non-rigid. It is impossible that the property that plays the redness-role does not play that role; and so, in a sense, redness could not have failed to be redness. Still the property that actually plays it might not have; and, so, in another sense, redness could have failed to be redness. For instance, the property that is in fact redness might not have disposed things to look red.

It seems to me that in ordinary discourse, we sometimes use 'redness' rigidly and sometimes use it non-rigidly. I see no decisive reason for thinking either use is primary. The description 'that property which disposes...' is used in a content-giving sense, rather than merely in a reference-fixing sense, in our functional analysis of redness. But that leaves open whether 'redness' is used rigidly or non-rigidly in the proposal. As concerns our basic proposal, if 'redness' is used rigidly in it, then while the proposal is a priori, it is contingent. If, however, 'redness' is used non-rigidly in it, then our proposal purports to be both a priori and necessary.[23] To fix our ideas, let us understand 'redness' to be used non-rigidly in the basic proposal. And let us hereafter always use 'redness' unqualified by a rigidifying expression such as 'actually' or 'in fact' in a non-rigid way, and use either the rigidified description 'the property that is actually redness' or the rigidified description 'the property that is in fact redness', when we want to pick out the same property in every possible world. Since 'redness' is used non-rigidly in our analysis, it entails that what property counts as redness can vary from one possible world to another. Thus, a statement of the form 'Φ is redness' would, like the

---

[22] Kripke (1980). As Kripke points out, the narrow/wide scope distinction can't do all of the work of the rigid/non-rigid distinction.

[23] To be precise, what purports to be a priori and necessary is the proposal that if redness exists, then redness is that property which disposes its bearers to look red to standard perceivers in standard circumstances and which is had by everything so disposed.

statement 'Benjamin Franklin is the inventor of bifocals', be a contingent statement of identification. But, even so, it is none the less necessary that if a property is redness, then it disposes its bearers to look red to standard perceivers in standard circumstances. The necessity here is *de dicto*, not *de re*, for the truth is a truth *de conceptu*, not *de re*. A property answers to our concept of redness only if it disposes its bearers to look red to standard perceivers in standard circumstances. It is not, however, an essential feature of the property (if any) that is in fact redness that it so dispose its bearers. On the contrary, that is a contingent feature of it, for the property (if any) that answers to our (unrigidified) concept of redness might not have.

7. The Role of Vision Science

It is compatible with our functional analysis, generalized to all colours, that colours are ontologically emergent properties, that is, fundamental, irreducible properties that emerge from microphysical properties of certain complex physical wholes.[24] There are, however, compelling, and often rehearsed, empirical reasons to deny that colours are fundamental properties. To note one such reason: as a matter of fact, to disposes its bearers to look some colour, a property will have to dispose them to causally produce visual experiences in a way that involves the behaviour of light. As physics is, among other things, the science of the behaviour of light, the fundamental properties that dispose things to produce effects by means of light are the concern of physics. But to explain the behaviour of light, physics has no need of the hypothesis that things are coloured; colours figure in no law of physics.[25] It remains open, however, that rather than fundamental, emergent properties of certain physical wholes, colours are in some sense derivative from microphysical properties of certain physical wholes. Indeed on the evidence, if there are colours, they are so derivative, for the properties that affect the behaviour of light are microphysical properties or properties derivative from them. Let us call properties that are derivative from microphysical properties, 'physical properties'.[26]

---

[24] The British Emergentists Alexander (1920) and Broad (1925) held such a position (see McLaughlin 1991); and, more recently, Cornman held this view (Cornman 1974, 1975). According to these emergentists, physical properties necessitate colour properties as a matter of law, but these laws are fundamental, and so irreducible. Emergentism entails that a world could be a minimal physical duplicate of the actual world and yet not contain the physical-colour laws in question. (For a discussion of the notion of 'a minimal physical duplicate' see Jackson 1996.)

[25] About that, Galileo was, of course, right.

[26] So-called functional properties—second-order properties such as being a property with such-and-such a causal role—would count as 'physical properties' in this broad sense if any minimal physical duplicate of the actual world must contain exactly the same pattern of distribution of functional properties as in the actual world.

Given that redness, if it exists, is such a derivative property, it is a job for vision science to identify the physical property in question and, thereby, to locate the place of redness in nature.[27] Vision science will do this by identifying the physical property that plays the redness-role. It is also a job for vision science to explain how the property in question fills the role. The explanation will include a description of the underlying mechanisms by means of which the property disposes its bearers to look red. It is thus a job for vision science to say (a) what physical property, if any, performs the redness-role, and, if there is such a property, (b) how it performs it. The tasks are related. For the explanation of how the property performs the role will figure in the justification for the theoretical identification of redness as that property.

Subtleties aside, if and when a filler of the redness-role is found, we can reason as follows: Redness is the property that plays the redness-role. Physical property Φ is the property that plays the redness-role. Thus, redness is physical property Φ. Redness will have, thereby, been located in nature.[28] It is thus, in the end, vision science that should tell us what property, if any, redness in fact is. The value of the armchair functional analysis is that it tells us where to look to locate redness in the story about colour vision that science hopes ultimately to tell. The property, if any, cast in the redness-role is the property that is in fact redness; likewise for the other colours.

8. Relations Among the Colours

According to our functional analysis, all it takes for a property to be redness is for it to play the redness-role. Some philosophers would object that this is not all that it takes, for colours participate in certain essential similarity and difference relationships. The relations in question include these:

Red is more similar to orange than it is to blue.
Blue is more similar to purple than it is to yellow.
Yellow is more similar to orange than it is to green.
Some reds are richer in redness than others.
Purple is reddish-blue.
Lime is yellowish-green.
Cyan is greenish-blue.
Some oranges are reddish-yellow, and some are yellowish-red.
There are no reddish-greens or greenish-reds.
There are no yellowish-blues or bluish-yellows.

[27] See the discussion of 'location problems' in Jackson (1998).
[28] Cf. Jackson and Pargetter (1987).

Such relationships are, it is claimed, essential to the colours in question.[29] If these relationships are indeed essential to the colours, then our functional analysis fails to state a sufficient condition for being redness. For it is possible for properties R, O, and B to play, respectively, the redness-role, the orangeness-role, and the blueness-role, and yet it not be the case that R is essentially more similar to O than it is to B. Thus, if these relationships are essential to the colours, then even if vision scientists succeed in identifying an occupant of the redness role, it would not follow that they have, thereby, succeeded in locating redness in nature. For the question would remain whether the property in question is essentially more similar to orangeness than it is to blueness.

Perhaps the leading *philosophical* objection to colour physicalism is that no physical properties that are even remotely plausible candidates for being the colours essentially participate in these patterns of relationships.[30] The problem of whether there are physical properties that so participate is called 'the problem of unity'.[31] The alleged problem is, I maintain, no problem whatsoever for colour-physicalism. And our functional analysis will do as it stands. Or so I'll now argue.

9. Colour Space and the Phenomenal Character of Colour Experiences

There are various systems for scaling surface colours. One is the Munsell System (Munsell 1905/46), another is the Swedish Natural Colour System, which is based on Herring's unique/binary distinction (1878/1964). I'll focus on the latter for illustration. The Natural System classifies every colour by its degree of resemblance to white, black, and the four so-called 'unique hues': pure red (red that is not at all bluish or yellowish), pure green (green that is

[29] Meinong took such relations to be 'internal relationships' among the colours (see Mulligan 1991), as did Wittgenstein (1921/61) following him. Thus, in 4.123 of the *Tractatus*, Wittgenstein tells us: 'A Property is internal if it is unthinkable that its object should not possess it' and he gives an example involving colour: 'This shade of blue and that one stand, eo ipso, in the internal relation of lighter to darker. It is unthinkable that these objects should not stand in that relation' (ibid 27). Similarly, Moritz Schlick (1979: 293–4) asserts: 'relations which hold between the elements of the systems of colours are, obviously, internal relations, for it is customary to call a relation internal if it relates two (or more) terms in such a way that the terms cannot possibly exist without the relation existing between them—in other words, if the relation is necessarily implied by the very nature of the terms'. (Wittgenstein and Schlick are quoted in Thompson 1995: 270–1.) More recent authors that seem to take the relationships to be essential include Campbell (1969); Hardin (1988/93); Boghossian and Velleman (1991); Johnston (1992); Maund (1995); and Thompson (1995).

[30] See Hardin (1988/93); Boghossian and Velleman (1991); Johnston (1992); Maund (1995); and Thompson (1995).

[31] See K. Campbell (1969) and Johnston (1992).

not at all bluish or yellowish), pure yellow (yellow that is not at all greenish or reddish), and pure blue (blue that is not at all greenish or reddish). The other hues (purple, orange, etc.) are 'binary' since each is a 'mixture' or 'blend' of two unique hues.[32] For instance, shades of purple are reddish-blue or bluish-red, and shades of orange are reddish-yellow or yellowish-red. 'Balanced' orange is characterized as a mixture of 50 per cent red and 50 per cent yellow. In contrast, unique red, for instance, contains no percentage of any other hues. Since there are no reddish-greens or greenish-reds, red and green are called 'opponent colours'; and, similarly, since there are no yellowish-blues or bluish-yellows, yellow and blue are also opponent colours. Colours of a given hue can vary in what are generally referred to as lightness and saturation. The resemblances among colours are in respect of hue, saturation, and lightness.[33] The hue attribute is scaled by the degree of redness, blueness, greenness, and yellowness of shades of colours. The saturation attribute is scaled by the proportion of hue (redness, blueness, etc.) relative to the central grey axis. And the lightness attribute runs from light to dark (in the case of achromatic colours, from white through various greys to black).

The Natural System for scaling surface colours generates a three-dimensional colour space that has the shape of a double-cone with the most intense colour (Herring's *Vollforbe*) at one apex of the constant hue triangles forming the double cone. Lightness is represented by the vertical axis of the double-cone, with white represented at the top end point, black at the other, shades of grey in between, and with middle grey represented by the mid-point (the centre of the double-cone). Saturation is represented by the horizontal axis of the double-cone as a result of the triangular Herring-type arrangement of constant hue colours in terms of blackness and whiteness content. Points on the central circumference of the double-cone, called 'the hue circle', represent hues of maximal saturation. Unique hues are arranged at 90° angle intervals

---

[32] As Hardin (1988/93: p.xxviii) accurately reports: 'The classic experiment is by Sternheim and Boynton (1966), in which it is demonstrated that subjects who are forbidden the use of the label "orange" are able fully to describe orange-looking stimuli by using the labels "yellow" and "red", whereas denying them the use of, say, "yellow" while permitting "red", "orange", and "green" results in a deficiency in the description of the stimuli that look yellow. Subsequent studies using the Sternheim–Boynton method showed that red and blue are also elemental. However, Fuld, Werner, and Wooten (1983) concluded that brown might be an elemental colour... although this conclusion was subsequently re-examined, retested, and rejected by Quinn, Rosano, and Wooten (1988).'

[33] Actually, in the NCS system, an implicit variable is chromaticness, rather than saturation. Chromaticness is the degree of resemblances to the four basic chromatic colours: red, blue, yellow, and green. As Hardin notes (1988/93: 119), 'the term "saturation" is used in the NCS system, but refers to increasing chromatic proportion'. Also rather than the attribute of lightness, that of blackness is used. This difference makes for differences in the represented relationships among chromatic colours. None of this, however, will make any difference to the claims that I make below.

on the hue circle. Opponent hues are represented on opposite sides of the circle at 180°, blue opposite yellow, red opposite green.

The colour double-cone represents all the similarity and difference relationships among colours listed in the preceding section. For instance, the fact that red is more similar to orange than it is to blue is represented by the fact that the volume of the double-cone representing shades of red is closer to the volume representing shades of orange than it is to the volume representing shades of blue; similarly for the fact that blue is more similar to purple than it is to yellow. The richer a shade of red is in redness, that is to say, the more saturated the shade is, the closer its representation will be to the surface of the circumference of the double-cone. The geometry of the double-cone and these assignments of representations exclude the possibility of would-be representations of reddish-greens, greenish-reds, bluish-yellows, or yellowish-blues.[34]

The colour double-cone was designed to reflect human colour discriminations according to the selected attributes.[35] The data about human colour discriminations is collected from the discriminations people make when instructed to compare samples on the basis of the way they look according to the selected attributes. The unique/binary distinction is, moreover, drawn phenomenologically; the relevant notion of 'mixing' or 'blending' is entirely phenomenological.[36] It thus has nothing to do, for instance, with mixing pigments or lights. Even though a mixture of blue and yellow pigments will make a green pigment, blue and yellow are opponent colours because nothing looks bluish-yellow or yellowish-blue. Similarly, even though the mixing of red light that is somewhat yellowish with green light that is somewhat yellowish will produce yellow light,[37] no shade of yellow appears reddish-green or greenish-red—indeed it seems that nothing appears reddish-green or greenish-red.[38] It is because there is a shade of yellow that things can look

[34] It isn't claimed by those who maintain these comparative relationships are essential to the colours that a colour can be defined by its position in the colour double-cone. And that is all to the good since there are many other colour spaces. There is, at present, no consensus in vision science as to what all the dimensions of colour are.

[35] The same is true of the irregular sphere generated in the Munsell colour scaling system, where the attributes are hue, lightness, and chroma.

[36] Herring (1878/1964).

[37] If the red light and green light are both neutral, then the mixture will be desaturated red, desaturated green, or white, depending on the mixture ratio.

[38] The claim that nothing appears reddish-green is, it should be noted, controversial, and the claim that nothing *could* appear reddish-green, even more so. Crane and Piantanida (1983) conducted an experiment in which they claim the boundary between two bars, one red the other green, could be made to appear reddish-green by stabilizing the eyes in a certain way. But their results are controversial. Hardin (1993: p. xxix) reports: 'At an Optical Society conference on colour appearance . . . I was able to interview four visual scientists, including Piantanida, who had looked at the boundary between the red and green bars as it was stabilized by means of the eye-tracker. I asked them to describe, in as much detail as they could, the colour appearance they had seen. Piantanida's reply was unequivocal: It was unproblematically a texture-free red-green.

without looking at all greenish or reddish (or any other combination of hues), that that shade, pure yellow, counts as a unique hue. Orange is a binary hue in that things that look orange look somewhat reddish and somewhat yellowish; orange is characterized as a 'perceptual mixture' of red and yellow. Visual experiences of the unique hues and of white and black serve as the basis of comparison of visual experiences of all other colours along the dimensions of hue, saturation, and lightness.

The important point for our purposes is that the facts represented in the colour double-cone are, in the first instance, about what it is like for things to look the colours in question, and only derivatively about the colours themselves. These derivative facts about the colours are, moreover, captured by our functional analysis as it stands. Consider, once again, the fact that

Red is more similar to orange than it is to blue.

This comparative fact holds in virtue of the fact that:

Red is more similar to orange than it is to blue in respect of what it is like for something to look the ways in question.

All else being equal (i.e. all other dimensions of visual experience held equal), what it is like for something to look red is more similar to what it is like for something to look orange than it is to what it is like for something to look

The answers from the other three were considerably more guarded. One said that it had a muddy, brownish quality, looking rather like certain regions of a post-Christmas poinsettia leaf in transition from red to green. (This is very similar in appearance to the autumn leaf my wife produced one day when I asked her if there could be reddish green. The surface of such leaves is of course an intermingling of tiny red spots and green spots.) Two others agreed that it was a colour, and not quite like any they had seen before. However, they were not immediately inclined to label it "reddish green", as they would have been immediately inclined to label an orange "reddish yellow", or a cyan "greenish-blue". Rather, when they were pressed to attach a colour name to it, "reddish green" seemed to them to be more appropriate than any other label, since the quality region seemed to resemble the red bar that was on the red side but also seemed to resemble the green bar that was on the other. More than one person saw it as dark and muddy and remarked that the hues of dark and muddy colours are typically difficult to judge. Although nobody believed that what is known of the workings of the human colour-vision system absolutely rules out the possibility of such visual experience as the one Piantanida claimed to have had, none of the three seemed sufficiently impressed by what he or she had seen to want to bother replicating the experiment, even though eye-trackers are now more common than they were at the time. There have been no published follow-up studies by Piantanida or by anyone else.' There has recently been a follow-up study by Billock, Gleason, and Tsou (2001) that supports Crane's and Piantanida's findings. But the issue is not yet definitively settled. I've not myself seen the bars. (I have, however, examined poinsettia leaves in transition from red to green and while they indeed have an intermingling of red and green spots, I can say with complete confidence that they don't look reddish-green or greenish-red.) I've spoken to one vision scientist who has seen the bars, and he reported that the boundary between them appeared dark and muddy and was difficult to classify. He also said it produced 'a surprising visual sensation', but added that it was not the most surprising sensation he had ever had. When asked what *was* the most surprising sensation he had ever had, he replied 'My first orgasm'.

blue. The comparative claim about red, orange, and blue is thus true in virtue of a comparative fact about the visual experiences in question. Colours themselves participate in the similarity and difference relationships derivatively—in virtue of the participation of the visual experiences that they dispose their bearers to produce.[39]

All else being equal, what it is like for something to look red is more similar to what it is like for something to look orange than it is to what it is like for something to look blue. That is to say, all else equal, visual experiences of red are more similar to visual experiences of orange than they are to visual experiences of blue—more similar, that is, in their phenomenal characters. *If* this similarity is an essential similarity, then it is necessarily the case that the kind of experience that red would dispose its bearers to produce (in standard perceivers in standard circumstances of observation) is more similar to the kind orange would dispose its bearers to produce than it is to the kind blue would dispose its bearers to produce. But the necessity of this claim about red, orange, and blue would be *de dicto*, not *de re*.[40] This *de dicto* necessary truth (assuming that it is a necessary truth) does not entail that the property that is in fact redness *essentially* participates in this comparative relation. Rather, it entails that to be redness a property must be such that the kind of experience that it disposes its bearers to produce is more similar in phenomenal character to the kind orange would dispose its bearers to produce than it is to the kind blue would dispose its bearers to produce. A physical property will meet this condition if it plays the redness-role, for it will, then, dispose its bearers to look red. If it is *de dicto* necessary that the kind of experience that red would dispose its bearers to produce is more similar in phenomenal character to the kind orange would dispose its bearers to produce than it is to the kind blue would dispose its bearers to produce, that would be because the truth is *de conceptu*: properties would answer to our concepts of redness, orangeness, and blueness only if they met this condition. That fact would be captured by the claim that redness, orangeness, and blueness must play, respectively, the redness-role, the orangeness-role, and the blueness-role.

Our functional analysis captures facts of unique-binary relations as it stands. To be orange, for example, a property *must* meet the following condition: it must be such that the things that have it are disposed to look somewhat similar in hue to the way red things would look and somewhat similar in hue to the way yellow things would look. This does not entail that it

---

[39] Cf. McLaughlin (1999).

[40] As I noted earlier, I'm assuming in this chapter that properties don't have their causal roles essentially. If properties have their causal roles essentially, then the comparative claim in question is *de re* necessary, for the colour properties would be essentially similar in respect of certain of their causal roles.

is an essential property of orange itself that it be such. The necessity is *de dicto*, not *de re*, for the truth is *de conceptu*, not *de re*. The condition is one that a physical property must meet to satisfy our concept of orangeness. A property will meet this condition if it plays the orange-role, for to play that role it must disposes its bearers to look orange; and that will guarantee that it meets the condition. As concerns opponent colours, if, for instance, red and green are indeed opponent colours, and so there is no reddish-green or greenish-red, then that fact would be captured by the fact that no property disposes its bearers to look reddish-green or greenish-red. And if, as now seems quite controversial (see n. 38), nothing could look reddish-green or greenish-red, then there couldn't be a property that disposes its bearers to look reddish-green or greenish-red, and so it would be impossible for reddish-green or greenish-red to exist.

It may be that some of the claims we've been discussing (e.g. that there is no reddish-green, that nothing looks reddish-green) will be disproved by experience. But should it prove to be the case that the properties that are in fact the colours do not essentially participate in the similarity and difference relationships in question that alone would give us no reason to reject any of the comparative claims about the colours. Nothing we could learn about the properties that are in fact the colours that is independent of how they dispose things to look would refute any of these claims, for if the comparative claims are true, they are so in virtue of what it is like for things to look the colours in question.

Of course, it could turn out that the property that is in fact redness is essentially overall more intrinsically similar to the property that is in fact orangeness than it is to the property that is in fact blueness; likewise, it could turn out that the property that is in fact orangeness is in some sense a 'mixture' or 'blend' or 'combination' of the properties that are in fact yellowness and redness. There could be a structure of essential relationships among the properties that are in fact the colours that is isomorphic to the structure of essential relationships among colour experiences.[41] But if that proved to be the case, it would be a happy coincidence. The fate of colour-physicalism does not depend on it.

In summary, then, the comparative facts about colours listed in s. 8 pose no problem whatsoever for the view that colours are physical properties. And that is all to the good since, as we'll now see, colour-physicalism faces problems enough.

---

[41] Several philosophers have claimed that triples of integrated reflectances will participate in the relevant essential relationships: see e.g. Hilbert (1987); Gibbard (1996); Hilbert and Bryne (1997); Lewis (1997); and Tye (2000). But the case has not been made in any detail. Of triples of integrated reflectances, more later.

10. The Problem of Standard Variation

Empirical investigation has led some prominent colour scientists to colour irrealism.[42] The reason, I submit, is that their investigations have led them to despair of finding physical properties that play the colour-roles. If our basic proposal is on the right track, then there are three basic problems that a defence of colour-realism faces. I'll call the first 'the problem of standard variation', the second 'the problem of common ground', and the third 'the problem of multiple grounds'. Let us begin with the problem of standard variation. (The other problems will be discussed in s. 12.)

Recall our first-pass understanding of standard visual perceivers and standard circumstances of visual observation as, respectively, the kinds of visual perceivers and circumstances that count as normal by actual everyday standards. There are variations in the state of adaptation of eyes and/or in lighting conditions, surrounds, intervening media, and the like, that count as within the normal range by our actual everyday standards yet which will affect certain ways things look in colour. By a basic way something looks in colour, I'll mean a way something looks in colour but not by means of looking some other way in colour. A basic shade of colour is a shade of which there are no more determinate shades. Whenever something looks some colour to us, it looks some basic shade of colour to us. For instance, something will look red by looking some basic shade of red. The point to note for present purposes, then, is that as concerns the basic ways things look in colour that are affected by the variations in question, there will be no physical properties that play the relevant colour-roles. The reason is that for no such way will there be a physical property that disposes its bearers to look that way in colour to *all* perceivers that count as normal in *every* circumstance that counts as normal by actual ordinary standards.

A wide variety of lighting conditions fall within the normal range by actual everyday standards. As lighting conditions change over the course of a typical sunny summer afternoon, a particular tomato may look, perhaps, a dozen different basic shades of red due to shifts in lighting that fall within the normal range.[43] Suppose that red_{12} is one of the basic shades in question. Then, there is no property that disposes its bearers to look red_{12} to all perceivers that count as normal in every circumstance that counts as normal by our actual ordinary standards. The same is true of most non-basic shades. Unique blue (blue that is not at all greenish or reddish) isn't a basic shade since there are shades of unique blue that vary in saturation (the amount of blue in them) and lightness (how light or dark they are). The dress may look

---

[42] See e.g. Kuehni (1997).
[43] This is true even though there is some colour constancy.

one shade of unique blue in the lighting of the shop, another in the bright sunlight of the street, and yet another by the light inside the restaurant, even though each lighting condition falls within what counts as the normal range by actual ordinary standards. These changes in colour appearance in the different lighting conditions are due to changes in the state of adaptation of the perceiver's eyes, more specifically, to changes in the photopigments in the perceiver's cones. Coming in from the sunlight, the protopigments will be bleached, and so the chair might look pinkish until one's eyes adjust to the different light, at which point it looks more reddish, yet both states of adaptation fall within the normal range. Usually, lighting conditions are continually varying and, as a result, so are the states of adaptation of the eyes of perceivers. The result is subtle shifts in the colours things look.[44]

The effects of surround on colour appearance should be familiar to anyone concerned with colour co-ordination of clothes, furniture, accessories, or the like.[45] Before you choose the tile for your floor on the basis of its colour, hold one of the tiles near a wall in the room in which you intend to place them. The colour the tiles look in the store may be sufficiently different from the colour they would look when placed in the room to affect your desire to purchase them. Before you paint the outside trims of the front windows of your house a certain way, take note of how the paint will affect the colour appearance of the house. The paint might 'bring out' a tinge in the house that you'll find unattractive.[46] Such changes in colour appearance are usually undramatic. But a colour scientist skilled at putting coloured pieces of crêpe paper against larger pieces to provide surrounds that affect colour appearance can produce fairly dramatic shifts.[47] There need be nothing 'abnormal' by ordinary standards in any of the arrangements of crêpe paper the scientist places before your eyes. You might come across any of the arrangements on any worktable in a pre-school classroom.

[44] To acquaint yourself or reacquaint yourself with the affects of adaptation, follow Clark's (1993: 167) advice: 'close one eye, stare at a bright colour for 30 seconds, and then blink your eyes successively, you will note shifts in the chromatic appearance of most things. The adaptation difference between the two eyes vanishes quickly, so the effects will soon disappear. While they last, however . . . discriminations made with the adapted eye will match those made with the unadapted eye. Any two items that present different hues to the unadapted eye will present different hues to the adapted eye. Matching items will continue to match as well. But the apparent hue of everything shifts.'

[45] Goethe discussed contrast effects due to surround (see Ribe 1985); earlier the Count of Rumford and the French geometrician Gaspard Monge discussed such effects. For a recent philosophical discussion, see Hardin (1988/93).

[46] It is in part because of the effects of surround on colour appearance that industry must employ definite (conventional) standards so as to ensure uniformity in filling orders for coloured materials or paints. See Judd and Wyszecki (1975).

[47] While the effects of contrast are stronger if one surface surrounds another, colour contrast can arise from distant surfaces. See Jameson and Hurvich (1955).

These colour shifts due to surround are called 'simultaneous contrast effects'. It should be noted that it won't do to count all colour experiences that result, in part, from such effects as illusory. Black, white, brown, navy blue, and olive are 'contrast colours'. Nothing looks any of these colours when seen in isolation. In a complete darkness, things look (what vision scientists call) brain-grey, not black.[48] Viewed in one's hand, a chocolate bar will appear brown; viewed through a reduction tube (a thin tube with black felt lining), that same bar will look orange.[49] When viewed through a reduction tube, nothing looks olive or navy blue.[50]

11. A Relativist Response to the Problem of Standard Variation

Much has been written about the relativity of colour, especially in the vast literature on dispositionalism.[51] While our ordinary colour talk presupposes

[48] Tye (2000: 157) is sceptical: 'This view seems to me stipulative. After all, in ordinary life, we certainly say things like "It's pitch black in here" with respect to totally dark rooms, presumably because that is the way such rooms look to us. Let us, then, distinguish between black and BLACK. In the dark room, one experiences black but not BLACK.' There is, of course, no sharp cut-off between where greys leave off and blacks begin. But I invite you to do the following. First, cover your open eyes with one hand and then cover that hand with another. Wait a moment. Then focus your visual attention on how things look. I'm betting that you won't think they look black (lower case), you'll think they look a dark grey (perhaps with some light fuzzy streaks). That look is what vision scientists call 'brain grey'.

[49] Hardin (1988/93).

[50] Tye (2000: 158) is sceptical of the idea that brown, for instance, is a contrast colour in some other sense than all colours are since they all 'disappear' in a Ganzfeld. A Ganzfeld is typically a uniformly painted dome that one's head can be placed under or the two halves of a ping-pong ball with uniformly painted interiors that can cover one's eyes. Now it is true that after a period of time in a Ganzfeld (usually a minute or so), nothing will look any colour but brain grey. But it is worthwhile noting first of all that the Ganzfeld effect is explained by receptoral mechanisms (see e.g. Coren et al. 1994), while the effects of simultaneous contrast on colour appearance is explained by later stages of processing (see Wandell 1995). Moreover, Tye (2000: 158) is mistaken when he says: 'it seems…false to assert unequivocally that one cannot experience brown without an appropriate contrast. Consider, for example, the case in which one is surrounded by a light brown fog. Of course, in such a Ganzfeld, the brown will "wash out" of one's phenomenal field very quickly. But then the same is true for colours such as red and blue.' Tye is misled here by his visual imagination. There are no visual experiences (as) of only light brown fog.

[51] Bennett's (1965) gustatory example is much discussed. He claims that phenyl-thio-urea (now known as thiocarbamide, PTC) tastes bitter to a minority of the human population, but is tasteless to the majority. If this is right, it seems that we could reverse the majority and minority by selective breeding. It thus seems natural to say that phenyl-thio-urea is bitter for the minority of the population and tasteless for the majority. While Jackson has himself appealed to this example to justify relativization (Jackson and Pargetter 1987), he has recently remarked that it may be that phenyl-thio-urea produces a chemical in the mouths of the minority and that it is this chemical that they taste, not phenyl-thio-urea (Jackson 1998). I believe that that is not in

notions of a normal perceiver and normal circumstances, folks don't normally assume that there is some circumstance that is revelatory of the true colours of things to certain perceivers whose experiences are wholly objectively authoritative. Upon reflection, folks can recognize that any notion of a standard observer and standard circumstance of observation is at least to some extent arbitrary, a matter of choice rather than discovery.

Still the idea that colours are relative might be resisted. A colour absolutist will insist that the colours things have are not relative to kinds of perceivers and kinds of circumstances. A colour absolutist can hold, following Mohan Matthen (1988), that 'normal misperception' is possible, where colour perception is concerned. In a case of normal misperception, the colour something actually has is different from the colour it would look to a normal perceiver in normal circumstances. Unless the true colours of things are perceptually inaccessible, however, which seems absurd, it should be possible for things to look their true colours to some kind of perceiver in some kind of circumstance. The colour absolutist needn't deny that colours are perceptually accessible. The absolutist can maintain that there are optimal circumstances in which the true colours of things, as opposed to 'illusory colours' or 'fool's colours', are revealed to optimal perceivers whose experiences are authoritative about their presence.[52]

In response, it seems fair to ask the colour absolutist what kind of perceivers and circumstances are optimal. If, in reply, the absolutist says that they are the kinds of perceivers to whom the true colours of things are revealed in the kinds of circumstances in question, then it seems fair to ask how the true colours of things are to be identified. On pain of circularity, an absolutist cannot identify them as the properties that would dispose things to look the colours they are to optimal perceivers in optimal circumstances. But how, then, one wonders, could the true colours of things be identified in a way that is entirely independent of visual experience? If we already knew that colours were certain sorts of physical properties, we could of course determine which of the physical properties in question things had without appeal to visual experience. But the issue is how to determine which physical properties, if any, are which colours.

Suppose that a proponent of the absolutist view in question provides a characterization of optimal perceivers and circumstances that would enable

---

fact the case. However, even if it were, it would none the less be the case that were it phenyl-thio-urea itself that tasted bitter to a minority and was tasteless to a majority, it would seem right to say that it is bitter for some, tasteless for others.

[52] The idea isn't of course that true colours are the colours *for* optimal perceivers in optimal circumstances. The absolutist rejects the idea of 'colours for'. The idea is, rather, that there are perceivers and circumstances that are optimal in that the colours things look to those perceivers in those circumstances are their true colours.

us, in principle, to identify them without having to identify, independently, the true colours of things. And let's suppose that the kind of perceiver identified is a kind of human perceiver. One issue, then, is whether there are colours of things that aren't revealed to such a perceiver because of limitations in the kinds of visual experiences human perceivers can have. Couldn't it be that the colours there are outrun the kinds of visual experiences humans can have? Normal humans are trichromats.[53] Pigeons have four kinds of photopigments in their cones, but five different types of cone-oil droplets combinations; as a result, they may be pentachromats.[54] In any event, pigeons sharply visually discrimin-ate samples that look the same shade of green to us.[55] On the evidence, they do so on the basis of the way the samples appear to them in colour, and so the samples that look the same shade of green to us look some other colour to them. Given that the optimal perceiver is a kind of human perceiver, she'll miss the colours that pigeons are seeing. It would be species chauvinism to say that pigeons are discriminating 'a fool's colour'. (And it would be unduly self-deprecating to say that we are.) There is wide variation in colour perception throughout the animal kingdom; there is every reason to think there are colours that are perceptually inaccessible to humans.[56] Colour absolutists will, however, acknowledge all that. They need not claim that there is a kind of perceiver and kind of circumstance such that *all* the true colours of things are experientially revealed to that kind of perceiver in that kind of circumstance. They can acknowledge, for instance, that there are colours that are perceptually inaccessible to even an optimal human perceiver in optimal circumstances of human observation. They maintain, however, that the colours things look to such a perceiver in such a circumstance are their true colours, in that they are at least among their true colours.

Note that either the optimal circumstances of human observation and/or optimal human perceivers can vary in ways that can affect colour experience, or else not. If there can be such variation, then this proposal faces the problem of standard variation. As concerns the specific variable ways in question that things can look in colour, there will be no property that disposes its bearers to look that way in colour to *all* optimal human perceivers in *every* optimal circumstances of human visual observation. So, it would be possible for optimal perceivers to have colour illusions in optimal circumstances. To avoid this result, the notions of optimal circumstances and optimal observers

[53] As Newton recognized, any colour we can visually discriminate can be matched using at most only three kinds of lights. That is why we count as trichromats. (I should mention here that there is evidence that some women are tretrachromats. See Mollon 1992.)

[54] Bowmaker (1977). Normal humans have three kinds of photopigments in their cones (see s. 13).

[55] Thompson (1995).

[56] See Matthen (2000).

will have to be such that no such variation is possible. The notions of optimal circumstances and optimal observers will have to be so specific as to exclude any variation in such observers or circumstances that could affect the way things can look in colour to them in such circumstances. It would almost certainly be the case then, that at the very most only one human being would be an optimal perceiver (and then, only at a time), and the optimal circumstance would almost certainly be one that none of us has ever been in. Given that we're members of the same species, would it follow that the rest of us have only been experiencing fool's colours?

Suffice it to note that it seems absurd to think that the colours things look to such completely specific kinds of perceivers in such specific kinds of circumstances are objectively true colours of things *simpliciter*. Rather, given how natural it is to think of colours as relativized, it seems appropriate to say that how things look in colour to them in such circumstances is how things are in colour *for them in such circumstances*. But to say that is of course to relativize colours to kinds of perceivers and kinds of circumstances, not to treat colours as absolute.

Radical relativization seems to me the right response to the problem of standard variation. Rather than embracing colour irrealism, we should handle the problem by radically relativizing the colours; that is, we should relativize them to kinds of perceivers and circumstances so specific as to leave no room for variation in colour appearance.[57] Thus, we can offer the following refined functional analysis:

> *Relativized Colours*. Redness for a visual perceiver of type P in circumstances of visual observation C is that property which disposes its bearers to look red to P in C, and which had by everything so disposed.

Here the type of perceiver is to be specified not only in terms of the kind of visual system possessed, but also in terms of very specific states of the system, including, for instance, the state of adaptation of the perceiver's cones; and the circumstances are to be specified in terms of exact lighting conditions, distance, intervening medium, angle, surround, and so on. The type of perceiver, P, and type of circumstances, C, should be as specific, but no more specific, than is required for it to be the case that exactly the same kinds of things would be disposed to look exactly the same way in colour to any perceiver of type P in any circumstance of type C.

Completely relativized colours are akin to such highly relative properties as being too heavy to lift, being too high to jump over, being too small to fit in, being a path, and the like.[58] Moreover, our ordinary talk of the colours of

---

[57] Cf. K. Campbell (1982, 1993); Jackson and Pargetter (1987).
[58] Cf. Campbell (1993: 251).

things should be given a semantic treatment analogous to the treatment of our ordinary talk of things being too heavy to lift, too high to jump over, etc. But the details of such a semantic treatment are complicated, so I leave them for another occasion.[59]

The claim that the only colours that exist are completely relativized colours (hereafter, simply 'relativized colours') is, of course, compatible with colour hallucination and colour illusion. Someone suffering from delirium tremens might visually hallucinate a pink elephant in the middle of the room. The person's visual experience of pink is not the manifestation of any object's disposition to look pink (even to that person in the circumstances in question), so there doesn't exist anything that looks pink to the person. Similarly, since it involves having an after-image, the Bidwell's Ghost phenomenon (Bidwell 1901) would count as a localized hallucination of colour. While it appears as if there is an instance of a certain colour on the spinning disk, it is not the case that the spinning disk looks the colour in question to the observer. The situation is, rather, like one in which one has a red after-image while staring at a white wall after having viewed something that has a saturated green colour. In such a situation, despite the fact that there appears to be an instance of colour (a red patch) in the vicinity of the wall, it is not the case that anything in the vicinity of the wall looks red to one. One's colour experience is not the manifestation of any object's disposition to look red (even to one in the circumstances in question). Such a colour experience is hallucinatory.[60] Colour illusion is also possible. One undergoes a colour illusion when something looks to one some colour that it isn't. From the fact that something looks red to P in C, it does not follow that it is red for P in C. For, if our analysis is correct, a further condition must be met for it to be red for P in C. The further condition is that some property that disposes it to looks red to P in C be shared by everything (i.e. every nomologically possible thing) that is so disposed.

Saul Kripke is reported to have raised the possibility of a 'killer red', a kind of red that would dispose something to kill a perceiver before the perceiver could see it. A property that did not dispose its bearers to look red to any kind of perceiver in any kind of circumstance would not be red for any kind of perceiver in any circumstance. It is, however, at least logically possible that a property that disposes its bearers to look red to a P in C would dispose its bearers to kill a P* in C before the P* could see its bearer. Perhaps things that

---

[59] One issue is what factors (if any) determine what proposition is being expressed when someone says 'That's red'; an analogous problem arises for 'That's too heavy to lift'.

[60] A colour physicalist must, of course, deny that when one is having a red after-image, it is thereby the case that there exists something such that one is seeing it and it is red. Having after-images must be treated as hallucinatory experiences (or radical illusions); otherwise physicalism is false.

have the property in C would supply light to the eyes of a P* that would burn holes right through them to the centre of the P*'s brain, thereby killing the individual. (Think of what some laser beams would do to our eyes.) So, red for Ps in C might be killer red for P*s in C (or even for Ps in C*). Killer red for P*s in C would not, however, be red for P*s in C; rather, red for Ps in C would lethal to P*s in C.[61]

12. The Problem of Common Ground and the Problem of Multiple Grounds

The so-called problem of metamers is much discussed in the literature on colour physicalism. When different physical properties dispose their bearers to look the same colour to a type of perceiver, P, in a type of circumstance, C, the properties are metameric in C for P. (Metameric matching is in respect of hue, saturation, and lightness.) On the evidence, no matter how specific the type of human perceiver, P, and type of circumstances, C, if one physical property can dispose its bearers to look some colour to P in C, more than one physical property can. The term 'the problem of metamers' suggests that the existence of metamers is itself a problem for colour physicalism. It isn't. The existence of metamers doesn't entail that there are no properties that play the relativized colour-roles. For to play the role of being (say) red for P in C, more is required than being a property that disposes its bearers to look red to P in C. It must also be the case that the property in question is common to everything so disposed. Thus, from the fact that there is no unique physical

---

[61] Consider another sort of case. Our functional analysis of relativized colours has the consequence that if a property R is red for P in C, then R disposes its bearers to look red to P in C. Suppose that something could have R and also have another property Q, with the result that it is nomologically impossible for the thing to look red to P in C since it is nomologically impossible for exemplifications of Q, P, and C to be co-present. Since, then, a bearer of R could at the same time be a bearer of Q, would R be such that its bearers—all its bearers, including ones that are also bearers of Q—are disposed to look red to P in C? If the answer is 'no' then a revision of our proposal is called for. We could revise it this way: redness for P in C is that property which disposes its kinds of bearers that are (to use a Liebnizian term) com-nomologically-possible with P in C to look red to P in C. Another possible response, however, is that the answer to the question is 'yes': bearers of R that are also bearers of Q are disposed to look red to P in C. This second possible answer would require us to reject a counterfactual analysis of dispositions according to which the fact that R disposes its bearers to look red to P in C entails that were an R in C and a P-type perceiver present, then the R would look red to the P-type perceiver. (The counterfactual would be a counter-legal since, by hypothesis, it is nomologically impossible for there to be an R in C and a P-type perceiver present.) One could reject this counterfactual analysis on the grounds that something could have the disposition yet the counterfactual be false because a standing condition for its manifestation is absent, namely a P in C. Suffice it to note that either avenue of response is available.

property that disposes its bearers to look red to P in C, it doesn't follow that no physical property plays the role of being red for P in C. The real problem here for colour physicalism is that there may be no basis for the disposition to look red to P in C that is common to everything so disposed. This is the common ground (basis) problem, the second basic problem for colour physicalism.

Of course, just as there may be no common basis for the disposition to look red to P in C, there may also be more than one. If there is more than one, then it's not the case that there is some property that is *the* property that disposes its bearers to look red to P in C and is common to all things so disposed. This is the multiple grounds problem, the third basic problem for colour physicalism.

As concerns the multiple grounds problem, if there is more than one common basis for the disposition to look red to P in C, but the bases participate in relations of determinable to determinate, then we can happily revise our functional analysis to say that redness for P in C is that most determinate property that disposes its bearers to look red to P in C and is common to everything so disposed. What, however, if the multiple common bases do not all participate in relations of determinable to determinate? Then, it seems the thing to say is that our relativized colour concepts suffer from indeterminacy of reference.

Such indeterminacy, I think, is in fact to be expected if there is a common basis; for if there is one, then, due to vagueness, there'll be more than one property that is an equally good candidate for being the common basis. An under-appreciated lesson of Unger's (1980) problem of the many is that virtually all our ordinary terms (and concepts) fail of determinate reference. Let me illustrate the problem as it arises for reference to objects. Consider Sparky, an atom right on the periphery of Kilimanjaro. Let 'Kilimanjaro (+)' to be the body of land constituted, in the way mountains are constituted by their constituent atoms, by the atoms that make up Kilimanjaro together with Sparky. Thus, if Sparky is a part of Kilimanjaro, then Kilimanjaro and Kilimanjaro(+) are identical; otherwise, Kilimanjaro(+) is ever so slightly larger than Kilimanjaro. Let Kilimanjaro(−) be the body of land constituted, in the way mountains are constituted by their constituent atoms, by the atoms that make up Kilimanjaro other than Sparky. Thus, either Kilimanjaro(−) is identical to Kilimanjaro or it is a body ever so slightly smaller than Kilimanjaro. Assuming, for simplicity, that we can be confident that Kilimanjaro doesn't contain part but not all of Sparky,[62] we have: If Sparky is a part of Kilimanjaro, Kilimanjaro = Kilimanjaro(+). If Sparky isn't part of Kilimanjaro, Kilimanjaro = Kilimanjaro(−). Consequently, either

---

[62] If we don't assume this, matters are worse.

Kilimanjaro = Kilimanjaro(+) or Kilimanjaro = Kilimanjaro(−).[63] Because Kilimanjaro(+) is not identical with Kilimanjaro(−), only one of the disjuncts can obtain, and so exactly one of Kilimanjaro(+) and Kilimanjaro(−) is the referent of 'Kilimanjaro'. The problem is that there seems to be no fact of the matter whether Kilimanjaro = Kilimanjaro(+) or Kilimanjaro = Kilimanjaro(−). And there's nothing special about Sparky in this. Countless billions of atoms are in Sparky's predicament, singly or in groups, so there are countless billions of bodies of land that have an equally good claim to being the referent of 'Kilimanjaro'. The reference of 'Kilimanjaro' is radically indeterminate.[64]

Suffice it to note that supervaluationism will see us through these straits.[65] And it will do likewise if there's more than one candidate common basis for the disposition to look red to P in C. That won't pose the threat of colour irrealism if the claim that colours exist is true on every way of resolving the referential indeterminacy, and so are 'supertrue'[66] or 'determinately true'.[67] The platitude that something is red if and only if it has the property that plays the redness-role will be determinately true since it will be true on any way of resolving the indeterminacy. So will the claim that 'redness' refers to redness if redness exists.[68] Moreover, such indeterminacy is compatible with the determinate truth of 'There is a unique physical property that plays the redness-role' and of 'The unique physical property that plays the redness-role is redness'. Indeed such indeterminacy is compatible with the determinate truth of a claim of the form 'Φ is redness', where 'Φ' refers to a physical property. I shall, then, discuss the problem of multiple common grounds no further.

The really serious problem for colour-realism is, I believe, the problem of common ground. If anything is disposed to look red to P in C, there will be many heterogeneous chemical properties that dispose their bearers to look red to P in C; many heterogeneous chemical properties will be metameric with respect to a given type of perceiver P in a given circumstance C.[69] Indeed many heterogeneous chemical properties will be isomeric for (a completely specific kind of perceiver) P, that is, whatever way in colour the one disposes its bearers to look to P in a (completely specific) observational circumstance

---

[63] Here I assume classical logic. For a defence of classical logic in the face of semantic indeterminacy, see McGee and McLaughlin (1995, 1998, 2000).

[64] Unger (1980) himself would not take this to be the lesson of the problem of the many here. He'd take the lesson to be that there are either trillions of mountains at 3.07° S, 37.35° E, or else there is no mountain there. But I can't myself say that I think geologists have much to learn from the problem of the many.

[65] See McGee and McLaughlin (2000).

[66] Supertruth is introduced in Fine (1975).

[67] Determinate truth is explicated in McGee and McLaughlin (1995, 1998, 2000).

[68] See McGee and McLaughlin (2000).

[69] See Nassau (1980, 1983).

C, the other will disposes its bearers to look to P in that C.[70] While the disjunction of all such chemical properties (if there are disjunctive properties) will be common to everything so disposed, the heterogeneous disjunctive property will not dispose anything to look red to P in C.[71] Thus, vision scientists look to more abstract properties such as light-dispositions.

A disposition to reflect or emit light predominately of a certain wavelength will be a basis for the disposition to look a certain colour to P, pretty much only in aperture settings in which contextual elements are eliminated, and so only in an extremely narrow range of specific circumstances. (In a typical aperture setting, the subject is looking through an aperture and the subject's entire field of vision consists of lights of various wavelengths on a white background.) Moreover, metamerism is rampant as concerns such light-dispositions in such settings. As Hardin (1988/93: 198) notes, 'if an observer's unique yellow were at 575 nm on the spectrum [in such a setting], an appropriate mixture of spectral 550 nm and 650 nm light would match it exactly'. Indeed there will be indefinitely many heterogeneous light-dispositions of the sort in question that will dispose something to look unique yellow (yellow that is not at all greenish or reddish) to P in such a circumstance.

Reflectance is measured by the ratio of reflected light to incident light (the light striking a surface). The spectral reflectance distribution of a surface is measured by the ratio of reflected light to incident light at each point on the surface throughout the visual spectrum (the range of electro-magnetic radiation from 380 to 750 nanometers).[72] Now certain kinds of surfaces are such

[70] The reason is that many heterogeneous chemical properties can endow a surface with exactly the same spectral reflectance, and certain sorts of surfaces with the same spectral reflectance distribution are such that whatever way the one sort of surface looks in colour to a P in a C the other will look in colour to that P in that C. (See the discussion below).

[71] The idea of identifying colours with disjunctions of physical properties was suggested by Smart (1961, 1963); see also Jackson and Pargetter (1987); Jackson (1996); Cohen (2000); and Ross (2001). Such theorists can claim that while it is not always the case that the disjunction of the bases of a disposition is itself a basis of the disposition, this is sometimes the case. Thus, it might be claimed that while disjunctions of 'heterogeneous bases' for a disposition are not themselves bases for the disposition, disjunctions of 'homogeneous bases' are. Here they might appeal to the 'naturalness' of the disjunction. If this idea can be defended, then there may be a common disjunctive base for the disposition to look red to P in C; whether there is will depend on whether the kinds of things that have the disposition have bases that are 'homogeneous', so that the disjunction of them is appropriately natural. This seems the way for so-called 'disjunctive physicalists' to go. If it works, all well and good from my point of view, I'd like to see colour realism vindicated. But I'm sceptical of this disjunctive strategy. First, I find the notion of disjunctive properties problematic, where 'property' is used in a non-pleonastic sense (see Armstrong 1979). Second, I find no clear cases of something's having a disposition D in virtue of having either A or B that aren't simply cases in which, strictly speaking, something has D either in virtue of having A or in virtue of having B.

[72] Grandy (1989) and Hilbert (1987) defend the view that physical surfaces' colours are spectral reflectances.

that when two of them have exactly the same spectral reflectance distribution, they will be isomeric. Metamerism, however, is rampant. Two such surfaces can have different spectral reflectances and yet look the same in colour to a certain kind of perceiver in a certain kind of circumstance. Moreover, it is not in general true that if two surfaces have exactly the same spectral reflectance distribution, then they are isomeric. Fluorescent and phosphorescent surfaces emit light as well as reflect it.[73] A non-fluorescent surface can have the same spectral reflectance as a fluorescent one yet the surfaces not look the same in colour to P in C since the fluorescent surface emits light in addition to what it reflects, so that its reflectance has limited effect on its colour appearance; and similarly for non-phosphorescent and phosphorescent surfaces. Moreover, translucent volumes such as a volume of red wine and red sunsets have spectral transmission distributions.[74] If two translucent volumes share exactly the same spectral transmission distribution, they will look exactly the same in colour to P in C. However, once again, metamerism is rampant. For a given perceiver P and circumstance C, there may well be many distinct spectral transmission distributions that are metameric for P in C. Neither spectral reflectance distributions nor spectral transmission distributions play even the relativized colour-roles. We must look elsewhere to find the colors.

13. A Promising Strategy for Solving the Problem of Common Ground

We're primarily concerned here with whether *our* colours are real—whether there exist colours for humans. We're primarily concerned with the prospects of what David Hilbert (1987) calls 'anthropocentric realism for colors'.

---

[73] Luminescence is the disposition to emit light when exposed to light. While phosphorescence is a 'slow' luminescence (light emission starts relatively slowly and subsides slowly, so that a phosphorescent surface can glow for a while in the dark), the luminescence of a fluorescent surface is immediate. Whiteners remove the yellowish look from old white shirts by adding fluorescence in the short wavelength range (Nassau 1983: 18). Thus the surfaces of white shirts treated with whiteners are fluorescent; so are the surfaces of red marks made by highlighting pens. The surfaces of some emeralds, for example, are phosphorescent. (Jakab 2001 cites the example of emeralds.)

[74] It might be thought that the redness of a sunset is an illusion. It is often said that the blueness of the sky is. I myself see no reason to say that. We can see translucent volumes. A volume of the atmosphere can have a property that disposes it to look blue to us. The scattering of short light waves in the volume of atmosphere causes the blue appearance. We can see blue eyes; when we do, we see a translucent volume. The blue appearance of the eyes is likewise due to the scattering of short light waves. Of course, it is enormously vague where the volume of atmosphere that we see begins and ends. But after the discussion of Unger's problem of the many it should be clear that it is also vague where the volume of blue eye that we see begins and ends; indeed it is vague where anything we see begins and ends. I see no reason to say either that the redness of a sunset or the blueness of the sky is an illusion.

Normal humans have three kinds of cones.[75] Due to differences in the photopigments in each, the cones differ in their spectral sensitivities. So-called L-cones absorb more light of longer wavelengths (within the visual spectrum) than do the others; M-cones absorb more light of medium wavelength; and S-cones absorb more light of short wavelengths. This fact about human vision makes it seem promising to look for light-distributions that somehow involve three bandwidths.

Triples of integrated reflectances are often characterized in the philosophical literature simply as certain portions of reflected light to incident light over three bandwidths, which are scaled and summed.[76] Some appeal to a physicalistic interpretation of Edwin Land's idea of computing colour by computing lightness within three bandwidths (Land 1977).[77] But the specifics of Land's idea so interpreted are unpromising.[78]

A more promising strategy is to appeal to results from opponent processing theory,[79] the leading neuro-computational theory of colour vision, to try to locate the colours among light-dispositions.[80] Opponent processing theory postulates computational mechanisms in the visual system that take as input the output of our three types of cones.[81] According to the theory, there are pairs of opponent information channels, where the activity in one channel inhibits activity in its opponent channel. The pairs of channels are the achromatic opponent channels WHITE and BLACK, the RED and GREEN opponent channels, and the BLUE and YELLOW opponent channels. Subtleties aside, the WHITE and BLACK channels involve a summing of the outputs of the L and M cones; the RED and GREEN channels involve a differencing of the outputs of the L and M cones; and the BLUE and YELLOW channels involve a summing of the outputs of the L and M cones and a differencing of that sum and the output of the S cones. Any spectral stimulus that affects the

[75] It should be noted that there is some evidence that some female humans have four types of cones; but I shall not discuss that here.

[76] Appeals to triples of integrated reflectances can be found in P. M. Churchland (1985, 1986); P. S. Churchland (1986); Hilbert (1987) (where the idea is appealed to in order to try to solve the problem of unity); Gibbard (1996); Jackson (1998); and Lewis (1997).

[77] See e.g. P. M. Churchland (1985, 1986); P. S. Churchland (1986); and Hilbert (1987: ch. 6). Land himself, it should be noted, was concerned with the appearance of lightness, while the proposal in question was concerned with lightness understood physicalistically as the ratio of reflected light to incident light. (Lewis 1997 and Jackson 1998 simply cite Hilbert 1987.)

[78] See Thompson (1995: ch. 3) for a discussion of why. Hilbert has rejected the idea because of Thompson's criticisms (see Bryne and Hilbert 1997: 285).

[79] See Jameson and Hurvich (1955, 1956), and Hurvich and Jameson (1955, 1956, 1957); and Hurvich (1981). For a very nice short tutorial on opponent processing theory (something I lack the space to provide here), see Hardin (1988/93: 26–36).

[80] This strategy is suggested by Bryne and Hilbert (1997: 265, 282 n. 9). Tye (2000) explores their suggestion in some detail. (See n. 84 below.)

[81] It should be noted that it is not known how opponent processing is implemented in the nervous system.

cones in such a way as to activate the RED channel, for instance, will inhibit its opponent channel, the GREEN channel; and likewise for the BLUE and YELLOW opponent channels. According to the opponent processing theory, that is why nothing looks reddish-green or bluish-yellow.[82]

Here is the basic strategy for appealing to opponent processing theory to locate colours among light-dispositions: as concerns any colour, C, look for a light disposition that, when activated, would affect the opponent processing system in a manner that will produce a visual experience of C. The strategy thus involves appealing to opponent processing theory to try to find 'structure in the light' (to use a Gibsonian phrase) that is supplied to the eyes. The idea is that colours are dispositions to supply light with the relevant structure. According to opponent processing theory, when the RED opponent channel is activated, the GREEN channel inhibited, and the YELLOW and BLUE channels are in equilibrium, the subject will have a visual experience of unique red. In rough outline, then, unique red is the property of being disposed to supply light of the sort that prompts cone responses that would trigger the activation of the RED channel and inhibition of the GREEN channel, while leaving the YELLOW and BLUE channels in equilibrium. We locate unique red among light dispositions by determining what light structure plays the role in question. Unique red is the property of being disposed to supply light with that structure.

Bryne and Hilbert (1997: 265) claim that in the case of surfaces, such dispositions will be types of spectral reflectances, and restrict the strategy to the colours of reflecting surfaces. Following their suggestion, Tye (2000) develops this idea in some detail, speaking of surface colours as such triples of integrated reflectances. Fluorescent and phosphorescent surfaces, we will recall, emit light as well as reflect it; and translucent volumes transmit light. The general strategy can, however, be extended to them, even though their reflectance properties have only a limited effect on their colour appearance. There is a technique in colour science for treating emitted or transmitted light as if it were part of the reflectance of a surface or transmittance of a volume in order to obtain cone responses: one can multiply the sum of reflectance, respectively transmittance and emission factors with the cone response function.[83] It is inaccurate, however, to talk of reflectances as what are integrated. In the case of fluorescent and phosphorescent surfaces, what is integrated for

---

[82] What about Crane's and Piantanida's claim that something can look reddish-green? As Hardin (1988/93) notes: 'Crane and Piantanida interpret [their] findings to mean that the opponent channels, which are the normal conduits of colour information, do not extend all the way up the visual processing chain, and that the opponency may be superseded by the filling-in mechanism which is known to lie within the brain itself.' In any case, their results are, as I noted, highly controversial.

[83] I owe thanks here to Rolf Kuehni.

cone responses is the spectral power of the light entering the eye weighted by the spectral cone sensitivity functions. The spectral power of the light supplied to the eye is affected by the spectral power of the light striking the surface, the surface's reflectance function, and the emission result from any fluorescent or phosphorescent properties; and comparably for translucent volumes. The point nevertheless remains that we can try to locate colours among light-dispositions by appeal to results from opponent processing theory. While fluorescent and non-fluorescent translucent volumes, fluorescent surfaces, phosphorescent surfaces, and non-fluorescent, non-phosphorescent surfaces all interact with light in different ways, they can all be disposed to interact with light in a way that prompts cone responses that trigger opponent processing mechanisms in a way which results in, for instance, a visual experience of unique red; and likewise for other colour experiences.

Recall the problem of standard variation. Because of the effects of lighting, surround, and the like, there is of course no single colour that any light-disposition of a surface or volume will dispose its bearers to look even to a completely specific kind of human visual perceiver in *every* observational circumstance that counts as normal by actual everyday standards. Moreover, there is no single colour that any light-disposition will dispose its bearers to look even in a completely specific kind of observational circumstances to *every* human visual perceiver that counts as normal by actual, everyday standards; for it's extraordinarily unlikely that any two normal human per-ceivers will have exactly the same cone-sensitivities, for instance; and cone-sensitivities will vary for an individual over time. Indeed it is unlikely that any two normal perceivers will have precisely the same opponent processing system. We've already seen, however, that the problem of standard variation can be handled by radical relativization. We've eliminated these concerns by relativizing colours to completely specific types of human perceivers and observational circumstances.

While many questions remain, it is, I believe, fair to say that given the promise of opponent processing theory, the strategy discussed above may well yield a solution to the problem of common ground for (completely) relativ-ized colours. Thus, while the issue has by no means been settled, there is, I believe, reason for optimism as concerns realism about relativized colours for humans.[84]

---

[84] The only detailed attempt to employ this strategy to locate colours among light-dispos-itions is Tye's attempt in Tye (2000). Following Bryne and Hilbert's (1997) brief suggestive remarks, Tye attempts to do this for red, green, yellow, blue, black, and white, and for the four broad ranges of binary hues: orange, purple, yellowish-green, and bluish-green. As Z. Jakab (2001) empirically demonstrates, however, Tye's proposals fail in their predictions about how coloured plastics and white ceramic tiles would look in colour. As I'll use the linguistic context '—/...', what occupies the dash position will be a description of a coloured item and what occupies the dots position will be the name of the colour that Tye's proposals predicts the item

This completes my discussion of colour. I turn now to the phenomenal character of colour experiences.

14. On the Possibility of a Certain Kind of Phenomenal Character Inversion

One traditional idea of 'colour spectrum inversion' is that the things that look one colour to one individual look its complementary colour to another, so that things that look red to the one look green to the other, things that look blue to the one look yellow to the other, and so on and so forth.[85] Such an inversion is, I believe, at least logically possible. If our functional analysis of colour is correct, then such an inversion is compatible with colour-physicalism. Given colour-physicalism, if the colour experiences of a perceiver P are so inverted relative to those of a perceiver P*, then the physical property that plays the redness-role for P would play the greenness-role for P*. One and the same physical property would be both redness for P in C and greenness for P* in C. More difficult questions are whether such an inversion is possible for two individuals who are exactly alike in their dispositions to peripheral behaviour, or in their microphysical constitution, or in their microphysical constitution and in the relationships they bear to the environment. Since I hold that visual experiences are types of neuroscientific states, I maintain that while the first kind of inversion is possible, the second two are impossible, despite being conceivable. This view of visual experiences is, however, strictly optional for a proponent of our functional analysis of colour. Our analysis of colour is compatible with a dualist view of visual experiences that allows for all three types of possibilities.

What I propose to do in this section is to raise the possibility of a different sort of inversion, one that has been the subject of discussion in recent years.

would be. Jakab's results, then, are these: red Lego block/orange, red plastic boat/orange, green Lego block/yellow, green plastic boat/yellow, yellow Lego block/orange, yellow plastic boat/ orange, blue Lego block/yellow, blue plastic boat/yellow, white ceramic tile/orange. Thus, Tye's proposals fail in their predictions. Now Tye says that his proposals stand or fall with opponent processing theory. However, opponent processing theory doesn't fall with his proposals. The main reason is that, as he himself notes, he frames his proposals by reference to the very oversimplified model of opponent processing described in Hardin (1988/93). That model does not specify the various non-linear computations performed by the opponent-processing system or take into account cone sensitivities (which are themselves non-linear). (Hardin (ibid. 35) lists the ways in which his model is oversimplified.) It should be noted, however, that proposals could be formulated that take into account the factors in question. Whose cone-sensitivities should be taken into account? On our relativized proposal, the cone-sensitivities will be determined by the choice of a specific type of perceiver P. To repeat: given the promise of opponent processing theory, there is reason for optimism as concerns realism about (completely) relativized colours for humans.

[85] This idea is found in Locke (1690/1975).

This will lead us back to the question of the relationship between how things look in colour and the phenomenal characters of visual experiences.

The central idea of the sort of inversion in question is that while whatever looks a certain colour to one individual looks that same colour to another, what it is like for something to look a certain colour to the one is what it is like for something to look the complementary colour to another, so that while whatever looks red to the one looks red to the other and whatever looks green to the one looks green to the other, it is none the less the case that what it's like for something to look red to the one is what it's like for something to look green to the other. Let us call such a would-be inversion 'a visual phenomenal character inversion'.[86] If such an inversion is possible, then there is no phenomenal character such that something looks a certain colour, C, to a subject only if the subject has an experience with that character. Thus, there is, for instance, no phenomenal character such that something looks red to a subject if and only if the subject has an experience with that character.[87]

Moreover, if such inversion is possible, then locutions such as 'what it is like for something to look red', 'what it is like for something to look green', etc., fail of determinate reference.[88] That, I should note, would pose no problem for my view of the colour double-cone presented in s. 9. The double-cone, in the first instance, represents patterns of relations among what it is like for something to look red, what it is like for something to look green, etc. If such inversion is possible, then there will be two equally good candidates for being the referent of 'what it is like for something to look red'; and so there will be indeterminacy of reference. Still the comparative claims about colour experiences discussed in ss. 8 and 9 would be true on either way of resolving the indeterminacy, and so would be 'supertrue' or 'determinately true'. For instance, on either way of resolving the indeterminacy, it would be true that what it is like for something to look red is more similar to what it is like for something to look orange than it is to what it is like for something to look blue. Moreover, on either way of resolving the indeterminacy, what it is like for something to look pure red would be unique, and what it is like for something to look orange would be binary. The possibility of visual

[86] C. I. Lewis (1929) held that phenomenal character inversion is possible. More recently, Shoemaker (1981) and Block (1990) have claimed it is possible; see also Strawson (1989, and forthcoming). See Lycan (1996) and Tye (2000) for challenges to the possibility of phenomenal character inversion.

[87] The inversion scenario in question is, however, compatible with the claim that there is a phenomenal character such that something looks red to a subject only if the subject has an experience with that character. For there may be a phenomenal character that is common to all colour experiences, or, more generally, to all sense experiences, so that while what it is like for something to look red to one individual is what it is like for something to look green to another, their experiences of red at least share the generic phenomenal character in question.

[88] See Strawson (1989, and forthcoming).

phenomenal character inversion would thus pose no problem for what I've said about the double-cone.

None the less, as we'll now see, whether such an inversion is possible raises important questions about the relationship between the phenomenal characters of colour experiences and how things look in colour.

15. Intentionalism

The possibility of phenomenal character inversion is incompatible with intentionalism about the phenomenal characters of experiences.[89] According to intentional theories of visual experience, there is a certain content such that something looks red to a subject if and only if the subject has a visual experience with that content.[90] Weak intentionalism entails that the phenomenal character of a visual experience supervenes on its content, strong intentionalism, that it is identical with its content. Both weak and strong intentionalism thus entail that phenomenal character inversion is impossible.[91]

I think that colour experiences have contents. If something looks red to one, then the question of whether the thing in question is the way it looks makes perfect sense. The experience has satisfaction conditions: the thing in question may or may not be the way the experience presents it as being. Some of the leading intentionalist theories maintain that the contents of experiences are non-conceptual contents, in that the subject of the experience needn't possess the concepts expressed in specifying the content.[92] I find that plausible. Something can look red to one, even if one lacks the concept of red. So, in specifying the satisfaction conditions for the experience, we do not presuppose that the subject of the experience has the concept(s) in question.[93] The content of the experience thus counts as 'non-conceptual content'. The

---

[89] What I call 'intentionalism' in this section is now often called 'representationalism'. I prefer 'intentionalism' since it draws attention to the connection between the view and Franz Brentano's doctrine that intentionality is the mark of the mental.

[90] See Harman (1990); Dretske (1995); Lycan (1996); and Tye (1995, 2000).

[91] Block's (1990) well-known Inverted Earth case, which is *not* a phenomenal inversion case, is a would-be counter-example to strong intentionalism. Or, more accurately, the case is a would-be counter-example to wide strong intentional theories of a sort to be discussed shortly. (Narrow intentionalism is the view that the phenomenal character of experiences supervenes on what's in the head; wide intentionalism denies that.) The inverted earth case is supposed to be one in which there is a difference in content, but no difference in phenomenal character. Weak intentionalism says only that there can be no difference in phenomenal character without a difference in content, and so seems immune from the case.

[92] See Dretske (1995) and Tye (2000).

[93] As we noted in n. 13, things can look basic shades of colours to us for which we have no concepts.

content is perhaps instead perceptual content, content borne by a percept, a certain kind of mental representation, rather than a concept. Perhaps what it is for an experience to be a visual experience of red is for it to contain as a constituent a visual percept that purports to represent redness (for the perceiver in the circumstances in question). In any event, it seems plausible that there is a kind of non-conceptual content such that something looks red to a subject if and only if the subject's experience has that content, for it seems plausible that there is a determinate satisfaction condition for the kind of experience in question and that the content is non-conceptual. I'll assume that this thesis is correct, and I'll call it 'the determinate-content thesis'. Given the determinate-content thesis, the central issue as concerns the possibility of phenomenal inversion is whether phenomenal character supervenes on non-conceptual content.

The main point to note for our present purposes is that it's open to a proponent of our functional analysis of colour to go either way on the issue of the possibility of phenomenal inversion. A proponent is free to reject weak intentionalism, thereby embracing the possibility of phenomenal inversion. A proponent is also free to accept weak intentionalism, thereby rejecting the possibility of phenomenal inversion.

A proponent of our functional analysis of colour could embrace weak intentionalism even if it turned out that there are no colours, and so that projectivism is true. The leading argument offered in favour of intentionalism is that it captures 'the transparency of visual experience'. The term 'transparency' suggests that we see through visual experiences; and indeed we do, in both senses of 'see through'. We see things in the scenes before our eyes through (by) having visual experiences, and we don't see our visual experiences; they don't look any way to us; they are not themselves objects of (direct) visual attention or visual awareness. These claims, however, are accepted by every theory of visual experience (including sense datum theory). The term 'transparency' is used differently in the defence of intentionalism. It is used to express the thesis:

Transparency Thesis. We are never directly aware of intrinsic aspects of our visual experiences.[94]

It might seem that if projectivism is true, then transparency is false. But that would be a mistake. The transparency thesis is a phenomenological thesis; it is defended entirely by appeal to the phenomenology of visual experience. The locution 'directly aware of' is used in the Transparency Thesis in its phenomenal sense, not its relational sense. In the relational sense of 'directly aware of' if one is directly aware of X, then X exists (occurs, obtains, etc.). In the phenom-

---

[94] See Harman (1990) and Tye (2000).

enal sense, it does not follow from the fact that one is directly aware of X that there exists (occurs, obtains, etc.) anything that one is aware of. The person who hallucinates a pink elephant is directly aware of a pink surface in the phenomenal sense, but is not directly aware of a pink surface in the relational sense.[95] Whether the awareness is phenomenal or relational, direct awareness is awareness that is not indirect, where one is indirectly aware of F if and only if one is aware of F by being aware of something else. As concerns colour at least, a colour-projectivist will insist on transparency. If we were directly phenomenally aware of colours as intrinsic aspects of our visual experiences, it would not be the case that colours are projected into scenes. According to the projectivist, we are never directly phenomenally aware of colours as aspects of our visual experiences, we are directly phenomenally aware of colours as in scenes. But, the projectivist also claims, what we are in fact relationally directly aware of are intrinsic aspects of our visual experiences.[96]

While a proponent of our analysis of colour can embrace weak intentionalism, and so reject the possibility of phenomenal inversion, a proponent cannot of course embrace the claim that being an experience of something's looking red consists in being an experience that bears an appropriate relationship to the property of redness. For, as noted in our discussion of the Euthyphro question, if our analysis is correct, then a property's being redness consists in its bearing an appropriate relationship to the experience of something's looking red. It follows that a proponent of our analysis cannot accept a certain version of intentionalism. I'll call the version 'denotational-intentionalism'. According to denotational-intentionalism, the non-conceptual content of an experience must be (or include as a component) the property that it represents. On this brand of intentionalism, non-conceptual contents are 'property involving'.

It so happens that the currently leading intentional theories of phenomenal experience are denotational theories. Moreover, they are wide intentional theories since they hold that the non-conceptual content of an experience fails to supervene on intrinsic properties of the subject.[97] Further, they are

---

[95] Harman (1990) is very explicit that he is using 'directly aware of' in its phenomenal, rather than its relational sense. He says, at one point of Eloise, who is viewing a tree, 'suppose that her experience [of the tree] is realized by a particular physical event and that certain intrinsic features of the event are in this case responsible for certain intentional features of Eloise's experience. Perhaps there is then a sense in which Eloise is aware of this physical process and aware of those intrinsic features, although she is not aware of them as the intrinsic features that they are' (ibid. 42). And when he uses the term 'see', he emphasizes that he is using it in its phenomenal, rather than its relational sense (ibid. 36–7). Tye (2000) also understands this thesis to be a phenomenological thesis and the relevant use of 'directly aware of' to be phenomenal; that's why he thinks the thesis can be defended on phenomenological grounds alone.

[96] Does phenomenology support intentionalism? That's a subject of heated debate that remains unresolved. I discuss this issue in McLaughlin (forthcoming b).

[97] Of course, narrow denotational-intentionalism is a possible view.

strong intentionalist theories since they imply that phenomenal character is non-conceptual content. I have in mind Dretske's (1995, 2000) and Tye's (2000) intentionalist theories of phenomenal character.[98] They both embrace denotational versions of wide strong intentionalism. The claim that while colours are properties of surfaces, volumes, and light-sources, these very same properties figure—along with such properties as shape, distance, angle, and the like—as constituents (presumably predicative-constituents) of the non-conceptual contents of visual experiences and that the characters of such experiences are identical with their non-conceptual contents.[99]

The issue of denotationalism separates from the issue of intentionalism. One can hold that the content of a colour experience includes a denoted colour property and yet reject even weak intentionalism. Indeed Block (1990), who is a leading opponent of even weak intentionalism, seems to embrace denotationalism. He rejects intentionalism since he holds that visual phenomenal character inversion is possible; indeed he thinks that for all we know it is actual.[100] On a phenomenal inversion scenario, while whatever looks red

[98] Lycan (1996) too holds a denotational theory of non-conceptual content. But his theory, unlike Dretske's and Tye's, is not a pure intentionalist theory since he doesn't hold that qualia (the phenomenal characters of experiences) supervene on non-conceptual content alone; for this reason, I omit discussion of this theory.

[99] If shapes themselves are predicative-constituents of the phenomenal characters of visual experiences, why is what it's like to see a circular shape different from what it's like to feel a circular shape? Their answer is that the phenomenal character of visual experiences of shape will also contain colours as predicative-constituents, and tactual experiences of shape won't. In visual experience shape is always accompanied by colour, in tactual experience it is never accompanied by colour. But why, then, is what it's like to see a circle different from what it's like to visually imagine a circle? Here again, they will, presumably, appeal to a property that is invariably a predicative-constitutent of the one sort of experience but never of the other. One wants to say visually imagining a circle is less vivid than seeing a circle, but Tye and Dretske owe us an account of this in terms of environmental properties that figure as constitutents of contents.

[100] Block (1990: 55–60) points out that 'looks red' has a meaning in English, and claims that it can't matter whether the 'quale' one competent English speaker associates with 'looks red' is the same quale another associates with 'looks green', so long as the phenomenal inversion is thorough and systematic. For all we know, the qualia of female English speakers are inverted in relation to those of male English speakers. (C. I. Lewis 1929 held the same view of qualia. One is reminded here, of course, of Wittgenstein's image of 'the beetle in a box'. Cf. Strawson 1986.) I find this reasoning unconvincing. It may very well be that phenomenal character inversion (or 'qualia inversion') is possible for two individuals that have exactly the same dispositions to verbal and non-verbal behaviour and who are such that the environment (both proximal and distal) has always impinged upon them in exactly the same way. But it is also conceivable (at least) that two individuals might have exactly the same dispositions to verbal and non-verbal behaviour and be such that the environment has always impinged upon them in exactly the same way, yet the one have a normal human conscious life and the other be a zombie devoid of consciousness. For 'all we know' (to use Block's expression), there may be prominent (at least apparent) members of our language community that are zombies. (I find it conceivable that I was a zombie until just five minutes ago.) Perhaps a zombie could be a member of our linguistic community. But could a zombie understand 'looks red' or 'pain'? Suffice it to note that I find it deeply unintuitive that a zombie could fully understand either of these locutions. (See the discussion of concepts and subjectivity in s. 18.)

to Dick looks red to Jane and whatever looks green to Dick looks green to Jane, what it's like for something to look red to Dick is what it's like for something to look green to Jane. This invites the question, what is it for something to look red to a subject? Block cannot answer that it is for the subject to have a visual experience with a certain phenomenal character, for if phenomenal inversion is possible, then there is no phenomenal character such that something looks red to a subject if and only if the subject has a visual experience with that character. He in fact maintains, instead, that it is for the subject to have a visual experience with an appropriate content. He thus plausibly embraces the determinate-content thesis. But that invites the question, what is it for an experience to have the kind of content necessary and sufficient for being an experience of something's looking red? His answer is denotationalist.[101] Despite the fact that the phenomenal character of Dick's experience when a red Christmas bulb looks red to him is the same as the phenomenal character of Jane's experience when an otherwise visually indistinguishable green Christmas bulb looks green to her, red Christmas bulbs look red to them both because their experiences of red Christmas bulbs bear an appropriate relationship to the property of redness. Block thus seems to agree with his denotational-intentionalist opponents that the correct psychosemantics for the contents of experiences is denotational. His disagreement with them is over intentionalism, that is, over the relationship content bears to phenomenal character. They hold that the phenomenal character of an experience is its (non-conceptual) content. He holds that the phenomenal character of an experience fails even to supervene on its content.

While I reject denotationalism itself, I'll spend ss. 16 and 17 focusing on Dretske's and Tye's brands of wide strong denotational-intentionalism. In s. 16, I'll briefly present their wide strong denotational accounts of the phenomenal characters of colour experiences. Then, in s. 17, I'll argue that they are committed to an untenable view of colour.

16. Colour and Tye's and Dretske's Wide Strong Denotational-Intentionalism

Dretske and Tye agree that the phenomenal character of a colour experience is its non-conceptual content, and that such a content will contain a colour property as a predicative constituent. They disagree, however, over what it is for an experience to have such a non-conceptual content. They both offer

---

[101] Block (1990: 55) embraces P. M. Churchland's (1979) calibration theory of content for experiences.

information-theoretic accounts of the non-conceptual contents of experiences,[102] but Dretske's account appeals to evolution, while Tye's is ahistorical. Subtleties aside (the precise details won't matter here), according to Dretske (1995: 15), what it is for an experiential state type of an organism O to have a non-conceptual content that contains a certain colour as a predicative constituent is for the state to have the function of representing the colour for members of O's species. A state type has the function of representing a certain colour for the members of a species, Dretske claims, just in case, during the evolutionary history of the species, the state type came to have a certain functional role in members of the species because it indicated the presence of the colour. Subtleties aside (again, the precise details won't matter), according to Tye (1995, 2000), what it is for an experiential state type to have a non-conceptual content that contains a certain colour as a predicative constituent is for the state type to track instances of the colour in optimal conditions.

Tye (2000) rejects Dretske's evolutionary account on the grounds that it denies Swampman (and even Swampchild and Swampgrandchild) phenomenal consciousness.[103] Tye's ahistorical account of sensory representation is free of that consequence. As Joseph Levine (this volume) points out, however, Tye's own account denies Swampbrain-in-a-vat phenomenal consciousness. Like Levine, I find that equally unintuitive. If an exact duplicate of my brain spontaneously formed in a vat of nutrients, I would deem it phenomenally conscious. I won't pursue issues about their respective brands of information-theoretic semantics here, however, since our interest lies in the role of colours in their accounts of the phenomenal characters of colour experiences.

Both Tye's and Dretske's versions of wide strong denotational-intentionalism place a heavy burden on colour realism. Their theories entail that colour irrealism is incompatible with realism about colour experiences. As I see it, one could be a colour irrealist without being an irrealist about colour experiences. But on their view, if there are no colours, then there are no colour experiences. Now if there are no colour experiences, there are no visual experiences, for all visual experiences are or include visual experiences of colour (in a broad sense of colour). Thus, on their view, if there are no colours, there are no visual experiences. If they are right, then whether there are visual experiences depends on the truth of colour-realism. This is a heavy burden for colour-realism.

I maintain that if there are colours, they are physical properties. I hold, on broad theoretical grounds, that colour-realism stands or falls with colour-physicalism. Tye and Dretske hold that too. They are colour-physicalists. Since, on their view, realism about visual experience stands or falls with

---

[102] And they both offer functional role accounts of what makes a state type an experience.
[103] Swampman is introduced in Davidson (1986).

colour-realism and colour-realism stands or falls with colour-physicalism, their view entails that visual experience realism stands or falls with colour-physicalism. Because of the problem of common ground, it seems to me an open question whether colour-physicalism is true. Suffice it to note that their account of the phenomenal characters of colour experiences places a heavy burden on colour-physicalism.

17. Dretske's and Tye's Commitment to Colour Absolutism

In discussing Tye's theory of phenomenal character, Block (1999) notes that a sample that looks unique green to one normal (by everyday standards) perceiver in a certain normal (by everyday standards) circumstance might look green tinged with blue to another normal perceiver in that same circumstance. Block notes, moreover, that it would be arbitrary to count one of them as representing the colour of the sample correctly and to count the other as not. One thing that Tye (2000: 92–3) says in response is that what seems to be a difference in unique green for each may really be a difference in the visual discrimination capacities of the perceivers. He says that the experiences of one of the perceivers may be more finely discriminating of colours than the experiences of the other, with the result that they are not visually discriminating the same physical property of the sample.[104]

But what would exclude the possibility that the perceivers are visually discriminating the same physical property of the same surface of the sample? There is in fact evidence that a physical property that disposes its bearers to look a certain unique hue to one normal (by ordinary standards) human perceiver can dispose its bearers to look some colour other than that unique hue to another normal (by ordinary standards) human perceiver in a given circumstance due to differences in the cone-sensitivities of the perceivers or differences in their opponent-processing systems.[105] It is possible that the

---

[104] For the situation to be as Tye describes, the perceivers would have to be seeing different surfaces of the sample in question, for a surface has at most one triple of reflectances. Now it may seem that an object has at most one overall surface. But the relevant notion of surface here is that of a visual surface. A given object can have different visual surfaces relative to different visual resolutions. A molecular surface grid can count as a visual surface relative to one degree of resolution for a certain kind of visual system, but not relative to another degree of resolution for that visual system. A sweater might look red from a few feet away, but look red and white (because it is made of red and white threads) from very close up (see Hilbert 1987). One sees one surface from a few feet away, another from close up. (To take a more dramatic case, think of Bishop Berkeley's example of blood under a microscope.) Tye might claim that in the Block case the two perceivers are seeing different surfaces. But, presumably, Block means to be describing a case in which the perceivers are seeing the same visual surface of the sample.

[105] See Kuehni (1997); see also Jakab (2001). This sort of phenomenon is discussed in Hardin (1988/93).

perceivers are visually discriminating the very same physical property of the very same surface of the sample. Tye and Dretske can appeal to the notion of normal misperception (discussed in s. 11) to try to handle cases of this sort. But the problem is precisely that, in the sort of case in question, it seems arbitrary which perceiver is to count as misperceiving the surface.[106]

At one point in his response to Block, Tye (2000: 92–3) appeals to relativism. He says:

Since colors comprise or include many shades, in representing something X as having a certain color, my experience effectively classifies it along with many other things whose color shades I can discriminate from X. Such classifications will certainly vary somewhat from person to person, and these classifications will be reflected in differences in verbal and nonverbal behavior. Given these differences, there can be no difficulty in allowing that a thing can be both more red than orange (for me) and more orange than red (for you). For it suffices that the red (orange) classifications at play in our experiences range over slightly different sets of shades. If a shade in my category of red is in your category of orange, something can look more red than orange to me while looking more orange than red to you. And we can both be right. Likewise, for the case of unique green and green tinged with blue.

It is important to note that Tye is talking here about experiential classification of colour (classification of colour by visual experience), not lexical categorization (see ibid. 93); he is using 'looks' in the phenomenal sense. Thus, he seems to allow that the physical property (on his view, 'the triple of integrated reflectances') that is unique green for one perceiver may be green tinged with blue for another.

Of course by my lights, this move to relativism is right. For a physical property counts as a certain colour only relative to a type of perceiver. The physical property that is unique green for one perceiver may be green tinged with blue for another perceiver. Indeed I urge the relativization of colours to observational circumstances as well since, for the reasons I gave earlier, I believe there is no non-arbitrary way of distinguishing certain environmental conditions (surrounds, certain lighting conditions, etc.) as colour illusion-inducing and others as not.

Unfortunately, however, it is not open to Tye or to Dretske to hold that a physical property counts as a certain colour only relative to the experience of a perceiver. On their view, it can't be that what makes a physical property unique green is the relationship it bears to experiences of unique green—or

---

[106] Dretske (1995: 71–2) treats the Clark example described in the quotation from Clark in n. 44 as illustrating a difference in discrimination. But the example is one of a rotation in hues due to adaptation, not an example of differences in discrimination. The case poses the problem for Dretske (and Tye) of how to distinguish states of adaptation that induce illusions of basic shades of colour from states of adaptation that do not. As should be clear, I see no way to do that that isn't to some extent arbitrary.

experiences with a certain phenomenal character; for on their view, what makes an experience an experience of unique green—or an experience with the relevant phenomenal character—is the fact that it represents unique green. On both of their theories, a subject's having a visual experience of unique green consists in the subject's having an experience with a non-conceptual content in which unique green itself—a certain physical property—enters. They can't hold that a given physical property enters the non-conceptual content of the experience of one perceiver as unique green and enters the non-conceptual content of the experience of another perceiver as green tinged with blue.

Tye and Dretske are colour objectivists. So am I, at least conditionally: I think that if there are colours (and I'm optimistic that there are), they are objective physical properties. But their theories of the phenomenal characters of colour experiences commit them to colour absolution. For the reasons discussed above and in s. 11, I think that colour absolutism is untenable.

18. Phenomenal Characters, Subjectivity, and Direct Acquaintance

While I reject denotational intentionalist theories of the phenomenal characters of experiences, I'm nevertheless a physicalist about phenomenal characters. As I noted earlier, I think that they are neuroscientific properties. I cannot defend that view here, however. In what remains, I'll set myself a more modest task. The doctrine of Revelation for the phenomenal characters of experiences, you will recall, is the doctrine that the nature of the phenomenal character of an experience is revealed to us when we have the experience. I'll try to articulate the intuitive considerations behind this doctrine of Revelation and then say why they don't entail the doctrine, and why they leave open whether phenomenal characters are neuroscientific properties.

Bertrand Russell (1927: 389) tells us that 'It is obvious that a man who can see knows things which a blind man cannot know; but a blind man can know the whole of physics. Thus the knowledge which other men have and he has not is not a part of physics.' Among the things sighted people know that (congenitally) blind people don't, is what it's like to see colours. Russell is right that no physics book could convey such knowledge, but the reason is more general than he suggests. It is that no book could. Whatever 'the true book of the world', whether it is a physics book, a Cartesian Dualist book, a neutral-monist book, an emergentist book, or a panpsychist book, a blind person couldn't learn what it is like to see colours by studying its contents, for such knowledge is not 'book learning'.[107] As concerns knowledge of what it is like see colours, there is no substitute for experience.

The phenomenal character of an experience is subjective in that we can know what it's like to have an experience with that character only if we've had the sort of experience in question or we're at least able to imagine the sort of experience in question or one appropriately similar in character. Recognition of the subjectivity of the phenomenal characters of experiences is, I believe, one of the two main sources of intuitive support for the doctrine of Revelation for the phenomenal characters of experiences. The second source of intuitive support is the recognition that in introspection, we are acquainted with the phenomenal characters of our experiences in a way that leaves no room for illusion. Introspection isn't a kind of inner vision, or even a kind of inner perception, since we don't introspect our experiences by having experiences of them; hence the often-made point that introspection has no phenomenology of its own. Our introspective access to our experiences is direct, unmediated by other experiences. We experience our experiences, but we do so by having them, not by having experiences of them; we are thus not introspectively aware of our experiences by having experiences of them. Our introspective awareness is a kind of cognitive awareness, not a kind of experimential awareness. Since our experiences don't experientially appear any way to us, there is no possibility of their presenting an illusory appearance.[108] The fact that the phenomenal characters of our experiences are subjective and the fact that we have a kind of access to them that leaves no room for an illusory appearance do not, however, jointly entail the doctrine of Revelation for the phenomenal characters of experiences. Indeed these facts are, I believe, compatible with the view that the phenomenal characters of our experiences are neuroscientific properties, even though this is not revealed to us when we have the experiences.

But how, one might well wonder, could the phenomenal character of an experience be a neuroscientific property? Neuroscientific properties are objective. How could a subjective property be an objective property? Note first of all that concepts are one thing, properties another.[109] The same property can answer to two concepts that are not a priori linked; witness the concept of

---

[107] D. Lewis (1990) observed that learning what it is like to have an experience is not book learning. Of course, a book might contain a picture of something red, but then it conveys knowledge of what it is like to see red by inducing an experience of red.

[108] This does not, of course, entail that our beliefs about what experiences we are having are incorrigible or indubitable.

[109] I reject the radical externalist view that concepts are properties that figure predicatively in thoughts and experiences.

being water and the concept of being H$_2$O. Secondly, the subjective/objective distinction is, in the first instance, epistemic. It is concepts that are, in the first instance, subjective or objective, not properties. A property is subjective or objective only under a conceptualization, i.e. under a concept.[110] The concepts under which properties count as objective differ in their a priori possession conditions from those under which properties counts as subjective. Some concepts are such that full possession of them a priori requires being able to apply them directly in introspection. We may call such concepts 'introspective concepts'. The concept of pain is an introspective concept; and so is the concept of what it is like to see red. Introspective concepts are subjective concepts; but not all concepts that count as subjective are introspective concepts. Non-introspective concepts can be linked to introspective ones in the sense that full possession of a non-introspective concept can a priori require full possession of an introspective one. A concept can be more or less subjective depending on the extent and nature of its links to introspective concepts. A concept is wholly objective if and only if it is not linked to any introspective concept. While subjective concepts are distinct from wholly objective ones, it is at least an open question whether a property might be both subjective (even introspective) and wholly objective, subjective under one concept and wholly objective under another.

Frank Jackson (1983) tried to pose a problem for physicalism by presenting the case of Mary, who knows all the physical facts about colour and colour experience, but has spent her life in a black and white room never seeing (chromatic) colours. Upon leaving the room and encountering something red, she can learn what it is like to see red. So, Jackson claims, she can come to know a fact about colour and colour experience that she did not know before. For this reason, Jackson concludes that physicalism is false.[111]

---

[110] This idea can be found in Loar (1990/7) and Sturgeon (1994), but I develop the idea differently from the way they do.

[111] Broad (1925: 71–2) once asked: 'Would there be any theoretical limit to the deduction of the properties of chemical elements and compounds if a mechanistic theory of chemistry were true? Yes. Take . . . e.g. "Nitrogen and Hydrogen combine when an electric discharge is passed through a mixture of the two. The resulting compound contains three atoms of Hydrogen to one of Nitrogen; it is a gas readily soluble in water, and possessed of a pungent and characteristic smell." If the mechanistic theory be true . . . a mathematical archangel could deduce from his knowledge of the microscopic structure of atoms all these facts but the last. He would know exactly what the microscopic structure of ammonia must be; but he would be totally unable to predict that a substance with this structure must smell as ammonia does when it gets into the human nose. The utmost that he could predict on this subject would be that certain changes would take place in the mucous membrance, the olfactory nerves and so on. But he could not possibly know that these changes would be accompanied by the appearance of a smell in general or of the peculiar smell of ammonia in particular, unless someone told him so or he has smelled it for himself.'

Mary's knowledge of what it is like to see red involves knowledge-that.[112] After leaving the room, Mary learns something she could express by saying, 'So this is what it's like to see red.' She comes to know that something is the case that she did not know to be the case before. She acquires new propositional knowledge; of that, I believe, there should be no question. Whether this new propositional knowledge is knowledge of a previously unknown fact is, however, controversial. The controversy turns, in part, on what is meant by a fact. On a conception of facts according to which they are obtaining states of affairs that are constituted by properties (and sometimes by objects as well), Mary does not learn a new fact—at least according to the physicalist. However, on a conception of facts according to which they individuate finely enough to individuate knowing-that states in a way that meets the strictest demands of rational explanation up to indexicality and demonstration, Mary indeed learns a new fact.[113] On this fine-grained conception of facts, facts contain concepts as constituents. On this conception, the fact that water puts out fire is distinct from the fact that H_2O puts out fire.

Let us call facts that contain a subjective concept as a constituent, 'subjective facts', and other facts 'wholly objective facts'. The fact Mary learns after leaving the room is subjective because it contains a subjective concept as a constituent, namely, the concept of what it's like to see red. The real moral of the considerations behind 'the Knowledge Argument' is, then, best made by the argument:

Premiss 1.   Before leaving the room, Mary knew all of the wholly objective facts about colour and colour experience.

Premiss 2.   After leaving the room and seeing something red, Mary learned a new fact about colour and colour experience.

Conclusion   Not all facts are wholly objective facts.

---

[112] Nemirow (1990) and D. Lewis (1990) argue that it is know-how, rather than knowledge-that. But see e.g. Loar (1990/7); Lycan (1996); Tye (2000); Deutsch (2001); and Crane (forthcoming).

[113] Essentially this notion of facts is, I believe, appealed to in the discussion of Jackson's argument in Lycan (1996), Deutsch (2001), and in Crane (forthcoming). This is a pleonastic notion of fact, rather than the metaphysical notion of an obtaining state of affairs. I add the qualification that such facts individuate knowledge-that states up to indexicality and demonstration. The qualification is needed since it seems to me that on any notion of fact, if I know that I've written a paper on colour and consciousness and you know that Brian McLaughlin has written a paper on colour and consciousness, we know the same fact. But the *de se* content of my knowledge plays a role in rationalizing explanation not played by the content of your knowledge. Likewise, if I know that that (where the second 'that' demonstrates Tom's car) is Tom's car and you know that Tom's car is Tom's car, then we know the same fact on any notion of fact, yet there are differences in the contents of our knowledge-that states that matter to rationalizing explanation.

On the fine-grained conception of facts in question, this argument strikes me as sound.

The argument poses no problem for physicalism, however. Subjective facts are not expressible in the theoretical vocabulary of microphysics because such scientific terms express wholly objective concepts. But it is not required by physicalism, as I understand it, that all facts—certainly in this extremely fine-grained sense of fact—be expressible in the vocabulary of microphysics. I take physicalism to require that *all there is is whatever there must (of metaphysical necessity) be for the actual world to be exactly as it is microphysically.*[114] This requirement has no such implication. Moreover, even if this is not a sufficient condition for physicalism,[115] there is no reason to think that physicalism requires that all facts be expressible in the vocabulary of microphysics. While they are ontological monists, physicalists can be, and should be, conceptual pluralists.

As noted above, a concept can be more or less extensively linked to introspective concepts; let's express this by saying that a concept can be more or less extensively linked with subjectivity. The concept of H_2O seems wholly objective, not at all linked with subjectivity. It is, however, less certain whether the concept of water is to some extent linked with subjectivity. It may be that full possession of the concept of water a priori requires full possession of a concept that is nowadays called 'the concept of watery stuff'[116]—i.e. the concept of the transparent, tasteless, potable liquid that falls from the sky when it rains, etc. While the concept of watery stuff is certainly not an introspective concept, it seems linked to such concepts, and so linked with subjectivity; for full possession of the concept of watery stuff a priori requires full possession of the concept of a taste and the concept of transparency, and these concepts seemed linked to introspective concepts. If full possession of the concept of water a priori requires full possession of the concept of watery stuff, then the concept of water too is linked with subjectivity, though less directly than the concept of watery stuff since it is so linked via its link to the concept of watery stuff. Still even if the concept of water is linked with subjectivity while the concept of H_2O is wholly objective, it is none the less

---

[114] This claim about physicalism entails Jackson's (1996) claim that physicalism is true only if any minimal physical duplicate of the actual world is a duplicate *simpliciter* of the actual world. But it is stronger than this claim of Jackson. A minimal physical duplicate of the actual world may fail to contain Frank Jackson or me since it may, instead, contain physical duplicates of us. But given that Jackson and I exist, if all there is is whatever there must be for the actual world to be exactly as it is microphysically, then Jackson and I must exist given the way the actual world is microphysically; and so must my *de re* beliefs about Jackson.

[115] If God is a necessary being, then the existence of God is compatible with the fact that all there is is whatever there must be for the actual world to be exactly as it is microphysically. But it seems that the existence of God should be incompatible with physicalism. (See Jackson 1996 for a discussion of this sort of issue.)

[116] Chalmers (1996).

the case that water = H_2O. Moreover, given that water = H_2O and that the watery stuff on Earth is water: (a) the totality of microphysical facts, nomological and otherwise, (b) the fact that it is the totality of microphysical facts, and (c) the (contingent) assumption that all there is is whatever there must be for the actual world to be exactly the way it is microphysically, jointly entail that the watery stuff on Earth is H_2O. However, (a)–(c) will fail to entail a priori that the watery stuff on Earth is H_2O, or even that some of the watery stuff on Earth is H_2O; for it will not be a priori that H_2O is watery stuff, let alone that it is the watery stuff on Earth. The entailment in question will be a posteriori.

It may well be that most of the concepts that are part of the 'manifest image' to use Wilfred Sellars's term, or part of our conception of 'the world of lived experience' to use Edmund Husserl's term, are at least to some extent linked with subjectivity, hence the problem of reconciling the manifest image with the scientific image, or the world of lived experience with the world of science. But given that subjectivity and objectivity are concept relative, from the fact that a concept is linked with subjectivity, it does not follow that the property that answers to it cannot also answer to a wholly objective concept.

Consider again the fact that we are directly acquainted with the phenomenal characters of our experiences in a way that leaves no room for illusion. Consideration of this fact invites the thought that the natures of the phenomenal characters of our experiences are revealed to us by the experiences themselves; and so, that we are able to come to know the natures of the phenomenal characters of our experiences by attending to them. The distinction between concepts and properties is, however, important here too, as is the structure of our cognitive architecture. Our access to the phenomenal characters of our experiences is indeed direct, not via a contingent mode of presentation of them or via some aspect of them. And to be sure, no matter how carefully one attends to it, introspection will not reveal the phenomenal character of an experience to be a neuroscientific property. But there is a distinction between *not being revealed as* an F and *being revealed as otherwise than* an F.[117] Introspection-as involves the exercise of concepts; introspecting something as an F involves the exercise of the concept of F. In introspection, the phenomenal characters of experiences are not revealed as neuroscientific properties because neuroscientific concepts are not introspective concepts: we can't deploy them introspectively (at least not directly); thus phenomenal characters cannot be *introspected as* neuroscientific properties. But it doesn't follow that introspection reveals the phenomenal characters of our experiences to be otherwise than neuroscientific properties.

---

[117] Recall Arnauld's response to Descartes.

Primitive introspective concepts are called 'phenomenal concepts'.[118] Deploying such concepts in introspection, we can recognize when we are having an experience with a certain phenomenal character, and recognize similarities and dissimilarities among phenomenal characters. However, phenomenal concepts don't enable us to acquire knowledge of the natures of the phenomenal characters of our experiences; or, if (controversially) acquaintance is a kind of knowledge, then phenomenal concepts don't enable us acquire descriptive knowledge of the natures of the phenomenal characters of our experiences. The dualist agrees. The reason that is so, the dualist claims, is that phenomenal characters are non-structural, intrinsic properties. Were phenomenal characters non-structural, intrinsic properties, then that would explain why we can have no descriptive knowledge of their natures. But I myself reject that explanation. I think the explanation lies rather in the fact that phenomenal concepts have no descriptive content; they function in thought somewhat like non-descriptive names. The dualist agrees that phenomenal concepts have no descriptive content, but goes on to say that the properties to which they answer are non-structural, intrinsic properties. That assumption isn't required, however, to explain why we can't have descriptive introspective knowledge of the natures of the phenomenal characters of our experiences; the fact that phenomenal concepts lack descriptive content is sufficient to explain why we can't. This explanation leaves open whether the properties that answer to our phenomenal concepts are structural or even relational properties. Indeed it leaves open whether they are neuroscientific properties.[119]

For these reasons, then, I think that the intuitive considerations behind the doctrine of Revelation for the phenomenal characters of experiences—the subjectivity of the phenomenal characters of our experiences and the fact that we are directly acquainted with them in a way that leaves no room for illusion—don't jointly entail the doctrine.

Unlike our concepts of sensory qualities, our phenomenal concepts do not admit of functional analyses. Analytical functionalism is false for the phenomenal characters of experiences. Thus, the sort of strategy we employed for trying to locate colours in nature cannot be employed to try to locate the phenomenal characters of experiences in nature. Still we can look for nomological correlations. And, where the phenomenal characters of colour experiences are concerned, opponent processing offers the hope that we can

---

[118] For discussions of phenomenal concepts see e.g. Loar (1990/7); Hill and McLaughlin (1999), McLaughlin (2001*a*); a related, though I think non-equivalent, notion of phenomenal concepts is discussed in Tye (2000).

[119] For the record, I believe that phenomenal characters are intrinsic, structural neuroscientific properties; I'm a type-materialist about the phenomenal characters of experiences, not a psychofunctionalist.

find neuroscientific nomological correlates.[120] I believe that if nomological correlates of the phenomenal characters of experiences are found, then on grounds of overall coherence and theoretical simplicity, the best explanation of the correlations would be that the correlates are identical. To be sure, such identity claims face well-known philosophical challenges.[121] I've here focused on only two such challenges. The fact that phenomenal characters are subjective and that we have direct access to them in introspection does not close the issue of the truth of such identity claims.[122]

REFERENCES

ALEXANDER, S. (1920), *Space, Time, and Deity*, 2 vols. (London: Macmillan).

ARMSTRONG, D. M. (1968), *A Materialist Theory of Mind* (London: Routledge & Kegan Paul).

—— (1979), *A Theory of Universals*, 2 vols. (Cambridge: Cambridge University Press).

BALDWIN, T. (1992), 'The Projective Theory of Sensory Content', in T. Crane (ed.), *The Contents of Experience* (Cambridge: Cambridge University Press), 177–95.

BENNETT, J. (1965), 'Substance, Reality and Primary Qualities', *American Philosophical Quarterly*, 2.

—— (1968), 'Substance, Reality, and Primary Qualities', in C. B. Martin and D. M. Armstrong (eds.), *Locke and Berkeley: A Collection of Critical Essays* (New York: Anchor Books).

BERKELEY, G. (1710/1965), *A Treatise Concerning the Principles of Human Knowledge*, in *Berkeley's Writings*, ed. D. M. Armstrong (New York: Macmillan).

BIDWELL, S. (1901), 'On Negative After-Images and their Relation to Certain Other Visual Phenomena', *Proceedings of the Royal Society of London B*, 68: 262–9.

BILLOCK, T., GLEASON, J., and TSOU, S. (2001), 'Perception of Forbidden Colors in Retinally Stabilized Equiluminant Images', *Journal of the Optical Society of America*, 18: 2398–403.

BLOCK, N. (1990), 'Inverted Earth', in J. Tomberlin (ed.), *Philosophical Perspectives* (Northridge, Calif.: Ridgeview), 53–80.

—— (1999), 'Sexism, Racism, Ageism, and the Nature of Consciousness', in *The Philosophy of Sydney Shoemaker, Philosophical Topics*, 26.

BOGHOSSIAN, P. A., and VELLEMAN, J. D. (1989), 'Colour as a Secondary Quality', *Mind*, 98: 81–103.

—— —— (1991), 'Physicalist Theories of Color', *Philosophical Review*, 7: 67–106.

---

[120] Cf. Hardin (1988/93).

[121] Some are addressed in Hill and McLaughlin (1999) and in McLaughlin (2001*a*).

[122] I'm grateful to Margaret Atherton, Jonathan Cohen, Larry Hardin, John Hawthorne, Frank Jackson, Rolf Kuehni, Cynthia Macdonald, Mohan Matthen, Barry Maund, Galen Strawson, and Zoltan Jakab for enormously helpful written comments on drafts of this chapter. I also thank Troy Cross, Tim Crane, Chris Hill, Terry Horgan, Peter Ross, Daniel Stoljar, and Adam Wager for helpful discussions.

150 Intentionality and Phenomenal Content

BOWMAKER, P. (1977), 'The Visual Pigments, Oil Droplets, and Spectral Sensitivity of the Pigeon', *Vision Research*, 17: 1129–38.

BROAD, C. D. (1925), *The Mind and Its Place in Nature* (London: Routledge & Kegan Paul).

BRYNE, A., and HILBERT, D. R. (1997), 'Colors and Reflectances', in A. Bryne and D. R. Hilbert (eds.), *Readings on Color*, i. *The Philosophy of Color* (Cambridge, Mass.: MIT Press), 263–88.

CAMPBELL, J. (1994), 'A Simple View of Colour', in J. Haldane and C. Wright (eds.), *Reality, Representation, and Projection* (Oxford: Clarendon Press).

CAMPBELL, K. (1969), 'Colours', in R. Brown and C. D. Rollins (eds.), *Contemporary Philosophy in Australia* (London: Allen & Unwin).

—— (1982), 'The Implications of Land's Theory of Colour Vision', in L. J. Cohen (ed.), *Logic, Methodology, and Philosophy of Science* (Amsterdam: North Holland)

—— (1993), 'David Armstrong and Realism about Colour', in J. Bacon, K. Campbell, and L. Reinhardt (eds.), *Ontology, Causality and Mind: Essays in Honour of D. M. Armstrong* (Cambridge: Cambridge University Press).

CHALMERS, D. (1996), *The Conscious Mind* (New York: Oxford University Press).

CHISHOLM, R. (1957), *Perceiving: A Philosophical Study* (Ithaca, NY: Cornell University Press).

CHURCHLAND, P. M. (1979), *Scientific Realism and the Plasticity of Mind* (Cambridge: Cambridge University Press).

—— (1985), 'Reduction, Qualia, and the Direct Introspection of Brain States', *Journal of Philosophy*, 82: 8–28.

—— (1986), 'Some Reductive Strategies in Cognitive Neurobiology', *Mind*, 279–309.

CHURCHLAND, P. S. (1986), *Neurophilosophy* (Cambridge, Mass.: MIT Press).

CLARK, A. (1993), *Sensory Qualities* (Oxford: Clarendon Press).

COHEN, J. (2000), 'Color Properties and Color Perception: A Functionalist Account', Doctoral Dissertation, Rutgers University.

—— 'Subjectivism, Physicalism, or None of the Above? Comments on Ross's "The Location Problem for Color Subjectivism"', in *Consciousness and Cognition*, 10: 94–104.

COREN, B., WARD, B., and ENNS G. (1994), *Sensation and Perception* (New York: Harcourt Brace), 370–72.

CORNMAN, J. (1974), 'Can Eddington's "Two" Tables be Identical?' *Australasian Journal of Philosophy*, 52: 22–38.

—— (1975), *Perception, Common Sense and Science* (New Haven: Yale University Press).

COSMIDES, L., and TOOBY, J. (1995), Foreword to S. Baron-Cohen, *Mindblindness* (Cambridge, Mass.: MIT Press).

CRANE, H., and PIANTANIDA, T. P. (1983), 'On Seeing Reddish Green and Yellowish Blue', *Science*, 221: 1078–80.

CRANE, T. (forthcoming), 'Subjective Facts'.

DAVIDOFF, J. (1991), *Cognition Through Color* (Cambridge, Mass.: MIT Press).

DAVIDSON, D. (1987), 'Knowing One's Mind', *Proceedings of the American Philosophical Association*, 60: 44–58.

Descartes, R (1954), *Philosophical Writings*, trans. G. E. M. Anscombe and P. Geach (London: Nelson).

Deutsch, M. (2001), 'The World Knot: The Problem of Consciousness and Revamped Materialism', Ph.D. Dissertation, Rutgers University.

Dretske, F. (1995), *Naturalizing the Mind* (Cambridge, Mass.: MIT Press).

—— (2000), *Perception, Knowledge and Belief: Selected Essays* (Cambridge: Cambridge University Press).

Evans, R. (1948), *An Introduction to Color* (New York: Wiley).

Fine, K. (1975), 'Vagueness, Truth, and Logic', *Synthese*, 30: 265–300.

Fuld, K., Werner, J. S. et al. (1983), 'The Possible Elemental Nature of Brown', *Vision Research*, 23: 631–7.

Gibbard, A. (1996), 'Visual Properties of Human Interest Only', in E. Villenueva (ed.), *Philosophical Issues* (Atascadero, Calif.: Ridgeview).

Grandy, R. E. (1989), 'A Modern Inquiry into the Physical Reality of Colors', in D. Weissbord (ed.), *Mind, Value and Culture: Essays in Honour of E. M. Adams* (Atascadero, Calif.: Ridgeview).

Hardin, C. L. (1988/93), *Color for Philosophers: Unweaving the Rainbow* (Indianapolis and Cambridge, Mass.: Hackett).

—— (1990), 'Perception and Physical Theory', in W. C. Lycan (ed.), *Mind and Cognition: A Reader* (Oxford: Blackwell).

Harman, G. (1990), 'The Intrinsic Quality of Experience', *Philosophical Perspectives*, 4: 31–52.

Herring, E. (1878/1964), *Outlines of a Theory of the Light Sense*, trans. L. M. Hurvich and D. Jameson (Cambridge, Mass.: Harvard University Press).

Hilbert, D. (1987), *Color and Color Perception: A Study in Anthropocentric Realism* (Stanford, Calif.: Stanford University Center for the Study of Language and Information).

Hill, C., and McLaughlin, B. P. (1999), 'There are Fewer Things than are Dreamt of in Chalmers's Philosophy', *Philosophy and Phenomenological Research*, 2: 445–54.

Hurvich, L. M. (1981), *Color Vision* (Sunderland, Mass.: Sinauer).

—— and Jameson, D. (1955), 'Some Quantitative Aspects of an Opponent-Colors Theory: II. Brightness, Saturation and Hue in Normal and Dichromatic Vision', *Journal of the Optical Society of America*, 45: 602–12.

—— —— (1956), 'Some Quantitative Aspects of an Opponent Colors Theory: IV. A Psychological Color Specification System', *Journal of the Optical Society of America*, 46: 416–21.

—— —— (1957), 'An Opponent-Process Theory of Color Vision', *Psychological Review*, 64: 384–408.

Indow, T. (1988), 'Multidimensional Studies of Munsell Color Solid', *Psychological Review*, 95: 456–70.

Jackson, F. (1977), *Perception* (Cambridge: Cambridge University Press).

—— (1996), 'The Primary Quality View of Color', *Philosophical Perspectives*, 10: 199–219.

—— (1998), *From Metaphysics to Ethics: A Defense of Conceptual Analysis* (Oxford and New York: Oxford University Press).

JACKSON, F., and PARGETTER, R. (1987), 'An Objectivist Guide to Subjectivism about Color', *Revue Internationale de Philosophie*, 160: 129–41.

JAKAB, Z. (2001), 'Color Experience: Empirical Evidence Against Representational Externalism', Doctoral Dissertation, Carleton University.

JAMESON, D., and HURVICH, L. M. (1955), 'Some Quantitative Aspects of Opponent-Colors Theory: 1. Chromatic Responses and Spectral Saturation', *Journal of the Optical Society of America*, 45: 546–52.

—————— (1956), 'Some Quantitative Aspects of an Opponent-Colors Theory: III. Changes in Brightness, Saturation and Hue with Chromatic Adaptation', *Journal of the Optical Society of America*, 46: 405–15.

JOHNSTON, M. (1992), 'How to Speak of Colors', *Philosophical Studies*, 68: 221–64.

JORDAN, G., and MOLLON, J. D. (1993), 'A Study of Women Heterozygous for Colour Deficiencies', *Vision Research*, 33: 1495–508.

JUDD, D. B., and WYSZECKI, G. (1975), *Color in Business, Science and Industry* (New York: John Wiley).

KRIPKE, S. (1980), *Naming and Necessity* (Cambridge, Mass.: Harvard University Press).

KUEHNI, R. (1997), *Color* (New York: J. Wiley).

LAND, E. (1977), 'The Retinex Theory of Color Vision', *Scientific American*, 237: 108–28.

LEWIS, C. I. (1929), *Mind and World Order* (New York: Dover).

LEWIS, D. (1990), 'What Experience Teaches', in W. Lycan (ed.), *Mind and Cognition: A Reader* (Oxford: Basil Blackwell).

—— (1997), 'Naming the Colours', *Australasian Journal of Philosophy*, 75: 325–42.

LOAR, B. (1990/7), 'Phenomenal States', in N. Block, O. Flanagan, and G. Güzeldere (eds.), *The Nature of Consciousness* (Cambridge, Mass.: MIT Press).

LOCKE, J. (1690/1975), *An Essay Concerning Human Understanding*, ed. P. H. Nidditch (Oxford: Oxford University Press).

LYCAN, W. G. (1996), *Consciousness and Experience* (Cambridge, Mass.: MIT Press).

McDOWELL, J. (1985), 'Values and Secondary Qualities', in T. Honderich (ed.), *Morality and Objectivity* (London: Routledge & Kegan Paul).

McGEE, V., and McLAUGHLIN, B. P. (1995), 'Distinctions without a Difference', *Vagueness Spindel Conference, Southern Journal of Philosophy*, 33: 203–51.

—————— (1998), Review of Timothy Williamson's *Vagueness*, *Linguistics and Philosophy*, 21: 221–35.

—————— (2000), 'Lessons of the Many', *Philosophical Topics*, 28: 129–51.

McGINN, C. (1983), *The Subjective View* (Oxford: Oxford University Press).

MACKIE, J. L. (1976), *Problems from Locke* (Oxford: Clarendon Press).

McLAUGHLIN, B. P. (1984), 'Perception, Causation, and Supervenience', *Midwest Studies in Philosophy*, 9: 569–91.

—— (1991), 'The Rise and Fall of British Emergentism', in A. Berckermann, H. Flohr, and J. Kim (eds.), *Emergence or Reduction: Essays on the Prospects of Nonreductive Physicalism* (Berlin: de Gruyter).

—— (1995), 'Dispositions', in J. Kim and E. Sosa (eds.), *A Companion to Metaphysics* (Oxford: Blackwell).

—— (1996), 'Lewis on What Distinguishes Perception from Hallucination', in K. Akins (ed.) *Problems in Perception* (Oxford: Oxford University Press), 198–231.

—— (1999), 'Colors and Color Spaces', *Epistemology*, 5: 83–9.

—— (2001*a*), 'In Defense of New Wave Materialism', in Barry Loewer (ed.), *Physicalism and Its Discontents* (Cambridge: Cambridge University Press).

—— (2001*b*), 'Physicalism and Its Alternatives', in *Encyclopedia of the Social and Behavioural Sciences* (Amsterdam: Elsevier), 11422–7.

—— (forthcoming *a*), 'The Place of Color in Nature', in R. Mausfeld and D. Hieter (eds.), *From Light to Object* (Oxford: Oxford University Press).

—— (forthcoming *b*), 'Intentionalism and the Relativity of Color'.

MAGEE, B., and MILLIGAN, M. (1995), *On Blindness* (Oxford: Oxford University Press).

MATTHEN, M. (1988), 'Biological Functions and Perceptual Content', *Journal of Philosophy*, 85: 5–27.

—— (2000), 'The Disunity of Color', *Philosophical Review*, 108: 47–84.

MAUND, B. (1991), 'The Nature of Color', *History of Philosophy Quarterly*, 8: 253–63.

—— (1995), *Colours: Their Nature and Representation* (Cambridge: Cambridge University Press).

MOLLON, J. D. (1992), 'Worlds of Difference', *Nature*, 356: 378–9.

MULLIGAN, K. (1991), 'Colours, Corners and Complexity', in W. Spohn (ed.), *Existence and Explanation* (Dordrecht: Kluwer), 45–9.

MUNSELL, A. H. (1905/46), *A Color Notation*, 14th edn. (Baltimore, Md.: Munsell Color Co.).

NASSAU, K. (1980), 'The Causes of Color', *Scientific American*, 242 n. 10, and 124–54.

—— (1983), *The Physics and Chemistry of Color* (New York: Wiley).

NEMIROW, L. (1990), 'Physicalism and the Cognitive Role of Acquisition', in W. Lycan (ed.), *Mind and Cognition: A Reader* (Oxford: Basil Blackwell).

NOZICK, R. (1980), *Philosophical Explanations* (Cambridge, Mass.: Harvard University Press).

PEACOCKE, C. (1984), 'Color Concepts and Color Experience', *Synthese*, 58: 365–82.

PERKINS, M. (1983), *Sensing the World* (Indianapolis: Hackett).

PRICE, H. H. (1957), *Thinking and Experience* (Cambridge: Cambridge University Press).

QUINN, P. C., ROSANO, J. L., and WOOTEN, B. R. (1988), 'Evidence that Brown is not an Elementary Color', *Perception and Psychophysics*, 43: 156–64.

RAFFMAN, D. (1995), 'On the Persistence of Phenomenology', in T. Metzinger (ed.), *Conscious Experience* (Berlin: Imprint Academic), 293–308.

RIBE, N. M. (1985), 'Goethe's Critique of Newton: Reconsideration', *Studies in History and Philosophy of Science*, 16: 315–35.

ROSS, P. (2001), 'The Location Problem for Color Subjectivism', *Consciousness and Cognition*, 10: 42–58.

RUSSELL, B. (1912), *The Problems of Philosophy* (London: Oxford University Press).

—— (1927), *Outline of Philosophy* (London: Routledge).

SCHLICK, M. (1979), 'Form and Content: An Introduction to Philosophical Think-ing', in Henk L. Mulder and Barbara Vele-Schlick (eds.), *Moritz Schlick: Philosoph-ical Papers*, ii. *1925–1936* (Dordrecht: D. Reide).

SHEPARD, R. N. (1987), 'Evolution of a Mesh between Principles of the Mind and Regularities of the World', in John Dupré (ed.), *Beyond the Best: Essays on Evolution and Optimality* (Cambridge, Mass.: MIT Press).

—— (1990), 'A Possible Evolutionary Basis for Trichromacy', in M. Brill (ed.), *Per-ceiving, Measuring, and Using Color: Proceedings of the SPIE/SPE Symposium on Electronic Imaging: Science and Technology*, 1250: 301–9.

SHOEMAKER, S. (1981), 'The Inverted Spectrum', *Journal of Philosophy*, 74: 357–81.

—— (1998), 'Causal and Metaphysical Necessity', *Pacific Philosophical Quarterly*, 79: 59–77.

SMART, J. J. C. (1961), 'Colours', *Philosophy*, 36: 128–42.

—— (1963), *Philosophy and Scientific Realism* (London: Routledge & Kegan Paul).

STERHEIM, C. S., and BOYTON, R. M. (1966), 'Uniqueness of Perceived Hues Investigated with a Continuous Judgmental Technique', *Journal of Experimental Psychology*, 72: 770–6.

STEWART, D. (1822), *The Works of Thomas Reid*, i (New York: N. Bangs and T. Mason, for the Methodist Episcopal Church).

STRAWSON, G. (1989), ' "Red" and red', *Synthese*, 78: 198–232.

—— (forthcoming), 'Knowledge of the World', *Philosophical Topics*.

STROUD, B. (2000), *The Quest for Reality: Subjectivism and the Metaphysics of Colour* (New York: Oxford University Press).

STURGEON, S. (1994), 'The Epistemic View of Subjectivity', *Journal of Philosophy*, 91/5: 221–35.

THOMPSON, E. (1995), *Colour Vision: A Study in Cognitive Science and the Philosophy of Perception* (London and New York: Routledge).

TYE, M. (1995), *Ten Problems of Consciousness: A Representational Theory of the Phenomenal Mind* (Cambridge, Mass.: MIT Press).

—— (2000), *Consciousness, Color, and Content* (Cambridge, Mass.: MIT Press).

UNGER, P. (1980), 'The Problem of the Many', *Midwest Studies in Philosophy*, 5: 411–67.

WANDELL, B. (1995), *Foundations of Vision* (Sunderland, Mass.: Sinauer), 100–1.

WIGGINS, D. (1987), 'A Sensible Subjectivism', in *Needs, Values, Truth* (Oxford: Blackwell).

WITTGENSTEIN, L. (1921/61), *Tractatus Logic-Philosophicus*, trans. D. F. Pears and Brian McGuinness (London: Routledge & Kegan Paul).

—— (1977), *Remarks on Colour*, ed. G. E. M. Anscombe (Oxford: Blackwell).

Part Two

Knowing Mental States

6. How to Read Your Own Mind: A Cognitive Theory of Self-Consciousness

SHAUN NICHOLS AND STEPHEN STICH

1. Introduction

The topic of self-awareness has an impressive philosophical pedigree, and sustained discussion of the topic goes back at least to Descartes. More recently, self-awareness has become a lively issue in the cognitive sciences, thanks largely to the emerging body of work on 'mind-reading', the process of attributing mental states to people (and other organisms). During the last fifteen years, the processes underlying mind-reading have been a major focus of attention in cognitive and developmental psychology. Most of this work has been concerned with the processes underlying the attribution of mental states to *other* people. However, a number of psychologists and philosophers have also proposed accounts of the mechanisms underlying the attribution of mental states to *oneself*. This process of reading one's own mind or becoming self-aware will be our primary concern in this chapter.

We'll start by examining what is probably the most widely held account of self-awareness, the 'theory theory' (TT). The basic idea of the TT of self-awareness is that one's access to one's own mind depends on the same cluster of cognitive mechanisms that plays a central role in attributing mental states to others. Those mechanisms include a body of information about psychology, a theory of mind (ToM). Though many authors have endorsed the theory theory of self-awareness (Gopnik 1993; Gopnik and Wellman 1994; Gopnik and Meltzoff 1994; Perner 1991; Wimmer and Hartl 1991; Carruthers 1996; C. D. Frith 1994; U. Frith and Happé 1999), it is our contention that advocates of this account of self-awareness have left their theory seriously underdescribed. In the next section, we'll suggest three different ways in which the TT account might be elaborated, all of which have significant shortcomings. In s. 3, we'll present our own theory of self-awareness, the monitoring mechanism theory, and compare its merits to those of the TT. Theory theorists argue that the TT is supported by evidence about psychological development and psychopathologies. In s. 4 we will review the arguments from psychopathologies and argue that none of the evidence favours the TT over our monitoring mechanism theory.[1] Indeed, in the fifth section we will exploit evidence on psychopathologies to provide an argument in favour of the monitoring mechanism theory. On our account, but not on the TT, it is possible for the mechanisms subserving self-awareness and reading other people's minds to be damaged independently. And, we will suggest, this may well be just what is happening in certain cases of schizophrenia and autism. After making our case against the TT and in favour of our theory, we will consider two other theories of self-awareness to be found in the recent literature. The first of these, discussed in s. 6, is Robert Gordon's (1995, 1996) 'ascent routine' account, which, we will argue, is clearly inadequate to explain the full range of self-awareness phenomena. The second is Alvin Goldman's (1993a, 1993b, 1997, forthcoming) phenomenological account which, we maintain, is also underdescribed and admits of two importantly different interpretations. On both of the interpretations, we'll argue, the theory is singularly implausible. But before we do any of this, there is a good deal of background that needs to be set in place.

Mind-reading skills, in both the first-person and the third-person cases, can be divided into two categories which, for want of better labels, we'll call *detecting* and *reasoning*.

1. *Detecting* is the capacity to *attribute* current mental states to someone.
2. *Reasoning* is the capacity to *use* information about a person's mental states (typically along with other information) to make predictions about the person's past and future mental states, her behaviour, and her environment.

So, for instance, one might *detect* that another person wants ice cream and that the person thinks the closest place to get ice cream is at the corner shop. Then one might *reason* from this information that, since the person wants ice cream and thinks that she can get it at the corner shop, she will go to the shop. The distinction between detecting and reasoning is an important one because some of the theories we'll be considering offer integrated accounts on which

---

[1] Elsewhere, we consider the evidence from development (Nichols and Stich forthcoming *a*, *b*). Nichols and Stich (forthcoming *b*) is intended as a companion piece to this chapter. In that article, we argue that a closer inspection of the developmental evidence shows that the developmental argument for TT is unworkable and that the evidence actually poses a problem for the TT. Of necessity, there is considerable overlap between this chapter and Nichols and Stich (forthcoming *b*). In both places we consider whether the evidence favours the TT or the monitoring mechanism theory, and the theoretical background against which the arguments are developed is largely the same in both papers. As a result, readers familiar with Nichols and Stich (forthcoming *b*) might skip ahead to s. 4.

detecting and reasoning are explained by the same cognitive mechanism. Other theories, including ours, maintain that in the first person case, these two aspects of mind-reading are subserved by different mechanisms.

Like the other authors we'll be considering, we take it to be a requirement on theories of self-awareness that they offer an explanation for:

(a) The obvious facts about self-attribution (e.g. that normal adults do it easily and often, that they are generally accurate, and that they have no clear idea of how they do it).

(b) The often rather unobvious facts about self-attribution that have been uncovered by cognitive and developmental psychologists (e.g. Gopnik and Slaughter 1991; Ericsson and Simon 1993; Nisbett and Wilson 1977).

However, we *do not* take it to be a requirement on theory building in this area that the theory address philosophical puzzles that have been raised about knowledge of one's own mental states. In recent years, philosophers have had a great deal to say about the link between content externalism and the possibility that people can have privileged knowledge about their own propositional attitudes (e.g. McLaughlin and Tye 1998).[2] These issues are largely orthogonal to the sorts of questions about underlying mechanisms that we will be discussing in this chapter, and we have nothing at all to contribute to the resolution of the philosophical puzzles posed by externalism. But in the unlikely event that philosophers who worry about such matters agree on solutions to these puzzles, we expect that the solutions will fit comfortably with our theory.

There is one last bit of background that needs to be made explicit before we begin. The theory we'll set out will help itself to two basic assumptions about the mind. We call the first of these *the basic architecture assumption*. What it claims is that a well-known commonsense account of the architecture of the cognitive mind is largely correct, though obviously incomplete. This account of cognitive architecture, which has been widely adopted both in cognitive science and in philosophy, maintains that in normal humans, and probably in other organisms as well, the mind contains two quite different kinds of representational states, beliefs and desires. These two kinds of states differ 'functionally' because they are caused in different ways and have different patterns of interaction with other components of the mind. Some beliefs are caused fairly directly by perception; others are derived from pre-existing

---

[2] Content externalism is the view that the content of one's mental states (what the mental states are about) is determined at least in part by factors external to one's mind. In contemporary analytic philosophy, the view was motivated largely by Putnam's Twin Earth thought experiments (Putnam 1975) that seem to show that two molecule-for-molecule twins can have thoughts with different meanings, apparently because of their different external environments.

beliefs via processes of deductive and non-deductive inference. Some desires (like the desire to get something to drink or the desire to get something to eat) are caused by systems that monitor various bodily states. Other desires, sometimes called 'instrumental desires' or 'sub-goals', are generated by a process of practical reasoning that has access to beliefs and to pre-existing desires. In addition to generating sub-goals, the practical reasoning system must also determine which structure of goals and sub-goals is to be acted upon at any time. Once made, that decision is passed on to various action-controlling systems whose job it is to sequence and co-ordinate the behaviours necessary to carry out the decision. Figure 6.1 is a sketch of the basic architecture assumption.

We find diagrams such as Fig. 6.1 to be very helpful in comparing and clarifying theories about mental mechanisms, and we'll make frequent use of

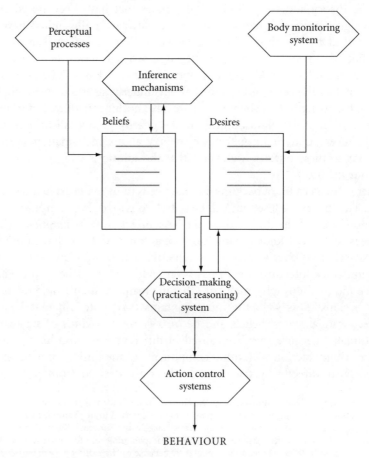

FIG. 6.1. Basic cognitive architecture

them in this chapter. It is important, however, that the diagrams not be misinterpreted. Positing a 'box' in which a certain category of mental states are located is simply a way of depicting the fact that those states share an important cluster of causal properties that are not shared by other types of states in the system. There is no suggestion that all the states in the box share a spatial location in the brain. Nor does it follow that there can't be significant and systematic differences among the states within a box. When it becomes important to emphasize such differences, we use boxes within boxes or other obvious notational devices. All this applies also to processing mechanisms, like the inference mechanism and the practical reasoning mechanism, which we distinguish by using hexagonal boxes.

Our second assumption, which we'll call *the representational account of cognition*, maintains that beliefs, desires, and other propositional attitudes are relational states. To have a belief or a desire with a particular content is to have a representation token with that content stored in the functionally appropriate way in the mind. So, for example, to believe that Socrates was an Athenian is to have a representation token whose content is *Socrates was an Athenian* stored in one's Belief Box, and to desire that it will be sunny tomorrow is to have a representation whose content is *It will be sunny tomorrow* stored in one's Desire Box. Many advocates of the representational account of cognition also assume that the representation tokens subserving propositional attitudes are linguistic or quasi-linguistic in form. This additional assumption is no part of our theory, however. If it turns out that some propositional attitudes are subserved by representation tokens that are not plausibly viewed as having a quasi-linguistic structure, that's fine with us.

We don't propose to mount any defence of these assumptions here. However, we think it is extremely plausible to suppose that the assumptions are shared by most or all of the authors whose views we will be discussing.

2. The Theory Theory

As noted earlier, the prevailing account of self-awareness is the theory theory. Of course, the prevailing account of how we understand *other minds* is also a TT. Before setting out the TT account of reading one's own mind, it's important to be clear about how the TT proposes to explain our capacity to read other minds.[3]

---

[3] In previous publications on the debate between the TT and simulation theory, we have defended the TT of how we understand other minds (Stich and Nichols 1992; Stich and Nichols 1995; Nichols et al. 1995; Nichols et al. 1996). More recently, we've argued that the simulation/theory theory debate has outlived its usefulness, and productive debate will require more detailed proposals and sharper distinctions (Stich and Nichols 1997; Nichols and Stich 1998).

2.1. The Theory Theory Account of Reading Other People's Minds

According to the theory theory, the capacity to *detect* other people's mental states relies on a theory-mediated inference. The theory that is invoked is a theory of mind (ToM) which some authors (e.g. Fodor 1992; Leslie 1994) conceive of as a special purpose body of knowledge housed in a mental module, and others (e.g. Gopnik and Wellman 1994) conceive of as a body of knowledge that is entirely parallel to other theories, both commonsense and scientific. For some purposes the distinction between the modular and the just-like-other-(scientific)-theories versions of the TT is of great import-ance. But for our purposes it is not. So in most of what follows we propose to ignore it (but see Stich and Nichols 1998). On all versions of the TT, when we detect another person's mental state, the theory-mediated inference can draw on perceptually available information about the behaviour of the target and about her environment. It can also draw on information stored in memory about the target and her environment. A sketch of the mental mechanisms invoked in this account is given in Fig. 6.2.

The theory that underlies the capacity to *detect* other people's mental states also underlies the capacity to *reason* about other people's mental states and thereby predict their behaviour. Reasoning about other people's mental states is thus a theory-mediated inference process, and the inferences draw on beliefs about (*inter alia*) the target's mental states. Of course, some of these beliefs will themselves have been produced by detection inferences. When detecting and reasoning are depicted together we get Fig. 6.3.

2.2. Reading One's Own Mind: Three Versions of the Theory Theory Account

The TT account of how we read other minds can be extended to provide an account of how we read our own minds. Indeed, both the TT for understand-ing other minds and the TT for self-awareness seem to have been first proposed in the same article by Wilfrid Sellars (1956). The core idea of the TT account of self-awareness is that the process of reading one's own mind is largely or entirely parallel to the process of reading someone else's mind. Advocates of the TT of self-awareness maintain that knowledge of one's own mind, like knowledge of other minds, comes from a theory-mediated infer-ence, and the theory that mediates the inference is the same for self and

In the first five sections of this chapter we've tried to sidestep these issues by granting the theory theorist as much as possible. We maintain that even if *all* attribution and reasoning about other minds depends on theory, that still won't provide the theory theorist with the resources to accommodate the facts about self-awareness. So, until s. 6, we will simply assume that reasoning about other minds depends on a theory.

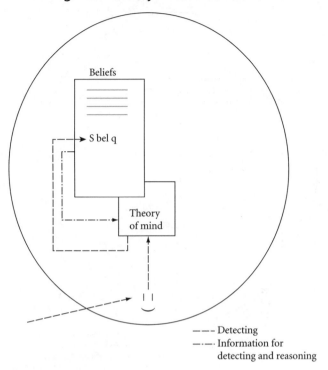

Fig. 6.2. Theory theory of detecting the mental states of others

other—it's the theory of mind. In recent years many authors have endorsed this idea; here are two examples:

Even though we seem to perceive our own mental states directly, this direct perception is an illusion. In fact, our knowledge of ourselves, like our knowledge of others, is the result of a theory, and depends as much on our experience of others as on our experience of ourselves.   (Gopnik and Meltzoff 1994: 168)

if the mechanism which underlies the computation of mental states is dysfunctional, then self-knowledge is likely to be impaired just as is the knowledge of other minds. The logical extension of the ToM [Theory of Mind] deficit account of autism is that individuals with autism may know as little about their own minds as about the minds of other people. This is not to say that these individuals lack mental states, but that in an important sense they are unable to reflect on their mental states. Simply put, they lack the cognitive machinery to represent their thoughts and feelings as thoughts and feelings.   (Frith and Happé 1999: 7).

As we noted earlier, advocates of the TT account of self-awareness are much less explicit than one would like, and unpacking the view in different ways

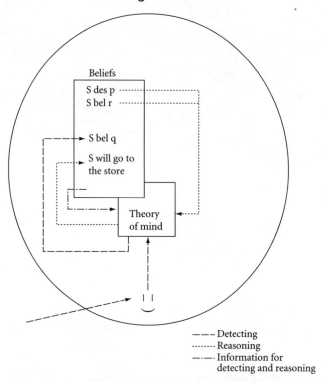

FIG. 6.3. Theory theory of detecting and reasoning about the mental stares of others

leads to significantly different versions of the TT account. But all of them share the claim that the processes of reasoning about and detecting one's own mental states will parallel the processes of reasoning about and detecting others' mental states. Since the process of *detecting* one's own mental states will be our focus, it's especially important to be very explicit about the account of detection suggested by the TT of self-awareness. According to the TT:

1. Detecting one's own mental states is a theory-mediated inferential process. The theory, here as in the third-person case, is ToM (either a modular version or a just-like-other-(scientific)-theories version or something in between).

2. As in the third-person case, the capacity to detect one's own mental states relies on a theory-mediated inference that draws on perceptually available information about one's own behaviour and environment. The inference also draws on information stored in memory about oneself and one's environment.

At this point the TT account of self-awareness can be developed in at least three different ways. So far as we know, advocates of the TT have never taken explicit note of the distinction. Thus it is difficult to determine which version a given theorist would endorse.

2.2.1 Theory Theory Version 1   Theory theory version 1 (for which our code name is *the crazy version*) proposes to maintain the parallel between detecting one's own mental states and detecting another person's mental states quite strictly. The *only* information used as evidence for the inference involved in detecting one's own mental state is the information provided by perception (in this case, perception of oneself) and by one's background beliefs (in this case, background beliefs about one's own environment and previously acquired beliefs about one's own mental states). This version of TT is sketched in Fig. 6.4.

Of course, we typically have much more information about our own minds than we do about other minds, so even on this version of the TT we may well have a *better* grasp of our own mind than we do of other minds (see e.g. Gopnik 1993: 94). However, the mechanisms underlying self-awareness are

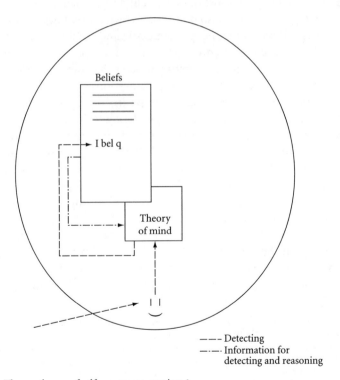

FIG. 6.4. Theory theory of self-awareness, version 1

supposed to be the same mechanisms that underlie awareness of the mental states of others. Thus this version of the TT denies the widely held view that an individual has some kind of special or privileged access to his own mental states.

We are reluctant to claim that anyone actually advocates this version of the TT, since we think it is a view that is hard to take seriously. Indeed, the claim that *perception of one's own behaviour* is the prime source of information on which to base inferences about one's own mental states reminds us of the old joke about the two behaviourists who meet on the street. One says to the other, 'You're fine. How am I?' The reason the joke works is that it seems patently absurd to think that perception of one's behaviour is the best way to find out how one is feeling. It seems obvious that people can sit quietly without exhibiting any relevant behaviour and report on their current thoughts. For instance, people can answer questions about current mental states such as 'What are you thinking about?' Similarly, after silently working a problem in their heads, people can answer subsequent questions such as 'How did you figure that out?' And we typically assume that people are correct when they tell us what they were thinking or how they just solved a problem. Of course, it's not just one's current and immediately past *thoughts* that one can report. One can also report one's own current desires, intentions, and imaginings. It seems that people can easily and reliably answer questions such as: 'What do you want to do?' 'What are you going to do?' 'What are you imagining?' People who aren't exhibiting much behaviour at all are often able to provide richly detailed answers to these questions.

These more or less intuitive claims are backed by considerable empirical evidence from research programmes in psychology. Using 'think aloud' procedures, researchers have been able to corroborate self-reports of current mental states against other measures. In typical experiments, subjects are given logical or mathematical problems to solve and are instructed to 'think aloud' while they work the problems.[4] For instance, people are asked to think aloud while multiplying 36 times 24 (Ericsson and Simon 1993: 346–7). Subjects' responses can then be correlated with formal analyses of how to solve the problem, and the subject's answer can be compared against the real answer. If the subject's think-aloud protocol conforms to the formal task analysis, that provides good reason to think that the subject's report of his thoughts is accurate (ibid. 330). In addition to these concurrent reports,

---

[4] To give an idea of how this works, here is an excerpt from Ericsson and Simon's (1993: 378) instructions to subjects in think-aloud experiments: 'In this experiment we are interested in what you think about when you find answers to some questions that I am going to ask you to answer. In order to do this I am going to ask you to THINK ALOUD as you work on the problem given. What I mean by think aloud is that I want you to tell me EVERYTHING you are thinking from the time you first see the question until you give an answer'.

researchers have also explored retrospective reports of one's own problem solving.[5] For instance Ericsson and Simon discuss a study by Hamilton and Sanford in which subjects were presented with two different letters (e.g. R–P) and asked whether the letters were in alphabetical order. Subjects were then asked to say how they solved the problem. Subjects reported bringing to mind strings of letters in alphabetical order (e.g. LMNOPQRST), and reaction times taken during the problem solving correlated with the number of letters subjects recollected (ibid. 191–2).

So, both commonsense and experimental studies confirm that people can sit quietly, exhibiting next to no overt behaviour, and give detailed, accurate self-reports about their mental states. In light of this, it strikes us as simply preposterous to suggest that the reports people make about their own mental states are being inferred from perceptions of their own behaviour and information stored in memory. For it's simply absurd to suppose that there is enough behavioural evidence or information stored in memory to serve as a basis for accurately answering such questions as 'What are you thinking about now?' or 'How did you solve that math problem?' Our ability to answer questions such as these indicates that version 1 of the TT of self-awareness can't be correct since it can't accommodate some central cases of self-awareness.

2.2.2   Theory Theory Version 2   Version 2 of the theory theory (for which our code name is *the underdescribed version*) allows that in using ToM to infer to conclusions about one's own mind there is information available *in addition to* the information provided by perception and one's background beliefs. This additional information is available only in the first-person case, not in the third-person case. Unfortunately, advocates of the TT say very little about what this alternative source of information is, and what little they do say about it is unhelpful, to put it mildly. Here, for instance, is an example of the sort of thing that Gopnik (1993: 11) has said about this additional source of information: 'One possible source of evidence for the child's theory may be first-person psychological experiences that may themselves be the consequence of genuine psychological perceptions. For example, we may well be equipped to detect certain kinds of internal cognitive activity in a vague and unspecified way, what we might call "*the Cartesian buzz*".' We have no serious

---

[5] For retrospective reports, immediately after the subject completes the problem, the subject is given instructions such as: 'Now I want to see how much you can remember about what you were thinking from the time you read the question until you gave the answer. We are interested in what you actually can REMEMBER rather than what you think you must have thought. If possible I would like you to tell about your memories in the sequence in which they occurred while working on the question. Please tell me if you are uncertain about any of your memories. I don't want you to work on solving the problem again, just report all that you can remember thinking about when answering the question. Now tell me what you remember' (ibid. 378).

idea what the 'Cartesian buzz' is, or how one would detect it. Nor do we understand how detecting the Cartesian buzz will enable the ToM to infer to conclusions like: *I want to spend next Christmas in Paris* or *I believe that the Brooklyn Bridge is about eight blocks south of the Manhattan Bridge.* Figure 6.5 is our attempt to sketch version 2 of the TT account.

We won't bother to mount a critique against this version of the account, apart from observing that without some less mysterious statement of what the additional source(s) of information are, the theory is too incomplete to evaluate.

2.2.3   Theory Theory Version 3   There is, of course, one very natural way to spell out what's missing in version 2. What is needed is some source of information that would help a person form beliefs (typically true beliefs) about his own mental states. The obvious source of information would be the mental states themselves. So, on this version of the TT, the ToM has access to information provided by perception, information provided by background beliefs, *and information about the representations contained in the Belief Box, the Desire Box, etc.* This version of the TT is sketched in Fig. 6.6.

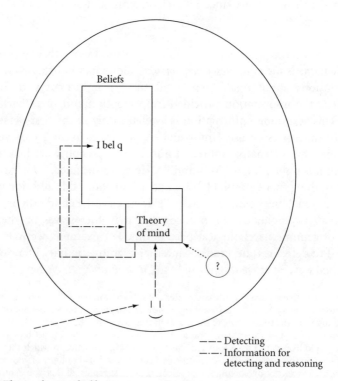

FIG. 6.5. Theory theory of self-awareness, version 2

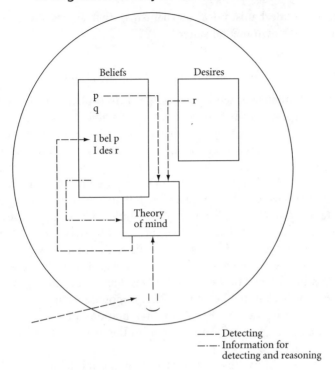

FIG. 6.6. Theory theory of self-awareness, version 3

Now at this juncture one might wonder why the ToM is *needed* in this story. If the mechanism subserving self-awareness has access to information about the representations in the various attitude boxes, then ToM has no serious work to do. So why suppose that it is involved at all? That's a good question, we think. And it's also a good launching pad for our theory. Because on our account Fig. 6.6 has it wrong. In detecting one's own mental states, the flow of information is *not* routed through the ToM. Rather, the process is subserved by a separate self-monitoring mechanism.

3. Reading One's Own Mind: The Monitoring Mechanism Theory

In constructing our theory about the process that subserves self-awareness we've tried to be, to borrow a phrase from Nelson Goodman (1983: 60), 'refreshingly non-cosmic'. What we propose is that we need to add another component or cluster of components to the basic picture of cognitive architecture, a mechanism (or mechanisms) that serves the function of monitoring one's own mental states.

3.1. The Monitoring Mechanism and Propositional Attitudes

Recall what the theory of self-awareness needs to explain. The basic facts are that when normal adults believe that p, they can quickly and accurately form the belief *I believe that p*; when normal adults desire that p, they can quickly and accurately form the belief *I desire that p*; and so on for the rest of the propositional attitudes. In order to implement this ability, no sophisticated ToM is required. All that is required is that there be a monitoring mechanism (MM) (or perhaps a set of mechanisms) that, when activated, takes the representation *p* in the Belief Box as input and produces the representation *I believe that p* as output. This mechanism would be trivial to implement. To produce representations of one's own beliefs, the monitoring mechanism merely has to copy representations from the Belief Box, embed the copies in a representation schema of the form: *I believe that*—, and then place the new representations back in the Belief Box. The proposed mechanism would work in much the same way to produce representations of one's own desires, intentions, and imaginings.[6] This account of the process of self-awareness is sketched in Fig. 6.7.

Although we propose that the MM is a special mechanism for detecting one's own mental states, we maintain that there is no special mechanism for what we earlier called *reasoning about* one's own mental states. Rather, reasoning about one's own mental states depends on the same theory of mind as reasoning about others' mental states. As a result, our theory (as well as the TT) predicts that, *ceteris paribus*, where the ToM is deficient or the relevant information is unavailable, subjects will make mistakes in reasoning about their own mental states as well as others. This allows our theory to accommodate findings such as those presented by Nisbett and Wilson (1977). They report a number of studies in which subjects make mistakes about their own mental states. However, the kinds of mistakes that are made in those experiments are typically not mistakes in *detecting* one's own mental states. Rather, the studies show that subjects make mistakes in *reasoning about* their own mental states. The central findings are that subjects sometimes attribute

---

[6] Apart from the cognitive science trappings, the idea of an internal monitor goes back at least to David Armstrong (1968) and has been elaborated by William Lycan (1987) among others. However, much of this literature has become intertwined with the attempt to determine the proper account of consciousness, and that is not our concern at all. Rather, on our account, the monitor is just a rather simple information-processing mechanism that generates explicit representations about the representations in various components of the mind and inserts these new representations in the Belief Box.

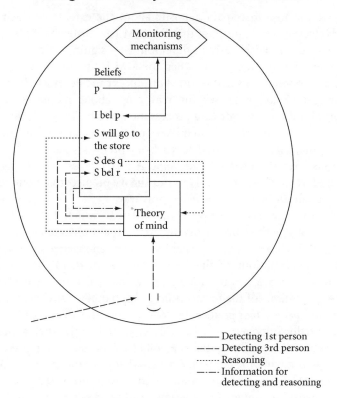

FIG. 6.7. Monitoring mechanism theory of self-awareness

their behaviour to inefficacious beliefs and that subjects sometimes deny the efficacy of beliefs that are, in fact, efficacious. For instance, Nisbett and Schacter (1966) found that subjects were willing to tolerate more intense shocks if they were given a drug (actually a placebo) and told that the drug would produce heart palpitations, irregular breathing, and butterflies in the stomach. Although being told about the drug had a significant effect on the subjects' willingness to take shocks, most subjects denied this. Nisbett and Wilson's (1977) explanation of these findings is, plausibly enough, that subjects have an incomplete theory regarding the mind and that the subjects' mistakes reflect the inadequacies of their theory. This explanation of the findings fits well with our account too. For on our account, when trying to figure out the *causes* of one's own behaviour, one must reason about mental states, and this process is mediated by the ToM. As a result, if the ToM is not up to the task, then people will make mistakes in reasoning about their own mental states as well as others' mental states.

Here we propose to remain agnostic about the extent to which ToM is innate. However, we do propose that the MM (or cluster of MMs) is innate and comes on line fairly early in development—significantly before ToM is fully in place. During the period when the MM is up and running but ToM is not, the representations that the MM produces can't do much. In particular, they can't serve as premises for reasoning about mental states, since reasoning about mental states is a process mediated by ToM. So, for example, ToM provides the additional premises (or the special purpose inferential strategies) that enable the mind to go from premises such as *I want q* to conclusions like: *If I believed that doing A was the best way to get q, then (probably) I would want to do A*. Thus our theory predicts that young children can't reason about their own beliefs in this way.

Although we want to leave open the extent to which ToM is innate, we maintain (along with many theory theorists) that ToM comes on line only gradually. As it comes on line, it enables a richer and richer set of inferences from the representations of the form *I believe (or desire) that p* that are produced by the MM. Some might argue that early on in development, these representations of the form *I believe that p* don't really count as having the content: *I believe that p*, since the concept (or 'proto-concept') of belief is too inferentially impoverished. On this view, it is only after a rich set of inferences becomes available that the child's *I believe that p* representations really count as having the content: *I believe that p*. To make a persuasive case for or against this view, one would need a well-motivated and carefully defended theory of content for concepts. And we don't happen to have one. (Indeed, at least one of us is inclined to suspect that much recent work aimed at constructing theories of content is deeply misguided (Stich 1992, 1996).) But, with this caveat, we don't have any objection to the claim that early *I believe that p* representations don't have the content: *I believe that p*. If that's what your favourite theory of content says, that's fine with us. Our proposal can be easily rendered consistent with such a view of content by simply replacing the embedded mental predicates (e.g. '*believe*') with technical terms 'bel', 'des', 'pret', etc. We might then say that the MM produces the belief that *I bel that p* and the belief that *I des that q*; and that at some point further on in development, these beliefs acquire the content *I believe that p*, *I desire that q*, and so forth. That said, we propose to ignore this subtlety for the rest of the chapter.

The core claim of our theory is that the MM is a distinct mechanism that is specialized for detecting one's own mental states.[7] However, it is important to

---

[7] As we've presented our theory, the MM is a mechanism that is distinct from the ToM. But it might be claimed that the MM that we postulate is just a *part* of the ToM. Here the crucial question to ask is whether it is a 'dissociable' part which could be selectively damaged or

note that on our account of mind-reading, the MM is not the *only* mental mechanism that can generate representations with the content *I believe that p*. Representations of this sort can also be generated by ToM. Thus it is possible that in some cases, the ToM and the MM will produce *conflicting* representations of the form *I believe that p*. For instance, if the theory of mind is deficient, then in some cases it might produce an inaccurate representation with the content *I believe that p* that conflicts with accurate representations generated by the MM. In these cases, our theory does not specify how the conflict will be resolved or which representation will guide verbal behaviour and other actions. On our view, it is an open empirical question how such conflicts will be resolved.

3.2. The Monitoring Mechanism and Perceptual States

Of course, the MM theory is not a complete account of self-awareness. One important limitation is that the MM is proposed as the mechanism under-lying self-awareness of one's propositional attitudes, and it's quite likely that the account cannot explain awareness of one's own perceptual states. Percep-tual states obviously have phenomenal character, and there is a vigorous debate over whether this phenomenal character is fully captured by a repre-sentational account (e.g. Tye 1995; Block forthcoming). If perceptual states can be captured by a representational or propositional account, then perhaps the MM can be extended to explain awareness of one's own perceptual states. For, as noted above, our proposed MM simply copies representations into representation schemas, e.g. it copies representations from the Belief Box into the schema 'I believe that —'. However, we're sceptical that perceptual states can be entirely captured by representational accounts, and as a result, we doubt that our MM Theory can adequately explain our awareness of our own perceptual states. None the less, we think it is plausible that some kind of monitoring account (as opposed to a TT account) might apply to awareness of one's own perceptual states. Since it will be important to have a sketch of such a theory on the table, we will provide a brief outline of what the theory might look like.

In specifying the architecture underlying awareness of one's own perceptual states, the first move is to posit a 'Percept Box'. This device holds the percepts produced by the perceptual processing systems. We propose that the Percept Box feeds into the Belief Box in two ways. First and most obviously, the contents of the Percept Box lead the subject to have beliefs about the world

selectively spared. If the answer is 'no', then we'll argue against this view in s. 5. If the answer is 'yes' (MM is a dissociable part of ToM) then there is nothing of substance left to fight about. That theory is a notational variant of ours.

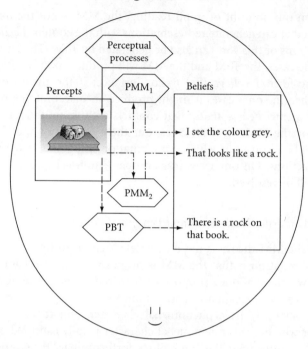

FIG. 6.8. Percept-monitoring mechanism theory

around her, by what we might call a percept-to-belief mediator. For instance, if a normal adult looks into a quarry, her perceptual system will produce percepts that will, *ceteris paribus*, lead her to form the belief that *there are rocks down there*. Something at least roughly similar is presumably true in dogs, birds, and frogs. Hence, there is a mechanism (or set of mechanisms) that takes percepts as input and produces beliefs as output. However, there is also, at least in normal adult humans, another way that the Percept Box feeds into the Belief Box—we form beliefs *about our percepts*. For example, when looking into a quarry I might form the belief that *I see rocks*. We also form beliefs about the similarity between percepts—e.g. *this toy rock looks like that real rock*. To explain this range of capacities, we tentatively propose that there is a set of percept-monitoring mechanisms (PMMs) that take input from the Percept Box and produce beliefs about the percepts.[8] We represent this account in Fig. 6.8. Note that the PMM will presumably be a far more

___

[8] How many PMMs are there? A thorough discussion of this is well beyond the scope of this chapter, but evidence from neuropsychology indicates that there might be numerous PMMs that can be selectively impaired by different kinds of brain damage. For instance, 'achromatopsia' is a condition in which some subjects claim to see only in black and white, but can in fact

complex mechanism than the MM. For the PMM must take perceptual experiences and produce representations about those perceptual experiences. We have no idea how to characterize this further in terms of cognitive mechanisms, and as a result, we are much less confident about this account than the MM account.

4. Autism and the Theory Theory

The theory theory of self-awareness is widely held among researchers working on mind-reading, and there are two prominent clusters of arguments offered in support of this account. One widely discussed set of arguments comes from developmental work charting the relation between performance on theory of mind tasks for self and theory of mind tasks for others.[9] This is an important set of arguments, but an adequate treatment of these arguments requires a close and lengthy inspection of the developmental data, a task we take up in the companion piece to this article (Nichols and Stich forthcoming b). Here we focus on the other central cluster of arguments for the TT of self awareness. Several prominent advocates of TT have appealed to evidence on autism as support for a TT account of self-awareness (Baron-Cohen 1989; Carruthers 1996; Frith and Happé 1999). On our view, however, the evidence from autism provides no support at all for this theory of self-awareness. But before we plunge into this debate, it may be useful to provide a brief reminder of the problems we've raised for various versions of the TT account:

1. Version 1 looks to be hopelessly implausible; it cannot handle some of the most obvious facts about self-awareness.

make some colour discriminations. 'In cases of achromatopsia ... there is evidence that some aspects of color processing mechanisms continue to function ... However ... there is no subjective experience of color' (Young 1994: 179). Similarly, prosopagnosiacs claim not to recognize faces; however, many prosopagnosiacs exhibit covert recognition effects in their electrophysiological and behavioural responses (Young 1998: 283–7). Achromatopsia and prosopagnosia are, of course, independent conditions. Prosopagnosiacs typically have no trouble recognizing colours and patients with achromatopsia typically have no trouble recognizing faces. So, it's quite possible that prosopagnosia involves a deficit to a PMM that is not implicated in colour recognition and that achromatopsia involves a deficit to a distinct PMM that is not implicated in face recognition. This issue is considerably complicated by the fact that some theorists (e.g. Dennett 1991) maintain that neuropsychological findings such as these can be explained by appealing to the mechanisms that build up the multiple layers of the percept itself. We won't treat this complicated issue here. Our point is just that if achromatopsia and prosopagnosia do involve deficits to percept-monitory mechanisms, it is plausible that they involve deficits to independent PMMs.

[9] The label 'theory of mind tasks' is used to characterize a range of experiments that explore the ability to attribute mental states and to predict and explain behaviour. For example, as we will discuss later, one prominent theory of mind tasks is the 'false belief task'.

2. Version 2 is a mystery theory; it maintains that there is a special source of information exploited in reading one's own mind, but it leaves the source of this additional information unexplained.

3. Version 3 faces the embarrassment that if information about the representations in the Belief Box and Desire Box is available, then no theory is needed to explain self-awareness; ToM has nothing to do.

We think that these considerations provide an important prima-facie case against the TT account of self-awareness, though we also think that, as in any scientific endeavour, solid empirical evidence might outweigh the prima-facie considerations. So we now turn to the empirical arguments.

To explicate the arguments based on evidence from autism, we first need to provide a bit of background to explain why data about autism are relevant to the issue of self-awareness. Studies of people with autism have loomed large in the literature in mind-reading ever since Baron-Cohen et al. (1985) reported some now famous results on the performance of autistic individuals on the false belief task. The original version of the false belief task was developed by Wimmer and Perner (1983). In their version of the experiment, children watched a puppet show in which the puppet protagonist, Maxi, puts chocolate in a box and then goes out to play. While Maxi is out, his puppet mother moves the chocolate to the cupboard. When Maxi returns, the children are asked where Maxi will look for the chocolate. Numerous studies have now found that 3-year-old children typically fail tasks like this, while 4-year-olds typically succeed at them (e.g. Baron-Cohen et al. 1985; Perner et al. 1987). This robust result has been widely interpreted to show that the ToM (or some quite fundamental component of it) is not yet in place until about the age of 4. Baron-Cohen and colleagues compared performance on false belief tasks in normal children, autistic children, and children with Down's syndrome. What they found was that autistic subjects with a mean chronological age of about 12 and mean verbal and non-verbal mental ages of 9;3 and 5;5 respectively failed the false belief task (Baron-Cohen et al. 1985). These subjects answered the way normal 3-year-olds do. By contrast, the control group of Down's syndrome subjects matched for mental age performed quite well on the false belief task. One widely accepted interpretation of these results is that *autistic individuals lack a properly functioning ToM.*

If we assume that this is correct, then, since the TT account of self-awareness claims that ToM is implicated in the formation of beliefs about one's own mental states, the TT predicts that autistic individuals should have deficits in this domain as well. If people with autism lack a properly functioning ToM and a ToM is required for self-awareness, then autistic individuals should be unable to form beliefs about their own beliefs and other mental states. In recent papers both Carruthers (1996) and U. Frith and Happé (1999) have maintained that autistic individuals do indeed lack self-awareness, and that this supports the TT account. In this section we will consider three different arguments from the data on autism. One argument depends on evidence that autistic children have difficulty with the appearance/reality distinction. A second argument appeals to introspective reports of adults with Asperger's syndrome (autistic individuals with near normal IQs), and a third, related, argument draws on autobiographical testimony of people with autism and Asperger's syndrome.

4.1. Autism and the Appearance/Reality Distinction

Both Baron-Cohen (1989) and Carruthers (1996) maintain that the perform-ance of autistic children on appearance/reality tasks provides support for the view that autistic children lack self-awareness, and hence provides evidence for the TT. The relevant studies were carried out by Baron-Cohen (1989), based on the appearance/reality tasks devised by Flavell and his colleagues. Using those tasks, Flavell and his colleagues found that children have diffi-culty with the appearance/reality distinction until about the age of 4 (Flavell et al. 1986). For instance, after playing with a sponge that visually resembles a piece of granite (a 'Hollywood rock'), most 3-year-olds claim that the object both is a sponge and looks like a sponge. Baron-Cohen found that autistic subjects also have difficulty with the appearance/reality distinction. When they were allowed to examine a piece of fake chocolate made out of plastic, for example, they thought that the object both looked like chocolate and really was chocolate. 'In those tasks that included plastic food,' Baron-Cohen reports, 'the autistic children alone persisted in trying to eat the object long after discovering its plastic quality. Indeed, so clear was this perseverative behavior that the experimenter could only terminate it by taking the plastic object out of their mouths' (Baron-Cohen 1989: 594).

Though we find Baron-Cohen and Flavell et al.'s work on the appearance/reality distinction intriguing, we are deeply puzzled by the suggestion that the studies done with autistic subjects provide support for the TT account of self-awareness. And, unfortunately, those who think that these studies do support the TT have never offered a detailed statement of how the argument is supposed to go. At best they have provided brief hints such as:

[T]he mind-blindness theory would predict that autistic people will lack adequate access to their own experiences as such . . . and hence that they should have difficulty in negotiating the contrast between *experience* (appearance) and *what it is an experi-ence of* (reality).   (Carruthers 1996: 260–1)

[Three-year-old children] appear unable to represent both an object's real and appar-ent identities simultaneously. . . . Gopnik and Astington (1988) argued that this is also an indication of the 3-year-old's inability to represent the distinction between their representation of the object (its appearance) and their knowledge about it (its real identity). In this sense, the A–R distinction is a test of the ability to attribute mental states to oneself.   (Baron-Cohen 1989: 591)

The prediction that this would be an area of difficulty for autistic subjects was supported, and this suggests that these children ... are unaware of the A–R distinction, and by implication unaware of their own mental states. These results suggest that when perceptual information contradicts one's own knowledge about the world, the autistic child is unable to separate these, and the perceptual information overrides other representations of an object.   (ibid. 595)

How might these hints be unpacked? What we have labelled Argument I is our best shot at making explicit what Carruthers and Baron-Cohen might have had in mind. Though we are not confident that this is the right interpretation of their suggestion, it is the most charitable reading we've been able to construct. If this *isn't* what they had in mind (or close to it) then we really haven't a clue about how the argument is supposed to work.

Argument I. If the TT of self-awareness is correct then ToM plays a crucial role in forming beliefs about one's own mental states. Thus, since autistic subjects do not have a properly functioning ToM they should have considerable difficulty in forming beliefs about their own mental states. So autistic people will typically not be able to form beliefs with contents such as:

(1) I believe that that object is a sponge.

and

(2) I am having a visual experience of something that looks like a rock.

Perhaps (2) is too sophisticated, however. Perhaps the relevant belief that they cannot form but that normal adults can form is something more like:

(2a) That object looks like a rock.

By contrast, since ToM is *not* involved in forming beliefs about the non-mental part of the world, autistic subjects should not have great difficulty in forming beliefs such as:

(3) That object is a sponge.

To get the correct answer in an appearance/reality task, subjects must have beliefs with contents such as (3) and they must also have beliefs with contents such as (2) or (2a). But if the TT of self-awareness is correct then autistic subjects cannot form beliefs with contents such as (2) or (2a). Thus the TT predicts that autistic subjects will fail appearance/reality tasks. And since they do in fact fail, this counts as evidence in favour of the TT.

Now what we find puzzling about Argument I is that, while the data do indeed indicate that autistic subjects fail the appearance/reality task, they fail it in exactly the *wrong* way. According to Argument I, autistic subjects should have trouble forming beliefs such as (2) and (2a) but should have no trouble in forming beliefs such as (3). In Baron-Cohen's studies, however, just the opposite appears to be the case. After being allowed to touch and taste objects made of plastic that looked like chocolate or eggs, the autistic children gave no indication that they had incorrect beliefs about what the object *looked like*. Quite the opposite was the case. When asked questions about their own perceptual states, autistic children answered *correctly*. They reported that the fake chocolate looked like chocolate and that the fake egg looked like an egg. Where the autistic children apparently *did* have problems was just where Argument I says they should *not* have problems. The fact that they persisted in trying to eat the plastic chocolate suggests that they had not succeeded in forming beliefs such as (3)—beliefs about *what the object really is*. There are lots of hypotheses that might be explored to explain why autistic children have this problem. Perhaps autistic children have difficulty updating their beliefs on the basis of new information; perhaps they perseverate on first impressions;[10] perhaps they privilege visual information over the information provided by touch and taste; perhaps the task demands are too heavy. But whatever the explanation turns out to be, it is hard to see how the sorts of failures predicted by the TT of self-awareness—the inability to form representations such as (1), (2), and (2a)—could have any role to play in explaining the pattern of behaviour that Baron-Cohen reports.

All this may be a bit clearer if we contrast the performance of autistic children on appearance/reality tasks with the performance of normal 3-year-olds. The 3-year-olds also fail the task. But unlike the autistic children who make what Baron-Cohen (1989: 594) calls 'phenomenist' errors, normal 3-year-olds make what might be called 'realist' errors on the same sorts of tasks. Once they discover that the Hollywood rock really is a sponge, they report that it *looks like* a sponge. Since there is reason to believe that ToM is not yet fully on line in 3-year-olds, one might think that the fact that 3-year-olds make 'realist' errors in appearance/reality tasks supports a TT account of self-awareness. Indeed, Alison Gopnik (1993: 93) appears to defend just such a view. The appearance/reality task, she argues,

is another case in which children make errors about their current mental states as a result of their lack of a representational theory [i.e. a mature ToM] ... Although it is not usually phrased with reference to the child's current mental states, this question depends on the child's accurately reporting an aspect of his current state, namely, the

---

[10] It's worth noting that perseveration is quite common in autistic children in other domains as well.

way the object looks to him. Children report that the sponge-rock looks to them like a sponge. To us, the fact that the sponge looks like a rock is a part of our immediate phenomenology, not something we infer. . . . The inability to understand the idea of false representations . . . seems to keep the child from accurately reporting perceptual appearances, even though those appearances are current mental states.

For our current purposes, the crucial point here is that Gopnik's argument, unlike Argument I, is perfectly sensible. Three-year-olds are not at all inclined to make 'phenomenist' errors on these tasks. Once they have examined the plastic chocolate, they no longer believe that it really is chocolate, and they have no inclination to eat it. Where the 3-year-olds go wrong is in reporting what plastic chocolate and Hollywood rocks look like. And this is just what we should expect if, as the TT insists, ToM is involved in forming beliefs about one's own perceptual states.

At this point, the reader may be thinking that we have jumped out of the frying pan and into the fire. In using Gopnik's argument to highlight the shortcomings of Argument I, have we not also provided a new argument for TT, albeit one that does not rely on data about autistic subjects? Our answer here is that Gopnik's argument is certainly one that must be taken seriously. But her explanation is not the only one that might be offered to account for the way in which 3-year-olds behave in appearance/reality tasks. The hypothesis we favour is that though the PMMs that we posited in s. 3.2 are in place in 3-year-olds, the usual appearance/reality tasks sidestep the PMMs because young children rely on a set of heuristic principles about appearance and reality, principles such as:

HP: For middle-sized objects, if an object is an X, then it looks like an X.

If a 3-year-old relies on such a heuristic, then her answers to the questions posed in appearance/reality tasks may not engage the PMMs at all. Of course, if this defence of our PMM hypothesis is right, then there should be other ways of showing that the young children really can detect their own perceptual states. One way to explore this is by running experiments on children's understanding of appearances, but with tasks that would not implicate the above heuristic. To do this, one might ask the child questions about the relations between her perceptual mental states themselves. So, for instance, one might let children play with two different Hollywood rocks and a plain yellow sponge, then ask the children which two look most alike. It would also be of interest to run a similar experiment based more closely on the Flavell task: show children a plain yellow sponge, a Hollywood rock, and a piece of granite, then ask them which two look most alike. If children do well on these sorts of tasks, that would provide evidence that they can indeed detect their own perceptual states, and hence that the PMM is intact and functioning even though ToM is not yet on line.

Let us briefly sum up this section. Our major conclusion is that, while the data about the performance of autistic subjects on appearance/reality tasks are fascinating, they provide no evidence at all for the theory theory of self-awareness. Moreover, while the data about the performance of normal 3-year-olds on appearance/reality tasks is compatible with the TT, there is an alternative hypothesis that is equally compatible with the data, and there are some relatively straightforward experiments that might determine which is correct.

4.2. Introspective Reports and Autobiographies from Adults with Asperger's Syndrome

The next two arguments we will consider are much more direct arguments for the Theory Theory, but, we maintain, no more convincing. Carruthers (1996) and Frith and Happé (1999) both cite evidence from a recent study on introspective reports in adults with Asperger's syndrome (Hurlburt et al. 1994). The study is based on a technique for 'experience sampling' developed by Russell Hurlburt. Subjects carry around a beeper and are told, 'Your task when you hear a beep is to attempt to "freeze" your current experience "in mind," and then to write a description of that experience in a . . . notebook which you will be carrying. The experience that you are to describe is the one that was occurring at the instant the beep began' (Hurlburt 1990: 21).

Hurlburt and his colleagues had three Asperger's adults carry out this experience sampling procedure (Hurlburt et al. 1994). All three of the subjects were able to succeed at simple theory of mind tasks. The researchers found that the reports of these subjects were considerably different from reports of normal subjects. According to Hurlburt and colleagues, two of the subjects reported only visual images, whereas it's common for normal subjects also to report inner verbalization, 'unsymbolized thinking',[11] and emotional feelings. The third subject didn't report any inner experience at all in response to the beeps.

Carruthers (1996: 261) maintains that these data suggest 'that autistic people might have severe difficulties of access to their own occurrent thought processes and emotions'. Frith and Happé (1999: 14) also argue that the evidence 'strengthens our hypothesis that self-awareness, like other awareness, is dependent on ToM'.

---

[11] Hurlburt and colleagues describe 'unsymbolized thoughts' as 'clearly-apprehended, differentiated thoughts that occurred with no experience of words, images, or others symbols that might carry the meaning. Subjects sometimes referred to the phenomenon as "pure thought". In such samples the subjects could, in their sampling interviews, say clearly what they had been thinking about at the moment of the beep, and thus could put the thought into words, but insisted that neither those words nor any other words or symbols were available to awareness at the moment of the beep, even though the thought itself was easily apprehended at that moment' (Hurlburt, Happé, and Frith 1994: 386).

As further support for the TT account of self-awareness, Frith and Happé (1999) appeal to several autobiographical essays written by adults with autism or Asperger's syndrome. They argue that these autobiographies indicate that their authors have significant peculiarities in self-consciousness. Here are several examples of autobiographical excerpts quoted by Frith and Happé (ibid. 15–17):

'When I was very young I can remember that speech seemed to be of no more significance than any other sound.... I began to understand a few single words by their appearance on paper.'   (from Jolliffe *et al.* 1992: 13)

'I had—and always had had, as long as I could remember—a great fear of jewellery... I thought they were frightening, detestable, revolting.'
(from Gerland 1997: 54)

'It confused me totally when someone said that he or she had seen something I had been doing in a different room.'   (from ibid. 64)

4.3. What Conclusions Can We Draw from the Data on Introspection in Autism?

We are inclined to think that the data cited by Carruthers (1996) and Frith and Happé (1999) provide a novel and valuable perspective on the inner life of people with autism. However, we do not think that the evidence lends any support at all to the TT account of self-awareness over the MM theory that we advocate. Quite to the contrary, we are inclined to think that if the evidence favours either theory, it favours ours.

What the data do strongly suggest is that the inner lives of autistic individuals differ radically from the inner lives of most of us. Images abound, inner speech is much less salient, and autistic individuals almost certainly devote much less time to thinking or wondering or worrying about *other people's* inner lives. As we read the evidence, however, it indicates that people with autism and Asperger's syndrome *do* have access to their inner lives. They are aware of, report, and remember their own beliefs and desires as well as their occurrent thoughts and emotions.

4.3.1 Hurlburt, Happé, and Frith (1994) Revisited

In the experience sampling study, there were a number of instances in which subjects clearly did report their occurrent thoughts. For example, one of the subjects, Robert, reported that

he was 'thinking about' what he had to do today. This 'thinking about' involved a series of images of the tasks he had set for himself. At the moment of the beep, he was trying to figure out how to find his way to the Cognitive Development Unit, where he had his appointment with us. This 'trying to figure out' was an image of himself walking down the street near Euston station.   (p. 388)

On another occasion, Robert reported that he was

'trying to figure out' why a key that he had recently had made did not work. This figuring-out involved picturing an image of the key in the door lock, with his left hand holding and turning the key... The lock itself was seen both from the outside... and from the inside (he could see the levers inside the lock move as the blades of the key pushed them along).   (p. 388)

A second subject, Nelson, reported that

he was 'thinking about' an old woman he had seen earlier that day. This thinking-about involved 'picturizing' (Nelson's own term for viewing an image of something) the old woman.... There was also a feeling of 'sympathy' for this woman, who (when he actually saw her earlier) was having difficulty crossing the street.   (p. 390).

In all three of these cases it seems clear that the subjects are capable of reporting their current thinking and, in the latter case, their feelings. Though, as we suggested earlier, it may well be the case that the inner lives that these people are reporting are rather different from the inner lives of normal people.

Perhaps even more instructive is the fact that Hurlburt and his colleagues claim to have been surprised at how well the subjects did on the experience sampling task. Hurlburt et al. (1994: 393) write: 'While we had expected a relative inability to think and talk about inner experience, this was true for only one of the subjects, Peter, who was also the least advanced in terms of understanding mental states in the theory of mind battery.' Moreover, even Peter, although he had difficulty with the experience sampling method, could talk about his current experience. Thus Frith and Happé (1999: 14) report: 'Although Peter was unable to tell us about his past inner experience using the beeper method, it was possible to discuss with him current ongoing inner experience during interviews.' So, far from showing that the TT account of self-awareness is correct, these data would seem to count *against* the TT account. For even Peter, who is likely to have had the most seriously abnormal ToM was capable of reporting his inner experiences.

It is true that all the subjects had some trouble with the experience sampling task, and that one of them could not do it at all. But we think that this should be expected in subjects whose ToM is functioning poorly, *even if*, as we maintain, *the ToM plays no role in self-awareness*. Advocates of TT maintain that ToM plays a central role in detecting mental states in other people and in reasoning about mental states—both their own and others'. And we are in agreement with both these claims. It follows that people who have poorly functioning ToMs will find it difficult or impossible to attribute mental states to other people and will do little or no reasoning about mental states. So thoughts about mental states will not be very useful or salient to them. Given the limited role that thoughts about mental states play in the lives of people with defective ToMs, it is hardly surprising that, when asked to describe their experience, they sometimes do not report much. An analogy may help to make the point. Suppose two people are asked to look at a forest scene and report what they notice. One of the two is an expert on the birds of the region and knows a great deal about their habits and distribution. The other knows very little about birds and has little interest in them. Suppose further that there is something quite extraordinary in the forest scene; there is a bird there that is rarely seen in that sort of environment. We would expect that bird to figure prominently in the expert's description, though it might not be mentioned at all in the novice's description. Now compared to autistic individuals, normal subjects are experts about mental states. They know a lot about them, they think a lot about them, and they care a lot about them. So it is to be expected that autistic subjects—novices about mental states—will often fail spontaneously to mention their own mental states even if, like the person who knows little about birds, they can detect and report their own mental states if their attention is drawn to them by their interlocutor. Not surprisingly then, research on spontaneous language use in autism indicates that autistic children tend not to talk about certain mental states. Tager-Flusberg (1993) found that among children whose Mean Length of Utterance is 5 words, autistic children talk about desire and perception a good deal, and in any case much more than the children in a mental-age matched sample of children with Down's syndrome. By contrast, however, the autistic children scarcely talked about 'cognitive' mental states (e.g. believing, pretending, thinking), whereas the Down's kids did talk about such mental states.[12]

4.3.2. Autobiographies Revisited   In the cases of autobiographical reflections, again, we maintain, a number of the examples cited by Frith and Happé are prima facie incompatible with the conclusion they are trying to establish. In the autobiographies, adults with autism or Asperger's syndrome repeatedly claim to recall their own childhood thoughts and other mental states. This is evident in the three quotes from Frith and Happé that we reproduced in s. 4.2, and in this respect, the passages from Frith and Happé are not at all unusual.

---

[12] While Tager-Flusberg's findings are compatible with our theory they do raise an interesting further question: Why do these autistic subjects talk so much more about desire and perception than about belief and the other 'cognitive' mental states? The answer, we think, is that attributing mental states to other people involves several separate mechanisms, some of which are spared in autism. The details make for a long story which we present elsewhere (Nichols and Stich, forthcoming *a*).

Here are three additional examples of autobiographical comments from adults with Asperger's syndrome:

'I remember being able to understand everything that people said to me, but I could not speak back.... One day my mother wanted me to wear a hat when we were in the car. I logically thought to myself that the only way I could tell her that I did not want to wear the hat was to scream and throw it on the car floor.'   (Grandin 1984: 145)

'When I was 5 years old I craved deep pressure and would daydream about mechanical devices which I could get into and be held by them.... As a child I wanted to feel the comfort of being held, but then I would shrink away for fear of losing control and being engulfed when people hugged me.'   (ibid. 151)

'I didn't talk until I was almost five, you know. Before I started talking I noticed a lot of things, and now when I tell my mother she is amazed I remember them. I remember that the world was really scary and everything was over-stimulating.'

(Reported in Dewey 1991: 204)

If these recollections are accurate, then these individuals must have been aware of their own mental states even though, at the time in question, they could not reliably attribute beliefs to other people.

5. Double Dissociations and the Monitoring Mechanism Theory

We've argued that the evidence from autism does not support the theory theory of self-awareness over our theory. Indeed, it seems that the evidence provides support for our theory over the Theory Theory. In this section, we want to argue that the monitoring mechanism theory provides a natural explanation of a range of evidence on autism and certain other psychopathologies.

One important difference between our MM theory and all versions of the TT account of self-awareness is that on the MM theory there are two quite distinct mechanisms involved in mind-reading. ToM is centrally involved in

1. detecting other people's mental states
2. reasoning about mental states in other people, and
3. reasoning about one's own mental states.

MM is the mechanism that underlies

4. detecting one's own mental states.

On the TT account, by contrast, ToM is centrally involved in *all four* of these capacities.

Thus on our theory, though not on the TT, it is possible for the mechanism underlying (1)–(3) to malfunction while the mechanism responsible for (4) continues to function normally. It is also possible for the opposite pattern of breakdowns to occur. This would produce deficits in (4) while leaving (1)–(3) unaffected. One way to confirm our theory would be to find a 'double dissociation'—cases in which subjects have an intact MM but a defective ToM and cases in which subjects have an intact ToM but a defective MM. If such cases could be found, that would provide evidence that there really are two independent mechanisms.

Do 'double dissociations' of this sort occur? We propose that they do. In autism, we maintain, the ToM is seriously defective, though the MM is functioning normally. In patients exhibiting certain 'first-rank' symptoms of schizophrenia, by contrast, MM is malfunctioning though ToM is functioning normally.

5.1. Intact MM but Damaged ToM

As we have already noted, it is widely agreed that autistic people have a serious ToM deficit. They fail a number of mind-reading tasks, including the false belief task (see e.g. Baron-Cohen 1995). And there is evidence that autistic individuals find minds and mental states puzzling. This comes out vividly in a famous passage from Oliver Sacks (1995: 259), discussing Temple Grandin:

She was bewildered, she said, by *Romeo and Juliet* ('I never knew what they were up to'), and with *Hamlet* she got lost with the back-and-forth of the play. Though she ascribed these problems to 'sequencing difficulties,' they seemed to arise from her failure to empathize with the characters, to follow the intricate play of motive and intention. She said that she could understand 'simple, strong, universal' emotions but was stumped by more complex emotions and the games people play. 'Much of the time,' she said, 'I feel like an anthropologist on Mars.'

Grandin herself writes: 'My emotions are simpler than those of most people. I don't know what complex emotion in a human relationship is. I only understand simple emotions, such as fear, anger, happiness, and sadness' (Grandin 1995: 89). Similarly, although autistic children seem to understand simple desires, they have significantly more difficulty than mental-aged peers on tasks that require inferring implicit desires (Phillips et al. 1995). For instance, Phillips and her colleagues showed two comic strips to autistic children and controls. In one strip, the child is first pictured shown standing next to the pool, in the next frame the child is jumping into the pool, and in the third frame the child is standing on the deck dripping wet. The other strip is basically the same as the first strip, except that in the second frame, the child is shown falling into the pool. The children are asked, 'Which boy meant to get wet?' (ibid. 157). The researchers found that autistic children did considerably worse than mentally handicapped children on this task. These observations and findings might reflect a difficulty in autistic individuals' ability to reason about mental states, but in any case, they certainly indicate a serious deficiency in Theory of Mind.[13] The standard view is that, unlike normal children, autistic children lack a ToM (Baron-Cohen 1995). We are sceptical that the evidence shows anything quite this strong. None the less, autism seems to involve a profound deficit in ToM.

Although there is abundant evidence that autism involves a deficit in ToM abilities, none of the evidence reviewed in s. 4 suggests that autism involves a deficit in the monitoring mechanism. Indeed, some of the data suggested just the opposite. The adults with Asperger's syndrome who were asked to recount their immediate experiences did show an appreciation of what was happening in their minds (Hurlburt et al. 1994). Further, in the autobiographical excerpts, the adults claim to recall their own beliefs and thoughts from childhood. Also, there is no evidence that autistic children or adults have any trouble recognizing their thoughts and actions as their own. (The importance of this point will emerge below.) Thus, in autism, while we have good reason to think that there is a deficit in ToM, we have no reason to think that there is a deficit in the MM. All these facts, we maintain, indicate that while autistic people suffer a serious ToM deficit, they have no deficit in the MM posited by our theory.

5.2. Intact ToM but Damaged MM

We have suggested that in autism we find a deficit in ToM but an intact MM. Are there cases in which we find the opposite pattern? That is, are there individuals with an intact ToM but a deficit in the MM? Although the data are often fragmentary and difficult to interpret, we think there might actually be such cases. Schizophrenia has recently played an important role in discussion of ToM, and we think that certain kinds of schizophrenia might involve a damaged MM but intact ToM.

There is a cluster of symptoms in some cases of schizophrenia sometimes referred to as 'passivity experiences' or 'first rank symptoms' (Schneider 1959) 'in which a patient's own feelings, wishes or acts seem to be alien and under external control' (C. Frith 1992: 73–4).

---

[13] Since the detection/reasoning distinction hasn't been explicitly drawn in the literature, it's sometimes hard to tell whether the tasks show a deficit in detection or a deficit in reasoning. For instance, there are two standard ways to ask the false belief task question in the Maxi-task, one that is explicitly about detection (e.g. where does Maxi think the candy is?) and one that involves reasoning (e.g. where will Maxi look for the candy?). If one can't solve the detection task, then that alone would preclude one from solving the reasoning task in the right way, since one would have to detect the mental states in order to reason to the right conclusion. So, for many of the results that seem to show a deficit in reasoning about mental states, it's not yet clear whether the deficit can simply be explained by a deficit in detection. This raises a number of important issues, but fortunately, for our purposes we don't need to sort them out here.

One 'first-rank' symptom of schizophrenia is delusions of control, in which a patient has difficulty recognizing that certain actions are her own actions. For example, one patient reported:

'When I reach my hand for the comb it is my hand and arm which move, and my fingers pick up the pen, but I don't control them. . . . I sit there watching them move, and they are quite independent, what they do is nothing to do with me. . . . I am just a puppet that is manipulated by cosmic strings. When the strings are pulled my body moves and I cannot prevent it.'   (Mellor 1970: 18)

Another first-rank symptom is 'thought withdrawal', the impression that one's thoughts are extracted from one's mind. One subject reported: 'I am thinking about my mother, and suddenly my thoughts are sucked out of my mind by a phrenological vacuum extractor, and there is nothing in my mind, it is empty' (ibid. 16–17).

At least some symptomatic schizophrenics have great difficulty in reporting their current thoughts. Russell Hurlburt had four schizophrenic patients participate in a study using Hurlburt's experience sampling method (see s. 4.2). Two of these subjects reported experiences and thoughts that were strange or 'goofed up'. One of the patients, who was symptomatic throughout the sampling period (and whose symptoms apparently included first-rank symptoms), seemed incapable of carrying out the task at all. Another patient was able to carry out the task until he became symptomatic, at which point he could no longer carry out the task. Hurlburt (1990: 239) argues that these two subjects, while they were symptomatic, did not have access to their inner experience. He writes:

What we had expected to find, with Joe, was that his inner experiences were un-usual—perhaps with images that were 'goofed up' as Jennifer had described, or several voices that spoke at once so that none was intelligible, or some other kind of aberrant inner experience that would explain his pressure of speech and delusions. What we found, however, was no such thing; instead, Joe could not describe *any* aspects of his inner experience in ways that we found compelling.   (ibid. 207–8)

What's especially striking here is the contrast between this claim and Hurlburt *et al.*'s claim about the adults with Asperger's syndrome. Hurlburt (1990) expected the symptomatic schizophrenics to be able to report their inner experiences, and Hurlburt et al. (1994) expected the adults with Asperger's syndrome to be unable to report their inner experiences. What they found, however, was just the opposite. The symptomatic schizophrenics could not report their inner experiences, and the adults with Asperger's syndrome could (see s. 4).

These findings on schizophrenia led Christopher Frith (e.g. 1992: 81–2) to suggest that in schizophrenics with first-rank symptoms, there is a deficit in 'central monitoring'.[14] Frith's initial account of central monitoring doesn't specify how the monitoring works, but in recent work, Frith (1994) has sharpened his characterization by connecting the idea of central monitoring with the work on ToM. He suggests that the way to fill out his proposal on central monitoring is in terms of ToM.

Many of the signs and symptoms of schizophrenia can be understood as arising from impairments in processes underlying 'theory of mind' such as the ability to represent beliefs and intentions.   (ibid. 148)

To have a 'theory of mind', we must be able to represent propositions like 'Chris believes that "It is raining"'. Leslie (1987) has proposed that a major requirement for such representations is a mechanism that decouples the content of the proposition (It is raining) from reality... I propose that, in certain cases of schizophrenia, something goes wrong with this decoupling process.... Failure of this decoupling mechanism would give rise... to ... the serious consequence... that the patient would no longer be able to represent mental states, *either their own or those of others*. I have suggested previously (Frith 1987) that patients have passivity experiences (such as delusions of control and thought insertion) because of a defect in central monitoring. Central monitoring depends on our being aware of our intention to make a particular response before the response is made. In the absence of central monitoring, responses and intentions can only be assessed by peripheral feedback. For example, if we were unable to monitor our intentions with regard to speech, we would not know what we were going to say until after we had said it. I now propose that this failure of central monitoring is the consequence of an inability to represent our own mental states, including our intentions.   (ibid. 154; emphasis added)

---

[14] Indeed, Frith put his suggestion to the empirical test, using a series of error correction experiments to test the hypothesis that passivity experiences result from a deficit in central monitoring. Frith and colleagues designed simple video games in which subjects had to use a joystick to follow a target around a computer screen. The games were designed so that subjects would make errors, and the researchers were interested in the subjects' ability to correct the errors without external (visual) feedback indicating the error. Normal people are able rapidly to correct these errors even when they don't get feedback. Frith takes this to indicate that normal people can monitor their intended response, so that they don't need to wait for the external feedback. Thus, he suggests, 'If certain patients cannot monitor their own intentions, then they should be unable to make these rapid error corrections' (1992: 83). Frith and others carried out studies of the performance of schizophrenics on these video game tasks. The researchers found that 'acute schizophrenic patients corrected their errors exactly like normal people when visual feedback was supplied but, unlike normal people often failed to correct errors when there was no feedback. Of particular interest was the observation that this disability was restricted to the patients with passivity experiences: delusions of control, thought insertion and thought blocking. These are precisely the symptoms that can most readily be explained in terms of a defect of self-monitoring' (ibid.). Mlakar et al. (1994) found similar results. Thus, there seems to be some evidence supporting Frith's general claim that passivity experiences derive from a defect in central monitoring.

Hence, Frith (1994) now views the problem of central monitoring in schizophrenia as a product of a deficit in Theory of Mind. Indeed, Frith characterizes schizophrenia as late-onset autism (ibid. 150).

Although we are intrigued by Frith's initial suggestion that passivity experiences derive from a deficit in central monitoring, we are quite sceptical of his
claim that the root problem is a deficit in ToM. We think that a better way to
fill out Frith's hypothesis is in terms of the MM. That is, we suggest that
certain first-rank symptoms or passivity experiences might result from a
deficit in the MM that is quite independent of any deficit in ToM. And,
indeed, Frith's subsequent empirical work on schizophrenia and ToM indicate
that schizophrenics with passivity experiences do *not* have any special difficulty
with standard theory of mind tasks. Frith and Corcoran (1996) write, 'It is
striking that the patients with passivity features (delusions of control, thought
insertion, etc.) could answer the theory of mind questions quite well. This was
also found by Corcoran et al. (1995) who used a different kind of task' (Frith
and Corcoran 1996: 527). Of course, this is exactly what would be predicted
by our theory since we maintain that the mechanism for detecting one's own
intentions is independent of the mechanism responsible for detecting
the intentions of others. Hence, there's no reason to think that a deficit in
detecting one's own intentions would be correlated with a deficit in detecting
intentions in others.

We maintain that, as with autism, our theory captures this range of data on
schizophrenia comfortably. *Contra* Frith's proposal, schizophrenia does not
seem to be a case in which ToM is damaged; rather, it's more plausible to
suppose that in schizophrenia, it's the theory-independent MM that is not
working properly. So, it's plausible that there are cases of double dissociation.
Autism plausibly involves a damaged ToM without a damaged MM. And
schizophrenic subjects with first-rank symptoms may have a damaged MM
but don't seem to have a damaged ToM. And this, we think, provides yet
another reason to prefer the MM theory to the TT account of self-awareness.[15]

---

[15] The idea that a monitoring mechanism can be selectively damaged while the analogous
ToM ability is intact might apply to mental states other than propositional attitudes such as
beliefs and desires. For instance, alexithymia is a clinical condition in which subjects have great
difficulty discerning their own emotional states. One researcher characterizes the condition as
follows: 'When asked about feelings related to highly charged emotional events, such as the loss
of a job or the death of a family member, patients with alexithymia usually respond in one of
two ways: either they describe their physical symptoms or they seem not to understand the
question' (Lesser 1985: 690). As a result, patients with this condition often need to be given
instruction about how to interpret their own somatic sensations. 'For instance, they need to
understand that when one is upset or scared, it is normal to feel abdominal discomfort or a
rapid heart beat. These sensations can be labeled "anger" or "fear" ' (p. 691). Thus alexithymia
might be a case in which subjects have selective damage to a system for monitoring one's own
emotions. Of course, to make a persuasive case for this, one would need to explore (among
other things) these subjects' ability to attribute emotions to other people. If it turns out that

6. The Ascent Routine Theory

Although the theory theory is the most widely accepted account of self-awareness in the recent literature, there are two other accounts that are also quite visible, though neither seems to have gained many advocates. In this section and the next we will briefly consider each of these accounts.

Our MM account appeals to an innate cognitive mechanism (or a cluster of mechanisms) specialized for detecting one's own mental states. One might want to provide an account of self-awareness that is more austere. One familiar suggestion is that when we're asked a question about our own beliefs, 'Do you believe that p?' we treat the question as the simple fact-question: 'p?'. This kind of account was proposed by Evans (1982), but in recent years it has been defended most vigorously by Robert Gordon. He labels the move from belief-question to fact-question an 'ascent routine' and even tries to extend the account to self-attributions of pain (Gordon 1995, 1996). Gordon (1996: 15) writes: 'self-ascription relies . . . on what I call *ascent routines*. For example, the way in which adults ordinarily determine whether or not they believe that p is simply to ask themselves the question whether or not p.'

This account has the virtue of emphasizing that, for both children and adults, questions like 'Do you think that p?' and 'Do you believe that p?' may not be interpreted as questions about one's mental state, but as questions about p. Similarly, statements like 'I believe that p' are often guarded assertions of p, rather than assertions about the speaker's mental state.[16] These are facts that must be kept in mind in interpreting the results of experiments on mind-reading and self-awareness.

Alongside these virtues, however, the ascent routine also has clear, and we think fatal, shortcomings. As Goldman (forthcoming: 23) points out, the ascent routine story doesn't work well for attitudes other than belief.

Suppose someone is asked the question, 'Do you hope that Team T won their game yesterday?' (Q_1). How is she supposed to answer that question using an ascent routine? Clearly she is not supposed to ask herself the question, 'Did Team T win their game yesterday?' (Q_2), which would only be relevant to belief, not hope. What question is she supposed to ask herself?

patients with alexithymia can effectively attribute emotions to others but not to themselves, that would indicate that alexithymia might indeed be caused by damage to a MM. We think that these kinds of questions and experiments only become salient when we get clear about the distinction between theory of mind and MMs. (We are grateful for Robert Woolfolk suggesting this interpretation of alexithymia.)

[16] Claims like this are, of course, commonplace in the philosophical literature on the 'analysis' of belief. For example, Urmson (1956: 194) maintains that 'believe' is a 'parenthetical verb' and that such verbs *are not psychological descriptions*. Rather, 'when a man says, "I believe that he is at home" or "He is, I believe, at home", he both implies a (guarded) claim of the truth, and also implies a claim of the reasonableness of the statement that he is at home' (ibid. 202).

Furthermore, even for beliefs and thoughts, the ascent routine strategy doesn't work for some central cases. In addition to questions like 'do you believe that p?', we can answer questions about current mental states such as 'What are you thinking about?' But in this case, it is hard to see how to rework the question into an ascent routine. Similarly, as we noted earlier, people can give accurate retrospective reports in response to such questions as 'How did you figure that out?' We can see no way of transforming these questions into fact-questions of the sort that Gordon's theory requires. This also holds for questions about current desires, intentions, and imaginings, such questions as: 'What do you want to do?' 'What are you going to do?' 'What are you imagining?' Our ability to answer these questions suggests that the ascent routine strategy simply can't accommodate many central cases of self-awareness. There is no plausible way of recasting these questions so that they are questions about the world rather than about one's mental state. As a result, the ascent routine account strikes us as clearly inadequate as a general theory of self-awareness.

7. The Phenomenological Theory

For the last several years, Alvin Goldman has been advocating a 'phenomeno-logical model for the attitudes' (Goldman 1993b: 23; see also 1997, forthcoming). According to Goldman, in order to detect one's own mental states, 'the cognitive system [must] use...information about the *intrinsic* (nonrelational) and *categorical* (nondispositional) properties of the target state' (1993a: 87). Goldman then goes on to ask 'which intrinsic and categorical properties might be detected in the case of mental states?' His answer is as follows: 'The best candidates, it would seem, are so-called *qualitative properties* of mental states—their phenomenological or subjective *feelings* (often called "qualia")' (ibid.).[17] So, on this view, one detects one's own mental states by discerning the phenomenological properties of the mental states, the way those mental states feel.

Goldman is most confident of this phenomenological approach when the mental states being detected are not propositional attitudes but rather what he calls 'sensations'. 'Certainly,' he argues, 'it is highly plausible that one classifies such sensations as headaches or itches on the basis of their qualitative feel' (ibid. 87). Goldman suggests that this account might also be extended to propositional attitudes, though he is rather more tentative about this application.

---

[17] Since Goldman regards these phenomenological properties as 'intrinsic', he rejects the higher-order account of consciousness advocated by Rosenthal (1992) and others (see Goldman, forthcoming: 17).

Whether the qualitative or phenomenological approach to mental concepts could be extended from sensations to attitudes is an open question. Even this prospect, though, is not beyond the bounds of credibility. There is no reason why phenomenological characteristics should be restricted to sensory characteristics, and it does indeed seem to 'feel' a particular way to experience doubt, surprise, or disappointment, all of which are forms of propositional attitudes.   (ibid. 88; see also 1993*b*: 25, 104)

We are inclined to think that the idea of extending the phenomenological approach from sensations to propositional attitudes is much less of an 'open question' than Goldman suggests. Indeed, as a general theory of the self-attribution of propositional attitudes, we think that it is quite hopeless.

7.1. Two Versions of Goldman's Proposal

Let us begin by noting that there are two quite different ways in which Goldman's proposal might be elaborated:

(*a*) *The Weaker Version* claims that we (or our cognitive systems) detect or classify the *type* of a given mental state by the qualitative or phenomenological properties of the mental state in question. It is the qualitative character of a state that tells us that it is a belief or a desire or a doubt. On the weaker version, however, the qualitative properties of propositional attitudes do not play a role in detecting the *content* of propositional attitudes.

(*b*) *The Stronger Version* claims that we (or our cognitive systems) detect or classify *both* the *type* and *the content* of a given mental state by the qualitative or phenomenological properties of the mental state in question. So it is the qualitative character of a state that tells us that it is a belief or a desire and it is also the qualitative character that tells us that it is the belief *that there is no greatest prime number* or the desire that the Democrats win the next election.

If one speaks, as we just did, of qualitative or phenomenological qualities 'telling us' that a state is a belief or that its content is *that there is no greatest prime number*, it is easy to ignore the fact that this is a metaphor. Qualitative states don't literally 'tell' anybody anything. What is really needed, to make a proposal like Goldman's work, is a mental mechanism (or a pair of mental mechanisms) which can be thought of as transducers: They are acted upon by the qualitative properties in question and produce, as output, *representations* of these qualitative properties (or, perhaps more accurately, representations of the kind of state that *has* the qualitative property). So, for example, on the weaker version of the theory, what is needed is a mechanism that goes from the qualitative property associated with belief or doubt to a representation that the state in question is a belief or doubt. On the stronger version, the transducer must do this for the content of the state as well. So, for instance, on the stronger version, the transducer must go from the qualitative property of the content *there is no greatest prime number* to a representation that the state in question has the content *there is no greatest prime number*. Figure 6.9 is an attempt to depict the mechanisms and processes required by Goldman's theory.

7.2. Critique of Goldman's Theory

As we see it, the weaker version of Goldman's proposal is not a serious competitor for our MM theory, since it does not really explain some of the crucial facts about self-awareness. At best, it explains how, if I know that I have a mental state with the content p, I can come to know that it is a belief and not a hope or desire. But the weaker version doesn't even try to explain how I know that I have a mental state with the content p in the first place. So as a full account of self-awareness of propositional attitudes, the weaker version is a non-starter.

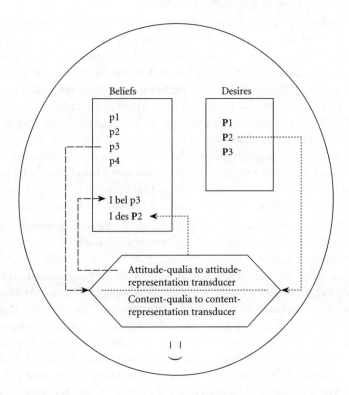

p Mental representation with belief-qualia

P Mental representation with desire-qualia

FIG. 6.9. Phenomenological model of self-awareness

The stronger version of Goldman's model *does* attempt to provide a full account of self-awareness of propositional attitudes. However, we think that there is no reason to believe the account, and there is good reason to doubt it.

The stronger version requires a phenomenological account of the awareness of content as well as a phenomenological account of the awareness of attitude type. Goldman does not provide a detailed argument for a phenomenological account of content, but he does sketch one argument in its favour. The argument draws on an example proposed by Keith Gunderson (1993). Goldman (1993*b*: 104) discusses the example:

If I overhear Brown say to Jones, 'I'm off to the bank,' I may wish to know whether he means a spot for fishing or a place to do financial transactions. But if *I* say to someone, 'I'm off to the bank,' I cannot query my own remark: 'To go fishing or to make a deposit?' I virtually always already know... The target article mainly supported a distinctive phenomenology for the attitude types. Gunderson's example supports distinctive phenomenology for different *contents*.

We think this argument is wholly unconvincing. It's true that we typically know the interpretation of our own ambiguous sentences. However, this doesn't even begin to show that belief contents have distinctive phenomenologies. At best it shows that we must have *some* mechanism or strategy for obtaining this knowledge. The MM theory can quite comfortably capture the fact that we typically know the interpretations of our own ambiguous sentences, and it does so without resorting to phenomenological features of content. As far as we can tell, then, there is no reason to adopt the phenomenological account of content. Moreover, there are two rather obvious reasons to prefer the MM account to the stronger version of the phenomenological theory.

On an account such as Goldman's there must be mechanisms in the mind that are sensitive to phenomenological or qualitative properties—i.e. mechanisms that *are causally affected by* these qualitative properties in a highly sensitive and discriminating way. The qualia of a belief must lead the mechanism to produce a representation of belief. The qualitative properties of states with the content *Socrates is wise* must cause the mechanism to produce representations with the content *Socrates is wise*. Now we don't wish to claim that there are no mechanisms of this sort or that there couldn't be. But what is clear is that no one has a clue about how such mechanisms would work. No one has even the beginning of a serious idea about how a mechanism could be built that would be differentially sensitive to the (putative) qualitative properties of the contents of propositional attitude states. So, for the moment, at least, the mechanisms that Goldman needs are quite mysterious. The mechanism that *our* theory needs, by contrast, is simple and straightforward. To generate representations of one's own beliefs, all that the MM has to do is copy representations in the Belief Box, embed them in a representation schema of the form: *I believe that* —, and then place this new representation back in the Belief Box. The analogous sort of transformation for representations in a computer memory could be performed by a simple and utterly *un*mysterious mechanism.[18]

The preceding argument is simply that it would be trivial to implement a mechanism such as the MM whereas no one has the faintest idea how to implement the mechanisms required for Goldman's account or how such mechanisms could work. Of course, this is just a prima-facie argument against Goldman's account. If it were independently plausible that phenomenology is the basis for awareness of one's own propositional attitudes, then the mysteriousness of the transducers would simply pose a challenge for cognitive scientists to figure out how such a mechanism could work. However, far from being independently plausible, it seems to us that the phenomenological account is *phenomenologically implausible*. To take the stronger version of Goldman's proposal seriously, one would have to assume that there is a distinct feel or qualia for every *type* of propositional attitude, *and* a distinct qualia for every content (or at least for every content we can detect). Now perhaps others have mental lives that are very different from ours. But from our perspective this seems to be (as Jerry Fodor might say) *crazy*. As best we can tell, believing that 17 is a prime number doesn't feel any different from believing that 19 is a prime number. Indeed, as best we can tell, neither of these states has any distinctive qualitative properties. Neither of them feels like much at all. If this is right, then the stronger version of the phenomenological theory is every bit as much a non-starter as the weaker version.

8. Conclusion

The empirical work on mind-reading provides an invaluable resource for characterizing the cognitive mechanisms underlying our capacity for self-awareness. However, we think that other authors have drawn the wrong conclusions from the data. Contrary to the claims of theory theorists, the evidence indicates that the capacity for self-awareness does not depend on the theory of mind. It's much more plausible, we have argued, to suppose that self-awareness derives from a monitoring mechanism that is independent of

---

[18] It might be argued that the PMM that we posit in s. 3.2 is just as mysterious as the mechanism that Goldman's theory requires. However, nothing in our account of the PMM requires that it is sensitive to *qualitative* properties of percepts. But even if it turns out that the PMM is sensitive to qualitative properties, we are inclined to think that the objection that we are proposing in this paragraph still has some force, since Goldman's account invokes a rather mysterious mechanism when a very unmysterious one would do the job.

the ToM. The intriguing evidence from autism has been used to support the TT. But we've argued that the evidence from psychopathologies actually suggests the opposite. The available evidence indicates that the capacity for understanding other minds can be dissociated from the capacity to detect one's own mental states and that the dissociation can go in either direction. If this is right, it poses a serious challenge to the TT, but it fits neatly with our suggestion that the MM is independent of the ToM. Like our MM theory, the ascent routine and the phenomenological accounts are also alternatives to the TT; but these theories, we have argued, are either obviously implausible or patently insufficient to capture central cases of self-awareness. Hence, we think that at this juncture in cognitive science, the most plausible account of self-awareness is that the mind comes pre-packaged with a set of special-purpose mechanisms for reading one's own mind.[19]

REFERENCES

ARMSTRONG, D. (1968), *A Materialist Theory of the Mind* (London: Routledge & Kegan Paul).

BARON-COHEN, S. (1989), 'Are Autistic Children "behaviorists"?' *Journal of Autism and Development Disorders*, 19: 579–600.

—— (1995), *Mindblindness* (Cambridge, Mass.: MIT Press).

—— LESLIE, A., and FRITH, U. (1985), 'Does the Autistic Child Have a Theory of Mind'? *Cognition*, 21: 37–46.

BLOCK, N. (forthcoming). 'Mental paint'.

CARRUTHERS, P. (1996), 'Autism as Mind-Blindness: An Elaboration and Partial Defence', in P. Carruthers and P. Smith (eds.), *Theories of Theories of Mind* (Cambridge: Cambridge University Press).

CORCORAN, R., FRITH, C., and MERCER, G. (1995), 'Schizophrenia, Symptomatology and Social Inference: Investigating "Theory of Mind" in People with Schizophrenia', *Schizophrenia Research*, 17: 5–13.

DENNETT, D. (1991), *Consciousness Explained* (Boston: Little, Brown).

DEWEY, M. (1991), 'Living with Asperger's Syndrome', in Uta Frith (ed.), *Autism and Asperger Syndrome* (Cambridge: Cambridge University Press).

ERICSSON, K., and SIMON, H. (1993), *Protocol Analysis: Verbal Reports as Data* (Cambridge, Mass.: MIT Press).

EVANS, G. (1982), *The Varieties of Reference* (Oxford: Oxford University Press).

[19] We would like to thank Peter Carruthers, Catherine Driscoll, Luc Faucher, Trisha Folds-Bennett, Christopher Frith, Gary Gates, Rochel Gelman, Alison Gopnik, Robert Gordon, Alan Leslie, Brian Loar, Dominic Murphy, Brian Scholl, Eric Schwitzgebel, and Robert Woolfolk for discussion and comments on earlier drafts of this chapter. Earlier versions were presented as a paper at a conference sponsored by the Center for Philosophical Education in Santa Barbara, California, at the Rutgers University Center for Cognitive Science, and at the Institute for the Study of Child Development, Robert Wood Johnson Medical School. We are grateful for the constructive feedback offered by members of the audience on all these occasions.

FLAVELL, J., GREEN, F., and FLAVELL, E. (1986), *Development of Knowledge about the Appearance–Reality Distinction* (Chicago: Society for Research in Child Development).

FODOR, J. (1992), 'A Theory of the Child's Theory of Mind', *Cognition*, 44: 283–96.

FRITH, C. D. (1987), 'The Positive and Negative Symptoms of Schizophrenia Reflect Impairment in the Perception and Initiation of Action', *Psychological Medicine*, 17: 631–48.

——(1992), *The Cognitive Neuropsychology of Schizophrenia* (Hillsdale, NJ: Lawrence Erlbaum).

——(1994), 'Theory of Mind in Schizophrenia', in A. David and J. Cutting (eds.), *The Neuropsychology of Schizophrenia* (Hillsdale, NJ: Lawrence Erlbaum).

——and CORCORAN, R. (1996), 'Exploring "Theory of Mind" in People with Schizophrenia', *Psychological Medicine*, 26: 521–30.

FRITH, U., and HAPPÉ, F. (1999), 'Theory of Mind and Self-Consciousness: What is it Like to be Autistic?' *Mind & Language*, 14: 1–22.

GERLAND, G. (1997), *A Real Person: Life on the Outside*, trans. from the Swedish by J. Tate (London: Souvenir Press).

GOLDMAN, A. (1993a), *Philosophical Applications of Cognitive Science* (Boulder: Westview Press).

——(1993b), 'The Psychology of Folk Psychology', *Behavioral and Brain Sciences*, 16: 15–28, 101–13.

——(1997), 'Science, Publicity, and Consciousness', *Philosophy of Science*, 64: 525–46.

——(forthcoming), 'The Mentalizing Folk', in D. Sperber (ed.) *Metarepresentation* (Oxford: Oxford University Press).

GOODMAN, N. (1983), *Fact, Fiction & Forecast*, 4th edn. (Cambridge, Mass.: Harvard University Press).

GOPNIK, A. (1993), 'How We Know Our Own Minds: The Illusion of First-Person Knowledge of Intentionality', *Behavioral and Brain Sciences*, 16: 1–14.

——and ASTINGTON, J. (1988), 'Children's Understanding of Representational Change and its Relation to the Understanding of False Belief and the Appearance–Reality Distinction', *Child Development*, 59: 26–37.

——and MELTZOFF, A. (1994), 'Minds, Bodies, and Persons: Young Children's Understanding of the Self and Others as Reflected in Imitation and Theory of Mind Research', in S. Parker, R. Mitchell, and M. Boccia (eds.), *Self-awareness in Animals and Humans* (New York: Cambridge University Press).

——and SLAUGHTER, V. (1991), 'Young Children's Understanding of Changes in their Mental States', *Child Development*, 62: 98–110.

——and WELLMAN, H. (1994), 'The Theory Theory', in S. Gelman and L. Hirschfeld (eds.), *Mapping the Mind* (Cambridge: Cambridge University Press).

GORDON, R. (1995), 'Simulation without Introspection or Inference from Me to You', in T. Stone and M. Davies (eds.), *Mental Simulation: Evaluations and Applications* (Oxford: Blackwell).

——(1996), 'Radical Simulationism', in P. Carruthers and P. Smith (eds.), *Theories of Theories of Mind* (Cambridge: Cambridge University Press), 11–21.

GRANDIN, T. (1984), 'My Experiences as an Autistic Child and Review of Selected Literature', *Journal of Orthomolecular Psychiatry*, 13: 144–75.

—— (1995), *Thinking in Pictures* (New York: Doubleday).

GUNDERSON, K. (1993), 'On Behalf of Phenomenological Parity for the Attitudes', *Behavioral and Brain Sciences*, 16: 46–7.

HURLBURT, R. (1990), *Sampling Normal and Schizophrenic Inner Experience* (New York: Plenum Press).

—— and HAPPÉ, F., & FRITH, U. (1994), 'Sampling the Form of Inner Experience in Three Adults with Asperger Syndrome', *Psychological Medicine*, 24: 385–95.

JOLLIFFE, T., LANSDOWN, R., and ROBINSON, C. (1992), 'Autism: A Personal Account', *Communication*, 26: 12–19.

LESLIE, A. (1994), 'ToMM, ToBY and Agency: Core Architecture and Domain Specificity', in L. Hirschfeld and S. Gelman (eds.), *Mapping the Mind* (Cambridge: Cambridge University Press), 119–48.

LESSER, I. (1985), 'Current Concepts in Psychiatry', *The New England Journal of Medicine*, 312: 690–2.

LYCAN, W. (1987), *Consciousness* (Cambridge, Mass.: MIT Press).

MCLAUGHLIN, B., and TYE, M. (1998), 'Is Content Externalism Compatible with Privileged Access?' *Philosophical Review*, 107: 349–80.

MELLOR, C. (1970), 'First Rank Symptoms of Schizophrenia', *British Journal of Psychiatry*, 117: 15–23.

MLAKAR, J. JENSTERLE, J., and FRITH, C. (1994), 'Central Monitoring Deficiency and Schizophrenic Symptoms', *Psychological Medicine*, 24: 557–64.

NICHOLS, S., and STICH, S. (1998), 'Rethinking Co-cognition', *Mind & Language*, 13: 499–512.

—— (forthcoming *a*), *Mindreading* (Oxford: Oxford University Press).

—— (forthcoming *b*), 'Reading One's Own Mind: Self-Awareness and Developmental Psychology', in R. Stainton, M. Ezcurdia, and C. Viger (eds.), *Language, Mind and World*.

—— —— and LESLIE, A. (1995), 'Choice Effects and the Ineffectiveness of Simulation: Response to Kuhberger et al.', *Mind & Language*, 10: 437–45.

—— —— —— and KLEIN, D. (1996), 'Varieties of Off-Line Simulation', in P. Carruthers and P. Smith (eds.), *Theories of Theories of Mind* (Cambridge: Cambridge University Press) 39–74.

NISBETT, R., and SCHACTER, S. (1966), 'Cognitive Manipulation of Pain', *Journal of Experimental Social Psychology*, 21: 227–36.

—— and WILSON, T. (1977), 'Telling More Than We Can Know', *Psychological Review*, 84: 231–59.

PERNER, J. (1991), *Understanding the Representational Mind* (Cambridge, Mass.: MIT Press).

—— LEEKAM, S., and WIMMER, H. (1987), 'Three-Year-Olds' Difficulty with False Belief: The Case for a Conceptual Deficit', *British Journal of Experimental Child Psychology*, 39: 437–71.

PHILLIPS, W., BARON-COHEN, S., and RUTTER, M. (1995), 'To What Extent Can Children with Autism Understand Desire?' *Development and Psychopathology*, 7: 151–69.

PUTNAM, H. (1975), 'The Meaning of Meaning', in *Mind, Language and Reality: Philosophical Papers*, ii (Cambridge: Cambridge University Press).

ROSENTHAL, D. (1992), 'Thinking That One Thinks', in M. Davies and G. Humphreys (eds.), *Consciousness* (Oxford: Blackwell).

SACKS, O. (1995), *An Anthropologist on Mars* (New York: Alfred A. Knopf).

SCHNEIDER, K. (1959), *Clinical Psychopathology*, trans. M. Hamilton (New York: Grune & Stratton).

SELLARS, W. (1956), 'Empiricism and the Philosophy of Mind', *Minnesota Studies in the Philosophy of Science*, 1 (Minneapolis: University of Minnesota Press). Reprinted in Sellars (1963), *Science, Perception and Reality* (London: Routledge & Kegan Paul).

STICH, S. (1992), 'What Is a Theory of Mental Representation?' *Mind*, 101: 243–61.

—— (1996), *Deconstructing the Mind* (New York: Oxford University Press).

—— and NICHOLS, S. (1992), 'Folk Psychology: Simulation or Tacit Theory', *Mind & Language*, 71: 35–71.

—— (1995), 'Second Thoughts on Simulation', in A. Stone and M. Davies (eds.), *Mental Simulation: Evaluations and Applications* (Oxford: Blackwell), 87–108.

—— (1997), 'Cognitive Penetrability, Rationality, and Restricted Simulation', *Mind and Language*, 12: 297–326.

—— (1998), 'Theory Theory to the Max: A Critical Notice of Gopnik & Meltzoff's *Words, Thoughts, and Theories*', *Mind & Language*, 13: 421–49.

TAGER-FLUSBERG, H. (1993), 'What Language Reveals about the Understanding of Minds in Children with Autism', in S. Baron-Cohen, H. Tager-Flusberg, and D. Cohen (eds.), *Understanding Other Minds: Perspectives from Autism* (Oxford: Oxford University Press).

TYE, M. (1995), *Ten Problems of Consciousness: A Representational Theory of the Phenomenal Mind* (Cambridge, Mass.: MIT Press).

URMSON, J. (1956), 'Parenthetical Verbs', in A. Flew (ed.), *Essays in Conceptual Analysis* (London: Macmillan).

WIMMER, H., and HARTL, M. (1991), 'The Cartesian View and the Theory View of Mind: Developmental Evidence from Understanding False Belief in Self and Other', *British Journal of Developmental Psychology*, 9: 125–8.

—— and PERNER, J. (1983), 'Beliefs about Beliefs: Representation and Constraining Function of Wrong Beliefs in Young Children's Understanding of Deception', *Cognition*, 13: 103–28.

YOUNG, A. (1994), 'Neuropsychology of Awareness', in A. Revonsuo and M. Kamppinen (eds.), *Consciousness in Philosophy and Cognitive Neuroscience* (Hillsdale, NJ: Lawrence Erlbaum).

—— (1998), *Face and Mind* (Oxford: Oxford University Press).

7. Knowing Mental States: The Asymmetry of Psychological Prediction and Explanation

KRISTIN ANDREWS

1. Introduction

The Machiavellian intelligence hypothesis promotes the view that cognition, and with it consciousness, is an evolutionary adaptation that arose owing to the complexities of social life (Humphrey 1976; Whiten and Byrne 1988). According to this view, we have knowledge of our own minds because we needed to have knowledge of others' minds. We needed to be able to predict what others were going to do in the future so that we could act to thwart their behaviours when they interfered with our own goals. If the Machiavellian intelligence hypothesis is right, our self-consciousness cannot be understood without also understanding our consciousness of others' mental states.

Some interpretations of the two major theories of how minds understand minds, the theory theory and the simulation theory, conform to this requirement of the Machiavellian intelligence thesis. Though both the theory theory and the simulation theory originated as accounts of how we understand other minds, it has been suggested that both simulation theory (e.g. Bolton 1995; Gordon 1995) and the theory theory (e.g. Frith and Happé 1999; Bolton 1995; Gopnick and Meltzoff 1994; Carruthers 1996) can also provide an account of how we understand our own minds. The classical account of how we know the contents of our own minds emphasized the role of introspection, and it was thought that we have private and direct access to mental states. However, in recent years a significant amount of evidence about the human tendency towards self-deception, overconfidence, bias, and rationalization has served to undermine the view that we are infallible with regard to our own mental states (Mele 2001; Gilovich 1991; Nisbett and Wilson 1977).

We can be wrong about our own mental states (e.g. one might deny being jealous even though it is clear to everyone else that she is jealous), we can make incorrect predictions about what we would do in a counterfactual situation, and we can generate incorrect explanations for the things we have already done (e.g. one might think she hired Smith because he was the best candidate for the job, though her action was considerably affected by her unacknowledged racism). Given this, a number of suggestions have come from the theory of mind literature to suggest that we know our own mental states the same way we know the mental states of others, through appeal to a theory or by using mental simulation. The role played by introspection, given both these accounts, is very limited.

I contend, however, that neither the simulation theory nor the theory theory provide us with an acceptable account of how we understand our minds or the minds of others. Both theories fail owing to their dependence on what I refer to as the symmetry of psychological prediction and explanation.

When a person predicts what someone else is going to do next, she demonstrates some understanding of that person. And when a person explains why someone acted in a certain way, she also demonstrates understanding. The same point can be made about understanding oneself. If a person had no competence in predicting or explaining her own behaviour, we would be inclined to say that she didn't know her own mind.

Perhaps because both explanation and prediction are key components to understanding, philosophers and psychologists often portray these two abilities as though they arise from the same competence, and sometimes they are taken to *be* the same competence. When explanation and prediction are associated in this way, they are taken to be two expressions of a single cognitive capacity that differ from one another only pragmatically. If the difference between prediction and explanation of human behaviour is merely pragmatic, then anytime I predict someone's future behaviour, I would at that moment also have an explanation of the behaviour. The same mechanism is used to generate both predictions and explanations, and something is a prediction rather than an explanation only if my goal were to predict rather than explain. On this view, explanations are nothing more than 'backward predictions' (Robinson and Mitchell 1995), and we can describe this thesis as the symmetry of psychological explanation and prediction.

Following from this line of reasoning, some have thought that any account of understanding must be able to handle both prediction and explanation (e.g. Churchland 1995, 1989; Gordon 1995, 2000; Stich and Ravenscroft 1996; Fodor 1987, 1991). Both the simulation theory and the theory theory are used to explicate prediction and explanation. Stich and Ravenscroft write, 'The simulation theory provides a real alternative to the prevailing explanatory strategy in cognitive science [i.e. the theory theory] for explaining our capacity to *predict and explain* other people's behaviour' (1996: 133, my emphasis). Though Stich and Ravenscroft reject the simulation theory as the best account of psychological prediction and explanation, underlying their discussion is the implicit acceptance of the symmetry thesis. The inputs used to predict a behaviour, regardless of whether the prediction is generated through a simulation or through appeal to a theory, become the explanation of that behaviour. If the symmetry thesis is correct, whenever we make a correct prediction of behaviour, we have at that moment an explanation of the behaviour in hand.

If we look at prediction and explanation in the physical world, we see that humans are able to predict that many things occur in a certain way without having an explanation of the phenomenon. I understand that there is a force of gravity, and that dropped objects fall to the ground. I expect that solid objects will not pass through other solid objects, and I expect that the sun will rise tomorrow. I can base these predictions on my experience of the world, and on the things that I have been taught. We would not assume that the method I use to predict the rising sun will provide an explanation of why the sun rises every morning. I can make this prediction through statistical induction, however induction will not tell me that the earth spins on its axis, and so it cannot give me an explanation for the rising sun. Prediction and explanation are not symmetrical in our folk physics, so why should we expect things to be any different in our folk psychology?

The symmetry thesis should be rejected in folk psychology, just as it was rejected in the philosophy of science half a century ago. I will argue that psychological prediction and explanation are not symmetrical, and in so doing I will make clear that there is no paradigm case of explanation. Instead, we provide different kinds of explanations given different circumstances. Because there are different sorts of explanations, we can have no clean mapping from explanation to prediction; there is no isomorphism between all cases of prediction and explanation. A major problem with past work in this area is that generalizations have been made about explanation *simpliciter* based on characteristics of one particular variety of explanation. To understand fully the ability to generate explanations, we must first recognize the different varieties of explanation.

I will also argue that there are different methods of predicting behaviour. Contrary to the dominant positions, we do not always need to attribute beliefs and desires in order to predict what a person will do next. Though this may be obvious in the case of predicting one's own behaviour, it may not be as obvious in the case of predicting the behaviour of others. In both cases it often suffices to refer to past events, and use statistical induction to conclude that a person will behave in the future the way she did in the past. Because predictions made on the basis of statistical induction will not offer a reason for why someone behaved as she did, statistical induction about behaviour is not symmetrical with explanation.

2. The Symmetry Thesis

Like people in the social world, scientists are concerned with both explaining and predicting the occurrences in the natural world. However, there has rarely been much agreement about what a scientific explanation looks like. For a short while, the symmetry thesis was embraced by philosophers of science with the introduction of Hempel and Oppenheim's (1948) deductive-nomological account of explanation. They argued that an explanation consists of a general covering law and initial conditions, the explanans, which deductively entails the phenomenon to be explained, the explandum. One can also use the explanans to predict an occurrence of the phenomenon, for the explandum follows logically from it. To both explain and predict the explandum, one needs merely to refer to the relevant initial conditions and general law that deductively entails it.

However, soon enough several counter-examples to the symmetry thesis were found. For one, not all predictions that fit this model acted as explanations. For example, sailors understood that there is a constant conjunction between the phases of the moon and the tides, and they used this law to predict the tides. However, until Newton, no one knew why there was this constant conjunction, and there was no explanation of the movement of the tides. Another celebrated counter-example to the symmetry thesis in scientific explanation is Bromberger's flagpole. Though the length of the flagpole's shadow can be explained by reference to the height of the pole, the position of the sun, and the general law of rectilinear propagation of light, the height of the flagpole is not itself explained by these other facts. These facts do not resolve the question of why the flagpole is a certain height. However, this information can be used to deduce, or predict, the height of the flagpole.[1] Thus, not all predictions serve as explanations. The symmetry thesis was further damaged with the realization that not all scientific explanations allow us to make predictions about how things will be in the future. To make this point, Scriven noted that though evolutionary biology explains what has evolved in the past, it does not serve to predict what will evolve in the future. Thus, not only is it the case that not all predictions provide explanations, but it is also true that not all explanations allow us to predict what will happen. Scriven (1959) gave us an example of an explanation that

[1] For a discussion of many other problems with the symmetry thesis in scientific explanation, see Salmon (1989).

does not have any predictive force. Once it was realized that there are predictions that do not provide explanations, and explanations that do not serve to make predictions, the symmetry thesis was rejected.

However, when we turn to psychological prediction and explanation, it seems that the symmetry thesis is widely accepted. For example, according to Daniel Dennett's intentional stance, in order for us to predict the behaviour of other people (and other intentional systems generally) we must recognize their goals, beliefs, and desires (Dennett 1987). From that we can infer how they will behave in the future. Thus, in order to explain why someone acted as she did, we need only to refer to her appropriate goal, belief, and desire. For Dennett, reference to the appropriate beliefs and desires serves both to predict and to explain.

Implicit advocacy of the symmetry thesis can also be seen in Fodor's writing when he speaks of 'explanation/prediction' (1991: 19), and when he moves from a discussion of 'predictive adequacy' to 'explanation' in such a way to present them as if they were one and the same (Fodor 1987). In Schiffer's criticism of Fodor, he notes the requirement of symmetry for the theory theory when he writes 'the conceptual roles of our propositional-attitude concepts secure that typically when we move directly from a belief that a person has such-and-such attitudes to a belief that he will do a certain act we also move to the belief that the person will do the act *because* he has those attitudes' (Schiffer 1991: 12–13). It is the 'because' that provides the explanation, according to Schiffer.

If I use the theory theory to predict what a person will do by appealing to initial belief/desire conditions C and the relevant theory T, I can infer with some degree of probability that the person will engage in the behaviour B. In contrast, when I explain behaviour B, I look for appropriate initial conditions C and a theory T that implies B. Instead of using beliefs and desires as the input, as is the case in prediction, the behaviour is the input, and the theory is used to determine which sets of beliefs and desires can cause that behaviour. Thus, for the theory theory, prediction of intentional behaviour and psychological explanation are symmetrical.

The simulation theory also advocates symmetry of prediction and explanation. Somewhat early in the debate between simulation theory and the theory theory, Paul Churchland (1989) criticized the simulation theory by suggesting that even if it describes an excellent method for predicting behaviour, simulation cannot be used to offer an explanation of behaviour. He argued that an appropriate explanation cannot be generated until we learn why the simulation model behaves as it does, and the real explanation of human behaviour would come from an understanding of the model's function. Churchland thought that for the simulation theory to be a viable alternative to theory theory, it must also provide for explanations of behaviour. This is because one of the simulation theory's strengths over theory theory was thought to be its relative simplicity. However, simulation would not be simpler if it were unable to account for explanation, but merely prediction. Because humans do explain *and* predict, if simulation only accounted for our ability to provide predictions, and the theory theory accounted for both prediction and explanation, any claim that simulation was simpler would have to be abandoned given that an entirely new account of explanation would be required to exist alongside the simulation account of prediction. Thus, symmetry of prediction and explanation became a virtue that any account of folk psychology must demonstrate.

Both Goldman (1995) and Gordon (1995) accepted the requirement of symmetry when they took pains to defend simulation from Churchland's criticism. They both argued that Churchland was wrong; simulation does provide explanations of behaviour by generating a number of possible belief/ desire sets that could have caused the action, and thus, like the theory theory, enjoys the virtue of symmetry.

Goldman, for example, writes, 'explanation can consist of telling a story that eliminates various alternative hypotheses about how the event in question came about, or could have come about. This is done by citing a specific set of goals and beliefs, which implicitly rules out the indefinitely many alternative desire-and-belief sets that might have led to the action' (Goldman 1995: 89). That is, one generates a number of possible belief/desire sets that could have caused the action and then tests these by using them as inputs in a simulation. When we arrive at a set of beliefs and desires that does produce the behaviour in question, we take that set as a possible explanation of the behaviour.

Gordon offers a similar account of explanation. He shows how model simulations can explain the behaviour of what is being modelled because models are manipulable. If we have a model that can be manipulated until the object behaviour is exhibited, we can determine which features interact to cause the behaviour. He writes 'in explaining one's own behaviour, it would seem that one can—without invoking or using laws or theories—simulate *in imagination* various counterfactual conditions and test their influence by methods akin to Mill's . . . And one can perform such thought experiments not just in one's own case but also within the context of a simulation of another' (Gordon 1995: 115). Gordon has argued that explanations of intentional behaviour need not refer to a person's psychological state, but that facts about a person's 'epistemic horizon' can and do serve equally well as explanations (Gordon 2000). Thus, even versions of simulation theory that take facts about a person's situation rather than her beliefs and desires as inputs to the simulation can provide satisfactory explanations. Thus both Gordon and

Goldman take simulation theory, like theory theory, to be consistent with the view that explanation is merely backwards prediction.

The requirement of symmetry is strongly advocated by other defenders of simulation theory as well. Boterill writes:

Perhaps the most commonly urged ground for regarding a theory as implicit in our folk psychological practices is that we use our knowledge of folk psychology to *explain* and *predict* the actions and reactions of others. Certainly explanation and prediction are two of the chief functions of theories. Yet this falls well short of providing a compelling case for theory-theory. Give or take the availability of the specific information required for predictive success, we can say: no theory without explanation and prediction. But we should hesitate to assert: no explanation or prediction without theory.   (Boterill 1996: 107)

This quote shows the force of the virtue criterion, and also the fallacy: since we use folk psychology to both predict and explain behaviour, any viable theory of our folk psychology must provide for both prediction and explanation. The fallacy comes from thinking that the same mechanism *must* be at work in both cases. Boterill points out the reason why simulation theorists have worked to develop simulation accounts of explanation. His reasoning is that any good theory must both predict and explain, and the theory theory seems to have a natural advantage in the explanation condition. In order to avoid losing the battle, the responses from Goldman and Gordon were to develop simulation accounts of explanation. However, there is another solution, and this is to deny the symmetry of prediction and explanation.

3. Prediction

According to our commonsense understanding of the mind, beliefs and desires cause our behaviours, and so we can predict the behaviour of other people by determining what beliefs and desires they have. Discussions of folk psychology normally begin by noting how successful humans are at predicting behaviour. And we are quite good, in many cases. We predict behaviour all the time, even sometimes when we're not aware of it. In most of our daily interactions with people on the street, we are in a continual state of anticipating behaviour. When walking down a city street we are confronted with hundreds of people with whom we interact, however briefly. We must dodge people approaching us, and move aside for those who want to pass. Our verbal and non-verbal interaction with other people is a constant dance choreographed by our society and our human impulse to anticipate similarity. If we were not skilled at predicting behaviour, we would be paralysed in the world, unable even to order a cup of coffee.

But how good are we, really, at predicting behaviour? How far do these abilities stretch? I can predict, with reasonable accuracy, that if you say you will bring a bottle of wine over for dinner, that you will arrive with a bottle of wine. I may even be able to predict to some extent what kind of wine you will bring. If I tell you that I am preparing steak for dinner, I might think that you will bring a bottle of red wine. If I know that you are a traditional wine drinker, who chooses red for beef and white for fish, then this prediction is easy to make. In making such predictions I rely on my knowledge of your habits, and I need not know anything about your wine-beliefs. Maybe the correct explanation for your behaviour is that you believe drinking red wine with beef is socially required, or perhaps you believe that the fruit and tannins of a robust red accentuate the taste of the meat. Perhaps you want to have the best possible aesthetic experience, so you buy the rare Bordeaux, or maybe instead you buy it with the desire to impress me with your good taste and financial success. I can predict what you will do, if I know your habits, but I may not have a very good understanding of why you buy a certain variety of wine. I could generate any number of possible explanations for your behaviour, even if I were able to predict that behaviour with great success.

In other cases, it is much more difficult to predict behaviour. If you have never been to dinner before, I may be unable to predict what variety of wine you will bring. And if we were walking down the street on the way to the wine store when a mugger confronted us, I would have very little idea of how either of us would behave. We might run, or hand over our money, or try to speak to the potential mugger, or one of us might try a self-defence move. In unfamiliar situations, we have difficulties predicting behaviour. If I have never observed a person in a particular situation, such as drinking wine or being confronted by a mugger, I won't have a good idea of how that person might behave in those respective situations, just as I would have a hard time predicting how I might act in a strange or complex situation.

We are most successful when predicting simple behaviours; that you will do what you say you will do, and that you will behave in the future as you have behaved in the past. When we start trying to predict what someone will do in complex or unusual situation, our success rate drops.

For example, suppose I need to get $100 from the bank. I can go inside the bank, and fill out a withdrawal slip, and ask the bank teller for $100 from my account. Because I've done this many times before, and because I was taught that this is normal behaviour, I can predict that the teller will give me $100. I know what the teller is going to do because I know that tellers generally honour withdrawal requests by giving the requested amount of money, so long as the customer has sufficient funds to cover the withdrawal. I don't need to attribute beliefs to the teller in order to predict his behaviour, and I don't need to imagine being him. I know that the teller will give me the money in the same way that I know that the automatic teller machine will give me the requested funds: they always (or, at least usually) have in the past. And I know it for the same reasons: we learn to expect a particular action in a particular circumstance after having experienced many cases of the conjunction. If I wanted to *explain* the teller's willingness to give me $100, I might well appeal to his beliefs and desires. But it doesn't follow that we need to attribute beliefs and desires to predict his behaviour.

The bank teller story is an example of a very simple prediction of behaviour, and it is true that we are much more successful when predicting simple behaviours than complex behaviours. Dennett (1987: 24), in defending the intentional stance account of prediction, recognizes its limitations when he writes '[The intentional stance] is notoriously unable to predict the exact purchase and sell decisions of stock traders, for instance, or the exact sequence of words a politician will utter when making a scheduled speech, but one's confidence can be very high indeed about slightly less specific predictions: that the particular trader *will not buy utilities today*, or that the politician *will side with the unions against his party*, for example'. However, we wouldn't need to attribute beliefs and desires to predict that the trader will not buy utilities today if we know that she never buys utilities when they are over $50 a share, even if we have no idea why. In fact, if we were to attribute beliefs and desires to the trader, we must first be familiar with her past behaviour; we need to understand the trader, and understanding will only come with exposure to regularities, either of the individual or of the kind of trader she is. We need to have some understanding of a person before we are able to make correct belief/desire attributions.

We are good at simple predictions, and not so good with complex or detailed predictions, I contend, because we use past regularities to make the large bulk of our predictions. We do not need to simulate or to appeal to a theory of folk psychology when walking down a city street, or expecting a person to pick up a dropped wallet, because we know that these are the sorts of things that we do. And, given that we use fewer variables when we predict behaviour using statistical induction about behaviour than we do when attributing beliefs and desires, our predictive power when using the inductive methodology is greater. This is not to say that all predictions of human actions can be made through statistical induction, because not all behaviour is predictable through appeal to past regularities. We sometimes appeal to our own behaviour in order to predict the behaviour of others, and use an overt simulation in order to predict behaviour, asking ourselves 'What would I do if I were him?' And we also frequently predict behaviour by attributing beliefs and desires, especially in complex or unusual circumstances. For example, a realtor who is trying to sell a house may try to discover the desires and beliefs of the customer in order to make the most convincing case for buying that particular house. There are many different kinds of behaviour that we are capable of predicting to different degrees. It is easier to predict the behaviour of the teller in the bank than it is to predict what he would do when confronted with a moral dilemma. It is often easier to predict one's own behaviour, or what one's family and friends will do, than to predict what strangers would do in the same situation. And it is not always easier to predict the behaviour of someone similar to oneself than someone dissimilar. If I saw a racist in a position where she could save only one of two drowning children equidistant from her, I would predict that she would save the child of her own race, and leave the other. If I placed myself in the same situation, I have little faith in any self-prediction I could now make.

My goal in this section is not to resolve the simulation theory/theory theory debate by arguing that we use neither strategy. Rather, I only mean to point out what most people already accept, namely that we often use induction when making predictions of behaviour. Perhaps we also use a folk-psychology theory, or perhaps we also simulate, or perhaps our cognitive mechanisms consist of a theory–simulation hybrid.

However, my point has not generally been accepted. Though Goldman recognizes that we do use induction to make predictions, on his account simulation is prior to induction. He writes, 'I am not saying, it should be emphasized, that simulation is the *only* method used for interpersonal mental ascriptions, or for the prediction of behaviour. Clearly, there are regularities about behaviour and individual differences that can be learned purely inductively' (Goldman 1995: 83). And later he adds, 'When a mature cognizer has constructed, by simulation, many similar instances of certain action-interpretation patterns, she may develop generalizations or other inductively formed representations (schemas, scripts, and so forth) that can trigger analogous interpretations by application of those "knowledge structures" alone, *sans* simulation' (ibid. 88). On Goldman's view, the work done by statistical induction about behaviour depends on having previously engaged in successful simulations. Because of this, our ability to predict through induction is derived from our prior simulations, and simulation remains fundamental.

The sort of induction I am talking about is not derivative of simulation or theory or anything else but recognition of past behaviour. I can predict that you will buy a double espresso every day at noon, not because I ever had to simulate your coffee-buying behaviour, but because I *noticed* that you have bought an espresso every day at noon, and I have no reason to think today will be any different. I can predict your behaviour the same way I can predict the leaves falling from the trees in autumn: it's always (or usually) been like that before.

For some predictions we make, it is simplest to use the inductive method, and in some cases it will be necessary to use the inductive method. For example, if I am trying to predict the behaviour of someone utterly unlike me, such as a visiting alien from another planet, I will not know what his beliefs and desires are, and I will need to study the subject for a while in order to determine what his behaviours are like. Simulation theory should only work with agents who are relevantly similar to oneself, and belief attribution should only work with agents to whom we can reliably attribute beliefs and desires. However, we can become quite good at predicting the behaviour of agents quite unlike ourselves. For example, we often predict the behaviour of non-human animals, and we can do this after observing them and determining how they actually do behave. We know that vervet monkeys run into the bushes when they hear a certain warning cry, and we can predict that any particular monkey will engage in this behaviour in such a situation. We know this because ethologists have observed vervet monkey behaviour, and they have seen this pattern of behaviour time and time again. However, we don't know *the* explanation for this behaviour. For those who are inclined to see animal behaviour as minded behaviour, an obvious explanation would be that the vervet monkey doesn't want to be eaten by the eagle, or that the vervet is afraid of the eagle. And for those inclined to think of animals as automata, an explanation may be given in stark behavioural reinforcement terms, or evolutionary terms. Whichever way one is inclined, a number of explanations suggest themselves, and it becomes difficult to adjudicate between them.

The goal of this section is to point out that some predictions of intentional behaviour appeal to statistical induction about behaviour, and do not take the mentality of the subject into account, either through simulation or through the use of a theory. It also seems that the predictions made through induction, because they are simple and involve fewer variables, are quite reliable. In complex situations, our ability to predict accurately breaks down, and it is in these situations that the inductive method fails as well.

4. Explanation

Explanation has typically played a less central role in the discussions of folk psychology. For the most part, empirical studies relating to this area have focused on the human ability to predict behaviour, and accounts of psychological explanation are derived from those results. Though there have been a few studies comparing our ability to predict and explain behaviour, it seems to me that the varieties of explanation have been glossed over. There is a distinctive pragmatic nature to explanations that doesn't seem to be addressed in this literature.

A few years ago, a number of psychologists presented the hypothesis that explanation is cognitively less demanding than prediction (Mitchell 1994; Robinson 1994; Robinson and Mitchell 1995; Moses and Flavell 1990; Riggs et al. 1998; Bartsch 1998). This view was meant to challenge previous findings coming from prediction-based tasks that concluded children do not develop an understanding of other people's beliefs until about 4 years old. These psychologists thought that children begin to understand others at an earlier age, and that their understanding derives at least in part from their ability to explain rather than predict human behaviour. Various reasons were given for thinking that explanation is simpler than prediction. Moses and Flavell, for example, argued that explanation is cognitively less demanding than prediction because when children see someone behaving in a way that is inconsistent with a desire the child expects the actor to have, that anomalous behaviour will serve as a clue to the actor's belief (Moses and Flavell 1990). However, we don't only offer explanations when a person behaves unexpectedly. Sometime we need to offer an explanation when trying to show that the behaviour is justified, or to help someone who doesn't know the person to understand him better. Moses and Flavell's reason for thinking that explanation is cognitively simpler is only true for cases of explaining anomalous behaviour. They do not show that explanation as a whole is simpler than prediction.

It seems that we need to understand the activity of psychological explanation better before drawing any conclusions about the relative difficulty of prediction and explanation, or about symmetry of prediction and explanation. Explanation of intentional behaviour involves a complex set of abilities, and appropriate explanations require an understanding of what information is being requested.

The criticisms of Hempel's D-N model of explanation and later criticisms of the inductive-statistical models of scientific explanations gave rise to a growing concern that scientific explanations are not arguments. It seems that there are similar problems with the view of psychological explanation as arguments, given that arguments have been unable to deal with the pragmatic issues that are involved in the generation of good explanations. Explanation of behaviour is in some sense less an objective phenomenon than prediction of actual behaviour. To judge a prediction as correct or incorrect one has an objective criterion—the actual behaviour. I can easily verify my prediction of someone's behaviour as long as I'm there to observe it. Explanations are not as easy to verify. The explanations that refer to a person's psychological state will be unverifiable in principle. I can't be certain that George W. Bush really wants to be president, even though he says he does, but I still use this belief to give a partial explanation of why he ran for the office.

There are varieties of explanations for one's behaviour; some are psychological and refer to propositions or desires, and others may refer to historical or environmental circumstances. Suppose I ask, 'Why did Kurt kill himself?' You might answer, 'His wife had just left him,' or perhaps 'He had just come out of drug rehab,' or instead you might say 'He was clinically depressed.' None of these explanations refers to Kurt's beliefs or desires. The last explanation gives a medical diagnosis that refers to his brain chemistry, and though it may help us understand why he killed himself, it is not psychological in the sense we are interested in here because it does not refer to Kurt's specific mental content. The context of the question might help decide which of these explanations would be acceptable at a given time. Many different sorts of explanations could be appropriate, and often no one is better than another. However, some explanations would not be satisfactory at all. Suppose you answered my why-question by saying 'Because he shot himself in the head.' That wouldn't satisfy me at all, though this action does give a sort of explanation.

The same point can be made about the explanations one generates for his own actions. Suppose a student is asked why he is taking Professor P's philosophy class. The student might refer to his beliefs: 'I think P is a good teacher,' or 'I am very interested in philosophy.' Or he might give other explanations such as 'It fits into my schedule,' or 'My adviser told me to.' Given that these explanations are consistent with one another, they might all be accurate explanations for the student's behaviour.

Van Fraassen, recognizing the pragmatic nature of explanation in the sciences, proposed the following account of an explanation: 'An explanation is not the same as a proposition, or an argument, or list of propositions; it is an *answer*' (Van Fraassen 1980: 137). More specifically, an explanation is an answer to a why-question. Thus, an account of explanation in the sciences must be an account of why-questions. Van Fraassen gives a story that undermines the universality of Bromberg's criticism of the D-N model of scientific explanation, because in some cases the length of the shadow *can* explain the height of a tower: suppose a mad Chevalier wanted to build a tower to commemorate an ill-fated relationship he had with his maid. He erects a tower at the spot where he killed her, and makes it tall enough so the shadow will cover the place where he first declared love to her. Given this story, we *can*, contrary to Bromberg, explain the height of the tower by referring to the (in this case necessary) length of the shadow (Van Fraassen 1980). Thus, explanations are not context-independent, but the correctness of the explanation depends on the context in which the question is being asked.

Let's apply Van Fraassen's ideas to psychological explanation. Suppose I use theory theory to predict that John will hide in a closet when he sees a person in the house. I make this prediction because I know that John is afraid and he wants to feel safe, and he feels safe in the closet. I can explain why John hid by referring to his belief and desire (that he thinks there is a burglar in the house, and he doesn't want to be shot), but if the why question is 'Why did John hide rather than attack the intruder?' the reference to the belief and desire I used to make the prediction does not answer the question. Nor would that response be a good answer to the question, 'Why did John hide to avoid the burglar rather than run out of the house?' To give a good explanation, I need to know what sort of explanation is called for. If John had told me that he hides when he is frightened, or if I had seen him hide in another instance when he was afraid, I may be able to predict that he will hide in this case. However, generating this explanation does not give me any understanding of why he hides rather than runs. Unfortunately for those who seek symmetry in folk psychology, not every appropriate explanation will refer to those mechanisms used to make the prediction.

This point may be clearer for theory theory than simulation, for most versions of the theory theory do seem to accept the covering law model of prediction and explanation. The symmetry in theory theory is explicit; those features I use to predict can also be used to explain. However, the same problem arises for the simulation theory. The explanation of John's behaviour is formed by generating reasons why John would hide in the closet given that there is a burglar in the house. Perhaps I know that John has certain beliefs and desires, and when I input these into the simulation, I see that he would hide in the closet because he was afraid of the burglar. Or perhaps I know that John will hide in the closet simply because there is a burglar in the house. The same problem of pragmatics arises regardless of whether you start the simulation with beliefs and desires or facts about the situation. If I explain John's behaviour by saying that he was afraid, I don't have an answer to *all* why-questions one might ask about John's behaviour. Perhaps I don't understand why John is afraid of the burglar, given that he is a brave fellow who has demonstrated his bravery time and time again. My why-question might not be satisfied by reference to John's fear, because I want to understand why he feels fear. An explanation in terms of the situation falls prey to the same problems. If I didn't know there was a burglar in the house, an appropriate explanation would be 'Because there is a burglar in the house.' But, of course, this would only be a good explanation if there really were a burglar in the house; if the noises John had heard were caused by a squirrel, the appropriate explanation would be neither 'Because there is a burglar in the house' or 'Because there is a squirrel in the house.' To be a good explanation, we would have to refer to John's mistaken belief about there being a burglar in the house. And if there really were a burglar in the house, the explanation of John's behaviour that cites this fact wouldn't explain why he hid rather than doing something else. One sees symmetry of prediction and explanation when looking at certain kinds of cases, but because there are many kinds of why-questions, not all of them will be answered through reference to the inputs of the simulation that allowed the behaviour to be predicted.

This point follows from Churchland's original criticism of the simulation theory's ability to offer explanations. It is true, given Goldman's and Gordon's responses, that simulation can answer *some* why questions. But Churchland pointed out that simulation cannot offer explanations of why one has those beliefs and desires, or how the situation causes one to act in a certain way. Simulation doesn't provide information about the causal interaction of the inputs of the simulation and the behaviour, and because of this certain why-questions such as 'Why did John feel afraid now when he had never been afraid before' may not be answered through appeal to simulation.

The asymmetry is also present when I use a statistical induction about behaviour to predict what someone will do. Suppose John lives in a bad neighborhood, and his house has been broken into many times while he was home. If in the past he had always hidden in the closet, I can predict using statistical induction that John will hide in the closet again this time. However, I will need to appeal elsewhere to develop a plausible explanation. Most of us won't be satisfied by the explanation 'He always does that,' for when we ask for a psychological explanation we often do want to know what beliefs and desires caused the behaviour we're interested in explaining.

A defender of symmetry might respond by saying, 'You predicted that John would hide because he thought there was a burglar in the house. If someone who didn't know about the burglar saw John hide, her question "Why did John hide?" would be easily answered with the response "John thinks there is a burglar in the house."' And I would agree with this. I am not claiming that reference to a belief or desire that one uses to generate a prediction will *never* be the correct answer to a why-question. Rather, I am pointing out that some why-questions cannot be answered in this way, and because of this, the perceived symmetry between prediction and explanation is an illusion. Symmetry exists between two things if it exists in all instances; if they are partially symmetrical, or sometimes symmetrical, then they are not symmetrical at all.

5. Asymmetry of Prediction and Explanation

I will introduce one last example (Table 1) to make the asymmetry of prediction and explanation clear. Kelly has just arrived home from work after a long day of fixing teeth. The three theories can produce the same prediction of Kelly's behaviour, but note the different explanations for her next action.

TABLE 1

	Theory theory	Simulation Theory	Statistical Induction
Prediction	Kelly gets a beer from the refrigerator	Kelly gets a beer from the refrigerator	Kelly gets a beer from the refrigerator
Explanation	Kelly thinks there is a beer in the fridge and desires a beer	Kelly thinks there is a beer in the fridge and desires a beer OR Kelly just got home from work	Kelly always gets a beer from the fridge when she gets home from work

The reference to Kelly's belief and desire doesn't provide a very full explanation of why she gets the beer. We have no information about the intention that leads her to drink a beer. Maybe she wants to relax after her hard day, or maybe she wants to forget about work, and intends to drink until she is drunk. If Kelly wanted to stop drinking, and went to a counsellor to help her stop, none of the explanations given above provide a *reason* why she was drinking after work, and without that understanding the counsellor might not be able to help her.

Due to the pragmatic nature of explanation, it is difficult to imagine any one-to-one correlation between a prediction and an explanation. An explanation can be a request for the beliefs and desires one had before acting, or the immediate causal story, or for a cause of the tendency being exhibited. Not all explanations of human behaviour will refer to mental events, as Gordon has made clear (Gordon 2000), though theory theory and some accounts of simulation theory take mental events as an integral to both prediction and explanation.

The case for symmetry becomes even weaker if you accept that many of our predictions are made by statistical induction about behaviour. If it is true that we do often appeal to simple regularities to predict, then the symmetry thesis is certainly false, for inductive generalizations do not usually provide explanations. However, in some cases a generalization about behaviour will be all the explanation there is. For example, you meet a fellow who often twirls his beard, and you ask his old friend why he twirls his beard. The friend might respond, 'Oh, it's just a habit.' This explanation, though it does not make reference to mental states, may be satisfactory, because it indicates that there are no beliefs or desires associated with the behaviour. There may be no further psychological reason for the behaviour.

If I answer a why-question by stating that things are always like that, I am either reporting on my epistemic state, or I am claiming that there is no further explanation. Explanations, like justifications, must come to an end somewhere, and there are some things that we have no further explanation for. Perhaps the final explanation may refer to the laws of nature, and if you ask me to explain why the laws of nature exist as they do, you are asking a question that I cannot answer if we understand laws of nature as necessary.

I have argued that there are different kinds of psychological explanations, and that one method we use to make predictions, statistical induction about behaviour, will often not automatically generate an explanation for the behaviour. Psychological prediction and explanation is only symmetrical if we use the same mechanisms to predict and explain behaviour, and if the act of making a prediction automatically results in an explanation.

Churchland's observation that simulation theory is not able to account for psychological explanations should not be taken as a criticism of simulation theory, because we should not expect symmetry between our ability to make predictions and our ability to provide explanations. Only after it has been accepted that these are two distinct activities can the investigation into our understanding of other minds proceed.

This conclusion not only undermines both theory theory and simulation theory as accounts of how we know *others'* mental states, but it also demonstrates that neither theory can provide a plausible account of how we know *our own* mental states. Simply knowing that I will do something does not help to illuminate the reasons I might have for acting as I do, nor need this knowledge provide any indications of my true beliefs and desires.

REFERENCES

BARTSCH, K. (1998), 'False Belief Prediction and Explanation: Which Develops First and Why it Matters', *International Journal of Behavioral Development*, 22: 423–8.

BOLTON, DEREK (1995), 'Self-Knowledge, Error, and Disorder', in Martin Davies and Tony Stone (eds.), *Mental Simulation* (Oxford: Blackwell), 209–34.

BOTERILL, GEORGE (1996), 'Folk Psychology and Theoretical Status', in Peter Carruthers and Peter K. Smith (eds.), *Theories of Theories of Mind* (Cambridge: Cambridge University Press), 105–18.

CARRUTHERS, PETER (1996), 'Autism as Mind-Blindness: An Elaboration and Partial Defence', in Peter Carruthers and Peter K. Smith (eds.), *Theories of Theories of Mind* (Cambridge: Cambridge University Press), 257–73.

CHURCHLAND, PAUL (1989), 'Folk Psychology and the Explanation of Human Behavior', *Philosophical Perspectives*, 3: *Philosophy of Mind and Action Theory*, 225–41.

DENNETT, DANIEL (1987), *The Intentional Stance* (Cambridge, Mass.: MIT Press).

FODOR, JERRY (1987), *Psychosemantics* (Cambridge, Mass.: MIT Press).

—— (1991), 'You Can Fool Some of the People All of the Time, Everything Else Being Equal: Hedged Laws and Psychological Explanations', *Mind*, 100: 19–34.

—— (1992), *A Theory of Content and Other Essays* (Cambridge Mass.: MIT Press).

FRITH, UTA, and HAPPÉ, FRANCESCA (1999), 'Theory of Mind and Self-Consciousness: What is it Like to be Autistic?' *Mind and Language*, 14/1: 1–22.

GILOVICH, THOMAS (1991), *How We Know What Isn't So* (New York: Free Press).

GOLDMAN, ALVIN (1995), 'Interpretation Psychologized', in Martin Davies and Tony Stone (eds.), *Folk Psychology* (Oxford: Blackwell), 74–99. Repr. from *Mind and Language*, 7/1–2 (1989), 161–85.

GOPNICK, ALISON, and MELTZOFF, A. N. (1994), 'Minds, Bodies, and Persons: Young Children's Understanding of the Self and Others as Reflected in Imitation and Theory of Mind Research', in S. Parker, R. Mitchell, and M. Boccia (eds.), *Self-Awareness in Animals and Humans* (New York: Cambridge University Press).

—— (2000), 'Simulation and the Explanation of Action', in H. Kölger and K. Stueber (eds.), *Empathy and Agency: The Problem of Understanding in the Human Sciences* (Boulder: Westview), 62–82.

GORDON, ROBERT (1995), 'The Simulation Theory: Objections and Misconceptions', in Martin Davies and Tony Stone (eds.), *Folk Psychology* (Oxford: Blackwell), 100–22. Repr. from *Mind and Language*, 7/1–2 (1992), 11–34.

HEMPEL, C. G., and OPPENHEIM, P. (1948), 'Studies in the Logic of Explanation', *Philosophy of Science*, 15: 135–75.

HUMPHREY, N. K. (1976), 'The Social Function of Intellect', in P. P. G. Bateson and R. A. Hinde (eds.), *Growing Points in Ethology* (Cambridge: Cambridge University Press), 303–21.

MELE, ALFRED R. (2001), *Self-Deception Unmasked* (Princeton and Oxford: Princeton University Press).

MITCHELL, P. (1994), 'Realism and Early Conception of Mind: A Synthesis of Phylogenetic and Ontogenetic Issues', in C. Lewis and P. Mitchell (eds.), *Children's Early Understanding of Minds: Origins and Development* (Hillsdale, NJ: Lawrence Erlbaum).

MOSES, L. J., and FLAVELL, J. H. (1990), 'Inferring False Beliefs from Actions and Reactions', *Child Development*, 61: 929–94.

NISBETT, RICHARD, and WILSON, TIMOTHY (1977), 'Telling More Than We Can Know', *Psychological Review*, 84: 231–59.

RIGGS, KEVIN, PETERSON, DONALD, ROBINSON, ELIZABETH J., and MITCHELL, PETER (1998), 'Are Errors in False Belief Tasks Symptomatic of a Broader Difficulty with Counterfactuality?' *Cognitive Development*, 13: 73–90.

ROBINSON, E. J. (1994), 'What People Say, What They Think, and What is Really the Case: Children's Understanding of Utterances as Sources of Knowledge', in C. Lewis and P. Mitchell (eds.), *Children's Early Understanding of Minds: Origins and Development* (Hillsdale, NJ: Lawrence Erlbaum).

—— and MITCHELL, P. (1995), 'Masking of Children's Early Understanding of the Representational Mind: Backwards Explanation versus Prediction', *Child Development*, 66: 1022–39.

SALMON, WESLEY C. (1989) 'Four Decades of Scientific Explanation', in P. Kitcher and W. C. Salmon (eds.), *Minnesota Studies in the Philosophy of Science* (Minneapolis: University of Minnesota Press).

SCHIFFER, STEPHEN (1991), '*Ceteris paribus* Laws', *Mind*, 100: 1–17.

Scriven, Michael (1956), 'Explanations, Predictions, and Laws', *Minnesota Studies in the Philosophy of Science* (Minneapolis: University of Minnesota Press).

—— (1959), 'Explanation and Prediction in Evolutionary Theory', *Science*, 130: 477–82.

Stich, Stephen, and Ravenscroft, Ian (1996), 'What is Folk Psychology?', in S. Stich, *Deconstructing the Mind* (Oxford: Oxford University Press).

Van Fraassen, Bas (1980), *The Scientific Image* (Oxford: Oxford University Press).

Whiten, A., and Byrne, R. W. (1988), 'The Machiavellian Intellect Hypotheses', in R. W. Byrne and A. Whiten (eds.), *Machiavellian Intelligence* (Oxford: Oxford University Press), 1–9.

8. The Content and Epistemology of Phenomenal Belief

1 Introduction

Experiences and beliefs are different sorts of mental states, and are often taken to belong to very different domains. Experiences are paradigmatically phenomenal, characterized by what it is like to have them. Beliefs are paradigmatically intentional, characterized by their propositional content. But there are a number of crucial points where these domains intersect. One central locus of intersection arises from the existence of phenomenal beliefs: beliefs that are about experiences.

The most important phenomenal beliefs are *first-person* phenomenal beliefs: a subject's beliefs about his or her own experiences, and especially, about the phenomenal character of the experiences that he or she is currently having. Examples include the belief that one is now having a red experience, or that one is experiencing pain.

These phenomenal beliefs raise important issues in metaphysics, in the theory of content, and in epistemology. In metaphysics, the relationship between phenomenal states and phenomenal beliefs is sometimes taken to put strong constraints on the metaphysics of mind. In the theory of content, analysing the content of phenomenal beliefs raises special issues for a general theory of content to handle, and the content of such beliefs has sometimes been taken to be at the foundations of a theory of content more generally. In epistemology, phenomenal beliefs are often taken to have a special epistemic status, and are sometimes taken to be the central epistemic nexus between cognition and the external world.

My project here is to analyse phenomenal beliefs in a way that sheds some light on these issues. I will start by focusing on the content of these beliefs, and will use the analysis developed there to discuss the underlying factors in virtue of which this content is constituted. I will then apply this framework to the central epistemological issues in the vicinity: incorrigibility, justification, and the dialectic over the 'Myth of the Given'.[1]

1.1. Phenomenal Realism

The discussion that follows is premised upon what I call 'phenomenal realism': the view that there are phenomenal properties (or phenomenal qualities, or qualia), properties that type mental states by what it is like to have them, and that phenomenal properties are not conceptually reducible to physical or functional properties (or equivalently, that phenomenal concepts are not reducible to physical or functional concepts). On this view, there are truths about what it is like to be a subject that are not entailed a priori by the physical and functional truth (including the environmental truth) about that subject.

The phenomenal realist view is most easily illustrated with some familiar thought experiments. Consider Frank Jackson's case of Mary, the neuroscientist who knows all relevant physical truths about colour processing, but whose visual experience has been entirely monochromatic (Jackson 1982). On the phenomenal realist view, Mary lacks factual knowledge concerning what it is like to see red. Views that deny this deny phenomenal realism. Or consider cases in which a hypothetical being has the same physical, functional, and environmental properties as an existing conscious being, but does not have the same phenomenal properties. Such a being might be a zombie, lacking experiences altogether, or it might be an inverted being, with experiences of a different character. On the phenomenal realist view, some such duplicates are coherently conceivable, in the sense that there is no a priori contradiction in the hypothesis in question. Views that deny this deny phenomenal realism.

(What if someone holds that functional duplicates without consciousness are coherently conceivable, but that physical duplicates without consciousness are not? Such a view would be in the spirit of phenomenal realism. This suggests that we could define phenomenal realism more weakly as the thesis that the phenomenal is not conceptually reducible to the functional, omitting mention of the physical. I do not define it this way, for two reasons. First, I think if functional duplicates without consciousness are conceivable, physical duplicates without consciousness must be conceivable too, as there is no reasonable possibility of a conceptual entailment from microphysical to phenomenal that does not proceed via the functional. Second, it is not easy to give a precise account of what functional duplication consists in, and

---

[1] The analysis presented here is a development of a brief discussion in Chalmers (1996: 203–8).

stipulating physical identity finesses that question. But if someone disagrees, everything that I say will apply, with appropriate changes, on the weaker view.)

Phenomenal realism subsumes most varieties of dualism about the phenomenal. It also subsumes many varieties of materialism. In particular it subsumes what I have called 'type-B' materialism (see Chalmers 2002*a*): views that hold that there is an a posteriori necessary entailment from the physical to the phenomenal, so that there is an epistemic or conceptual gap between the physical and phenomenal domains, but no ontological gap. Views of this sort typically allow that Mary gains factual knowledge when she sees red for the first time, but hold that it is knowledge of an old fact known in a new way; and they typically hold that the duplication cases mentioned above are conceptually coherent but not metaphysically possible.

Phenomenal realism excludes what I have called 'type-A' materialism: views that hold that all phenomenal truths are entailed a priori by physical truths. Such views include eliminativism about the phenomenal, as well as analytical functionalism and logical behaviourism, and certain forms of analytic representationalism. Views of this sort typically deny that Mary gains any knowledge when she sees red for the first time, or hold that she gains only new abilities; and they typically deny that the duplication cases mentioned above are coherently conceivable.

Those who are not phenomenal realists might want to stop reading now, but there are two reasons why they might continue. First, although the arguments I will give for my view of phenomenal beliefs will presuppose phenomenal realism, it is possible that some aspects of the view itself may be tenable even on some views that deny phenomenal realism. Second, some of the most important arguments *against* phenomenal realism are epistemological arguments that centre on the connection between experience and belief. I will be using my analysis to help rebut those arguments, and thus indirectly to support phenomenal realism against its opponents.

A note on modality: because I am assuming phenomenal realism but not property dualism, all references to necessity and possibility should be taken as invoking conceptual necessity and possibility. Similarly, talk of possible worlds can be taken as invoking conceivable worlds (corresponding to the epistemically constructed scenarios of Chalmers (forthcoming); see also the appendix to this chapter), and talk of constitutive relations should be taken as invoking conceptually necessary connections. If one accepts a certain sort of link between conceptual and metaphysical possibility (e.g. the thesis that ideal primary conceivability entails primary possibility), then these references can equally be taken as invoking metaphysical possibility and necessity.

A note on phenomenal properties: it is natural to speak as if phenomenal properties are instantiated by mental states, and as if there are entities, experiences, that bear their phenomenal properties essentially. But one can also speak as if phenomenal properties are directly instantiated by conscious subjects, typing subjects by aspects of what it is like to be them at the time of instantiation. These ways of speaking do not commit one to corresponding ontologies, but they at least suggest such ontologies. In a *quality-based* ontology, the subject–property relation is fundamental. From this one can derive a subject–experience–property structure, by identifying experiences with phenomenal states (instantiations of phenomenal properties), and attributing phenomenal properties to these states in a derivative sense. In a more complex *experience-based* ontology, a subject–experience–property structure is fundamental (where experiences are phenomenal individuals, or at least something more than property instantiations), and the subject–property relation is derivative. In what follows, I will sometimes use both sorts of language, and will be neutral between the ontological frameworks.

2. The Content of Phenomenal Concepts and Phenomenal Beliefs

2.1. *Relational, Demonstrative, and Pure Phenomenal Concepts*

Phenomenal beliefs involve the attribution of phenomenal properties. These properties are attributed under phenomenal concepts. To understand the content of phenomenal beliefs, we need to understand the nature and content of phenomenal concepts.

I look at a red apple, and visually experience its colour. This experience instantiates a phenomenal quality R, which we might call phenomenal redness. It is natural to say that I am having a red experience, even though of course experiences are not red in the same sense in which apples are red. Phenomenal redness (a property of experiences, or of subjects of experience) is a different property from external redness (a property of external objects), but both are respectable properties in their own right.

I attend to my visual experience, and think *I am having an experience of such-and-such quality*, referring to the quality of phenomenal redness. There are various concepts of the quality in question that might yield a true belief.[2]

---

[2] I take concepts to be mental entities on a par with beliefs: they are constituents of beliefs (and other propositional attitudes) in a manner loosely analogous to the way in which words are constituents of sentences. Like beliefs, concepts are tokens rather than types in the first instance. But they also fall under types, some of which I explore in what follows. In such cases it is natural to use singular expressions such as 'the concept' for a concept-type, just as one sometimes uses expressions such as 'the belief' for a belief-type, or 'the word' for a word-type. I will use italics for concepts and beliefs throughout.

We can first consider the concept expressed by 'red' in the public-language expression 'red experience', or the concept expressed by the public-language expression 'phenomenal redness'. The reference of these expressions is fixed via a relation to red things in the external world, and ultimately via a relation to certain paradigmatic red objects that are ostended in learning the public-language term 'red'. A language learner learns to call the experiences typically brought about by these objects 'red' (in the phenomenal sense), and to call the objects that typically bring about those experiences 'red' (in the external sense). So the phenomenal concept involved here is *relational*, in that it has its reference fixed by a relation to external objects. The property that is referred to need not be relational, however. The phenomenal concept plausibly designates an intrinsic property rigidly, so that there are counterfactual worlds in which red experiences are never caused by red things.

One can distinguish at least two relational phenomenal concepts, depending on whether reference is fixed by relations across a whole community of subjects, or by relations restricted to the subject in question. The first is what we can call the *community relational concept*, or red_C. This can be glossed roughly as *the phenomenal quality typically caused in normal subjects within my community by paradigmatic red things*. The second is what we can call the *individual relational concept*, or red_I. This can be glossed roughly as *the phenomenal quality typically caused in me by paradigmatic red things*. The two concepts red_C and red_I will co-refer for normal subjects, but for abnormal subjects they may yield different results. For example, a red/green-inverted subject's concept red_C will refer to (what others call) phenomenal redness, but his or her concept red_I will refer to (what others call) phenomenal greenness.

The public-language term 'red' as a predicate of experiences can arguably be read as expressing either red_C or red_I. The community reading of 'red' guarantees a sort of shared meaning within the community, in that all uses of the term are guaranteed to co-refer, and in that tokens of sentences such as 'X has a red experience at time t' will have the same truth-value whether uttered by normal or abnormal subjects. On the other hand, the individual reading allows a subject better access to the term's referent. On this reading, an unknowingly inverted subject's term 'red' will refer to what she think it refers to (unless the inversion was recent), while on the community reading, her term 'red' may refer to something quite different, and her utterance 'I have had red experiences' may even be unknowingly quite false.[3] In any case, we need not settle here just what is expressed by phenomenal predicates in public language. All that matters is that both concepts are available.

---

[3] These cases may not be entirely hypothetical. Nida-Rümelin (1996) gives reasons, based on the neurobiological and genetic bases of colour-blindness, to believe that a small fraction of the population may actually be spectrum-inverted with respect to the rest of us. If so, it is natural to wonder just what their phenomenal expressions refer to.

Phenomenal properties can also be picked out indexically. When seeing the tomato, I can refer indexically to a visual quality associated with it, by saying 'this quality' or 'this sort of experience'. These expressions express a demonstrative concept that we might call E. E functions in an indexical manner, roughly by picking out whatever quality the subject is currently ostending. Like other demonstratives, it has a 'character', which fixes reference in a context roughly by picking out whatever quality is ostended in that context; and it has a distinct 'content', corresponding to the quality that is actually ostended—in this case, phenomenal redness. The demonstrative concept E rigidly designates its referent, so that it picks out the quality in question even in counterfactual worlds in which no one is ostending the quality.

The three concepts red_C, red_I, and E may all refer to the same quality, phenomenal redness. In each case, reference is fixed relationally, with the referent characterized in terms of its relations to external objects or acts of ostension. There is another crucial phenomenal concept in the vicinity, one that does not pick out phenomenal redness relationally, but rather picks it out directly, in terms of its intrinsic phenomenal nature. This is what we might call a *pure phenomenal concept*.

To see the need for the pure phenomenal concept, consider the knowledge that Mary gains when she learns for the first time what it is like to see red. She learns that seeing red has such-and-such quality. Mary learns (or reasonably comes to believe) that red things will typically cause experiences of such-and-such quality in her, and in other members of her community. She learns (or gains the cognitively significant belief) that the experience she is now having has such-and-such quality, and that the quality she is now ostending is such-and-such. Call Mary's 'such-and-such' concept here R. (Note that the phenomenal concept R should be distinguished from the phenomenal quality R (unitalicized) that it refers to.)

Mary's concept R picks out phenomenal redness, but it is quite distinct from the concepts red_C, red_I, and E. We can see this by using cognitive significance as a test for difference between concepts. Mary gains the belief $red_C = R$—that the quality typically caused in her community by red things is such-and-such—and this belief is cognitively significant knowledge. She gains the cognitively significant belief $red_I = R$ in a similar way. And she gains the belief $E = R$—roughly, that the quality she is now ostending is such-and-such.

Mary's belief $E = R$ is as cognitively significant as any other belief in which the object of a demonstrative is independently characterized: e.g. my belief *I am David Chalmers*, or my belief *that object is tall*. For Mary, $E = R$ is not a priori. No a priori reasoning can rule out the hypothesis that she is now ostending some other quality entirely, just as no a priori reasoning can rule out the hypothesis that I am David Hume, or that the object I am pointing to is short. Indeed, nothing known a priori entails that the phenomenal quality R is ever instantiated in the actual world.

It is useful to consider analogies with other demonstrative knowledge of types. Let $this_S$ be a demonstrative concept of shapes ('this shape'). Jill might tell Jack that she is about to show him her favourite shape. When she shows him a circle, he might form the thought *Jill's favourite shape is $this_S$*. This is a demonstrative thought, where this instance of $this_S$ picks out the shape of a circle. He might also form the thought *Jill's favourite shape is circle*. This is a non-demonstrative thought: instead of a demonstrative concept, the right-hand side uses what we might call a *qualitative* concept of the shape of a circle. Finally, he might form the thought *$this_S$ is circle*. This is a substantive, non-trivial thought, taking the form of an identity involving a demonstrative concept and a qualitative concept. Here, as in the examples above, one conceives the object of a demonstration *as* the object of a demonstration ('this shape, whatever it happens to be'), and at the same time attributes it substantive qualitative properties, conceived non-demonstratively.

Of course Jack's concept *circle* (unlike Mary's concept R) is an old concept, previously acquired. But this is inessential to Jack's case. We can imagine that Jack has never seen a circle before, but that on seeing a circle for the first time, he acquires the qualitative concept of circularity. He will then be in a position to think the qualitative thought *Jill's favourite shape is circle*, and to think the substantive demonstrative-qualitative thought *$this_S$ is circle*.

Mary's situation is analogous. Where Jack thinks the substantive thought *$this_S$ is circle*, Mary might think the substantive thought $E = R$ ('this quality is R'). Like Jack's thought, Mary's thought involves attributing a certain substantive qualitative nature to a type that is identified demonstratively. This qualitative nature is attributed using a qualitative concept of phenomenal redness, acquired upon having a red experience for the first time. Her thoughts $red_C = R$ and $red_I = R$ are substantive thoughts analogous to Jack's thought *Jill's favourite shape is circle*. Her crucial thought $E = R$ is a substantive thought involving both a demonstrative and a qualitative concept, and is as cognitively significant as Jack's thought *$this_S$ is circle*.

So the concept R is quite distinct from red_C, red_I, and E. We might say that unlike the other concepts, the pure phenomenal concept characterizes the phenomenal quality *as* the phenomenal quality that it is.

The concept R is difficult to express directly in language, since the most natural terms, such as 'phenomenal redness' and 'this experience', arguably express other concepts such as red_C and E. Still, one can arguably discern uses of these terms that express pure phenomenal concepts; or if not, one can stipulate such uses. For example, Chisholm (1957) suggests that there is a 'non-comparative' sense of expressions such as 'looks red'; this sense seems to express a pure phenomenal concept, whereas his 'comparative sense' seems to express a relational phenomenal concept.[4] And at least informally, demonstratives are sometimes used to express pure phenomenal concepts. For example, the belief that $E = R$ might be informally expressed by saying something like 'this quality is *this* quality'.

It may be that there is a sense in which R can be regarded as a 'demonstrative' concept. I will not regard it this way: I take it that demonstrative concepts work roughly as analysed by Kaplan (1989), so that they have a reference-fixing 'character' that leaves their referent open. This is how E behaves: its content might be glossed roughly as 'this quality, whatever it happens to be'. R, on the other hand, is a substantive concept that is tied a priori to a specific sort of quality, so it does not behave the way that Kaplan suggests that a demonstrative should. Still, there is an intimate relationship between pure and demonstrative phenomenal concepts that I will discuss later; and if someone wants to count pure phenomenal concepts as 'demonstrative' in a broad sense (perhaps regarding E as 'indexical'), there is no great harm in doing so, as long as the relevant distinctions are kept clear. What matters for my purposes is not the terminological point, but the more basic point that the distinct concepts E and R exist.

The relations among these concepts can be analysed straightforwardly using the two-dimensional framework for representing the content of concepts. A quick introduction to this framework is given in an appendix; more details can be found in Chalmers (2002c). The central points in what follows should be comprehensible if matters involving the two-dimensional framework are skipped, but the framework makes the analysis of some crucial points much clearer.

According to the two-dimensional framework, when an identity $A = B$ is a posteriori, the concepts A and B have different epistemic (or primary) intensions. If A and B are rigid concepts and the identity is true, A and B have the same subjunctive (or secondary) intensions. So we should expect that the concepts red_C, red_I, E, and R have different epistemic intensions, but the same subjunctive intension. And this is what we find. The subjunctive intension of each picks out phenomenal redness in all worlds. The epistemic intension of red_C picks out, in a given centred world, roughly the quality typically caused by certain paradigmatic objects in the community of the subject at the centre of the world. The epistemic intension of red_I picks

---

[4] The distinction also roughly tracks Nida-Rümelin's (1995; 1997) distinction between 'phenomenal' and 'non-phenomenal' readings of belief attributions concerning phenomenal states. 'Phenomenal' belief attributions seem to require that the subject satisfies the attribution by virtue of a belief involving a pure phenomenal concept, while 'non-phenomenal' attributions allow that the subject can satisfy the attribution by virtue of a belief involving a relational phenomenal concept.

out roughly the quality typically caused by those objects in the subject at the centre.

As for the demonstrative concept E: to a first approximation, one might hold that its epistemic intension picks out the quality that is ostended by the subject at the centre. This characterization is good enough for most of our purposes, but it is not quite correct. It is possible to ostend two experiences simultaneously and invoke two distinct demonstrative concepts, as when one thinks *that quality differs from that quality*, ostending two different parts of a symmetrical visual field (see Austin 1990). Here no descriptive characterization such as the one above will capture the difference between the two concepts. It is better to see E as a sort of indexical, like I or *now*. To characterize the epistemic possibilities relevant to demonstrative phenomenal concepts, we need centred worlds whose centres contain not only a 'marked' subject and time, but also one or more marked experiences; in the general case, a sequence of such experiences.[5] Then a concept such as E will map a centred world to the quality of the 'marked' experience (if any) in that world. Where two demonstrative concepts E_1 and E_2 are involved, as above, the relevant epistemic possibilities will contain at least two marked experiences, and we can see E_1 as picking out the quality of the first marked experience in a centred world, and E_2 as picking out the quality of the second. Then the belief above will endorse all worlds at which the quality of the first marked experience differs from the quality of the second. This subtlety will not be central in what follows.

The epistemic intension of R is quite distinct from all of these. It picks out phenomenal redness in all worlds. I will analyse this matter in more depth shortly; but one can see intuitively why this is plausible. When Mary believes *roses cause R experiences*, or *I am currently having an R experience*, she thereby excludes all epistemic possibilities in which roses cause some other quality (such as G, phenomenal greenness), or in which she is experiencing some other quality: only epistemic possibilities involving phenomenal redness remain.

The cognitive significance of identities such as $red_C = R$, $red_I = R$, and $E = R$ is reflected in the differences between the concept's epistemic intensions. The first two identities endorse all epistemic possibilities in which paradigmatic objects stand in the right relation to experiences of R; these are only a subset of the epistemic possibilities available a priori. The third identity endorses all epistemic possibilities in which the marked experience at the centre (or the ostended experience, on the rough characterization) is R. Again, there are many epistemic possibilities (a priori) that are not like

---

[5] In the experience-based framework: if experiences do not map one-to-one to instances of phenomenal properties, then instances of phenomenal properties should be marked instead.

this: centred worlds in which the marked experience is G, for example. Once again, this epistemic contingency reflects the cognitive significance of the identity.

Phenomenal realists (e.g. Loar 1997; Hawthorne 2002) analysing what Mary learns have occasionally suggested that her phenomenal concept is a demonstrative concept. This is particularly popular as a way of resisting anti-materialist arguments, as it is tempting to invoke the distinctive epistemic and referential behaviour of demonstrative concepts in explaining why the epistemic gap between the physical and phenomenal domains does not reflect an ontological gap. But on a closer look it is clear that Mary's central phenomenal concept R (the one that captures what she learns) is *distinct* from her central demonstrative concept E, as witnessed by the non-trivial identity $E = R$, and is not a demonstrative concept in the usual sense. This is not just a terminological point. Those who use these analyses to rebut anti-materialist arguments typically rely on analogies with the epistemic and referential behaviour of ordinary (Kaplan-style) demonstratives. In so far as these analyses rely on such analogies, they mischaracterize Mary's new knowledge. Something similar applies to analyses that liken phenomenal concepts to indexical concepts (e.g. Ismael 1999; Perry 2001). If my analysis is correct, then pure phenomenal concepts (unlike demonstrative phenomenal concepts) are not indexical concepts at all.

2.2. Inverted Mary

We can now complicate the situation by introducing another thought experiment on top of the first one. Consider the case of *Inverted Mary*, who is physically, functionally, and environmentally just like Mary, except that her phenomenal colour vision is red/green inverted. (I will assume for simplicity that Inverted Mary lives in a community of inverted observers.) Like Mary, Inverted Mary learns something new when she sees red things for the first time. But Inverted Mary learns something different from what Mary learns. Where Mary learns that tomatoes cause experiences of (what we call) phenomenal redness, Inverted Mary learns that they cause experiences of (what we call) phenomenal greenness. In the terms given earlier, Mary acquires beliefs $red_C = R$, $red_I = R$, and $E = R$, while Inverted Mary acquire beliefs $red_C = G$, $red_I = G$, and $E = G$ (where G is the obvious analogue of R). So Mary and Inverted Mary acquire beliefs with quite different contents.

This is already enough to draw a strong conclusion about the irreducibility of content. Recall that Mary and Inverted Mary are physical/functional and environmental twins, even after they see red things for the first time. Nevertheless, they have beliefs with different contents. It follows that belief content does not supervene conceptually on physical/functional properties. And it follows from this that intentional properties are not conceptually supervenient on physical/functional properties, in the general case.

This is a non-trivial conclusion. Phenomenal realists often hold that while the phenomenal is conceptually irreducible to the physical and functional, the intentional can be analysed in functional terms. But if what I have said here is correct, then this irreducibility cannot be quarantined in this way. If the phenomenal is conceptually irreducible to the physical and functional, so too is at least one aspect of the intentional: the content of phenomenal beliefs.

At this point, there is a natural temptation to downplay this phenomenon by reducing it to a sort of dependence of belief content on reference that is found in many other cases: in particular in the cases that are central to externalism about the content of belief. Take Putnam's case of Twin Earth. Oscar and Twin Oscar are functional duplicates, but they inhabit different environments: Oscar's contains H_2O as the clear liquid in the oceans and lakes, while Twin Oscar's contains XYZ (which we count not as water but as twin water). As a consequence, Oscar's *water* concept refers to water (H_2O), while Twin Oscar's analogous concept refers to twin water (XYZ). Because of this difference in reference, Oscar and Twin Oscar seem to have different beliefs: Oscar believes that water is wet, while Twin Oscar believes that twin water is wet. Perhaps the case of Mary and Inverted Mary is just like this?[6]

The analogy does not go through, however. Or rather, it goes through only to a limited extent. Oscar and Twin Oscar's *water* concepts here are analogous to Mary and Inverted Mary's relational phenomenal concepts (red_C or red_I), or perhaps to their demonstrative concepts. For example, the relational concepts that they express with their public-language expressions 'red experience' will refer to two different properties, phenomenal redness and phenomenal greenness. Mary and Inverted Mary can deploy these concepts in certain beliefs, such as the beliefs that they express by saying 'Tomatoes cause red experiences', even before they leave their monochromatic rooms for the first time. Because of the distinct referents of their concepts, there is a natural sense (Nida-Rümelin's 'non-phenomenal' sense) in which we can say that Mary believed that tomatoes caused red experiences, while Inverted Mary did not; she believed that tomatoes caused green experiences. Here the analogy goes through straightforwardly.

The pure phenomenal concepts R and G, however, are less analogous to the two *water* concepts than to the chemical concepts H_2O and XYZ. When Oscar learns the true nature of water, he acquires the new belief *water = H_2O*, while Twin Oscar acquires an analogous belief involving *XYZ*. When Mary learns the true nature of red experiences, she acquires a new belief $red_C = R$, while Inverted Mary acquires an analogous belief involving G. That is, Mary and

[6] This sort of treatment of phenomenal belief is suggested by Francescotti (1994).

Inverted Mary's later knowledge involving R and G is fully lucid knowledge of the referents of the concepts in question, analogous to Oscar and Twin Oscar's knowledge involving the chemical concepts H_2O and XYZ.

But here we see the strong disanalogy. Once Oscar acquires the chemical concept H_2O and Twin Oscar acquires XYZ, they will no longer be twins: their functional properties will differ significantly. By contrast, at the corresponding point Mary and Inverted Mary are still twins. Even though Mary has the pure phenomenal concept R and Inverted Mary has G, their functional properties are just the same. So the difference between the concepts R and G across functional twins is something that has no counterpart in the standard Twin Earth story.

All this reflects the fact that in standard externalist cases, the pairs of corresponding concepts may differ in reference, but they have the same or similar *epistemic* or *notional* contents. Oscar and Twin Oscar's *water* concepts have different referents (H_2O *v.* XYZ), but they have the same epistemic contents: both intend to refer to roughly the liquid around them with certain superficial properties. Something like this applies to Mary's and Inverted Mary's relational phenomenal concepts, which have different referents but the same epistemic content (which picks out whatever quality stands in a certain relation), and to their demonstrative concepts (which pick out roughly whatever quality happens to be ostended).

In terms of the two-dimensional framework, where epistemic contents correspond to epistemic intensions: Oscar's and Twin Oscar's *water* concepts have the same epistemic intension but different subjunctive intensions. A similar pattern holds in all the cases characteristic of standard externalism. The pattern also holds for Mary's and Inverted Mary's relational phenomenal concepts, and their demonstrative phenomenal concepts.

But Mary's concept R and Twin Mary's concept G have *different* epistemic contents. In this way they are analogous to Oscar's concept H_2O and Twin Oscar's concept XYZ. But again, the disanalogy is that R and G are possessed by twins, and H_2O and XYZ are not. So the case of Inverted Mary yields an entirely different phenomenon: a case in which *epistemic* content differs between twins.

This can be illustrated by seeing how the concepts in question are used to constrain epistemic possibilities. When Oscar confidently believes that there is water in the glass, he is not thereby in a position to rule out the epistemic possibility that there is XYZ in the glass (unless he has some further knowledge, such as the knowledge that water is H_2O). The same goes for Twin Oscar's corresponding belief. For both of them, it is equally epistemically possible that the glass contains H_2O and that it contains XYZ. Any epistemic possibility compatible with Oscar's belief is also compatible with Twin Oscar's belief: in both cases, these will be roughly those epistemic possibilities in which a sample of the dominant watery stuff in the environment is in the glass.

Epistemic content reflects the way that a belief constrains the space of epistemic possibilities, so Oscar's and Twin Oscar's epistemic contents are the same. Something similar applies to Mary and Inverted Mary, at least where their pairwise relational and demonstrative phenomenal concepts are concerned. When Mary confidently believes (under her relational concept) that her mother is having a red experience, for example, she is not thereby in a position to rule out the epistemic possibility that her mother is having an experience with the quality G. Both Mary's and Inverted Mary's beliefs are compatible with any epistemic possibility in which the subject's mother is having the sort of experience typically caused in the community by paradigmatic red objects. So their beliefs have the same epistemic contents.

But Mary's and Inverted Mary's pure phenomenal concepts do not work like this. Mary's concept R and Inverted Mary's concept G differ not just in their referents but also in their epistemic contents. When Mary leaves the monochromatic room and acquires the confident belief (under her pure phenomenal concept) that tomatoes cause red experiences, she is thereby in a position to rule out the epistemic possibility that tomatoes cause experiences with quality G. The only epistemic possibilities compatible with her belief are those in which tomatoes cause R experiences. For Inverted Mary, things are reversed: the only epistemic possibilities compatible with her belief are those in which tomatoes cause G experiences. So their epistemic contents are quite different.

Again, the epistemic situation with R and G is analogous to the epistemic situation with the concepts H_2O and XYZ. When Oscar believes (under a fully lucid chemical concept) that the glass contains H_2O, he is thereby in a position to rule out all epistemic possibilities in which the glass contains XYZ. For Twin Oscar, things are reversed. This is to say that H_2O and XYZ have different epistemic contents. The same goes for R and G.

So in the case of the pure phenomenal concepts, uniquely, we have a situation in which two concepts differ in their epistemic content despite the subjects being physically identical. So phenomenal concepts seem to give a case in which even epistemic content is not conceptually supervenient on the physical.

Using the two-dimensional framework: the epistemic intension of a concept reflects the way it applies to epistemic possibilities. We saw above that the epistemic intensions of Oscar's and Twin Oscar's *water* concepts are the same, as are the epistemic intensions of Mary's and Inverted Mary's relational and demonstrative phenomenal concepts. But R and G differ in the way they apply to epistemic possibilities, and their epistemic intensions differ accordingly: the epistemic intension of R picks out phenomenal redness in all worlds, and the epistemic intension of *G* picks out phenomenal greenness in all worlds. When Mary thinks *I am having an R experience now*, the epistemic intension of her thought is true at all and only those worlds in which the being at the centre is having an R experience.

Something very unusual is going on here. In standard externalism, and in standard cases of so-called 'direct reference', a referent plays a role in constituting the subjunctive content (subjunctive intension) of concepts and beliefs, while leaving the epistemic content (epistemic intension) unaffected. In the pure phenomenal case, by contrast, the quality of the experiences plays a role in constituting the *epistemic* content of the concept and of the corresponding belief. One might say very loosely that in this case, the referent of the concept is somehow present inside the concept's sense, in a way much stronger than in the usual cases of 'direct reference'.

We might say that the pure phenomenal concept is *epistemically rigid*: its epistemic content picks out the same referent in every possible world (considered as actual). By contrast, ordinary rigid concepts are merely *subjunctively rigid*, with a subjunctive content that picks out the same referent in every possible world (considered as counterfactual). Epistemically rigid concepts will typically be subjunctively rigid, but most subjunctively rigid concepts are not epistemically rigid. Pure phenomenal concepts are both epistemically and subjunctively rigid.[7]

One might see here some justification for Russell's claim that we have a special capacity for direct reference to our experiences.[8] Contemporary direct-reference theorists hold that Russell's view was too restrictive, and that we can make direct reference to a much broader class of entities. But the cases they invoke are 'direct' only in the weak sense outlined above: the subjunctive content depends on the referent, but the epistemic content of the

---

[7] Further: epistemically rigid concepts will usually be subjunctively rigid *de jure*, which entails that they are what Martine Nida-Rümelin calls (in a forthcoming article) *super-rigid*: they pick out the same referent relative to all pairs of scenarios considered as actual and worlds considered as counterfactual. When represented by a two-dimensional matrix, super-rigid concepts have the same entry at each point of the matrix.

[8] Russell also held that direct reference is possible to universals, and perhaps to the self. It is arguable that for at least some universals (in the domains of mathematics or of causation, perhaps), one can form an epistemically rigid concept whose epistemic content picks out instances of that universal in all worlds. So there is at least a limited analogy here, though it seems unlikely that in these cases the content of such a (token) concept is directly constituted by an underlying instance of the universal, in the manner suggested below. There is no analogous phenomenon with the self. There may, however, be a different sense in which we can make 'direct reference' to the self, to the current time, and to particular experiences: this is the sort of direct indexical reference that grounds the need to build these entities into the centre of a centred world fully to characterize epistemic possibilities. We can refer to these 'directly' (in a certain sense) under indexical concepts; but we cannot form concepts whose epistemic contents reflect the referents in question. This suggests that direct reference to particulars and direct reference to properties are quite different phenomena.

concept does not. In the phenomenal case, the epistemic content itself seems to be constituted by the referent. It is not hard to imagine that some such epistemic requirement on direct reference is what Russell had in mind.

3.   The Constitution of Phenomenal Beliefs

3.1.   Direct Phenomenal Concepts and Beliefs

We have seen that the content of phenomenal concepts and phenomenal beliefs does not supervene conceptually on physical properties. Does this content supervene conceptually on some broader class of properties, and if so, on which? I will offer an analysis of how the content of pure phenomenal concepts is constituted. I will not give a knockdown argument for this analysis by decisively refuting all alternatives, but I will offer it as perhaps the most natural and elegant account of the phenomena, and as an account that can in turn do further explanatory work.

To start with, it is natural to hold that the content of phenomenal concepts and beliefs supervenes conceptually on the combination of physical and phenomenal properties. Mary and Inverted Mary are physical twins, but they are phenomenally distinct, and this phenomenal distinctness (Mary experiences phenomenal redness, Inverted Mary experiences phenomenal greenness) precisely mirrors their intentional distinctness (Mary believes that tomatoes cause R experiences, Inverted Mary believes that tomatoes cause G experiences). It is very plausible to suppose that their intentional distinctness holds in virtue of their phenomenal distinctness.

The alternative is that the intentional content of the phenomenal concept is conceptually independent of both physical and phenomenal properties. If that is so, it should be conceivable that two subjects have the same physical and phenomenal properties, while having phenomenal beliefs that differ in content. Such a case might involve Mary and Mary' as physical and phenomenal twins, who are both experiencing phenomenal redness for the first time (while being phenomenally identical in all other respects), with Mary acquiring the belief that tomatoes cause R experiences while Mary' acquires the belief that tomatoes cause G experiences. It is not at all clear that such a case is conceivable.

Another possibility is that the intentional content of Mary's phenomenal concept in question might be determined by phenomenal states *other* than the phenomenal redness that Mary is visually experiencing. For example, maybe Mary's belief content is determined by a faint phenomenal 'idea' that goes along with her phenomenal 'impression', where the former is not conceptually determined by the latter, and neither is conceptually determined by the physical. In that case, it should once again be conceivable that twins Mary and Mary' both visually experience phenomenal redness upon leaving the room, with Mary acquiring the belief that tomatoes cause R experiences while Mary' acquires the belief that tomatoes cause G experiences, this time because of a difference in their associated phenomenal ideas. But again, it is far from clear that this is conceivable.

There is a very strong intuition that the content of Mary's phenomenal concept and phenomenal belief is *determined* by the phenomenal character of her visual experience, in that it will vary directly as a function of that character in cases where that character varies while physical and other phenomenal properties are held fixed, and that it will not vary independently of that character in such cases. I will adopt this claim as a plausible working hypothesis.

In particular, I will take it that in cases such as Mary's, the content of a phenomenal concept and a corresponding phenomenal belief, is partly *constituted* by an underlying phenomenal quality, in that the content will mirror the quality (picking out instances of the quality in all epistemic possibilities), and in that across a wide range of nearby conceptually possible cases in which the underlying quality is varied while background properties are held constant, the content will co-vary to mirror the quality. Let us call this sort of phenomenal concept a *direct phenomenal concept.*

Not all experiences are accompanied by corresponding direct phenomenal concepts. Many of our experiences appear to pass without our forming any beliefs about them, and without the sort of concept formation that occurs in the Mary case. The clearest cases of direct phenomenal concepts arise when a subject attends to the quality of an experience, and forms a concept wholly based on the attention to the quality, 'taking up' the quality into the concept. This sort of concept formation can occur with visual experiences, as in the Mary case, but it can equally occur with all sorts of other experiences: auditory and other perceptual experiences, bodily sensations, emotional experiences, and so on. In each case we can imagine the analogue of Mary having such an experience for the first time, attending to it, and coming to have a concept of what it is like to have it. There is no reason to suppose that this sort of concept formation is restricted to entirely novel experiences. I can experience a particular shade of phenomenal redness for the hundredth time, attend to it, and form a concept of what it is like to have that experience, a concept whose content is based entirely on the character of the experience.

Direct phenomenal concepts can be deployed in a wide variety of beliefs, and other propositional attitudes. When Mary attends to her phenomenally red experience and forms her direct phenomenal concept *R*, she is thereby in a position to believe that tomatoes cause R experiences, to believe that others have R experiences, to believe that she previously had no R experiences, to desire more R experiences, and so on.

Perhaps the most crucial sort of deployment of a direct phenomenal concept occurs when a subject predicates the concept of the very experience responsible for constituting its content. Mary has a phenomenally red experience, attends to it, and forms the direct phenomenal concept R, and forms the belief *this experience is R*, demonstrating the phenomenally red experience in question. We can call this special sort of belief a *direct phenomenal belief.*

We can also cast this idea within an experience-free ontology of qualities. In this framework, we can say that a direct phenomenal concept is formed by attending to a quality and taking up that quality into a concept whose content mirrors the quality, picking out instances of the quality in all epistemic possibilities. A direct phenomenal belief is formed when the referent of this direct phenomenal concept is identified with the referent of a corresponding demonstrative phenomenal concept, e.g. when Mary forms the belief that *this quality is R*. The general form of a direct phenomenal belief in this framework is $E = R$, where E is a demonstrative phenomenal concept and R is the corresponding direct phenomenal concept.

3.2.   Some Notes on Direct Phenomenal Beliefs

1. For a direct phenomenal belief, it is required that the demonstrative and direct concepts involved be appropriately 'aligned'. Say that Mary experiences phenomenal redness in both the left and right halves of her visual field, forms a direct phenomenal concept R based on her attention to the left half, forms a demonstrative concept of phenomenal redness based on her attention to the right half, and identifies the two by a belief of the form $E = R$. Then this is not a direct phenomenal belief, even though the same quality (phenomenal redness) is referred to on both sides, since the concepts are grounded in different instances of that quality. The belief has the right sort of content, but it does not have the right sort of constitution.

To characterize the required alignment more carefully we can note that all direct phenomenal concepts, like all demonstrative phenomenal concepts, are based in acts of attention to instances of phenomenal qualities. A direct phenomenal concept such as R does not characterize a quality *as an object* of attention, but it nevertheless requires attention to a quality for its formation. The same act of attention can also be used to form a demonstrative phenomenal concept E. A direct phenomenal belief (in the quality-based framework) will be a belief of the form $E = R$ where the demonstrative phenomenal concept E and the direct phenomenal concept R are *aligned*: that is, where they are based in the same act of attention.

One can simplify the language by regarding the act of attention as a demonstration. We can then say that both demonstrative and direct phenomenal concepts are based in demonstrations, and that a direct phenomenal belief is a belief of the form $E = R$ where the two concepts are based in the same demonstration.[9]

2. As with all acts of demonstration and attention, phenomenal demonstration and attention involves a cognitive element. Reference to a phenomenal quality is determined in part by cognitive elements of a demonstration. These cognitive elements will also enter into determining the content of a corresponding direct phenomenal concept.

Consider two individuals with identical visual experiences. These individuals might engage in different acts of demonstration—e.g. one might demonstrate a red quality experienced in the right half of the visual field, and the other a green quality experienced in the left half of the visual field—and thus form distinct direct phenomenal concepts. Or they might attend to the same location in the visual field, but demonstrate distinct qualities associated with that location: e.g. one might demonstrate a highly specific shade of phenomenal redness, and the other a less specific shade, again resulting in distinct direct phenomenal concepts. These differences will be due to differences in the cognitive backgrounds of the demonstrations in the two individuals. I will be neutral here about whether such cognitive differences are themselves constituted by underlying functioning, aspects of cognitive phenomenology, or both.

One can imagine varying the visual experiences and the cognitive background here independently. Varying visual experiences might yield a range of cases in which direct phenomenal concepts of phenomenal redness, greenness, and other hues are formed. Varying the cognitive background might yield a range of cases in which direct phenomenal concepts of different degrees of specificity (for example) are formed.

Along with this cognitive element comes the possibility of failed demonstration, if the cognitive element and the targeted experiential elements mismatch sufficiently. Take Nancy, who attends to a patch of phenomenal colour, acting cognitively as if to demonstrate a highly specific phenomenal shade. Nancy has not attended sufficiently closely to notice that the patch has a non-uniform phenomenal colour: let us say it is a veridical experience of a square coloured with different shades of red on its left and right side.[10]

[9] Gertler (2001) has independently developed a related account of phenomenal introspection, according to which a phenomenal state is introspected when it is 'embedded' in another state, and when the second state constitutes demonstrative attention to the relevant content by virtue of this embedding. On my account, things are the other way around: any 'embedding' holds in virtue of demonstrative attention, rather than the reverse.

[10] This sort of case was suggested to me by Delia Graff and Mark Johnston.

In such a case, the demonstrative phenomenal concept will presumably refer to no quality at all: given its cognitive structure, it could refer only to a specific quality, but it would break symmetry for it to refer to either instantiated quality, and presumably uninstantiated qualities cannot be demonstrated.

What of any associated direct phenomenal concept? It is not out of the question that the subject forms *some* substantive concept where a direct phenomenal concept would normally be formed; perhaps a concept of an intermediate uninstantiated shade of phenomenal red, at least if the instantiated shades are not too different. Like a direct phenomenal concept, this concept will have a content that depends constitutively on associated qualities of experience (Inverted Nancy might form a concept of an intermediate phenomenal green), but it will not truly be a direct phenomenal concept, since its content will not directly mirror an underlying quality.

This possibility of cognitive mismatch affects the path from demonstration to a demonstrated phenomenal quality, but given that a phenomenal quality is truly demonstrated, it does not seem to affect the path from demonstrated phenomenal quality to a direct phenomenal concept. That is, as long as a phenomenal quality is demonstrated, and the cognitive act typical of forming a direct phenomenal concept based on such a demonstration is present, a direct phenomenal concept will be formed.

We might call a concept that shares the cognitive structure of a direct phenomenal concept a *quasi-direct* phenomenal concept; and we can call a belief with the same cognitive structure as a direct phenomenal belief a *quasi-direct* phenomenal belief. Like a direct phenomenal concept, a quasi-direct phenomenal concept arises from an act of (intended) demonstration, along with a characteristic sort of cognitive act. Unlike a direct phenomenal concept, a quasi-direct phenomenal concept is not required to have a content that is constituted by an underlying quality. Nancy's concept above is a quasi-direct phenomenal concept but not a direct phenomenal concept, for example.

We can call a quasi-direct phenomenal concept that is not a direct phenomenal concept a *pseudo-direct* phenomenal concept, and we can define a pseudo-direct phenomenal belief similarly. If the suggestion above is correct, then the only pseudo-direct phenomenal concepts are like Nancy's, in involving an unsuccessful demonstration. As long as a quasi-direct phenomenal concept is grounded in a successful demonstration, it will be a direct phenomenal concept. I will return to this claim later.

3. All direct phenomenal concepts are pure phenomenal concepts, but not all pure phenomenal concepts are direct phenomenal concepts. To see this, note that Mary may well retain some knowledge of what it is like to see tomatoes even after she goes back into her black-and-white room, or while she shuts her eyes, or while she looks at green grass. She still has a concept of

phenomenal redness than can be deployed in various beliefs, with the sort of epistemic relations to relational and demonstrative phenomenal concepts that is characteristic of pure phenomenal concepts. Inverted Mary (still Mary's physical twin) has a corresponding concept deployed in corresponding beliefs that *differ* in content from Mary's. As before, their corresponding beliefs *differ* in epistemic content, including and excluding different classes of epistemic possibilities. Mary's concept is still a concept of phenomenal redness as the quality it is, based on a lucid understanding of that quality, rather than on a mere relational or demonstrative identification. So as before, it is a pure phenomenal concept. But it is not a direct phenomenal concept, since there is no corresponding experience (or instantiated quality) that is being attended to or taken up into the concept. We can call this sort of concept a *standing* phenomenal concept, since it may persist in a way that direct phenomenal concepts do not.

There are some differences in character between direct and standing phenomenal concepts. Direct phenomenal concepts may be very fine-grained, picking out a very specific phenomenal quality (a highly specific shade of phenomenal redness, for example). Standing phenomenal concepts are usually more coarse-grained, picking out less specific qualities. One can note this phenomenologically from the difficulty of 'holding' in mind specific qualities as opposed to coarser categories when relevant visual experiences are not present; and this is also brought out by empirical results showing the difficulty of reidentifying specific qualities over time.[11] It usually seems possible for a direct phenomenal concept to yield a corresponding standing phenomenal concept as a 'successor' concept once the experience in question disappears, at the cost of some degree of coarse-graining.

As with direct phenomenal concepts, the content of standing phenomenal concepts does not conceptually supervene on the physical (witness Mary and Inverted Mary, back in their rooms). A question arises as to what determines their content. I will not try to analyse that matter here, but I think it is plausible that their content is determined by some combination of (1) nonsensory phenomenal states of a cognitive sort, which bear a relevant relation to the original phenomenal quality in question—e.g. a faint Humean phenomenal 'idea' that is relevantly related to the original 'impression'; (2) dispositions to have such states; and (3) dispositions to recognize instances of the phenomenal quality in question. It is not implausible that Mary and Inverted Mary (back in their rooms) still differ in some or all of these respects, and that these respects are constitutively responsible for the difference in the content of their concepts.

---

[11] See Raffman 1995 for a discussion of these results in an argument for an anti-representationalist 'presentational' analysis of phenomenal concepts that is very much compatible with the analysis here.

One might be tempted to use the existence of standing phenomenal concepts to argue against the earlier analysis of direct phenomenal concepts (that is, of concepts akin to those Mary acquires on first experiencing phenomenal redness) as constituted by the quality of the relevant instantiated experience. Why not assimilate them to standing phenomenal concepts instead, giving a unified account of the two? In response, note first that it remains difficult to conceive of the content of direct phenomenal concepts varying independently of the phenomenal quality in question, whereas it does not seem so difficult to conceive of the content of standing phenomenal concepts varying independently. And second, note that the difference in specificity between direct and standing phenomenal concepts gives some reason to believe that they are constituted in different ways.

The lifetime of a direct phenomenal concept is limited to the lifetime of the experience (or the instantiated quality) that constitutes it. (In some cases a specific phenomenal concept might persist for a few moments due to the persistence of a vivid iconic memory, but even this will soon disappear.) Some might worry that this lack of persistence suggests that it is not a concept at all, since concepthood requires persistence. This seems misguided, however: it is surely possible for a concept to be formed moments before a subject dies. The concepts in question are still predicable of any number of entities, during their limited lifetimes, and these predications can be true or false (e.g. Mary may falsely believe that her sister is currently experiencing R). This sort of predicability, with assessibility for truth or falsehood, seems sufficient for concepthood; at least it is sufficient for the uses of concepthood that will be required here.

4. As with pure phenomenal concepts generally, we do not have public language expressions that distinctively express the content of direct phenomenal concepts. Public reference to phenomenal qualities is always fixed relationally, it seems: by virtue of a relation to certain external stimuli, or certain sorts of behaviour, or certain demonstrations. (Recall Ryle's remark that there are no 'neat' sensation words.) Of course Mary can express a pure phenomenal concept by introducing her own term, such as 'R', or by using an old term, such as 'red', with this stipulated meaning. But this use will not be public, at least in the limited sense that there is no method by which we can ensure that other members of the community will use the term with the same epistemic content. One can at best ensure that they pick out the same quality by picking it out under a different epistemic content (e.g. as the quality Mary is having at a certain time), or by referring through semantic deference (as the quality that Mary picks out with 'R'). In this sense it seems that any resulting language will be 'private': it can be used with full competence by just one subject, and others can use it only deferentially. (An exception may arguably be made for terms expressing *structural* pure phenomenal concepts—e.g.

phenomenal similarity and difference and perhaps phenomenal spatial rela-tions—which arguably do not rely on relational reference-fixing.)

Of course the view I have set out here is just the sort of view that Wittgenstein directed his 'private language' argument against. The nature of the private language argument is contested, so in response I can say only that I have seen no reconstruction of it that provides a strong case against the view I have laid out. Some versions of the argument seem to fall prey to the mistake just outlined, that of requiring a strong sort of 'repeatability' for concept possession (and an exceptionally strong sort at that, requiring the recognizability of correct repeated application). A certain sort of repeatability is required for concept possession, but it is merely the 'hypothetical repeat-ability' involved in *present* predicability of the concept to actual and hypo-thetical cases, with associated truth-conditions. Another reconstruction of the argument, that of Kripke (1981), provides no distinctive traction against my analysis of direct phenomenal concepts: any force that it has applies to concepts quite generally.

(One might even argue that Kripke's argument provides *less* traction in the case of direct phenomenal concepts, as this is precisely a case in which we can see how a determinate application-condition can be constituted by an under-lying phenomenal quality. Kripke's remarks about associated phenomenal qualities (ibid. 41–51)—e.g. a certain sort of 'headache'—being irrelevant to the content of concepts such as addition apply much less strongly where *phenomenal* concepts are concerned. Of course there is more to say here, but in any case it is a curiosity of Kripke's reconstruction of the argument that it applies least obviously to the phenomena at which Wittgenstein's argument is often taken to be aimed.)

4. The Epistemology of Phenomenal Belief

4.1. Incorrigibility

A traditional thesis in the epistemology of mind is that first-person beliefs about phenomenal states are *incorrigible*, or *infallible* (I use these terms equivalently), in that they cannot be false. In recent years such a thesis has been widely rejected. This rejection stems from both general philosophical reasoning (e.g. the suggestion that if beliefs and experiences are distinct existences, there can be no necessary connection between them) and from apparent counter-examples (e.g. a case where someone, expecting to be burnt, momentarily misclassifies a cold sensation as hot). In this light, it is interest-ing to note that the framework outlined so far supports an incorrigibility thesis, albeit a very limited one.

Incorrigibility Thesis: A direct phenomenal belief cannot be false.

The truth of this thesis is an immediate consequence of the definition of direct phenomenal belief. A direct phenomenal concept by its nature picks out instances of an underlying demonstrated phenomenal quality, and a direct phenomenal belief identifies the referent of that concept with the very demonstrated quality (or predicates the concept of the very experience that instantiated the quality), so its truth is guaranteed.

If we combine this thesis (which is more or less true by definition) with the substantive thesis that there are direct phenomenal beliefs (which is argued earlier), then we have a substantive incorrigibility thesis, one that applies to a significant range of actual beliefs.[12]

The thesis nevertheless has a number of significant limitations. The first is that most phenomenal beliefs are not direct phenomenal beliefs, so most phenomenal beliefs are still corrigible. The most common sort of phenomenal belief arguably involves the application of a *pre-existing* phenomenal concept (either a relational phenomenal concept or a standing pure phenomenal concept) to a new situation, as with the beliefs typically expressed by claims such as 'I am having a red experience' or 'I am in pain'. These are not direct phenomenal beliefs, and are almost certainly corrigible.

There are also cases in which a direct phenomenal concept is applied to a quality (or an experience) other than the one that constituted it, as when one forms a direct phenomenal concept R based on a quality instantiated in the left half of one's visual field, and applies it to a quality instantiated in the right half. These are also not direct phenomenal beliefs, and are again almost certainly corrigible.

(The second sort of case brings out a further limitation in the incorrigibility thesis: it does not yield incorrigibility in virtue of content. If the left and right qualities in the case above are in fact the same, then the resulting non-direct phenomenal belief will arguably have the same content as the corresponding direct phenomenal belief, but the incorrigibility thesis will not apply to it. The domain of the incorrigibility thesis is constrained not just by content, but also by underlying constitution.)

It is plausible that all the standard counter-examples to incorrigibility theses fall into classes such as these, particularly the first. All the standard

---

[12] Pollock (1986: 32–3) entertains a version of this sort of view as a way of supporting incorrigibility, discussing a 'Containment Thesis' according to which experiences are constituents of beliefs about experiences. He rejects the view on the grounds that (1) it does not support incorrigibility of negative beliefs about experiences (e.g. the belief that one is not having a given experience), which he holds to be required for incorrigibility in general, and (2) that having an experience does not suffice to have the relevant belief, so having the belief also requires thinking about the experience, which renders the incorrigibility thesis trivial. I discuss both these points below.

counter-examples appear to involve the application of pre-existing phenomenal concepts (*pain, hot, red experience*). So none of the standard counter-
examples apply to the incorrigibility thesis articulated here.

There is a natural temptation to find further counter-examples to the
incorrigibility thesis. For example, one might consider a case in which a
subject's experience changes very rapidly, and argue that the corresponding
direct phenomenal concept must lag behind. In response to these attempted
counter-examples, the most obvious reply is that these cannot truly
be counter-examples, since the truth of the incorrigibility thesis is guaranteed
by the definition of direct phenomenal belief. If the cases work as described,
they do not involve direct phenomenal beliefs: they either involve a concept
that is not a direct phenomenal concept, or they involve a direct phenomenal
concept predicated of a quality other than the one that constitutes it. At best,
they involve what I earlier called pseudo-direct phenomenal beliefs: beliefs
that share the cognitive structure of direct phenomenal beliefs (and thus
are quasi-direct phenomenal beliefs) but that are not direct phenomenal
beliefs.

One need not let matters rest there, however. I think that these counter-
examples can usually be analysed away on their own terms, so that the
purported pseudo-direct phenomenal beliefs in question can be seen as direct
phenomenal beliefs, and as correct. In the case of a rapidly changing experience, one can plausibly hold that the content of a direct phenomenal concept
co-varies immediately with the underlying quality, so that there is no moment
at which the belief is false. This is just what we would expect, given the
constitutive relation suggested earlier. We might picture this schematically
by suggesting that the basis for a direct phenomenal concept contains within
it a 'slot' for an instantiated quality, such that the quality that fills the slot
constitutes the content. In a case where experience changes rapidly, the filler
of the slot changes rapidly, and so does the content.

Something similar goes for many other examples involving quasi-direct
phenomenal beliefs. Take a case where a subject attends to two different visual
qualities (demonstrating them as E_1 and E_2), and mistakenly accepts $E_1 = E_2$.
In this case, someone might suggest that if the subject forms specific quasi-
direct phenomenal concepts R_1 and R_2 based on the two acts of attention,
these must have the same content, leading to false quasi-direct phenomenal
beliefs (and thus to pseudo-direct phenomenal beliefs). But on my account,
this case is better classified as one in which R_1 and R_2 are direct phenomenal
concepts with different contents, yielding two correct direct phenomenal beliefs $E_1 = R_1$ and $E_2 = R_2$. The false beliefs here are of the form
$E_1 = R_2$, $E_2 = R_1$, and $R_1 = R_2$. The last of these illustrates the important
point that identities involving two direct phenomenal concepts, like identities
involving two pure phenomenal concepts more generally, are not incorrigible.

Other cases of misclassification can be treated similarly. In the case in which a subject expecting to be burnt misclassifies a cold sensation as hot, someone might suggest that any quasi-direct phenomenal concept will be a concept of phenomenal hotness, not coldness. But one can plausibly hold that if a quasi-direct phenomenal concept is formed, it will be a concept of phenomenal coldness and will yield a correct direct phenomenal belief. The subject's mistake involves misclassifying the experience under standing phenomenal concepts, and perhaps a mistaken identity involving a direct and a standing phenomenal concept.

It is arguable that most cases involving quasi-direct phenomenal beliefs can be treated this way. The only clear exceptions are cases such as Nancy's, in which no phenomenal quality is demonstrated and so no substantive direct phenomenal concept is formed. It remains plausible that as long as a quality is demonstrated, the cognitive act in question will yield a direct phenomenal concept with the right content, and a true direct phenomenal belief. If that is correct, one can then accept a broader incorrigibility thesis applying to any quasi-direct phenomenal belief that is based in a successful demonstration of a phenomenal quality. I will not try to establish this thesis conclusively, since I will not need it, and since the incorrigibility thesis for direct phenomenal beliefs is unthreatened either way. But it is interesting to see that it can be defended.

One might suggest that the incorrigibility thesis articulated here (in either the narrower or the broader version) captures the *plausible core* of traditional incorrigibility theses. A number of philosophers have had the sense that there is something correct about the incorrigibility theses, which is not touched by the counter-examples. This is reflected, for example, in Chisholm's distinction between 'comparative' and 'non-comparative' uses of 'appears' talk, where only the non-comparative uses are held to be incorrigible. I think that this is not quite the right distinction: even non-comparative uses can be corrigible, when they correspond to uses of pure phenomenal concepts outside direct phenomenal beliefs. But perhaps a thesis restricted to direct phenomenal beliefs might play this role.

Certainly the analysis of direct phenomenal beliefs shows why the most common general philosophical argument against incorrigibility does not apply across the board. In the case of direct phenomenal beliefs, beliefs and experiences are *not* entirely distinct existences. It is precisely because of the constitutive connection between experiential quality and belief that the two can be necessarily connected.

Another limitation: sometimes incorrigibility theses are articulated in a 'reverse' or bidirectional form, holding that all phenomenal states are incorrigibly known, or at least incorrigibly knowable. Such a thesis is not supported by the current discussion. Most phenomenal states are not attended to, and are not taken up into direct phenomenal concepts, so they are not the subjects of direct phenomenal beliefs. And for all I have said, it may be that some phenomenal states, such as fleeting or background phenomenal states, *cannot* be taken up into a direct phenomenal concept, perhaps because they cannot be subject to the right sort of attention. If so, they are not even incorrigibly knowable, let alone incorrigibly known.

Incorrigibility theses are also sometimes articulated in a 'negative' form, requiring that a subject cannot be mistaken in their belief that they are *not* having a given sort of experience. No direct phenomenal belief is a negative phenomenal belief, so the current framework does not support this thesis, and I think the thesis is false in general.

A final limitation: although direct phenomenal beliefs are incorrigible, subjects are not incorrigible about whether they are having a direct phenomenal belief. For example, if I am not thinking clearly, I might misclassify a belief involving a standing phenomenal concept as a direct phenomenal belief. And in the Nancy case above, if Nancy is philosophically sophisticated she might well think that she is having a direct phenomenal belief, although she is not.

One could argue that this lack of higher-order incorrigibility prevents the first-order incorrigibility thesis from doing significant epistemological work. The matter is delicate: higher-order incorrigibility is probably too strong a requirement for an epistemologically useful incorrigibility thesis. But on the other side, *some* sort of further condition is required for a useful thesis. For example, any member of the class of true mathematical beliefs is incorrigible (since it is necessarily true), but this is of little epistemic use to a subject who cannot antecedently distinguish true and false mathematical beliefs. A natural suggestion is that some sort of higher-order accessibility is required.

Intermediate accessibility requirements might include these: for the incorrigibility of a direct phenomenal belief to be epistemologically significant, a subject must know that it is a direct phenomenal belief, or at least be justified in so believing; or a subject must be capable of so knowing on reflection; or direct phenomenal beliefs must be cognitively or phenomenologically distinctive as a class relative to non-direct phenomenal beliefs.

I am sympathetic with the sufficiency of a requirement appealing to cognitive or phenomenological distinctiveness, if properly articulated. Whether such a requirement holds of direct phenomenal beliefs turns on questions about quasi-direct and pseudo-direct phenomenal beliefs. If there are many pseudo-direct phenomenal beliefs, and if there is nothing cognitively or phenomenologically distinctive about direct phenomenal beliefs by comparison, then direct phenomenal beliefs will simply be distinguished as quasi-direct phenomenal beliefs with the right sort of content, and the incorrigibility claim will be relatively trivial. On the other hand, if pseudo-direct phenomenal beliefs are rare, or if direct phenomenal beliefs are a cognitively or phenomenologically distinctive subclass, then it is more likely that incorrigibility will be non-trivial and carry epistemological significance.

If pseudo-direct phenomenal beliefs are restricted to cases in which no phenomenal quality is demonstrated, such as the case of Nancy (as I have suggested), then the incorrigibility thesis will hold of a class of beliefs that can be distinctively and independently characterized in cognitive and phenomenological terms: the class of quasi-direct phenomenal beliefs which are based in a successful demonstration. This would render the incorrigibility claim entirely non-trivial, and it would make it more likely that it could do epistemological work. But I will not try to settle this matter decisively here, and I will not put the incorrigibility thesis to any epistemological work in what follows.

It might be thought that the incorrigibility thesis suffers from another problem: that direct phenomenal beliefs are incorrigible because they are *trivial.* After all, beliefs such as *I am here* or *this is this* are (almost) incorrigible, but only because they are (almost) trivial. ('Almost' is present because of the arguable non-triviality of my existence and spatial locatedness in one case, and because of the possibility of reference failure for the demonstrative in the other.)

The analogy fails, however. The trivial beliefs in question are (almost) cognitively insignificant: they are (almost) a priori, containing (almost) no cognitively significant knowledge about the world. This is reflected in the fact that they hardly constrain the class of a priori epistemic possibilities: they are true of (almost) all such possibilities, considered as hypotheses about the actual world. (Two-dimensionally: these beliefs have an epistemic intension that is (almost) conceptually necessary.) A direct phenomenal belief, by contrast, is cognitively significant: it heavily constrains the class of a priori epistemic possibilities, and is false in most of them (considered as actual). For example, Mary's direct phenomenal belief, on leaving her room, is false of all worlds (considered as actual) in which the subject is not experiencing phenomenal redness. (Two-dimensionally: the epistemic intension of a direct phenomenal belief is conceptually contingent.) So direct phenomenal beliefs, unlike the beliefs above, are entirely non-trivial.

So: the incorrigibility thesis articulated here has a number of limitations, but it nevertheless applies to a significant class of non-trivial phenomenal beliefs.

4.2. *Acquaintance and Justification*

At this point is natural to ask: if we can form this special class of incorrigible, distinctively constituted beliefs where phenomenal states and properties are concerned, why cannot we do so where other states and properties are concerned? Why cannot we form direct height concepts, for example, whose epistemic content is directly constituted by our height properties, and which can be deployed in incorrigible direct height beliefs? Or similarly for direct chemical beliefs, direct age beliefs, direct colour beliefs, and so on?

At one level, the answer is that we simply cannot. If one tries to form a direct height concept—one whose content depends constitutively on an instantiated height—the best one can do is form a relational height concept (*my height, the height of my house*) or a demonstrative height concept. But these are not pure height concepts at all. They are analogous only to red_C or E, in that their subjunctive content may depend on the property in question but their epistemic content does not.

It is arguable whether pure height concepts exist at all: that is, whether there is any concept whose epistemic content picks out a certain height (say, 2 metres) in any epistemic possibility. But even if there are pure height concepts, they are not direct height concepts. Perhaps one can independently form a pure height concept of a given height (2 metres), which might coincide with an instantiated height, but it will not depend constitutively on an instantiated height. The best one can do is attend to an object, have an experience or judgement concerning its height, and use this experience or judgement as the epistemic content of a 'pure' height concept. But here the instantiated height property is not constitutively relevant to the concept's content, but only causally relevant: it is the height experience or judgement that is constitutively relevant, and the experience or judgement is only causally dependent on the height. In no case does the epistemic content of a height concept depend constitutively on a demonstrated height property, or on any instantiated height property at all.

Proponents of certain direct realist views may hold that it is possible to form a direct concept of a height property (or other perceivable external properties), by demonstrating it and taking it up into a concept in a manner analogous to the manner suggested for phenomenal properties. I think that this is implausible. In a case where an object is 2 metres tall but appears to be 1 metre tall, any 'pure' height concept formed as a result will be a concept of 1 metre, not of 2 metres. There may be a demonstrative concept of 2 metres, but that is not enough. More generally, considering a range of cases in which height and experience are varied independently, we can see that any contribution of the height to a pure concept is 'screened off' by the contribution of the experience. This suggests that if anything is playing a constitutive role in the concept's content, it is the experience and not the external property.[13]

---

[13] There may be further moves available to the direct realist. For example, a direct realist might hold that the constitutive role of external properties is restricted to cases of veridical

The same goes for chemical concepts, age concepts, and external colour concepts. Although we can form many such concepts, in no case is it possible to form a direct concept: that is, a concept whose epistemic content depends constitutively on a demonstrated property. It seems that only phenomenal properties can support direct concepts.

This conclusion is apparently revealed by an examination of cases; but it would be preferable not to leave it as a brute conclusion. In particular, it is natural to suggest that the conclusion holds because we bear a special relation to the phenomenal properties instantiated in our experience: a relation that we do not bear to the other instantiated properties in question, and a relation that is required in order to form a direct concept of a property in the manner described. This relation would seem to be a peculiarly intimate one, made possible by the fact that experiences lie at the heart of the mind rather than standing at a distance from it; and it seems to be a relation that carries the potential for conceptual and epistemic consequences. We might call this relation *acquaintance*.

As things stand, acquaintance has been characterized only as that relation between subjects and properties that makes possible the formation of direct phenomenal concepts; so it is not yet doing much explanatory work. But having inferred the relation of acquaintance, we can put it to work. As characterized, acquaintance is a relation that makes possible the formation of pure phenomenal concepts, and we have seen that pure phenomenal concepts embody a certain sort of lucid understanding of phenomenal properties. So acquaintance is a relation that makes this sort of lucid understanding possible. As such, it is natural to suppose that the relation can also do work in the epistemic domain. If so, the result will be an attractive picture in which the distinctive conceptual character and the distinctive epistemic character of the phenomenal domain have a common source.

It is independently plausible to hold that phenomenal properties and beliefs have a distinctive epistemic character. Many have held that phenomenal properties can (at least sometimes) be known with a distinctive sort of justification, or even with certainty; and many have held that phenomenal beliefs have a special epistemic status. Even those who explicitly deny this will

perception, and that non-veridical perception must be treated differently. I think that this sort of restriction threatens to trivialize the constitution thesis, as any causal connection might be seen as a 'constitutive' connection by a relevantly similar restriction. (If A causes B which necessitates C, then A is contingently connected to C; but if we restrict attention to cases where A causes B, then A necessitates C relative to this restriction.) And the case remains formally disanalogous to the case of direct phenomenal concepts, in which there is no factor distinct from the quality that even looks as if it screens off the contribution of the quality to the concept. But there is undoubtedly more to say here. In what follows I will assume that the direct realist view is incorrect, but direct realists are free to hold that what I say about phenomenal properties applies equally to the relevant external properties.

often tacitly concede that there is at least a prima-facie case for this status: for example, it is striking that those who construct sceptical scenarios almost always ensure that that phenomenal properties are preserved. So it is arguable that simply having a phenomenal property provides the potential for a strong sort of phenomenal knowledge. Something similar is suggested by the Mary case: Mary's experience of the phenomenal property R allows her to have not just a distinctive phenomenal belief, but also distinctive phenomenal knowledge. Some element of this distinctive epistemic character can be captured in the present framework.

One natural suggestion is the following: direct phenomenal beliefs are always justified. Certainly Mary's belief on leaving her room seems to be justified, and most other examples seem to fit this thesis. This thesis has to be modified slightly. There are presumably subjects who are so irrational or confused that none of their beliefs qualify as justified, so that their direct phenomenal beliefs are not justified either. And perhaps there could be subjects who are so confused about phenomenology that they accept not just direct phenomenal beliefs but their negations, casting doubt on whether either belief is truly justified. To meet this sort of case, we might adjust the thesis to say that all direct phenomenal beliefs have some prima-facie justification, where prima-facie justification is an element of justification that can sometimes be overridden by other elements, rendering a belief below the threshold for 'justification' *simpliciter*. Something similar presumably applies to other features of a belief that might seem to confer justification, such as being inferred from justified beliefs by a justified rule of inference.

Assuming that something like this is right: it is nevertheless one thing to make the case that direct phenomenal beliefs are (prima facie) justified, and another to give an account of what this justification consists in. It may be tempting to appeal to incorrigibility; but incorrigibility alone does not entail justification (as the mathematical case shows), and while certain higher-order accessibility theses might close the gap, it is not obvious that they are satisfied for direct phenomenal beliefs.

A better idea is to appeal to the acquaintance relation, thus unifying the distinctive conceptual and epistemic character of phenomenal beliefs. In particular, one might assert:

> *Justification Thesis*: When a subject forms a direct phenomenal belief based on a phenomenal quality, then that belief is prima facie justified by virtue of the subject's acquaintance with that quality.

Certainly many philosophers, including especially sense-datum theorists and more recent foundationalists, have appealed to a relation of acquaintance (or 'direct awareness') in supporting the special epistemic status of phenomenal beliefs. The current account offers a more constrained version of such a thesis, suggesting that it holds for a special class of phenomenal beliefs (on which the epistemic content of a predicated concept is required to mirror and be constituted by the acquainted quality, to which it is applied), and on the basis of a relation whose existence we have made an independent case for.

Some philosophers (e.g. Russell 1910; Fumerton 1995) have held that we are 'acquainted with acquaintance', and have made the case of its existence that way. I think there is something to the idea that our special epistemic relation to experience is revealed in our experience, but I note that the proponent of acquaintance is not forced to rely on such a thesis. It is equally possible to regard acquaintance as a theoretical notion, inferred to give a unified account of the distinctive conceptual and epistemic character that we have reason to believe is present in the phenomenal domain.

Acquaintance can be regarded as a basic sort of epistemic relation between a subject and a property. Most fundamentally, it might be seen as a relation between a subject and an *instance* of a property: I am most directly acquainted with *this instance* of phenomenal greenness. This acquaintance with an instance can then be seen to confer a derivative relation to the property itself. Or in the experience-based framework, one might regard acquaintance as most fundamentally a relation between a subject and an experience, which confers a derivative relation between the subject and the phenomenal properties of the experience. But I will usually abstract away from these fine details. What is central will be the shared feature that whenever a subject has a phenomenal property, the subject is acquainted with that phenomenal property.

Even if acquaintance is a theoretical notion, it clearly gains some pre-theoretical support from the intuitive view that beliefs can be epistemically grounded in experiences, where experiences are not themselves beliefs but nevertheless have an epistemic status that can help justify a belief. One might view acquaintance as capturing that epistemic status.

In certain respects (though not in all respects), the justification of a direct phenomenal belief by an experience can be seen as analogous to the justification of an inferred belief by another belief. For an inferred belief to be prima facie justified, there are three central requirements: one concerning the content of the belief in relation to the justifying state, one concerning the natural connection between the belief and the justifying state, and one concerning the epistemic status of the justifying state. First, the epistemic content of the belief must be appropriately related to that of the belief that it is inferred from. Second, the belief must be appropriately caused by the justifying belief. Third, the justifying belief must itself be justified.

In the prima-facie justification of a direct phenomenal belief by an experience, there are three factors of the same sort. First, content: the epistemic content of the direct phenomenal belief must mirror the quality of the experience. Second, a natural connection: the phenomenal belief must be appropriately constituted by the experience. And third, epistemic status: the subject must be acquainted with the justifying quality. The details of the requirements are different, as befits the difference between belief and experience, but the basic pattern is very similar.

It is plausible that a subject can have phenomenal properties without having corresponding concepts, or corresponding beliefs, or corresponding justification.[14] If so, the same goes for acquaintance. Acquaintance is not itself a conceptual relation: rather, it makes certain sorts of concepts possible. And it is not itself a justificatory relation: rather, it makes certain sorts of justification possible. Phenomenal concepts and phenomenal knowledge require not just acquaintance, but acquaintance in the right cognitive background: a cognitive background that minimally involves a certain sort of attention to the phenomenal quality in question, a cognitive act of concept formation, the absence of certain sorts of confusion and other undermining factors (for full justification), and so on. But it is acquaintance with the quality or the experience itself that does the crucial justifying work.

Some philosophers hold that only a belief can justify another belief. It is unclear why this view should be accepted. The view has no pre-theoretical support: pre-theoretically, it is extremely plausible that experiences (e.g. a certain experience of phenomenal greenness) play a role in justifying beliefs (e.g. my belief that there is something green in front of me, or my belief that I am having a certain sort of experience), even though experiences are not themselves beliefs. And the view has no obvious theoretical support. Perhaps the central motivation for the view comes from the idea that inference is the only sort of justification that we understand and have a theoretical model for, and that we have no model for any other sort of justification. But this is obviously not a strong reason, and the account I have just sketched suggests a

---

[14] Nothing I have said so far requires that experiences can exist without concepts; at most, it requires that experiences can exist without phenomenal concepts. So what I have said may be compatible with views on which experiences depend on other concepts in turn. Still, I think it is independently plausible that experiences do not require concepts for their existence, and I will occasionally assume this in what follows. This is not to deny that *some* experiences depend on concepts, and it is also not to deny that experiences have representational content. My own view is that at least for perceptual experiences (and perhaps for all experiences), experiences have representational content by virtue of their phenomenology, where this content is sometimes conceptual and sometimes non-conceptual. This yields an interesting possibility (developed in forthcoming work): the constitutive relation between phenomenal states and phenomenal concepts might be extended to yield a similar constitutive relation between perceptual phenomenal states and a special class of perceptual concepts, by virtue of the phenomenal states' representational content. Such an account might yield some insight into the content and epistemology of perceptual belief.

theoretical model of how experiences can justify beliefs that fits well with our pre-theoretical intuitions. So it seems that the cases of justification of beliefs by other beliefs and by experiences are on a par here.

Another motivation for the view comes from the thesis that for a state to justify another state, it must itself be justified (along with the claim that only beliefs can be justified. But again, it is unclear why this thesis should be accepted. Again, it is pre-theoretically reasonable to accept that beliefs are justified by experiences, and that experiences are not themselves the sort of states that can be justified or unjustified. And there is no obvious theoretical reason to accept the thesis. It may be that for a state to justify, it must have *some* sort of epistemic status, but there is no clear reason why the status of acquaintance should be insufficient.

(BonJour (1978) suggests that the denial that justifying states must be justified is an ad hoc move aimed at stopping the regress argument against foundationalism. But considerations about foundationalism and about regress arguments have played no role in my claims: the claims are independently supported by observations about the epistemic and conceptual relations between belief and experience. BonJour also claims that a justifying state must involve assertive content; but again, there is no clear pre-theoretical or theoretical reason to accept this. Pre-theoretically: experiences can justify beliefs without obviously involving assertive content. Theoretically: acquaintance with a property makes the property available to a subject in a manner that makes concepts and assertions involving the property possible, and that enables these assertions to be justified. There is no reason why this requires acquaintance to itself involve an assertion.)

A number of epistemological issues remain. One concerns the strength of the justification of phenomenal beliefs. It is often held that phenomenal beliefs are (or can be) *certain*, for example. Can the present framework deliver this? It can certainly deliver incorrigibility, but certainty requires something different. I think that the relevant sense of certainty involves something like *knowledge beyond scepticism*: intuitively, knowledge such that one's epistemic situation enables one to rule out all sceptical counterpossibilities. There is an intuition that phenomenal belief at least sometimes involves this sort of knowledge beyond scepticism, as the standard construction of sceptical scenarios suggests.

This epistemic status might be captured by a claim to the effect that acquaintance with a property enables one to eliminate all (a priori) epistemic possibilities in which the property is absent. If so, then in the right cognitive background (with sufficient attention, concept formation, lack of confusion, and so on), the justification of a direct phenomenal belief P by acquaintance with a property will sometimes enable a subject not just to know that P by the usual standards of knowledge, but to eliminate all sceptical counterpossibilities in which *P* is false. This matter requires further exploration, but one can see at least the beginnings of a reasonable picture.[15]

A second further issue: can the justification thesis be extended to all pure phenomenal concepts, including standing phenomenal concepts? There is some intuitive appeal in the idea that application of a standing phenomenal concept to an instantiated quality may also carry some justification by virtue of acquaintance with the quality (perhaps under the restriction that the content of the standing concept match the quality, and that there be an appropriate natural connection between the quality and the belief). If this belief were justified directly by acquaintance, however, we would need an account of justification by acquaintance that does not give a central role to constitution. Such an account is not out of the question, but it is worth noting that justification for beliefs involving standing phenomenal concepts can also be secured indirectly.

Indirect justification for such beliefs can be secured by virtue of the plausible claim that any belief of the form $S = R$ is (prima facie) justifiable, where S and R are standing and direct phenomenal concepts with the same epistemic content. This is an instance of the more general claim that any belief

---

[15] I argued in *The Conscious Mind* (1996) that something like acquaintance is required to secure certainty, and that a mere causal connection or reliable connection cannot do the job. If the justification of a belief is based solely on a reliable or causal connection, the subject will not be in a position to rule out sceptical scenarios in which the connection is absent and the belief is false, so the belief will not be certain. In response, a number of philosophers, including Bayne (2001), have argued that acquaintance accounts can be criticized in a similar way. Bayne notes that acquaintance alone is compatible with the absence of certainty (e.g. in conditions of inattention), so certainty requires background factors in addition to acquaintance; but we cannot be certain that these factors obtain, so we cannot rule out sceptical scenarios in which they fail to obtain, so a phenomenal belief cannot be certain. This argument stems from a natural misreading of my argument against reliabilist accounts. The argument is not: certainty requires certainty about the factors that enable certainty, and a reliabilist account cannot deliver this sort of certainty. That argument would require a strong version of a CJ thesis, that certain justification requires certainty about the basis of certain justification (analogous to the KJ thesis that justification requires knowledge of justification). I think such a thesis should clearly be rejected. The argument is rather: certainty about P requires (first-order) 'knowledge beyond scepticism', or an epistemic state that enables a subject to rule out all sceptical scenarios in which P is false. Reliabilism by its nature cannot do this: there will always be sceptical scenarios in which the reliable connection fails and in which P is false.

Bayne's argument against acquaintance gives an analogue of the invalid CJ argument. At most this establishes that we cannot rule out scenarios in which the belief is uncertain. Even this is unclear, as it is not obvious that certainty about certainty requires certainty about the factors enabling certainty. But even if this point is granted, the existence of sceptical scenarios in which the belief is uncertain does not entail the existence of sceptical scenarios in which P is false. Acquaintance yields certainty about experiences, not about beliefs: it enables one directly to rule out sceptical scenarios in which P is false, whether or not it enables one to rule out sceptical scenarios in which a belief is uncertain. In cases of justification by a reliable connection, there are separate reasons to hold that sceptical scenarios in which P is false cannot be ruled out, but in the case of acquaintance, these reasons do not apply. (Note: the published version of Bayne's article takes these points into account and offers some further considerations.)

of the form $A = B$ is justifiable when A and B have the same epistemic content. (This thesis may need some restriction to handle cases of deep hyperintensionality, but it is plausibly applicable in this case.) Such beliefs are plausibly justifiable a priori: experience may enter into a grasp of the concepts involved in such a belief, but it does not enter into the belief's justification. If so, then beliefs involving standing phenomenal concepts can inherit justification by a priori inference from direct phenomenal beliefs, which will be justified in virtue of the Justification Thesis.

Finally, a note on ontology: talk of acquaintance often brings sense-datum theories to mind, so it may be worth noting that a commitment to phenomenal realism and to acquaintance does not entail a commitment to sense-data. First, the picture is entirely compatible with an 'adverbial' subject–property model, and with other quality-based ontologies on which there are phenomenal properties but not phenomenal individuals. Second, even if one accepts the existence of phenomenal individuals such as experiences, one might well reject a sense-datum model of perception, on which one perceives the world by perceiving these entities.

It is also worth noting that one need not regard the acquaintance relation that a subject bears to a phenomenal property as something ontologically over and above the subject's instantiation of the property, requiring a subject–relation–quality ontology at the fundamental level. It is arguable that it is a conceptual truth that to have a phenomenal quality is to be acquainted with it (at least in so far as we have a concept of acquaintance that is not wholly theoretical). Certainly it is hard to conceive of a scenario in which a phenomenal quality is instantiated but no one is acquainted with it. If so, then the picture I have sketched is combined with a simple subject–quality ontology, combined with this conceptual truth. The ontological ground of all this might lie in the nature of phenomenal qualities, rather than in some ontologically further relation.

4.3. Epistemological Problems for Phenomenal Realism

Phenomenal realism, especially property dualism, is often thought to face epistemological problems. In particular, it is sometimes held that these views make it hard to see how phenomenal beliefs can be justified or can qualify as knowledge, since the views entail that phenomenal beliefs do not stand in the right sort of relationship to experiences. If what I have said so far is right, this cannot be correct. But it is worth looking at the arguments more closely.[16]

---

[16] I discussed these arguments at length in ch. 5 of *The Conscious Mind*, on 'The Paradox of Phenomenal Judgment'. I now think that discussion is at best suboptimal. The final section of the chapter put forward a preliminary and sketchy version of the view of phenomenal concepts

The most influential arguments of this sort have been put forward by Sydney Shoemaker (1975). Shoemaker's arguments are intended as an argument against a view that admits the conceptual possibility of 'absent qualia': an experience-free functional duplicate of an experiencing being. The view under attack is slightly stronger than phenomenal realism (a phenomenal realist could admit inverted qualia without absent qualia), is slightly weaker than a view on which zombies (experience-free physical duplicates) are conceptually possible, and is weaker than property dualism. But for the purposes of the argument, it will not hurt to assume a property dualist version of the view on which zombies are metaphysically possible. This has the effect of making Shoemaker's arguments harder to answer, not easier. The answers can easily be adapted to weaker versions of phenomenal realism.

The starkest version of Shoemaker's epistemological argument runs as follows:

(1) If phenomenal realism is true, experiences are causally irrelevant to phenomenal beliefs.

(2) If experiences are causally irrelevant to phenomenal beliefs, phenomenal beliefs are not knowledge.

(3) If phenomenal realism is true, phenomenal beliefs are not knowledge.

Some phenomenal realists might deny the first premiss: a type-B materialist could hold that experiences have effects on beliefs by virtue of their identity with physical states, and a property dualist could hold that these effects proceed through a fundamental causal connection between the phenomenal and physical domains, or through a fundamental causal connection among non-physical mental states. But for the purposes of the argument, I will assume the version of phenomenal realism that makes answering the argument as hard as possible, so I will rule out these responses. In particular, I will assume epiphenomenalism, according to which the phenomenal has no effects on the physical domain.[17]

The view I have outlined makes it easy to see why this argument fails, even against an epiphenomenalist. Whatever the status of the first premiss, the second premiss is false. The second premiss assumes that a causal connection between experience and phenomenal belief is required for the latter to count as knowledge. But if what I have said is correct, the connection between

I have discussed here, but I did not give it a central epistemological role (except in a tentative suggestion on pp. 207–8). I now think that this view of phenomenal concepts is central to the epistemology. So the present discussion can be viewed in part as a replacement for that chapter.

[17] I am not endorsing epiphenomenalism, but I regard it as one of the three serious options that remain once one accepts phenomenal realism and rules out type-B materialism and idealism. The other two are interactionism and a Russellian 'panprotopsychism'. See Chalmers (2002a).

experience and phenomenal belief is tighter than any causal connection: it is constitution. And if a causal connection can underwrite knowledge, a constitutive connection can certainly underwrite knowledge too.

Even without appealing to constitution, the epiphenomenalist can respond reasonably to this argument by appealing to the notion of acquaintance, and arguing that a subject's acquaintance with experience can non-causally justify a phenomenal belief. (I used this strategy in *The Conscious Mind*.) But when the role of constitution is made clear, the reply becomes even stronger. Acquaintance and constitution together enable a theoretical model of the justification of phenomenal belief (as above), a model that is compatible with epiphenomenalism. And any residual worries about the lack of an appropriate connection between the experience and the belief are removed by the presence of a constitutive connection.

This first argument is only a subsidiary argument in Shoemaker's discussion. Shoemaker's main argument specifically concerns the possibility of absent qualia. His argument involves functional duplicates and conceptual possibility, but as before I will modify these details to involve physical duplicates and metaphysical possibility, thus making the argument harder to answer. The modified argument runs roughly as follows:

(1) If phenomenal realism is true, then every conscious being has a possible zombie twin.

(2) If zombies are possible, they have the same phenomenal beliefs as their conscious twins, formed by the same mechanism.

(3) If zombies are possible, their phenomenal beliefs are false and unjustified.

(4) If it is possible that there are beings with the same phenomenal beliefs as a conscious being, formed by the same mechanism, where those phenomenal beliefs are false and unjustified, then the conscious being's phenomenal beliefs are unjustified.

(5) If phenomenal realism is true, every conscious being's phenomenal beliefs are unjustified.

Some phenomenal realists could respond by denying premiss 1 and holding that zombies are impossible. But even the conceptual possibility of functional duplicates with absent qualia is arguably enough to make an analogous argument go through, if there are no other problems. Premiss 3 is relatively unproblematic. Perhaps one could argue that a zombie's phenomenal beliefs have some sort of justification, but the conclusion that our phenomenal beliefs are no more justified than a zombie's would be strong enough for an opponent. Disputing premiss 4 holds more promise. If one accepts an acquaintance model of justification, one might hold that the justification of a phenomenal belief does not supervene on its mechanism of formation. (I used this strategy in *The Conscious Mind*.) But given what has gone before, by far the most obvious reply is to dispute premiss 2. There is no reason to accept that zombies have the same phenomenal beliefs as their conscious twins, and every reason to believe that they do not.

It is by no means obvious that zombies have beliefs at all. The basis of intentionality is poorly understood, and one might plausibly hold that a capacity for consciousness is required for intentional states. But even if we allow that zombies have beliefs, it is clear that a zombie cannot share a conscious being's phenomenal beliefs. The content of a conscious being's direct phenomenal beliefs is partly constituted by underlying phenomenal qualities. A zombie lacks those qualities, so it cannot have a phenomenal belief with the same content.

Let us take the case of Zombie Mary, where we recombine thought experiments in the obvious way. Assuming that Zombie Mary has a belief where Mary has a direct phenomenal belief, what sort of content does it have? Mary has a belief with the content $E = R$, and Inverted Mary has a belief with the content $E = G$. Let us focus on the direct phenomenal concepts R and G, and their zombie counterpart. It is obvious that Zombie Mary's concept is neither R nor G: if it has content at all, it has a different content entirely. I think that the most plausible view is that the zombie's concept is *empty*: it has no content. On the view I have been outlining, a phenomenal quality can be thought of as filling a slot that is left open in the content of a direct phenomenal concept, and thus contributing its content. If there is no phenomenal quality to fill the slot, as in Zombie Mary's case, the concept will have no content at all.

What about Zombie Mary's analogue of Mary's direct phenomenal belief $E = R$? It is not obvious that a zombie can possess a demonstrative phenomenal concept: for a start, a concept whose content is that of 'this experience' seems to require a concept of experience, which a zombie may lack. But even if a zombie could possess a demonstrative phenomenal concept, any such concept would fail to refer (like failed demonstratives in other domains). And more importantly, the other half of the identity (the zombie's analogue of R) would be empty. So Zombie Mary's belief would be entirely different from Mary's belief.

It is natural to wonder about the truth-value of Zombie Mary's belief. Clearly her belief is not true. I would say that it is either false or empty, depending on one's view about beliefs involving empty concepts. The latter view is perhaps the most plausible, since it seems that Zombie Mary's belief has no propositional content to evaluate. As for Zombie Mary's 'new knowledge': it is clear that she gains no propositional knowledge (though she may think that she does). One might see her as in the position that type-A materialists, and in particular proponents of the 'ability hypothesis', hold that we are in the actual world. When Zombie Mary first sees a flower, she may gain certain abilities to recognize and discriminate, although even these abilities will be severely constrained, since they cannot involve experiences.

This is enough to see that the epistemological argument against phenomenal realism does not get off the ground. A zombie clearly does not have the same phenomenal beliefs as its conscious twin in general; and its corresponding beliefs are not even formed by the same mechanism, since constitution by a phenomenal quality plays a central role in forming a direct phenomenal belief. So the second premiss is false, and there is no bar to the justification of direct phenomenal beliefs.[18]

What about other phenomenal beliefs? We have seen that standing phenomenal concepts differ between twins, and that their content is plausibly constituted either by phenomenal properties or by dispositions involving those properties. A zombie lacks all phenomenal properties, so it is plausible that its analogues of standing phenomenal concepts will be empty, too. So beliefs involving standing phenomenal concepts are also immune from this argument.

What about the standing concept of *experience* (or *qualia*, or *phenomenal consciousness*) generally? In this case there is no difference in content between conscious twins. But it remains plausible that phenomenal properties and the capacity to have them play a crucial role in constituting its content, just as they do for specific standing phenomenal concepts. And it is equally plausible that the zombie's analogue of this standing concept is empty.[19] So beliefs involving the standing concept of experience (such as *I am conscious*) are equally unthreatened by this argument. The same goes for beliefs involving concepts in which the concept *experience* plays a part, such as relational phenomenal concepts, and perhaps demonstrative phenomenal concepts.

---

[18] Conee (1985) and Francescotti (1994) also respond to Shoemaker's argument by denying the equivalent of premiss 2, although for somewhat different reasons.

[19] This is relevant to an argument against conceivability arguments for property dualism given by Balog (1999). Balog maintains that a zombie could make a conceivability argument with the same form, with true premisses and a false conclusion, so the argument form must be invalid. Balog's argument requires as a premiss the claim that a zombie's assertion 'I am phenomenally conscious' (and the like) expresses a truth. But the discussion here suggests that it is much more plausible that the assertion is false or truth-valueless. This is plausible on independent grounds: in a zombie world, when a zombie realist asserts (an analogue of) 'Qualia exist', and a zombie eliminativist asserts 'Qualia do not exist', it seems clear that the zombie eliminativist is closer to being correct. If so, Balog's argument fails. Balog also discusses 'Yogis', creatures that make a form of direct reference to brain states without this being mediated by phenomenology. I think it is clear that Yogis have at most a sort of demonstrative concept (roughly: '*this* inner state'), and do not have the analogue of pure phenomenal concepts. For these concepts, no analogous epistemic gap arises. For example, given full physical and indexical information, Yogis will be in a position to know all truths involving the concepts in question.

How are these beliefs justified? For beliefs involving standing phenomenal concepts, such as $E = S$, we have seen that one reasonable model involves inference from $E = R$ and $R = S$. Here, the former belief is justified by acquaintance and constitution, and the second belief is justified a priori by virtue of its content. These two beliefs combine by virtue of the common element R to justify the belief $E = S$. (One can also hold that $E = S$ is justified directly by acquaintance, at cost of losing the special contribution of constitution.) One can justify general beliefs of the form *E is a phenomenal property* in much the same way, given that *R is a phenomenal property* is a priori.

From here, beliefs such as *I am conscious* are a short leap away. The leap is non-trivial, as there are distinctive problems about the epistemology of the self: witness Hume's scepticism about the self, and Lichtenberg's point that in the *cogito*, Descartes was entitled only to *there is thought*, not to *I think*. I have nothing special to say about these epistemological problems. But assuming that these problems can be solved, it is not implausible that a belief such as *if E exists, I have E* is justified (perhaps a priori). Then the whole range of first-person phenomenal beliefs lies within reach.

(If one takes direct phenomenal beliefs as truly foundational, one might even suggest that the *cogito* should have a three-stage structure: from $E = R$ (or some such), to *I have E*, to *I exist*!)

As for beliefs involving relational phenomenal concepts: presumably beliefs such as $S = red_I$, where S is a standing pure concept of phenomenal redness, will be justified a posteriori, perhaps by inference from the observation that the relevant paradigmatic objects typically cause one to experience instances of S. And beliefs of the form $S = red_C$ will be justified at least in so far as $red_I = red_C$ is justified. Of course for the first sort of belief to be justified, sceptical problems about the external world (and about the self) must be overcome, and for the second sort of belief to be justified, sceptical problems about other minds must be overcome. I have nothing special to say about these problems here. But assuming that these problems can be dealt with, then both general relational phenomenal beliefs (e.g. $S = red_C$) and particular relational phenomenal beliefs (e.g. $E = red_C$) will be justified straightforwardly.

It seems, then, that a wide range of phenomenal beliefs can be justified by inference from direct phenomenal beliefs (such as $E = R$), a priori phenomenal beliefs (such as $R = S$ and perhaps *if E exists, I have E*), and a posteriori phenomenal beliefs such as ($S = red_I$ and $S = red_C$). I have given a model for the justification of direct phenomenal beliefs. Phenomenal realism, and even epiphenomenalism, seem to pose no particular problem for the justification of the a priori phenomenal beliefs (or at least no distinctive problem that does not arise for a priori justification on any view). And the same goes for the justification of the a posteriori phenomenal beliefs. Even if experience plays no causal role, this does not matter. Experiences have no special role in justifying the a priori beliefs, and the justification of the a posteriori beliefs can be seen as derivative on beliefs of the form $E = S$ (which are already accounted for), plus general methods of external observation and inductive inference.

So all we need to justify all these beliefs is the justification of direct phenomenal beliefs, the justification of a priori beliefs in virtue of their content, and the justification involved in inference, observation, and induction. There are no special problems in any of these matters for the phenomenal realist. One might think that inference poses a problem for the epiphenomenalist: how do $E = R$ and $R = S$ justify $E = S$ if the content of R is partly constituted by an epiphenomenal quality, and if inference requires causation? But this is no problem: R acts as a middle term and its content is not required to play any special causal role. We can think of the inference in question as being *E is R, which is S, so E is S*. Here the content of R is inessential to the validity of the inference: as long as the premises are justified, the conclusion will be justified.

Perhaps the main residual epistemological issue concerns the persistence of standing phenomenal concepts. One might worry if S is partly constituted by an element that is epiphenomenal, then even if one acquires a justified belief—say of the form *roses cause S*—at one time, it is not clear how this justification carries over to instances of a belief with that content at a later time. It is plausible that more than a match in content is required for justification: the later belief must be in some sense the 'same' belief, or at least a 'descendant' belief, involving the 'same' (or 'descendant') concepts. The same sort of issue arises with inference of the sort in the previous paragraph. Whether or not *E is S* is wholly distinct from the two premises, we certainly want later beliefs of the form *that was S* to be justified, and to play a role in further inferences in turn. But this arguably requires that the later concept be a 'descendant' of the earlier concept in a sense that allows beliefs involving the later concept to inherit justification from beliefs involving the earlier concepts.

In response: I have no good account of what it is for one token of a concept to be a 'descendant' of another, in a manner that allows it to inherit justification.[20] Nor, I think, does anyone. Clearly more than sameness in content is required: if a new concept with the same content were to be formed *de novo*,

---

[20] This sort of persistence relation among tokens is central to our use of concepts and beliefs, but has received less discussion than it might have. In effect, it introduces a 'typing' of concepts and beliefs that is more fine-grained than a mere typing by content, but less fine-grained than a typing by numerical identity of tokens. This sort of typing was already tacit in my earlier discussion, when I said that direct phenomenal concepts do not persist beyond the lifetime of an experience, but that standing phenomenal concepts do.

no justification would be inherited. So some sort of natural connection between concept tokens is required. But it is plausible that this sort of connection need only require an appropriate causal connection between the physical vehicles of the concept, along with an appropriate match in content: it is not required that the elements constituting the content of the initial concept do any distinctive causal work.

To see this, consider the persistence of concepts on an externalist view, where content is constituted by external factors that may lie in the distant past. Here, the factors that constitute the content of two tokens of the concept will play no distinctive role in causally connecting the tokens, since those factors lie in the distant past. The persistence will instead be supported by appropriate connections between the tokens' physical vehicles. It is plausible that the phenomenal realist, and the epiphenomenalist, can say something similar: conceptual persistence is underwritten by natural connections among vehicles, perhaps along with an appropriate match in content. Of course it would be desirable to have a full positive account of this sort of conceptual persistence, but it seems that there is no distinctive problem for the phenomenal realist here.

Further questions concern the justification of beliefs about the representational content of experiences, and the role phenomenal beliefs might play in justifying beliefs about the external world. I will not say anything about these issues here. But it is plausible that these issues pose mere challenges for the phenomenal realist to answer, rather than posing distinctive arguments against it. The distinctive epistemological problems for phenomenal realism have been removed.

4.4. 'The Myth of the Given'

A traditional view in epistemology and the philosophy of mind holds that experiences have a special epistemic status that renders them 'given' to a subject. This epistemic status is traditionally held to give phenomenal beliefs a special status, and sometimes to allow experiences to act as a foundation for all empirical knowledge. In recent years, this sort of view has often been rejected. The *locus classicus* for this rejection is Wilfrid Sellars's 'Empiricism and the Philosophy of Mind' (1956), which criticized such views as involving 'The Myth of the Given'. Sellars's (deliberately abusive) term for the view has caught on, and today it is not uncommon for this label to be used in criticizing such views as if no further argument is necessary.

I do not know whether my view is one on which experiences are 'given'. It does not fit Sellars's official characterization of the given (as we will see), and there are other characterizations that it also does not fit. But the term 'given' (and in particular 'myth of the given') often shifts to encompass many different views, and it may well be that my view shares something of the spirit of the views that were originally criticized under this label. So rather than trying to adjudicate the terminological issue, we can simply ask: are any of the arguments that have been put forward against the 'given' good arguments against the view I have put forward here?

Here one runs up against the problem that clear arguments against the 'given' are surprisingly hard to find. There are many suggestive ideas in Sellars's paper, but few explicit arguments. When arguments appear, they often take the form of suggesting alternative views, rather than directly criticizing an existing view. But there is at least one clear argument against the 'given' in Sellars's paper. This is his famous 'inconsistent triad'. This was intended as an argument against sense-datum theories, but it clearly applies to a wider class of views.

It is clear from the above analysis, therefore, that classical sense-datum theories ... are confronted by an inconsistent triad made up of the following three propositions:

A. *x senses red sense content s* entails *x non-inferentially knows that s is red.* B. The ability to sense sense contents is unacquired. C. The ability to know facts of the form *x is phi* is acquired.

A and B together entail not-C; B and C entail not-A; A and C entail not-B.   (Sellars 1956: s. 6)

It is clear how the view I have put forward should deal with this inconsistent triad: by denying A. I have said nothing about just which mental capacities are acquired or unacquired, but on the view I have put forward, it is clearly possible to have experiences without having phenomenal beliefs, and therefore without having knowledge of phenomenal facts. On my view, phenomenal beliefs are formed only rarely, when a subject attends to his or her experiences and makes judgements about them. The rest of the time, the experiences pass unaccompanied by any phenomenal beliefs or phenomenal knowledge.

Underlying Sellars's critique is the idea that knowledge requires concepts, and that experiences do not require concepts, so that having experiences cannot entail having knowledge. The view I have put forward is compatible with all this. On my view, experiences require little cognitive sophistication, and in particular do not require the possession of concepts. There may be some experiences that require concepts (for example, the experience of a spoon as a spoon), but not all experiences do. No concepts are required to experience phenomenal redness, for example. Knowledge of facts requires belief, however, and belief requires the possession of concepts. So experience does not entail knowledge.

Sellars associated the 'given' most strongly with the acceptance of (A), and the denial of (A) is what he argues for himself. In discussing the possibility that a sense-datum theorist might deny (A), all he says is: 'He can abandon A, in which case the sensing of sense contents becomes a non-cognitive fact—a non-cognitive fact, to be sure which may be a necessary condition, even a logically necessary condition, of non-inferential knowledge, but a fact, nevertheless, which cannot constitute this knowledge.'

On my view, all this is correct. Experiences do not, on their own, constitute knowledge. They play a role in *justifying* knowledge, and they play a role in *partly* constituting the beliefs that qualify as knowledge, in combination with other cognitive elements. But experiences themselves are to be sharply separated from beliefs and from items of knowledge. So none of this provides any argument against my view.

(On my reading, a number of the sense-datum theorists also deny (A), making clear distinctions between the sort of non-conceptual epistemic relation that one stands in by virtue of having an experience and the sort of conceptual epistemic relation that one has when one knows facts. Such theorists clearly avoid the conflation between experience and knowledge that Sellars accuses sense-datum theorists of making.)

Curiously, Sellars never discusses the possibility that experiences could justify knowledge without entailing knowledge. It seems clear that he would reject such a view, perhaps because he holds that only conceptual states can enter into justification, but this is never made explicit in his article.[21]

Although Sellars does not argue explicitly against this sort of view, such arguments have been given by a number of later philosophers writing in the same tradition. In particular, there is a popular argument against any view on which experiences are non-conceptual states that play a role in justifying beliefs. This argument, which we might call the *justification dilemma*, has been put forward by BonJour (1969), Davidson (1986), and McDowell (1994), among others. We can represent it as:

---

[21] The one further part of Sellars's article that may be relevant to the view I have put forward is part VI (ss. 26–9), where he addresses the traditional empiricist idea that experience involves awareness of determinate repeatables. This is closely related to my claim that experience involves acquaintance with properties. Sellars does not provide any direct argument against this view, however. He simply notes (ss. 26–8) that Locke, Berkeley, and Hume take this thesis as a presupposition rather than a conclusion (they use it to give an account of how we can be aware of determinable repeatables). And then he asserts (s. 29) that this awareness must either be mediated by concepts (e.g. through the belief that certain experiences resemble each other, or that they are red) or be a purely linguistic matter. He gives no argument for this claim, which I think should be rejected. On my view, our acquaintance with qualities requires neither concepts nor language.

(1) There can be no *inferential* relation between a non-conceptual experience and a belief, as inference requires connections within the conceptual domain.

(2) But a mere *causal* relation between experience and belief cannot justify
the belief; so

(3) Non-conceptual experiences cannot justify beliefs.

The first premiss is plausible, as it is plausible that inference is mediated by
concepts. The status of the second premiss is much less clear. While it is
plausible that the mere existence of a causal connection does not suffice to
justify a belief, it is far from clear that the right *sort* of causal connection could
not serve to justify a belief. McDowell says that a causal connection 'offers
exculpation where we wanted justification'. But clearly causal connections
cannot involve mere exculpation simply by virtue of being causal connections, as the case of inference shows: here a causal connection of the right kind
between states can be seen to justify. So further argument is required to show
that no other sort of causal connection (perhaps with subtle constraints on
the content of a belief and on the relationship between belief and experience)
can provide justification.

But in any case, even if the two premisses are accepted, the conclusion does
not follow. An option has been missed: inference and causation do not
exhaust the possible justifying relations between non-conceptual experiences
and beliefs. On my view, the relation in question is not inference or causation,
and neither is it identity or entailment, as on the views that Sellars criticized.
Rather, the relation is partial constitution.

I have already given a model of how the justification of a direct phenomenal
belief by an experience works, involving three central elements that parallel
the three central elements in the case of inference. The analogue of the
causal element is the constitutive connection between experience and belief;
the analogue of the content element is the match between epistemic content
of belief and quality of experience; and the analogue of the epistemic element is
the subject's acquaintance with the phenomenal quality. If the model of
justification by inference is accepted, there is no clear reason why this
model should be rejected.

Some philosophers hold that only a conceptual state can justify another
conceptual state. But as with the thesis that only a belief can justify
another belief, it is not clear why this thesis should be accepted. It is not
supported pre-theoretically: pre-theoretically, there is every reason to hold
that experiences are non-conceptual and can justify beliefs. And there is no
clear theoretical support for this claim, either. Proponents sometimes talk of
'the space of reasons' in this context, but the slogan alone does not convert
easily into an argument. McDowell suggests that justifications for our beliefs

should be *articulable*, which requires concepts; but as Peacocke (2001) points out, we can articulate a justification by referring to a justifying experience under a concept, whether or not the experience itself involves concepts. Perhaps the central motivation for the thesis lies in the fact that we have a clear theoretical model for conceptual justification, but not for other sorts of justification. But again, this is a weak argument, and again, the exhibition of a theoretical model ought to remove this sort of worry.

In any case: the view I have put forward avoids Sellars's central version of the given (an entailment from experience to knowledge), and BonJour's, Davidson's, and McDowell's central version of the given (a mere causal connection), along with the arguments against those views. It may be that the view I have put forward accepts a 'given' in some expanded sense. But the substantive question remains: are there good arguments against the given that are good arguments against this view? I have not been able to find such arguments, but I would welcome candidates.

5   Further Questions

I have drawn a number of conclusions about the content and epistemology of phenomenal beliefs. It is natural to ask whether these conclusions apply more generally.

First, regarding content: I have argued that the content of pure phenomenal concepts and phenomenal beliefs is conceptually irreducible to the physical and functional, because this content itself depends on the constitutive role of experience. Does this sort of irreducibility extend to other concepts or beliefs? Is the content of concepts and beliefs irreducible to the physical and functional quite generally?

There is one class of concepts for which such a conclusion clearly follows. This is the class of concepts that have phenomenal concepts as constituents. Such concepts might include *the tallest conscious being in this room, the physical basis of consciousness*, and *the external cause of R*, where R is a pure concept of phenomenal redness. More generally, in so far as a concept has conceptual ties with phenomenal concepts, so that claims involving that concept conceptually and non-trivially entail claims involving pure phenomenal concepts, then the content of such a concept will be irreducible in a similar way.

It is arguable that many or most of our perceptual concepts have this feature. At least some concepts of external colours can be analysed roughly as *the property causally responsible for C in me*, where C is a pure concept of a phenomenal colour. Things are more complex for community-level concepts. Here it is more plausible that an external colour concept might be analysed in terms of community-wide relations to a non-specific phenomenal concept: perhaps *the property causally responsible for the dominant sort of visual experience caused by certain paradigmatic objects in this community*, or something like that. But this still has the concept of visual experience as a constituent, and so will still have functionally irreducible content. The alternative is that external colour concepts might be analysed in terms of their relations to certain *judgements* or other non-experiential responses, in which case the reducibility or irreducibility will not be so clear. I will not adjudicate this matter here, but my own view is that while there may be some perceptual concepts without an obvious phenomenal component, many or most of the perceptual concepts that we actually possess have such a component.

One might try to extend this further. In the case of theoretical concepts from science, for example, one can argue that these have conceptual ties to various perceptual concepts (as the Ramsey–Lewis analysis of theoretical concepts suggests). If so, and if the perceptual concepts in question have irreducible content, it is arguable that these concepts have irreducible content. And one might argue for conceptual ties between intentional concepts and phenomenal concepts, and between social concepts and intentional concepts, so that a wide range of social concepts will turn out to have irreducible content. If this is right, then a being without consciousness could have at best impoverished versions of these concepts, and perhaps no such concepts at all.

This sort of argument will not work for all concepts. Many mathematical or philosophical concepts have no obvious tie to phenomenal concepts, for example. And in fact there is good reason to think that some concepts do not have a phenomenal component. If all concepts have a phenomenal component, it would be hard to avoid the conclusion that all concepts are *entirely* constituted by phenomenal concepts, which would lead naturally to phenomenalism or idealism. My own view is that certain central concepts, such as that of causation, have no deep phenomenal component at all. Once this is recognized, it becomes clear that even if a wide range of concepts have a phenomenal component, only a small number of them are entirely phenomenal.

Even if some concepts have no phenomenal component, it is not out of the question that their content might still be irreducible. One intriguing possibility is that something about a subject's phenomenal states could be central to a subject's *possessing* a concept such as that of causation, or certain mathematical concepts, even though these concepts do not refer to phenomenal states as part of their content. (Compare a reductive view on which neural states might constitute the content of concepts that do not refer to neural states.) There is at least some intuition that a capacity for consciousness may be required to have concepts in the first place; and it is not obviously false that phenomenology plays a role in the possession of even non-phenomenal concepts.

Such a thesis would require much further argument, of course, and I am not certain whether it is true. But even if it is false, the more limited thesis that phenomenology plays a role in constituting the content of phenomenal concepts, and that phenomenal concepts play a role in determining the content of a wide range of other concepts, has significant consequences. If even the more limited thesis is true, then the project of giving a functional analysis of intentionality cannot succeed across the board, and a central role must be given to phenomenology in the analysis of intentional content.

Second, epistemology: I have in effect argued for a sort of limited foundationalism within the phenomenal domain. Direct phenomenal beliefs are in a certain sense foundational: they receive justification directly from experience, and their prima-facie justification does not rely on other beliefs. And I have argued that direct phenomenal beliefs can justify at least some other phenomenal beliefs in turn, when aided by various sorts of a priori reasoning. Does this give any support to foundationalism about a broader class of empirical beliefs, or about empirical knowledge in general?

Nothing I have said implies this. This gap between phenomenal knowledge and knowledge of the external world remains as wide as ever, and I have done nothing to close it. The framework here is compatible with various standard suggestions: that phenomenology might justify external beliefs through inference to the best explanation, or through a principle that gives prima-facie justification to a belief that endorses an experience's representational content. But so far, the framework outlined here does nothing special to support these suggestions or to answer sceptical objections. And the framework is equally compatible with many alternative non-foundationalist accounts of our knowledge of the external world.[22]

Still, this framework may help to overcome what is sometimes taken to be the largest problem for foundationalism: bridging the gap between experience and belief. I have argued that an independently motivated account of the role of experience in phenomenal belief, and of subject's epistemic relations to them, has the resources to solve this problem, by exploiting the paired notions of constitution and acquaintance.

---

[22] A particular problem in extending this account to a general foundationalism is that we do not usually form direct phenomenal beliefs associated with a given experience, so such beliefs are not available to help in justifying perceptual beliefs. (Thanks to Alvin Goldman for discussion on this point.) Here there are a few alternatives: (1) deny that perceptual beliefs are usually justified in the strongest sense, but hold that such justification is available; (2) hold that the mere availability of justifying direct phenomenal beliefs confers a sort of justification on perceptual beliefs; or (3) extend the account so that perceptual experiences can justify perceptual beliefs directly, through a constitutive connection to perceptual concepts analogous to the connection to phenomenal concepts. I explore the third possibility in forthcoming work on the content of perceptual experience and perceptual belief.

Any plausible epistemological view must find a central role for experience in the justification of both beliefs about experience and beliefs about the world. If what I have said here is correct, then we can at least see how experience gains a foothold in this epistemic network. Many other problems remain, especially regarding the relationship between experience and beliefs about the external world. But here, as in the case of phenomenal belief, a better understanding of the relationship between experience and belief may take us a long way.[23]

Appendix

What follows is a brief and simplified introduction to the two-dimensional semantic framework as I understand it. See also Chalmers (2002c; forthcoming).

Let us say that S is epistemically possible in the broad sense if the hypothesis that S is the case is not ruled out a priori. Then there will be a wide space of epistemic possible hypotheses (in the broad sense; I will usually omit the qualifier in what follows). Some of these will conflict with each other; some of them will be compatible with each other; and some will subsume each other. We have a systematic way of evaluating and describing epistemic possibilities that differs from our way of evaluating and describing subjunctive counterfactual possibilities. It is this sort of evaluation and description that is captured by the first dimension of the two-dimensional framework.

It is epistemically possible that water is not H_2O, in the broad sense that this is not ruled out a priori. And there are many specific versions of this epistemic possibility: intuitively, specific ways our world could turn out such that if they turn out that way, it will turn out that water is not H_2O. Take the XYZ-world, one containing superficially identical XYZ in place of H_2O. It is epistemically possible that our world is the XYZ-world. When we consider this epistemic possibility—that is, when we consider the hypothesis that *our* world contains XYZ in the oceans, and so on—then this epistemic possibility can be seen as an instance of the epistemic possibility that water is not H_2O. We can rationally say 'if our world turns out to have XYZ in the oceans (etc.), it will turn out that water is not H_2O'. The hypothesis that the XYZ-world is actual rationally entails the belief that water is not H_2O, and is rationally inconsistent with the belief that water is H_2O.

[23] I have presented versions of this paper (starting in 1997) at Antwerp, ANU, Arizona, Delaware, Fribourg, Miami, Munich, Princeton, Sydney, UC Santa Cruz, the APA (Pacific Division), Metaphysical Mayhem (Syracuse), and the World Congress of Philosophy (Boston). Thanks to many people in audiences there, and elsewhere. Special thanks to Mark Johnston, Martine Nida-Rümelin, Susanna Siegel, and Daniel Stoljar for lengthy discussions.

Here, as with subjunctive counterfactual evaluation, we are considering and describing a world, but we are considering and describing it in a different way. In the epistemic case, we consider a world *as actual*: that is, we consider the hypothesis that our world is that world. In the subjunctive case, we consider a world as *counterfactual*: that is, we consider it as a way things might have been, but (probably) are not. These two modes of consideration of a world yield two ways in which a world might be seen to make a sentence or a belief true. When the XYZ-world is considered as actual, it makes true 'water is XYZ'; when it is considered as counterfactual, it does not.

In considering a world as actual, we ask ourselves: what if the actual world is really that way? In the broad sense, it is *epistemically* possible that Hesperus is not Phosphorus. This is mirrored by the fact that there are specific epistemic possibilities (not ruled out a priori) in which the heavenly bodies visible in the morning and evening are distinct; and upon consideration, such epistemic possibilities are revealed as instances of the epistemic possibility that Hesperus is not Phosphorus.

When we consider worlds as counterfactual, we consider and evaluate them in the way that we consider and evaluate subjunctive counterfactual possibilities. That is, we acknowledge that the character of the actual world is fixed, and say to ourselves: what if the world *had been* such-and-such a way? When we consider the counterfactual hypothesis that the morning star might have been distinct from the evening star, we conclude not that Hesperus would not have been Phosphorus, but rather that at least one of the objects is distinct from both Hesperus and Phosphorus (at least if we take for granted the actual-world knowledge that Hesperus is Phosphorus, and if we accept Kripke's intuitions).

Given a statement S and a world W, the *epistemic intension* of S returns the truth-value of S in W considered as actual. (Test: if W actually obtains, is S the case?) The *subjunctive intension* of S returns the truth-value of S in W considered as counterfactual. (Test: if W had obtained, would S would have been the case?) We can then say that S is *primarily possible* (or 1-possible) if its epistemic intension is true in some world (i.e. if it is true in some world considered as actual), and that S is *secondarily possible* (or 2-possible) if its subjunctive intension is true in some world (i.e. if it is true in some world considered as counterfactual). Primary and secondary necessity can be defined analogously.

For a world to be considered as actual, it must be a *centred* world—a world marked with a specified individual and time—as an epistemic possibility is not complete until one's 'viewpoint' is specified. So an epistemic intension should be seen as a function from centred world to truth-values. For example, the epistemic intension of 'I' picks out the individual at the centre of a centred world; and the epistemic intension of 'water' picks out, very roughly, the clear drinkable (etc.) liquid in the vicinity of the centre. No such marking of a centre is required for considering a world as counterfactual, or for evaluating subjunctive intensions.

Epistemic and subjunctive intensions can be associated with statements in language, as above, and equally with singular terms and property terms. The intension of a statement will be a function from worlds to truth-values; the intension of a term will be a function from worlds to individuals or properties within those worlds. (In some cases, intensions are best associated with linguistic tokens rather than types.)

Epistemic intensions can also be associated in much the same way with the (token) concepts and thoughts of a thinker, all of which can be used to describe and evaluate epistemic possibilities as well as subjunctive counter-factual possibilities. In 'The Components of Content' (2002c) I argue that the epistemic intension of a concept or a thought can be seen as its 'epistemic content' (a sort of internal, cognitive content), and that the subjunctive intension captures much of what is often called 'wide content'.

A crucial property of epistemic content is that it reflects the rational relations between thoughts. In particular, if a belief A entails a belief B by a priori reasoning, then it will be epistemically impossible (in the broad sense) for A to be true without B being true, so the epistemic intension of A entails the epistemic intension of B. Further, if an identity $a = b$ is a posteriori for a subject, then it is epistemically possible for the subject that the identity is false, and there will be an epistemic possibility in which the referents of the two concepts involved differ, so the subject's concepts a and b will have distinct epistemic intensions. This applies even to beliefs expressed by a posteriori necessities such as 'water is H_2O' and 'Hesperus is Phosphorus': the epistemic intensions of these beliefs are false at some worlds, so the concepts involved have different epistemic intensions. So epistemic intensions behave something like Fregean senses, individuating concepts according to cognitive significance at least up to the level of a priori equivalence.

(A complication here is that on some philosophical views, there may be 'strong necessities' whose epistemic intension is false at no world. An example might be 'A god exists', on a theist view on which a god exists necessarily but not a priori, or 'Zombies do not exist', on a type-B materialist view on which zombies are conceivable but metaphysically impossible. These necessities go well beyond Kripkean a posteriori necessities, and I have argued elsewhere (Chalmers 2002b) that there are no such necessities. If they exist, however, the present framework can accommodate them by moving to a broader class of conceptual or epistemic possibilities, which need not correspond to meta-physical possibilities (see Chalmers (forthcoming) for more details). In the cases above, for example, there will be at least a conceptually possible world (or 'scenario') in which there is no god, and one in which there are zombies.

More generally, any a posteriori belief will have an epistemic intension that is false at some such world.)

In the work presented here, the two-dimensional framework is being applied rather than being discussed or justified in its own right. The discussion here indicates important distinctions among phenomenal concepts whose analysis requires the idea of epistemic content. And importantly, there are epistemological distinctions that turn on these distinctions in content. This reflects a more general phenomenon: the sort of possibility that is most crucial in epistemology is epistemic possibility, and the sort of content that is correspondingly most crucial is epistemic content.

REFERENCES

AUSTIN, D. F. (1990), *What's the Meaning of 'This'?* (Ithaca, NY: Cornell University Press).

BALOG, K. (1999), 'Conceivability, Possibility, and the Mind-Body Problem', *Philosophical Review*, 108: 497–528.

BAYNE, T. (2001), 'Chalmers on the Justification of Phenomenal Judgments', *Philosophy and Phenomenological Research*, 62: 407–19.

BONJOUR, L. (1969), 'Knowledge, Justification, and Truth: A Sellarsian Approach to Epistemology', Ph.D. Dissertation, Princeton University. <http://www.ditext.com/bonjour/bonjour0.html>.

——— (1978), 'Can Empirical Knowledge Have a Foundation?' *American Philosophical Quarterly*, 15: 1–13.

CHALMERS, D. J. (1996), *The Conscious Mind: In Search of a Fundamental Theory* (New York: Oxford University Press).

——— (2002a), 'Consciousness and its Place in Nature', in S. Stich and F. Warfield (eds.), *The Blackwell Guide to the Philosophy of Mind* (Oxford: Blackwell). <http://consc.net/papers/nature.html>.

——— (2002b), 'Does Conceivability Entail Possibility?', in T. Gendler and J. Hawthorne (eds.), *Conceivability and Possibility* (Oxford: Oxford University Press). <http://consc.net/papers/conceivability.html>.

——— (2002c), 'The Components of Content', in D. Chalmers (ed.), *The Philosophy of Mind: Classical and Contemporary Readings* (New York: Oxford University Press). <http://consc.net/papers/content.html>.

——— (forthcoming), 'The Nature of Epistemic Space'. <http://consc.net/papers/espace.html>.

CHISHOLM, R. (1957), *Perceiving: A Philosophical Study* (Ithaca: Cornell University Press).

CONEE, E. (1985), 'The Possibility of Absent Qualia', *Philosophical Review*, 94: 345–66.

DAVIDSON, D. (1986), 'A Coherence Theory of Truth and Knowledge', in E. Lepore (ed.), *Truth and Interpretation: Perspectives on the Philosophy of Donald Davidson* (Oxford: Blackwell).

FRANCESCOTTI, R. M. (1994), 'Qualitative Beliefs, Wide Content, and Wide Behaviour', *Nous*, 28: 396–404.

FUMERTON, R. (1995), *Metaepistemology and Scepticism* (Lanham, Md.: Rowman & Littlefield).

GERTLER, B. (2001), 'Introspecting Phenomenal States', *Philosophy and Phenomenological Research*, 63: 305–28.

HAWTHORNE, J. (2002), 'Advice to Physicalists', *Philosophical Studies*, 101: 17–52.

ISMAEL, J. (1999), 'Science and the Phenomenal', *Philosophy of Science*, 66: 351–69.

JACKSON, F. (1982), 'Epiphenomenal Qualia', *Philosophical Quarterly*, 32: 127–36.

KAPLAN, D. (1989), 'Demonstratives', in J. Almog, J. Perry, and H. Wettstein (eds.), *Themes from Kaplan* (New York: Oxford University Press).

KRIPKE, S. A. (1981), *Wittgenstein on Rules and Private Language* (Cambridge, Mass.: Harvard University Press).

LOAR, B. (1997), 'Phenomenal States (Second Version)', in N. Block, O. Flanagan, and G. Güzeldere (eds.), *The Nature of Consciousness* (Cambridge, Mass.: MIT Press).

McDOWELL, J. (1994), *Mind and World* (Cambridge, Mass.: Harvard University Press).

NIDA-RÜMELIN, M. (1995), 'What Mary Couldn't Know: Belief about Phenomenal States', in T. Metzinger (ed.), *Conscious Experience* (Exeter: Imprint Academic).

——(1996), 'Pseudonormal Vision: An Actual Case of Qualia Inversion?' *Philosophical Studies*, 82: 145–57.

——(1997), 'On Belief about Experiences: An Epistemological Distinction Applied to the Knowledge Argument', *Philosophy and Phenomenological Research*, 58: 51–73.

PEACOCKE, C. (2001), 'Does Perception Have a Non-Conceptual Content?' *Journal of Philosophy*, 98: 239–64.

PERRY, J. (2001), *Knowledge, Possibility, and Consciousness* (Cambridge, Mass.: MIT Press).

POLLOCK, J. (1986), *Contemporary Theories of Knowledge* (Lanham, Md.: Rowman & Littlefield).

RAFFMAN, D. (1995), 'On the Persistence of Phenomenology', in T. Metzinger (ed.), *Conscious Experience* (Exeter: Imprint Academic).

RUSSELL, B. (1910), 'Knowledge by Acquaintance and Knowledge by Description', *Proceedings of the Aristotelian Society*, 11: 108–28.

SELLARS, W. (1956), 'Empiricism and the Philosophy of Mind', *Minnesota Studies in the Philosophy of Science*, 1: 253–329. Repr. as *Empiricism and the Philosophy of Mind* (Cambridge, Mass.: Harvard University Press, 1997).

SHOEMAKER, S. (1975), 'Functionalism and Qualia', *Philosophical Studies*, 27: 291–315.

WITTGENSTEIN, L. (1953), *Philosophical Investigations* (Oxford: Blackwell).

9. Privileged Access

1. Privileged Access: Gilbert Ryle

As part of his rejection of Cartesianism, Ryle discounts the importance and distinctiveness of self-knowledge, knowledge of one's own mental or psychological episodes, states, moods, traits, and so on. He argues that the difference between how we know our own minds and how we know other minds is vastly overrated. Mostly we know others in the same ways we know ourselves. We need to see patterns in our behaviour, for example, in order to discern a character trait, or a mood, or a motive. Where you know yourself better than do others, moreover, it's through the richer bank of data derived from your closer and more steady proximity to yourself. But such data are also accessible to others. And character flaws are in fact more easily discerned by others than by the flawed.

While aware of the difference between episodes and traits, Ryle presses his attack even against that Cartesian citadel, *episodic* consciousness. The famous central chapter of *The Concept of Mind* (1949), on 'Self Knowledge', defines his target with unusual closeness and formality:

It is often held...(1) that a mind cannot help being constantly aware of all the supposed occupants of its private stage, and (2) that it can also deliberately scrutinise by a species of non-sensuous perception at least some of its own states and operations. Moreover both this constant awareness (generally called 'consciousness'), and this non-sensuous inner perception (generally called 'introspection') have been supposed to be exempt from error. A mind has a twofold Privileged Access to it own doings, which makes its self-knowledge superior in quality, as well as prior in genesis, to its grasp of other things. I may doubt the evidence of my senses but not the deliverances of consciousness or introspection. (p. 154)

While rejecting any fundamentally mental episodes as ghostly phenomena in the machine, Ryle objects to the doctrine of privileged access in ways mostly independent of that ontological issue. Unfortunately, his main distinctive arguments are weak. His attack against part 1 of the doctrine of privileged access, for example, presupposes that 'supposed occupants of the private stage' include the following: knowing a certain fact, having a certain motive, being irritated or excited, being awake, and dreaming. But Cartesian defenders of privileged access would hardly suppose any of these to be a conscious *episode* of the sort to which we supposedly enjoy privileged access. So these are mere skirmishes outside the citadel.

2. Privileged Access: Other Accounts

Has Wittgenstein settled the issue? Some find the solution in a doctrine of avowals according to which pain reports have an expressive function and purport to state no facts. But this is subject to the 'Geach point', that the language of supposed avowals seems semantically much richer than any purely expressive vocabulary such as 'Ouch!' Thus the declarative 'I am in pain' can figure in antecedents of conditionals, as in 'When I am in pain, I normally take some aspirin.' Crispin Wright (1998) has shown how this objection can be blunted by taking avowals to be truth-evaluable expressions with a performative use, as with 'I promise'. But he concludes that the approach through avowals remains incredible even so, because of its unacceptable implications. For example, it implies that torturers can know about the pains inflicted better than the tortured, since they are better positioned to see the outward signs.

The approach is incredible, but it is not Wittgenstein's, or so Wright would have us believe. Wittgenstein's proposal is said to be rather this: that privileged access is not a consequence of the nature of our psychological states, but is involved constitutively in the conditions of identification of what a subject believes. 'According to the Default View, it ... is simply basic to the competent ascription of the attitudes that, in the absence of good reason to the contrary, one must accord correctness to what a subject is willing to avow, and limit one's ascriptions to her to those she is willing to avow.' (ibid. 41)

However, it is hard to see how the default view can amount to much more than just a dogmatic stance. At the core of the onion we would find a peel with the disappointing inscription, 'This language game is played.'

I agree with Wright about this: we have found in Wittgenstein (*as interpreted*) no acceptable resolution of our issue: neither in expressivism of avowals nor in the default view.

Christopher Peacocke (1998), for his part, focuses on how conscious states themselves rationally ground introspective beliefs, drawing on his broader view about conditions for concept-possession, and in particular labour conditions for possession of the concept of belief. Appeal to such conditions can illuminate how the occurrent belief that p can so appropriately prompt the self-attribution of that very belief. The possession of the concept of belief itself requires such self-attribution. This proposal is also under suspicion of dogmatism, however, in the way of the default view. Don't we need some reason at least to believe that in self-ascribing beliefs we are not likely to go wrong? Michael Martin (1998: 116) raises a related worry:

[We] ... can see Peacocke's account as implicitly offering to delimit in part the range of ... beliefs about which we have authority: namely, those which we can ascribe on the basis of conscious thoughts. But ... this is too broad a basis for authoritative self-ascription ... A too familiar phenomenon in philosophical enquiry is the realization that the proposition that one felt that one had a real conviction was so, turns out to be not the proposition that one identified initially, but really another proposition, which is a close cousin.

Martin goes on to appeal, with Peacocke, to insights due to Gareth Evans, who writes: 'The crucial point is [this] ... in making a self-ascription of belief, one's eyes are, so to speak, or occasionally literally, directed outwards—upon the world' (Evans 1982: 225). According to Martin (1998: 117), there is perhaps a moral to be drawn from Evans's approach:

When the subject has her eyes directed outwards, they are directed on the world, as it is for her. Now, we should not assume that all of a subject's conscious states form part of the world as it is for her, not even all of her conscious beliefs. So, we might say, what we expect is that a subject should at least have authority with respect to those mental states which comprise in part her point of view on the world. Peacocke himself endorses a close link here between consciousness and the subjective point of view when he claims that 'The requirement that the reason-giving state is one which is, or could become, conscious is intimately related to our conception of an agent as someone with a point of view, one whose rational actions make sense to the subject himself ... given that point of view' (p. 96).

Despite the insights contained in this approach, it cannot be a complete account, however, not even of the restricted field of states that make up one's subjective point of view. A gaping deficiency in the account suggests a different approach, one that will not explain the authority of such beliefs by noting that they are rationalized through the support of corresponding conscious states.

The gap concerns our knowledge that we do *not* believe such and such, and our knowledge that we do *not* intend such and such, and our knowledge that we do *not* seem to see anything red or any triangle. In no such case is our knowledge to be arrived at by means of first-order enquiry or deliberation of any sort; nor is our knowledge based on some conscious state that rationalizes it. On the contrary, it is precisely the *absence* of a relevant belief or intention or experience that makes it a case of knowledge. Moreover, our belief that the state is absent seems clearly *not* to be based on any conscious state to which it is appropriately responsive.

We must distinguish between believing that not-p and not believing that p, between desiring that not-p and not desiring that p, between experiencing as if not-p and not experiencing as if p. Nevertheless, we enjoy privileged access to both sides of each such pair. The more general problem for the approach in terms of an intermediate conscious state is this: we enjoy privileged access both to what is present in our consciousness and to what is absent therefrom. What explains the one is unlikely to differ dramatically and fundamentally from what explains the other. So, even if the account of what is present to consciousness must invoke some relevantly distinguished conscious states that help rationalize our pertinent beliefs, something deeper must explain what is shared in common between that case of privileged access and our equally privileged access to what is absent from consciousness. We need therefore a deeper and closer look.

3. Acquaintance and Awareness

Consider first Leibniz: 'Our direct awareness of our own existence and of our thoughts provides us with the primary truths a posteriori, the primary truths of fact.... [They can be called "immediate"] because there is no mediation between the understanding and its objects.'[1] Compare Russell: 'We shall say that we have *acquaintance* with anything of which we are directly aware, without the intermediary of any process of inference or any knowledge of truths.'[2] An ambiguity is shared here by Leibniz and Russell. One's consciousness contains experiences that go unnoticed; unnoticed altogether, or at least unnoticed as experiences with an intrinsic, experiential character that they nevertheless do have. Just as one automatically jumps one's jumps, smiles one's smiles, and dances one's dances, however, so one experiences one's experiences. And since experiencing is a form of awareness, one is thus in one sense automatically aware of one's experiences, precisely in experiencing them. One is so aware even of experiences that escape one's notice and of which one is hence *un*aware, in another sense. What is more, it is not only her smile that the Mona Lisa smiles; she smiles her specifically enigmatic smile. Similarly, one experiences not just one's experiencing but also one's experiencing in the specific ways in which one does experience.

Which kind of awareness do Leibniz and Russell intend: (a) noticing, intellectual awareness, whereby one occurrently believes or judges the thing noticed to be present, as characterized a certain way; or (b) experiential

---

[1] *New Essays Concerning Human Understanding*, bk. IV, ch. 9.
[2] *Problems of Philosophy* (Oxford: Oxford University Press, 1997), 46. (First published in 1912.)

awareness, whereby one is 'aware' directly of an experience of a certain specific sort simply in virtue of undergoing it?

That distinction—between n(oticing)-awareness, and e(xperiencing)-awareness—is important as follows. From the fact that one is e-aware of something it does not follow that one is n-aware of it. To notice a fact about one's experience at a given time is to believe correctly that it is so, but just a guess will not do: the correct belief must also be at a minimum justified, or reasonable, or epistemically appropriate, or some such thing. So, what sort(s) of experience can be discerned with epistemic justification through believing it (them) to be present to one's consciousness at the time?

Foundationalists through the ages have tried to understand how we can be justified foundationally in a certain belief. And they have appealed crucially to what is 'given' in one's experience, or to what is 'present' to one's consciousness. So they have appealed to what we are 'directly' aware of. But this requires that we be clear on the kind of awareness that is here invoked: in particular, is it e-awareness or is it n-awareness? The latter will *not* enable the desired explanation, since the concept of 'noticing' is itself epistemic in a way that unsuits it for the explanatory work that it is being asked to do. What we want is an explanation in non-epistemic terms of how a non-inferential, foundational belief can acquire epistemic status in the first place, so that holding it is not just arbitrary, so that conclusions drawn from it can inherit epistemic status. Our explanation hence cannot properly rest with 'noticings' that are supposed to have epistemic status *already*. The question will remain as to how *these* beliefs constitutive of the 'noticings' have acquired their status.[3]

Thus are foundationalists led to mental phenomena epistemically more primitive than any 'noticings' or beliefs, to conscious states 'given in' or 'present to' consciousness. In our terminology, what foundationalists are thus led to is e-awareness: that is, to states constitutive of the subject's total mental life-slice, including both those noticed and also those which escape her notice. But we now face the 'Problem of the Speckled Hen', which worried Roderick Chisholm (1942) when he published a paper so titled. The problem, which is found in Ayer's *Foundations of Empirical Knowledge*, concerns the gap between e-awareness and n-awareness.

Much in the intricate character of our experience can, again, escape our notice, and can even be mischaracterized, as when one takes oneself to be able to tell at a glance that an image has ten speckles although in actual fact it has eleven rather than ten. If the classical foundationalist wishes to have a theory and not just a promissory note, he needs to tell us *which* sorts of features of our states of consciousness are the epistemically effective ones, the ones such

---

[3] Of course one can believe that such and such, and the mere presence of this occurrent belief might largely account for one's justification for self-attributing it, *even without the object belief being itself justified*. The present discussion in the main text abstracts from such cases.

that it is *by corresponding to them specifically* that our basic beliefs acquire epistemically foundational status. Having a visual image with forty-eight speckles seems not to qualify, whereas having a visual image with three speckles might (at least when the speckles are large and separate enough). What is the relevant difference?[4] The full dimensions of this problem for foundationalist epistemology have not yet been properly appreciated, or so I will argue.

Our distinction between e-awareness and n-awareness also reveals a further limitation of Ryle's definition of privileged access, whose first clause reads again as follows:

> (1) that a mind cannot help being constantly aware of all the supposed occupants of its private stage.

The question is now as to the kind of awareness involved in this clause: is it e-awareness or is it n-awareness? If the former, then the clause is trivially empty, amounting only to the claim that a mind cannot help undergoing whatever experiences it undergoes. If the latter, then the claim is absurdly strong, and not something that any sensible form of privileged access can require: surely one is not required actually to notice every aspect, nor even every constitutive or internal or intrinsic aspect, of every experience one undergoes. Much of the intricacy of our visual experience escapes our notice at any given time.

So the question naturally arises as to how privileged access is to restrict its claim (1) within more defensible bounds. What distinguishes those occupants of one's consciousness that one can properly know to be present 'by direct inspection'? Or, to put the question another way: What is the kind of state which by being given in or present to one's consciousness becomes a source of foundational status for a corresponding belief?

4. Knowledge of the Given: Through Thick and Thin

If one affirms a declarative, meaningful, indexical-containing sentence, thus producing an utterance none of whose indexicals misfires, one's utterance will have a content and thus will be true or false. By affirming such an indexical affirmable in the right way, in appropriate circumstances, one endows one's affirmation with content in such a way that it will be true or false, relative to its context of affirmation, depending on the truth or falsity of its content.

---

[4] When he introduces the problem, by the way, Ayer acknowledges that he owes it to another philosopher. Ironically, that philosopher was Gilbert Ryle. The objections pressed by Ryle against the possibility of privileged access are weak, whereas he also spots a much more serious problem, one that he fails to press.

Thus I might say 'This pen is black' as I show the pen, thereby endowing my utterance with a content, composed of my pen and the property of being black, such that my affirmation will be true if and only if my pen then has that property. If I mumble those same words while tossing and turning half-asleep, or if I affirm them as an actor in a play, however, my utterance may lack both determinate content and, therefore, truth value.

Consider the great variety of ways of being or acting: ways of being shaped, ways of being coloured, ways of thinking, ways of tying one's shoes, ways of waving goodbye, and so on. Such ways are among the things one can refer to by means of indexicals. Thus: 'This is the way I tie my shoe, or I tie my shoe this way, or I tie my shoe thus.' 'This is how I wave goodbye, or I wave goodbye like this, or I wave goodbye thus.' 'This is how a pencil looks when immersed in water.' Et cetera.

Such ways of being or acting are made salient when one points to an exemplification, or perhaps when one saliently *produces* an exemplification. The way thus made salient is then the referent of the appropriate utterance of 'this way' or of 'thus'.

Indexical affirmations occur not only in speech but also in thought. And our points remain true, *mutatis mutandis*, for such affirmations in thought as for their correlates in speech. Thus one may have the thought 'This itch has been bothering me longer than that itch,' where one's attending to the respective itches takes the place of physical pointing as when, pointing, one says: 'This book has been here longer than that book.' Selective attention is the index finger of the mind.[5]

Consider now the progression from . . . to . . . . to . . . . ., etc., to . . . . At some point in this progression from 3-membered linear arrays to 4-membered ones, etc., one will hit arrays that one can no longer classify numerically at a glance. Let us focus on a well-lit 11-membered array (Fig. 9.1). Here we can distinguish:

(*a*) One's 'seeing' an 11-membered linear array (as when Macbeth in his hallucination could 'see' a dagger).

(*b*) One's believing that one is 'seeing' an 11-membered linear array.

A1 • • • • • • • • • • •

FIG. 9.1. Well-lit 11-membered linear array.

---

[5] I assume here that the conditions of contextual reference through the use of 'thus' enable its use, aided by some mechanism of attention, to pick out a colour or shape as present in that very image. Of course the requirement of such a mechanism of attention would seem to import a need for some presupposed *non-demonstrative* concepts to give content to the attention, which means that such demonstrative reference could not be conceptually fundamental.

This second is the sort of 'conceptual' belief whose content—11-membered linear array—permits such inferences as: linear array with less than 12 members; array with half as many members as a 22-membered linear array; etc.

> (*c*) One's believing that one is 'seeing' *thus*, where one selectively attends to the way in which that array (A1) now presents itself in one's visual experience.

Compare A1 with A2 (Fig. 9.2). Here again we can make analogous distinctions. Thus:

> (*d*) One's 'seeing' an 11-membered hourglass array.
> (*e*) One's believing that one is 'seeing' an 11-membered hourglass array.
> (*f*) One's believing that one is 'seeing' *thus*.

Let's focus on (*c*) and (*f*), while assuming for simplicity that in visual experience one 'sees' particular images (whatever their ontological status may be). Thus my images when I dream or hallucinate are different from yours. And let's assume visual images to have certain definite features: e.g. of shape and cardinality. Thus the images one has while focusing on A1 and A2 have certain definite features of shape and cardinality.

Consider now beliefs expressible in terms such as those of (*c*) and (*f*). But let's now put it as follows:

One's believing that *this* is *thus*.

One such belief simply picks out an image and attributes to it the properties of shape and cardinality exemplified in it, where one picks out these properties *as* exemplified in that image. In that case, assuming I have picked out an image, I cannot go wrong in the shape and cardinality that I attribute to it. However, that is quite compatible with my failing to know that the image is *11-membered* in either case. The 'phenomenal' concepts used in such a belief that 'this is thus' are more primitive than even the simple arithmetical ones involving cardinality of 11. But we need to take account of a difference between A1 and A2.

So far the kind of statement or thought we are considering is just like 'I exist' or 'This exists' in that the conditions of reference guarantee truth.

A2

FIG. 9.2. Eleven-membered hourglass array

However, the guarantee of truth comes with a corresponding conceptual lightness.

From the *cogito* not much follows logically about one's nature. One could be a body, a soul, the World Spirit, whatever. And similarly little follows logically from the fact that 'this is thus' as we are understanding this statement or thought *vis-à-vis*, e.g., A1. Not much can be derived about how this is from the fact that it is 'thus'. The concept involved here is a very thin indexical one, with minimal conceptual content.

The thinness of such beliefs may be appreciated by comparing A1 and A2. Thus consider your discriminatory and recognitional capacities *vis-à-vis* these patterns. Or compare your recognition of a familiar face with your knowledge that you see a façade with a certain specific look, though one you could not distinguish in all its specificity from many very similar façades; or, better yet, consider a highly irregular pattern that you would be unable to discriminate a minute later from many similar ones.

There is a difference between (a) having just an *indexical concept* which one can apply to a perceptible characteristic, and (b) having a thicker *perceptual concept* of that characteristic. What is the difference? The latter involves discriminatory and recognitional capacities. It is not enough that one be able to believe correctly that this is thus, that one be able to use indexical concepts such as *this* or *thus* in order to capture a fact that one has an image of a certain specific sort, or the like. Such indexical concepts are highly portable all-purpose conceptual tools by means of which we can capture a great variety of facts by situating ourselves appropriately to use the indexical involved. But they are also, again, very thin; not much follows from their mere content.

Thicker perceptual concepts go beyond thin indexical ones at least in requiring some ability to recognize the commonality in a diversity of items that co-exemplify some feature. Possession of such a perceptual concept would involve sensitivity, when appropriately situated, to the presence or absence of that feature. It may be thought that full grasp of the concept would require that one be able to recognize the feature as the same again when it reappears, but this implies absurdly that concepts cannot be lost. For if the concept is lost then one may of course lose the ability to recognize the feature as the same again. What we may require for possession of the concept *at a given time* is rather this: that within a certain set of possible alternative settings one would *at that same time* have recognized the pattern if *then* presented; one *would* have classified the instances of the features appropriately, and would not have mischaracterized instances of other, distinct, patterns as instances of this one. This is what seems missing once we reach the level of 11 linearly arrayed dots, as above. If we had *right now* been on the next page, where there are 10 similar dots, or 12, we would not have been sensitive to these differences and might too easily have responded intellectually and linguistically as we do now when we see 11 dots. This is in contrast to the 11-membered hourglass pattern that again we may have no word or symbol for, but that we can think to be present not just as the figure being *thus* patterned, but also as a specific phenomenally grasped pattern that we can go on to recognize on another page as the same, that we would have recognized now had we been looking at that page.

Grasping such a phenomenal concept comes with a certain guarantee of reliability, then, since it is defined in part by sensitivity to the relevant feature of which it is a concept. It is defined in part by the ability to tell when that feature is present and when absent in our experience. So we must be sufficiently reliable in the application of the concept in order to so much as grasp it. Again, therefore, the conditions for giving our thought such 'thicker' conceptual content, automatically require that we be reliable in forming and sustaining beliefs by use of such concepts, so long as the conditions of application are undefective for their use. Thus our thick perceptual concepts enjoy a certain guarantee of reliability, as do those that are thinly indexical. What makes *introspective* beliefs with both varieties of concept so reliable is that in both cases we rely so little on conditions of application that might be defective. In these cases there is precious little in the way of medium or channel through which the relevant faculties or mechanisms operate. There is no dependence on light or air or the quality of these. Reliability is at a maximum because the very grasp of the concepts requires reliability in the right circumstances and the circumstances are nearly always right, leaving little scope for possible failure.

We move beyond such concepts already with the theoretically richer concepts of arithmetic and geometry. When we form beliefs as to whether *these* concepts apply to our present experience, we can easily go wrong, in the way of a claim ventured about the number of dots in linear array A1. So here the question remains as to which of *such* beliefs we can be justified in holding foundationally, unsupported by reasons or inferences, or in any case independently of any such support.

Classical foundationalists need some such beliefs with arithmetical or geometrical content, since from purely indexical or phenomenal concepts very little could be inferred, even allowing some explanatory induction from the given to the external. Has foundationalism been able to explain how we are justified through taking what is given in sheer sensory experience? More specifically, has it vindicated our justified application of the thicker concepts required if we are to move adequately from the given to what lies beyond consciousness itself? For example, has it explained how we might be justified foundationally in applying arithmetical and geometric concepts to our experience? No, its lack of any such explanation is a serious problem for classical foundationalism. Might it be overcome in due course? I myself cannot see how.

5. Recourse to Attention

Let us distinguish among three sorts of concepts: indexical ones; phenomenal ones; and simple geometric and arithmetical ones: 'SGA concepts', for short. All three can be applied to our experience. The former two—indexical concepts and phenomenal ones—come with a certain guarantee of reliability. To grasp them is at least in part to be able to apply them correctly to one's experience, in ways sketched above. SGA concepts differ from phenomenal ones in this respect: no guarantee of reliability in applying them to experience derives simply from understanding them. SGA concepts differ from indexical ones because their conditions of reference fail to guarantee their correct application. However, the mere application to experience of indexical or phenomenal concepts will not provide a rich enough foundation for the empirical know-ledge enjoyed by a normal human. Yet classical foundationalism seems unable to account for how more contentful concepts, such as SGA concepts, might be applied with foundational justification. Here for example is one attempt:

> An SGA belief that one's experience has feature F (an SGA feature) is foundationally justified so long as (a) one's experience does have feature F, and (b) one believes that one's experience has feature F.

But the Speckled Hen Case shows the inadequacy of this attempt.

It may be argued that classical foundationalism *can* provide an account of how we are foundationally justified in applying phenomenal concepts. Far from denying this, I have myself suggested it above. Regarding indexical and phenomenal concepts my doubt is rather this: that they seem too thin, not thickly contentful enough to provide what is needed in a foundation of empirical knowledge.[6]

Next it may be argued that classical foundationalism *can* after all give an account of the foundational status not only of some introspective indexical and phenomenal beliefs, but also of some introspective SGA beliefs. We need only add to our account a further clause requiring that the believer 'attend' to the SGA feature F. An intriguing idea,[7] this recalls our invoking attention in

---

[6] And if one prefers an observationalist foundation in perceptual judgements about one's surroundings, a similar problematic will attach to the modified classical foundationalist view that such judgements derive their justification from the mere fact that they are judgements that attribute an observational characteristic to a perceived object on the basis of the presentation of that characteristic in one's sensory experience. The problem will be that this seems wrong for the cases where one's judgement does fit the observational characteristic of the perceived object *and* its presentation in one's sensory experience, while nevertheless *one is generally inept in making such judgements*, and rarely gets them right.

[7] This was suggested as worth considering by Richard Feldman in his comments on an earlier version of this chapter, a paper delivered at the APA Eastern Division meetings of 1999, (comments that I have found characteristically excellent and stimulating).

the conditions required if one is to pick out an aspect of one's experience by saying or thinking that one is experiencing 'thus'. Somehow one must zero in on the target aspect of one's experience, to be picked out as 'experiencing thus'—which is to 'attend' to that aspect.

Are foundationally justified beliefs perhaps those that result from attending to our experience and to features of it or in it?

Consider again the hourglass 11-membered pattern of dots. Suppose you have a grasp of a corresponding phenomenal concept (which requires that you would have been able to recognize this pattern if it had occurred suitably within your experience), and that you would have been able to detect its absence.[8] This is compatible with your not having counted the dots, however, while by assumption only counting can make you justified in believing that there are 11. Your phenomenal concept of that 11-membered array is then *not* an arithmetical concept, and its logical content will not yield that the dots in it do number 11. (If the hourglass pattern with 11 dots does not establish the point, we can substitute an hourglass pattern with 19 dots, or one with 29, etc.)

What is worse, one *can* attend to a pattern in one's experience without having a phenomenal concept of it. Suppose you see a well-lit white decagon against a black background in an otherwise darkened room. You can attend to that shape, you can focus on it and see it stand out clearly from its background. All of that you *can* do despite lacking a phenomenal concept of that property, which would require at a minimum that you would have been able to spot other exemplifications of it in appropriate conditions, and would have been able to spot its lack as well. You may simply lack this sort of ability; thus, you may be unable to attach a label to the pattern so as to be able to apply that label with systematic correctness in enough otherwise dissimilar cases where the pattern was also present.

Consider now a *modified classical foundationalism*:

An SGA belief that one's experience has feature F (an SGA feature) is foundationally justified so long as (a) one's experience does have feature F, (b) one believes that one's experience has feature F, and (c) one attends to feature F.

Our example of the decagon shows this to be inadequate. One would not be foundationally justified in believing the white figure in one's visual field to

---

[8] This second requirement is by the way particularly stringent and difficult for those who appeal to graspings of features *as featured* in one's experience; when a feature is absent it cannot be grasped thus, and hence our correct denials of the concept in those cases will not be amenable to the same kind of explanation of our reliability.

be a decagon, despite it's being one, and despite one's then attending to that shape as it appears in one's visual experience.[9]

6. Experience, Concepts, and Intentionality

Might things look different to two people in otherwise similar perceptual circumstances simply because one has a phenomenal concept that the other lacks? This is trivially true in intellectual senses of 'looks', as for example in a sense involving simply an inclination to believe (an inclination requiring possession of the constitutive concepts). The more interesting question is whether, *in a sensory sense of 'looks'*, possession of a phenomenal concept could make a difference to how things 'look'. If so, it may be claimed, accordingly, that if one lacks a certain phenomenal concept then one's experience will *not* in fact have the feature corresponding to that phenomenal concept. Anyone who *does* have a given phenomenal concept, whose experience has moreover

---

[9] Richard Fumerton has a further proposal. He proposes a special relation of acquaintance which he explicitly distinguishes from any intentional propositional attitude. He then writes: 'If my being acquainted with the fact that P is part of what justifies me in believing P and if acquaintance is a genuine relation that requires the existence of its relata, then when I am acquainted with the fact that P, P is true. The fact I am acquainted with is the very fact that makes P true. The very source of justification includes that which makes true the belief. In a way it is this idea that makes an acquaintance foundation theory so attractive. I have no need to turn to other beliefs to justify my belief that I am in pain because the very fact that makes the belief true is unproblematically before consciousness, as is the correspondence that holds between my thought and the fact. Again, everything one could possibly want or need by way of justification is there in consciousness' (*Metaepistemology and Scepticism* (Rowman & Littlefield, 1995), 76). A page earlier he had required for the non-inferential justification of one's belief B with content P, that one be acquainted with three things: first, one's belief B; second, the fact that P; and, third, the correspondence holding between that belief and that fact. Now we must ask what Fumerton means by acquaintance. Is it enough for one to be acquainted with an item that it figure in one's consciousness, perhaps at its surface? If so then it would seem that one would be automatically acquainted with one's occurrent beliefs and with one's conscious sensory experiences.

Take a case where one sees a black figure against a white background. One sees an image, a triangular image I, say. So there is one's experience E of seeing that image just then. In addition suppose one also has an occurrent belief B that one sees that triangular image. Both E and B figure in one's consciousness, then, at its surface. In addition, there is the fact that B corresponds to E, at least in the sense that E makes B true. Does this also figure in one's consciousness? Well, if one had two images I1 and I2, both triangular, would it not figure in one's consciousness that the two are isomorphic? Or, at least, their being isomorphic? That would seem to be also constitutive of one's consciousness at the time. And, if so, it could also plausibly be held that the correspondence of B to E, both items in one's consciousness at a given time, would also figure in one's consciousness at that time. And so, if it is enough, for one to be 'acquainted' with an item, that it figure in one's consciousness (at its surface, perhaps) at the time, then all that is required for one to satisfy Fumerton's three conditions is that E and B figure in one's consciousness and that B correspond to E. But this runs against the Problem of the Speckled Hen.

the corresponding feature, plausibly *will* believe, and believe reliably, that it does, since part of what is involved in possession of such a phenomenal concept is the ability to tell when the corresponding feature *is* present in one's experience.

How plausible is it that those who have and those who lack a given phenomenal concept differ in the way specified. Here now are some arguments against that dubious idea.

Suppose I am presented with an appropriately sized, well-lit, regular decagon that stands out from a black background, and suppose I focus on this image at the centre of my visual field. As it happens, I myself *lack* any such phenomenal concept of a decagon, so that, for example, I am unable to tell decagons by simple inspection. Yet that image surely has a definite shape in my visual field. But what shape could that be other than that of a decagon? But if that is the shape of the image in my visual field, does it not follow that the image looks sensorily to me like a decagon?

That is a first argument; here is a second. Consider the arrays in Fig. 9.3. Your cardinality judgements for the top half or so of the horizontal arrays are quite reliable even before you count, unlike your judgement for the bottom half (that's how it is for me, anyhow, and we could surely modify the example so that it is also true of just about anyone... except maybe one of Oliver Sacks's idiot-savants).

Consider now the images of one-line horizontal arrays that you have as you stare at that large pattern. One might think that the top half or so of these imaged arrays have a determinate cardinality, unlike the others, towards the bottom. But is it not determinate that each array has one more dot than its

FIG. 9.3. Series of linear arrays

predecessor as we move down from the top to the bottom array? As we consider any pair of proximate imaged arrays, can we not see clearly that the successor has one more member than its predecessor? And, if so, does it not follow that if (a) the first array has, determinately, two dots, and if (b) each array has, determinately, one more than the preceding array, then (c) the tenth array must have, determinately, eleven dots?

We could also reason similarly with the imaged arrays corresponding to the fragment of our pattern at Fig. 9.4. Here the reasoning would be as follows:

1. The top imaged array has, determinately, 6 dots.
2. There are, determinately, five imaged arrays from top to bottom.
3. Each imaged array has, determinately, one more dot than its predecessor.
4. Therefore, the fifth array must have, determinately, 10 dots.

It may be replied that experience is intentional in a way that makes our argument questionable. Thus one might experience that there are lots of speckles, more than a dozen, without experiencing that there are specifically 48, or any other nearby number of dots. Even if experience is indeed intentional, however, my argument still goes through in some form, or so it seems to me. Here I will not be able to go into that in greater detail. Instead I will try to turn the argument from intentionality on its head, by showing that, even at the heart of the intentional, the argument against classical foundationalism still goes through.

I grant that even while thinking that there is a triangular item in a box B, one need not think that there is an isosceles one, or an equiangular one, or an equilateral one, etc. Nevertheless, intentional facts can still be metaphysically determinate. What is determinately so in the case before us is that I am 'predicating' or 'invoking' the property of triangularity. Such determinacy suffices for my main point, as suggested by the following, which moves beyond sensory experience to occurrent thought. My main point about the fallibility and unreliability of introspection can be made about as plausibly in terms of occurrent thought as in terms of experience.

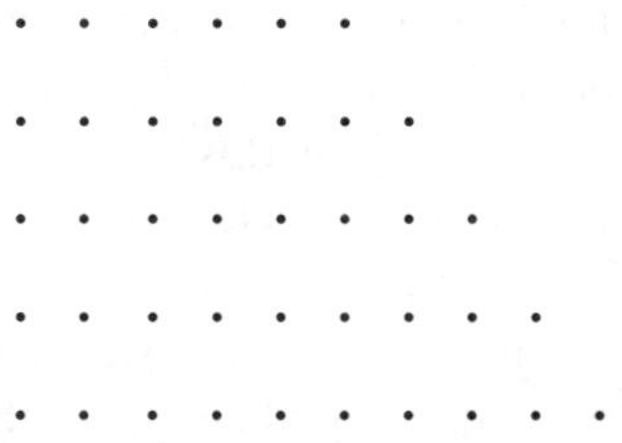

FIG. 9.4. Second series of linear arrays

Suppose you are having right now the occurrent thought:

(T1) That if squares have more sides than triangles, and pentagons more than squares, and hexagons more than pentagons, and heptagons more than hexagons, then heptagons have more sides than triangles.

Presumably one can affirm that complex conditional occurrently, which requires that it be the content of one's affirmation at the time one affirms it. Compare this occurrent thought:

(T2) That if squares have more sides than triangles, then squares have more sides than triangles.

We can know about each of these that it is a conditional thought, and how many atomic conditions make up its antecedent, and how many geometric figures are specified in each. Take just the last of these: how many geometric figures are specified. Most of us can know this about T2 immediately, but to know it about T1 we would need to count. Consider now a nonchalant judgement about one's T1 occurrent, conscious thought, unaided by counting. Is there not a way in which this judgement is unreliable and therefore unjustified while the corresponding judgement about T2 is not?

Something similar could be done with any thought that involves a multiplicity of properties (or concepts, depending on your view of thought). Thus you might right now occurrently think (T3) that if everything blue is spherical, and everything red is cubical, and nothing is spherical and cubical, then nothing is red and blue. Now quick: How many simple colour or shape properties are you thinking about? Can you tell right off, without counting? Can you make an honest mistake? But isn't there a determinate number of such colour or shape properties that your (intentional) thought is about, even before you count? Otherwise how do you attribute to your thought a given logical form, with a certain content involving the predication of certain properties, etc.?

Our antigivenist argument is not restricted to experiences, then, but may be framed with similar plausibility in terms of thoughts. Some intrinsic features of our thoughts are attributable to them directly, or foundationally, while others are attributable only based on counting or inference. How will the classical foundationalist specify which features belong on which side of that divide? It is hard to see how this could be done without appealing to intellectual virtues or faculties seated in the subject. For example, an attribution of a feature to an experience or thought is perhaps foundationally justified only when it derives from the operation of a reliable virtue or faculty. This may then yield the important difference between the claim about our thought T3 that it is about two shapes, on the one hand, and on the other the claim about our thought T1 that it is about seven.[10]

7. Knowledge by Acquaintance

We have been offered various accounts of how beliefs can be *foundationally* justified through sticking to the character of the subject's own conscious experience at the time. None of these has been successful, or so it seems to me. Although discussing earlier failures can be illuminating, in the space at my disposal I would like to sketch instead a positive view that seems more promising.

What distinguishes the case of 48 speckles where one guesses right, and does not know, from the case of 3 speckles, where one does know foundationally, by acquaintance? We need to appeal not just

(a) to the specific phenomenal character of the experience, and
(b) to the propositional content of the occurrent thought as one judges the image to contain so many speckles, and
(c) to the fit between that phenomenal character and that propositional content.

For in the case of the 48-speckled image, where one guesses right in taking the image to contain that many speckles, all of those conditions are met, and the judgement does fit the character of the image. Yet one fails to know by acquaintance.

It is hard to resist the conclusion that what we require, in addition to (a)–(c), is a further appeal to the following:

(d) to some causal or counterfactual connection between the character of the experience and the propositional content of the judgement.

This is abetted by the thought that if the judgement (with its content) is to be rationalized by the experience (with its relevant character), then the former must be appropriately sensitive to the latter, in such a way that variations in the latter would have led to corresponding variations in the former. Or perhaps it will suffice for appropriate sensitivity that not easily might one have so believed without that belief's being then accompanied by one's experiencing in a corresponding way.

Accordingly, what seems required is that one's judgement as to the phenomenal character of one's experience be appropriately causally or

---

[10] At least that seems to be so except perhaps for idiot-savants who can tell directly the number of figures involved in thoughts like T1 or even in those involving many more figures than that.

counterfactually (and reliably) related to the character of the experience. If this is right, it is fascinating to find at the heart of givenist, internalist, classical foundationalism a need for the sort of relation so often used by its externalist opponents, over the course of recent decades, for their various externalist alternatives. Some have invoked straight causation of a belief by the fact that is its content, others a requirement of non-accidentality, others a counterfactual tracking requirement, and others yet a requirement of reliable generation and sustainment of the belief. These have been proposed mostly as requirements that a belief must satisfy in order to qualify as knowledge, whereas our main focus here has been on how a belief gets to be epistemically justified. But there is a close connection between the two concerns, though this has yet to be spelled out in satisfactory detail, given the unclarity and ambiguity in the relevant terminology of 'epistemic justification'.

I will conclude with a sketch of the sort of requirements that seem to me most promising. How then would one distinguish

(1) an *unjustified* 'introspective' judgement, say that one's image has 48 speckles, when it is a true judgement, and one issued in full view of the image with that specific character,

from

(2) a *justified* 'introspective' judgement, say that one's image has 3 speckles?

The relevant distinction is that the latter judgement is both (a) *safe* and (b) *virtuous*, or so I wish to suggest. It is 'safe' because in the circumstances not easily *would* one believe as one does without being right. It is 'virtuous' because one's belief derives from a way of forming beliefs that is an intellectual virtue, one that in our normal situation for forming such beliefs would tend strongly enough to give us beliefs that are safe.

One does not know foundationally that one's image contains 48 speckles even if one's image *does* in fact containt 48 speckles, and one's belief hence corresponds precisely to what is then given in one's consciousness. One fails to know in that case because too easily one might have believed that one's image had 48 speckles while it had one more speckle or one less. But that is not so for the belief that one's image has 3 speckles.

It is not sufficient, however, that one's belief be thus *safe*. Consider the belief that $4,567,888 + 3,767,923 = 8,335,811$. Not easily would anyone believe this without being right, since not possibly would anyone believe it without being right. Nevertheless, if the way one arrives at one's belief is by a method according to which the sum of any two seven-digit numbers is any seven-digit number, then one fails to know, despite one's belief's being perfectly 'safe', in the sense defined.

For that reason, knowledge requires one's belief to be not only safe but also virtuously generated and sustained, through the use of a reliable method or faculty, through an 'intellectual virtue'.[11]

It might be argued, finally, that we are missing the point, that *justification* is not just whatever must be added to true belief in order to attain knowledge. Justification may be said to answer to its own requirements, and to have its own separate intuitive basis. This basis is more closely allied to concepts of reasonableness and rationality. Thus what one is assessing in calling a belief justified is rather the worth of the mind of the believer in respect of holding that belief with the basis that it has and in the internal circumstances in which it is held. Thus the relevant focus of evaluation is rather the relevant coherence of that mind, either at that moment or over the stretch of its history that is relevant to the acquisition and sustainment of that belief.

Nevertheless, my basic point remains. It is not enough that one's beliefs at that time jibe in logical respects with the experiences one is then undergoing. For the belief that one has an image with 48 speckles could hardly jibe better with that image's indeed having exactly that many speckles, while yet the belief remains unjustified despite such impressive coherence. What is missing here and present in the case where one believes that one's image has 3 speckles, at a time when that is exactly how many speckles it has? Once again what matters seems quite plausibly to be one's virtuous ability to discern cases of 3 speckles from those that have fewer speckles, or more, by contrast with one's inability to discriminate comparably as to 48 speckles.

In evaluating that proposal, however, recall that we seek to understand a source of *epistemic justification* (in a sense allied with rationality and reasonableness) that will be *foundational*, i.e. that will not derive from any inference, implicit or explicit, or at least one that will not derive wholly from that. It is a mistake, therefore, to object to the present proposal by arguing that someone *could* be justified in self-attributing an experience of 48 speckles despite lacking a virtuous ability to discriminate such experiences directly: by arguing, for example, that someone *could* be thus justified simply by inferring from a directly introspected inclination to so believe, along with a well-justified belief that such inclinations almost always turn out correct. This *would* explain a source of epistemic justification for that belief all right, even absent any virtuous ability to discriminate such experiences directly, but that justification would be inferential, not foundational.

[11] Of course these notions need to be clarified, and their virtues need to be displayed more fully in dialectical interplay with main competitors—which must, however, remain a project for another occasion.

REFERENCES

AYER, A. J. (1940), *Foundations of Empirical Knowledge* (London: Macmillan).

CHISHOLM, RODERICK (1942), 'Problem of the Speckled Hen', *Mind*, 1: 368–73.

EVANS, GARETH (1982), *The Varieties of Reference* (Oxford: Oxford University Press).

FUMERTON, RICHARD (1995), *Metaepistemology and Scepticism* (Totowa, NJ: Rowman & Littlefield).

MARTIN, MICHAEL (1998), 'An Eye Directed Outward', in Wright, Smith, and Macdonald (1998).

PEACOCKE, CHRISTOPHER (1998), 'Conscious Attitudes, Attention, and Self-Knowledge', in Wright, Smith, and Macdonald (1998).

RUSSELL, BERTRAND (1997), *Problems of Philosophy* (Oxford: Oxford University Press).

RYLE, GILBERT (1949), *The Concept of Mind* (London: Taylor & Francis).

WRIGHT, CRISPIN (1998), 'Self-Knowledge: The Wittgensteinian Legacy', in Wright, Smith, and Macdonald (1998).

—— SMITH, B. C., and MACDONALD, C. (eds.) (1998), *Knowing Our Own Minds* (Oxford: Oxford University Press).

Part Three

Consciousness and the Brain

Part Three

10. Consciousness and Cognition: Semiotic Conceptions of Bodies and Minds

JAMES H. FETZER

A comprehensive and complete theory of mentality, including an account of the nature of consciousness and of cognition, would have to include at least the following three ingredients familiar from classical philosophy of mind, namely: a theory of mind, a solution to the mind–body problem, and a resolution of the problem of other minds. This enquiry has the purpose of providing a summary of the theory of minds as *sign-using (or 'semiotic') systems* and to explain how this approach can solve the mind–body problem (by means of a nomological theory of mind–body interaction) and can resolve the problem of other minds (on the basis of epistemic principles supplied by inference to the best explanation).

This approach appears to fulfil the desideratum advanced by Jerry Fodor—namely, that a cognitive theory aims at connecting the *intensional properties* of mental states with their *causal properties vis-à-vis* behaviour—by employing the concept of a sign as something that stands for something else in some respect or other for somebody as a foundation for understanding the nature of a mind, where minds are those kinds of things for which something can stand for something else in some respect or other. It successfully connects the intensional properties of mental states with their causal properties *vis-à-vis* behaviour, but it also contradicts the popular view of minds as digital machines (Fetzer 1990, 1996*a*).

Virtually from conception, the discipline of cognitive science has been dominated by the computational paradigm, according to which cognition is

This chapter is a revised and expanded version of a paper, 'Consciousness and Cognition: Semiotic Conceptions', presented to the Semiotics and Communication Symposium held at The Catholic University of São Paulo, São Paulo, Brazil, 18–23 August 1998.

nothing more than computation across representations. Minds are symbol systems (in the sense of Newell and Simon 1976), the relation of minds and bodies is that of software to hardware, and the problem of other minds is resolved by means of the Turing test. John Haugeland has formulated the theses that sustain this conception by observing that, on this approach, thinking is reasoning, reasoning is reckoning, reckoning is computation, and the boundaries of computability define the boundaries of thought (Haugeland 1981). It is an appealing conception.

1. The Chinese Room (Again)

The conception is also deeply entrenched. Even recent work by Daniel Dennett (1996), David Chalmers (1996), and Igor Aleksander (1996) takes the computational conception for granted—with significant differences, of course. In order to motivate the adoption of an alternative account, especially one that implies that computers (at least, digital machines of the kind that Turing defined) are incapable of consciousness and cognition, not merely good but strong reasons have to be produced to make a choice both definable and defensible. The semiotic approach is preferable only if thinking is not reducible to reasoning, reasoning is not reducible to computation, and computability does not define the boundaries of thought.

A familiar, but still useful, point of departure is the Chinese Room argument, advanced by John Searle (1980). Searle distinguishes between two scenarios but here I shall distinguish three. The first involves a fluent speaker of Chinese, situated in a room, where strings of Chinese symbols are sent in for processing and strings of Chinese symbols are sent out in response. The second involves similar arrangements, except that the occupant of the room is not fluent in Chinese, but possesses a look-up table that offers instructions (in English) about which strings of Chinese symbols should be sent out in response to specific strings being sent in. The third replaces the room's human occupant with an automated look-up table.

Searle implies that there are important differences between systems of these three kinds, where their modes of operation are not the same. Although each of them might produce the same strings of symbols (as output) in response to receiving the same strings of symbols (as input), that does not provide an adequate foundation to make them systems that implement the same procedures (as programs). And, indeed, that each of these systems has the ability to produce the same outputs in relation to the same inputs has been assumed as a hypothesis in the construction of these scenarios. Yet it should be apparent that generating those outputs from those inputs occurs by utilizing quite different processes or procedures.

2. Simulation and Replication

The Chinese Room thus invites distinctions between systems that *simulate* by producing the same outputs in relation to the same imputs, systems that *replicate* by producing the same outputs in relation to the same inputs by employing the same processes or procedures, and systems that *emulate* by producing the same outputs in relation to the same inputs by employing the same processes or procedures *and* are made out of the same or at least similar material (or 'stuff') (Fetzer 1990: 17–18). The force of Searle's Chinese thought experiment thus emanates from introducing a case in which systems produce the same outputs in relation to the same inputs, but do so utilizing different processes or procedures.

These three conceptions are successively stronger and stronger, which means that systems that emulate also replicate and systems that replicate also simulate, necessarily, but not vice versa. The Chinese Room thus exemplifies systems that stand in relations of simulation without also standing in relations of replication by virtue of implementing different processes or procedures. When the first occupant (a fluent speaker of Chinese) is identified with a thinking thing and the third (an automated look-up table) with an inanimate machine, then from the perspective of ontology, Searle's thought experiment suggests that important—even crucial—differences may remain even when inanimate machines can simulate thinking things.

From the point of view of epistemology, moreover, Searle's Chinese Room functions as a counter-example—indeed, as a decisive refutation—of the Turing test as a criterion for the existence of other minds. The test itself measures the extent to which the symbol-manipulating behaviour of an inanimate machine has the ability to simulate that of a thinking thing. But if relations of simulation are not sufficient to guarantee the existence of similar processes or procedures that generate output from input, then passing the Turing test cannot guarantee that an inanimate machine has a mind. Thus, even if 'minds' could be suitably defined as thinking things, the Turing test would remain an inadequate evidential indicator of their existence.

3. Chalmers's Conception

A fascinating rejoinder to this position has been advanced by David Chalmers, who contends that, 'for some properties, simulation is replication', in particular, 'a simulation of X is an X when the property of being an X is an *organizational invariant*' (Chalmers 1996: 328). According to this conception, any system that has the same fine-grained functional organization will have qualitatively identical experiences, where the 'functional organization' of a system determines (at a suitable level of description) its behavioural capacities (ibid. 248–9). While he agrees that (computer) simulations of hurricanes are not hurricanes, he maintains that (computer) simulations of conscious minds can be conscious minds.

Chalmers's defence of this position hinges upon his introduction of the notion of *combinatorial-state automata*, which are like *finite-state automata* with structured internal states. This condition thus captures the idea of systems that not only produce the same outputs from the same inputs but do so by means of the same processes or procedures. Thus, a physical system *P* implements a combinatorial-state automata *M* when there is a one-to-one correspondence between input–output relations *and* the processes or procedures that produce those outputs from those inputs correspond, so that for every state transition rule, inputs of kind *I* will produce corresponding shifts between states $S1, \ldots, Sn$ and corresponding states $S'1, \ldots, S'n$ to outputs of kind *O*, which reliably causes *P* to implement *M* (ibid. 318).

While this characterization simplifies Chalmers's account in certain respects, his notion of combinatorial-state automata appears to reflect the distinction between simulation and replication, where simulation requires only that different systems produce the same outputs *O* in response to the same inputs *I*, while replication requires that those outputs be derived from those inputs by means of the same processes or procedures. These processes are thus captured by the state transitions from $S1, \ldots, Sn$ (in *M*) and $S'1, \ldots, S'n$ (in *P*), which guarantee that, at that level of description, the implementation of *M* by *P* will 'reliably cause' output *O* to be derived from the input *I*, provided such an outcome will be brought about at all.

4. Chalmers's Misconception

If we take Chalmers's symbols *M* and *P* to stand for mental and physical functional organization, respectively, then he may appear to have found the way to relate mental to physical properties and relations, thereby resolving the mind–body problem. Indeed, Chalmers (ibid. 321) at this juncture maintains the thesis:

There is a rich causal dynamics inside a computer, just as there [is] in the brain. Indeed, in an ordinary computer that implements a neuron-by-neuron simulation of my brain, there will be real causation going on between voltages in various circuits, precisely mirroring patterns of causation between the neurons. For each neuron, there will be a memory location that represents the neuron, and each of these locations will be physically realized in a voltage at some physical location. It is the causal patterns among these circuits, just as it is the causal patterns among the neurons in the brain, that are responsible for any conscious experience that arises.

On this basis, Chalmers completes his defence of the thesis that computers can be the possessors of conscious minds when they are executing appropriate programs.

This position, of course, is known as that of 'strong AI', as opposed to the alternative position of 'weak AI', which holds that computers are simply useful tools for the study of the mind (Searle 1980; cf. Fetzer 1990: 61). Chalmers's defence of strong AI, however, appears to depend upon certain misconceptions. The first is that 'an ordinary computer that implements a neuron-by-neuron simulation of [his] brain' would not be 'an ordinary computer'; indeed, such systems are sufficiently rare that none exist at present. The second is that ordinary computers are complex systems that 'reliably cause' shifts from inputs I to outputs O because their state transitions are controlled by programs, which implement algorithms.

Suppose, however, that human thought processes are non-algorithmic, as the semiotic conception suggests. Then Chalmers's argument will have neglected to consider one of the fundamental differences between human beings and digital machines. Moreover, Chalmers takes for granted that conscious experiences are mental properties that supervene on physical properties, where 'M properties' supervene on 'P properties' if and only if no situations could be identical with respect to their P properties and differ in relation to their M properties (Chalmers 1996: 33). But he does nothing to show that specific mental properties such as consciousness are among those that supervene on these physical properties.

5. Chalmersian Supervenience

Chalmers acknowledges that the existence of laws of supervenience that relate consciousness to physical systems is the foundation of his theory of consciousness (ibid. 213). He also acknowledges the logical possibility that systems that are physically identical might have different properties of consciousness. The crucial distinction, therefore, is that, although it *is* logically possible for systems that are physically identical to have different properties of consciousness, it is *not* physically possible for systems that are physically identical to have different properties of consciousness (ibid. 38). This contention, which seems to be correct, however, depends upon a defensible conception of supervenience.

In order to appreciate the difficulties of Chalmers's position—which, it should be acknowledged, are encountered by every other theoretician who makes use of the notion of supervenience—recall that M-properties supervene on P-properties if and only if no situations could be identical with respect to their P-properties and differ in relation to their M-properties. The force of 'could' here needs to be explained. If it is a matter of logical possibility, then it appears to be well understood, but it is also trivial. If it is a matter of physical possibility, then it is not trivial, but it is also not well understood. In this context, supervenience poses a problem rather than providing a solution to whether machines can have minds.

That Chalmers has actually bitten off more than he can chew, moreover, becomes apparent in relation to his defence of strong AI. The contention that physical systems that implement the same fine-grained functional organization will possess the same mental properties depends upon three factors: (1) the specific mental properties under consideration, (2) the specific physical properties under consideration, and (3) whether those physical properties include every property whose presence or absence makes a difference to those mental properties. Thus, when Chalmers characterizes combinatorial-state automata, he simply takes for granted that supervenient properties of M will be supervenient properties of P.

6. Chalmers's Sleight-of-Hand

The class of cases in which simulations are replications appears to be a very special class. It would presumably include representations of representations, since any simulation of a representation is itself a representation. Chalmers's example is that a simulation of a system with a causal loop would be a system with a causal loop (ibid. 328). But that appears to be a mistake. The requirements of simulation are those imposed by input–output relations exclusively. A system with a causal loop, presumably, is one for which any input yields no output at all. But that could be done by means of processes or procedures that do not resort to causal loops. Chalmers is trading in replications, not in simulations.

Moreover, the truth of psychophysical laws relating mental and physical properties may depend upon considerations that transcend those relevant to replicating the processes or procedures involved in getting from input I to output O. In particular, suppose that the combinatorial-state automota under consideration is one for constructing proofs of theorems within well-defined logico-mathematical contexts. Under those conditions, a human proof (call it an M-proof) of theorem T from axiom A might proceed with intermediate steps $S1, S2, \ldots, Sn$, and a machine proof (call it a P-proof) of T from A take place with the same intermediate steps $S'1, S'2, \ldots, S'n$. Yet their respective experiences might not be the same at all.

Just because a machine proof replicated a human proof, for example, would not show that they felt the same way about it. The system responsible for the *M*-proof might be overjoyed to have accomplished such a feat, while the system responsible for the *P*-proof might be incapable of emotions as an inanimate machine. That is, after all, what we would expect. Chalmers's presumption that simulations of processes or procedures that produce an output *O* from an input *I* are going to bring conscious experiences along with them as an effect of psychophysical laws, after all, presupposes the existence of such laws for the systems he considers. Combinatorial-state automata might replicate some human traits without replicating them all.

7. Maximal Specificity

Chalmers ignores the full range of conditions that might make a difference to the occurrence of conscious experience. Aleksander (1996), for example, has proposed the conjecture that consciousness may be solely a property of neurons as a product of the process of evolution. If Aleksander is correct, then even a highly successful replication of human reasoning by means of combinatorial-state automata instantiated by inanimate machines could not be expected to possess corresponding conscious experiences, because they are not made out of the right 'stuff'. It appears ironic, in view of Chalmers's studies, that not only are simulations not enough for replications, but that some replications may depend upon emulations.

At the very least, it depends upon the level of description (the fine-grainedness), the completeness of the description, and the nature of the outcome under consideration. Working backwards, the experience of the qualities of a stop sign with respect to its colour, shape, size, and relative location are those of perceptual systems that are capable of perceiving colours, shapes, sizes, and relative locations. In order to construct a system that could have those experiences, it would be essential to consider every property that makes a difference to its perceptual capabilities, which are those that are causally relevant to outcomes of this kind. Perceptual abilities of systems thus depend upon their casually relevant properties.

Even a fine-grained analysis of a system might be expected to capture system laws for the occurrence of specific outcome phenomena, including consciousness, for example, only when it takes into account every property that makes a difference to their occurrence. If only neurons are capable of consciousness—a possibility I am discussing rather than endorsing—then any attempt to formulate psychophysical laws that does not take that factor into account necessarily fails. The truth of lawlike sentences thus requires that their antecedents must be *maximally specific* by implying the presence or the absence of every property that makes a difference to the occurrence of their outcomes (Fetzer 1981, 1993, 1996a).

8. A Broader Approach

When the material (or 'stuff') of which systems are composed makes a difference to their internal or external behaviour with respect to specific outcomes, then corresponding laws must take that into account, on pain of sacrificing their truth. If the difference between chips made of silicon or of chocolate would affect their capacity to conduct electrons, on the one hand, or in making a tasty snack, on the other, then the laws for silicon chips and for chocolate chips must differ. There is no good reason to suppose that psycho-physical laws that obtain for arrangements of neurons, for example, are going to coincide with those that obtain for arrangements of software and hardware, however seductive the computational paradigm.

Not the least of the objections that might be raised to Chalmers's account, moreover, is that he embraces a relatively narrow, though not therefore unusual, conception of consciousness, which he characterizes as 'the subject-ive quality of experience' (Chalmers 1996: 4). However interesting it might be, this conception ultimately appears to be peripheral to alternative concepts of greater importance. Distinctions need to be drawn between sentience, aware-ness, and self-awareness, which he considers to be of less significance (ibid. ch. 1). Accounting for the phenomenal qualities of experience poses an important problem, but it also seems secondary to analysing the contribution of con-sciousness to cognition.

A complete and comprehensive account of human cognition would have to take consciousness (in this phenomenal sense) into consideration, but a much broader and far richer conception seems to be required that might apply to various forms of thinking, including sensing, perceiving, dreaming, day-dreaming, learning, memorizing, remembering, conjecturing, hypothesizing, arguing, reasoning, criticizing—without assuming these are distinct and independent activities—where most if not all of these appear to involve consciousness and cognition in senses that go beyond the phenomenal sense. In the sections that follow, therefore, broader conceptions of conscious-ness and cognition will be introduced and their ramifications explored.

9. Minds as Semiotic Systems

The theory of signs (or 'semiotic') introduced by Charles S. Peirce provides a foundation for the conception of minds as sign-using (or 'semiotic') systems.

On this approach, *there are at least three kinds of minds*, corresponding to Peirce's distinction between three kinds of signs, iconic, indexical, and symbolic, where minds of each of these kinds use signs of corresponding kinds. These appear to be successively stronger kinds of minds, in so far as minds that are indexical are also iconic and minds that are symbolic are also indexical (Fetzer 1988, 1990, 1996a). In so far as mentality has presumably emerged through a process of evolution, systems that are lower on the evolutionary scale ought to have weaker mental abilities, while those that are higher should have stronger mental abilities.

On Peirce's account, a *sign* is a something that stands for something (else) in some respect or other for somebody (Hartshorne and Weiss 1960: ii. 247–9, and 274–308). As I have elsewhere explained, the use of 'somebody' seems to imply that the kind of thing for which something can stand for something else has to be human. An appropriate conception of *minds* as sign-using (or semiotic) systems thus requires generalizing and inverting this triadic relationship in order to define minds as the kinds of things for which things can stand for other things. Three ways in which things can stand for other things thus include relations of resemblance, relations of cause-and-effect, and relations of habitual association.

The conception of minds as semiotic systems invites conceptions of consciousness according to which systems are conscious when they have the ability to use signs of specific kinds and not incapacitated from the exercise of that ability. This implies that *consciousness is relative to signs of specific kinds*, such that a system may be said to be conscious (with respect to signs of that kind) when it is able to use signs of that kind and not incapacitated from exercising that ability. The counterpart conception of cognition thus maintains that *cognition occurs as a consequence of causal interactions* between systems that are conscious (with respect to signs of specific kinds) and the presence of signs of those specific kinds in suitable causal proximity. Cognition is therefore an effect of a causal process.

10. Iconic Mentality

Iconic mentality, which is the most elementary kind and the most primitive from an evolutionary point of view, depends upon the ability to distinguish different instances of things as instances of things of the same kind. A criterion of the existence of iconic mentality thus appears to be the ability for type/token recognition, which is the ability to recognize different instances (tokens) of the same kind (type) (Fetzer 1988: 142). Because every specific instance of any property at any time is a unique event with infinitely many relations to other instances of other properties at other times, this ability depends upon presupposed points of view demarcating aspects of those events as the relevant kind.

Familiar examples include statues, photographs, and drawings, when they are realistically construed, which thereby presupposes a point of view. Your passport photograph, for example, when viewed from the front, may look like you, perhaps on a bad day. But viewed from the side, it may not look like you at all, because you are just not that thin. Michelangelo's statue 'David' presumably resembles its subject with respect to his features, his proportions, and his appearance, but not with respect to his weight, or his temperature, or the stuff of which he is made. Conventions commonly define the respects that are to be preserved by different forms of art, but sometimes those constraints are violated. Picasso's work is a striking example of successful contraventions of conventions.

The *E. coli* bacterium affords an example of a primitive life form that appears to possess iconic mentality. These organisms possess receptor proteins on their cell surfaces that combine with specific chemotactic substances to induce motion towards twelve different attracting substances and away from eight different repellants by the rotation of their flagella (Bonner 1980: 63). Assuming that the substances toward which *E. coli* are attracted are beneficial while those by which they are repelled are harmful, the bacterium appears to have an evolved ability to identify different instances of these chemotactic substances as instances of different kinds. It thus should be apparent that not all semiotic abilities are learned.

11. Indexical Mentality

Indexical mentality depends on the existence of causal connections between instantiations of properties of different kinds, such as heat, ashes, and smoke as effects of fire. The presence of smoke, ashes, or heat thus stand for the presence of fire as effects of such a cause. Since other causes can bring about some of the same effects—hot water in radiators radiating heat, for example—these signs are usually reliable but not therefore infallible indicators of the presence of a corresponding cause. For complex systems that possess various internal states, such as 'motives' and 'beliefs', broadly construed, as variables whose values make a difference to a sign's significance, their discriminatory capacity may be considerable.

Their ability to use echolocation provides an especially intriguing example of indexical mentality in the case of bats. By emitting high-frequency sounds and sensing subtle differences in their echoed effects, bats are able to navigate their way through complex environments that include hundreds or even thousands of other bats. Donald Griffin has speculated that 'when bats detect and identify insects by echolocation, they perceive not a special pattern of echos but rather the presence, position, and location of an object with certain properties—such as an edible insect or a falling leaf' (Griffin 1992: 238). The process of perception thus may not depend on the specific sensory modality by which it is exercised.

That indexical mentality implies iconic mentality can be demonstrated in many different ways, because similar causes are expected to produce similar effects, which presupposes the ability to classify different instantiations of properties as similar. That this is indeed the case emerges even from classic philosophical analyses of causation. According to Hume, the relation of causation obtains between two events of kinds C and E just in case events of kind E occur in spatial proximity with events of kind C, events of kind C temporally precede events of kind E, and events of kind E are constantly conjoined with events of kind C, the recognition of which depends on being able to identify events of similar kinds.

12. Symbolic Mentality

The words and sentences that occur in ordinary languages, such as English, German, and Portuguese, for example, are the most familiar examples of symbols that are used by human beings. Although primitive languages are rudimentary in relation to contemporary languages, the words and sentences they employ are merely habitually associated with those things for which they stand. Words such as *schnee* and *weiss*, for example, do not resemble those things for which they stand, namely, *snow* and *white*, nor are they causes or effects of things of those kinds. The sentence 'Schnee ist weiss' (in German) has the same meaning as the sentence 'Snow is white' (in English), but their meanings depend on conventions.

Conventions are best understood as habitual associations between signs and things that are supported by customs, traditions, and practices, which might or might not be formally institutionalized. The vervet monkeys, for example, use several different alarm calls, at least three of which are distinctive in relation to specific kinds of predators: a snake call, a leopard call, and an eagle call. Whenever they hear these specific calls, their behavioural responses tend to be similar; in particular, 'Animals hearing the leopard call rush up into the trees, they respond to the eagle call by running down to the ground and hiding in thickets, and the snake call leads them to approach and look down' (Slater 1985: 155–6).

Of course, their behaviour is not always the same. Those who have strayed off into the bush may not hear the alarm call and remain vulnerable to attack, while those who are suffering from physical impairment—such as poor hearing due to a bad cold or physical infirmities from broken limbs, for example—may not display the same behaviour as other monkeys not suffering from those incapacities. These alarm calls function as causes in relation to bringing about such behaviours as an effect for monkeys who are able to use signs of those kinds and who are not inhibited from the exercise of that ability by related incapacities, where behaviour of one kind or another comes about relative to considerations of context.

13. Language and Mentality

Examples such as these involving the chemotactical sensitivies of bacteria, the echolocation abilities of bats, and the alarm calls utilized by monkeys display the untenability of theories of mentality that make the ability to use an ordinary language a precondition for having a mind. The most striking case of this kind has been advanced by a leading cognitive scientist in the form of his *language of thought* hypothesis, which maintains that humans could not learn any ordinary language unless they possessed prior linguistic understanding of the phenomena thereby described to which its words might be attached, which entails either an infinite regress or an innate, species-specific, 'base' language.

What Jerry Fodor overlooks is the possibility that the requisite kind of prior understanding of the phenomena described by the words of that language might be *non-linguistic* (Fodor 1975). Indeed, since the words that occur in ordinary language are symbols and symbols are only one among the three basic kinds of signs, it would be peculiar indeed if the ability to use signs of any of these kinds presupposed the ability to use signs of the highest kind. A more promising avenue toward understanding sign-using phenomena generally thus appears to be provided by the realization that the meaning of signs has to be understood dispositionally by means of the contextual influence of those signs upon behaviour.

Babes-in-arms, toddling tots, and infant children learn to suck the nipples of bottles, to play with balls, and to draw with crayons long before they learn that the words for those activities are 'sucking on nipples of bottles', 'playing with balls', and 'drawing with crayons'. What they acquire through experience with things of these kinds are physical habits concerning the kinds of things that can be done with bottles, with balls, and with crayons, some of which are activities, such as rolling them down the stairs, throwing them in the house, and writing on the walls, of which most mothers in particular would not approve (Fetzer 1991).

14. Concepts and Cognition

Once a youngster has acquired the concept of a bottle, a ball, or a crayon, by learning a possibly complex set of physical habits concerning what can be done with things of that kind, it becomes trivial to associate those concepts with language through the further acquisition of linguistic habits. Thus, sounds (as phonemes) thereby become *infused with meaning* (as morphemes) and inscriptions that would otherwise be meaningless marks become written words instead. As children acquire more and more concepts, therefore, they are able to learn more and more words, until new words can be associated with old words in a process that yields new linguistic habits without having to acquire new physical habits.

Some uses of signs, however, may be innate and unlearned, as displayed by the iconic abilities of *E. coli* bacteria and the echolocation abilities of bats. Either way, consciousness is always relative to specific classes of signs. *E. coli* bacteria may be conscious with respect to twenty specific chemotactic substances, in so far as they have the ability to use signs of that kind when they are not incapacitated from its exercise, but are not conscious with respect to high-frequency sounds, which they are unable to detect. Bats may be conscious with respect to high-frequency sounds, by comparison, which they can use when they are not incapacitated, but they are not conscious with respect to vervet monkey alarm calls.

Automobile drivers are nice examples of semiotic systems relative to those signs that govern the use of highways. For those who are qualified as drivers by virtue of having mastered the rules of the road (as physical habits) and signs of the road (as mental habits), the occurrence of a red light at an intersection has an established meaning, namely: apply the brakes and come to a halt, only proceeding when the light changes to green and it is safe to do so. Notice, especially, that the meaning of a stop sign of this kind is provided by a set of physical habits and mental habits, which combine to reflect, at least in part, the concept of a stop sign. Perception, on this view, thus appears to involve the subsumption of experiences by means of concepts, which situate those experiences within complexes of habits.

15. Dennett's Alternative

Dennett has introduced an alternative scheme of classification. In Dennett (1996), for example, he differentiates between *Darwinian creatures*, which are the products of natural selection, *Skinnerian creatures*, which are capable of operant conditioning, *Popperian creatures*, which are capable of preselection between possible behaviours, and *Gregorian creatures*, which are capable of the evolution of culture. As in relation to his previous discussion of things of these kinds (Dennett 1995), Dennett insists that human beings are not merely Skinnerian creatures who are capable of operant conditioning but also Darwinian creatures who benefit from inherited hardwiring, and Popperian creatures who can represent their options (Dennett 1996: 92, for example).

What ought to be considered most interesting about Popperian creatures, I think, is they they are capable of *representing* their environments and their choices before they act, a capacity that Dennett ascribes to many different kinds of animals: 'We do not differ from all other species in being Popperian creatures then. Far from it: mammals and birds, reptiles, amphibians, fish, and even many invertebrates exhibit the capacity to use general information they obtain from their environments to presort their behavioral options before striking out' (ibid. 92–3). Somewhat surprisingly, in view of his commitments to computational conceptions, Dennett appears to contradict the notion that the distinctive ability of minds is *the capacity to utilize and manipulate representations*. Those who approach the problem from this perspective are likely to take Popperian creatures as thinking things.

If Popperian creatures are thinking things, human mentality has evolutionary origins. Dennett (ibid. 99–101), however, contends that only Gregorian creatures can be thinking things, because they are capable of the use of tools, including language, especially. The conception of human beings as distinctive toolmakers and tool-users is an early anthropological conception that has been superseded by research in cognitive ethology. Anyone more familiar with the state of current research would not be drawn to such a view, which ignores or distorts the evolution of communication and the nature of animal mind. (For recent work, see Ristau 1991; Dawkins 1993; Beckoff and Jamieson 1996; and Fetzer 1996*b*.)

16. Action and Meaning

In so far as *consciousness* (with respect to signs of a specific kind) entails the ability to use signs of that kind and the absence of an incapacity to exercise the ability, *cognition* occurs when a system that is conscious (with respect to signs of a specific kind) encounters a sign of that kind within suitable causal proximity (within appropriate spatio-temporal parameters). The effects that may be brought about thereby, however, may or may not be immediate in their manifestations. Some mental states induced by the process of cognition may have only distant or intermittent behavioural manifestations, whose occurrence may depend upon the presence of other factors that are rarely if ever encountered.

What this means is that the theory of meaning (what signs mean) must be embedded within the theory of action (why organisms act as they do). Within this framework, it should be apparent that the more complex the inner states of an organism, the more complex the explanations for its behaviour. Human beings, for example, are the most complicated species with which we are presently familiar and may be the most complicated species within the physical universe. Thus, the totality of kinds of factors that can affect the behaviour of human beings includes *motives, beliefs, ethics, abilities, capabilities*, and *opportunities*, where opportunities concern how things are (truth) rather than believed to be (belief).

These variables matter to explanations of human behaviour just in case their values make a difference to the behaviour that people display. Theoretically, the difference they make can be measured by the differences in behaviour that are brought about by varying their values systematically, one by one. Thus, taking adult humans as reference subjects, having a strong sex drive, for example, turns out to be explanatorily relevant to a specific instance of behaviour just in case the value of that variable (which might be weak, average, or strong) makes a difference to that behaviour (including its duration, intensity, and frequency). In most cases (shopping for groceries, for example), it might not make a difference at all.

17. The Meaning of Mental States

Precisely the same pattern of analysis can be applied to specify the meaning, intension, or sense of attributions of beliefs, ethics, abilities, and capabilities via this broadly dispositional approach, according to which factors of each of these kinds can best be understood on the basis of their causal influence on behaviour. The meaning of a *specific belief B1*, for example, such as that dry ice can bring about suffocation, could then be explained by stipulating the difference that this specific belief would make to a person's—any person's—behaviour relative to *various contexts C1, ..., Cn* that fix the values of the other relevant variables that affect behaviour, which includes their degrees of rationality of action and belief.

Thus, since these relationships are completely general and characterize the behaviour that would be (invariably or probably) expected under complete sets of relevant conditions $C1, ..., Cn$, they might be formally expressed by means of *subjunctive* conditionals '... $\Longrightarrow$ —' about what would happen '—' if something '...' were the case and *causal* conditionals '... $= n \Rightarrow$ —' about the effects '—' that would be brought about (invariably or probably) within that particular context (where n indicates the strength of the corresponding tendency), namely:

(M1) $(x)(t)[C1xt \implies (B1xt = n \Rightarrow R1xt^*)];$

(M2) $(x)(t)[C2xt \implies (B1xt = m \Rightarrow R2xt^*)];\ldots$

which mean that, if x were in context $C1$ at time t, having belief $B1$ at t would bring about (with strenth n) the behavioural response $R1$ at time t^*; and so forth.

A similar pattern of analysis could be applied to motives, other beliefs, ethics, abilities, and capabilities, where their contribution to a human being's behaviour could thereby be made explicit. These formulations can be fashioned in at least two different ways, moreover, where by assuming a constant context $C1$, the difference made by the acquisition of various beliefs $B1,\ldots,$ Bn can be specified:

(M3) $(x)(t)[B1xt \implies (C1xt = n \Rightarrow R1xt^*)];$

(M4) $(x)(t)[B2xt \implies (C1xt = m \Rightarrow R2xt^*)];\ldots$

which mean that, if x were to acquire belief $B1$ at t, then being in context $C1$ at t would bring about (with strength n) the behavioural response $R1$ at time t^*; etc.

18. The Role of Rationality

The role of rationality, moreover, should not be misunderstood. Rationality comes in at least two varieties, namely: rationality of action and rationality of belief. A system has high *rationality of action* when it tends to adopt means that are appropriate to attain its goals, given its motives, beliefs, ethics, abilities, and capabilities. A system displays high *rationality of belief* when it tends to adopt beliefs that are well supported by the relevant evidence at its disposal. The appropriate standards of rationality of both kinds are normative in so far as they characterize how systems in specific causal states would function. Either of them might be induced as a consequence of evolution or of learning.

Thus, evolution by natural selection tends to produce systems that are at least fairly well adapted to their environments. The survival of the fittest is a process that tends to enhance prospects for survival and reproduction when allowances are made for random occurrences and chance events. Analogously, the process of education by academic selection tends to produce systems that are at least fairly capable of rational deliberation. One of the benefits of a college education appears to be its capacity to enhance a student's rationality of belief. It would be a mistake to suppose that causation precludes rationality.

The role of *opportunities* (how the world is as opposed to our beliefs about it) frequently tends to account for differences between success and failure in actions. A recent story in the local paper, for example, reported that a woman tried to kill her husband three times without success (Hanners 1998). First, she tried to suffocate him by placing dry ice under his bed, but she only made the room a bit colder. Second, she dropped a clock-radio into his bath, but it had a ground-fault interrupter, which functioned as a circuit breaker. Third, she tried to hire a hit-man, but he turned out to be an undercover cop. She was game and her ethics did not inhibit her, but opportunities for success were just not there.

19. Psychophysical Laws

A distinction can be drawn between permanent and transient properties that clarifies the nature of supervenience and of psychophysical laws. In particular, an attribute A is a *permanent* property of a reference property R if and only if, although the possession of A is not part of the definition of R, there is no process or procedure, natural or contrived, by means of which something that has R could lose A without also losing R. Properties that things that are R could lose while remaining things that are R, however, are only *transient* (Fetzer 1981, 1990, 1993). When attribute A is a permanent property of property R, there can be no instance of R that is not an instance of A as a matter of natural instead of logical necessity.

Thus, the melting point, boiling point, and specific gravity of things that are gold, when 'gold' is defined by means of its atomic number, which is 79, are among its permanent properties, which things that are gold could only lose by no longer having atomic number 79. The size, shape, and selling price of things that are gold, however, are among their transient properties. Permanent properties of things are therefore properties that supervene on their reference properties, in so far as nothing that has the same reference property could differ with respect to its permanent properties. Mental properties therefore supervene on physical properties just in case they are permanent properties of those same physical properties.

The logical contingency of the permanent property relation must be preserved. When attribute M is a permanent property of property P, a corresponding subjunctive conditional obtains, since for all x, if x were P, then x would be M, as follows:

(PP) (x) (t) $(Pxt \Longrightarrow Mxt)$

but not as a logical truth. Thus, employing the *material* conditional '... → —' and box '□' as the symbol for logical necessity, the following claim must be false:

(LT) □ (x) (t) (Pxt → Mxt).

Provided the presence or absence of these properties can be ascertained, under suitable conditions, permanent property hypotheses may be tested by efforts to disconfirm them as an aspect of inference to the best explanation (Fetzer 1993).

20. Minds and Brains

The importance of this distinction becomes apparent relative to the difference between minds and mind-states, on the one hand, and brains and brain-states, on the other. Let us adopt the conception of brains as neural networks of numerous nodes that are capable of activation. These nodes can be connected to other nodes where, depending upon their levels of activation, they may bring about increases or decreases in the levels of activation of those other nodes (Rumelhart et al. 1986). Some of these patterns of activation may arise in response to the function of sense receptors (for taste, touch, sight, smell, and hearing, for example), and others may control the function of muscle and sound activators (for motion and speech).

The patterns of activation between these nodes may be probabilistic or deterministic, depending upon their fine-grained causal character. But if *brain states* are envisioned as specific patterns of neural activation, then *brains* must be those things that are capable of possessing brain states, where brain states themselves may be permanent or transient properties of brains. And if *mind states* are envisioned as specific semiotic states (reflecting the causal influence of signs across different contexts), then *minds* must be those things that are capable of possessing mind states, which may be permanent or transient properties of minds. And minds of different kinds may be permanent properties of various kinds of brains.

This conception supports the possibility that minds are species-specific dispositions for the acquistion and utilization of signs of specific kinds. *E. coli* bacteria, for example, may be the possessors of iconic mentality of a highly restricted variety, which only permits the activation of patterns of neurons in response to the presence of specific chemotactic substances. Bats may be the possessors of indexical mentality of a rather special type, which includes the activation of patterns of neurons in response to high-frequency sound vibrations. Vervet monkeys may be the possessors of symbolic mentality that allows the activation of patterns of neurons in response to specific patterns of sound that function for them as alarm calls.

21. Mind–Body Interaction

These considerations strongly suggest that the relationship between the body and the mind (or the brain and the mind) must be *interactive*. This possibility is supported by even our most commonplace experience. Consider, for example, going to a lecture. During the lecture, you are exposed to various sounds, some of which are familiar as phonemes, others familiar as morphemes. Processing them by means of your senses, specific patterns of neurons are subjected to activation. The activation of some patterns may (invariably or probabilistically) bring about the activation of other patterns. These transitions between patterns of activation may bring about associated transitions in sequences of thoughts from $T1, \ldots, Tn$.

Assume that brains of specific kinds B^* have minds of specific kinds M^* among their permanent properties, which may be formalized thus:

(LC1) (x) (t) $(B^*xt \Longrightarrow M^*xt)$.

Then minds of kind M^* presumably have innate capacities for acquiring semiotic abilities, say, learning a language L, under suitable environmental conditions EFi:

(LC2) $(x)(t)[M^*xt \Longrightarrow (EFixt = n \Rightarrow Lxt^*)]$,

which might be a deterministic or a probabilistic consequence of those conditions. Then anyone in a specific context $C1$, including such semiotic abilities, might be in conditions where hearing a lecture might bring about the acquisition of belief $B1$:

(LC3) $(x)(t)$ $[C1xt \Longrightarrow (EFjxt = m \Rightarrow B1xt^*)]$;

where $B1$ is (invariably or probabilistically) brought about under conditions EFj.

That changes in brain states have been brought about by hearing a lecture becomes obvious when we consider that we not only remember having been present on that occasion but also can even recollect its content. This implies not only that specific patterns of neurons were activated at the time of the lecture but that we have the ability to reactivate those patterns under suitable conditions. The capacities for sensation, perception, memory, and recollection thus appear to be amenable to understanding on the basis of the assumption of the existence of psychophysical laws that relate specific mind states as permanent properties of corresponding brain states to their transient manifestations under suitable conditions.

22. Brains and Behaviour

The number of neurons in the human brain appears to be on the order of 10^{12} (or one trillion), where the number of connections that those neurons can establish with other neurons is approximately 1,000. This means that there are 10^{15} (or one quadrillion) possible states of the brain defined by distinct arrangements of patterns of activation. The activation of some of these patterns brings about the activation of others as innate properties that no normal brain could be without, while others may come about as acquired properties that normal brains could be without. The capacity to learn a language (within the range of humanly learnable languages), for example, appears to be inborn, while actually knowing English, German, and Portuguese is acquired.

Some brain states interact with other internal states to bring about transitions to successive brain states, while others activate specific sequences of motor behaviours, which may include speech. The factors that affect these effects include every property that makes a difference to these transitions, which constitute its neural context. Our interest in these patterns of activation derives from their causal contribution to speech and other behaviour, however. Motives and beliefs, for example, refer to the energizing and directive factors that influence behaviour and speech, while ethics refers to a special subset that tends to inhibit certain kinds of behaviour and speech under certain kinds of conditions. Abilities even have specific modular neural locations.

The acquisition of different habits of action and habits of mind as an effect of our life histories thus tends to determine our capacity to subsume various experiences by means of corresponding concepts. Those with restricted opportunities to learn and to acquire concepts are therefore inhibited from interacting with their environments in ways that might maximize their fitness. A community that wants to benefit all its members, therefore, should maximize their opportunities for diversified experiences that will enhance their acquisition of concepts. Every neurologically normal human being may have the same innate potential to learn language and acquire other semiotic abilities, yet only actually acquire them under specific environmental conditions.

23. The Nature of Perception

The key to understanding consciousness and cognition specifically and mentality in general thus appears to be their distinctively semiotic dimension.

Processes that involve the use of signs are properly qualified as *mental activities*, while those that do not are not. The term 'sentience' appears to be perfectly appropriate in relation to the capacity to experience sensations. But unless those sensations are subsumed, in turn, by sets of habits of action and habits of thought with distinctively semiotic character, it does not properly qualify as 'consciousness'. And forms of consciousness that entail an awareness of the use of signs by a system, especially through the use of signs that stand for consciousness itself, may properly qualify as higher order.

Thus, if Dennett (1996) were right—if there were no more to sentience (as the lowest level of consciousness) than sensitivity—then his own examples of sensitivity *without* consciousness—photographic film, thermometers, and litmus paper—have to be conscious, after all, which is not an enviable position to defend. The missing ingredient x whose existence he doubts appears to be the subsumption of sensations by means of specific sets of habits of action and habits of thought. The reason why his examples are such appropriate illustrations of non-conscious things is that no one would be inclined to suppose that any causal interactions between photographic film and light (thermometers and heat, and so on) involve any subsumption by concepts.

The highest order of consciousness, from this point of view, may involve not only awareness of the use of signs by a system, but that system's own awareness that it is the system using those signs as 'self-consciousness', a capacity that does not seem to be the exclusive prerogative of human beings. Thus, *E. coli bacteria* swim towards twelve chemotactic substances and away from eight others (Bonner 1980), an evolved response that at least exemplifies sentience. *Bats* employ echolocation by means of high-frequency sound vibrations (Griffin 1984), an evolved response that appears to exemplify consciousness. And *chimpanzees* display forms of self-awareness that seem properly to qualify as kinds of self-consciousness (Cheyney and Seyfarth 1990).

24. Icons, Indices, Symbols

None of these forms of consciousness—from sentience to self-consciousness—appears to be reducible to mere sensitivity. But it is fascinating to discover that precisely the same sensation as a pattern of activation of neurons in the brain might be interpreted iconically, indexically, or symbolically. Consider again, for example, a red light at an intersection. It might be taken *iconically* when the sensations that it brings about cause mental transitions to other patterns of activation that stand for other things that resemble its colour (its shape, and so on), such as the dress that his wife wore the night before. Taken *indexically* it might cause a repairman to think about possible reasons why it is not working properly. Taken *symbolically* it might cause a driver to stop.

Indeed, as a generalization, it appears to be the case that for something to stand for something for a system presupposes a *point of view* relative to which something experienced as a pattern of neural activation becomes identified, classified, or categorized as a thing of a certain kind. This function, of course, can be fulfilled when the system possesses corresponding concepts, in the absence of which it has no 'point of view'. These sets of habits of action and habits of thought occur as pre-exisiting inner states of that system, which affect the tendency for the activation of one pattern of neurons to bring about the activation of another, which might be iconic, indexical, or symbolic. The strength of the tendency for specific patterns of neural activation to bring about other specific patterns thus has the nature of a propensity (Fetzer 1996*a*).

As properties of semiotic systems, mental dispositions might be deterministic or probabilistic. They are *deterministic* when, under precisely the same (internal and external) conditions of stimulation, the system would respond in precisely the same way by effecting the same transitions between mental states and bringing about the same behaviour as an outcome. They are *probabilistic* when, under precisely the same (internal and external) conditions of stimulation, the system would respond by effecting one or another transition between mental states and bringing about two or more behaviours as its outcome, each with constant probabilities. The system, in this case, possesses mental and behavioural *propensities* as probabilistic dispositional properties.

25. Turing Machines

In a broad sense, motives, beliefs, ethics, abilities, and capabilities can all be qualified as mental properties to whatever extent they involve the use of signs. They may also be qualified as physical properties to the extent to which they are properties of systems in space–time. What makes physical properties into mental properties is that they involve the use of signs. The difference between the mental and the physical is not a difference in causal capability but rather a difference in the kind of causal capability they possess. From the perspective of the conception of minds as semiotic systems, any system that has the ability to use signs has a mind, no matter whether it is human, (other) animal, or machine.

If we return to the Chinese Room, then it should be apparent that what distinguishes these scenarios is the semiotic ability (or lack thereof) of the three occupants: a fluent speaker of Chinese, a non-fluent speaker using a look-up table, and an automated look-up table, respectively. For the fluent speaker of Chinese the Chinese symbols sent in were meaningful for her and the symbols she sent out were appropriate in response. For the non-fluent speaker, those same symbols were meaningless strings, where her responses were determined by following the look-up table without understanding them. For the automated machine, those otherwise meaningless strings were causally processed into other strings.

Digital machines have the ability to process strings even though they do so on the basis of their physical properties alone, including the shapes, sizes, and relative locations of the marks of which they are composed. This should come as no surprise in view of the nature of Turing machines, which have the ability to make marks, to remove marks, to move one cell forward and to move one cell backward in relation to a segmented tape of arbitrary length. Even if the state of the system before its instructions are executed is called 'input' and the state of the system after its instructions have been executed is called 'output', there is nothing to suggest that any of those marks stand for anything for the machine.

26. The Static Difference

We have discovered that Chalmers's defence of strong AI depends upon making the assumption that psychophysical laws guarantee that systems that stand in relations of simulation also stand in relations of replication, when those simulations involve organizational invariants. When the fallacious foundation for his argument has been exposed, it becomes apparent that the kinds of systems that remain are no more than symbol systems (in Newell and Simon's (1976) sense), which makes them mark-manipulating or string-processing systems in the classic sense of digital computers as instantiations of Turing machines. Chalmers has offered no good reasons for concluding that digital machines possess conscious minds.

The fundamental difference between digital machines as symbol systems or as string-processing or as mark-manipulating systems, therefore, is that nothing stands for anything for systems of this kind. The triadic relation between signs, sign-users, and that for which they stand encompassing causal relations betwen signs and sign users (which must be in suitable causal proximity), semantic relations between signs and that for which they stand (which must be grounded in resemblance relations, cause-and-effect connections, or habitual associations), and pragmatic relations (between signs, sign users, and what they stand for) are not present. The grounding relations, most importantly, are completely missing.

That the symbols, marks, and strings that digital computers manipulate have no meaning for those systems themselves might be obscured by failing to draw a distinction between signs that are meaningful for *users of* a system and signs that are meaningful for *use by* a system (Fetzer 1990, 1996*a*). The reason why these digital machines can be so valuable in relieving us of mental labour, just as the steam engine (and later the petrol engine) has been so valuable in relieving us of physical labour, is because we design them to perform tasks on our behalf. Their successful performance of those tasks does not require that the symbols, marks, or strings they process possess any meaning for them at all.

27. The Dynamic Difference

Another difference that appears to be at least equal in importance is that digital machines are governed by *programs*, which are causal implementations of *algorithms* as procedures that are definite (you always get an answer), reliable (you always get a correct answer), and completable (you always get a correct answer in a finite number of steps). These procedures exemplify what has been called 'disciplined step satisfaction', where one step is followed by another in an orderly sequence to bring about a solution to a problem. The transitions between states $S1, \ldots, Sn$, therefore, are under the control of programs in ways in which human thought processes do not appear to be regulated or constrained.

Consider dreams and daydreams, for example. They have no definite starting or stopping points and normally do not solve problems. Even under Freudian interpretations, they do not follow specific steps to secure solutions to problems. They therefore do not display disciplined step satisfaction (Fetzer 1994, 1997*b*, 1998). Indeed, the transitions between mental states are affected by our experiences in life and other subjective factors that differ from person to person and from time to time. Sitting at a stop sign may cause me to think of other occasions when I sat at stop signs and effects that were brought about on those occasions, their consequences, and conversations I have had about them.

Indeed, distinctions between intensions and extensions are commonly drawn in relation to words, where *intensions* specify the conditions that must be satisfied for those words to apply, while *extensions* include everything that satisfies those conditions. Distinctions may also be drawn between connotations and denotations, however, where *connotations* are the emotions and attitudes associated with things of a certain kind, and *denotations* are members of the extensions of words with which you are personally acquainted. Transitions between human thoughts $T1, \ldots, Tn$ thus appear to be at least as strongly affected by subjective connotations and denotations as they are by objective intensions and extensions.

28. Ordinary Human Thought

Having suggested that dreams, daydreams, and ordinary thought processes are semiotic and non-algorithmic, a detailed example may be appropriate. Not long ago, as my wife and I were driving from Minneapolis to Madison on I-94, I noticed that the green hills of Wisconsin looked strikingly like the green hills of Virginia, where we lived while I taught at UVA. That made me think of the song, 'Country Road', which alludes to the Blue Ridge Mountains and the Shenandoah Valley, which are located, not in West Virginia, but in western Virginia, and of the songwriter and singer, John Denver. This made me think of his recent death while he piloted an experimental aircraft over the Pacific Ocean, an ironic demise for someone who extolled the virtues of nature and the outdoors.

This train of thought can easily be understood as a semiotic phenomenon. The transition from observing the green hills of Wisconsin to thinking about the green hills of Virginia, of course, was brought about by an iconic relation of resemblance. That setting has been praised by symbols in a song that has become familiar through repetition, a habitual association. I thought of how West Virginians have thought it misdescribed their state, where the symbols used did not correspond to the things for which they stand. The song itself, of course, was an effect of the efforts of the songwriter, to whom it stands in an indexical relationship. The songwriter (in one context) resembles himself (in another), which led me to think about his demise while flying over the ocean, something that must have brought great pleasure but also brought him death.

This train of thought appears to be typical, normal, adult, human cognition. It is not algorithmic. There is no completable, definite, and reliable effective decision procedure that underlies these causal transitions, which appear to be influenced at least as much by past experience and emotional connotations as they are by logic and reasoning. No reckoning at all is involved. There is nothing here to support the inference that thought processes are governed by finite sets of effective rules. And this is not peculiar to thinking of this specific kind. Even perception and memory fail to qualify as activities that are governed by mental algorithms. Wanting to perceive something and trying to remember something are certainly problems we encounter in life. But they are problems for which life, alas, provides no effective solutions (Fetzer 1997b: 360–1).

29. Inference to the Best Explanation

Since minds and mental states are non-observable properties of brains and brain states, their existence and properties must be approached inferentially. Inference to the best explanation is a species of inductive inference that involves selecting one member from a set of alternative hypotheses as the one that provides the best explanation for the available evidence. Alternatives that explain more of the available evidence are preferable to those that explain less, while those that are preferable when sufficient evidence is available are also acceptable. Acceptable hypotheses may still be false, which makes such reasoning fallible, but are the most rational of the alternatives under consideration.

This approach is perfectly general and applies to scientific enquiries generally (Fetzer 1993). As we have discovered, a complete and comprehensive account of human cognition would apply to various forms of thinking, including sensing, perceiving, dreaming, daydreaming, learning, memorizing, remembering, conjecturing, hypothesizing, arguing, reasoning, criticizing, where most if not all of these appear to involve consciousness and cognition in senses that go beyond the phenomenal sense. As we have also discovered, these activities appear to involve properties that transcend or contravene the characteristics that would be imposed upon human thought processes by the specific features that distinguish digital machines.

If specific patterns of neural activation are connected to specific dispositions toward behaviour within specific contexts for various kinds of systems, then the semiotic conception would appear to have the resources to solve the mind–body problem. An advantage that it enjoys in relation to alternative conceptions, no doubt, is that it provides a foundation for understanding the nature of thought as a semiotic activity in which something stands for something else in some respect or other for a system. This approach thereby supplies a framework for investigating various kinds of thoughts, different kinds of minds, and the various species that may possess them. The nature of thought is no longer mysterious.

30. The Problem of Other Minds

If 'consciousness' or 'cognition' were left as primitives within an account of this kind, then that would pose a serious objection. The concepts of consciousness and of cognition presented here, however, strongly support the theory of minds as semiotic systems. Indeed, perhaps the fundamental advantage of this approach over its computational alternatives is that it supplies a more credible account of what it means to be 'a thinking thing' (namely, a semiotic system) and of what it means to be 'a conscious thinking thing' (namely, a semiotic system that is not incapacitated from the exercise of its abilities). But it also provides a framework for pursuing the problem of other minds in its varied guises.

When the behaviour of a system is sufficiently non-complex as to be explainable without attributing mentality to that system, then it should not be attributed, nor should stronger forms if lesser will do. That *E. coli* bacteria swim towards twelve specific chemotactic substances and away from eight others may count as evidence that *E. coli* possesses iconic mentality, but it could not support inferences to any stronger kind. That bats navigate on the basis of echolocation and that vervet monkeys make at least three distinct alarm calls, by comparison, supplies evidence of more complex behaviours, which supports inferences to higher modes of indexical and of symbolic mentality, respectively.

Ultimately, it may be important to draw distinctions between different kinds of consciousness, where *consciousness1* is the ability to use signs when it is not incapacitated, *consciousness2* is consciousness1 with awareness and articulation, and *consciousness3* is consciousness2 with self-awareness (or self-knowledge). It may also be important to distinguish consciousness from sensitivity and sentience (Fetzer 1997*a*). But nothing considered here suggests that such problems as these—including qualitative experience, which may depend upon the 'stuff' of which things are made—cannot be resolved within this framework. This study shows that the conception of minds as semiotic systems can explain more of the available evidence than its alternatives and thus provides a preferable theory.

REFERENCES

ALEKSANDER, I. (1996), *Impossible Minds* (London: Imperial College).

BECKOFF, M., and JAMIESON, D. (eds.) (1996), *Reading in Animal Cognition* (Cambridge, Mass: MIT Press).

BONNER, J. T. (1980), *The Evolution of Culture in Animals* (Princeton, NJ: Princeton University Press).

CHALMERS, D. (1996), *The Conscious Mind* (New York: Oxford University Press).

CHENEY, D., and SEYFARTH, R. (1990), *How Monkeys See the World* (Chicago: University of Chicago Press).

DAWKINS, M. S. (1993), *Through Our Eyes Only? The Search for Animal Consciousness* (New York: William Freeman).

DENNETT, D. (1995), *Darwin's Dangerous Idea* (New York: Simon & Schuster).

—— (1996), *Kinds of Minds* (New York: Basic Books.).

FETZER, J. H. (1981), *Scientific Knowledge* (Dordrecht: D. Reidel).

FETZER, J. H. (1988), 'Signs and Minds: An Introduction to the Theory of Semiotic Systems', in J. H. Fetzer (ed.), *Aspects of Artificial Intelligence* (Dordrecht: Kluwer), 133–61.

—— (1990), *Artificial Intelligence: Its Scope and Limits* (Dordrecht: Kluwer).

—— (1991), 'Primitive Concepts: Habits, Conventions, and Laws', in J. H. Fetzer *et al.* (eds.), *Definitions and Definability* (Dordrecht: Kluwer), 51–68.

—— (1993), *Philosophy of Science* (New York: Paragon House).

—— (1994), 'Mental Algorithms: Are Minds Computational Systems?' *Pragmatics & Cognition*, 2: 1–29.

—— (1996*a*), *Philosophy and Cognitive Science*, 2nd edn. (Minneapolis: Paragon House).

—— (1996*b*), 'Are there Animal Minds? Discussion Review: M. S. Dawkins, *Through Our Eyes Only: The Search for Animal Consciousness*', *Journal of Social and Evolutionary Systems*, 19: 187–92.

—— (1997*a*), 'Review of Daniel Dennett, *Kinds of Minds*', *Philosophical Psychology*, 10: 113–15.

—— (1997*b*), 'Thinking and Computing: Computers as Special Kinds of Signs', *Minds and Machines*, 7: 345–64.

—— (1998), 'People are Not Computers: (Most) Thought Processes are Not Computational Procedures', *Journal of Experimental and Theoretical AI*, 10: 371–91.

FODOR, J. (1975), *The Language of Thought* (Cambridge, Mass.: MIT Press).

GRIFFIN, D. R. (1992), *Animal Minds* (Chicago: University of Chicago Press).

—— (1984), *Animal Thinking* (Cambridge, Mass.: Harvard University Press).

HANNERS, D. (1998), 'Wife fails 3 times to kill husband', *Duluth News-Tribune* (28 June 1998), 1A and 11A.

HARTSHORNE, P., and WEISS, P. (eds.) (1960), *The Collected Papers of Charles S. Peirce*, 2 vols. (Cambridge, Mass.: Harvard University Press).

HAUGELAND, J. (1981), 'Semantic Engines: An Introduction to Mind Design', in J. Haugeland (ed.), *Mind Design* (Cambridge, Mass.: MIT Press), 1–34.

NEWELL, A., and SIMON, H. (1976), 'Computer Science as Empirical Inquiry: Symbols and Search', repr. in J. Haugeland (ed.), *Mind Design* (Cambridge, Mass.: MIT Press, 1981), 35–66.

RISTAU, C. (ed.) (1991), *Cognitive Ethology* (Hillsdale, NJ: Lawrence Erlbaum).

RUMELHART, D., et al. (1986), *Parallel Distributed Processing* (Cambridge, Mass.: MIT Press).

SEARLE, J. (1980), 'Minds, Brains, and Programs', *Behavioral and Brain Sciences*, 3: 417–57.

SLATER, P. J. B. (1985), *An Introduction to Ethology* (New York: Cambridge University Press, 1985).

11. Maps, Gaps, and Traps

Robert Van Gulick

The explanatory gap metaphor occurs so often in the recent discussion of consciousness that we might easily lose sight of its metaphoric status, but we would be unwise to do so. Indeed, we would do well to step back and reflect a little about what points of view might lie behind it.

1. Gaps in the Background

The problem has been with us longer than the label. The problematic link between subjective mind and objective physical world has been front and centre stage since at least 1974, when Thomas Nagel famously asked us to imagine what it's like to be a bat as a means of illustrating the subjective/objective gulf. Nagel (1974) wrote, 'At the present time the status of physicalism is similar to that which the hypothesis that matter is energy would have if uttered by a Presocratic philosopher. We do not have the beginnings of a conception of how it might be true.' One thinks also of Wittgenstein in the *Philosophical Investigations* (1953) 'clutching his forehead' and saying in a tone of mock amazement, 'THIS, is supposed to be produced in the brain!' Earlier in that section (I. 412) he writes, 'The feeling of an unbridgeable gulf between consciousness and brain processes . . . This idea of a difference in kind is accompanied by slight giddiness—which occurs when we are performing a piece of logical sleight-of-hand.' Though he seems to be subverting rather than endorsing the asking of such questions, the question none the less was clearly on the table.

During the early days of the identity theory, Herbert Feigl (1958) worried about 'nomological danglers', i.e. about lawful links between the mental and physical unsecured by more basic underlying nomic connections or explanations. In the fanciful speculations of the time, philosophers imagined a 'cerebrescope' that could monitor a person's brain activity as she passed through a series of conscious states. One point of the exercise was to show that empirically established correlations—no matter how regular and lawful—would not by themselves suffice to resolve the perplexity of the mind–body question. A deeper explanation was needed of *how* and *why* the relevant neural states might be identical with their mental correlates, rather than merely linked.

Forty years later, the decade of the brain saw the spectacular rise of just such data, as thousands of brain imaging studies—using PET, fMRI, EEG, or MEG—provided us with brilliantly colour-coded brain maps that show in just which areas neural activity rises during specific mental acts. A specific region in extrastriate cortex (known as the fusiform place area—FPA) 'lights up' when a subject sees, imagines, or remembers a face. Activity shifts to a distinct extrastriate region (the parahippocampal place area—PPA) if the subject shifts her attention to a perceptual, imagery, or memory task involving places or scenes, such as thinking about the layout of her office or looking at a picture of Buckingham Palace (Kanwisher 2000). Moreover, the neural correlates track not merely the basic processing but the content of awareness itself. Experiments that separate the two using a binocular rivalry method (face to one eye, place to the other) show that the active neural area is the one associated with the content of the consciously attended percept, even though both images are being processed to a high level of informational and conceptual detail as can be shown by various implicit measures.

The data are impressive and the temporal and spatial resolution of the images continues to improve. None the less, there are lots of technical questions about such research, e.g. about the subtractive and filtering techniques used to construct the images; the brain is a very noisy system and far more of it is active at any given moment than the images might suggest to the naïve observer. The images generally depict *changes in activity* relative to some baseline rather than absolute levels. Thus when one carries out a given task, e.g. imagines a face, activity may rise in the fusiform gyrus, but it would be wrong to conclude that all the work is being done locally in that one elevated region. More likely the task relies upon interactions between that hot spot and multiple regions that contribute as well to lots of other tasks, and thus may not show up as specially enhanced during the specific task. This seems especially probable with conscious states since they are perhaps the least likely to have purely local neural substrates; most models focus instead on the global integration and binding of multiple simultaneously interactive regions (von der Marlsburg 2000; Varela 2000).

These limits on interpreting the data are well known to those in the field, and most would admit—at least in candid moments when not applying for grant renewal—that the ability to generate data has far outpaced the ability to interpret it. We have ever more trees, but at best a murky view of the mind–brain forest. It has taken just forty years for scientific fact to catch up with philosophical science fiction, but our *de facto* cerebrescopes have run up against the explanatory limits imagined in the 1950s. Maps of spatio-temporal mind–brain correlations are no doubt of great value and interest, but in themselves they do not get us very far in undangling nomological mind–brain links.

Though the gap (gulf) problem entered the conversation long before the gap locution did, labels and metaphors make a difference. They structure how we look at problems. They can frame an issue in a way that reveals otherwise hidden aspects, but also veils from view assumptions and possibilities that recede into the background. The explanatory gap metaphor, coined by Joseph Levine in 1983, has focused the psychophysical debate in useful ways. But just because it's been so influential, we should pause and ask about the metaphor itself and how it shapes our thinking. Despite its value and its power (indeed perhaps because of its power) it can lead the unwary into philosophical traps. Thus I will post warnings of five such traps along the way as we map through the metaphor and its uses.

2. Mapping the Metaphor

The idea of an explanatory gap is ambiguous in at least two ways: one lexical, the other syntactic. In ordinary contexts, the word 'gap' has varied uses: some quite literally spatial, others originally metaphoric but now so entrenched as to count as literal themselves. My online *American Heritage Dictionary* (1992) gives the following entry for 'gap'.

gap n.
1. a. An opening in a solid structure or surface: a cleft or breach.
    b. A break in a line of defense.
2. An opening through mountains; a pass.
3. A space between objects or points; an aperture.
4. An interruption in continuity.
5. a. A conspicuous difference or imbalance; a disparity.
    b. A problematic situation resulting from such a disparity.

The first, fourth, and fifth definitions seem immediately relevant. Although the first refers literally to a break in a surface, it has obvious metaphoric application. The explanatory gap is supposed to exist against a background of otherwise unbroken explanatory links. The fourth as well ties into that assumption of explanatory continuity. The psychophysical gap is presented to us as an interruption in the normal state of affairs: a puzzle, an anomaly, an absence where there ought to be a presence. And the void may seem unfillable; consciousness appears so unlike any candidate substrate that we are left with just the sort of conspicuous disparity to which the fifth definition refers. It is no wonder that the gap metaphor so readily grabs attention, given that it bundles so many potent intuitions in a single, spatial, and almost tangible package.

The second ambiguity is less obvious and syntactic rather than lexical. As a matter of grammar, an 'explanatory gap' might be either a gap *in our explanations* or a gap *that explains*. Clearly Joe Levine (1983) meant the former, and that's how the phrase is understood in the literature, but I think we should be open to the possibility of unintended but none the less apt meanings. Even if it's not what's standardly meant, perhaps the psychophysical gap is in fact *a gap that explains*, a gap from which one might learn something interesting about consciousness and its relation to the physical.

This syntactic alternative even suggests a way in which the two lexical options we ignored above might yet come into play, namely definitions 2 and 3:

2. An opening through mountains; a pass.
3. A space between objects or points; an aperture.

Again the application is metaphoric not literal. The psychophysical gap might serve as an opening, an aperture through which we look to see something important about consciousness, or it might provide a route that takes us through a barrier to understanding as a pass leads us through mountains. It's worth noting that mountain gaps are of two types: wind gaps and water gaps. Rivers flow through the latter, but only wind blows through the former. More interestingly water gaps typically explain themselves. The river causes the gap and often flowed where it does before the mountains rose, wearing them down as they went up. Wind gaps, in contrast, are rarely caused by wind; their explanations must be sought elsewhere. What of the psycho-physical gap? Might it be not only a gap that explains, but also one that explains itself? (Or helps at least to do so?) Perhaps that's just wishful thinking, but maybe not; I'll have more to say nearer the end of the chapter about some ways in which it might be so.

The explanatory gap takes many forms in the literature, and two inter-related but distinct questions may help to sort them out:

1. *Where* is the gap alleged to occur? (i.e. *what items* does it separate?)
2. *What sort of lack* creates the gap that keeps them apart?

I'll focus explicitly on answering the first question, but in the course of doing so the second will be addressed as well.

Psycho-physical gaps can be of two kinds: objective gaps that occur in the world and subjective gaps that occur in our representation of the world (Fig. 11.1). Each has many subtypes. Objective mental/physical gaps might be causal, metaphysical, or ontological in nature (see Fig. 11.2), though the distinctions blur a bit at the boundaries. An *objective causal gap* would exist

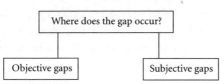

FIG. 11.1. Two kinds of gap

if as a matter of *natural law* no physical substrate nomically sufficed to produce consciousness, or in a somewhat more restricted version if no combination of *physical laws* plus physical substrate nomically sufficed (leaving open the possibility that natural but non-physical laws might do so). Even if there were no *nomic* gaps of either sort, there might be *practical* causal gaps if technical limits (perhaps even inevitable and unavoidable ones) prevented us from producing consciousness by any physical process within our control.

Objective *metaphysical gaps*, like nomic causal gaps, might be matters of non-necessitation. If there are forms of metaphysical necessity distinct from those of natural law (a controversial but not obviously false supposition), then psycho-physical gaps might occur in the absence of such metaphysically necessary links binding mind and matter.

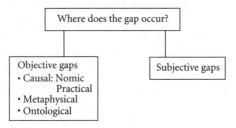

FIG. 11.2. Objective gaps

Even if the mental and physical were necessarily linked, either by natural law or some other metaphysical tie, an objective *ontological gap* might still exist in so far as consciousness and its linked physical correlate remained distinct items. If consciousness were not strictly identical with anything physical but something more, then the world would be divided ontologically no matter how tightly tied its two sides were. Indeed avoiding such ontological dualism has kept materialists busy looking for a specification of the mind–body relation that is short of type–type identity but none the less strong enough to secure their materialist monism (Kim 1999). A variety of options have been offered, including many varieties of supervenience, logical dependence, composition, and realization. I view such matters from a teleo-pragmatic slant (Van Gulick 1992) which makes me a kind of functionalist;

thus I find realization the most promising candidate: all instances of mental properties are fully realized by organized complexes of underlying physical properties. But that is not an issue we need to address in detail here. (For more see Kim 1999; Van Gulick 1992.)

What then of subjective gaps? Gaps in our representation of the world also come in many types including conceptual gaps, theoretical gaps, gaps in our models (and maps), and gaps in our understanding, practical or otherwise (see Fig. 11.3).

Unsurprisingly there are no sufficient a priori links between our physical concepts and our concept(s) of consciousness. Mere a priori reflection on the nature of the former will not suffice to deduce the existence or nature of any conscious state. This is a familiar point that goes back at least to the 1950s and the early days of the identity thesis whose supporters described it as a factual claim rather than a conceptual or semantic one (Smart 1959). More recently, some neodualists (e.g Jackson 1982; Chalmers 1997) have tried to use the absence of any such a priori link as an initial premiss in reaching an anti-physicalist conclusion. I believe such arguments are unsound, and will say more about that below.

Theoretical links might seem to hold more promise in tying the physical and the conscious. Systems for representing, describing, and calculating based on empirical evidence and theoretical construction should offer better tools for explaining how these two seemingly disparate aspects of the world fit together. However, here too explanatory gaps are alleged to be the psycho-physical norm. As Joseph Levine (1993) argues, we can give a plausible and intuitively satisfying explanation of why a collection of H_2O molecules at 20°C is liquid, but we cannot give anything comparable in the case of consciousness and its possible physical substrates. Here we come up against a theoretical blank wall; or so at least the gap supporters claim. It's not merely that we don't have a true detailed account of how consciousness might depend upon the brain, but we allegedly lack even an understanding of how such a thing might be possible. We have no remotely adequate theoretical

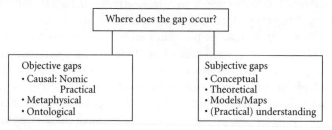

FIG. 11.3. Objective and subjective gaps

resources for imagining how the the psychophysical gap might be bridged. Or so at least it's claimed.

Some have tried to run what we can call 'boomerang arguments', arguments that reach over to the subjective side and then swing back to the objective, inferring the existence of gaps in the world from alleged gaps in our representation of it. Neodualist arguments based on the supposed conceivability of zombie worlds (i.e. worlds just like the actual world in all physical respects but lacking consciousness) fit this general pattern (Chalmers 1996), and I will have more to say about them shortly. Frank Jackson's (1982) famous Mary case aims to throw a boomerang as well. Mary, the hypothetical super colour-scientist, supposedly learns something new when she first experiences red despite having known beforehand all the physical facts about doing so. Jackson draws an objective antiphysicalist conclusion from Mary's imagined subjective gap, but it's far from clear that his boomerang can make a valid return trip. Indeed, I and many others (Churchland 1985; Loar 1990; Lycan 1990; Van Gulick 1993) have denied that it can, but I won't repeat those criticisms here. I will focus instead on the zombie form of the boomerang (the zoomerang?). But first we should complete our survey of the subjective answers to our question of *where* the gap occurs.

The two alternatives we have already considered—conceptual and theoretical gaps—give the issue an intellectual slant. Concepts and theories provide the basis for propositional knowledge, but the subjective domain includes other modes of representing and understanding the world, and we should be open to the possibility that gaps might occur there as well. We use many kinds of structures to guide us in our practical dealings with the world, e.g. many sorts of models and maps. Although models are often associated with theories, we should not ignore the differences between the two and the types of gaps that may occur in each. Philosophers often think of theories as formalized sets of sentences closed under logical implication. Given such a view, it is natural to suppose that *if* the facts described by theory T1 are entirely dependent on those described by theory T2, *then* it should be possible to derive T1 from T2. The form of the representation leads us to interpret the notion of dependence as a matter of formal (or logical) derivation. Because we tend to think of theories as descriptions of the world—perhaps even as linguistic depictions of it—we tend also to expect that objective dependence relations will have to be reflected in our subjective representations of the items that they link. If we look hard enough we should be able to see them, and if they are not there then we face an anomalous gap. Objective links imply subjective links, or so at least it seems given such a picture view of theories.

However, if we focus on models rather than theories that presumption seems less plausible. Imagine a complex system S with many levels of organization and patterned regularity, an organism or perhaps an economy. I might construct an effective and reliable model M_i that allows me to successfully predict and interact with some higher level aspect or feature of S, call it H_i. I might also have a model M_l that provides me with equally effective interactive causal access to the lower level organization of S on which H_i ultimately depends. It need not follow that I can translate back and forth between the two models or use M_l as a tool to guide my interactions with S in ways that mimic those I can achieve with M_i, nor would I expect to do so. Because we view models more as practical tools than as pictures, we more readily accept gaps between them. Whether one tool does its job well rarely turns on whether we can use it to do the job of another.

By contrast, the notion of a map carries a powerfully spatial connotation whether literal or merely metaphoric. Thus when we think of our subjective representation of the world as a map of reality, the existence of gaps may seem deeply puzzling. How can we have two regions depicted on a map without any path that connects the one with the other; the very notion of a space in the mathematical sense would seem to imply that all points are connected or reachable from each other. Thus how puzzling we find the gaps within our representation of the world will depend in part upon the sorts of representations we are considering. Gaps in maps may seem especially problematic, but gaps in models (or between models) may seem much less so. And how we feel about intertheoretical gaps may depend upon whether we view them as more like intra-map gaps or inter-model ones. I think the second is apt far more often than is commonly realized.

Despite their differences maps, models, theories, and concepts share a common status as constructs used by cognitive agents, but our fourth and final subjective gap location falls in a different category. Understanding is an activity that minds participate in, a success-loaded form of cognitive achievement rather than a tool used in its pursuit. Gaps in our understanding may result from gaps in the means by which we pursue it, but we should be cautious about inferring the one from the other. As I will argue below, an inability to explain of the sort that might result from gaps in our theories or other cognitive constructs need not entail an equivalent lack of understanding. In particular we must be cautious about inferring understanding gaps from explanatory gaps.

3. Zombies and Boomerangs

Having completed our quick survey of the objective and subjective answers to our *where* question, let us return to the zombie argument as an example of how boomerang reasoning aims to derive an objective gap from a subjective one. I regard it as Trap 1; so let the unwary take care.

Dualists since Descartes have tried to use conceivability arguments to show the non-materiality of mind. Descartes famously claimed that he could clearly and distinctly conceive of his conscious mind continuing to exist in the total absence of his physical body (*Med.* VI). He thus concluded that the two could not be one and the same. In recent years imagined zombie cases have been called upon to play a similar argumentative role. David Chalmers (1996) for example asks us to imagine a world W2 satisfying the following conditions:

1. There are beings who are molecule-for-molecule duplicates of conscious humans in the actual world.
2. Our molecule-for-molecule *doppelgängers* in W2 are not conscious.
3. The physical laws that hold in W2 are the same as those that hold in the actual world.

(To be more precise, Chalmers claims that upon rational reflection he can conceive of such a world in what he calls the primary positive sense; however I will ignore those qualifications here since they would not make any difference to the outcome of our critical evaluation.)

On the basis of this claim about what he can *conceive* Chalmers concludes that such molecule-for-molecule zombies are *logically possible*. He then argues in familiar Kripkean style that the mere logical possibility of mental and physical separation shows the two must in fact be separate and distinct. If they were not, i.e. if mental properties were identical to physical properties or logically supervenient on them, then there could be no logically possible world in which the one occurred but not the other. The existence of even one such world suffices to show their non-identity.

The standard reply distinguishes between two senses of conceivability: a weak or merely apparent sense and a strong or strictly logical sense. The zombie argument and its kin rely on two premises or claims: first a claim that the existence of one sort of property without the other is indeed conceivable, and second a linking premiss asserting that what is conceivable is logically possible. For example,

(P1)   I can conceive of a without b (e.g. zombie world)
(P2)   Whatever is conceivable is logically possible or more specifically
(P2*) If I can conceive of a without b then it is logically possible for a to exist without b.
(C3)   Therefore it is logically possible for a to exist without b.
(P4)   If it is logically possible for a to exist without b, then a is distinct from b (not identical with b)
(C5)   Thus a is distinct from b (not identical with b).

(Again to be precise, Chalmers would qualify 'conceivable' throughout as 'conceivable in the primary positive sense', but also again the qualifications

do not affect the outcome, and so I will stick with the simpler formulation.)

Such an argument must either equivocate in its use of the word 'conceivable' or fail to support at least one of its first two premises. To make (P1)
plausible, one needs to read it in the weak sense of saying only that one can
conceive of a in the absence of b, without seeming to contradict oneself, i.e.
one can tell oneself what seems to be a coherent story in which a exists but b
does not. But though this makes P1 plausible, it undercuts the next step (P2),
which links conceivability to logical possibility. That an imagined state of
affairs does not *seem to involve* a contradiction does not entail that it *in fact
involves* none. If we strengthen the notion of conceivability and require that
there in fact be no contradiction (as opposed to merely seeming such) the link
to logical possibility goes through directly. But then the initial claim (P1) that
one can conceive of a without b begs the question. One can say in the strong
sense whether one can or cannot conceive of minds without matter (Descartes's disembodied minds) or brains without minds (zombies) only if one
has already settled the question of whether minds and brains are in fact
distinct. Thus if we read 'conceivable' strongly we lose P1, if we read it weakly
we lose P2, and if we equivocate the inference to C3 is invalid. Thus the
argument is unsound.

This line of criticism is often illustrated with familiar scientific examples
such as those of water and H_2O or heat and molecular kinetic energy. The fact
that a chemically ignorant person might conceive (in the weak sense) of water
existing without H_2O shows nothing about their non-identity, and because
water *is* H_2O—as established a posteriori—it is not logically possible for the
one to exist without the other.

Chalmers is fully aware of these objections but believes his own arguments
escape such criticism. He uses 'logical possibility' with a sense that would
rehabilitate the move to C3 but leave the overall argument unsound. 'Logical
possibility' for him means little more than conceivability, what he calls
'a priori possibility' and which concerns only what we can infer from the
concepts involved by a priori means. If logical possibility is read in that way,
P2 becomes more or less a tautology even on the weak reading of 'conceivable',
and the move to C3 is automatic. The original problem, however recurs at the
next step (P4). If the 'logical possibility' of separation means merely its a
priori conceivability then, as the scientific cases show, it does not entail
distinctness. P4 comes out false, and the general argument again fails. Chalmers acknowledges this and, unlike some of his predecessors, does not rely on
any general linking principle such as P4. Moreover he acknowledges that a
priori conceivability (what he calls logical possibility) does not in itself entail
what he calls 'metaphysical possibility', the strong relation needed to license
the move from *possibility of separation* to *non-identity*.

In analysing the familiar scientific examples, he carefully distinguishes between what he calls primary and secondary intensions associated with terms. The primary intension of the word 'water' involves having various watery characteristics (colour, liquidity, taste, smell, etc.). However, through its use in context by our linguistic group to refer to the stuff around here that has those characteristics, it acquires the secondary intension (H_2O). Thus when someone in our linguistic community claims to be imagining a situation with water but without H_2O, she is misdescribing her state; when she uses 'water' it means H_2O (secondary intension). Such a person is in fact imagining a situation in which some substance satisfies the primary intension associated with 'water' without being water.

However, according to Chalmers the analogy breaks down in the psycho-physical case. The disanalogy is this: anything that satisfied the primary intension associated with 'consciousness' would *be* a case of consciousness. Thus if one can conceive of that concept (primary intension) being satisfied in a world that lacks the materialist's proposed physical properties, then consciousness must be distinct from them. More importantly, if one can conceive of the primary intension associated with 'consciousness' *not* being satisfied in a world that contains all the relevant physical properties, then consciousness cannot be identical with them nor logically supervenient on them.

To be exact, what Chalmers claims is just a bit weaker: namely that as a matter of a priori/logical possibility the phenomenal aspect associated with the primary intension can exist independently of any supposed physical basis and thus must be distinct from it. But since that aspect involves the existence of phenomenal awareness, whether or not we identify it outright with consciousness matters little. What counts is the supposed logical possibility that phenomenal what-it's-like-to-be-ness can exist or not exist independently of the physical facts.

However, even if Chalmers succeeded in using two-level semantics to weaken the analogy with certain examples (e.g. water/H_2O) that are standardly used to *illustrate* the problems with modal conceivability arguments, that in itself would not solve those problems. Though some analogies are broken, others remain that still suffice to undermine the zombie thought experiment. More importantly, there are residual questions about the adequacy of the concepts that Chalmers and the neodualists use in their thought experiments. Are those concepts well enough developed and anchored to support the argumentative use to which they are put? I think not.

Consider the analogies kept and broken. There are allegedly two sorts of worlds. First are those in which the primary intension of 'consciousness' (which concerns its phenomenal aspect) is satisfied despite the absence of the materialist's purported physical referent. These are worlds analogous to those in which there is watery XYZ without any H_2O. This is where the disanalogy intrudes; although we can imagine something watery that is not water, we can't imagine something that involves phenomenal awareness without imagining what amounts to consciousness in the philosophically important sense. The primary intension of 'water' refers to relatively superficial properties that demonstratively link us to its referent in context. But the primary intension of 'consciousness' incorporates so much that its imagined satisfaction in the absence of its materialist counterpart shows the two to be distinct.

But this wouldn't suffice to refute materialism; it shows that consciousness can be realized by multiple substrates, but that's a materialist platitude. To get a dualist result, one needs to claim that one can imagine consciousness occurring in the absence of *any* physical substrate at all—a true Cartesian disembodied mind. Materialists typically and justifiably accuse such claims of begging the question. If being in a state of phenomenal awareness is in fact a matter of being in a special sort of dynamically organized physical state, then when one imagines a world with phenomenal awareness, one imagines some physical substrate whether one recognizes that one is doing so or not. If 'being a something that-it's-like-to-be' is a matter of being a certain sort of physical system that interacts with itself in a special way, then when one imagines the former, one imagines the latter whether one conceives of it *as such* or not. The materialist may be wrong, but to *show* him so one needs assumptions that don't prejudge the issue.

Imagined worlds of the second sort are even more problematic; these are the zombie worlds in which our exact physical duplicates completely lack consciousness. The materialist will reply that this is just as contradictory as imagining a world in which there is a substance that is physically and behaviourally just like the water in Lake Erie for some extended stretch of time, but that is not liquid. Obviously when one imagines the Lake Erie *doppelgänger*, one in effect imagines its liquidity. Though it may be less obvious, the materialist claims we do the same when we imagine our physical duplicates; whether we realize it or not, when we imagine our physical doubles we imagine conscious beings just as we imagine liquid lakes when we imagine microphysical duplicates of Lake Erie. Is he right? That remains an open question, but to assume he's wrong again seems to beg the question.

The neodualist will deny the parallel. With Lake Erie, we can reductively explain just why and how the underlying physical substrate satisfies all the functional conditions to count as liquid, but we can't do the same for consciousness. Indeed we cannot at this time come close to doing so, but that need reflect only the poverty of our current theories and concepts. It shows we have a current representational or subjective gap in our system of explanations, but no objective metaphysical implications follow. The fault may lie not in the world but in our concepts of it.

We come thus to the second and more general question about the dualist's thought experiments. Are the concepts that he uses adequate to the task to which he puts them? Is our concept of phenomenal consciousness or our concept of its possible physical basis well enough developed to allow us to draw metaphysical conclusions about their relation? As I said above, I think they are not.

Consider for comparison a non-mental example, the familiar case of vitalism. In particular imagine a mid-nineteenth-century vitalist who argues as follows:

1. I can conceive of creatures that are just like actual creatures (say actual cats) in all physical respects but that have no ability to reproduce.
2. Therefore the ability to reproduce does not logically supervene on a creature's physical structure.

With the benefit of late twentieth-century science we know the vitalist's conclusion is dead wrong; the ability to reproduce *does* logically supervene on physical structure. More interestingly we can see diagnostically where the vitalist went wrong; he had neither an adequate concept of reproduction nor an adequate concept of the total physical structure of a living organism, and he also lacked an adequate theory of how the two might fit together. He had no idea of the way in which reproduction involves the replication and transfer of genetic information, and he had not the slightest grasp of what we now know to be the biochemical basis of that process, of how genetic information can be coded by sequences of DNA and RNA. What was conceivable from the vitalist's perspective shows little if anything about what is logically (or metaphysically) possible in matters reproductive and physical. The vitalist might have conjoined *his concept* of the total physical structure of a cat with the negation of *his concept* of the ability to reproduce without generating any a priori contradictions, but given the radical incompleteness of his concepts *vis-à-vis* the natures of the two phenomena to which he applied them, nothing really follows regarding what relations of logical (or metaphysical) possibility or dependence might or might not hold between those phenomena themselves.

Are the concepts used by Chalmers and the neodualist more adequate than the vitalist's? First we must ask, 'What specific concepts do they use?' On the mental side they use a concept of experience derived from our first-person awareness of our own conscious mental states and processes. The nature of these concepts derives from their representational and regulatory role in the monitoring and control of our conscious mental life. They surely meet conditions of adequacy relative to that role. But in what other respects might they be adequate or inadequate? For the neodualist's purposes his concept of conscious experience, call it CCE, must be adequate to limn the boundaries of consciousness; whatever satisfies CCE in any world must be an instance of consciousness and whatever fails to fall under CCE must equally fail to be an instance of consciousness. The neodualist treats his concept CCE as a Protagorean norm, i.e. as a universal standard of consciousness, but doing so seems less than plausible or at least problematic. Why should that concept of experience, whose nature derives from its role in regulating our specific form of consciousness, provide a characterization sufficiently general to determine the logically possible boundaries of consciousness? Please note that I am not saying the neodualist assumes that all logically possible conscious experience must involve the same specific phenomenal properties associated with human consciousness; he most surely and rightly does not say that. But what he does implicitly assume, though more modest, is still upon reflection implausible: namely that the concepts of consciousness that we command on the basis of their application within our own self-awareness can provide us with a general means of delimiting the logically possible boundaries of consciousness.

Moreover, the neodualist's concept of consciousness is inadequate in another respect that is directly relevant to his thought experiment. The question is whether or not that concept is adequate for assessing whether and how it might be instantiated by a material substrate. Recall the vitalist's concept of reproduction, which failed to include the idea of information transfer. Given the incompleteness of the vitalist's concept it is not surprising that he could not see how reproduction might be a fully material process. The situation, I believe, is comparable with respect to the neodualist's concept of consciousness. Here too our current understanding of consciousness *qua consciousness* is far too incomplete for us to say with any justified confidence how it might or might not be physically realized.

This conceptual inadequacy on the mental side is compounded by the fact that the concepts that the neodualist invokes on the physical side of his conceivability experiment are terribly non-specific and even less adequate to the task at hand. Indeed the physical concepts used are often little more than dummy concepts, such as 'beings like actual conscious humans in all physical respects'. No real detailed concepts that might characterize the physical substrate of consciousness are given. It's akin to the vitalist's blanket claim about the possibility of physically identical creatures without the ability to reproduce. The vitalist really knew nothing in any specific way about what the physical substrate of inheritance might be; he knew nothing of biochemistry, nothing of nucleic acids or their structure or operation within the cell.

The vitalist had no remotely adequate or detailed concept of the physical basis of reproduction. He lacked an adequate conception of what reproduction required. And thus he couldn't understand how to fit together the two inadequately conceptualized pieces of his puzzle. It is the same for the neodualist.

Chalmers explicitly denies that there is any valid analogy between his conceivability argument and vitalist arguments for antimaterialism. However, he never considers basing the analogy on the parallel conceptual inadequacies in the two cases, and so his denials do not speak directly to the analogy as laid out just above. He appeals instead to the functional nature of all the phenomena that the vitalist saw as beyond physical explanation. According to Chalmers, what the vitalist couldn't see was how any physical structures or processes could perform the requisite functions. To refute the vitalist we needed only to show how they could in fact do so.

Chalmers, however, denies that the same might happen with respect to consciousness and the physical because on his reckoning—and this is a key claim—consciousness is *not* a fundamentally functional process. He admits that consciousness and conscious mental states *perform* various functions, but he denies that an account of such roles can explain what consciousness *is*, i.e. he denies we can *analyse* or *explicate* the nature of consciousness in functional terms. To support his claim, he considers various functional roles that have been proposed for consciousness—information-processing roles or behaviour-regulating roles, executive roles, or metacognitive roles—and he argues that in each case we can conceive or imagine that role being filled in the complete absence of phenomenal consciousness. In effect, he appeals to a variety of absent qualia intuitions directed at each of the various functional roles proposed for consciousness. But here again we need to ask about the adequacy of the concepts that Chalmers uses to reach his general antifunctionalist conclusion. I agree that consciousness does not logically supervene on the specific functional phenomena that he considers, but that reflects negatively only on the specific inadequate functionalist proposals he considers not on the general prospects for functionally explicating consciousness. The functionalist is left with a large IOU to pay, but having such a debt is not at all the same as having been refuted, and that as yet the functionalist has not been.

Moreover, even if Chalmers were right that consciousness involves an essentially non-functional element, that disanalogy *per se* would not undercut the parallels between his zombie argument and the vitalist's. What tripped up the vitalist was the inadequacy of his concepts, not their functionality. Thus the core question remains: are the neodualist's concepts of consciousness and its material substrate up to the job of deciding what sorts of dependence and independence are logically possible in the strong sense? And to that the answer is: most probably not.

Thus the zombie version of the boomerang (the zoomerang) fails to establish an objective dualism of mind and body; it provides no way of reaching back and deriving an objective gap from a subjective one. It's an attractive trap, but a trap none the less and all the more reason to beware of it.

WARNING: To avoid Trap 1, watch out for boomerangs and be sceptical of claims to derive objective gaps from subjective ones.

4. Who's Afraid of the Big Bad Gap?

However, even if the neodualists can't prove their view with a boomerang, the physicalist seems left in a far from comfortable position. She still confronts what appears to be a deep and puzzling gap in her story of how consciousness might turn out to be just a special part of the physical world. Nomological danglers threaten with a vengeance, and she is left to repeat ever more hollow-sounding general claims about how everything mental ultimately depends upon (and is realized by) the physical. Unless she can cash those claims with some more specific and explanatory links, she is in danger of appearing little more than a dogmatic true believer in the universal physical faith. Many gap-touting philosophers, including Joe Levine himself and Colin McGinn (1989), have been content to make a merely epistemological point about the principled inadequacy of our understanding of the psychophysical link, without drawing any metaphysical conclusions. Though less radical than the neodualists' direct attack, this supposed epistemological gulf threatens to reduce physicalism to the status of a position we cannot really understand; the materialist may understand no more than Nagel's Presocratic trying to make sense of relativity. Or so at least it's claimed, but is it really so? A thorough enquiry may turn up some surprises along with our four remaining traps.

There are clearly gaps in our current understanding of the psychophysical link, but how great are they? And are they different in kind from other gaps in our understanding that cause us less metaphysical and epistemological distress? There is much we do not understand about the relations between mind and matter—between brain and conscious thought. But likewise there is a lot we do not understand about how life depends upon its biochemical substrate. Since the early 1950s we have had a general understanding of the genetic code and how it gets translated into proteins and more complex structures. The intervening decades have seen an explosion of detailed data and technological applications, but no one would claim that we are even close to a comprehensive understanding of how a complete organism develops from the genetic 'blueprint' encoded in the DNA of the single-celled zygote. Our ignorance is not regarded as a matter of philosophical importance; it's just a mundane fact about the early stage of an ongoing scientific programme.

Why are we supposed to regard the gaps in our psycho-physical understanding differently? In the psychophysical case, it's claimed we don't have even the beginning of an idea of how the two halves of the divide might fit together. Moreover, they are of such different natures, there may be some in-principle bar to our ever coming to grasp the link. Colin McGinn (1989, 1995) for example, has argued that our intellectual and conceptual capacities are unsuited to the explanatory task; he claims that our physical concepts are inevitably spatial and that consciousness cannot be understood in terms of spatial processes (or at least not without radically revising our understanding of the nature of space). According to McGinn, the mind–body link retains an almost magical air of mystery; using yet another water analogy, he claims we cannot imagine how the trick is done of turning the 'water of brain into the wine of consciousness' (1991).

Rather than assess such theories of why a special gap exists, I suggest we take a somewhat sceptical look at the underlying assumption that the gap is all that special. As noted above, Joe Levine asks us to contrast our ability to explain the liquidity of water in terms of its molecular structure with our inability to explain the phenomenal experience of red in terms of its neural substrate. That comparison may make our psycho-physical situation seem very poor indeed. The gap partisans ask, 'How could we ever hope to gain the sort of intuitive satisfaction about the psychophysical link that we get in the liquidity of H_2O case?'

Two responses are in order: the first a minor factual one, the second more substantial and philosophical. Based on an admittedly unscientific random sample, it seems to me that most people, including many with a good deal of higher education, understand little about why H_2O is liquid at 20 °C. Indeed, it is surprising that it is, given its low molecular weight; it would be a gas at room temperature were it not for the powerful electrical attractions among its highly bipolar molecules. And only very recently (1999) have chemists dis-covered that the hydrogen bonds between H_2O molecules involve a weak form of covalent bonding and sharing of electrons. So even the supposed paradigm case of obvious explanatory clarity turns out to be more of a puzzle than its use as a philosophical example would suggest.

More importantly as a philosophical matter, I believe the comparison misleads us into regarding our psychophysical prospects as far less promising than we should. In support of that view, consider three issues:

1. the disanalogies between the psychophysical and H_2O/liquidity cases;
2. the prospects for future explanation of the psychophysical relation;
3. the implicit understanding we may already have of that link if physical-ism is in fact true.

There are at least two disanalogies that make it misleading to compare our psychophysical explanations with those we can give of the liquidity of H_2O; each is seductive and easily lost sight of so I'd better mark them as our next two traps. More descriptively we can label them

Trap 2 *The multiple levels problem*
Trap 3 *The right relata problem*

The first concerns the fact that in the water case, our explanations need to bridge only a single interlevel gap, but in the psychophysical case there will probably be many levels of organization intervening between neurophysiological processes and conscious experience. It might be more apt to compare the psycho-physical case with trying to understand the life and behaviour of a complex organism—a moose or a duck—in terms of its underlying biochemical substrates. One will not forge interesting and explanatory links in a single step across such disparate levels of organization; one must instead construct good models of the many levels of increasing complexity and organization that intervene. The male greylag goose may perform the particular type of courtship ritual that it does (responding only to what it regards as a conspecific lying low and prone in the water) because its nervous system has the specific biochemical structure that it does and that in turn may have been 'blueprinted' in its genes (Lorenz 1965). But we have no real hope of giving an intuitively satisfying account of how the former depends upon the latter unless we take account of the many levels of organization that intervene between the two, including those that make essential reference to the goose's natural environment since its mating ritual is partly determined by learning and imprinting. The H_2O/liquidity example may seduce us with its very simplicity and directness of connection. The explandum and the explanans lie at immediately adjacent levels of organization, and thus it is not difficult to 'see' in an intuitively satisfying way how the one can produce the other. Given the many levels of explanation needed to tie consciousness to a neural substrate, we should not expect the same sort of intuitive satisfaction; that sense of simple and immediate comprehension is not likely when we must project our understanding across so many different links.

WARNING: To avoid Trap 2 pay attention to the plurality and diversity of levels in complex systems. Don't expect to link high-level features with micro-substrates by a simple, direct, and easily surveyable explanation of the type we get in the water/H_2O example.

The second disanalogy is the right relata problem (Trap 3); in the psychophysical case, unlike the liquidity/H_2O case, it's not obvious what is supposed to stand on the two sides of the explanatory bridge, especially on the conscious side. In the explanatory gap literature we are often asked to consider explanations that tie together a specific phenomenal property or type of conscious state and an isolated neural substrate (the firings of a specific group or type of neurons). We are then asked to consider how or why such a substrate could possibly be responsible for that particular hue of phenomenal red, or for an experience of it. Unsurprisingly we find ourselves looking at an explanatory blank wall. Part of the problem is that the phenomenal property is presented as a simple entity identified demonstratively: that particular red. If we can't say anything about it beyond its being the colour that it is, it shouldn't surprise us that we find it difficult to attach any explanatory hooks to it. There's nothing there to grab on to, no structure or relations that one might hope to explain by appeal to correlated or isomorphic structures or relations in the substrate. That's what we normally do in cases of interlevel explanation, and it works in the liquidity/H_2O case. But if the phenomenal property were just an unstructured simple, any correspondence between it and the physical would seem inevitably arbitrary and brute. Why qualia Q_1 rather than Q_3 or Q_n? That's just the way it is. Brute facts like that leave us wanting more, while nomological danglers loom on all sides.

In reply, one needs to shift the explandum (the psychic side of the link) away from single isolated phenomenal properties towards entities with significant internal relational structure. Following C. L. Hardin (1988) and others, the first move is from single colours to the structured colour space. Colours, phenomenal colours, exhibit a great many relations of difference and similarity as well as containment, exclusion, and location along multiple parameters suchy as the hot/cold, active/passive dimension. The phenomenal colour space is also asymmetric, exhibiting far fewer minimally different hues of yellow than of green, a pattern not replicated in the comparable transition from red to blue. Given such a structured entity as the phenomenal colour space, one can look for non-arbitrary links to neural substrates. Reds and yellows can combine phenomenally to form oranges (some more reddish, some more yellowish), but no hue in our experience can similarly contain as elements both red and green; that fact can be understood as a natural consequence of the double-opponent process model of colour vision, on which red and yellow are the respective maximal outputs of two distinct channels, while red and green are mutually exclusive outputs of one and the same channel in response to opposite levels of stimulation. Of course, there is still a lot to be explained, but none the less we can see a general result: in so far as what one wishes to explain can be characterized relationally we can hope to succeed, but facts about phenomenal simples (if there are such) are likely to resist explanation, just because they are simples.

The next move up in explananda is to locate specific forms of experience within the larger context of a conscious experiencing subject. Colour experiences, structured or otherwise, don't exist in isolation, but as the passing experiences of a conscious experiencing self. To put the point in old-fashioned quasi-scholastic terminology, they are modes or modulations of a thinking experiencing being, apart from whom they could no more exist than could the waves without the sea. The right relata for the project of psychophysical explanation is thus not the pair of isolated neural firings and specific instance of phenomenal red, but rather that of functioning globally active brain and conscious experiencing subject. If the beginnings of that story could be told—admittedly a very big 'if'—then more local answers might be fitted within that larger model. We may not ever produce such a model, but at least to my eye the possibility of doing so doesn't seem so hopeless as that of the original puzzle requiring us to explain local psychophysical links considered in isolation.

WARNING: To avoid Trap 3 make sure you're trying to relate the right relata. In particular pay attention to relata defined in terms of the larger system and to relations between minds and brains as dynamic interactive wholes, rather than focusing on all-too-familiar puzzles about how isolated mental and physical items might be intelligibly linked.

Our consideration of the right relata problem has carried us from our first issue (the disanalogies) into our second: the prospects for future progress in bridging the gap. Structural isomorphisms such as those between the organization of the phenomenal colour space and underlying neural structure may provide powerful predictive models for detailed psychophysical dependence. The correspondences might hold between psychophysical entities with very similar quantitative descriptions, e.g. both might be modelled as multidimensional vector spaces (Clark 1993).

None the less, champions of the gap might concede the possibility or even probability of such results, but still deny that they would fill the gap or suffice to quell explanatory concerns. If absent and inverted qualia are possible, as many gap supporters believe, then no relational model alone will suffice to explain qualitative consciousness. Any such model will have possible realizations that lack qualia (or lack the proper qualia); relational factors alone can't constrain the realizations space to include only conscious systems. Hence relational models can't provide a deductive bridge from realizing substrate to conscious experience, and a problematic explanatory gap remains.

What might be said in reply? First, it's far from obvious that absent qualia are possible in every relational case. Paralleling what was said above in reply to the neodualist's antifunctionalist claim, we should not draw general antifunctionalist conclusions from the failings of specific functional proposals. Absent qualia may be possible for the sorts of models proposed to date (i.e. those specified in terms of computational or highly abstract causal roles), but that does exclude the possibility of better relational models in the future. The challenge is to specify roles that could be filled only by qualitative states (without just begging the question by building explicit qualitative conditions into the definitions of the roles). We have no such models at present, but claims about their impossibility would have to shoulder the heavy burden of establishing a modal negative existential, which they have as yet not done.

A second reply attacks the assumption (Trap 4) upon which the last move in the argument relies: that the absence of a deductive bridge leaves a problematic explanatory gap. Not all gaps gape. Returning to the literal basis of the metaphor, there are many ways to link across a real gap short of bridging it. One might throw a line across, not strong enough to be a bridge but able to establish contact and allow some limited transfer back and forth. Or one might simply send signals, messages, or information from one side to the other. Similarly we might build links across the psychophysical divide even if we could not construct a strictly deductive bridge that we could walk across in thought with logically sufficient licence. We don't reject an empirically successful economic model of trade and currency values just because the relational structure of the model could be realized in non-economic processes. We don't require that formal economic models have only economic realizations. Why then should we demand that relational models of consciousness do any more. Various sorts of partial explanatory links might help to eliminate the gap even if no logically sufficient deductive bridge is ever built.

> WARNING: To avoid Trap 4 resist from the outset the sceptic's claim that nothing short of a strict deduction counts as explanation; remember, 'Not every link need be a bridge.'

Having considered both the disanalogies and prospects for future explanatory success, we come at last to our third and final item: the possibility that we may already implicitly understand far more about the psychophysical link than any of the parties to gap debate imagine. This also happily brings us back to the discussion promised far above of the final answer to our first question: Where does the gap occur? The answer is: as a gap in our understanding. We'll also look at our fifth and final trap, which can snare us if we fail to appreciate the difference between understanding and explaining.

Of the two notions, understanding is the more basic, with explanations serving as means or tools to achieve it. A successful explanation provides us with understanding, but the inability to explain x does not entail the absence of all understanding of x. To explain, we must lay out matters in an explicit, articulate way (an idea echoed by its Latin etymology: *explanare*, literally to spread out or lay flat before one). We can lack that ability but still have significant implicit understanding. Not being able to explain does not entail that one does not understand.

> WARNING: To avoid Trap 5, don't conflate an inability to explain with the total absence of understanding; the former does not entail the latter.

Keeping that fact in mind, I ask you to consider a hypothetical. For the sake of the exercise, assume the truth of physicalism; i.e. assume that phenomenal consciousness is a complex higher order feature of certain sorts of active organized physical systems, one that is logically supervenient on its underlying physical substrate. In fact, I believe that's true, but I won't argue for that nor ask you to accept it. I ask you only to *assume* it in order to answer the following question: If it were true, what sorts of implicit understanding would we already have of the materiality (physicality) of consciousness?

I believe we would have at least three types of implicit psychophysical understanding, which to make a little acronymic joke we can label:

Genetic
Autopoietic
Poetic.

Let me say something brief about each.

Genetic. The genetic material of an organism contains a complete self-actualizing blueprint of all the structures and systems to be built in the mature organism. It also implicitly contains information about the operation and function of those systems and how both depend upon its structure and organization. Thus our human genetic material embodies an implicit understanding of how human conscious mental processes depend upon the brain. That understanding is the result of our genetic blueprint's having been adapted through natural selection to produce just the right sort of physical organization needed for conscious mentality. The relevant understanding is practical in nature; it's embedded in biological procedures that are effective only in the context of the developing organism within an appropriately supportive environment. But to put it in a slogan, 'They get the job done.' Of course this sort of embedded practical understanding gives us no ability to explain how it's done, but as already noted the inability to explain need not entail the absence of all related understanding.

Autopoietic. Our embedded understanding of the psychophysical link is not restricted to the genetic domain. Being conscious involves a great deal of self-control, not in the ethical sense of resistance from temptation and discipline in action, but in all the many ways that conscious minds as active dynamic systems must monitor themselves, modulate themselves, and transform themselves. Whenever I engage in conscious inference, redirect my attention, call up a mental image, or reflect on a philosophical puzzle I exercise informed and able control over the flow and development of my own conscious mental processes. If our physicalist hypothetical is true, then whenever I regulate my conscious life, I am also monitoring, modulating, and transforming the physical processes on which my consciousness depends.

The self-directed control processes that are essentially required for the dynamically self-modulating nature of consciousness must at some level be implemented in procedures that adaptively reflect the detailed structure of the psychophysical link. If our physicalist assumption is true, then whatever practical causal access we have to the conscious properties of our own minds must in the end be grounded in the properties of the physical substrate on which they depend. We can get the causal leverage that we need to monitor or modify those conscious properties only through physically implemented procedures that are specifically adapted to the detailed structure of the psychophysical nexus.

As an analogy, consider the way in which you deal with the PC on your desk. You give it high-level commands, and it executes them. Perhaps you are using word processing to edit a document; you highlight a passage, copy it, delete it, and move it to a new location. The cut-and-paste operations are all you see and all you ever explicitly deal with. But those commands can do their job only because your computer includes compilers that convert or translate those commands into machine commands that operate on the basic binary machine code and their physical electronic embodiment. The operation of the virtual word-processing machine, indeed its very existence, depends upon those compilers. They in turn can do their jobs only if their own organization implicitly but accurately reflects (and in some sense procedurally 'understands') the links that hold between the higher- and lower-level features of the system.

The application to the mind–brain case is immediate. If as, per our assumption, consciousness is physical, then our ability to exercise the mental control we do in conscious thought requires the ability to implement our mental actions in the underlying neural substrate. At the conscious level, I can call up a mental image of my house and rotate it in my mind's eye as I count the windows in it. But given our physicalist assumption, I can exercise such self-control only if the overall mind–brain system embodies the required implicit self-understanding about how those conscious phenomena are neurally realized and how those actions are to be physically implemented. Thus the dynamic self-controlling nature of consciousness entails that the mind–brain system carries a great deal of implicit understanding of the psychophysical link procedurally embedded in its underlying organization.

We can call this form of implicit understanding 'autopoietic' borrowing a term used by biologists to refer to self-modifying processes or systems. As in the genetic case, most of this autopoietic understanding is opaquely embedded in practical procedures, and those procedures can perform their functions effectively only if their organization embodies a great deal of implicit psychophysical information or understanding. Extensive though that understanding must be, it is generally not in a form that we could make explicit as we need to do when we explain. I suspect some readers will be reluctant to use the term 'understanding' in reference to either genetic or autopoietic information; they will regard it as too great a reach from ordinary use. I concede that there are lots of important differences; indeed if there weren't the whole point of understanding without the ability to explain would be moot. We should not think of the DNA having little beliefs about how conscious pain depends upon its neural substrate, but none the less I think we are more than justified in regarding such highly adapted systems of control as carriers of evolution-arily derived information about the link. Adaptation—the highly improbable match of action and object—should not be regarded as mere coincidence, but seen as the result of a long process of evolution and selection through which biological information or understanding about the object (in this case the psychophysical link) has been acquired. Thus I believe we are justified in saying that both genetically and autopoietically we understand a lot, at least implicitly, about the pscho-physical links on which our existence as conscious beings depends.

As a bonus, this supplies a way in which we might apply the alternative syntactic reading raised above, that which parses 'explanatory gap' as *gap that explains.* I promised earlier to say a bit about how that might be, so here's one way it might go.

Our recognition of the gap leads us to reflect on why we can't link our mental and physical concepts by a priori or deductive means. In doing so, it brings us to see the way in which our subjective phenomenal concepts are anchored and defined by their roles within the interactive arena of our conscious lives as continuously self-modifying mental systems. The pragmatic contexts in which our subjective concepts are embedded are so unlike those from which our third-person concepts derive their contents that a gap between the two is very likely, indeed all but inevitable. The causal interactive contexts within which those representational systems operate and by which they get interpreted are so dissimilar and the modes of causal access through which they each engage the world so disparate, that it's unlikely we could establish any tight correspondence between the concepts defined by those two schemes, as we would need for a priori deduction or reductive explanation. Thus, as I've shown in detail elsewhere (1985, 1992, 2001) we obtain a powerful argument for the predictable occurrence of the gap itself and in favour of non-reductive physicalism.

The gap explains in a second sense as well by teaching us something important about the nature of consciousness, specifically about how the existence of conscious minds depends upon their nature as self-modifying mental systems. Once we recognize the active causal roles played by first-person concepts in the dynamic arena of our lives as self-conscious beings, we can't help but see as well that the coherent flow of phenomenal experience depends essentially upon the continuous self-modifying and self-generating activity of our conscious minds as physically realized self-understanding systems. In this way too the gap qualifies as a *gap that explains*. Reflecting upon it leads us by a series of direct and simple steps to a recognition of the central respects in which consciousness depends upon pragmatically implemented self-understanding, a fact generally not otherwise recognized or appreciated.

Thus the subjective psychophysical gap turns out to be a gap that explains in both the senses given above. It helps *explain consciousness* by leading us to see the essentially self-understanding aspect of its nature as an autopoietically dynamic mental process. And secondly it even helps *explain itself*. Reflecting on the gap and why it exists, leads us to recognize it as an all-but-inevitable consequence of the differing pragmatic contexts in which our first- and third-person concepts are anchored. Thus, though the variant syntactic meaning was intended neither by Levine nor those who followed him, it yet seems apt and worth attending to, whether intended or not.

A metaphoric link with water gaps also now appears; let's indulge a bit and run with it to see how far unmeant analogy might take us. As we saw earlier, the psychophysical gap is unlike the water/H_2O gap in important ways; yet surprisingly it may turn out to share important features with the other type of water gap we talked of above, the kind that flows through mountains. Water gaps, we said, explain themselves by being their own causes; the river often flowed where it does before the mountains rose and wore them down as they went up, creating the gap through which it passes. The flow of conscious experience and the implicit psychophysical self-understanding on which it depends long predate the rise of the more explicit forms of understanding—both subjective and objective—that we use when we explain. The phenomenal order of experience already in itself displays our implicit understanding of the subject/object duality of consciousness; even if we cannot explicate it, we understand it in some inarticulate way as we create it.

Our more explicit modes of understanding—both subjective and objective—find their source in the inchoate form of self-awareness that's embodied in the orderly flow of our phenomenal experience. Those explicit forms rise through a long, slow process of abstraction that draws our understanding out from the procedures in which it lies embedded, transforming implicit mental contours into conceptual shapes that can themselves become objects visible and graspable by thought. But even as those tangible forms evolve, their content still rests upon the interactive bonds by which they link pragmatically with consciousness itself.

Just as the contours of a water gap's two sides reflect the history of their causal interplay with the river that shaped them on their upward passage, so too the conceptual slopes of the subjective and objective modes in which we understand our minds are shaped and formed by their past and present active, practical engagement with self-reflective consciousness itself. Though those abstractive mental structures are, by definition, 'pulled away' (*ab tractus*) from the process that they aim to be about, they none the less depend upon their causal bonds to consciousness for their interpretation. And as we saw above, the ties that bind the two sides of the psychophysical gap to their common conscious target are too disparate to make those concepts match as tightly as we need to lead us through a priori deductions or reductive explanations.

Rivers shape each side of their passage in its own distinctive way; thus the upper slopes of a water gap raised long ago and high above the flow show at best a loose reflection of each other. They are not like Dennett's famous torn Jello box used by spies as the perfect cipher (Dennett 1991), because each part's random jagged edge has it precise complement in the other's border. That might be true of a mountain rift torn by a sudden seismic shift, where one past unitary form was broken on a common line; there one might find a Jello-boxlike match. But in river gaps, each side has its own evolving history, and the shapes and forms that the river's flow gives to one side are only rarely reflected in the other, especially when the river bends and twists in passage.

Reciprocation makes that even more the case, as the ever-sculptured shore in turn reforms the river's flow; each reshapes the other. Just as the flow and course of the river is changed by the shape of the gap to which itself gives form, so too the subjective and objective concepts by which we explicate our minds evolve in a reciprocal interplay with the flow of phenomenal experience. Those concepts in their own particular ways give us self-understanding access to our minds, and in the process give new form to consciousness itself. Our conscious minds in turn continually reshape those concepts better to engage their ever-changing dynamic reality. Thus we see that, like a water gap, the psychophysical divide exists and takes the form it does because a river flows through it, the river of self-awareness.

There's probably no bridge that we can walk across with simple inferential stride from slope to slope, nor any theoretical boat that might float us clear across the river without getting wet. To grasp properly how the two sides of the gap fit together we may need to get into the river itself. There may be ways of understanding consciousness and its psychophysical duality that only conscious selves can have and only through their way of being conscious. The mental constructs that we use when we explain—the concepts, models, maps, and theories—no doubt enhance our understanding. But they are merely tools of mind and not themselves active experiential agents. If there are ways in which conscious minds understand their consciousness by actively *being it* rather than merely *representing it* to themselves, then it may well be impossible to reproduce those forms of understanding using only relations among our mental tools and constructs. No relation among models or concepts would suffice to capture that active form of self-understanding. We may not be able to lay it out flat and explain it even though we understand it in our own way of being self-aware. No image of the river sculpted in the rocky slope—not even if reflected back upon the river's face—will suffice to replicate the order of its flow. So too our constructs, shaped of mental shale and gneiss, might reflect a lot of consciousness but never hope to capture all that we understand about ourselves in being self-aware.

But some while back—at least a few river bends ago—we crossed a subtle line between philosophy and poetry, so perhaps it's time to pass on to our last topic.

Poetic. To complete the GAP acronym we need a P word, and 'poetry' comes from the same Greek root as -*poiesis*, the verb *poiein*, which means to make or create. But bringing in poetry here is more than just a gimmick to make an alphabetic joke. Poets have always engaged ideas and themes that go to the heart of the psychophysical question. What has the poet to tell us of coming to be and passing away? And what of the place of self and mind in space and time? Our conscious minds range far in thought across the actual world and realms of possibility, but they themselves are actually bound quite locally in body, space, and time (or so at least they seem on our assumption.) In this duality of location, as glimpsed through our reflective self-awareness of it, lies one of the oldest, deepest sources of the poetical imagination. How much good verse flows from the triple intersect of self and time and mind?

Poetry reflects our duality not only in its content but also in its mode of expression. It exists within the space created by the interplay of words as particular concrete things with rhythms, sounds, and colours—and words as general bearers of meaning, both in what they signify or point at and also how and with what tones or feels they do so (Koch 1998). Good verse slides back and forth almost unnoticed between ideas and images and the particular locally sounded words with which we give them voice. One can say in verse things one cannot say in prose, and what one can say one can in general think. Thus if poetic speech is an expression of mind, what sort of mental states does it express? What intentional mental modes with what sort and range of meanings might poetic speech express? In rational agent psychology, assertions are taken to express propositional thoughts or beliefs. By analogy, what might poetry be taken to express, and how might it contribute to our understanding of ourselves as conscious beings?

I hope it's not too wild to suggest that part of what we understand through poetry is our own materiality. The double aspect of the poem implicitly reflects the local/general duality of our being and the intimacy and intricacy of their interdependence. Poets create structures in speech and mind that in their special way express the deepest of concerns by what they are as well as what they mean. Poets traditionally engage themes of coming to be and passing away, of self and space and time. So too do philosophers. But what the poet creates expresses those concerns not only by what it means but in the structure of its being, and perhaps it's just in that—in the mutual expressive interplay of being and meaning—that poetry most succeeds in giving us a way of understanding consciousness we cannot get by other means. If we are what we've assumed, namely conscious physical systems, then we are what we are in large part because we understand ourselves as such. We make ourselves as physical systems into conscious beings through the self-forming autopoietic understanding of our own interdependent duality as both physical and mental. Poets too are physical on our assumption, and it may be not only in their themes but also in the intertwined duality of their creations that they implicitly understand and express their own psychophysicality.

It's not a common practice to end a philosophical essay with a poem; indeed I don't know of any that do. But in this case it seems apt to make an exception, and so I'll end with a poem of my own. Though it expresses some of the poet's familiar general concerns, it was written about a very specific moment. One recent autumn term, I had a student in my course who had missed a lot of classes and failed to hand in several assignments. I asked her to come and see me, and when she arrived at my office she explained that her father had died during the summer and she was still wrestling with dark and powerful emotions. I expressed my sympathy, and we made all the arrangements to accommodate her situation. Our business was done, but she did not leave. She continued to sit in my office through sometimes awkward silences, expecting or hoping for something more that I might say or do. But I found I had nothing to offer. In time she left, and as I sat at my desk quietly thinking, my eye fell on a photo taken just a few months back, and this poem is about that.

Still Life with Flashback and Daisies

> The mother and her daughter stand
> beside the table with a tall
> > blue vase of daisies in a
> summer snapshot.
> > The father, unseen photographer
> who stood before the scene
> > behind the lens and with
> > his shutter
> made the stuttering day stand still,
> > > > > appears
> > > as just a small white spot
> reflected
> > in a distant window
> > > down a hall
> > > behind the happy family.

> The mirroring glass shows nothing of
> the camera or its holder,
> > but just the instantaneous flash,
> that bright white spot
> > > > that
> > > was so quickly there and not,
> unnoticed until now
> > > > in a still life moment.

REFERENCES

American Heritage Electronic Dictionary of the English Language (1992) (New York: Houghton Mifflin).

CHALMERS, DAVID (1996), *The Conscious Mind* (Oxford: Oxford University Press).

CHURCHLAND, PAUL (1985), 'Reduction, Qualia and the Direct Introspection of Brain States', *Journal of Philosophy*, 82: 8–28.

CLARK, AUSTEN (1993), *Sensory Qualities* (New York: Oxford University Press).

DENNETT, DANIEL (1991), *Consciousness Explained* (New York: Little Brown).

FIEGL, HERBERT (1958), The '*Mental*' and the '*Physical*', Minnesota Studies in the Philosophy of Science, 2 (Minneapolis: University of Minnesota Press), 390–497.

HARDIN, CLYDE (1988), *Color for Philosophers* (Indianapolis: Hackett).

JACKSON, FRANK (1982), 'Epiphenomenal Qualia', *Philosophical Quarterly*, 32: 12–36.

KANWISHER, NANCY (2000), 'Neural Correlates of Changes in Perceptual Awareness in the Absence of Changes in the Stimulus', *Consciousness Research Abstracts/ Journal of Consciousness Studies*, 82.

KIM, JAEGWON (1999), *Mind in a Physical World* (Cambridge, Mass.: MIT Press).

Koch, Kenneth (1998), 'The Language of Poetry', *The New York Review of Books* (14 May), 44–7.

Levine, Joseph (1983), 'Materialism and Qualia: The Explanatory Gap', *Pacific Philosophical Quarterly*, 64: 354–61.

—— (1993), 'On Leaving Out What It's Like', in M. Davies and G. Humphreys (eds.), *Consciousness* (Oxford: Blackwell), 121–36.

Loar, Brian (1990), 'Phenomenal properties', *Philosophical Perspectives*, 4: 81–108.

Lorenz, Konrad (1965), *Evolution and the Modification of Behavior* (Chicago: University of Chicago Press).

Lycan, William (1990), 'What is the Subjectivity of the Mental?' *Philosophical Perspectives*, 4: 109–30.

McGinn, Colin (1989), 'Can we Solve the Mind–Body Problem?' *Mind*, 98: 349–66.

—— (1991), *The Problem of Consciousness* (Oxford: Blackwell).

—— (1995), 'Consciousness and Space', in T. Metzinger (ed.), *Conscious Experience* (Thorverton: Imprint Academic), 149–64.

Nagel, Thomas (1974), 'What is it Like to be a Bat?' *Philosophical Review*, 83: 435–50.

Smart, J. J. C. (1959), 'Sensations and Brain Processes', *The Philosophical Review*, 68: 141–56.

Van Gulick, Robert (1985), 'Physicalism and the Subjectivity of the Mental', *Philosophical Topics*, 12: 51–70.

—— (1992), 'Emergence, Reduction and Intertheoretical constraint', in A. Beckerman, H. Flohr, and J. Kim (eds.), *Reduction or Emergence* (New York: de Gruyter), 157–79.

—— (1993), 'Understanding the Phenomenal Mind: Are We All Just Armadillos?' in M. Davies and G. Humphreys (eds.), *Consciousness* (Oxford: Blackwell), 137–54.

—— (2001), 'Nichtreductiver Materialismus—noch immer das beste Angebot auf dem Leib–Sele Basar (Nonreductive Physicalism: Still the Best Buy at the Mind–Body Bazaar)', in Michael Pauen (ed.), *Phaenomenales Bewustein: Entstehung und Erklarg* (Berlin: Mentis Verlag), 297–326.

Varela, Francisco (2000), 'Neural Synchrony and the Lived Present', *Consciousness Research Abstracts/Journal of Consciousness Studies*, 91.

von der Marlsburg, Christoph (2000), 'The Unity of Consciousness: Binding and the Integration of Subsystems', *Consciousness Research Abstracts/Journal of Consciousness Studies*, 90.

Wittgenstein, Ludwig (1953), *Philosophical Investigations* (New York: Macmillan).

12. Theories of Consciousness

DAVID PAPINEAU

1. Introduction

There are many theories of consciousness around, and my view is that they are all misconceived. Consciousness is not a normal scientific subject, and needs to be handled with special care. It is foolhardy to jump straight in and start building a theory, as if consciousness were just like electricity or chemical valency. We will do much better to reflect explicitly on our methodology first. When we do this, we will see that theories of consciousness are trying to answer a question that isn't there.

2. Consciousness as a Determinable Property

I begin with a useful distinction. We can think of *consciousness* as a determinable property, whose determinates are more specific modes of consciousness such as *being in pain, tasting chocolate, seeing an elephant,* and so on. By way of analogy, contrast the determinable property, *having a shape,* with the more specific (determinate) properties *square, triangular, elliptical.* Or again, contrast the determinable property *being a car,* with the determinates *being a Ford, a Rover, a Rolls-Royce,* and so on. The idea here is simply the notion of a genus, which then divides into a number of more restrictive species. In this way, then, *being conscious* is a general property, whose instances all have some more determinate conscious feature like *being in pain.*[1]

---

[1] When I talk about a mental 'state', I shall simply mean the instantiation of a mental property. I shall take the particulars which instantiate such properties to be ordinary organisms, like people or possibly cats. This means that my basic notion of consciousness is that of an organism being conscious at a given time. For those readers who prefer to focus on 'state consciousness', rather than 'creature consciousness', let me observe that, when an organism is conscious on my account, this will be in virtue of its being in one or more mental states that are determinates of the determinable, being conscious. These determinate mental states are thus naturally counted as 'conscious' states. (Compare: my car is coloured in virtue of being red, or green, or whatever; red and green and so on are thus colours.) As for 'consciousness of', the other notion that is sometimes taken to be basic, I do not assume that all conscious states have intentional objects (though some certainly do), nor that all intentional states are conscious.

The theories of consciousness that are my target in this chapter are theories of the determinable property of consciousness-as-such, not determinate conscious properties such as pain, or seeing an elephant, or whatever. Many theories of just this kind are on offer nowadays. Thus, to pick a quick sample, consider the identification of consciousness with quantum collapses in cellular microtubules (Penrose 1994), or with operations in the global workspace (Baars 1988), or with competition for action control (Shallice 1988), or with informational content (Chalmers 1996; Tye 1995; Dretske 1995), or, again with, higher-order thought (Armstrong 1968; Rosenthal 1996; Lycan 1996, Carruthers 2000). These are all theories of what it takes to be conscious at all, not of more determinate states such as feeling a pain and so on. My argument will be that theories of this kind are barking up the wrong tree.

Before discussing theories of the determinable property, being conscious, it will be useful first to explain at some length how I think of determinate conscious properties, as my analysis of general 'theories of consciousness' will be informed by this understanding.

3. Determinate Conscious Properties are Physical Properties

I am a physicalist about determinate conscious properties. I think that the property of being in pain is identical to some physical property. This is not because I want to be provocative, or because I am caught up by current philosophical fashion, but because I think that there is an overwhelming argument for this identification, namely, that conscious mental states would have no influence on our behaviour, which they clearly do, were they not identical with physical states.

This is not the place to analyse this argument in any detail, but three brief comments will be in order. First, you might want to ask, if so simple an argument can establish physicalism, why hasn't everybody always been persuaded by it. My answer is that it is a simple argument, but that until recently a crucial premiss was not available. This is the premiss that physical effects, like behaviour, are always fully determined, in so far as they are determined at all, by prior physical causes. This is a highly empirical premiss, and moreover one that informed scientific opinion didn't take to be fully evidenced until some time into this century. It is this evidential shift, and not any tide of philosophical fashion, that has been responsible for the recent rise of physicalism. (For more details on this history, see Papineau 2000.)

Second, let me say something about what I mean by 'physical'. I am happy to leave this quite vague in this chapter. In particular, I would like it to be read in such a way as to include 'functional' properties (like having-*some*-physical-property-produced-by-bodily-damage-and-causing-avoidance-behaviour), and physiological properties (like having your C-fibres firing), as well as strictly physical properties like mass, position, and quantum collapses. This is skating over a number of tricky issues (in particular the issue of whether functional and other higher-level properties can themselves really *cause* behaviour, if that behaviour always has full physical causes). Fortunately these issues are orthogonal to my concerns here. The important point for present purposes is only that I want to identify determinate conscious properties with independently identifiable properties of a general scientific-causal sort, with properties that *are not sui generis* irreducibly conscious properties. Given this, it doesn't matter here exactly which kind of properties we count as broadly 'physical' in this sense. (For more on this, see Papineau 1998.)

Third, and to forestall any possible confusion, I would like to emphasize that physicalism does not deny the 'what-it's-likeness' of conscious occurrences. To say that pain is identical with a certain physical property is not to deny that it is like something to be in pain. Rather, it is to affirm that it is like something to be in a certain physical state. Of course it is like something to experience pain, or to see red, or to taste chocolate. And these experiences matter, especially to their subjects. But, insists the physicalist, they are not non-physical things. They are just a matter of your having some physical property. They are how it is for you, if you have that physical property.

4. Phenomenal Concepts and Third-Person Concepts

While I am a physicalist about determinate conscious *properties*, I am a sort of dualist about the *concepts* we use refer to these properties. I think that we have two quite different ways of thinking about determinate conscious properties. Moreover, I think that is crucially important for physicalists to realize that, even if conscious properties are just physical properties, they can be referred to in these two different ways. Physicalists who do not acknowledge this, and there are some, will find themselves unable to answer some standard anti-physicalist challenges.

I shall call these two kinds of concepts 'phenomenal' concepts and 'third-person' concepts. The idea, then, is that we have two quite different ways of thinking about pain, say, or tasting chocolate, or seeing an elephant, both of which refer to the same properties in reality. By way of obvious analogy, consider the case where we have two names, 'Judy Garland' and 'Frances Gumm', say, both of which refer to the same real person.

The distinction between concepts is similar to David Chalmers's distinction between 'phenomenal' and 'psychological' concepts. The reason I have contrasted phenomenal concepts with 'third-person concepts' rather than with Chalmers's 'psychological concepts' is that I am not currently concerned to analyse our non-phenomenal ways of thinking about conscious states in any detail (though I will say a bit more on this below). Chalmers has specific views on this matter, which make him focus in the first instance on *functional* concepts of mental states, which he calls 'psychological' concepts (for example, the concept of having-some-physical-property-produced-by-bodily-damage-and-causing-avodiance-behaviour). While such psychological concepts are one instance of what I mean by 'third-personal' concepts, I want also to include here any other concepts that identify their referents as parts of the third-personal, causal world, including physiological concepts (C-fibres firing) strictly physical concepts (involving ideas of mass, position, and so on), and indeed such everyday descriptive concepts as 'his reaction to that bad news last Thursday' or 'the causes of his offensive behaviour'.

Third-personal concepts will thus be a broad category, but that doesn't matter, given that we don't really need a definition of the category beyond its contrast with 'phenomenal' concepts. These comprise the more interesting category. When we use phenomenal concepts, we think of mental properties, not as items in the third-personal causal world, but in terms of *what they are like*. Consider what happens when the dentist's drill slips and hits the nerve in your tooth. We can think of this third-personally, in terms of nerve messages, brain activity, involuntary flinching, and so on. Or we can think of it in terms of what it would be *like*, of how it would *feel* if that happened to you.

5. How Physicalists Can Stop Worrying and Learn to Love Phenomenal Concepts

Phenomenal concepts are normally introduced by antiphysicalist philosophers, by philosophers who want to resist the identification of phenomenal properties with physical properties. Such antiphysicalists aim to move from the existence of distinctive non-physical ways of *thinking* to the existence of distinctive non-physical ways of *being*.

Now some physicalists aim to resist this move by denying the existence of phenomenal concepts, by denying that there are any distinctive non-physical ways of thinking (Dennett 1991; Churchland and Churchland 1998). But this seems to me quite the wrong move. There is nothing in phenomenal concepts *per se* to worry the physicalist. In particular, they don't entail that there are distictive phenomenal properties.

A good way to show this is to consider Frank Jackson's story of Mary (Jackson 1986). Jackson takes this story to demonstrate the existence of distinctive phenomenal *properties*. But the physicalist can respond that, while the story is certainly a good way of demonstrating that there are distinctive phenomenal *concepts*, the further move to non-physical properties is invalid.

In Jackson's thought experiment, Mary is an expert on colour vision. She knows everything there is to know about the physics and physiology of peoples' brains when they see colours. However, Mary is peculiar in that she has never seen any colours herself. She has always lived in a house with an entirely black-and-white interior, she doesn't have a colour television, all her books have only black-and-white illustrations, and so on. Then one day Mary goes out and sees a red rose.

At this point, argues Jackson, she learns *about* something she didn't know before. As we say, she now '*knows* what it is like to see red'. And since she already knew about everything physical connected with colour experience, continues Jackson, this must involve her now knowing about some distinctive *phenomenal property* associated with red experiences, which she didn't have access to before she saw the rose.

However, as I suggested, physicalists who recognize phenomenal concepts needn't accept this argument. For they can respond that, while there is indeed a genuine before–after difference in Mary, this is just a matter of her acquiring a new *concept* of seeing red. The *property* she refers to with this concept is still a perfectly good physical property, the physical property, whatever it is, that is present in just those people who are seeing red, and which she could think *about* perfectly well, albeit using third-personal concepts, even before she saw the rose. (In the terminology of philosophical logic, we can say that Mary has a new Fregean thought, but not a new Russellian one.)

To fill out this suggestion, note that the essential change in Mary, now that she 'knows what it is like to see red', involves two things. First, she is now able to have memories, and other thoughts, that imaginatively *recreate* the experience, as when she recalls what it was like to see red, or anticipates what it will be like to see red. Second, she is also now able introspectively to *reidentify* other experiences as of that type, as when she thinks that she is now having the same experience as when she saw the rose.[2]

When I speak of Mary's acquiring a new phenomenal concept, I mean she is able to think new (Fregean) thoughts by using these new powers of recreation and reidentification. Thus she will be able imaginatively to recreate the experience in question, and thereby think such thoughts as, 'Having a ø [and here she imagines the experience] won't be possible for people who are colour-blind,' or 'Jim will have a ø in a minute.' Again, when she is actually having the experience in question, she will be able to think such thoughts as, 'This ø [here she identifies an aspect of her current experience] is a hallucination caused by what I ate,' or 'Looking at that square has made me have this ø after-image.' Thoughts of these kinds seem quite unproblematically

---

[2] Note that Mary will be able to make such reidentifications even if she doesn't have a word for the experience. Nor need she yet be able to identify the property she can now think about in phenomenal terms with any of the properties she could previously think about third-personally.

truth-evaluable, and in particular there seems no special difficulty in under-standing the contribution that the ø-element makes to the truth conditions of these thoughts. So we can think of the ø-element as a concept, in the familiar sense of an item that makes a systematic contribution to the truth conditions of the thoughts it enters into.

Now, as I said, Jackson and others take the existence of Mary's new phenomenal concept, and of phenomenal concepts in general, to imply the existence of distinctive phenomenal *properties*. The idea, presumably (though this is not often spelled out), is that the before–after difference in Mary (she now 'knows what it's like to see red', when before she didn't) somehow derives from her new-found *acquaintance* with the phenomenal features of her experi-ence. On this model, then, the possession of a phenomenal concept requires that the possessor previously be directly acquainted with some phenomenal property. This is why nobody can 'know what an experience is like' prior to having it.

However, given the suggestions I have made about the structure of phe-nomenal concepts, there is an obvious alternative physicalist story to be told, that accounts equally well for the fact that you can't 'know what an experience is like' prior to having it, and does so without invoking any special phenom-enal properties.[3]

Here is the obvious physicalist explanation. Coming to 'know what an experience is like' involves being able to imaginatively recreate and introspect-ively identify the experience. Let me take these in turn. Suppose first that imaginative recreation depends on the ability to reactivate (some of) the same parts of the brain as are activated by the original experience itself. Then it would scarcely be surprising that we can do this only with respect to types of experience we have previously had. We can't form replicas, so to speak, if external stimulation hasn't fixed a mould in our brains. Less metaphorically, we can reactivate just the parts of the brain required for the imaginative recreation of some experience E only if some actual instance of E has previously activated those parts. A similar story can be told for introspective identification. Suppose the introspective identification of some experience requires that it is compared with some model or template stored in the brain. Again, it would scarcely be surprising that we should need an original

---

[3] Nor, a fortiori, does the physicalist story rest anything on the dubious idea of direct acquaintance with such phenomenal properties. I find the antiphysicalist story especially puzzling at this point. In particular, how is the change in Mary (her now 'knowing what seeing red is like') supposed to be sustained after she stops having her new experience? Can she now recall the phenomenal property to her mind at will, so as to *reacquaint* herself with it? Or can her memory reach back through time to keep *acquainting* her with the earlier instance? Both these ideas seem odd, but something along these lines seems to be needed to explain why Mary continues to 'know what the experience is like' after the experience is over, if such knowing depends on acquaintance with a phenomenal property.

version of the experience in order to form the template for such compari-
sons.[4]

So this now gives us a physicalist account of what is involved in Mary's
coming to 'know what it is like' to see red. This account acknowledges that
Mary acquires a new phenomenal concept of seeing red. But it denies that this
new concept points to any new non-physical property. The change in Mary
does not involve any acquaintance with a phenomenal property. Rather, her
brain is lastingly altered in certain ways, and this now allows her imaginatively
to recreate and introspectively to reidentify an experience she could previously think about only in a third-person way. Seen in this way, it is clear there
is nothing in the idea of phenomenal concepts as such which bars them to
physicalists.

6. Kripkean Intuitions

Not only *can* physicalists happily accept the existence of distinctive phenomenal concepts, but they *should* accept them, otherwise they will have
trouble responding to Saul Kripke's famous argument against mind–brain
identity.

At its simplest, Kripke's argument starts from the imaginability of zombies.
Surely it makes sense to suppose that there could be a being physically just like
me, but with no feelings, an unconscious automaton. But if zombies are
imaginable, then they are possible. And, if they are possible, then it would
seem to follow that conscious properties are distinct from physical properties,
for it is precisely their lack of conscious properties, despite their sharing all
our physical properties, that creates the possibility of zombies.

Physicalists should object to the slide from imaginability to possibility.
Zombies may be imaginable, but they aren't possible. Even God could not
make a zombie. Since my conscious properties are nothing but a subclass of
my physical properties, any being that shares all my physical properties will
therewith share all my conscious properties.

---

[4] What is the status of the claim that you can know what an experience is like only once you
have had it yourself? It does seem, give or take a bit, that actual human beings cannot
imaginatively recreate or introspectively reidentify any conscious experiences that they have
not previously undergone. But note that the explanation I have given for this phenomenon
implies it to be a pretty contingent matter. There seems nothing impossible about creatures
being born with imaginative and introspective abilities, prior to any experience. (Simply
imagine that the 'moulds' or 'templates' involved, and the dispositions to use them, are 'hard-
wired', that is, grow independently of any specific experiences.) There is also an interesting
question here about the link between imaginative recreation and introspective reidentification
as such, whether or not these powers derive from prior experiences. Again, these seem to go
hand in hand in actual human beings (though here the explanation is not so obvious), while
once more there seems nothing impossible about creatures in whom they would come apart.

But if zombies aren't possible, as the physicalist must say, then how come they are imaginable, as clearly they are? This is where Kripke's argument bites. A natural explanation for our apparent ability to imagine many impossibilities (such as the impossibility that H_2O is not *water*) is that we are picking out an entity (water) via some contingent features it has in this world in (odourless, colourless, etc.), and then imagining the genuinely possible world in which H_2O (that is, *water*) does not have those contingent features. But no strategy like this is going to help physicalists with the mind–brain case, for if they try arguing that, in imagining zombies, we are imagining beings who really do have pain, and only lack those properties by which we pick out pain in this world (*hurtfulness*, perhaps, or *achiness*), then they can be challenged to explain how the physically identical zombies can lack these *further* properties, unless these properties are themselves non-physical.

We can see why physicalists get into trouble here. In effect, the imaginability of zombies shows that we have a concept of pain that is different from any possible third-personal concept: we can conceive of a being who does not satisfy the pain concept, however many third-personal concepts it satisfies. The water-H_2O analogy then invites the physicalist to explain the distinctive nature of this pain concept in terms of certain distinctive *properties* (hurtfulness, achiness) by which it picks out its referent. However, once this invitation is accepted, then the physicalist runs straight into trouble. For it seems that these supposed distinctive properties will do the job of explaining why the pain concept is distinct from all third-personal concepts only if they are themselves *non*-physical properties. After all, if the pain concept referred by invoking physical properties, this would seem to imply that it must be the same as some ordinary third-personal concept, which it isn't.

Physicalists shouldn't accept the invitation implicit in the water/H_2O analogy in the first place. That is, they shouldn't aim to explain the distinctive nature of the phenomenal pain concept as a matter of certain distinctive properties that that concept uses to pick out its referent. Instead they should argue that such concepts refer *directly*, without invoking any distinctive properties of their referents, and that their distinctive nature lies elsewhere, in the fact that their deployment involves exercises of imagination or introspection.

If this strikes you as ad hoc, note that some concepts of properties *must* refer to their objects directly, without invoking other properties, on pain of regress. It can't be that every concept of a property refers to that property *as* 'the property that has some other property F', or in any similar other-F-invoking way, since the concept that refers to this other property F will then need to invoke some further property G, and so on. So there must be some concepts of properties that refer directly, at least in the sense that they don't do so by invoking other properties. I do not claim that phenomenal concepts are the *only* such directly referring concepts of properties. In fact I think it likely that there are many such concepts. But all that matters for the moment is that there must be some, and that phenomenal concepts will feature among them.[5]

Some unfinished business remains. If phenomenal concepts pick out their referents without invoking contingent properties of those referents, then, once more, how do physicalists explain the imaginability of zombies? What exactly is the content of our thought when we imagine a physical duplicate that does not feel pain? The water/H_2O model is no longer available. Physicalists can't now say that in imagining all our physical properties, and yet no pains, we are imagining a world in which the relevant physical properties lack the contingent features by which we pick out pains. For we have now agreed that pain isn't picked out by any contingent features.

However, there is an obvious enough alternative solution. Instead of trying to identify some genuine possibility that we are imagining, physicalists can simply say that there is no real possibility associated with the thought that *pains are not C-fibres firing* (or any other physical property), and that the thinkability of this thought consists in nothing beyond the facts that we have a concept *pain*, a concept *C-fibres firing*, the concepts *are* and *not*, and the power to form a thought by joining them together.

Indeed, having come this far, we can see that we may as well have said the same thing about imagining the impossibility that H_2O is not water. There is no real need to tell the complicated Kripkean story about our really imagining something else, namely, a world in which H_2O (that is, water) lacks the properties that fix reference to water in this world. Why not simply say that 'water' and 'H_2O' are different concepts, which they clearly are for most people, and use this fact alone to explain how those people can, without conceptual inconsistency, think the 'impossible' thought that H_2O is not water? The point is that there is nothing difficult about thinking an impossible thought, once you have two terms for one thing. Just join them in a thought where they flank a term for non-identity, and there you are.

Of course, there remains a genuine disanalogy between the H_2O/water case and the mind–brain cases. Since 'water' still does arguably refer by invoking properties, there indeed is a genuine possibility in the offing here (the possibility that H_2O not be odourless, etc.), even if we don't *need* this

---

[5] What does make it the case that phenomenal concepts refer as they do? This is a further question, on which I shall not say much (though see n. 8 below). True, in the next section I shall make much of the fact that, when phenomenal concepts are deployed in imagination or introspection, their employment phenomenally resembles the experiences they refer to, and moreover that this resemblance is important for understanding the mind–brain issue. But I should like to make it clear that I certainly do not take this resemblance to account for the referential power of phenomenal concepts.

possibility to provide a content for '$H_2O \neq$ water' thoughts. By contrast, there is no genuine possibility corresponding to the thought that zombies might have no feelings. Since phenomenal concepts don't refer by invoking distinctive conscious properties, there is simply no possibility at all corresponding to the thought that a being may share your physical properties yet lack your conscious ones.

7. The Antipathetic Fallacy

There is a further reason why physicalists will do well to recognize a distinctive species of phenomenal concepts. It will help to explain why physicalism seems so implausible.

There is no denying that intuition weighs against physicalism. As noted, there is a strong argument for identifying conscious properties with physical properties, namely, that modern science shows that this is the only way of respecting the causal significance that we ordinarily ascribe to conscious states. Still, it is striking that, even in the face of this argument, many people continue to find it unbelievable that conscious states should be identical with physical states. This reaction contrasts with the response to other theoretical identifications. Thus, it is in a way surprising that water turned out to be H_2O, or heat to be molecular motion. But few people continue to resist these conclusions, once they appreciate the evidence. Mind–brain identification is different, in that intuition continues to object, even after the evidence is on the table. How can *pain* (which hurts so) possibily be the same thing as insensate molecules rushing around in nerve fibres? Or again, as Colin McGinn (1991) is so fond of asking, how can our vivid *technicolour phenomenology* (our experience of reds and purples and so on) possibly be the same as cellular activity in squishy *grey* matter?

The difference between phenomenal concepts and third-personal concepts yields a very natural explanation of these antiphysicalist intuitions. Consider the two ways in which phenomenal concepts can be deployed, that is, in imaginative recreations and in introspective identifications. Both these exercises of phenomenal concepts have the unusual feature that we effectively *use* the experiences being referred to in the act of referring to them. When we imaginatively recreate an experience, we activate a faint *copy* of the original experience (cf. Hume on ideas and impressions), and when we reidentify an experience, we think by bringing an *actual* experience under some comparison.

In both these cases the experience itself is in a sense being *used* in our thinking, and so is present in us. For this reason exercising a phenomenal concept will *feel* like having the experience itself. When you imagine a pain, or seeing red, or even more when you attend to these experiences while having them, versions of these experiences themselves will be present in you, and because of this the activity of thinking *about* pain or seeing red will introspectively strike you as sharing the subjective phenomenology of these experiences themselves.

Now compare exercises of some third-personal concept that, according to the physicalist, refers to just the same state. No similar feelings there. To think of C-fibres firing, or of some-physical-state-that-causes-damage-avoidance, doesn't in itself create any feeling like pain. Or, again, thinking of grey matter doesn't in itself make you experience colours.

So there is a intuitive sense in which exercises of third-personal concepts 'leave out' the experience at issue. They leave out the pain and the technicolour phenomenology, in the sense that they don't activate or involve these experiences. Now, it is all too easy to slide from this to the conclusion that, in exercising third-personal concepts, we are not thinking *about* the experiences themselves. After all, doesn't this third-personal mode of thought leave out the experiences, in a way that our phenomenal concepts do not? And doesn't this show that the third-personal concepts simply don't refer to the experiences denoted by our phenomenal concept of pain?

This line of thought is terribly natural, and I think it is largely responsible for widespread conviction that the mind must be extra to the brain. (Consider again the standard rhetorical ploy: 'How could this panoply of *feeling* arise from mere neuronal activity?') However, this line of thought is a fallacy (which elsewhere I have dubbed the 'antipathetic fallacy'). There is a sense in which third-personal concepts do leave out the feelings. Uses of them do not in any way activate the experiences in question, by contrast with uses of phenomenal concepts. But it simply does not follow that third-personal concepts leave out the feelings in the sense of failing to refer to them. They can still refer to the feelings, even though they don't activate them.

After all, most concepts don't use or involve the things they refer to. When I think of being rich, say, or having measles, this doesn't in any sense make me rich or give me measles. In *using* the states they refer to, pheneomenal concepts are very much the exception. So we shouldn't conclude on this account that third-personal concepts, which work in the normal way of most concepts, in not using the states they refer to, fail to refer to those states.

This then offers a natural account of the intuitive resistance to physicalism about conscious experiences. This resistance arises because we have a special way of thinking about our conscious experiences, namely, by using phenomenal concepts. We can think about our conscious experience using concepts to which they bear a phenomenal resemblance. And this then creates the fallacious impression that other, third-personal ways of thinking about those experiences fail to refer to the felt experiences themselves.[6]

8. Implicit Dualism

I now return to the main topic of this chapter, 'theories of consciousness', in the sense of theories of consciousness-as-such, of the determinable property of consciousness, rather than its determinates.

At first pass, I would say that much theorizing of this kind is motivated by more or less explicit dualism. Go back to determinate mental states like pain, seeing red, and so on, for a moment. If you are a dualist about such states, that is, if you think that in addition to their physical underpinnings these states also involve some distinct non-physical property, floating above the physical, as it were, then you will of course think that there is something terribly important common to all conscious states. They involve a special kind of non-physical property not found in the rest of the natural world. And if you think this, then of course you will want a theory about these special non-physical goings-on, a theory that tells you about the kinds of circumstances that will generate these extra non-physical states.

Some of those who trade in theories of consciousness are quite overt about their dualist motivations. David Chalmers, for example, argues explicitly that conscious properties are extra to any physical properties, and so actively urges that the task of a 'theory of consciousness' is to figure out which physical processes give rise to this extra realm. He compares the theory of consciousness with the nineteenth-century theory of electromagnetism. Early in the nineteenth century many scientists hoped that electromagnetism could be explained in terms of more basic mechanical processes. But James Clerk Maxwell and his contemporaries later realized that this was impossible, and so added electromagnetism to the list of basic elements of reality. Chalmers

---

[6] Some readers might not be persuaded that imaginative recreations of experience really feel like the experiences themselves. Does an imagined pain really feel like a real pain? I myself do think there is a real phenomenal resemblance, especially with pains and colour experiences, and that this is part of what seduces people into the antipathetic fallacy. But I do not need to insist on this. For I can restrict my diagnosis of antiphysicalist intuitions to the other kind of use of phenomenal concepts, namely, in thoughts that deploy introspective identifications, rather than imaginative recreations. These uses unquestionably feel like the experiences themselves, since they use actual experiences, brought under some categorization, and not just some imagined recreation. I would like to stress this point, given that my previous explanations of the 'antipathetic fallacy' have focused on imaginative recreations, rather than introspective identifications, for reasons that now escape me. It is perhaps also worth stressing that the points made about phenomenal concepts in earlier sections, and in particular my explanation of how they help physicalists to deal with Jackson and Kripke, are quite independent of my account of the antipathetic fallacy.

urges exactly the same move with respect to consciousness. We need to recognize conscious experience as an additional feature of nature, and figure out the theoretical principles governing its generation.

Not all theorists of consciousness are as upfront as Chalmers. Yet the same commitments can be discerned even among thinkers who would be disinclined to consider themselves dualists. Thus theorists who begin by explicitly disavowing any inclinations towards dualism will often betray themselves soon afterwards, when they start talking about the physical processes which 'generate' consciousness, or 'cause' it, or 'give rise to' it, or 'are correlated with' it. These phrases may seem innocuous, but they implicitly presuppose that conscious properties are some extra feature of reality, over and above all its physical features. That they come so readily to thinkers who do not see themselves as dualists only testifies to the strength of antiphysicalist intuition. You may recognize the theoretical difficulties that accompany dualism, and wish sincerely to avoid them. But the peculiar structure of phenomenal concepts will grip you once more, and persuade you that third-personal ways of thinking inevitably 'leave out' the crucial thing. So conscious feelings can't just *be* physical states, but must in some sense 'arise from' them, or be 'generated by' them. And then of course it will seem obvious, as before, that we need a 'theory of consciousness'. For what could be more important than to figure out which physical processes have the special power to 'generate' consciousness?

In this chapter I shall have no further interest in theories of consciousness motivated in this way. I take the points already made in earlier sections to show what is wrong with dualism, and therewith to discredit the enterprise of finding out which physical states 'give rise' to some extra realm of conscious being. There is no such extra realm, and so any theory seeking to identify its sources is embarking on a wild-goose chase.

9. Physicalist Theories of Consciousness

Rather, what I shall consider from now on is whether there is room for theories of consciousness within a serious physicalism that *identifies* determinate conscious properties with physical properties, and does not slip back into thinking of the physical properties as 'giving rise' to the conscious ones. Certainly there are plenty of serious physicalists who defend this possibility. They are quite clear that conscious properties are one and the same as physical properties, yet still want a theory that will tell us what is common to all cases of consciousness.

But I have severe doubts. I think that once we give up on dualism, the motivation for theorizing of this kind disappears. When we follow the argument right through, and make sure that dualists' thoughts are not allowed to intrude anywhere, then it will become unclear what such theories of consciousness-in-general are trying to do.

This conclusion is by no means obvious. The idea of a physicalist theory of consciousness-as-such certainly makes initial sense. It is perfectly normal for a scientific theory to identify the physical property that constitutes the real nature of some everyday kind. Thus science has shown us that water is H_2O, and that genes are sequences of DNA, and many other such things. So why shouldn't it show us which physical property constitutes the real nature of consciousness?

Physicalists can find another good model in nineteenth-century physics, to set against Chalmers's appeal to Maxwell's theory. Where Chalmers appeals to electromagnetism, they can appeal to temperature. In the case of temperature, physics went the other way. Instead of adding temperature to the fundamental components of reality, it explained it in terms of a more basic mechanical quantity, namely mean kinetic energy. Similarly, argue physicalists about consciousness-as-such, we need a scientific theory that will identify the underlying physical property common to all cases of consciousness, and thereby show us what consciousness really is.

However, I don't think that this programme can be carried through. This is because I am doubtful about the concept of consciousness-as-such, the concept of a state's being like something. I don't think that this notion succeeds in picking out any kind. So there is no possibility of a reductive scientific theory that identifies the essence of this kind. Such a theory will lack a target. We think our concept of consciousness gives us a good grasp of a real kind, but in fact there is nothing there.

At first this idea may seem absurd. What could be more obvious than the difference between states it is like something to have, and those it is not? Am I a zombie, that I don't know? But I would ask readers to bear with me. The notion of a state's 'being like something' is not a normal concept, and we shouldn't take it for granted that it works like other concepts.

Perhaps I should make it clear that I do not want to deny that there are certainly plenty of mental states that are like something for human beings, and plenty of other states that are not. But we need to treat the language involved in these claims with caution. I shall argue that the form of words, 'being like something', does not draw a line across the whole of reality, with the states that are like something on one side, and those that aren't on the other.

I am not going to try to convince you of this head-on, however. My strategy will be to creep up on this conclusion from behind, by considering the methodology adopted by those who trade in theories of consciousness. At first sight, these theorists look as if they are simply trying to do for consciousness what science has done for water or temperature. But when we look more closely at the precise methodology adopted by these theorists, we shall find that it doesn't really add up. This will lead me to reflect on the notion that defines the object of such theorizing, the notion of consciousness-as-such, and to my eventual conclusion that this notion does not have what it takes to pick out a kind.

As a preliminary to these explorations, it will be helpful briefly to compare the concept of consciousness-as-such with our concepts of specific conscious states, such as pain, or seeing red, or tasting chocolate. I am interested here in such concepts as we might possess *prior* to any scientific investigations. Once we have arrived at scientific findings about either the determinable, consciousness-as-such, or its determinates, such as pain, we might wish to incorporate these findings into augmented concepts of these properties. But before we can arrive at such scientific findings, we will need some everyday, pre-theoretical concepts, with which initially to pick out a subject matter for our scientific investigations.

In this connection, I would say that our pre-theoretical concepts of determinate conscious properties have a definiteness that is lacking from our concept of consciousness-as-such. In line with our earlier discussion, I take there to be two elements to such pre-theoretical everyday concepts. First, there are our phenomenal ways of thinking about determinate conscious states, our ways of thinking about those states by reactivating or reidentifying them. Second, I take there to be third-personal functional elements ('psychological' in David Chalmers's terms) in our everyday thinking about determinate conscious states.[7] Some of the ways of referring to mental states that I earlier included in the category of 'third-personal concepts' will clearly be posterior to scientific investigation, for example, identifications in terms of physiology or sub-personal cognitive architecture. But prior to such discoveries we will already have some grasp, in everyday terms, of the functional roles played by determinate conscious states, as when we think of pain, say, as something caused by bodily damage and giving rise to avoidance behaviour.[8]

---

[7] Should we think of our everyday word 'pain' as ambiguous, equivocally expressing separate phenomenal and functional concepts? I am not sure. An alternative would be to understand 'pain' as referring to that property, if any, that satisfies both concepts. (Note that, on this option, 'pain' would arguably end up non-referring if epiphenomenalism, rather than physicalism or interactionism, were true.) A further question that arises at this point is whether 'pure' phenomenal concepts must be augmented by at least some functional specifications if they are to have any power to refer determinately.

[8] Note that it would be a mistake to infer, from the fact that a concept is available prior to active scientific investigation, that it must be unconnected with *any* testable empirical theory. It may well derive its content from some empirical 'folk' theory. (Note also that in that case, as with all 'theoretical concepts', it won't be the concept's existence, so to speak, but its satisfaction, that depends on the truth of empirical theory. I can use 'pain' to express 'that property, if any, that results from damage and causes avoidance behaviour' even if it is empirically false that there is any such property. If there is no such property, then my term will still be meaningful, but will simply fail to refer to anything.)

Now I see no reason to suppose that our everyday concept of concscious-ness-as-such contains either the phenomenal or functional elements charac-teristic of our everyday concepts of determinate conscious states. Take first the question of whether we have a phenomenal concept of consciousness. It is difficult to know what to say here. Certainly we can imagine and recognize a list of determinate conscious states (pain, sadness, itches, and so on and on), and we can form some thought along the lines of 'one of *those*'. But whether this on its own amounts to any kind of concept, let alone a phenomenal concept akin to those we have for determinate conscious states, seems to me an open question. A list by itself does not tell us how to extrapolate to further cases. Because of this, I see no reason to regard the construction 'one of *those*' as in itself doing anything to pick out conscious from non-conscious states.

The situation with our pre-theoretical functional grasp on consciousness-as-such seems more straightforward. We have almost no such grasp. Everyday thinking contains scarcely any ideas about what consciousness *does*. True, there is the idea that if a subject is 'internally aware' of a state, then it is conscious, and (perhaps less strongly) that if any human state is conscious, then we will be 'internally aware' of it. This fact, and how exactly to under-stand 'internal awareness' in this context, will feature prominently in what follows. But beyond this connection with internal awareness, there is a surprising dearth of everyday ideas about any distinctive psychological role played by consciousness-as-such. We have no good a priori notion of any distinctive functional role played by all and only conscious states.

10. Testing Theories of Consciousness

I intend now to switch tack, and focus on the issue of how we *test* theories of consciousness. By asking this question, I hope to creep up on the concept of consciousness-as-such from behind. At least there seems to be an agreed methodology for testing theories of consciousness. By examining this meth-odology, we ought to be able to reconstruct the prior concept that identifies the subject matter of such theories. However, it will turn out that it is hard to make good sense of the agreed methodology for testing theories of conscious-ness. This will in turn reflect adversely on the concept of consciousness-as-such.

While it is not often explicitly discussed, I take the standard procedure for testing theories of consciousness to be as follows. We humans look into ourselves, and check whether the states *we are internally aware of* coincide with the states in us that *the theory identifies as conscious*. This strategy seems appropriate across the board, from philosophical theories such as Dretske's or Tye's intentionalism, through cognitive-functional theories such as Baar's global workspace model, to physiological theories such as Penrose's. We test the theory by seeing whether we can find states that we are internally aware of, but that don't fall under the theory's characterization of consciousness, or alternatively, whether *we have* states that do fall under the theory's characterization, but we aren't internally aware of. If there are states of either of these kinds, then this counts against the theory, while the absence of any such states counts in favour of the theory.

I will illustrate this briefly by considering intentionalist theories such as Tye's or Dretske's, which equate being conscious with being a representational state of a certain kind. Emotions are a prima-facie problem for such theories. For we are *internally aware* of our emotions, but they are not obviously representational. (What does anger represent, or elation?) The standard counter is to argue that emotions are representational after all, despite first appearances. (Perhaps anger represents certain actions as unjust, and elation represents things in general as very good.)

Intentionalist theories also face problems on the other side. For example, sub-personal representation (in early visual processing, say) is a prima-facie problem, since we are *not* internally aware of such sub-personal states, even though they are representational. And to this the standard counter is to refine the theory, so as to be more specific about the *kind* of representation that is being equated with consciousness (perhaps it should enter into decisions in a certain way), and thereby to make sure that the theory does not attribute consciousness to any states we are not internally aware of.

The details do not matter here. My current concern is simply to draw your attention to the fact that theories of consciousness-as-such answer to the class of states we are internally aware of. Such theories need to get the class of human states they identify as conscious to line up with the class of states we are internally aware of.

Now, you might wonder why I am belabouring this point. Isn't this the obvious way to test theories of consciousness? But I don't think it is obvious at all. On the contrary, I want to show you that there is something very puzzling here. It is not at all clear why a theory of consciousness should answer to the class of states we are *internally aware* of.

11. Internal Awareness and Phenomenal Concepts

As a first step, let us stop to ask what exactly is meant by 'internal awareness' in this context. A natural answer is that we are internally aware of just that range of states for which we have phenomenal concepts. What shows that we aren't internally aware of sub-personal representations, for instance, or high blood pressure, to take another example, is that we cannot identify these states introspectively when we have them, nor can we recreate them in imagination.

Let me be clear here. My claim is not that a state's being *conscious* should be equated with our having phenomenal concepts of that state. Whether this is so is a further issue, which will come into focus in a moment. My current claim is only about the notion of 'internal awareness' that I have been assuming when I have pointed out that theories of consciousness answer to what we are 'internally aware' of. I take it to be uncontentious that *this* notion at least can be equated with the availability of phenomenal concepts. To see this, suppose that there was some perceptual state, sensitivity to ultrasonic sound, say, that shared many of the features of paradigm conscious states (including guiding action and filling other higher cognitive functions), but for which we had no phenomenal concept whatsoever. That is, we were *never* able introspectively to identify it when it occurred, and we could *never* think about it by recreating it in imagination afterwards. It seems clear that a theory of consciousness that included such ultrasonic sensitivity among the class of conscious states would on this count be deemed to be deficient.

The puzzling feature of the standard methodology should now be apparent. Our methodological practice seems to rest on the assumption that the class of conscious human states coincides with the class of states for which we have phenomenal concepts. But, once we put this assumption on the table, it seems open to an obvious objection.

Let me pose this objection in terms that will be familiar, but that I have not used so far. A distinction is often made between *sentience* and *self-consciousness*. The standard assumption is that some animals, mice perhaps, and cats, are sentient without being self-conscious. They have states that are like something, they have feelings, but they don't think *about* those states. In particular, they don't introspectively identify those states as mental states of a certain sort, nor do they think about them by recreating them in imagination. These further abilities require self-consciousness, which is only present in humans and perhaps some higher primates. Self-consciousness requires concepts of conscious states, with which to think *about* conscious states, as well as just *having* conscious states.[9]

Now, if theories of consciousness are aiming to account for 'what-it's-likeness', as I have been assuming, then we need to understand them as aiming at the basic property of *sentience*, rather than the more sophisticated metarepresentational property of of self-consciousness. But if this is right, then the standard methodology for testing theories of consciousness stands in need

---

[9] Let this be a stipulation of what I mean by 'self-conscious'. There is also a weaker notion, that would be satisfied by creatures (some apes perhaps, or indeed people with 'theory of mind' deficiencies) who can think of themselves as one creature among others, but do not have any thoughts about mental states.

of further justification. For the availability of phenomenal concepts for certain states, while equivalent to the *self*-consciousness of those states, seems unnecessary for the *sentience* of those states. So now my worry is clear. If sentience is less than self-consciousness, as it seems to be, why should theories aiming at sentience be tested by seeing whether they correctly identify some category of states we are self-conscious of?

12. Sentience is Self-Consciousness

I can think of two possible answers to this question. The first assumes that consciousness requires higher-order thought, the second that internal awareness is a kind of observation. I shall consider these in turn.

The first answer in effect denies the distinction between self-consciousness and mere sentience, by arguing that it is a confusion to suppose that a state can be like something when it is not in some sense available to self-consciousness.

Note that, if this view is to help in the present context of argument, it needs to be upheld as an a priori thesis about our initial concept of consciousness, not as something we discover empirically. We are currently trying to understand the puzzling logic by which theories of consciousness are standardly tested against the empirical facts. So it would fail to address this issue to postulate that the coincidence of sentient consciousness with self-consciousness *emerges* from this kind of empirical investigation. Rather, we need to suppose that, prior to any empirical investigation, conceptual analysis tells us that 'consciousness', in the sense of what-it's-likeness, just *means* some kind of internal awareness or self-consciousness.[10]

Putting to one side for the moment the plausibility of this a priori claim, note that the kind of HOT (higher-order thought) theory needed in the present context of argument has at least one virtue. Let us distinguish, following Peter Carruthers (2000), between *dispositional* and *actualist* HOT theories of consciousness. Actualist HOT theories say that mental states are conscious only when they are actually the object of introspection. There are different versions of such actualist theories, depending on whether they conceive of introspection as more akin to thought, or as more akin to perception, but they share the feature that no particular mental occurrence

---

[10] The role of empirical investigation could then be to tell us which states are conscious (that is, objects of higher-order thought) in which creatures. This would indeed make good sense of much psychological research. Information about about 35–75 Hertz oscillations in the human sensory cortex, say, seems of no great relevance to our understanding of consciousness in any possible creature. But it could help identify those states that are objects of higher-order thought in human beings.

is conscious unless it is actually being introspectively judged to be of a certain kind at that moment. Dispositional HOT theories are not so restrictive about what it takes to be conscious. They allow that a given mental occurrence is conscious if it *can* be the object of introspection, even if it is not currently being so introspected. So the dull pain in your left foot, or your visual perception of the car in front, are both conscious, on a dispositional HOT theory, although you are not currently introspecting them, on the grounds that you are *capable* of such introspection, even if you are not doing it now.

It is clearly the less aggressive dispositional version of a HOT theory that we need to make sense of the methodology by which we test empirical theories of consciousness. When we check to see whether an empirical theory of consciousness correctly identifies the states that we are 'internally aware' of, we don't require it to pick out precisely those particular mental occurrences we are at some time *actually* internally aware of. Rather we want the theory to identify those *types* of mental states that we *can* be internally aware of, in the sense of having phenomenal concepts for states of that type. Thus, it would not be a problem for an empirical theory of consciousness that some of the particular occurrences it identifies as conscious do not happen to be introspectively identified or recreated in imaginative recall. All that is required is that those occurrences are of a kind that *can* so be objects of internal awareness.

Still, even if the kind of HOT theory currently needed is only a dispositional one, it still faces the obvious objection that its a priori standards for consciousness are unacceptably high.

To start with, note that standard HOT theories make consciousness a *relational* property of conscious states. For any standard HOT theory, determinate conscious states, such as being in pain, are conscious in virtue of the fact that their subjects are thinking about them, or at least *could* think about them. However, this then implies that just the same determinate states could occur (some organism could be in pain, say) but without any consciousness. Just keep everything else the same, but remove the higher-order thought. For example, consider a being such as a cat, which I assume cannot think about its mental states. Now suppose that this cat instantiates the property that I think about when I am internally aware of a pain. A HOT theory will imply that the cat is indeed in pain, but that this pain is not conscious.

Of course, a variant style of HOT theory could avoid a commitment to unconscious pains (and emotions, sensory experiences, and so on), by being more restrictive about what is required for pains and other experiences. For example, they could say that the property of being in pain *includes* the feature that some first-order property is being thought about. The cat would then not be in pain (it only has a proto-pain, we might say), precisely because its state is not conscious, in that it does not incorporate any higher-order thought about anything.

This seems to me a more natural way to develop HOT theories. Rather than admit non-conscious pains and other experiences, it seems neater to continue to keep all experiences as determinate modes of *consciousness*, simply by including consciousness as a necessary condition of their presence. However, the underlying difficulty remains. Perhaps HOT theories can avoid unconscious pains and other experiences simply by including higher-order thinking as part of what any such experiential state requires. But what they cannot avoid is the denial of consciousness to beings incapable of thinking higher-order thoughts. Whichever way we cut the cake, cats won't be conscious. Either they won't have pains at all, or they will have non-conscious pains. And the same goes for all other beings who are incapable of thought about mental states, including 1-year-old human infants.

I take this to rule out HOT-style theories, at least as an a priori analysis of our concept of consciousness. Perhaps some form of HOT theory could emerge as the *outcome* of empirical investigation into consciousness, and indeed I shall return to this possibility later. But remember that in the present context of argument we are still trying to make sense of the logic of such empirical investigations, and so are trying to figure out what prior idea of consciousness sets the empirical agenda. And in this context it is surely unacceptable to claim that consciousness requires higher-order thought. Whatever content our prior concept of consciousness may have, it surely isn't such as to make it *inconceivable* that 1-year-old children should have conscious experience. It makes little sense to suppose that pure conceptual reflection could show us that it isn't like anything to be a baby that has hurt itself.

13. Inner Observation

I now turn to my second possible explanation for the standard methodology for testing theories of consciousness. On this explanation, the role of inner awareness is to *observe* a sample of conscious states, and so provide a database against which we can test empirical theories of consciousness. After all, if we consider other reductive theories in science, such as the reduction of water to H_2O, or of temperature to molecular motion, they all rely on some pre-theoretical way of identifying instances of the target property, so as to provide a sample of cases against which to test the claim that all such instances possess the reducing property. So perhaps this is the role of internal awareness in testing theories of consciousness. Our internal awareness enables us to pick out, by directly observing their sentience, a sample of the sentient states that exist in the universe. And this then sets the stage for scientific investigation to identify some underlying property that constitutes the essence of these sentient states. (Having dismissed a priori HOT theories, I shall use 'sentience' as a variant for 'conscious' from now on.)

An initial set of queries about this observational model relates to the accuracy with which inner observation detects sentience. Other forms of observation are fallible in various ways. So it is natural to enquire whether inner observation of sentience is similarly fallible. More specifically, do we need to allow that this supposed faculty for observing sentience

(a) can make *errors*, in the sense of identifying some states as sentient when they are not, and

(b) be responsible for *ignorance*, in the sense of failing to register as sentient all human mental states that are sentient?

Now, questions of roughly this kind have been widely discussed in the philosophy of mind, under the heading of 'self-knowledge'. It is uncontentious that humans have some distinctive way of knowing about their own conscious mental states, and many philosophers have sought to explain how this works, and in particular to understand whether or not this faculty of self-knowledge is immune to mistakes.

Our current questions, however, are slightly different from the ones normally discussed under the heading of 'self-knowledge', in that we are interested in internal judgements about which *types* of mental state are conscious, rather than internal judgements to the effect that a *particular* conscious state of some type is occurring ('I am now in pain', 'I am now tasting chocolate'). That is, we are interested in whether internal awareness can go wrong in telling us positively that the property of being in pain, say, or seeing red, *is* conscious, and also in telling us negatively that the property of perceiving ultrasonically, say, or having high blood pressure, is *not* conscious. It wouldn't matter, from this perspective, if internal awareness went wrong now and then on particular mental states, classifying a particular sensation of cold as a pain, say, or failing to notice some particular conscious experiences at all. As long as it is right about which *types* of mental states are and are not conscious, it will provide accurate data against which to test reductive theories of consciousness.

Is internal awareness necessarily a good guide in this sense to which mental *types* are and are not conscious? Well, it seems hard to make sense of the idea that it could be prone to general *errors* of this kind, that is, that it could register instances of a certain mental type as conscious, while in fact they are not.[11] Perhaps the idea of inner awareness succumbing to *ignorance* is less

---

[11] Someone could, of course, make the *theoretical* mistake of holding that believings, say, are conscious, when they are not. But this may be just because they haven't introspected carefully enough. What does not seem possible is that inner awareness could itself mislead us on such a matter, by taking episodes of a certain type to be conscious when they are not.

problematic: maybe there should be room for certain kinds of perception, say, to count as sentient, even though we cannot introspectively identify or im- aginatively recreate them.

However, I shall not pursue these issues any further here. This is because a high degree of accuracy is not *essential* to the observational model of the role of inner awareness in testing theories of consciousness. Suppose it were allowed that inner observation could indeed succumb to ignorance, and fail to identify certain sentient human states as conscious. Or suppose even (harder though this is to make sense of) that inner observation could fall into error by presenting certain states as conscious when they aren't. Then the methodology for testing reductive theories of consciousness could simply be adjusted accordingly. If inner observation of sentience can be inaccurate, then to that extent a theory of consciousness is excused from lining up with its deliverances. (This would be in line with the standard scientific methodology for testing reductive scientific theories. While we need some pre-theoretical ability to identify water, or temperature, or whatever, to get the enterprise of reducing these kinds off the ground, these pre-theoretic identifications are not regarded as inviolable. It is perfectly acceptable to allow a reductive theory to *correct* some of our pre-theoretical judgements about what is and isn't water, if it is an otherwise attractive theory that fits the general run of cases.)

14. Is Consciousness a Kind?

My central worry about the observational model derives from different considerations. I doubt whether there is a kind, *conscious*, for inner awareness to detect. On the observational model, the role of inner awareness is to pick out those states that display the special property of consciousness. But I do not accept that there is any such special property.

I shall proceed by a kind of pincer movement. In this section I shall argue that there is no reason to suppose that any real kind is picked out by the description 'the essence common to those states we are internally aware of'. In the next section I shall then address the thought that, if inner awareness is a kind of observation, there *must be* such a kind, namely the kind observed by inner awareness. In response to this latter thought, I shall offer a non- observational account of the workings of inner awareness, which does not suppose that inner awareness detects some independently existing kind. That is, I shall show that inner awareness would work just as it does, even if there were no division in nature between the states that are like something and those that are not.

So my first target is the idea of '*the* real essence common to those states we are internally aware of'.

One intial problem here is whether we will find *any* interesting physical property (in the broad sense of 'physical') that is peculiar to the states of which humans are internally aware. The range of states we are internally aware of is quite heterogenous. As well as pains, itches, tickles, and the various modes of sense experience, there are emotions, cogitations, and moods. There seems no obvious reason, on the face of it, why there should be any physical property common to this whole genus. Each species within the genus may share some common physical characteristic, but there may be no further physical property binding them all together that they do not share with all manner of bodily states.

However, let me put this worry to one side, and suppose that there are indeed one or more interesting physical properties peculiar to those states that humans are internally aware of. The next worry is then whether any of these will be either necessary or sufficient for consciousness in *other* kinds of beings. In humans, perhaps we are aware of all and only those states which involve 35–75 Hertz oscillations in the sensory cortex. But should we conclude on this basis that consciousness in any being will coincide with 35–75 Hertz oscillations in sensory cortices? The same problem will arise if we switch from physiological properties to functional ones. Maybe humans are aware of all and only those states that have a certain kind of representational role. But why infer on this basis that consciousness will everywhere coincide with this representational role?

At first sight it might seem that this is simply a standard inductive difficulty, which will arise whenever we try to identify the essence of some kind on the basis of some limited sample. However, this is not the real problem. It is true that the restriction to the human case does radically limit our sampling, and that this accentuates the standard inductive difficulty. But the problem goes deeper than that. The real obstacle is that we have no hold on what *sort* of property sentience is supposed to be, no clues about what *sort* of extrapolation from our sample is called for.

Here there is a contrast with kinds like water or temperature. In these cases, we don't just have some bare means of recognizing instances. We also have some a priori idea of what the kinds *do*. Water is wet, colourless, odourless, and so on. Temperature increases with inputs of heat, finds an equilibrium in closed systems, yields boiling and freezing at extreme values, and so on. Such prior ideas play a crucial role in guiding identifications of the scientific essence of such kinds. We don't just look for any physical property common to our limited finite samples of water or temperature. We look specifically for some physical property that will be characteristic of anything that is wet, colourless, and so on, or some physical quantity that will characterize any object's absorption of heat, will tend to equilibriate, will identify boiling and freezing points, and so on.

With consciousness it is different. As I pointed out earlier, when contrasting our notion of consciousness-as-such with our concepts of determinate conscious states, we have no real a priori idea of what consciousness-as-such *does*. Beyond the minimal assumption that consciousness registers in internal awareness, we don't have a clue about what psychological role consciousness is supposed to play. The claim that a state is 'conscious' tells us nothing about its psychological operations. So nothing guides the extrapolation of sample properties towards a unique target, some essence common to all conscious states. Without some prior notion of a role played by consciousness, nothing decides what sort of property should be sought.

Of course, there are plenty of functionalist 'theories of consciousness', from representationalism to global workspace theories. However, given our lack of a priori ideas about the functional role played by consciousness, such theories can only be the *outcomes* of empirical investigation, arrived at by examining our introspected sample of conscious states, and identifying what they have physically in common. Yet it is precisely this kind of empirical investigation that is stymied, I am now arguing, by our lack of a priori ideas about the functional role of consciousness. Without some *prior* notion of what conscious states are generally supposed to do, the essence of consciousness cannot be fixed as one or other functional property that happens be common to the sample of states we are internally aware of.

The observational model of internal awareness offers the possibility of identifying the reference of 'conscious' as that essence that scientific investigation will reveal to be characteristic of the range of states we are internally aware of. But it turns out that scientific investigation does not have the wherewithal to complete this job. Without some prior specification of the psychological role consciousness is supposed play, the enterprise of identifying its scientific essence cannot get off the ground. And so the idea that 'conscious' refers to that essence turns out to be empty.

Perhaps this is too quick. Isn't there a case for bringing back HOT-style theories at this point? Even if such theories cannot be vindicated a priori, they certainly identify a salient broadly physical characteristic peculiar to the states we are internally aware of. After all, the one such feature that is uncontroversially peculiar to those states is that we can reidentify them introspectively and recreate them in imagination. So why not accept this as the underlying attribute that empirical investigation reveals to be essential to consciousness?

This suggestion has attractions, but it seems to me open to an objection based on the point made earlier against a priori HOT-style theories. There I urged that it is surely a conceptual possibility at least that beings without higher-order thought, such as human babies, may nevertheless have conscious states. So, if scientific investigation is going to show that this conceptual possibility is not actual, this will presumably be on the basis of positive

empirical evidence that non-reflective beings are not in fact conscious. However, the proposed route to an a posteriori HOT theory does not really invoke
any such positive evidence. It is entirely predetermined by the methodology
that the most obvious characteristic common to our sample of 'observed'
states will be that we are internally aware of them. Whatever scientific investigation may or may not discover about these states, we know beforehand that
they will all be states that we can introspectively reidentify and imaginatively
recreate, for this is simply what we are assuming is needed to 'observe' the
consciousness of those states. Given this, it would surely be wrong to regard
this fact alone as ruling out what we have already agreed to be a live conceptual possibility, namely, the possibility that something less than internal
awareness may be required for consciousness itself, as opposed to the observation of consciousness.

15. A Different Model of Internal Awareness

Some of you may feel that the conclusion being urged in the last section
comes close to a *reductio* of my overall stance. Surely I have followed the
argument too far, if I am in danger of concluding that those states that are *like*
something do not constitute a kind. Isn't it obvious that there must be such a
kind? Something must have gone wrong with my argument, you may feel, if it
forces us to deny this. Indeed perhaps my conclusion reflects back on my
initial physicalism. If the cost of physicalism is to deny the reality of consciousness, then surely we ought to take another look at dualism.

But let me ask you to bear with me for a moment. Perhaps our conviction
that there must be a kind here derives from too ready an acceptance of the
observational model, and on its accompanying idea that consciousness is *the*
kind that is there observed. For note that, once we start thinking of inner
awareness on the model of observation, then this accompanying idea becomes
irresistible. As soon as we embrace the observational model, we are forced to
think of inner awareness as a kind of scanner, searching through the nooks
and crannies of our minds, looking for those states with that special extra
spark, the feature of consciousness. The observational model thus automatically carries with it the idea of some kind to which the observational faculty
responds.[12]

However, there is another way of thinking about inner awareness, that
accounts happily for all the facts to the hand, but that doesn't trade on the

---

[12] Note also how any residual dualist inclinations will strongly encourage this observational
package. On the dualist picture, conscious states are peculiar in involving phenomenal aspects
of reality, and it is then very natural to think of inner awareness as sensitive precisely to this
property of phenomenality.

idea of inner observation, and so a fortiori doesn't commit us to the existence of a property that triggers such observations.

Suppose that there isn't anything special about the states that we are internally aware of (the states that we know to be 'like something'), *apart* from the fact that they are hooked up to higher-order thinking as they are, via introspection and imagination. That is, the only thing that is special about them is that we have phenomenal concepts for them. We can introspectively reidentify and imaginatively recreate them. On this suggestion, then, we are internally aware of certain states simply because they enter into our thinking in a special way. They don't enter into our thinking in this special way because they have some further special nature.

Let me draw out a natural, if somewhat striking, corollary. *Any* state that was similarly hooked up to our thinking would thereby be one that we knew what it was like to have. We are internally aware of certain states because they are used in our thinking, in a way that other states aren't. We think *with* them, when we deploy phenomenal concepts of them. This is what makes us pick them out as states that are 'like something'. But we don't need to suppose that there is anything else special about such states. Any state that was similarly used in our thinking would strike us as a state that is like something. Once a state is so used, its *being* gets into our thinking, so to speak, and its nature ('what it is like') thus becomes part of our mental life, in a way that is not true for other states of the world.

Here is an analogy. To think of inner awareness as observation of a special kind is like thinking of television as a medium that identifies a special kind of 'televisualizable' event. Imagine an innocent who thought that some worldly events display a special glow, a kind of luminance, and that television cameras were instruments somehow designed to detect this glow and transmit events with it to our screens. This would be a mistake. Even if some events are more suitable for televising than others, for aesthetic or commercial reasons, this plays no part in the mechanics of television transmissions. Any event can appear on your set, once it is appropriately linked to it via television cameras and transmission stations. Similarly, I say, with consciousness. Any event is capable of registering in internal awareness, once it is linked to it via introspection and imagination.

16. Conclusions

I have now argued against both possible explanations of the standard methodology for testing empirical theories of consciousness. The a priori equation of sentience with self-consciousness is unacceptable. And the idea of inner awareness as observation fails to pick out a kind, and is in any case unnecessary to account for the workings of inner awareness. I draw the moral that consciousness-as-such is an irredeemably vague concept. At first pass it is natural to suppose that it picks out some natural kind. But in fact it fails to draw any serious line between those things that are conscious and those that are not.

To see why this pessimistic conclusion should follow from the methodological analysis of the past few sections, let me summarize the problems facing attempts to construct scientific 'theories of consciousness'. There is indeed an unproblematic distinction associated with the methodology of such theories, namely, the distinction between self-consciousness and its absence. But theories of consciousness want to get beyond this distinction to some further boundary in reality, and unfortunately there is nothing there for them to find.

Consider first the unproblematic distinction between states that can be thought about phenomenally, and those that cannot. As I showed in earlier sections, a satisfactory physicalist account of this distinction is straightforward. Phenomenal thought is simply a matter of imaginative recreation and introspective reidentification. There seems no barrier to an understanding of how brains can generate recreations and reidentifications. So there is no difficulty for a physicalist about the difference between states that are objects of phenomenal thought and others.

Dispositional higher-order thought theories of consciousness want to equate the distinction between conscious and non-conscious states with the unproblematic difference between states that are objects of phenomenal thought and others. However, this is not faithful to our initial pre-theoretical concept of consciousness. There may not be very much to this pre-theoretical concept, as I have argued throughout, but it does at least resist the a priori identification of consciousness with higher-order thought. If there is one thing we can be confident about in this area, it is surely that it is conceptually possible for infants and animals to be conscious though not self-conscious.

Unfortunately, the pre-theoretical concept of consciousness then casts us adrift. Having pushed us away from the identification of consciousness with self-consciousness, it fails to offer any other hold on where the line between consciousness and non-consciousness might fall. The concept of consciousness-as-such thus turns out to be irredeemably vague. We have some clear examples, namely, the states that we humans are phenomenally aware of. But any attempt to delineate a kind on this basis fizzles out into nothing.

Can we rest here? Not happily. The notion of consciousness may be too thin to pick out any real kind, and so fail to point to anything beyond the category of phenomenal self-consciousness. But there remain serious further issues that are standardly taken to be bound up with questions of consciousness, and these issues seem to demand answers.

I am thinking here primarily of moral questions about the treatment of non-human creatures. What moral principles should govern our conduct towards cows, or fish, or lobsters, or indeed possible intelligent machines or extra-terrestrial organisms? It seems natural to suppose that answers here will hinge on whether such creatures are conscious. It would be all right to drop live lobsters into boiling water, for example, if they feel no conscious pain, but not if they do.

Perhaps some progress here can be made by switching back from the determinable, consciousness-as-such, to more specific determinates such as pain. That is, we might be able to establish that cows and lobsters, say, should be objects of moral concern, even in the absence of a general theory of consciousness-as-such, simply by establishing that they have pains.[13]

One issue that arises here is whether even our concepts of such determinate states as pain are contentful enough to pick out a real kind, and so determine which creatures are in pain. This is really the topic for another occasion. Let me simply make two comments. First, and in line with my discussion in earlier sections, I take it that our pre-theoretical concepts of determinate mental states are at least *more* contentful than our concept of consciousness-as-such. Second, I suspect than even these concepts will be infected by *some* degree of vagueness, with the result that it is to some extent indeterminate which real kinds they refer to. Given these two points, my guess is that cows can be shown definitely to experience pain, but that it may be indeterminate whether lobsters do, and even more indeterminate with exotic creatures from other parts of the universe and the technological future.

In any case, the strategy of trying to resolve the moral issues by switching from the determinable, consciousness-as-such, to determinates such as pain, can have only limited application. For it will yield a way of deciding issues of consciousness only in connection with those determinate conscious states for which we already happen to possess concepts with a phenomenal element. Yet it seems clear that there can be determinates of the determinable, consciousness-as-such, on which we humans have no phenomenal grasp. The experience of bats when they echolocate, for example, is arguably a determinate conscious property which we humans are unable to conceptualize phenomenally. And there would seem no limit in principle to similarly humanly unconceptualized modes of consciousness that could be present in intelligent machines or extra-terrestrial creatures.

Of course, we could always construct functional or other third-person concepts of such determinate alien states. But if these concepts include no phenomenal element, as would be the case if they referred to states radically

---

[13] We can take it at this stage that pains carry consciousness with them. The idea of non-conscious pains was an artefact of HOT theories' a priori equation of consciousness with self-consciousness, and we have rejected such theories precisely because this equation is mistaken.

removed from our own phenomenal experience, then there would be nothing in them to tell us that they referred to *conscious* states. Given that we would not be thinking about these states in phenomenal terms, and given that we lack any general theory of consciousness-as-such, we would have no reason to place these states on the side of things that are like something, rather than on the side of those that are not.

I am not at all sure how to make further progress at this stage. I do not want to rule out the possibility that further scientific knowledge will help us decide such tricky questions as whether it is morally permissible to immerse live lobsters in boiling water, and more generally to decide about appropriate moral dealings with psychologically distant creatures. By finding out more about the brains and cognitive mechanisms of lobsters and other alien creatures, we may be able to get further information that bears on the question of their proper treatment. However, I do not think that any such further information will direct us to moral conclusions *via* telling us whether the exotic creatures are conscious. Rather, my thought is that the scientific information may help resolve the moral treatment of unfamiliar creatures, independently of deciding whether they are conscious. For, if the arguments of this chapter are any good, the concept of consciousness is too vague to fix an answer to such questions as whether lobsters and other strange creatures are conscious, however much scientific knowledge becomes available.

REFERENCES

ARMSTRONG, D. (1968), *A Materialist Theory of the Mind* (London: Routledge & Kegan Paul).

BAARS, B. (1988), *A Cognitive Theory of Consciousness* (Cambridge: Cambridge University Press).

CARRUTHERS, P. (2000), *Phenomenal Consciousness* (Cambridge: Cambridge University Press).

CHALMERS, D. (1996), *The Conscious Mind* (Oxford: Oxford University Press).

CHURCHLAND, P., and CHURCHLAND, P. (1998), *On the Contrary* (Cambridge, Mass.: MIT Press).

CRICK, F. (1994), *The Astonishing Hypothesis* (London: Simon & Schuster).

DENNETT, D. (1991), *Consciousness Explained* (London: Allen Lane).

DRETSKE, F. (1995), *Naturalizing the Mind* (Cambridge, Mass.: MIT Press).

JACKSON, F. (1986), 'What Mary Didn't Know', *Journal of Philosophy*, 83.

LYCAN, W. (1996), *Consciousness and Experience* (Cambridge, Mass.: MIT Press).

McGINN, C. (1991), *The Problem of Consciousness* (Oxford: Basil Blackwell).

PAPINEAU, D. (1998), 'Mind the Gap', in J. Tomberlin (ed.), *Philosophical Perspectives*, 12.

—— (2000), 'The Rise of Physicalism', in B. Loewer (ed.), *Physicalism and its Discontents* (Cambridge: Cambridge University Press), and in M. Stone and J. Woolf (eds.), *The Proper Ambition of Science* (London: Routledge).

PENROSE, R. (1994), *Shadows of the Mind* (Oxford: Oxford University Press).

ROSENTHAL, D. (1996), 'A Theory of Consciousness', in N. Block, O. Flanagan, and G. Güzeldere (eds.), *The Nature of Consciousness* (Cambridge, Mass.: MIT Press).

SHALLICE, T. (1988), *From Neuropsychology to Mental Structure* (Cambridge: Cambridge University Press).

TYE, M. (1995), *Ten Problems of Consciousness* (Cambridge, Mass.: MIT Press).

13. Perspectival Representation and the Knowledge Argument

WILLIAM G. LYCAN

> ... this man wanted to be outside everything; to see everything hung in a
> vacuum, simply its own dead self.
>
> G. K. Chesterton, 'The Shadow of the Shark'

Someday there will be no more articles written about the 'Knowledge Argument' (Nagel 1974; Jackson 1982). That is beyond dispute. What is less
certain is, how much sooner that day will come than the heat death of the
universe.

I thought I had said my own last words on the topic (Lycan 1987: ch. 7, 1990*b*,
1996: ch. 3), but it seems not. There is at least a bit of unfinished business.

1. The Irrepressible Mary

Let us quickly review Jackson's version of the argument. He offers the now
painfully familiar example of Mary, the brilliant colour scientist trapped in an
entirely black-and-white laboratory. (Even she herself is painted black and
white. There are potential complications that would have been avoided had
Jackson made Mary temporarily colour-blind instead of merely confined to
her lab space, but I shall ignore those.) Working through her modem and
various black-and-white monitors, she becomes scientifically omniscient as
regards the physics and chemistry of colour, the neurophysiology of colour
vision, and every other conceivably relevant scientific fact; we may even
suppose that she becomes scientifically omniscient, period. Yet when she is
finally released from her captivity and ventures into the outside world, she
sees colours themselves for the first time; and she thereby learns something,
namely, she learns what it is like to see red and many of the other colours.
That is, she learns what it is like to experience subjective or *phenomenal*
redness, never mind the actual colours of the physical objects she encounters
(which, scientifically, she already knew).

And so she has acquired information that is—by hypothesis—outside the whole domain of science. It is intrinsically subjective phenomenal information, and what she has learned seems to be an intrinsically perspectival *fact*, that eludes the whole of science. According to materialist theories of mind, no fact about the mind is anything but a neurophysiological or otherwise scientific or 'objective' fact; so it would follow that materialism is false.

Actually there is a crucial distinction to be respected here. In Jackson's official formulation, the word 'fact' is not used; his conclusion is just that 'one can have all the physical information without having all the information there is to have' (Lycan 1990*a*: 472). This, he says, refutes the doctrine he calls 'Physicalism' (ibid. 469): 'All (correct) information is physical information.' But depending on how one construes the slippery term 'information', 'Physicalism' in this sense need not be taken to be an ontological claim at all (Horgan 1984). It is most naturally understood as being about *truths*, rather than about what kinds of things there are; Flanagan (1992: 98) calls it 'linguistic physicalism'. And taken in that way, it is not entailed by materialism about the mind. (Materialism says only that human beings are made entirely of physical matter and that their properties, and facts about them, consist in arrangements of that matter. It hardly follows that every sentence or proposition about a human being *means* something about physical matter.) However—witness his title—Jackson goes on to draw an explicitly ontological conclusion. I shall return to this distinction.

Here is a more formal statement of the Knowledge Argument, construed ontologically, as an objection to materialism.

(1) Before her release, Mary knows all the scientific and other 'objective' facts there are to know about colour and colour vision and colour experience, and every other relevant fact. [Stipulation.]

(2) Upon being released, Mary learns something, namely, she learns what it's like (w.i.l.) to experience visual redness. [Seems obvious.]

∴ (3) There is a fact, the fact of w.i.l. to experience visual redness, that Mary knows after her release but did not know prior to it. [1, 2]

(4) For any facts: if $F_1 = F_2$, then anyone who knows F_1 knows F_2. [Suppressed; assumes simple factive grammar of 'know'.]

∴ (5) There is a fact, that of w.i.l., that is distinct from every relevant scientific/'objective' fact. [1, 3, 4]

(6) If materialism is true, then every fact about colour experience is identical with some physiological, functional, or otherwise scientific/'objective' fact.

∴ (7) Materialism is not true. [5, 6]

Premiss (4) is supplied because without it there seems no way to get (5) from (1) and (3).

2. Perspectivalism

There are three main materialist responses to the Knowledge Argument. One is brutally to deny (2) (Churchland 1985; Dennett 1991; Akins 1993), and to insist that if Mary really did know *all* the scientific/'objective' facts, she would after all know w.i.1. to see red. A second is to grant (2) but baulk at (3), holding that Mary's acquisition is not a fact, but a mere ability, a knowing-*how* (Nemirow 1990; Lewis 1990) or a mere acquaintance (Conee 1994). The third is a generic response that is by now standard; I shall call it the 'perspectivalist' response. In one form or another, it has been suggested and/or defended by McGinn (1983); Horgan (1984); McMullen (1985); Churchland (1985); Van Gulick (1985); Tye (1986); Lycan (1987, 1990*b*, 1996); Loar (1990); Rey (1991); Levine (1998); and no doubt others. It is this third position that I shall continue to develop here.[1]

The perspectivalist begins by rejecting premiss (4), the suppressed principle according to which (to put it another way) if someone knows that P but does not know that Q, then the fact that P and the fact that Q are different facts.

That principle may at first seem obvious. It seems to be licensed by Leibniz's Law: If fact F_1 is known to Smith, and $F_1 = F_2$, then surely F_2 is known to Smith. But there are clear counter-examples to it: the fact of water splashing just is the moving of lots of H_2O molecules, but someone can know that water is splashing without knowing anything about H_2O; the fact of my being overpaid just is the fact of W.G.L.'s being overpaid, but someone (who does not know that I am W.G.L.) can know that W.G.L. is overpaid while having no idea whether I am overpaid.

What has gone wrong? As always and notoriously, Leibniz's Law fails for *representation-dependent* properties. That Oedipus wanted to marry Jocasta but did not want to marry his mother does not show that Jocasta was not his mother; the poor woman was his marriage-object under one description or mode of presentation but not under the other.[2] And *being known to Smith* is a representation-dependent property: Whether Smith knows a given fact depends on how Smith represents that fact. She may know it under one representation but not know it under a different one. That is just what is going on in the 'water' and 'overpaid' examples. One may see water splashing but lack the chemical perspective entirely; less commonly, a mad chemist might record a motion of H_2O molecules but be mentally so far removed from the perspective of everyday things and substances that she has no thought of water.

---

[1] For a battery of arguments against the Nemirow and Lewis 'ability' theory, see Lycan (1996: ch. 5).

[2] I here ignore two complications: that some theorists insist that a 'representation-dependent property' is no genuine property at all, and that Leibniz's Law does hold for properties incorporating representations when the representations are *de re*.

The 'overpaid' example is perspectival too, but a different kind of perspective is at work. Someone can know that W.G.L. is overpaid without knowing that I am overpaid, if that person has only a public, (non-auto)biographical perspective on me and is not in a position to refer to me more directly. Even if the person were to come into the room, point straight at me, and exclaim 'You are overpaid,' I might insist that the knowledge she thereby expresses is still not quite the same knowledge I have when I know that *I myself* am overpaid. (Especially if I believe that she is mistaken as to who I am.) As Hector Castañeda (1966) emphasized so many years ago,[3] if I myself am amnesic I may know many facts about W.G.L., including that he is overpaid, without knowing that I myself am overpaid; so it seems that what I know when I do know that I myself am overpaid is a different fact from any of those I could know while amnesic, and an intrinsically perspectival fact. In order to designate the person it is supposed to designate, a mental pronoun can be tokened only from a certain point of view; only I, W.G.L., can think 'I' and thereby designate W.G.L.

Clearly, *being known to Mary* is a representation-dependent property; whether Mary knows a given fact depends on how she represents that fact. Facts can be differently represented from differing perspectives, and that is why (4) is false. Without (4), seemingly, the Knowledge Argument collapses.

But that is not the end of the story.

3. Fine-grained 'Facts'

Now, sometimes philosophers do individuate 'facts' in a less chunky, more fine-grained sort of way. The late Roderick Chisholm (1976) used a version of principle (4) itself as a test for sameness of 'fact'.[4] In his sense, the water splashing is a different fact from the H_2O molecules moving, odd as it sounds to say that.

I do not think anyone could credibly insist that one of these two ways of counting 'facts'—the chunky or the Chisholmian—is *correct* to the exclusion of the other. I make the following terminological proposal. Let us continue to use the term 'fact' in the more usual chunky way with which we began, and let us call Chisholm-facts 'pieces of information'. The latter seems reasonable because Chisholm thinks of the things epistemically, as objects of conceptual knowledge rather than as chunks of the world. Thus, the fact of water splashing just is the moving of lots of H_2O molecules, but that water is

---

[3] Following Geach (1957); see also Perry (1979).
[4] Chisholm himself preferred to speak of *states of affairs*; for him, a fact is a state of affairs that (actually) obtains.

splashing and that H_2O molecules are moving are two different pieces of information. Likewise, according to the materialist, that such-and-such neural goings-on are taking place in a subject's brain and that it is like so-and-so for the subject to have an experience are the same fact but different pieces of information.

Once this distinction is introduced, the perspectivalist objection to the Knowledge Argument seems to have been blunted, for (by definition) (4) remains true at least of 'facts' in the fine-grained sense, i.e. of pieces of information. Have Nagel and Jackson not then proved that there is *information* that is not public, objective, scientific, etc. information?

I say they have: just plug in 'piece of information' for 'fact' in our official statement of Jackson's argument, and I believe, *pace* those who simply deny (2) and those who resist the inference from (2) to (3), that the resulting argument succeeds.

The existence of non-physical, subjective, intrinsically perspectival, etc. *information* may or may not be of metaphysical interest. But for purposes of philosophy of mind, here are two key ways in which it is not interesting: (1) The phenomenon is not specifically about the mind; it is everywhere. No amount of chemistry contains the information that *water* is splashing. No amount of economic etc. information contains the information that *I* am overpaid. And so forth. And/but (2) it does not follow in any of these cases that the object or stuff in question—water, or W.G.L.—has a non-physical or immaterial *property.* I believe Jackson tacitly makes this inference, from non-physical (piece of) information to non-physical property, and so commits a fallacy; otherwise, he has no argument for the existence of epiphenomenal qualia.

4. The Continuing Problem

The perspectivalist has rebutted the Knowledge Argument by showing that its fourth premiss is false of facts in the chunky sense. But, even once we have conceded and denigrated the point about non-physical pieces of information, that is not enough. For we have not yet *shown how* the case of Mary in particular can be seen as an instance of the foregoing kind of Leibniz's-Law failure—i.e. as a case of knowing a fact under one representation but not knowing it under a different one. Also, as Charles Hill has acutely pointed out to me,[5] we have so far left it open for Nagel or Jackson to repair the argument by *qualifying* (4).

---

[5] Hill's observation directly inspired this chapter; I thank him again for it.

These two reasons are closely related, both being grounded in the fact that Mary's predicament does not seem akin either to the 'water' example or to the 'overpaid' example.

To expand the second reason: though the 'water' example is indeed a counter-example to (4), it is irrelevant, because it is a case of scientific ignorance, and we have stipulated that Mary suffers from no relevant scientific ignorance at all. So instead of (4) in full generality, Jackson could substitute,

(4′) If $F_1 = F_2$, then anyone who knows F_1 *and is not suffering from scientific ignorance* knows F_2.

Premiss (2) already guarantees that Mary is not suffering from scientific ignorance, so this revised argument would defy the counter-example.

The 'overpaid' example seems irrelevant too, because Mary does not seem to differ from the rest of us in virtue of any inability to use pronouns. So we can restrict (4) still further:

(4″) If $F_1 = F_2$, then, *barring pronominal discrepancies*, anyone who knows F_1 and is not suffering from scientific ignorance knows F_2.

Neither the 'water' example nor the 'overpaid' example is a counter-example to (4″). So if we substitute (4″) for (4) and merely add the premiss (4+) 'Mary's deficit is not a pronominal discrepancy,' Jackson's argument goes through once more.

5. The Perspectivalist Approach to the Continuing Problem

To apply the standard two-perspectives explanation of Leibniz's-Law failure, we need a second perspective. That is, we already have Mary's scientific perspective on everything physical, neurophysiological, functional, etc. about seeing colours—all her various public, objective modes of representing the relevant facts. So what other perspective, what other mode of representation, could explain her failing to know w.i.l.?

My answer is: an introspective perspective.[6] As Nagel emphasizes, to know w.i.l., one must either have had the experience oneself, in the first person, from the inside, or been told w.i.l. by someone who has had it and is psychologically very similar to oneself. The descendants of Descartes of course champion that first-person perspective and believe it is the one we are stuck in whenever we philosophize about the mind. But what can a materialist say

---

[6] NB, rhymes with 'insective detective'.

about any first-person perspective? Materialists from Ryle onwards have seemed almost to deny the existence of such a thing.[7]

How might a materialist reverse that attitude, and implement an introspective perspective? Why, in good neural hardware. That is where theories of conscious awareness and introspection come in.

Occurrent mental or psychological states fall roughly into four categories: those whose subjects are consciously attending to them; those whose subjects are aware of being in them though not actively introspecting them; those whose subjects are not aware of being in them, but could have been had they taken notice; and those, such as language-processing states, that are entirely subterranean and inaccessible to introspection. A theory is needed to explain these differences.

D. M. Armstrong's (1968, 1981) Lockean 'inner sense' or 'higher-order perception' theory fills the bill admirably. (See also Lycan 1987: ch. 6, 1996: ch. 2, as well as the 'higher-order thought' theory defended by Rosenthal 1993.) According to such theories, a subject's awareness of her or his own mental state consists in a representing of that state itself. The 'inner sense' view has it that the representing is done quasi-perceptually, by a set of functionally specified internal attention mechanisms of some kind that scan or monitor 'first-order' mental/brain states. This theory explains the differences between our four categories of first-order state in the obvious way.

(If you are inclined to doubt whether awareness or introspection of a mental state really requires higher-order quasi-perception or at least representation, consider: awareness is intentional; it is always awareness of something. In particular, awareness of a mental state one is in has that mental state as its intentional object. If you doubt that such awareness consists in higher-order representation, i.e. in some representation of the first-order state in question, you are abandoning the thesis that intentionality is representation. In my view that is not an easy thesis to abandon. Descartes himself championed it.)

If there is something like an intra-mental sense modality, then it would come with an introspective mode of representation, and it would present its objects from a special, uniquely internal point of view. This introspective perspective would be unlike any public point of view available to Mary. The internal monitor would say such things as, 'You're having one of *those* again,' and '*This* is what it's like to have one of those' (except of course that it would not use English words, but would mobilize representations of its own proprietary kind).

On this view, the perspectival difference would after all be much like the pronominal discrepancies. 'You can know all the scientific stuff, but no amount of that will tell you what *this* is like' (said from the inside) sounds much like, 'You can know all the economic, biographical facts about W.G.L.,

---

[7] As is vociferously deplored by Searle (1992); see also Siewert (1998).

but no amount of that information will tell you anything about *me*' (said by an amnesic who is, in fact, W.G.L.), and like, 'You can know all about Caldwell Hall and all its rooms and offices and know that the meeting will be held in room 213, but no amount of that information will tell you that the meeting will be held *right here*.'

It is not just a matter of pronouns, of course, even if one of them is a mental pronoun. Introspection type-classifies mental states—that is, it classifies the various states it surveys into states of the same or different kinds—in its own distinctive way, under its own representations of them ('There's one of those *semanthas* again'). But those representations are not going to be synonymous with English words, because your internal monitors do not speak English or any other natural language. The introspective representations are not going to be deducible from neuroscience or from any other body of public information expressed in English. (Incidentally, that is why Levine (1983, 1993) is right to contend that there is an 'explanatory gap'. It is also why the gap exists in the first place.[8]) The introspective representations' contents are going to be non-physical pieces of information.

And that, says the perspectivalist, is why Mary can know all the scientific stuff about experiences of red and not know w.i.l. to experience red: It is because, never having had a first-order experience of red herself, she cannot represent that experience from the introspective perspective. She can represent other people's experiences of red, but only from the neuroscientific, the commonsensical, and other public perspectives. Once she is released and does experience red herself, she then does introspect and represent that experience in the distinctive first-person way—and that is when and how she comes to know w.i.l. to experience red, gaining a non-physical piece of information.

6. And (4″)?

If the difference between Mary Before and Mary After is not *just* pronouns, then it is not excluded under the 'pronominal discrepancy' clause. If 4″ is true, then, the argument would still go through. So the perspectivalist

---

[8] There are parallel explanatory gaps in the pronominal cases too. Notice that no extravagant metaphysical conclusions can be drawn from any of them, for much the same reason that non-physical pieces of information are metaphysically harmless: the gaps are due to there being intrinsically perspectival, non-physical pieces of information, which itself does not show that anything has a non-physical or immaterial property. (However, for an argument that there may be further metaphysical trouble, see Levine forthcoming.) I do not here deal with the far more elaborate antimaterialist argument based on the explanatory gap, due to Jackson (1993) and Chalmers (1996). See Lycan (1998), as well as Block and Stalnaker (1999) and Levine (forthcoming).

must argue that even 4″ is too strong. And she or he cannot do that by just insisting that 4″ is falsified by the case of Mary, because that would beg the question.

Let us talk of a 'quasi-perceptual' perspective. Sense organs and other detectors, monitors etc. are intrinsically perspectival and deliver only intrinsically perspectival representations, in that (a) they show the objects they detect only from particular points of view, (b) they key on different properties of the objects, (c) they give you different packets of information about the same objects, and (d) they offer their representational contents under different modes of presentation. Suppose you are in the forest at night and, very close by, a tree falls and crushes your Porsche.[9] The falling of a tree is, scientifically speaking, the complex motion of gazillions of cellulose etc. molecules (same fact). But that event can be thought of and described nonscientifically, under many different sensory modes of presentation: if you have good night vision, you see the tree, falling. What you hear is a great rending crash. You feel the impact of the shock wave in the air. (You can also think of the event as 'what destroyed my car'.) These are all different pieces of information, but each describes the same chunky event or fact, scientifically just the motion of molecules.

This refutes 4″, I believe. Without either scientific ignorance or pronominal discrepancy, someone could know that the tree had fallen without knowing that there had been an audible crash, etc., etc.

Armstrong's 'inner sense' is not exactly like an external sense such as sight, hearing, or touch. (The differences stem from the fact that its function is not to detect adaptively significant features of objects in the external environment.) But it is analogous; it is a *quasi*-perceptual faculty, a form of proprioception. And part of the analogy is that it gives a perceptual-type perspective on and mode of presentation of a brain fact, different ones from those of science itself, sight, hearing, touch, and so on. So if we were to restrict 4″ further, to exclude differences of sensory perspective, I would argue that quasi-sensory perspective should count as well.

Thus, were Jackson to replace (4″) by

(4‴) If $F_1 = F_2$, then, barring pronominal discrepancies *and differences of sensory or quasi-sensory perspective,* anyone who knows F_1 and is not suffering from scientific ignorance knows F_2.

he would have to add the premiss (4++) 'Mary's deficit is not the lack of some sensory or quasi-sensory perspective'; and this time his argument would

---

[9] Yes, I know that in real life you do not have a Porsche, or you would not be reading this article. Or, if you do actually own a Porsche, would you be willing to send me a cheque for $1,000?

not go through, because (4++) is not granted by the perspectivalist, and should not readily be granted by anyone.

7. A Curious Consequence

I said that before she was released, Mary could represent other people's experiences of red, but only from the various public perspectives and not introspectively. But perhaps that is only a contingent limitation. Assume that Mary has a perfectly good internal monitor or set of them, which she uses to introspect the first-order mental states she does have. Then we can imagine a futuristic surgical procedure in which we wire up the relevant internal monitors of Mary's into some other person's visual cortex. If that is possible in principle, then on the Inner Sense view, Mary would be able to introspect the other person's experiences of red, and find out in that way w.i.l. to see red. That seems quite plausible to me, but then I have been defending Armstrong's view for a long time. If it does not seem plausible to you, then you may find that you have an objection either to the Inner Sense view itself or to its incorporation into the perspectivalist theory of knowing w.i.l.

And of course, any objection to the Inner Sense view is an objection to the perspectivalist theory as formulated here. It is a further question whether the perspectivalist could swap Inner Sense for a different theory of conscious awareness, such as Rosenthal's, and still be able to make the perspectivalist move. I believe that would work, since I hold that all awareness is intentional and that all intentional states represent their intentional objects under distinctive modes of presentation; but I shall not try to make that case here.

REFERENCES

AKINS, K. (1993), 'What is it Like to be Boring and Myopic?' in B. Dahlbom (ed.), *Dennett and His Critics* (Oxford: Basil Blackwell).

ARMSTRONG, D. M. (1968), *A Materialist Theory of the Mind* (London: Routledge & Kegan Paul).

—— (1981), 'What is Consciousness?' in *The Nature of Mind* (Ithaca: Cornell University Press).

BLOCK, N., and STALNAKER, R. (1999), 'Conceptual Analysis, Dualism, and the Explanatory Gap', *Philosophical Review*, 108: 1–46.

CASTAÑEDA, H.-N. (1966), ' "He": A Study in the Logic of Self-Consciousness', *Ratio*, 8: 130–57.

CHALMERS, D. (1996), *The Conscious Mind* (Oxford: Oxford University Press).

CHISHOLM, R. (1976), *Person and Object* (London: George Allen & Unwin).

CHURCHLAND, P. M. (1985), 'Reduction, Qualia, and the Direct Introspection of Brain States', *Journal of Philosophy*, 82: 8–28.

CONEE, E. (1994), 'Phenomenal Knowledge', *Australasian Journal of Philosophy*, 72: 136–50.

DAVIES, M., and HUMPHREYS, G. (eds.) (1993), *Consciousness* (Oxford: Basil Blackwell).

DENNETT, D. C. (1991), *Consciousness Explained* (Boston: Little, Brown).

FLANAGAN, O. (1992), *Consciousness Reconsidered* (Cambridge, Mass.: MIT Press).

GEACH, P. (1957), 'On Belief about Oneself', *Analysis*, 18: 23–4.

HORGAN, T. (1984), 'Jackson on Physical Information and Qualia', *Philosophical Quarterly*, 34: 147–83.

JACKSON, F. (1982), 'Epiphenomenal Qualia', *Philosophical Quarterly*, 32: 127–36. Reprinted in Lycan (1990a).

—— (1993), 'Armchair Metaphysics', in M. Michael and J. O'Leary-Hawthorne (eds.), *Philosophy in Mind* (Dordrecht: Kluwer Academic Publishing).

LEVINE, J. (1983), 'Materialism and Qualia: The Explanatory Gap', *Pacific Philosophical Quarterly*, 64: 354–61.

—— (1993), 'On Leaving Out What It's Like', in Davies and Humphreys (1993).

—— (1998), 'Conceivability and the Metaphysics of Mind', *Noûs*, 32: 449–80.

—— (forthcoming), *Purple Haze: The Puzzle of Conscious Experience* (Oxford: Oxford University Press).

LEWIS, D. (1990), 'What Experience Teaches', in Lycan (1990a).

LOAR, B. (1990), 'Phenomenal States', in Tomberlin (1990).

LYCAN, W. G. (1987), *Consciousness* (Cambridge, Mass.: MIT Press).

—— (ed.) (1990a), *Mind and Cognition* (Oxford: Basil Blackwell).

—— (1990b), 'What is the "Subjectivity" of the Mental?' in Tomberlin (1990).

—— (1996), *Consciousness and Experience* (Cambridge, Mass.: MIT Press).

—— (1998), 'Against the New Apriorism in Metaphysics', Invited Lecture to the Twenty-Fourth Annual Meeting of the Society for Philosophy and Psychology, Minneapolis (June 1998).

McGINN, C. (1983), *The Subjective View* (Oxford: Oxford University Press).

McMULLEN, C. (1985), ' "Knowing What It's Like" and the Essential Indexical', *Philosophical Studies*, 48: 211–34.

NAGEL, T. (1974), 'What is it Like to Be a Bat?' *Philosophical Review*, 82: 435–56.

NEMIROW, L. (1990), 'Physicalism and the Cognitive Role of Acquaintance', in Lycan (1990a).

PERRY, J. (1979), 'The Problem of the Essential Indexical', *Noûs*, 13: 3–21.

REY, G. (1991), 'Sensations in a Language of Thought', in E. Villanueva (ed.), *Philosophical Issues, I: Consciousness* (Atascadero, Calif.: Ridgeview).

ROSENTHAL, D. (1993), 'Thinking that One Thinks', in Davies and Humphreys (1993).

SEARLE, J. (1992), *The Rediscovery of the Mind* (Cambridge, Mass.: MIT Press).

SIEWERT, C. (1998), *The Significance of Consciousness* (Princeton: Princeton University Press).

TOMBERLIN, J. E. (ed.) (1990), *Philosophical Perspectives, 4: Action Theory and Philosophy of Mind* (Atascadero, Calif.: Ridgeview).

TYE, M. (1986), 'The Subjective Qualities of Experience', *Mind*, 95: 1–17.

VAN GULICK, R. (1985), 'Physicalism and the Subjectivity of the Mental', *Philosophical Topics*, 13: 51–70.

14. McGinn on Consciousness and the Mind–Body Problem

ANTHONY BRUECKNER AND E. ALEX BEROUKHIM

> ...there is a great difference between mind and body, inasmuch as a body is by nature alway divisible, and the mind is entirely indivisible. For, as a matter of fact, when I consider the mind, that is to say myself inasmuch as I am only a thinking thing, I cannot distinguish in myself any parts, but apprehend myself to be clearly one and entire...But it is quite otherwise with corporeal and extended objects.
>
> René Descartes, *Meditations on First Philosophy*

> If we pretend that there is a machine whose structure makes it think, sense and have perceptions, then we can conceive it enlarged, but keeping to the same proportions, so that we might go inside it as into a mill. Suppose that we do: then if we inspect the interior we shall find there nothing but parts which push one another, and never anything which could explain a perception. Thus, perception must be sought in simple substance, not in what is composite or in machines.
>
> G. W. Leibniz, *Monadology*

Colin McGinn has attempted to provide a novel solution to the mind–body problem.[1] As McGinn points out, his attempted solution draws upon work by Noam Chomsky and Thomas Nagel.[2] In this chapter we will try to clarify how McGinn's solution is supposed to work, and then we will raise some problems.

---

[1] See his 'Can We Solve the Mind-Body Problem?', in *The Problem of Consciousness* (Cambridge: Blackwell, 1991). All page references in the text are to this article. See also his 'Consciousness and Content', 'Consciousness and the Natural Order', and 'The Hidden Structure of Consciousness', all in that volume of essays.

[2] See Chomsky's *Reflections on Language* (New York: Pantheon Books, 1975) and Nagel's 'What Is It Like To Be a Bat?' and 'Panpsychism' in his *Mortal Questions* (Cambridge: Cambridge University Press, 1979).

1. McGinn's Solution

For McGinn, *consciousness* is 'the hard nut of the mind-body problem'. This problem is: 'How is it possible for conscious states to depend upon brain states?' (p. 1). How does the brain *generate*, or *give rise to*, or (as McGinn sometimes misleadingly says) *cause* consciousness?[3] More flashily: 'How can technicolour phenomenology arise from soggy grey matter?... [How is] the water of the physical brain...turned into the wine of consciousness?' (ibid.).

A *constructive solution* to the mind-body problem is one that attempts to specify some 'natural property of the brain which explains how consciousness can be elicited from it' (p. 2). Functionalism, according to McGinn, is a classic example of such a solution, where the natural property in question is *playing a certain causal role*. It is misleading, though, for McGinn to say that functionalists attempt to explain, via such causal properties, how conscious states *arise from*, or are *generated by*, brain states. Functionalist token-token identity theorists, such as David Lewis, hold instead that conscious states (in us) are *identical* to brain states, since brain states themselves play the right causal roles, i.e. the roles that are definitive of conscious mental states.[4]

Cartesian dualism offers a different form of solution, according to which 'nothing merely natural could do the job' (ibid.). On this view, 'supernatural entities' are required in order to explain the link between the physical and consciousness. McGinn's thought here is presumably that on the Cartesian view, the physical brain causally interacts with an immaterial mental substance that is the subject of conscious states. McGinn deplores the Cartesian solution as being 'as extreme as the problem', in virtue of its abandonment of naturalism (ibid.).

His own solution, by contrast to both Cartesianism and constructive naturalism, is *non-constructive* and *naturalistic*. His view is that there is some natural property—call it *P*—instantiated by the brain, that is 'responsible for consciousness' (ibid.). *P* is neither mysterious nor miraculous—it is part of the natural order, just as much as is the property of being an electromagnetic wave. However, we cannot specify which property *P* is, since 'we are cut off by our very cognitive constitution from achieving a conception' of *P*. We cannot solve the mind-body problem constructively, and it would be a desperate mistake to acquiesce to occult Cartesian supernaturalism. McGinn's answer is to maintain that the psychophysical link is a feature of nature that we are congenitally barred from understanding.

The notion of *cognitive closure* is crucial to non-constructivity. A type of mind is said to be cognitively closed with respect to a property F iff such

---

[3] This is misleading because, as we will see, McGinn holds that nothing physical *explains* the presence of consciousness.

[4] See e.g. Lewis's 'An Argument for the Identity Theory', *Journal of Philosophy* (1966).

minds' concept-forming procedures 'cannot extend to a grasp of' F. (p. 3) According to McGinn's realist way of thinking, it is quite possible that there are some properties with respect to which human minds are cognitively closed: 'nothing... in the concept of reality shows that everything real is open to the human concept-forming faculty' (p. 4). Monkey minds are cognitively closed with respect to quantum-mechanical properties. It would be objectionably antirealist hubris to insist that there are no features of reality that stand to our minds as quantum fields stand to monkey minds. At this point, then, we should be open to the possibility that P, the property that connects the brain with consciousness, is among those properties with respect to which our minds are cognitively closed.

In earlier work, McGinn subscribed to a version of token-token physicaism according to which each particular mental event (in humans) is identical to some or other brain event.[5] On his earlier view, mental properties are not *reducible* to physical properties, in virtue of their multiple physical realizability: a given mental property can be instantiated by creatures that instantiate wildly different physical properties. However, suppose that a mental property M is realized in some physical basis, where B is the relevant realizing physical property. Then, according to McGinn's earlier view, there will exist a relation of supervenience of the following kind: necessarily, if a creature instantiates B, then it instantiates M. This holds for *all* the mental properties physically realized in a given creature. It follows that if two creatures are indistinguishable in respect of their physical properties, then they will also be indistinguishable in respect of their mental properties.

In his current thinking on consciousness, McGinn reaffirms the supervenience of consciousness (in us) upon the body and brain. In his review of David Chalmers's *The Conscious Mind*, he locates the chief problems for Chalmers in his denial of the 'logical supervenience' of consciousness upon the physical.[6] According to Chalmers's view, it is logically possible that there should be a physical duplicate of me who is a zombie altogether lacking conscious states. McGinn objects on two counts. First, when my zombie twin says, 'I am having conscious experience,' this utterance obviously cannot be explained by his having conscious experience. It follows, says McGinn, that *my* conscious experience is epiphenomenal with respect to my self-ascription of conscious experience. This is the first strike against Chalmers's position. Second, the denial of the logical supervenience in question, according to McGinn, entails the logical possibility of disembodied consciousness. In keeping with his general anti-Cartesian sentiments, McGinn does not wish

[5] See e.g. 'Mental States, Natural Kinds and Psychophysical Laws' and 'Philosophical Materialism', both in *The Problem of Consciousness*.

[6] See 'Chalmers: Wise Incomprehension', in McGinn's *Minds and Bodies* (New York: Oxford University Press, 1997).

to countenance that possibility: 'How would such disembodied experiences be connected to the rest of nature? What might their causal powers depend on? How could they have any dynamic role in anyone's psychology? Where would they *come* from?'[7]

McGinn holds, against Chalmers, that it is no objection to the supervenience thesis that it cannot be known by us in an a priori manner. The objection McGinn wishes to forestall would be that if the supervenience in question held, then it *would* be knowable a priori by us. But the conceivability of zombies shows that we do *not* know the alleged supervenience a priori. McGinn's reply is as follows:

Might we not . . . be confronted by a case of *opaque* logical supervenience? If that were so, then there would exist concepts of both the physical and the experiential, and of whatever relations might connect them, such that there is an a priori explanatory connection between those concepts—*even though they are not concepts we do or even could grasp.* . . . In other words, zombies *seem* possible to us only and precisely because we do not grasp the concepts that render them *im*possible.[8]

So we have the following picture. Consciousness properties are those whose possession by a thing entails that the thing is conscious (call them *C-properties*). The property of thinking about baseball and the property of visually experiencing are C-properties. Such properties supervene upon brain properties with respect to which we are cognitively *open* (call them *B-properties*), such as undergoing c-fibre stimulation. This supervenience does not hold in virtue of an identity between C- and B-properties. No C-property, for example, is identical to any property that we could conceive the brain as instantiating, including functional properties that physical things other than brains can instantiate. So we apparently have a mystery: in virtue of what does the supervenience hold? McGinn's answer is that the brain instantiates a natural property P that is *not* a B-property, since we are cognitively closed with respect to P (but not with respect to B-properties). It is in virtue of the brain's having P that consciousness exists in us and supervenes upon the brain's B-properties. P is what fits the brain for embodying consciousness in a supervenient manner.

2. McGinn's Argument for Cognitive Closure

Before getting to the main order of business—examining McGinn's argument to show that we are cognitively closed with respect to P—let us first note that McGinn needs to begin by giving us some reason to suppose that, hidden

---

[7] See ibid. 102.
[8] See ibid. One might well wonder how such an explanatory connection could be a priori, if that concept concerns how we come to *know* the truth of a proposition.

from us or not, there *is* some natural property that plays the role McGinn assigns to P, i.e. the role of grounding the supervenience of consciousness upon the brain. His reason is that the alternatives are too unattractive. One alternative is the non-naturalistic Cartesian one that McGinn has already rejected: conscious states are states of a non-physical substance that is merely contingently related to the brain and body. The other alternative shares an objectionable feature with Cartesianism. According to *emergentism*, consciousness does *not* reside in some supernatural mental substance. However, consciousness *is* contingently related to our neural organization. The psycho-physical correlations that in fact obtain are 'ultimate and inexplicable facts' that are *not necessitated* by any properties of the matter composing our brains and bodies (p. 6). These two alternatives, then, share a denial of the supervenience thesis we have been discussing.

Now let us turn to McGinn's reasons for thinking that even though P is a natural property, our minds are cognitively closed with respect to P. His master argument is Humean in character, in the sense that it canvasses the candidate sources for our acquiring an understanding of P and finds them all lacking.[9] Let us first consider introspection. To identify P, we might investigate consciousness directly. McGinn says that introspection affords us 'direct cognitive access to one term of the mind–brain relation, but we do not have such access to the nature of the link' (p. 8). McGinn treats this as being fairly obvious, saying, for example, 'Introspection does not present conscious states *as* depending upon the brain in some intelligible way' (p. 8).[10] So an understanding of P is not available via introspective examination of consciousness itself.

The remaining alternative is to try to find P by investigating the second term in the mind–brain relation, using perception and perceptually based theory construction. In attempting to show that perception is not up to the task at hand, McGinn's first step is to claim that consciousness is not a perceptible property of the brain. Just as introspection does not present conscious states as being brain states (or as depending upon them), perception does not present brain states as being conscious states. Thus 'we know that there are properties of the brain [namely consciousness properties] that are necessarily closed to perception of the brain' (p. 11). Maybe the same is true of the property of the brain we are seeking—P itself. McGinn maintains that P *is* closed to perception. In order to establish this, he proceeds by amplifying the reasons for thinking that *consciousness* is closed to perception.

---

[9] As we will see, McGinn's argument does not rest upon a Humean empiricism about the origin of concepts.

[10] McGinn has another reason for thinking that P is closed to introspection, based on Thomas Nagel's idea that 'one's form of subjectivity restricts one's concepts of subjectivity' (pp. 8–10). See Robert S. Kirk's 'Why Shouldn't we be Able to Solve the Mind–Body Problem?', *Analysis* (1991), for a critical discussion of McGinn's Nagelian argument.

He says that Kant was right in holding that the form of outer sense is spatial: 'the senses are geared to representing a spatial world; they essentially present things in space, with spatially defined properties' (p. 11). But consciousness is not spatial in character: '[it] does not seem made up out of smaller spatial processes' (p. 12). In a later piece, McGinn, again, says that 'consciousness is a nonspatial phenomenon'.[11] Compare this with the brain: 'There . . . [it] is, an object of perception, laid out in space, containing spatially distributed processes; but consciousness defies explanation in such terms' (pp. 11–12).

What of the linking property P? McGinn says that the non-spatiality of consciousness and the spatiality of perception together show that P is closed to perception (and thus closed to direct perceptual investigation of the brain). He says, 'We simply do not understand the idea that conscious states might intelligibly arise from spatial configurations of the kind disclosed by perception of the world' (p. 12). McGinn's reasoning is not perfectly clear here. He appears to be claiming that the property that links consciousness and the brain must share the non-spatiality of consciousness and is for that reason inaccessible to perception.

But this is not the end of the story. McGinn is not a Humean about concept-formation. Even if a property is perceptually closed off from us (e.g. the property of being a heterotic superstring), we may well be capable of forming an adequate concept of it via theory construction, employing inference to the best explanation. Perceptual closure does not imply cognitive closure. So McGinn needs to complete his master argument by ruling out the following possibility: '[given that] there is no compelling reason to suppose that the property needed to explain the mind–brain relation should be in principle perceptible . . . it might be essentially "theoretical", an object of thought not sensory experience' (ibid.).

McGinn argues first that consciousness itself can play no role in an inference to the best explanation involving B-properties as *explananda*:

Let me first note that consciousness itself could not be introduced simply on the basis of what we observe about the brain and its physical effects. If our data, arrived at by perception of the brain, do not include anything that brings in conscious states, then the theoretical properties we need to explain these data will not include conscious states either. Inference to the best explanation of purely physical data will never take us outside the realm of the physical, forcing us to introduce concepts of consciousness. Everything physical has a purely physical explanation. So the property of consciousness is cognitively closed with respect to the introduction of concepts by means of inference to the best explanation of perceptual data about the brain. (12–13)[12]

---

[11] See 'McGinn: Out of Body, Out of Mind', in *Minds and Bodies*, p. 108.
[12] McGinn cites the following quotation from Nagel's 'Panpsychism' (p. 183): 'It will never be legitimate to infer, as a theoretical explanation of physical phenomena alone, a property that includes or implies the consciousness of its subject.'

It is important to see that this passage rests upon the assumption that consciousness is not physical (and therefore cannot explain physical data about the brain). McGinn has already maintained that consciousness is not *spatial* in character. We take it that this is McGinn's ground for asserting the non-physicality of consciousness. He offers no other candidate reason.

Let us pause for a bit of an aside. It is at this point hard to see how McGinn can reasonably criticize Chalmers on the ground that his views regarding zombies render consciousness epiphenomenal. The current step in his own Humean argument, we just noted, is in effect the assertion of the epiphenomenality of consciousness with respect to brain data. Thus on McGinn's own view, his utterance of 'I have conscious states' cannot be seen as an expression of self-knowledge, since the occurrence of the utterance is not explained by the occurrence of a known conscious state.[13]

Before considering the final development of the Humean argument concerning P, let us return briefly to McGinn's earlier token-token physicalism. Given what we have just seen, McGinn's current view appears to preclude an identity between token mental states and brain states (in us). My current conscious state (a thought about baseball) cannot be identical to any brain state because, according to what seems to be McGinn's view, the thought differs in properties from any given brain state. The thought is non-physical and non-spatial, but brain states are physical and spatial.[14] The denial of token-token physicalism, though, is consistent with the supervenience thesis discussed above. We will return to this point a bit later.

Let us now turn to the question of whether P 'could ever be arrived at' by inference to the best explanation. McGinn answers in the negative, but his reasoning is rather obscure. According to McGinn, inference to the best explanation 'would no more serve to introduce P than it serves to introduce the property of consciousness itself'. He continues, 'To explain the observed physical data we need only such theoretical properties as bear upon those data, not the property that explains consciousness, which does not occur in the data. Since we do not need consciousness to explain those data, we do not need the property that explains consciousness' (p. 13). This is a puzzling passage. In the first sentence, McGinn seems to be saying that P, the property that 'explains consciousness', will not be needed to explain the physical brain data because that which P is fitted to explain—consciousness—'does not occur in the data'.

---

[13] I thank Ivan Fox for discussion of this point. He raised the question of how McGinn and Chalmers can account for knowledge of conscious states, given their epiphenomenality with respect to behaviour that is standardly seen as giving expression to such knowledge.

[14] Note that in 'Consciousness and the Natural Order', p. 60, McGinn says, 'I shall not fuss over distinctions of type and token, event and state, process and property. I use "consciousness" to cover all these.' Thus it is fair to transfer what McGinn says about consciousness to token conscious states such as thoughts.

But what precludes the possibility that P plays the *dual* role of *both* explaining consciousness *and* explaining the brain data? If P played this dual explanatory role, then the possibility would remain that P is a theoretically accessible property of the brain that *can* be arrived at by inference to the best explanation.

Perhaps the second sentence in the quoted passage will help us understand why McGinn would deny that possibility. He may have the following idea in mind. For reasons we have already discussed, consciousness is, according to McGinn, not fit to explain brain data. Now in order to play its defining role of explaining consciousness, P must share certain crucial characteristics with consciousness. McGinn says that in perception-based inference to the best explanation, 'we get . . . [theoretical concepts] by a sort of analogical extension of what we observe. Thus, for example, we arrive at the concept of a molecule by taking our perceptual representations of macroscopic objects and conceiving of smaller scale objects of the same general kind' (ibid.). Since consciousness is not physical and not spatial, P, the property that explains consciousness, must also lack those characteristics. But then P will be just as unfit to explain brain data as is consciousness itself: P will not bear upon those data. P will thus be shown to be incapable of playing the envisaged *dual* explanatory role. By holding that P is an 'analogical extension' of non-physical, non-spatial consciousness, McGinn can hold that P is sufficiently similar to consciousness to preclude it from explaining brain data.

3. McGinn's Cartesianism

We are now in a position to see how *Cartesian* McGinn's position turns out to be. His Humean master argument appears to require that both consciousness and the linking property P be non-physical and non-spatial in character. Otherwise, both would be candidates for explaining the physical, spatial brain data; P might therefore be accessible via theoretical inference. Further, McGinn would have no reason to hold that P is closed to perception.

But now what becomes of McGinn's claim to have given a *naturalistic* solution to the mind-body problem, a solution that is preferable to Cartesianism? McGinn might well say that by 'physical' he means, roughly, 'whatever physics will bring us next', in Nagel's phrase.[15] Since his main point is that P is closed to our best scientific endeavours, the view that P is non-physical in that Nagelian sense is just what McGinn intends.

To say that P is inaccessible to our best possible physicists' minds is one thing, but to say that P (along with consciousness) is non-spatial is another. If P is non-spatial in character, then it is hard to see what its being a *natural*

---

[15] See Nagel's 'Panpsychism', p. 183.

property comes to, if not just being a *real* property of things. According to the Cartesian, properties of non-physical mental states and substances are natural in *that* sense. Furthermore, if P and consciousness are non-spatial in character, then it is hard to see how the *brain*—'laid out in space'—could instantiate these properties. Remember that P, according to McGinn, is a property of the brain, the one that enables that organ to embody consciousness.

McGinn might respond to these accusations of Cartesianism by first re-affirming the token-token identity thesis. Conscious states, such as thoughts about baseball, he might say, are identical to brain states (in creatures such as us). We cannot understand how these token-token identities are possible, however, McGinn might continue. Since brain states are spatial and physical, thoughts also have these properties. But this is extremely puzzling, because even though thoughts are in fact spatial, introspection does not *present* them as being spatial, whereas perception necessarily presents brain states as being spatial. As McGinn says, 'Consciousness does not *seem* made up out of smaller spatial processes' (p. 12, my emphasis). This is consistent with conscious states *in fact* having a spatial nature. It is just that our epistemic route to consciousness—introspection—obscures that nature. An understanding of the property P would clear up the difficulty, since, according to this view, the puzzling token-token identities hold in virtue of the brain's instantiation of P. But such understanding is not forthcoming.

If McGinn were to take this position, then it would become unclear whether his Humean argument can succeed. We have seen that the argument crucially depends upon the thesis that consciousness is non-physical and non-spatial. This thesis is used to show that P is closed to perception and inference to the best explanation. If McGinn were to hold that consciousness is in fact physical and spatial, though it does not *seem* to be so, then the Humean argument would be stymied.

Let us now consider a different manoeuvre that McGinn might try. We will say that a property F is *space-implicating* iff necessarily, if x instantiates F, then x is spatial. *Being divisible by 3*, then, is not a space-implicating property, given the non-spatiality of the number 9. *Being a neuron*, on the other hand, is a space-implicating property. Now McGinn might say that consciousness properties, and P itself, are not space-implicating properties. He might say that even though consciousness, and P, are in fact instantiated (in me) by something that is spatial—namely, my brain—it is not *necessary* that these properties are instantiated by spatial things.

The next step would be to maintain that

(E1) In order to explain physical, spatial data regarding a thing, one must appeal to space-implicating properties of the thing.

E1 could be backed by this thesis about explanation:

(E2) A proper explanans will necessitate its explanandum.[16]

To see why E1 might hold, suppose that my possession of some property G that is not space-implicating explains my possession of a space-implicating property S. Since G is, by hypothesis, *not* a space-implicating property, there will be some possible world in which something x has G and yet is not spatial. That thing x would thus lack S, since S *is* space-implicating. Therefore, given E2, my possession of G turns out not to explain my possession of S, since the former does not necessitate the latter: x has G but lacks S.

Now if the above requirements on explanation did hold, then neither the non-space-implicating consciousness properties, nor the property P itself, could explain brain data, as maintained in the Humean argument. Still, according to the manœuvre we are considering, conscious states are in fact identical to physical, spatial brain states (in us). The charge of Cartesianism can thus apparently be met. Conscious states possess *both* space-implicating properties *and* non-space-implicating properties.

Is this position consistent with the supervenience thesis that McGinn wishes to defend? That is, is the view that consciousness properties and P are not space-implicating properties consistent with the supervenience thesis? The supervenience discussed above says that necessarily, if x and y share all the same B-properties (brain properties), then they share all the same C-properties (consciousness properties). This is compatible with e.g. the circumstance that in this world, my brain instantiates C-property C1 in virtue of instantiating B-property B1, while in world w, C1 is instantiated by a thing that is not spatial. There will be some such possible worlds as w if C1 is not a space-implicating property, and this is consistent with the view that every world in which B1 is instantiated is a world in which C1 is also instantiated.

We noticed earlier that McGinn chastises Chalmers for denying the supervenience thesis. One of McGinn's criticisms was that this denial opens up the Cartesian possibility of disembodied consciousness. But we have just seen that this possibility is *consistent* with McGinn's supervenience thesis, as we have been understanding it. It is worth noting, then, that affirming supervenience does not by itself ensure the anti-Cartesianism that McGinn desires.[17]

---

[16] See e.g. Nagel, 'Panpsychism', 185–7.

[17] In 'Philosophical Materialism', p. 181, McGinn states his supervenience thesis as follows: 'necessarily, for any mental property instantiated by a creature at a time, there is a physical property the creature instantiates such that, necessarily, if any creature instantiates that physical property, then it instantiates that mental property'. This is compatible with the possibility of mental properties that are instantiated but not by *creatures*. Though McGinn does not do so, one might formulate supervenience as the conjunction of (1) the thesis that he *calls* supervenience (roughly, that fixing the physical fixes the mental), and (2) the view that whenever a thing instantiates a consciousness property, it also instantiates a physical, spatial property. Obviously, such a supervenience thesis is inconsistent with the possibility of disembodied consciousness.

We now get to the moral of the story regarding the manœuvre we have been considering. It is that the manœuvre would be an incredibly bad idea for McGinn. It would be a bad idea to hold that C-properties, along with P, are not space-implicating properties in the sense we have been discussing. To hold *that* is to hold that these properties can be instantiated by things that are not spatial. In attempting the suggested manœuvre, McGinn would end up countenancing the possibilities of disembodied consciousness and disembodied P. His position, then, would be to that degree Cartesian. Naturalism would apparently go out of the window.

4. Conclusion

McGinn has attempted a naturalistic, non-constructive solution to the mind-body problem. We have seen that his Humean argument for non-constructivity, in which he attempts to show that we are cognitively closed with respect to the linking property P, raises problems for his naturalism. This argument depends upon claims about consciousness and about P that are Cartesian in character. The ways of resolving this problem that we have considered are all problematic. We conclude that McGinn has not succeeded in presenting a viable solution to the mind-body problem.

Part Four

Quantum Mechanics and Consciousness

Part Four

15. Why Cognitive Scientists Cannot Ignore Quantum Mechanics

QUENTIN SMITH

Introduction

There is something fundamentally disturbing about contemporary philosophy of mind and philosophical cognitive science. Almost without exception (exceptions such as Lockwood (1989) and Chalmers (1996, see esp. p. 349)), the philosophical theories are logically inconsistent with the most well-confirmed theory ever developed by humans, namely, quantum mechanics. Why do philosophers develop theories of the mind–brain as if quantum mechanics does not exist, or as if it is utterly irrelevant to theories of the mind–brain?

I believe this epistemic situation has arisen due to a series of questionable philosophical arguments about the role of philosophy of mind/cognitive science and quantum mechanics in our overall theoretical framework. In sect. 1 I explain some of these arguments and contend they are unsound.

A second factor is that the most epistemically warranted resolution of the conflict between philosophical theories of the mind–brain and quantum mechanics, namely, that current cognitive science and philosophies of mind be replaced by a quantum cognitive science, involves such a radical violation of the theory-forming criterion of 'conservativeness' (roughly 'change your old, most central beliefs to the minimal degree required by the new evidence or arguments'), that philosophers might think it is more reasonable to retain standard, non-quantum cognitive science and wait until a 'new science' is developed that allows the criterion of theoretical conservativeness to be more nearly met than would be the case if we made the transition from non-quantum to quantum cognitive science. This second factor is typically expressed in noting the 'bizarreness' (relative to our non-quantum background beliefs) of

I thank Peter Momchiloff, Barry Loewer, Michael Lockwood, Don Page, David Chalmers, Michael Tye, David Newman, and several anonymous referees for Oxford University Press for reading, commenting upon, or discussing the ideas in this chapter.

the various ontologies with which we are faced if we have to accept any of the presently known interpretations of quantum mechanics and their implications for cognitive science.

In fact, there may be an even more basic (and perhaps unique) problem that arises due to the highly non-conservative shift in thinking that a transition to quantum cognitive science would require. It may be that the quantum ontologies are so 'strange' that many, most, or virtually all philosophers find them psychologically impossible to believe. This may be a genetic problem, rather than merely a problem in the lack of intellectual acculturation in quantum ontology. For example, one of the ontological interpretations of quantum mechanics requires us to believe that each of our minds (conceived in terms of substance dualism) is regularly splitting into an infinite (continuum-many) number of distinct minds, each with the same body (so there is just one body or brain for all the minds), such that each of the minds is unaware of the other minds (e.g. a version of Albert and Loewer's 'many-minds' interpretation of quantum mechanics). Suppose, for the sake of argument, that this is the correct interpretation of quantum mechanics. It could be that many, most, or all of us are not psychologically capable of actually and sincerely believing this ontology. Varying on McGinn, it could be that we are not cognitively closed to *understanding* the mind–brain relation (for example), but that we can understand the true theory of this relation but are cognitively closed to *believing* it. This should not be surprising. Why should we expect that *homo sapiens sapiens* is genetically capable of finding epistemically plausible the ontology implied by the true cognitive science, especially if this ontology differs radically from both folk psychology and what Stich (1996: 11) calls 'our folk physics' (common sense beliefs, predictions, explanations, etc., about the nature of physical reality)? Believing such an ontology appears to confer no increase in our survival value; it may even decrease our 'fitness' to survive and reproduce. Would we still want to undertake the difficult task of raising offspring if we all knew and emotionally appreciated the significance of the fact that infinite sets of varying copies of ourselves were continually coming into existence? Admittedly, many of our beliefs have no firm explanatory link with enhanced reproductive success, but in the case of quantum mechanical beliefs the decrease in our 'fitness' seems much greater than with other beliefs.

Quantum cognitive science (in so far as it is presently developed) requires the rejection of both folk psychology and folk physics, but not in the name of eliminative materialism, reductive physicalism, or what the Churchlands call 'neuroscience' or 'neurophilosophy'. For these ontologies (e.g. Patricia and Paul Churchland's versions of eliminative materialism) are non-quantum ontologies and will have to be rejected for the same reasons that require the rejection of folk psychology and folk physics.

There will remain two positive aspects of non-quantum cognitive science or philosophy of mind (if my arguments for quantum cognitive science are sound).

One positive aspect is that non-quantum cognitive sciences, if interpreted instrumentally (and anti-realistically) can still have the theoretical virtue of being successful at predicting approximately accurate macroscopic observations. Although non-quantum theories are false if interpreted in terms of ontological realism, they are none the less highly useful for instrumentalist purposes.

The second positive aspect is that the non-quantum theories or theses can in some cases be 'quantized' and made consistent with quantum cognitive science and in these cases their quantized versions can be interpreted realistically and thereby can have the truth value of true (in the sense of 'correspondence' to reality).

These theses are argued for in sect. 1 of this chapter. In sect. 2 I outline a new version of quantum cognitive science that is capable of explaining the only available experimental, macroscopic evidence for quantum cognitive science, the Nunn–Clarke–Blott experiments. Note that the widely discussed Hammeroff–Penrose quantum theory of the physical basis of consciousness (they do not develop a theory of the nature of consciousness) is not put forward by Hammeroff and Penrose as an experimentally confirmed theory, but as a testable proposal that is not yet confirmed. Much of the criticism of their theory is based on the false assumption that they put it forward as a confirmed hypothesis.

1. A Response to the Standard Objections to Quantum Cognitive Science

1.1. Fallacious Reasoning about Prior and Posterior Probabilities of Non-Quantum Cognitive Science and Quantum Cognitive Science

Just as David Lewis's theory of possible worlds was once met with what Lewis called 'the incredulous stare' (which I take to be an informal logical fallacy, one species of the *ad hominem* fallacy), so quantum consciousness theories are 'dismissed with a hand wave' by most philosophers, even by some who know quantum mechanics. In this section I argue that this informal logical fallacy, 'the hand-wave dismissal', (a species of the *ignori elenchi* fallacy) is based on a tacit (because not explicitly formulated), formal logical failure to distinguish *the prior probability of quantum cognitive science* from *the probability of quantum cognitive science based on macroscopically observable evidence*. The kind of probability I am talking about is epistemic probability (see

Smith 2002*a*) and the probability of quantum cognitive science is the probability that some cognitive science is true by virtue of, and only by virtue of, the quantum mechanical ideas it contains. This quantum cognitive science need not yet exist in a completely developed (or even incompletely developed) form.

Let the hypothesis *h* be some quantum cognitive science (such that the hypothesis entails that some quantum cognitive science is true, where 'entails' is used in the sense of relevance logic). Let *k* be our background knowledge of the verification of quantum mechanics in microscopic physical experiments (about electrons etc.). Let *p* stand for probability. The prior probability of some quantum cognitive science *h* may thus be represented as $p(h/k)$, i.e. the probability of *h*, given *k*.

The posterior probability adds the evidence *e*, where *e* is our observational evidence at the macroscopic level, such that *e* is evidence about people's behaviour, the subjective, first-person experiences that you or I experience at each moment we are awake or are dreaming, EEG pen positions that are correlated to a brain, and other items that are discussed in cognitive psychology, neurophysiology, and related disciplines (e.g. descriptions of effects of anaesthetics, blindsight experiments, etc.). The posterior probability that some cognitive quantum science is true is thus $p(h/e + k)$.

My claim is that many philosophers have committed the hand-wave dismissal fallacy because they have *implicitly* failed to distinguish the posterior probability $p(h/e + k)$ from the probability of *h* given only *e*, that is, $p(h/e)$. Since $p(h/e)$ is very low, quantum cognitive science poses no large threat to non-quantum cognitive scientists or philosophers *if* $p(h/e)$ is the only relevant probability.

But $p(h/e)$ is not a significantly relevant probability, let alone the only or the most relevant probability. The probability with which we should be concerned is $p(h/e + k)$. Since $p(h/k)$, which is the prior probability that some quantum cognitive science is true, is much higher than the posterior probability of some non-quantum cognitive science (as I shall argue), the prior probability of some quantum cognitive science is the most important factor in the assessment. In this section I concentrate on arguing that $p(h/k)$ is considerably higher than non-quantum cognitive scientists or philosophers of mind believe. Further, I make the case that these arguments for the strength of $p(h/k)$ defeat the standardly offered justifiers for the belief in the superior plausibility of non-quantum cognitive science or non-quantum philosophy of mind. If my arguments are sound, then virtually every scientist or philosopher who works on consciousness and its relation to the brain, ranging from the eliminative materialists, e.g. the Churchlands, to the substance dualists, e.g. Richard Swinburne, hold unjustified beliefs about consciousness and the brain. Albert and Loewer, Bohm and Hiley, Chalmers, Eccles, Lockwood,

Page, Squires, Stapp, and Wigner on the other hand, are quantum consciousness theorists (at least in some of their writings, e.g. Loewer's co-authored
work with Albert) and they hold the justified belief h.

I address a different but closely related subject in sect. 2. There I argue that
the prevailing opinion among philosophers that $p(h/e) = 0$ is false, since
there is some macroscopic observational evidence e for h that gives $p(h/e)$ a
significant, non-zero value, even though it may be less than 0.5.

1.2. The Objection that Quantum Cognitive Science is Mere Speculation

There is a common belief among philosophers that quantum cognitive
science is mere speculation and thus can be safely ignored. This objection to
the relevance of quantum mechanics to cognitive science is implicitly based
on a fallacy, since it conflates particular claims (made by Penrose and Hammeroff, or Eccles, etc.) about certain brain–consciousness relations with the
different hypothesis that the brain and consciousness are governed by quantum mechanical laws. Are quantum wave-field collapses in tubulins the source
of consciousness (Hammeroff and Penrose)? This is a speculative hypothesis;
it is not confirmed, at least not yet. But it is not a speculative hypothesis that
quantum mechanics is very highly confirmed and applies to all physical
realities, including the brain. This is as hard a hard fact as one can get; no
theory has been confirmed to a greater degree than quantum mechanics. And
since most interpretations of quantum mechanics essentially involve theories
of consciousness, we may add that (on most interpretations of quantum
mechanics) it is a scientific fact (appearing even in undergraduate and
graduate textbooks) that quantum mechanics has implications for the nature
of consciousness.

It is invalid to infer from 'it is speculative that consciousness is due to
quantum field collapses in tubulins' to 'it is speculative that the brain–mind
relation (and the nature of consciousness) is quantum mechanical rather than
non-quantum mechanical'. This is obviously invalid and thus should be
considered as a tacitly assumed belief that influences the hand-wave dismissal
fallacy. A more accurate statement of this tacit belief would imply that it is
assumed in a more exhaustive manner (where 'exhaustive' has the sense it
does in the phrase 'the exhaustive and mutually exclusive class of Fs'), such
that the assumption or practice takes the following form.

The more general practice is to take a presently advocated, particular
version of quantum cognitive science, such as Hammeroff–Penrose's ($h1$),
Eccles's ($h2$), or Stapp's ($h3$), and produce arguments such as the one I will
construct shortly. In this argument, $h =$ some quantum cognitive science is
true, $n =$ some non-quantum cognitive science is true, $e =$ all macroscopic
evidence relevant to cognitive science, and $k =$ the background knowledge

that all microscopic evidence highly confirms quantum mechanics (as distinct from Einstein's relativity theory and Newtonism). The general argument tacitly used by non-quantum cognitive scientists or philosophers is typified by the argument:

(1) $p\ (h1/e\ \&\ k) << p\ (n/e\ \&\ k)$
(2) $p\ (h2/e\ \&\ k) << p\ (n/e\ \&\ k)$
(3) Etc., for each other presently advocated, particular version of quantum cognitive sciences, h3, h4, and so on.

Therefore,

(4) $p\ (h/k\ \&\ e) << p\ (n/e\ \&\ k)$.

The symbol '<' means *less than* and the symbol '<<' means *considerably less than*. There are at least two errors in the argument I have just presented. First, the probability of a presently advocated, particular version of quantum cognitive science, such as *h1* or *h2*, is compared with the probability of some non-quantum cognitive quantum science *n*, rather than with some particular, presently advocated version of non-quantum cognitive science, such as Fodor's *n1* or Dretkse's *n2*.

The second error is that the argument is based on the false assumption that it is not true that $p\ (h/k) >> p\ (n/e + k)$. The critics of quantum cognitive science do not realize that, by virtue of *k*, the prior probability that some quantum cognitive science is true is significantly greater than the posterior probability that some non-quantum cognitive science is true (as I shall argue in the next subsections). Even if some presently advocated, particular version of quantum cognitive science is so badly flawed that it is more likely that quantum mechanics is false than this version is true, it still is the case that the truth of *some* quantum cognitive science, be it currently existent in some form or not yet formulated at all, is much more probable than the truth of some non-quantum cognitive science.

1.3. The Objection that Cognitive Science is an Autonomous Science

The received view is that psychology, cognitive science, neuroscience, etc., have their own laws and they are not quantum laws. The various versions of non-reductivist physicalism, the predominant view today among philosophers of mind and philosophers of science in general, are associated with the belief that each distinct domain of science has non-reducible laws. A main contemporary way to conceive the autonomy of the psychological sciences is along the general lines of the 'unity of science' theory, presented as early as 1958 in Oppenheim and Putnam (1958), and given an especially clear formulation by Kim (1993: 337). This widely accepted kind of argument (which allows cognitive scientists justifiably to ignore quantum mechanics) goes thus: At the bottom level there are electrons, quarks, and other microscopic entities described by quantum mechanics (and its extensions in quantum field theories). The bottom level entities have certain kinds of properties, such as spin, energy, mass, etc., and whatever else we need to posit on some given interpretation of quantum mechanics. This is physics. We go up one level to chemistry and find at this higher level new kinds of property that emerge when we consider large wholes made up of the entities posited by physics. Kim gives the example of 'lumps of H_2O molecules, with [such] properties as transparency, power to dissolve sugar and salt, and their characteristic density and viscosity, and so on' (ibid.). At a still higher level, biology, we find wholes composed of carbon, water, oxygen, etc., and these wholes have new kinds of properties, such as photosynthesis, digestion, reproduction, and the like. Eventually we come to psychology or cognitive science, with its characteristic kinds of properties or relations, such as propositional attitudes and sensory qualia, or perhaps neural nets, nodes, and the like (if cognitive science is connectionism, as some hold).

The entities at each level are composed of entities on the immediately lower level, but have emergent properties that are different in kind than the properties at the lower level. The properties at each level are related to properties at a lower level by supervening upon them. These supervening properties enable cognitive science, for example, to form an autonomous domain, with laws connecting the supervenient properties that are distinctive to that domain. Therefore, the argument goes, *quantum mechanical cognitive science* is a contradiction in terms, or a 'domain fallacy' (to coin a phrase), or at least is empirically false since there is no macroscopic evidence *e* that the kinds of properties belonging to the autonomous domain of cognitive science are quantum mechanical in nature. The probability of quantum cognitive science, $p(h/e)$, is the only relevant one, for *e*, macroscopic evidence about human behaviour, EEG machines, etc., is the only evidence relevant to the autonomous cognitive science domain. The background knowledge *k* about the behaviour of electrons and photons, etc., is relevant only to lower-level kinds of properties, the kinds of properties possessed by electrons, photons, and the like. There are cognitive science or psychological causal laws (some, like Davidson, deny this, but not for reasons pertinent to my argument), and these laws are different in kind than quantum mechanical laws.

This objection to quantum cognitive science is unsound since *the kinds of properties at every level or domain are kinds of quantum mechanical properties*, regardless of whether the domain is physics, biology, or psychology. According to quantum mechanics, each and every item that exists obeys the laws of quantum mechanics, not just electrons, photons and the like. Each kind of domain-property is a subkind of the general kind of property,

Quantum Mechanical Property. If you say, 'Mechanics *by definition* is about matter and motion, not consciousness!', I respond, 'This may be true for the non-quantum mechanics, be it Newton's or Einstein's, but not for quantum mechanics. Indeed, according to some prevalent interpretations of quantum mechanics, there is no such thing as matter and motion!'

Exactly how this universal application of quantum mechanics is explained depends on the interpretation of quantum mechanics one is using. On some versions of the Copenhagen interpretation (say of Stapp, perhaps the leading contemporary quantum cognitive scientist who belongs to the Copenhagen tradition), the emergent, psychological property of *being a conscious state* is an actualization of a potential conscious state that exists in a quantum mechanical configuration space. There is no need to understand the technical notions of quantum mechanics to understand my point; one need merely know that 'configuration space', 'state vectors', 'wave functions', 'eigenvalues', etc. refer to very different kinds of abstract or concrete entities or properties than those posited by non-quantum cognitive science. On the Copenhagen interpretation (usually called 'the standard interpretation') that I am discussing here, in the context of Stapp's formulation, we have a specific theory of the nature of a conscious state. The nature of a conscious state is to be the actualization of a 'Hilbert space state vector' (Stapp 1998: 205). 'In this conception, the experienced reality is the coming into being of a psychologically felt command: Do X! This experiential reality, in its potential form, is represented (or embodied) in Hilbert space' (ibid.). 'Each actualization event has its physical side, which is just the "collapse" of the wave function itself, and also its experiential side. In a rational causal theory collapse must have a cause... *What is consciousness? It is the part of nature that... causes the physical state to collapse*' (ibid. 208–9: my italics). This is the fundamental principle of cognitive science, if this interpretation of quantum mechanics is correct. There is no reductionism to a lower level, since quantum mechanical properties are the only properties that are exemplified at each level in the hierarchy of the sciences, ranging from physics to cognitive science. Again, there is no need to understand quantum mechanics to understand my point; merely note that in the above quotation consciousness is defined (without being reduced to anything physical) in terms of quantum mechanical notions. We need to accept some interpretation of quantum mechanics, and on the standard (Copenhagen) interpretation Stapp correctly notes, I believe, that consciousness causes the physical state to collapse. Wigner in 1961 also realized, I believe, that the standard interpretation is led by the logic of its interpretation to the thesis that consciousness is the cause of the wave function collapse.

A very different interpretation of quantum mechanics is that of Everett, which was originally formulated (by deWitt) as a 'many worlds' theory, which has more recently and correctly been superseded by the 'many minds' (Albert and Loewer) or 'many perceptions' (Lockwood, Page) theory. Michael Lockwood (1989) and Don Page (1995; 1996) have developed the 'many perceptions' interpretation to the fullest degree. Consider how Lockwood explains the universal applicability of quantum mechanics (to every entity and state, including brain states and conscious states). Again it is not necessary to understand the complicated technical terms in this quotation to grasp my point. Lockwood (1989: 214) writes:

there will, at any given time, be some unique vector, in the cosmic Hilbert space, which represents the current state of the entire universe.... This state, in conjunction with a given designated state of the brain system, allows one to assign to any physical subsystem a unique state—represented by a vector in its own Hilbert space—which is its state relative to the designated state. Suppose I observe, say, the golf ball to be in the hole, or Schrödinger's cat to be alive and purring. Then what that really amounts to is the following. A particular state of my brain (or, more accurately, subsystem of my brain) is designated in the relevant act of awareness. And the perceived state of the system being observed—the nineteenth hole, or Schrödinger's cat—[is] its unique state, given the overall state of things as represented by the cosmic state vector, relative to that designated brain state.

If the reader prefers an Everett interpretation to the Copenhagen interpretation, she will still end up with consciousness as the basis of the theory. The readers unfamiliar with quantum mechanics and Lockwood's theory will not understand what this passage exactly means, but they will understand that it implies that the familiar 'autonomy of the sciences' and 'emergent non-quantum properties' argument for non-quantum cognitive science is in conflict with this (and other) interpretations of quantum mechanics.

The familiar 'autonomy of the sciences' argument against quantum cognitive science is based on a misunderstanding of quantum mechanics as being only about electrons and quarks and the like. On *no* interpretation does quantum mechanics have implications merely about electrons and other microscopic entities. It is not about only electrons, quarks, photons, etc.; it is about your consciousness, your brain, and everything else that exists. This applies, as I will later argue, even to antirealist interpretations of quantum mechanics.

Other interpretations of quantum mechanics also imply that the autonomy of the sciences argument fails because the background knowledge k in $p\,(h/e+k)$ entails that each level of kinds of properties in the hierarchy of the sciences contains only quantum mechanical kinds of properties. We recall that $k =$ our background knowledge of the verification of quantum mechanics in microphysical experiments, $e =$ our relevant evidence at the macroscopic level and $p\,(h)$ is the probability that a cognitive science has to include a substantial amount of quantum mechanical ideas in order correctly to describe its subject matter. Kim's idea that 'spin', but not 'consciousness', is a quantum mechanical property, is based on the false, tacit assumption that k does not entail that each level of kinds of properties in the hierarchy of the sciences contains only quantum mechanical kinds of properties.

Note that I am not denying that cognitive science is autonomous; it is not reducible to the quantum mechanics of electrons and quarks. I am saying that the cognitive science properties (the kind of properties that are distinctive to the autonomous level of cognitive science) are subkinds of quantum mechanical properties.

Fodor's position on this sort of situation has been one of the most influential. Fodor (1987: 9) writes: 'the (putative) generalizations of the (putative) completed physics would apply to the motions of organisms qua motions, but not qua organismic. Physics presumably has as little use for the categories of macrobiology as it does for the categories of commonsense psychology... What's left is atoms in the void.' He also presents another influential argument (ibid. 6): 'If the world is described as a closed causal system at all, it is so only in the vocabulary of our most basic science. From this nothing follows that a psychologist (or a geologist) needs to worry about.' If Fodor is talking about non-quantum physics, he is right. But he is wrong if he is talking about quantum physics, for this physics makes use of the categories of commonsense psychology, such as consciousness, experience, perception, observation, etc. These categories are borrowed from commonsense psychology and are 'regimented' (in Quine's sense) for use (to talk technically for a moment) in locating dimensions in configuration space or for specifying certain kinds of state vectors, observables, etc. Even on the most widely used formulation of the 'standard' (i.e. Copenhagen) interpretation of quantum mechanics, namely, von Neumann's, conscious experiences enter the basic axioms, for von Neumann's formulation essentially refers to consciousness. One of the basic axioms of the 'standard' interpretation (von Neumann's 'projection postulate') is that the collapse of the wave function occurs at some time in a measuring instrument, sense organ, or brain *before a mind becomes conscious of the measured result.* (Here consciousness does not collapse the wave function, but is defined as one of the temporal limits within which the collapse occurs.) On this standard interpretation 'no consciousness' implies 'no collapse' which implies 'quantum physics is false'. A basic axiom of physics ('the projection postulate') *essentially includes psychological vocabulary.* Fodor's theory of how the sciences related to each other is more appropriate to a Newtonian or Einsteinian world-view.

There is a more fundamental sense in which everything *is* quantum mechanical *and is nothing but quantum mechanical.* I am making an unusual but non-reductivist claim. How is everything nothing but quantum mechanical reality? Reality itself is nothing but configuration space, the wave function (quantum wave-field) of the universe, and/or some other *purely* quantum reality. This is nicely summarized by Albert (1996: 277) and his remarks deserve to be quoted: 'it has been essential to the project of quantum-mechanical realism (in whatever particular form it takes—Bohm's theory, or modal theories, or Everettish theories, or theories of spontaneous local-izations), to learn to think of wave functions as physical objects in and of themselves'. For example, 'on the GRW theory (or for that matter on any theory of collapse), the world will consist of exactly one physical object—the universal wave function' (ibid. 278). And

on Bohm's theory, for example, the world will consist of exactly two physical objects. One of those is the universal wave function and the other is the universal particle. And the story of the world consists, in its entirety, of a continuous succession of changes of shape of the former and of a continuous succession of changes in the position of the latter. (ibid.)

The individuals of which it [the world] consists on *Modal* theories are two fields like that [where the fields are wave-function fields at all points in configuration space]; and pinning the conditions of all those individuals down, on any of those theories, pins down *everything*. (ibid. 282 n. 7)

And of course the space those sorts of objects live in, and *therefore the space we live in*, the space in which any realist understanding of quantum mechanics is necessarily going to depict the history of the world as playing itself out (if space is the right name for it—of which more later) is configuration-space. *And whatever impression we have to the contrary (whatever impression we have, say, of living in a three-dimensional space, or in a four-dimensional space-time) is somehow flatly illusory.*

(Albert 1996: 277, my emphases)

This passage indicates how distant non-quantum cognitive science is from the quantum nature of reality. The brain, consciousness, and objects of perceptions are in reality very different from how they are represented in non-quantum cognitive science. Thought experiments such as the Twin Earth experiment make sense on the assumption that non-quantum physics is true, but are logically incoherent if placed in a quantum framework. Phase-entanglement alone (combined with a quantum big bang cosmology) would falsify a necessary assumption of the Twin Earth experiment, namely that each twin is a numerically distinguishable individual. (At the big bang, everything is phase entangled.) Furthermore, on the Bohmian particle inter-pretation mentioned by Albert, it would not be logically possible for two particles to exist, let alone two planets; the thought experiment would be an explicit logical contradiction. There are even broader worries. The super-venience of the mental on the physical, the wide content/narrow content distinction (and the related debate between Externalism and Internalism), the Representationalism versus Non-representationalism debate, the func-tionalism versus connectionism debate, and similar debates have yet to be shown to have any application or relevance to the nature of reality. For example, what could 'the representational theory of the mind' possibly mean if consciousness is what causes the wavefunction to collapse (Wigner, Stapp)? There would be no conceivable representations and no conceivable items that could be represented. 'The representational theory of the mind' would be a syntactic string without semantic content (or at least without empirical, semantic content). And what possible meaning could be attached to 'wide content' and 'Externalism' if an Everett–Squires one-mind interpretation of quantum mechanics is true? None. Functionalism and connectionism are false by definition if the many-perceptions interpretation or the Copenhagen interpretation of quantum mechanics is true, not to mention other interpretations that would imply the same. Functionalism and connectionism are formulated within a Newtonian theoretical framework. The notion of 'the supervenience of the mental on the physical' could not even be coherently formulated, let alone be true, if these or other (e.g. the many-minds or Everett–Squires one-mind interpretations) are true. On the so-called 'standard interpretation of quantum mechanics', the Copenhagen interpretation, the current theories of the physical supervenience basis would be literally a meaningless syntactic string without semantic content. According to the standard interpretation, it is meaningless to say that 'right now several billion humans have electrons travelling down the axons of their neurons'; to produce a syntactic string with semantic content, we need to say something such as 'there is an observation of an electron occupying a certain position', which would pertain only to the very few people whose pertinent neurons are currently being observed. Proceeding to another item, the coherency of the notion of 'narrow content' is no less endangered than the coherency of the notion of 'wide content'; for example, the notion of 'narrow content' would be a self-contradictory notion if a Bohm–Hiley interpretation of quantum mechanics is true (see Bohm and Hiley 1993: 386). Indeed, phase-entanglement (on most interpretations of quantum mechanics) would do away with 'narrow content' altogether. These sound like radical ideas, but they are less radical than they seem, for non-quantum cognitive sciences still serve useful functions.

The point is not that non-quantum cognitive sciences are without value (certainly an absurd suggestion); rather, I am trying to emphasize how much work needs to be done. The above-mentioned distinctions and debates that form the subject-matter of contemporary philosophical and scientific theories need to be *quantized*. However, if they still do not make realistic sense after being quantized and if, in addition, they are interpreted *non-instrumentally* (and *realistically*) then we have no choice but to 'cast them to the flames' (Hume). This is not an absurd suggestion. For we have the other option of developing an antirealist and instrumentalist interpretation of non-quantum cognitive sciences and this interpretation would have significant value and usefulness, just as Newtonism does in guiding rockets and most other large technological projects.

Alternatively, one could hope that one day quantum mechanics will be falsified, as tends to be the case with scientific theories (this hope would be a logically self-consistent position for a realist, non-quantum cognitive scientist to adopt). However there is no prospect of such a falsification in sight; the Vilenkin and Hartle–Hawking new quantum gravity theories, Penrose's twistor theory, the many different string or superstring theories, M-brane theories (e.g. Ed Witten's), etc., that are being developed incorporate quantum mechanical ideas.

1.4. *The Objection that Quantum Mechanics is Unnecessary for Predictive Success in Cognitive Science*

More objections to quantum cognitive science need to be answered before my above-stated theses can be adequately justified. I will here point out that the widely held (and true) claim that 'quantum mechanics is unnecessary for predictive success in cognitive science' is misused in the equally widespread but invalid inference from 'Non-quantum Predictive Success' to 'Non-quantum Reality'. Consider this argument:

(1) We can predict (approximately) the processes of neural networks, the occurrence of states of consciousness, behaviours of organisms, etc., using the assumption that neural nets, neurons, the brain, objects of external perception, as well as beliefs, desires, sensory qualia, etc. obey non-quantum laws of nature.
Therefore,

(2) The neural nets, sensory qualia, beliefs, etc. obey non-quantum physical laws, or non-quantum psychophysical laws, or non-quantum psychological laws.

This is invalid, since a theory T's approximate predictive success in some limited domain does not entail T's truth. Richard Grush and Patricia Churchland are two of the most severe critics of quantum cognitive science and quantum theories of the brain and they make this invalid inference; they think realistic neuroscience should be a non-quantum neuroscience since 'quantum-level effects are generally agreed to be washed out at the neuronal level' (Grush and Churchland 1998: 206). What this means is that the significant difference between a quantum behaviour and a non-quantum behaviour of entities does not *appear* at the neuronal level, and thus that a *description of the appearances, and predictions of future appearances*, need not mention QM (quantum mechanical) properties. The problem is that Grush and Churchland, like many other non-quantum cognitive scientists, bypass the next step their theory ought to take; they fail to realize that the non-quantum appearances are *deceptive appearances, that the neurons* (and consciousness) *appear to be something they really are not,* namely, non-quantum realities. And thus they are led to construct a theory of the mind–brain based on the misleading appearances, giving us at best an instrumentalist theory of the mind–brain that, if quantized, may give us some true propositions.

Put another way, how is it even possible that communications among neurons or mind–brain relations do not involve QM features such as collapses or pilot waves or splitting universes or many-minds or non-locality or the 'observations of eigenvalues', etc.? For example, to stay on the neural level, a neuron is governed by QM laws and its communication with other neurons is a QM communication. At best, the standard cognitive scientists can say: 'I can falsely describe neurons (and the associated conscious states) in non-quantum terms since I am making such vague, albeit useful, predictions that the falsity of my descriptions does not affect the approximate predicted answer for which I am looking.' But how is this different from using Ptolemy to describe the solar system? Ptolemy's theory has a significant degree of predictive success in a certain limited domain.

The problem is not confined to philosophers. For example, another manifestation of this invalid inference is present in the mathematician Alwyn C. Scott's (1998: 637) remark that 'there is no theoretical need for' quantum coherence in explaining the physical basis of conscious thought. 'We can't even construct Schrödinger's equation for a nerve impulse that is traveling along an axon. A nerve impulse is a *completely classical [non-quantum] phenomenon*'. Here the argument is:

(3) Humans lack the intelligence (intellectual complexity) to construct Schrödinger's equation for a nerve impulse.
    Therefore,
(4) The description of a nerve impulse in terms of Schrödinger's equation cannot be used in our theories of the movements of a nerve impulse.
    Therefore
(5) The nerve impulse is non-quantum in nature (and is instead completely classical).

This is invalid, since all that follows is that we do not use Schrödinger's equation to predict the future behaviour of what appears to us as nerve impulses, since it is too complex for us (not very intelligent *homo sapiens sapiens*) to construct QM equations for these impulses. Our predictive theories about nerve impulses do not include Schrödinger's equation. But it does not follow that the nerve impulse is a non-quantum entity obeying non-quantum Newtonian laws, non-quantum neurophysiological laws, etc. Predictive success in some limited domain does not entail truth. And our inability to construct a QM equation for a nerve impulse because the equation is too complex for our not very intelligent minds to construct does not in the least imply that the nerve impulse does not obey Schrödinger's equation. Indeed, it does obey Schrödinger's equation, and *every* real particle obeys it, regardless of whether or not we, with our limited mental abilities, can construct the relevant equation. Consciousness also obeys it, at least on such interpretations of QM as Lockwood's, Albert and Loewer's, Squires's, Page's, etc.

1.5. The Objection that Quantum Mechanics can be Interpreted Instrumentally, in which case Non-quantum Cognitive Science can be Realistic

Perhaps the non-quantum cognitive scientist can adopt the instrumentalist interpretation of quantum mechanics associated with the founders of the Copenhagen interpretation, such as Bohr. Instrumentalism about quantum mechanics is associated with the Copenhagen interpretation. But it is a mistake to think that this instrumentalist interpretation is consistent with holding that all reality is non-quantum in nature; or that it is consistent with dividing the universe into non-quantum (macroscopic) realities such as brains and quantum realities such as electrons. In fact, the Copenhagen interpretation holds that the macroscopic measuring instrument (including the brain of the observer) is, *in reality*, a quantum-mechanical system. Such an instrument is made up of quantum-mechanical entities and is itself such an entity; but that its quantum-mechanical nature can be bracketed (not described) for purposes of convenience and ease of description, since macroscopic systems appear similar enough to non-quantum entities that their quantum nature can be treated (for instrumentalist purposes) as if it were non-quantum (Bohr 1934: 85; 1945). On this interpretation, the laws of quantum mechanics imply that the macroscopic measuring instrument and the microscopic entity being measured themselves form a new, more complex quantum-mechanical reality (represented by another 'state vector in Hilbert space'), such that this macroscopic reality (the measuring instrument M) and the system S being measured constitute the quantum-mechanical reality represented $\Psi M + S$ (the state vector or wave function that represents a single quantum-mechanical state, one that can in turn be measured by another measuring instrument M'). In short, each microscopic or macroscopic subsystem of the universe, on the Copenhagen instrumentalist interpretation, is a measurable quantum-mechanical reality relative to some distinct macroscopic subsystem M' that is regarded instrumentally as a macroscopic instrument that measures a quantum system. 'The universe as a whole' is a meaningless expression on the instrumentalist interpretation (since nothing outside the universe can measure it), and there is no part of the universe that is not a quantum-mechanical reality. What's the catch? The catch is that the instrumentalist, antirealist interpretation of quantum mechanics (even if not of other theories) implies something about the nature of reality.

But the instrumentalist interpretation has even more drastic consequences for non-quantum cognitive science. On the instrumentalist interpretation, QM merely predicts certain perceptions (e.g. perceptions of point readings) and regards as meaningless sentences about an observation-independent reality. Thus, von Neumann talks of 'experimental propositions' to emphasize that meaningful talk is only about observations, and that it is meaningless to talk about whether propositions are (to quote Putnam's (1983: 255) apt summation) 'true or false in some realist sense when we aren't looking'. This antirealism entails subjective idealism, which is just as far from contemporary non-quantum cognitive science as any realist interpretation of quantum mechanics. Even the most elementary introductions to quantum mechanics note this point; for instance, Robert Pine (1989: 228) points out that this instrumentalism is in fact a version of metaphysical idealism: 'If an electron is not a thing until it is observed by [us, using] some instrument, does not this imply that reality depends on our observations and hence, ultimately, the thoughts we use to frame the world? Does this not imply that reality is created by human thought?'

Instrumentalism is the dominant belief among quantum physicists, except for those who are working out new interpretations of quantum mechanics, such as Gell-Mann and Hartle, Page, Albert and Loewer, Lockwood, Healey, Bohm and Hiley, Ghirardi, Rimini, and Weber. Instrumentalism is the view assumed in both undergraduate and graduate textbooks on quantum mechanics. But the emphasis is on QM enabling us merely to 'predict observations'; the 'metaphysical idealism' implied is 'left for philosophers to discuss'.

The reason for this instrumentalism is that the 'standard' or Copenhagen interpretation, if physically interpreted, seems logically incoherent. (But Wigner, Stapp, and other developers of this interpretation produce logically coherent non-instrumentalist versions of the Copenhagen interpretation, since they avowedly embrace a metaphysical view about the nature of reality, namely, that it is 'created by the human mind' in some technical sense.) Regarding the standard Copenhagen interpretation, the logical problem that results is that one would have to describe mind-independent reality in such sentences as: 'The electrons move from place x to place x' and P1 and P2 are the only paths from x to x'; the electrons do not take path P1 and they do not take path P2 and they do not take both of these paths and they do not take neither of these paths. However these four possibilities are all the conceivable possibilities or logical possibilities.' Richard Feynman reportedly replied to a question about why a graduate student in quantum physics dropped out of school and took up a non-intellectual vocation, by saying that the student made the mistake of trying to figure out what mind-independent reality must be like if quantum mechanics is true. Faced with such conundrums, most physicists agreed that it was not false, but 'meaningless' to talk about paths of electrons or any other mind-independent state of affairs; all we can talk about is the sensory observations or perceptual experiences we predict.

The consequence for cognitive science is that if talk about microscopic motions of particles, etc., is meaningless, then we cannot assert meaningfully that (or make true assertions that) there exist electrons travelling on paths among potassium and sodium ions in nerve cells and similar ontological claims essential to virtually all cognitive sciences today. Consciousness cannot supervene on brain states or any other physical states, and there cannot be physically realized functionalist or connectionist systems, since (given QM instrumentalism) such theses cannot have a truth value since they lack semantic content. The instrumentalist interpretation of QM leads ineluctably to a subjective idealism or phenomenalism, where all that exists are states of consciousness— 'experiences', 'observations', etc. Stapp, a physicist, captures the situation in a pithy manner: 'Thus the founders of quantum mechanics [who were instrumentalists] constructed the new physics as a theory of statistical correlations between *experiences*... The basic kinds of realities of the new physical science became... *experiences*' (Stapp 1998: 599, my emphasis). Compare this with Fodor's very widely accepted view that psychology, but not physics, is about *experiences*.

This indicates that non-quantum cognitive scientists cannot preserve their theories by adopting the standard instrumentalist interpretation of quantum mechanics. Virtually every single philosopher of mind or cognitive scientist today is a realist about the physical world; they believe stones, tables, and neural firings exist while they are not being looked at by somebody. They do not believe that neural firings are created by human consciousness and cease to exist when they are not being observed. The crucial point is that the instrumentalist interpretation of quantum mechanics does imply an ontology, by virtue of saying there are true statements about perceptual experiences but no meaningful statements about something that is not, in fact, being experienced. This is an ontology of subjective idealism or phenomenalism, or some other form of strong antirealism about the physical world.

Consequently, the contemporary, realist, non-quantum cognitive sciences cannot be held consistently with an instrumentalist interpretation of quantum mechanics. This should complete the trap for non-quantum cognitive science. Quantum mechanics is the most highly confirmed theory ever developed and it *implies* non-quantum cognitive science is false regardless of whether quantum mechanics is interpreted realistically or antirealistically.

1.6. Do Philosophers of Mind Need a Graduate Degree in Physics?

Philosophers ought not to give up work on non-quantum theories of the mind. Nor need they stop their work for ten years in order to learn quantum mechanics. The successful results of their non-quantum work will eventually be used as input to a 'quantizing box', which quantizes whatever of their results can be quantized, and the output of this box will be theories or theses in quantum cognitive science.

At present, one of the major reasons that non-quantum philosophers should keep working on the input side of the box is that the box quantizes the input in terms of some particular interpretation of quantum mechanics, and there are many different interpretations of quantum mechanics, with little prospect that one interpretation above others will be demonstrated to be the right one at any time in the near future. The input can be built up until the correct interpretation is determined, and then we can go to work into quantizing the input in terms of this correct interpretation, giving us a true (approximately true or highly confirmed) quantum cognitive science as the output. A change in behaviour or in research programmes is not being advocated in this chapter. Rather, merely a change in belief. Non-quantum philosophers of mind or cognitive scientists ought to realize that their theories, on pain of being evaluated as highly disconfirmed, must be interpreted anti-realistically and instrumentally.

2. Macroscopic Evidence for the Quantum Basis and the Quantum Nature of Consciousness

2.1. A New De Broglie/Bohm Quantum Consciousness Hypothesis

First, I will formulate, in outline form, a hypothesis about the nature of consciousness that I believe to have significant prior probability and to be testable. Second, I will argue that this hypothesis is significantly confirmed (but not to a degree greater than 0.5) by a series of experiments, the Nunn–Clarke–Blott experiments.

One goal of this section of the chapter is to show that the prevalent view that there is no macroscopic evidence for quantum consciousness is mistaken. A second goal is to sketch in outline form a new quantum cognitive science theory, one that is different from, but influenced by, David Bohm's interpretation of quantum mechanics and Roger Penrose's quantum cognitive science. The phenomenological theory of consciousness I use is presented in my earlier work (Smith 1986) and here I will use only some of its elementary ideas that can be generally expressed in the current jargon ('qualia', 'propositional attitudes', etc.)

Before I go into the physical aspect of the theory (the theory of the quantum functioning of the brain), I will present my ideas about the nature of consciousness that belong to the hypothesis h' I use to explain the macroscopic evidence.

I distinguish between acts (events or states) of being conscious ('intentional acts' in the Brentano tradition), which I divide into (a) sensings and propositional attitudes, and (b) the immediate contents of consciousness, which are phenomena with which I am immediately acquainted through my sensings and my propositional attitudes. Sensings are sensings of sensory qualia and propositional attitudes are attitudes to propositions (which I shall call 'thoughts' to emphasize that they are mental realities, not platonic realities). The folk-psychological interpretation of sensory qualia (e.g. as the pink surface of a cloud or as a pain in my toe) is a propositional attitude in which I grasp a singular or de re proposition (thought) that includes the sensory quale as a part, and includes the quale *qua* attributed to the property of being the pink surface of the cloud, such that the proposition (thought) is the singular thought or proposition

$<*, $ *being the pink surface of the cloud* $>$

where the asterisk, '*', is the sensory quale itself. The admittance of such singular propositions enables us to bypass the objection that some sensings of our qualia are non-propositional and merely involve applying a concept to the quale. Applying a concept to a quale is equivalent (on my account) to attributing a property to the quale, where the quale is the subject-constituent of the resultant singular proposition. The singular proposition,

$<*, $ *being a pain* $>$

is an example of such a proposition.

A corresponding QM interpretation would be the grasping of a thought such as

$<*, $ *having the amplitude n and phase n' in the such-and-such dimension of configuration space* $>$

For example, 'Pink clouds' are mere mental constructions produced by folk-psychological and folk-physical interpretations of the sensory qualia that exist in the mental dimensions of configuration space. The mental dimensions of configuration space neither are minds nor constitute a single 'Supermind' but instead are proper classes (in Menzel's (1986) sense) that include acts of consciousness, sensed qualia, thoughts, and possible (but unactualized) acts of consciousness, merely possible sensed qualia and merely possible thoughts. These possibilia are universals (properties or relations) that are 'not actualized' by a given human or minded-organism at a given time in the sense that the organism does not (at the time mentioned) instantiate the universal. This way of conceiving configuration space arguably carries the ontological commitment of a Tooleyian (1987) realism about universals, and a rejection of the Barcan (1946) formula and acceptance of a quantified modal logic, in the tradition stemming from Hintikka (1961), that implies that some possible worlds have domains including members that do not exist in the actual world.

A crucial part of my quantum consciousness hypothesis is the rejection of physical reductionism, since configuration space contains some physical dimensions and some non-reducible mental dimensions, such that conscious acts and the immediate contents of consciousness (qualia and thoughts) exist in the mental dimensions of configuration space.

Should we use the technical term 'configuration space'? Bohm and Hiley (1993) sometimes talk instead of 'information space' (but they conceive its mental dimensions differently, and also too ambiguously and vaguely to be usable in a testable hypothesis). The reason Bohm and Hiley use 'information space' is that many physicists use 'configuration space' to refer either to an abstract mathematical object (containing only numbers or classes) or else to a certain type of wholly physical reality.[1] But I shall use 'configuration space' since I wish to make the argumentative point that some physicists' narrower or different conception of configuration space should be reconceived in the way I am conceiving it.

The acts or states of being conscious (or, more strictly and technically, what I called 'feeling-awarenesses' (Smith 1986)) are *wave-forms* whose metaphorical 'flowing through configuration space' is literally a temporal succession of states of being conscious. The contents of consciousness (sensory qualia and thoughts) are the existents that are directed by the wave-forms. What does this mean? The wave (by virtue of its form) pilots or guides the existents, and thus is often called by quantum physicists 'the pilot wave' of the existent it is directing. In fact, the de Broglie–Bohm interpretation of quantum mechanics is often called 'the pilot wave theory'; see Valentini (1992; 1996) for a history-based justification of this name for the interpretation. *Wave-forms*, and the *directing* relation are basic ontological notions in Bohm and Hiley (1993) that I am borrowing and developing to apply to the mental dimensions of configuration space. Intentionality, I want to say, or 'intentional directedness' as Brentano, Husserl, etc. call it, is a *forming* of the immediate

[1] In Smith and Craig (1993) and in Smith (1997*a*) I said configuration space is an abstract mathematical object and concrete reality consists of what corresponds to certain trajectories in configuration space. But this was in the context of developing an interpretation of the Hartle–Hawking theory of quantum gravity. To correlate the terminology in my essays on the Hartle–Hawking theory with the present essay, I would say that there is an *abstract mathematical representation* (1993: 307) of the concretely real configuration space (and its occupants) I am discussing in the present chapter. In my essays on the Hartle–Hawking theory I used the phrase 'configuration space' to refer to this abstract mathematical representation of concrete reality.

contents of consciousness in such a way as to make them appearances of a humanly constructed 'objective world' (the constructed commonsense 'physical world' in case of perception and, in the case of abstract thinking, the constructed 'non-physical world' of numbers, truths, and the like). This objective world is a human construction, and it is constructed out of folk-psychological and folk-physical concepts that are applied to our sensory qualia. This constructed objective world, which we instinctively interpret our sensory qualia and propositions to be appearances of,[2] is in fact not a mind-independent world but a mental construction and it exists in the mental dimensions of configuration space. Reality, i.e. configuration space and its occupants, is *not* what we interpret our sensory qualia to be appearances of. And the propositional thoughts we immediately grasp (in commonsense thinking) are not propositions about the amplitudes and phases of the field wave in configuration space. Rather, our sensory qualia are interpreted to be appearances of an 'objective folk-physical world' that is supposed to be a mind-independent physical reality, but in fact it is not real but a mere folk-psychological and folk-physical construction. Reality is configuration space and its occupants, and it contains as parts our conscious acts, our sensory qualia and propositional thoughts; the constructed objective world does not exist except in the sense that the illusion of this 'objective folk-physical world' exists. The sense in which *the illusion* of the objective folk-physical world exists is the sense in which our folk-psychological and folk-physical thoughts, and sensory qualia, exist. The existence of an illusion is the existence of certain thoughts and qualia and these thoughts and qualia exist as occupants of the mental dimensions of configuration space.

---

[2] Something x *mediately* appears to us in a propositional thought p that is said to be about x, such that the proposition p *immediately* appears to us and x *mediately* appears to us via the immediately appearing proposition. See Smith (1986) for this distinction between immediate and mediate appearances. Since 'the objective folk world' is an illusion, our folk propositional thoughts are not mediate, accurate appearances *of* anything at all; rather, they are mistakenly believed in our everyday life to be mediate, *accurate* appearances *of* something. For this reason, our normal folk thoughts are typically false. None the less, these false thoughts are either useful or not useful for survival and reproduction and, in addition, they are the means by which Reality (configuration space, the pilot wave of the universe, and the universe) mediately and inaccurately appears to us. None the less, some philosophical or scientific thoughts about the quantum world are accurate, mediate appearances of Reality. Our most accurate immediate grasp of Reality is our temporal consciousness of what may be called The Presence, where The Presence is the universe that is constantly being guided through configuration space by the pilot wave of the universe. See Smith (2002b) for a non-scientific and purely philosophical discussion of The Presence. This allows us to make statements about the nature of philosophical contemplation such as: One can remain alone in one's study all one's life and still grasp Reality to the maximally humanly possible degree, merely (1) by grasping philosophical or scientific mediate appearances of the quantum mechanical world and (2) grasping immediate appearances of The Presence, The Presence that is constantly seeping through one's study, much as the light in Jan Vermeer's paintings is semiternally shining through his windows.

Configuration space (or, more simply, Reality) includes many dimensions, such as position, momentum, energy, and spin dimensions, but also many dimensions containing the different possible kinds of conscious acts (propositional attitudes and sensings) and conscious contents (sensory qualia and propositions). For example, a suitable reformulation of the Munsell colour tree and Land's colour solid (see Paul Churchland 1985; 1986; Lockwood 1989) would enable us to add to configuration space at least three dimensions of hue, luminance, and saturation (Munsell). Each possible hue, luminance, and saturation in the visual qualia dimensions of configuration space occupies a point in configuration space. As unactualized possibilities, these points and hues, etc. should be understood as abstract entities (unexemplified properties), but when they are actualized by a wave-form, they become concrete mental existents. (This is a major difference from Everett-type views, such as Page's, Lockwood's, and Albert and Loewer's, where each possibility is actualized.)

Speaking in general terms, my hypothesis is that the pilot wave of my consciousness directs my consciousness through configuration space in the sense of actualizing these possibilities; e.g. a possible hue becomes an actual content of my visual awareness by virtue of being actualized by a mental wave-form, in particular, an intentional act. More exactly, as we shall see below, it is the more complex wave-form produced by the entanglement of my brain's pilot wave with the pilot wave of my consciousness that simultaneously actualizes the sensory quale and a set of nerve cell firings. De Broglie–Bohm quantum mechanics requires absolute simultaneity and we can say that our temporal sense of the 'continuing presentness of everything' is our experience of the pilot wave of the universe's enduring in absolute time as it 'flows' through configuration space. The vague sense of an all-encompassing and enduring temporal presence is perhaps the nearest our instinctive folk-physical and folk-psychological interpretations allow us to get to a perceptual grasp of Reality. On the de Broglie–Bohm interpretation, there is only one wave-field, the pilot wave of the universe, and the pilot wave of my consciousness and the pilot wave of my brain are inseparable parts of the pilot wave of the universe that can be considered only in abstraction from the other parts of the universe's pilot wave. Although Durr, Goldstein, and Zanghi (1996) develop a version of the de Broglie–Bohm interpretation different than mine, I agree with them when they write:

Which systems should be governed by Bohmian mechanics? The systems which we normally consider are subsystems of a larger system—for example, the universe—whose behaviour (the behaviour of the whole) determines the behaviour of its subsystems (the behaviour of the parts). Thus for a Bohmian universe, it is only the universe itself which a priori [sic]—i.e., without further analysis, can be said to be governed by Bohmian mechanics.... Fix an initial wavefunction Ψ_0 of this universe.

Then since the Bohmian evolution is completely deterministic, once the initial configuration Q of this universe is also specified, all future events, including of course the results of measurements, are determined.   (Durr et al. 1996: 37)

The 'universe' here is of course not the universe of folk physics or Newtonian or Einsteinian classical mechanics; it exists in a de Broglie–Bohm configuration space. The phrase 'a priori—i.e., without further analysis' in the quoted passage is best replaced by 'without being considered in abstraction as a subsystem'.

How does this quantum consciousness hypothesis I am outlining relate to the quantum mechanics of physical reality, specifically to physical subsystems of the universe, e.g. particles? A physical particle is not mechanically caused to move by a pilot wave, but is instantaneously directed from a distance by the form of the particle's pilot wave. The wave-form directs the particle by instantaneously imparting to it a form, a form similar to the wave-form itself. A non-quantum or classical wave, by contrast, acts mechanically (transfers energy or momentum to push an object, for example) and produces effects that are proportional to the intensity of the wave. But the quantum wave is different. It has a 'quantum potential', which depends on the form of the wave and not on its strength or intensity (Bohm and Hiley 1993: 31). Instead of giving their equation, I will give an intuitive example they provide.

For example we may consider a ship on automatic pilot being guided by radio waves. Here, too, the effect of the radio waves is independent of their intensity and depends only on their form. The essential point is that this ship is moving with its own energy, and that the *form* of the radio wave is taken up to *direct* the much greater energy of the ship. We may therefore propose that an electron too moves under its own energy, and that the *form* of the quantum wave *directs* the energy of the electron.   (ibid. 31-2)

Thus in the example of the ship guided by the radio waves, one may say that these waves carry information about what is in the environment of the ship and that this information enters into the movements of the ship through its being taken up in the mechanism of the automatic pilot. Similarly we explain the interference properties by saying that the quantum field contains information, for example about the slits, and that this information is taken up in the movements of the particle. In effect we have in this way introduced a concept that is new in the context of physics—a concept that we shall call *active information*. The basic idea of active information is that a form having very little energy enters into and directs a much greater energy. The activity of the latter is in this way given a form similar to that of the smaller energy.... What is crucial here is that we are calling attention to the literal meaning of the word, to in-form, which is actively to put form into something or to imbue something with form.   (ibid. 35)

The fact that the particle is moving under its own energy, but being guided by the information in the quantum field [the wave-form], suggests that an electron or any other elementary particle has a complex and subtle inner structure (e.g. perhaps even comparable to a radio).   (ibid. 37)

Since the wave-form of the electron's pilot wave has this sort of non-mechanical, non-contactive, instantaneous, in-forming relation to the electron, we see that the 'physical' and 'mental' may be much closer together than they are in non-quantum physics.

Conscious acts do not direct or in-form across spatial distances, but actively inform sensory qualia by interpreting them in terms of the conceptual forms, the concepts, that are parts of propositional thoughts. For example, a sensory pinkness is in-formed (ascribed the property) of being the pink surface of a cloud by the conscious act of interpreting the sensory quale as this surface. The interpretation is the propositional attitude, in this case a perceptual judgement that ascribes to the quale the property of being a pink surface of the cloud. The act of perceptually judging (the conscious act that is the wave-form) in-forms the sensory quale by ascribing this property to it. Bohm and Hiley (1993: ch. 15) have a theory of the mental dimensions of configuration space, but it is not based on a sufficiently precise phenomenological theory of consciousness (see Smith 1986), and thus I follow them in principle here but not in details (they don't have details).

The basic, unique relation in the Bohm–Hiley theory is actively in-forming, which is a wave-form imparting a form to an existent, and by means of this in-forming relation instantaneously and non-contactively directs the existent that the wave-form is piloting. They take this as a primitive notion, but I analyse it into more basic notions: I define active in-forming as *an act*, either an act of consciousness or of a quantum potential, instantaneously, and without physical contact, of *ascribing a property or relation* to an existent (or bringing about the *instantiation* of a property or relation in the existent). This, among other things, is what is common to 'mind' and 'matter'. There is the question of how the same mathematics apply to both. For example, how can conscious acts be numerically described in terms of Schrödinger's wave equation and the guidance condition (the quantum potential, or with de Broglie, Bell, Valentini and others, a trajectory equation without the quantum potential), which pertains to a generalized gradient of the phase of the wave? I respond that Schrödinger's equation has already been applied to conscious experiences or conscious observations, in various ways, by Page, Lockwood, Albert and Loewer, Squires, Stapp, Wigner, and in effect by Bohr himself. Indeed, are not 'observations' precisely the subject-matter of the 'standard' or Copenhagen interpretation physicists have adopted since the late 1920s?

The mindlikeness of 'matter' (already mentioned), and the matterlikeness of 'mind' (existing in and obeying the quantum mechanical rules of configuration space) suggests a new way to outline the mind–brain relation, a way not recognized by Bohm and Hiley in their discussions of consciousness. My suggestion is that the pilot wave of the brain is phase-entangled with the pilot wave of consciousness in such a way that the new, combined, more complex wave-form simultaneity directs both the correlated neural firings and the contents of consciousness. There is no causal interaction between the mind and brain (interactionism and epiphenomenalism are thus ruled out), but there is a wave-form non-contactively and simultaneously in-forming both the mental contents and the neural firings, so parallelism (where there is no influence between the two) are ruled out. Further supervenience and emergentism are ruled out, since the mental does not supervene upon the physical but instead is directed simultaneously with the physical by the entangled pilot waves of both the mental and physical, such that they have equal status (i.e. one does not supervene upon the other). Further, there is no eliminative or reductive materialism, for the mind both exists and is neither reducible to nor identical with the physical. If we want a name for this theory of consciousness, we may call it 'the wave-entanglement theory of consciousness' and the new mind–brain relation it implies is an entangled wave-form simultaneously in-forming both the mental contents and the brain processes. For example, the entangled wave-form simultaneously, instantaneously, and without physical contact, in-forms pinkness (by ascribing to it the property of being the sensory surface of the sensed cloud that is present in my visual field) and in-forms the spiking frequencies in area V4 of the cortical system (by ascribing to them the properties and relations constitutive of a 95Hz/80Hz/80Hz/chord).

The pink surface of the sensory cloud in my visual field is a part of my commonsense constructed 'objective physical world'. On the view I am proposing, the sensory cloud neither is, nor represents, nor is caused by, a material thing in an 'objective physical world' composed of distinct material things. Very roughly and only in part, we have something like Sellars's 'manifest image/scientific image' distinction, or, even more roughly, Eddington's 'two tables' theory of the sensory field of consciousness and the physical field of scientific entities. But their theories are only distantly approximated, since their theories must be drastically altered to conform to both de Broglie-Bohm quantum mechanics and the wave-entanglement theory of consciousness where, for example, the relation between the physical scientific world and the sensory field of consciousness is not a causal or one-to-one representative relation but is instead a simultaneous, mutually in-forming relation based on the entanglement of the wave-forms of physical events and conscious acts. The pink cloud I am visually sensing exists, but it exists only as a part of some mental dimensions of configuration space and it may be said to be an 'illusion' inasmuch as I misinterpret what I am sensing to be a separable, non-abstracted, physical thing that is a part of a mind-independent objective physical world. What I am misinterpreting would be correctly interpreted as an inseparable abstraction from the one and only system, the universe, that occupies configuration space. The sensory pink cloud that is present in my visual field is in reality a mind-dependent construction based on folk-physical concepts. The sensory pink cloud occupies certain mental-content dimensions in configuration space, and occupies them only while I am mentally constructing it. On the view I am proposing, the commonsense (commonly sensed) 'objective physical world of separate things' is an illusion that we learned to perceive after the decline of the animistic world-interpretation and the infiltration of the Galilean and Newtonian mechanical world-view into commonsense beliefs. But just as humans learned how to perceptually reinterpret the world, from the animistic world-view to the sixteenth- and seventeenth-century mechanical world-view of separate, causally contactive things, they can relearn to perceive a de Broglie–Bohm world that includes entangled wave-forms that consciously construct the illusion of the commonsense mechanical world. If we accomplished this relearning, what would we perceive? What would really exist? If my version of the de Broglie–Bohm interpretation is correct, what really exists is *configuration space*, the *universe* that occupies configuration space, and the *universal pilot wave* that directs the universe. Since configuration space includes mental dimensions, the constructed illusions that everyday common sense takes to be 'separate parts of the objective, mind-independent physical world' also exist in configuration space; if there are illusions, then illusions exist, and these existents are in reality inseparable and abstracted parts of the universe that is directed by the universal pilot wave. These illusions neither represent nor are caused by separate mechanical parts of a physical world. Rather, they are delusive ways of appearing of certain inseparable abstractions of an existent that is neither a subsystem nor an abstraction, namely, *the universe*, the complete system that is piloted through configuration space by the pilot wave of the universe. The specific kinds of illusions that we are piloted or directed to perceive or think about in commonsense thinking are the kinds of illusions that are in large part sufficient to enable the abstracted subsystem, the human species, to survive and reproduce in the complete system, the universe. If each apparently separate thing is really an inseparable abstraction from the one thing that is not itself an abstraction, the universe, this is too definite to be known through a mystical experience but requires mathematical knowledge of the wave function of the universe and the associated guidance equation.

My goal here is not to present a theory of consciousness or an ontology, which would require at least a book, but to sketch a theory whose detailed working-out could be used to 'quantize' everything, i.e. not only non-quantum cognitive sciences, but all non-quantum theories and our folk physics and folk psychology. This sketch furthers the de Broglie–Bohm programme, since it provides a more precise, fleshed-out, and detailed theory of consciousness than that provided by Bohm and Hiley (1993). It should be added that Don Page (1996) outlines a de Broglie–Bohm theory of consciousness, which is also more precise than Bohm and Hiley's, but it is different than the one I present here; Page's outline is in part modelled on his 'sensible quantum mechanics'. One possible task in developing the phase-entanglement theory of consciousness I have outlined here is to compare it with Page's articulation of a 'Bohmian sensible quantum mechanics' and to explain the considerations that show one or the other of the two theories to be more justified. Page is not a Bohmian (he belongs to the Everett tradition) and in his (1996) his goal is to explain how his own 'sensible quantum mechanics' can be reformulated as a Bohmian sensible quantum mechanics.

The theory I am proposing consists of more than just the sketch I have offered here. A theory of the objects of singular and general propositional attitudes, namely singular propositions and general propositions, is developed in Smith (1993b) (see Nerlich (1998) for a clear summary and interesting critique). In addition, a phenomenology of *consciousness* (intentional conscious acts are argued to be feeling-awarenesses in an expanded sense of 'feeling') and a phenomenology of the various kinds of *contents* of consciousness (every content is argued to be either a feeling-sensation, a feeling-tonality, and/or a way of being important in an expanded sense of 'important') is developed in Smith (1986). The major, remaining task is to integrate these ideas into a version of the de Broglie–Bohm interpretation of quantum mechanics and to argue that this interpretation, in my version, is preferable to other interpretations of quantum mechanics. Some further ideas for a de Broglie-Bohm theory of consciousness and the brain will emerge in the next section as I explain the Nunn–Clarke–Blott experiments.

2.2. A Quantum-Brain Hypothesis

We recall that part of the aim of the second half of this essay is to discuss $p(h/e)$, that is, the probability of a quantum cognitive science being true given only some macroscopic evidence e, evidence of a general sort that is often used by non-quantum cognitive scientists in justifying their theories. Given the scarcity of such macroscopic evidence for quantum cognitive science, and the fact that the main evidence for quantum mechanics is $k = $ *the background knowledge of the evidence for the universal scope of quantum mechanics in general*, we should expect that $p(h/e)$ is not only much lower than $p(h/e \& k)$ but also much lower than $p(h/k)$. None the less, $p(h/e \& k)$ is higher than $p(h/k)$. Philosophers seem unaware that there is any macroscopic quantum mechanical evidence e, even though scientists who are interested in quantum cognitive science frequently refer to this evidence e as partial support for their theories. Accordingly, I aim to explain to philosophers of mind and philosophical cognitive scientists the quantum mechanical nature of this evidence e, and I aim to explain to quantum scientists a new way to interpret this evidence that is preferable to the other interpretations that are currently being discussed in the scientific literature. I must emphasize, however, that this evidence *e* is weak, since no one has attempted to replicate the experiment apart from the original experimenters themselves (Nunn, Clarke, and Blott 1994; 1996), and there has been only silence from non-quantum cognitive scientists about whether the experiments admit of a non-quantum interpretation. The original, pilot experiment and the replications are reported in the 1994 paper, of which the 1996 paper is a non-technical summary.

A specific aim of the Nunn, Clarke, and Blott (1994; 1996) experiments is to confirm or disconfirm whether increasing the gravitational force of a brain state (specifically, a state dependent on different ion shifts across cell membranes) can affect brain activity associated with consciousness. The quantum cognitive science hypothesis I am putting forward implies that a brain area involved in a conscious decision-making task should be altered by the electroencephalographic (EEG) activity of an EEG instrument. The EEG activities, the pen positions, record an activity from the relevant brain area. I claim that by increasing the gravitational field of that brain area, the brain activity should increase and the conscious decision-making should be more accurate or be more rapid. Of course, there would be no point in discussing the Nunn–Clarke–Blott experiments unless they confirmed the hypothesis I am advancing, so I can note at the outset that their experiments show that increased gravity alters brain activity in a way that is explicable (I argue) only by quantum cognitive science. Nunn, Clarke, and Blott (1994: 127) write:

taking an EEG from the area [of the brain] should modify the gravitational prerequisite for [effective] collapse, so affecting task performance. There are no non-quantum theories which could lead one to expect that taking an EEG could directly affect task performance by subjects. The results of both pilot and main experiments indicated that task performance was indeed influenced by taking an EEG from relevant brain areas. Control experiments suggest that the influence was quantum mechanical in origin.

Nunn–Clarke–Blott do not assume a de Broglie–Bohm interpretation of quantum mechanics, so they do not talk about 'effective collapses'; I am inserting the word 'effective' in the relevant passages. Collapses are merely 'effective' (can be treated as real collapses for predictive purposes) on the de Broglie-Bohm interpretation. Nunn, Clarke, and Blott (1994) assume a quantum cognitive science hypothesis proposed by Penrose (1989), which they believe is the only quantum cognitive science hypothesis that can explain the experiments. But I will show shortly that Penrose's quantum cognitive science is in principle flawed and should be replaced by a unique version of de Broglie-Bohm quantum cognitive science. My explanation of the experiments begins by noting the fact that the superposition of EEG pen positions is significant since the pens are *heavy* relative to the ions shifting across nerve cell membranes. Given the general background knowledge k of the evidence for quantum mechanics, we know there will be a *phase entanglement* between the pen positions and the measured brain regions; by means of this phase entanglement, I predict, the pen positions will *gravitationally* influence the brain regions with which they are correlated. Since there is no complete or widely agreed upon approach to quantum gravity theory, I will use only the most elemental notions about quantum gravity, specifically, the notion of a graviton that arises when we apply quantum field theory to gravity. A graviton is the smallest unit in quantum gravity theory and is roughly 'the smallest allowable force of gravity', which is defined in terms of Planck scales. The mathematics need not be rehearsed here. I predict that the effective collapse of a wave field occurs when there is a difference of one graviton or more between the alternatives in a superposition. The 'collapse due to a one-graviton difference' is a notion common to several scientists in the field of quantum gravity theory. For example, Penrose (1989) and others used this 'one-gravition criterion' as a part of their various, different quantum gravity theories. But now we are applying this criterion to develop a testable prediction about the brain and consciousness. The prediction is that the effective collapse criterion (namely, when there is a difference of one graviton or more between the alternatives in a superposition) will be exceeded sooner than usual in the measured brain regions, with consequences for the speed or accuracy of the consciously performed button pressing. Subjects whose EEG measurements are made from the relevant, active part of the brain, the right motor cortex, should have quicker or more accurate results on the button-pushing tasks. This is because the correlated EEG pen position will increase (at least) the gravitational field of the various, alternative *temporally initial parts* of the entire process in a nerve cell, and these parts are the elements that are in superposition. Superpositions of tubulin states or complete states of a nerve cell belong to Hammeroff's and Penrose's different hypotheses, which I shall criticize below. The gravitational increase will induce the temporally initial parts in superposition effectively to collapse onto one alternative or the other, allowing the 'chosen' alternative to evolve into part of an entire brain state that is accompanied by a decision to push (or not push) the button. (My hypothesis about 'the superposed initial phases of neural states' will be clarified below.) These predictions are confirmed by the Nunn–Clarke–Blott experiments. (Confirmation is not in general symmetrical to explanation, but in this particular case there is symmetry.) The pilot experiment was to involve the left side of the brain in a task; subjects press a button with their right thumb when 2, 5, or 8 appears in a series of numbers (0–9) flashed at random on the screen. The right brain was kept busy by playing music to the left ear only. A total of 28 subjects were used in the experiment. EEGs were taken in random sequence from the left or right sides of the brain. There were fewer misses when the EEG was taken from the right motor cortex (which was responsible for task performance) but more misses when it was taken from other areas on the right. My hypothesis is that the EEG pen positions increase the neural activity in the right motor cortex—increase the rate of effective collapses of the superposed initial temporal parts of possible neural processes. The initial temporal parts in superposition effectively collapse onto just one alternative, increasing the decision-making activity (e.g. the evolution of the process of certain nerve signals being transmitted down axons) and this alternative evolves into a part of a macroscopic brain state that underlies a conscious decision.

The experiments showed that the miss/non-miss proportions were significant only when the EEG frequencies were set at the EEG alpha rhythm (alpha activity is traditionally associated with changes in awareness). There were no effects in the 35–45 Hz range, suggesting that the 40 Hz activity important to perception is relevant to unconscious functions only (cf. Baringa 1990).

Non-quantum theories are ultimately physically based on the ontology of Einstein's General Theory of Relativity (Newtonism is disconfirmed and thus can only be used instrumentally at speeds that are slow compared to the velocity of light). There is a reason why an Einsteinian-based theory cannot explain this experiment, although this is not mentioned by Nunn–Clarke–Blott. According to the General Theory of Relativity, where *gravity = curvature of spacetime*, the curvature increase in the relevant brain parts, due to the pen's relations to the brain region, is much too small or insignificant to cause the observed alterations in the brain states. A much more massive body than a pen or pen tip would be needed to induce a suitably high degree of curvature in the brain regions where the recorded activities take place.

An even more basic reason why non-quantum theories cannot explain these results is that a significant increase in curvature would *reduce* (due to the effects of the curvature) the activity of the ions and electrons involved in nerve signalling, e.g. movements of ions and electrons would be slowed down relative to the reference frames of the pen positions and the buttons the subject presses. This conflicts with the recorded evidence, namely, that there is an *increase* in the activities of ions and electrons in the measured brain area, relative to the reference frames of the buttons and pen positions. This sheds further doubt on the possibility of providing a non-quantum cognitive science explanation of these experiments. Further, we have a reason given by Nunn–Clark–Blott: that there is no known or conceivable non-quantum cognitive science that leads to the predictions that are confirmed in the experiments.

There are additional, but similar, data that can be explained by my quantum cognitive science proposal. A second and more sophisticated experiment by Nunn, Clarke, and Blott (1994: 130) involving forty-two subjects showed similar results.

In our second experiment...we conducted control observations which showed that the experimental effect did not depend on programming errors or any electrical or acoustical feedback to the subjects, while the fact that the experiment was fully automated eliminated any possibility that the experimenter might have influenced the subject's performance. The over-all probability that these findings may be due to chance is around 1 in 500, small enough to be very suggestive but not conclusive.

Further experiments were done whose details I shall not recount, leading to Nunn, Clarke, and Blott's (ibid. 139) conclusion: 'In the absence of any alternative [non-quantum] explanation of the results, we are left with the conclusion that a quantum-mechanical effect was observed during these experiments and that it depended on the ability of the EEG pens to move.'

One problem with some of Nunn–Clarke–Blott's theoretical interpretations of their own results is that they used Penrose's (1989) ideas about quantum cognitive science. However, Penrose (1994: 355) correctly came to reject his 1989 theory since his assumption that the elements in superposition, an entire nerve cell that simultaneously exists in two spatially separated states, one of these states being a state of firing and a second state being a state of not firing, are too large to be consistent with the conjunction of the observational evidence and background knowledge about quantum theory. A nerve cell superposed in two spatially distant states, one of firing and one of not firing, are macroscopic entities (ibid.). Penrose does not elaborate upon his reasons for rejecting the 1989 theory, but I think there are several reasons. First, it ill comports with observation: we can observe nerve cells and we do not observe their states to be superposed; Penrose's realist interpretation of quantum mechanics requires the superposition of nerve cell states to be observable.

I agree that this theory should be rejected, but I do not think Penrose's (1994) solution is required, which is to identify the superposed elements as tubulin states in the microtubular filaments in nerve cells. The study of tubulins is most closely associated with Hammeroff and so this new theory is known as the Hammeroff–Penrose theory (1996). There is a widely pursued Marshall (1989) programme in quantum cognitive science, namely, to develop the idea that coherent quantum states (Bose–Einstein condensates) are involved in brain activity and perhaps even underlie, synchronize, or determine in some way the firings of nerve cells, but this added assumption makes the theory have less prior probability among competing quantum cognitive sciences. Why? Because now two independent theses, each controversial by themselves, need to be confirmed for the quantum cognitive science to be confirmed. First, we need to confirm that (real or effective) collapses of superpositions of brain parts underlie conscious states, and, second, we need to confirm the idea that tubulin states (rather than nerve cell firings) are the primary brain events underlying conscious awareness, in face of the massive data that nerve cell firings are the primary brain events underlying conscious awareness.

Thus, I suggest that we retain the standard idea that nerve cell firings are the basic physical processes associated with the occurrence of conscious experiences. States of entire nerve cells are too large to be in superposition (for the reasons given above), but I suggest that we now identify the superposed entities with spatial, neural parts that exist during the temporally initial slices of a nerve cell firing or not firing. Specifically, the superposed elements are the different possible states of the initial movements of the electrons in certain potassium ions, the ions that begin to be released through a potassium pump when neurotransmitters attach to synaptic clefts. If we identify the superposed components with positions of electrons, then the 'anti-quantum-cognitive-science arguments' I endeavoured to counter in section 1 can effectively be silenced, for even the severest critics would not deny that electrons are governed by quantum mechanical laws.

The next step is to replace Penrose's 'real' or 'objective' collapse or 'objective reduction' interpretation of quantum mechanics with the 'effective collapse' postulated by the de Broglie–Bohm interpretation. On a de Broglie–Bohm theory, there is no collapse of a wave field. But there is a 'measurement-like' interaction that 'effectively' (the standard technical term) appears partly similar to a collapse and can be treated like a real collapse (for instrumentalist or conveniently 'effective' predictive purposes) and this is technically called an 'effective collapse'. Collapse is, intuitively, when a wave field that is about to undergo a change, with several different possible outcomes of the change, each with a certain probability, collapses onto just one of the possible outcomes, making it the only actual outcome (so it has probability one). Bohm and Hiley's idea is that there are wave packets that are real, existent 'channels', intuitively, possible paths a particle may take, in the case of particle motion. In transition periods, of which a measurement-like interaction is one type, 'each of the possibilities [possible paths] ... constitutes a kind of a channel ... such that the apparatus particles initially on trajectories leading to one side of these points enter, for example, the mth channel, while others do not' (Bohm and Hiley 1993: 99). This unstable period ends quickly and the apparatus enters just one channel and the others are empty. (See also ibid. 257 and chs. 5 and 6.) Callender and Weingard (1996: 26) sum things up in the most pithy manner: 'Bohmian measurement theory then guarantees that when the wave function of a system evolves into a superposition of macroscopically distinct states, the particles will always be forced into one component of the superposition ["one channel"] or the other.' I think I would slightly rephrase this: when the quantum field wave (described by the mathematical wave function) evolves into a superposition of *microscopically* distinct states, then any further evolution into a superposition of *macroscopically* distinct states is always *prevented* by the particles being directed into one component (channel) of the superposition. One respect in which the collapse is effective rather than real is that the other components in the superposition remain in existence, even if empty. Aharonov and Vaidman (1996) offered experimental evidence for the continued existence of these empty channels.

How do the subjects' decision-making conscious experiences arise through such active in-forming relations? My hypothesis is: Some spatial parts of a nerve cell, parts that occur during the initial temporal parts of the cell's firing or not firing, are in an effective superposition, and when the difference in gravitational strength, the difference in the gravitational field (g1–g2) between the elements in the superposition reach the one-graviton threshold, there is an effective collapse and the nerve cell fires or does not fire. When such an effective collapse occurs in the requisite number of superposed subneural states, which stand in the requisite synchronization or order, then a conscious state occurs. The complex wave-form that directs the relevant, large aggregate of firing (or not firing) neurons is not only an entanglement of the many wave-forms of these neurons, but is also entangled with the wave-form of consciousness. In this case, the wave-form of consciousness is (identically) a decision-making propositional attitude or intentional act whose intentional content is the decision. This more complex, entangled, wave-form *simultaneously* directs the neuronal firings and directs (by actualizing) certain conscious contents, namely, certain sensory qualia and the decision, which is the propositional thought *press the button*. Is this really a proposition? As I earlier mentioned, it is usually thought that we consciously have non-propositional acts of consciousness. My theory can accommodate them in part by taking into account the illocutionary force of certain singular propositions, e.g. <B, Press!>, which may be understood as a singular proposition that includes the button B as the target of what is mentally commanded.

Note that the absolute simultaneity of the various in-formings performed by the wave-form, an anti-Einsteinian absolute simultaneity, is not something I am 'adding on' to the de Broglie–Bohm interpretation of quantum mechanics, but is entailed by it. If the de Broglie–Bohm interpretation is true, Einstein's Special Theory of Relativity is false and some neo-Lorentz theory is true (e.g. see Craig 2000).

There are more details about the experiments that make more plain the observable quantum gravity features. One graviton is the smallest unit allowed in (the proposed) quantum gravitational field theory. Based on some mathematical results by Abhay Ashekar, Penrose (1989) suggests the one-graviton criterion is reached at about one-hundredth of the Planck mass

$m_p = 10^{-5}$ grams (1/100,000 of a gram). The graviton level threshold would be reached at one ten-millionth of a gram. This estimate is partly speculative, and other estimates have been made, but we do not need the exact figure for the experiment, due to the great numerical differences that will appear and swamp any difference in the various estimates.

By measuring the EEG activity of the right motor cortex, which governs task performance, the superpositions of its nerve signal states are induced to effectively collapse sooner. In each pertinent superposition in the right motor cortex, the gravitational difference field (g1–g2) reaches the one-graviton threshold due to the increase in gravity from the massive EEG pen. The resulting nerve signals then evolve and lead to a brain state that is associated (via phase entanglement) with the conscious experience of perceiving the number flashed in the experiment and, later, to a brain state that is associated with deciding to press or not press the button. Since the measured subject will have more time and more brain activity involved in the button-pressing decision, she will be more likely to be accurate. The test results show this increased accuracy in the subjects' performance.

We can see now why the speculative hypotheses about the exact numerical figure of the graviton criterion or the gravitational difference field do not affect the result or implications of the experiments. The EEG is attached to the decision-making part of the brain, such that there is a phase entanglement of the effective wave for the decision-making part of the brain with the effective wave of the EEG pen-tip positions. This implies that if one of these effective waves undergoes an effective collapse the other undergoes an instantaneous effective collapse. The EEG pen mass of at least 4g undergoes an excursion through 0.5cm at its tip; the dipole moment change of at least 0.5g.cm is associated with this change in the EEG pen. This figure is considerably larger than the dipole moment of the brain region required for an effective collapse and the occurrence of the conscious decision when it is not connected to the EEG. Assume a 1 per cent w/w concentration of sodium ions in the intercellular fluid. Assume also a shift of the centre of gravity of these sodium ions (at the decision-making event), in relation to potassium ions, amounting to 10 per cent of their concentration with a length-scale of 0.5cm, maintained homogeneously over a volume of 50 ml. The resulting dipole moment is 5×10^{-2} g.cm. Obviously 5×10^{-2} g.cm (the figure without an EEG attachment) is much less than 0.5 g.cm (due to the pen movement). The decision-making brain activity associated with the dipole moment of 0.5 g.cm is thus measurably greater than the decision-making brain activity associated with the dipole moment of 5×10^{-2} g.cm, which correlates to the increase in accuracy of the conscious decisions. The greater dipole moment measurement and the increased conscious decision-making accuracy, due to the EEG pen movement of 0.5 cm, are 'macroscopic observational evidence' and this evidence (as I have indicated) has not been explained by non-quantum theories of cognitive science that are based on non-quantum theories of gravity (general relativity), but this evidence is both explained and predicted by an effective collapse of phase-entangled effective quantum field waves.

We can see this in terms of some relevant equations. We begin with the wave function of the universe at a time t = 0, written merely schematically (for example, we ignore the role of quantum statistics in requiring states not to be simple tensor products). On the de Broglie–Bohm theory, there is only the wave function of the universe, and a wave function representing some subsystem is an abstraction of an inseparable component of the wave function of the universe, an abstraction that enables us to examine the subcomponent. The wave function of the universe will be written as:

$$\psi(0) = \psi B(0) \otimes \psi C(0) \otimes \psi g(0) \otimes \psi E(0) \otimes R(0) \tag{1}$$

Here B = the brain; C = the relevant conscious state; g = the gravitational field; E = the EEG apparatus, and R = the rest of the universe. I use 'wave function' to refer to an equation and 'wave' to a quantum field described by the wave function. In the course of conscious decision-making, the wave for the brain state $\psi B(0)$ is expected (during the experiment) to evolve into a wave with varying, significant amplitudes at different parts of the wave, e.g. into $\psi B1 + \psi B2$. The gravitational field g is coupled to the brain state and (instantaneously) to all other matter, and the part of the wave function of the universe describing the brain and the gravity field g will be written (at some later time t > 0) as:

$$\psi B1(t) \otimes \psi g1(t) + \psi B2(t) \otimes g2(t) \tag{2}$$

At time t, the gravitational parts differ sufficiently for the effective collapse to take place, and the conscious decision-making state is realized. An EEG is connected to the decision-making part of the appropriate hemisphere so that it is correlated with the brain in such a way that $\psi B1(t)$ and $\psi B2(t)$ realize significantly different EEG pen traces. We need note that the initial state $\psi B(0) \otimes \psi E(0) \otimes \psi g(0)$ 'evolves to' or will be written at the later time as:

$$\psi B1(t) \otimes \psi E1(t) \otimes \psi' g1(t) + \psi B2(t) \otimes g2(t) \otimes \psi E2(t) \otimes \psi' g2(t). \tag{3}$$

We are considering microscopic superpositions that will eventually lead to a macroscopic neural realization of a conscious state. E1 and E2 must be microscopic states of the smaller parts of the EEG pen; the EEG pen is too big for its different possible states to go into superposition. The gravitational wave $\psi'g$ now reflects the EEG pen movements. By contrast, if the EEG is connected to the wrong hemisphere (not involved in decision-making), so the EEG is not correlated with the brain state involved in the decision, then $\psi B(0) \otimes \psi E(0) \otimes \psi g(0)$ evolves to the different state:

$$\psi B1(t) \otimes \psi E(t) \otimes \psi'g(t) + \psi B2(t) \otimes g2(t) \otimes \psi E(t) \otimes \psi'g(t) \tag{4}$$

Notice the difference in the E and g terms between equations 3 and 4. There is no (non-negligible) difference in the gravitational fields between equation 4 and equation 1, but there is a significant difference between the gravitational fields in equations 3 and 1. In the people whose brains were measured, conscious decision-making was significantly more accurate in case equation 3 than in case equation 4, indicating that the gravitational field has a predicted 'quantum mechanical effect' on the decision-making part of the brain.

What should I conclude from my explanation of the Nunn-Clarke-Blott experiments, an explanation in terms of my outline of a version of the de Broglie-Bohm interpretation of quantum mechanics? I have already said that the experimental evidence is relatively weak and thus does not make $p\,(h \,\&\, e/k)$ significantly greater than $p\,(h/k)$. Further, the ideas I used in my explanation are too sketchy to deserve the honorific title of 'a quantum cognitive science theory'. Rather, it is an outline whose details need to be filled in and which has yet to be shown to be more justified than other cognitive science theories. But some progress has been made and that is all we should expect at this early stage of the quantum cognitive science research programme. Quantum cognitive science is still undergoing its birth pangs and the most pertinent conclusion I can draw at this stage is that the ideas in this chapter should *either* stimulate more philosophers of mind or cognitive scientists to pursue further the various avenues of thought suggested in this essay *or* else to refute my arguments in an attempt to justify philosophers' continued reliance on non-quantum cognitive science for their understanding of consciousness and its relation to the brain.

REFERENCES

AHARONOV, Y., and VAIDMAN, L. (1996), 'About Position Measurements which do not Show the Bohmian Particle Position', in J. T. Cushing, A. Fine, and S. Goldstein (eds.), *Bohmian Mechanics and Quantum Theory: An Appraisal* (Dordrecht: Kluwer Academic Publishers).

ALBERT, D. (1996), 'Elementary Quantum Mechanics', in J. T. Cushing, A. Fine, and S. Goldstein (eds.), *Bohmian Mechanics and Quantum Theory: An Appraisal* (Dordrecht: Kluwer Academic Publishers).

—— and LOEWER, BARRY (1988), 'Interpreting the Many-Worlds Interpretation', *Synthese*, 77: 195–213.

BARCAN, R. (1946), 'A Functional Calculus of First Order Based on Strict Implication', *Journal of Symbolic Logic*, 11.

BARINGA, M. (1990), 'The Mind Revealed?', *Science*, 249: 856–8.

BOHM, D., and HILEY, B. (1993), *The Undivided Universe* (London: Routledge).

BOHR, N. (1934), *Atomic Theory and the Description of Nature* (Cambridge: Cambridge University Press).

CHALMERS, DAVID (1996), *The Conscious Mind* (Oxford: Oxford University Press).

CALLENDER, CRAIG, and WEINGARD, ROBERT (1996), 'Trouble in Paradise? Problems for Bohm's Theory', *The Monist*, 80: 24–43.

CHURCHLAND, P. M. (1985), 'Reduction, Qualia, and the Direct Introspection of Brain States', *Journal of Philosophy*, 82: 8–28.

—— (1986), 'Some Reductive Strategies in Cognitive Neurobiology', *Mind*, 95: 279–309.

CRAIG, W. L. (2000), *The Tensed Theory of Time* (Dordrecht: Kluwer Academic Publishers).

DURR, D., GOLDSTEIN S., and ZANGHI, N. (1996), 'Bohmian Mechanics as the Foundation of Quantum Mechanics', in J. T. Cushing, A. Fine, and S. Goldstein (eds.), *Bohmian Mechanics and Quantum Theory: An Appraisal* (Dordrecht: Kluwer Academic Publishers).

FODOR, J. (1987), *Psychosemantics* (Cambridge, Mass.: MIT Press).

GRUSH, R., and CHURCHLAND, PATRICIA (1998), 'Gaps in Penrose's Toilings', in Paul Churchland and Patrician Churchland, *On the Contrary* (Cambridge, Mass.: MIT Press).

HAMEROFF, S. R., and PENROSE, R. (1996), 'Orchestrated Reduction of Quantum Coherence in Brain Microtubules: A Model for Consciousness', in S. Hameroff *et al.* (eds.), *Toward a Science of Consciousness* (Cambridge, Mass.: MIT Press), i.

—— and WATT, R. C. (1982), 'Information Processing in Microtubules', *Journal of Theoretical Biology*, 98: 549–61.

HINTIKKA, J. (1961), 'Modality and Quantification', *Theoria*, 27: 119–28.

KIM, J. (1993), 'The Nonreductivist's Troubles with Mental Causation', in his *Supervenience and Mind* (Cambridge: Cambridge University Press).

LOCKWOOD, MICHAEL (1989), *Mind, Brain and the Quantum* (Oxford: Blackwell).

MARSHAL, IAN (1989), 'Consciousness and Bose-Einstein Condensates', *New Ideas in Psychology*, 7/1: 73–83.

NERLICH, G. (1998), 'Time as Spacetime', in R. Le Poidevin (ed.), *Questions of Time and Tense* (Oxford: Clarendon Press).

NUNN, C., CLARKE, C., and BLOTT, B. (1994), 'Collapse of a Quantum Field May Affect Brain Function', *Journal of Consciousness Studies*, 1: 127–39.

—— —— —— (1996), 'Collapse of a Quantum Field May Affect Brain Function', in S. Hameroff *et al.* (eds.), *Toward a Science of Consciousness* (Cambridge, Mass.: MIT Press), i. (This is a summary of the 1994 article of the same title.)

OPPENHEIM, P., and PUTNAM, H. (1958), 'Unity of Science as a Working Hypothesis', in H. Feigl, M. Scriven, and G. Maxwell (eds.), *Minnesota Studies in the Philosophy of Science* (Minneapolis: University of Minnesota Press), ii.

PAGE, DON (1995), 'Sensible Quantum Mechanics: Are Perceptions Only Probabilistic?', unpublished.

—— (1996), 'Attaching Theories of Consciousness to Bohmian Quantum Mechanics', in J. T. Cushing, A. Fine, and S. Goldstein (eds.), *Bohmian Mechanics and Quantum Theory: An Appraisal* (Dordrecht: Kluwer Academic Publishers).

PENROSE, ROGER (1989), *The Emperor's New Mind* (Oxford: Oxford University Press).

—— (1994), *Shadows of the Mind* (Oxford: Oxford University Press).

PINE, R. (1989), *Science and the Human Prospect* (Hawaii: University of Hawaii Press).

PUTNAM, H. (1983), *Philosophical Papers* (Cambridge: Cambridge University Press).

SCOTT, A (with Hameroff) (1998), 'A Sonoran Afternoon', in S. Hameroff et al., *Towards a Science of Consciousness* (Cambridge, Mass.: MIT Press), ii.

SMITH, QUENTIN (1977), 'On Husserl's Theory of Consciousness in the Fifth Logical Investigation', *Philosophy and Phenomenological Research*, 39: 433–47. For further published articles on phenomenology and consciousness, see QSmithWMU.com.

—— (1986), *The Felt Meanings of the World: A Metaphysics of Feeling* (West Lafayette, Ind.: Purdue University Press).

—— (1993), *Language and Time* (Oxford: Oxford University Press).

—— (1997*a*), *Ethical and Religious Thought in Analytic Philosophy of Language* (New Haven, Conn.: Yale University Press).

—— (1997*b*), 'The Ontological Interpretation of the Wave Function of the Universe', in B. Loewer (ed.), *Monist*, 80: 160–85. See also www.QSmithWMU.com.

—— (1998), 'Absolute Simultaneity and the Infinity of Time', in R. Le Poidevin (ed.), *Questions of Time and Tense* (Oxford: Oxford University Press).

—— (2000), 'Problems with John Earman's Attempt to Reconcile Theism with General Relativity', *Erkenntniss*, 52: 1–27. See also www.QSmithWMU.com.

—— (2002*a*): ' "Time Was Caused by a Timeless Point": An Atheist Explanation of Spacetime', in G. Gegansall and D. Woodruff (eds.), *God and Time* (New York: Oxford University Press).

—— (2002*b*), 'Time and Degrees of Existence', in C. Callender (ed.), *Time, Reality and Experience* (Cambridge: Cambridge University Press). See also www.QSmithWMU.com.

—— and CRAIG, WILLIAM LANE (1993), *Theism, Atheism and Big Bang Cosmology* (Oxford: Oxford University Press).

STAPP, HENRY (1998), 'The Evolution of Consciousness', in S. Hameroff et al. (eds.), *Toward a Science of Consciousness* (Cambridge, Mass.: MIT Press.), ii.

STICH, S. (1996), *Deconstructing the Mind* (Cambridge, Mass.: MIT Press).

TOOLEY, M. (1987), *Causation* (Oxford: Oxford University Press).

VALENTINI, A. (1992), 'On the Pilot-Wave Theory of Classical, Quantum and Subquantum Physics', unpublished Ph.D. thesis (International School for Advanced Studies, Trieste, Italy).

—— (1996), 'Pilot-Wave Theory of Fields, Gravitation and Cosmology', in J. Cushing et al. (eds.), *Bohmian Mechanics and Quantum Theory* (Dordrecht: Kluwer Academic Publishers).

16. Consciousness and the Quantum World: Putting Qualia on the Map

MICHAEL LOCKWOOD

Let me begin by nailing my colours to the mast. I count myself a materialist, in the sense that I take consciousness to be a species of brain activity. Having said that, however, it seems to me evident that no description of brain activity of the relevant kind, couched in the currently available languages of physics, physiology, or functional or computational roles, is remotely capable of capturing what is distinctive about consciousness. So glaring, indeed, are the shortcomings of all the reductive programmes currently on offer, that I cannot believe that anyone with a philosophical training, looking dispassionately at these programmes, would take any of them seriously for a moment, were it not for a deep-seated conviction that current physical science has essentially got reality taped, and accordingly, *something* along the lines of what the reductionists are offering *must* be correct. To that extent, the very existence of consciousness seems to me to be a standing demonstration of the explanatory limitations of contemporary physical science. On the assumption that some form of materialism is nevertheless true, we have only to introspect in order to recognize that our present understanding of matter is itself radically deficient. Consciousness remains for us, at the dawn of the twenty-first century, what it was for Newton at the dawn of the eighteenth century: an occult power that lies beyond the pool of illumination that physical theory casts on the world we inhabit.[1]

Having said that, we can only work with what we have. And for all its shortcomings, fundamental physics provides the currently most authoritative overall guide to the material world, which as I conceive it, has consciousness as an integral constituent. It is because material reality, as depicted by modern physics, is quantum-mechanical through and through, that I intend, shortly, to deploy quantum mechanics in an analysis of the contents of consciousness.

---

[1] I owe this way of putting it to Richard Gregory and Galen Strawson.

In recent years, a number of people have suggested that distinctively quantum-mechanical effects may be implicated in those brain processes that underlie consciousness. Over the past decade, indeed, such speculations (in which I myself have dabbled in the past) have developed into a major academic industry.[2] This chapter, however, is not intended as a contribution to that industry. My own starting point is the more modest thought that the difficulty we have in integrating mind into our overall world-view may in part be due to the lack of fit between the concepts we bring to bear on our own and others' inner lives, and those that we customarily apply to the material world. Specifically, I suggest that, rather than trying to make do with the conceptual currency of everyday discourse, philosophers of mind should avail themselves of the more finely honed concepts that modern physics has developed, for the purpose of rendering natural phenomena susceptible of illuminating mathematical analysis.

1. The Mind as a Physical System

One problem that the mind poses at the outset, is that it seems systematically to elude the categories that we employ in other contexts. From a common-sense perspective, the mind seems not to be an *object*, in the sense in which a chair or a rose bush is an object. Nor does it seem, as some have suggested, to be a *process* or set of processes. Rather, the mind, as we normally think of it, is that *in which* mental processes occur. In short, the categorial status of the mind seems—unsatisfactorily for the philosopher—to be *sui generis* as far as ordinary language is concerned. (This point was brought home to me some years ago, when I heard my eldest son, then aged 9, repeatedly referring to his *brain*, in talking about his thoughts and feelings. I put it to him that 'mind' was the right word to use—which in terms of standard English usage it undoubtedly was. Later the same evening, having reflected on what I'd said, he had a question for me: 'What *is* the mind?' he asked. 'It isn't a liquid and it isn't a gas, so what is it?')

Here, it seems to me, would-be materialists might profitably avail themselves of a concept that is central to modern physics—namely, that of a *physical* (or *dynamical*) *system*. This is a wonderfully versatile notion, which has proved extraordinarily fruitful. It encompasses, in a rigorous fashion, not only what we should normally think of as physical objects, such as paper-clips and petunias, but also functional aspects of physical objects, such as the transmission system of a car or the endocrine system of a frog, collections

<hr />

[2] See Penrose (1994) and Hameroff and Penrose (1996).

of physical objects such as the solar system, and things that fall into none of these categories, such as a magnetic field.

A physical system is defined by its *degrees of freedom*. These are quantities that can vary independently of each other, and that jointly define the instantaneous *configuration* of the system. Roughly speaking, one can think of a configuration as what is depicted by a snapshot, or a single frame of a movie (with no tell-tale blurring of the image to reveal movement). Consider, by way of illustration, a rigid three-dimensional object that is free to rotate and move around in any direction. This is a physical system with six degrees of freedom. Three of these degrees of freedom correspond to the three co-ordinates required to specify the location of the object's centre of mass, and the remaining three correspond to the three angles required to specify its spatial orientation. If you start with two or more physical systems, you can combine them, conceptually, to form a so-called *composite* system, of which the original systems are *subsystems*. Thus, a system composed of n rigid bodies, each of which can move independently of the others, has $6n$ degrees of freedom. Conversely, any physical system with more than one degree of freedom can be divided, conceptually, into subsystems, defined by subsets of the degrees of freedom of the original system. In classical physics, the *state* of a dynamical system, at any given time, can be specified by $2k$ numbers, where k is the number of degrees of freedom. For our rigid body, these numbers will comprise (a) the instantaneous values of the co-ordinates and angles defining the position and orientation of the body, and (b) for each of these values, a number giving the rate and direction of *change* of these values, multiplied by the body's mass—the instantaneous values, in other words, of the components of the body's linear and angular momentum.

Consider, now, a contraption consisting of a weight, or *bob*, suspended from a beam by a spring. If the bob is pulled down and then released, it will oscillate up and down. This system has one degree of freedom, corresponding to the height of the bob's centre of mass. And accordingly, we can represent the state of the system, at any given time, by a point in a two-dimensional *phase space*. By convention, the horizontal axis will represent the constantly shifting position of the bob, and the vertical axis will represent the system's *momentum*, the product of the mass of the bob and its velocity. This will be positive when the bob is moving downwards and negative when it is moving upwards. Likewise the position co-ordinate will be positive when the bob is below its equilibrium position and negative when it is above it. Where the two axes cross we have the zero point, or *origin*, which corresponds to the *equilibrium* position of the bob, i.e. the location of the bob's centre of mass when it is hanging motionless and the upward force exerted by the spring is precisely balanced by the pull of gravity.

In an idealized set-up in which the spring is attached to a totally rigid beam, and the whole system is enclosed in an evacuated chamber so that there is no friction with the air, the representative point will describe, indefinitely, a perfect ellipse within the phase space. (The further down the bob is pulled, before being released, the larger the ellipse will be.) In the real world, where there *is* friction with the air, and energy is lost, also, through the creation of vibrations in the beam, the representative point will instead, as the system runs down, describe an elliptical spiral that ends up at the origin.

Our bob on a spring is just one physical realization of what is known as the *simple harmonic oscillator* (see Fig. 16.1). But there are other such realizations. What is formally the same phase space, with a similar elliptical *orbit* (as the phase space trajectory is called) can equally well be used to describe a pendulum. In that application, the two dimensions correspond, respectively, to *angular* position and *angular* momentum.

More surprisingly, a formally identical phase space can also be used to describe a *tuned circuit*. Such a circuit, which is to be found in every radio and television, includes an *inductor* and a *capacitor*. The inductor, let us assume, is a coil; and the capacitor is a pair of parallel metal plates separated by a small gap. Suppose that the capacitor is briefly connected to a battery, with the result that one of the plates, plate *A*, becomes positively charged, and the other plate, plate *B*, becomes negatively charged. Current then flows from plate *A* to plate *B*, and on through the induction coil. There it generates a magnetic disturbance that has the effect of charging the capacitor, which is closely adjacent to it, in the *opposite* direction. Electricity then flows from plate *B* to plate *A* and through the coil, once more generating a magnetic disturbance that now causes plate *A* to become positively charged and plate *B* to become negatively charged, and so on, over and over again. The electricity thus flows back and forth in the form of an alternating current.

The *charge* in the capacitor and the *current* flowing through the circuit are here related to each other in a way that is formally analogous to the way in which the position of our bob is related to its linear momentum. In the oscillating circuit, energy is constantly converted, back and forth, between potential energy stored in the capacitor and kinetic energy embodied in the current flowing through the wire. The capacitor stores energy in the form of charge, which it subsequently releases in the form of electrical current, just as our bob on a spring, when away from its equilibrium position, stores energy (in the form of tension in the spring and/or gravitational potential energy) which it subsequently releases in the form of linear momentum.

Later in this chapter I shall introduce yet another realization of the simple harmonic oscillator, for which the foregoing account will provide a suitable preparation. But my primary purpose, here, is to give the reader a feel for what is meant by a physical system. For clearly, a functioning human brain

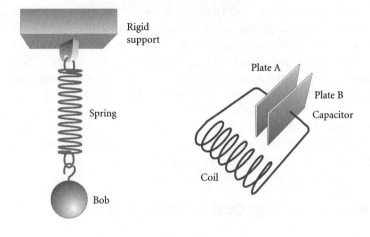

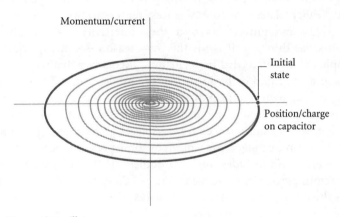

FIG. 16.1. Harmonic oscillator

may be regarded as a physical system, a system that is defined by the vast number of degrees of freedom corresponding to the independent ways in which the overall state of the brain can change. The mind associated with this brain may then, I suggest, be equated with a certain subsystem of the brain— specifically, the subsystem defined by the subset of the brain's internal degrees of freedom that are *constitutively*, and not merely *causally*, implicated in consciousness. The mind, that is to say, can be thought of as the smallest subsystem of the brain, appropriate functioning of which is *by itself* sufficient for the experiential life of the corresponding conscious subject. In philosopher's jargon, the mind is that subsystem of the brain on whose behaviour consciousness directly *supervenes*. If I bark one of my shins on a pedal while manœuvring my bicycle out of the shed (by no means a rare occurrence!) I shall feel pain. And this pain has a causal provenance that involves nerve transmission from my shin to the appropriate cortical primary projection area and beyond. But the message reaches my *mind*, in the sense just indicated, only with the occurrence of brain activity that, in the given cerebral context, is sufficient for me to feel the pain that I do *regardless of how it is caused*. Such brain activity could thus in principle be triggered—by an implanted electrode, say—in a manner that by-passes the normal causal route by which I come to have such a sensation.

2. Consciousness and Qualitative Content

Such is the success and prestige of the physical and biological sciences that we are tempted to think of them as having penetrated the very heart and core of external reality. These mature sciences represent, we think, a triumph of objectivity and universality over the subjectivity and parochialism of common-sense thinking. It is for this very reason that many scientists and philosophers have succeeded in persuading themselves that what science has to say about the mind or brain simply supersedes our common-sense conceptions of our own nature. But as I see it, this attitude is grounded in a fundamental misunderstanding of the metaphysical status of the models of reality that the relevant sciences are capable of generating. All we ultimately have to go on, in forming a conception of some part or aspect of the external world—which here includes our own bodies—is the evidence presented by our conscious perceptions. We make sense of these perceptions by construing them as the upshot of complex causal chains within an elaborate structure of which the sensorium of any given conscious being constitutes only a tiny fragment. But this assumed external structure is essentially just that: abstract *structure* or *form*, devoid of explicit qualitative *content*. This abstractness becomes manifest in the higher reaches of theoretical physics, where the language is one of vector spaces, differential operators, and so forth. But on reflection, it can be seen to be latently characteristic even of our most jejune common-sense conceptions. For anyone with the least scientific nous, it will become obvious, on reflection, that the exquisite hue and scent that we attribute to the rose are really *projections* on to external reality of goings-on in our own (and others') consciousness: goings-on triggered by the emission of a seductive combination of photons and aromatic hydrocarbons.

None of this is to deny that the physical world in general *possesses* intrinsic qualities. In its physical application, mathematics is merely a *language* that enables us to describe structure abstracted from content. Such content can be identified and labelled, but never directly intuited in the way that we directly intuit our own conscious states. Our only access to such content, in the world at large, is via interactions that, at some point, make an impact on the conscious mind. The only understanding I can have of any physical item belonging to the non-mental world is as a 'something I know not what' that occupies a particular node in a postulated causal network, in which certain of my own conscious events figure. I know what *pain* is, in itself. But I have no such knowledge in respect of such things as electric charge.

And now we get to the crux of the argument, which in essence is due to Bertrand Russell (1927).[3] If materialism is true, then the panoply of qualia that, in our waking lives and in our dreams, we encounter within our own fields of consciousness, are to be construed as manifestations of the qualitative character of the mind itself, considered as a subsystem of the brain! By courtesy of the inner illumination that is consciousness, a certain subsystem of my brain is enabled to be directly cognizant of aspects of its own intrinsic nature. As a conscious being, I encounter a slice of physical reality, in my own person, quite literally in the flesh, instead of through the mediation of a mental representation.

But this idea that consciousness, at any given time, confers an unmediated apprehension of some part or aspect of one's own being, qua subsystem of one's brain, runs up against an obvious objection. It is an objection that was eloquently expressed by the late Carl Sagan (1985: 235), through the medium of a television evangelist who figures in his novel, *Contact*: 'Think of what consciousness feels like, what it feels like this moment. Does that *feel* like billions of tiny atoms wiggling in place?' The problem, in a nutshell, is that there seems to be a profound structural mismatch between the contents of one's consciousness at any given time, and what science would tell us is simultaneously going on in the brain. In particular, the contents of consciousness would seem to be highly *coarse-grained*, in relation to the immensely intricate physical processes on which they ostensibly supervene. A philosopher who took this difficulty for materialism very seriously was Wilfrid Sellars (1965), who dubbed it the 'grain problem'.

Were qualia, contrary to what I argued just now, mere representations of brain activity, their relative lack of definition, with respect to the corresponding goings-on in the brain, would be unproblematic. Qualia could then be thought of as standing to the brain activity in a relation similar to that of an impressionist painting *vis-à-vis*, say, a row of poplars on a hillside in Provence. But according to the kind of materialism that Sellars has in mind, and which we are here exploring, qualia simply aren't *distanced* from brain activity

---

[3] An analysis of Russell's views, and the history of their development, are to be found in Lockwood (1981).

in the way that paintings are distanced from what they depict. They just *are* aspects of brain activity, apprehended, as it were, from the inside. In the currently fashionable psychobabble, people talk about 'getting in touch with their own feelings'. I don't deny that it may make sense to speak of *unconscious* feelings. But it is in the very *nature* of one's feelings, qua *qualia*, that one is *inescapably* in touch with them, in the most intimate sense possible.

The Concept of an Observable

What we want, here, are two things that are ostensibly mutually exclusive. On the one hand, we wish to construe qualia as *perspectives* on the neurophysiological reality, manifesting the relevant subsystem of the brain from a particular standpoint, and with relatively low definition. But on the other hand, we want qualia to be slices of neurophysiological reality in their own right—*ingredients* in this reality. Classical physics, as *normally* understood, is incapable of simultaneously satisfying these two seemingly incompatible requirements. Possibly one could reconcile them by radically reconstruing classical physics along the lines recommended by Leibniz, according to which all that exists is a continuous set of monads, each representing a distinct point of view, with the history of the physical world being ultimately *constituted* by the joint histories of the way things appear to these monads.[4] In Leibniz's metaphysics, reality itself becomes a sum of perspectives. But in the context of classical physics, I take it that most people would regard this metaphysical exercise as Procrustean in the extreme. What I now want to suggest, however, is that, by contrast with classical physics, quantum mechanics lends itself very naturally to an interpretation that has a certain affinity with Leibniz's project.

In order to apply a physical theory to the world, we obviously have to be able, in a systematic way, to associate elements of the theory with items in the world that lend themselves to being observed or measured. In classical physics, observation and measurement are regarded as unproblematic activities that, at the level of theory, can simply be taken for granted. In quantum mechanics, however, it has proved essential to pay attention to the very physics of observation itself. For observation and measurement lose the transparency that they possess in classical physics. To observe or measure some aspect of a physical system is to interact with it; and that interaction itself calls for theoretical analysis. And two things—two very non-classical things—emerge from this analysis. First, the *state* of a physical system, in the context of quantum mechanics, does not, as in classical mechanics, determine unique outcomes for all the observations or measurements we might carry

[4] See Leibniz (1898) (written 1714).

out on it. Knowledge of the state will in general allow us only to assign *probabilities* to various outcomes of a particular measurement. Secondly, if one considers a number of distinct measurements that one might carry out on a physical system, it turns out that the probability of getting a particular outcome for one such measurement can depend on what measurements have already been carried out. Famously, this is true of measurements of position and momentum. Neither of these can be measured *exactly*. But the more precise a measurement one makes of the position of a particle, the greater will be the statistical spread of the possible outcomes of a subsequent measurement of the momentum. And precisely the same holds of momentum *vis-à-vis* position: measurement of the one queers the pitch, as it were, for subsequent measurement of the other, and the more so, the smaller the mass of the particle being observed. (It's the same story, by the way, for current in relation to charge.)

In quantum mechanics, things that we can measure or observe are called *observables*. Every observable has a corresponding *spectrum*. The spectrum of an observable is the range of possible outcomes of measuring it, the results one could get. I like to think of an observable as a *question* that can be asked concerning a physical system—a question that one's measurement apparatus is capable of answering. Then the spectrum of the observable is a range of possible answers. The state of a physical system at any given time determines, for every observable on that system, the probability that a measurement of that observable at that time will yield a given outcome (or answer). One can represent each possible outcome by a number. Correspondingly, the spectrum of every observable (properly so-called) comprises a range of discrete numerical values, known as the observable's *eigenvalues*. Thus, if one measures the energy of our bob on a spring, the result of the measurement is guaranteed to be one of a set of spaced-out *energy eigenvalues*, representing distinct quantized energy levels. The position and momentum of the bob are not quantized in the same sense as is energy. For elementary quantum mechanics places no finite limit on how fine-grained a measurement of position or momentum can be. But the degree of precision that any given measurement of the instantaneous position or momentum of the bob can command is nevertheless bound to be finite. So one must envisage the position and momentum axes as being partitioned into small numbered segments, such that an outcome of a measurement of position or momentum amounts to a narrowing down of the position or the momentum to a specific segment of the corresponding axis. For our bob on a spring, there is thus an infinity of distinct position and momentum observables, corresponding to all possible sizes of the segments.

A set of observables is said to be a *compatible* set if a measurement of any one observable in the set leaves the probabilities of outcome of measuring any of the others unaffected. Whether or not a given pair of position and momentum observables, on a given object, constitutes a compatible set will thus depend on how fine-grained these observables are, in relation to the mass of the object in question. Moreover, the energy observable is compatible neither with (sufficiently) fine-grained position nor with fine-grained momentum.

4. Qualia and Quantum Physics

Measurement or observation, as it is understood in quantum mechanics, is strictly a transaction involving two distinct physical systems. But consciousness, as I conceive it, involves no such transaction: I would firmly repudiate the equation of consciousness with the notion of a 'self' or 'subject' somehow 'inspecting' its own mind or brain. It is merely that, given a developed living brain, there will, for much of the time, be 'something it is like to be' a certain subsystem of that brain. Consciousness, thus understood, is not *per se* observation or measurement, although it is often the *upshot* of observation—as with the deployment of our five senses on the external world. Nevertheless, I take it to be a very plausible conjecture that consciousness, *vis-à-vis* the brain states or processes on which it supervenes, is bound by the same restrictions that quantum mechanics imposes on measurement and observation. I am suggesting, in other words, that the contents of consciousness, at any given moment, correspond to a set of measurement outcomes that belong to the respective spectra of a compatible set of observables on the mind, construed as a subsystem of the brain. Were it otherwise, it would be impossible in principle, assuming psychophysical parallelism, for an outside observer—by means of a brain scanner, say—to ascertain, in their entirety, the momentary contents of another person's consciousness. For to do so would be to violate the rules of quantum measurement in the context of a measurement by the outside observer of the relevant subsystem of the other person's brain.

Assuming that consciousness is, in the sense just indicated, bound by the rules of quantum measurement theory, it follows inescapably that consciousness is irreducibly *perspectival* with respect to the underlying goings-on in the brain. The present contents of my consciousness, according to the view I have just been promoting, are defined by a set of answers to a set of mutually compatible questions regarding the current state of a certain subsystem of my own brain. But these answers, which jointly define what it is like to be me now, are answers to just *one* set of mutually compatible questions amongst a potential *infinity* of such sets. The claim that I am making, therefore, is that there is a set of questions (at any given time at least) that is *subjectively* preferred, in the sense that it corresponds to the mind's 'take' on itself.

With this, we are in a position to say what a *quale* is, from the standpoint of physics. On the theory that I am here putting forward, a quale is the objective correlate of a point in a certain *n*-dimensional abstract space—let's call it a *phenomenal space*—the dimensions of which correspond, respectively, to the spectra of *n* observables on the mind, that jointly constitute a compatible set. All hues, for example, can be located within an abstract three-dimensional colour space. So a patch of colour in one's visual field, too small for there to be detectable variations of hue within it, would presumably correspond to a set of eigenvalues belonging, respectively, to the spectra of each of a compatible set of mind observables that included, as a subset, three eigenvalues specifying the experienced hue. (The remaining eigenvalues would be associated with observables that jointly specified the perceived size, shape, and orientation of the patch, and its location within the visual field.)

5. Slices of Reality

I have already argued that the perspectival character of consciousness is demanded by quantum mechanics, which I am assuming to be universally applicable. Now, however, I am in a position to make good upon my earlier claim. For I can now show that, if we conceptualize the relevant subsystem of the brain in the way that quantum mechanics dictates, we are enabled to construe the momentary contents of consciousness as simultaneously *perspectives* on the reality of the brain and constituents of reality in their own right. This, as I earlier remarked, is an impossible combination from the standpoint of classical mechanics.

How, then, does quantum mechanics make this possible? Well, given any quantum-mechanical system, there will be an infinity of distinct compatible sets of observables on that system. Every such set defines a corresponding way of mathematically decomposing states of the system in question, enabling us to express each state as a weighted sum of terms that correspond one-to-one with distinct overall sets of measurement outcomes.

At this point, I shall introduce a homely analogy. Imagine that we have a block of wood, square at each end, with longer rectangular sides. This block, which here serves as an analogue of a quantum state, is a three-dimensional object that we can regard as being composed of a continuous infinity of appropriately ordered parallel *two-dimensional* slices. These slices correspond, in our analogy, to distinct possible outcomes of measuring the system, when it is in this state. Now there is, of course, an infinity of *distinct* ways of conceptually carving up the block into such slices—one way for every possible orientation of the notional blade that does the slicing. The different orientations here correspond to different compatible sets of observables. The block corresponds to a quantum state of the mind; and every two-dimensional cross-section of the block corresponds to a perspective on this quantum state. Crucially, the cross-sections of the block are no mere *representations* of the block: they are embedded within the block itself. Likewise, on the view adopted here, the contents of consciousness are no mere representations of the corresponding quantum state of the mind; they are, in their own right, encompassed by this quantum state.

Think, now, of the activity of measuring a compatible set of observables on a physical system as analogous to slicing the block along a certain plane and observing the corresponding pattern. (The same information could be acquired, without literally sawing the block in two, by employing the imaging technique known as *X-ray tomography.*) Measurements of different complete compatible sets of observables here correspond to slicing the block at different *angles.* Suppose one employs a method of slicing that allows one to choose the *orientation* of the slice, but not its *position* with respect to the block's long axis, which hinges on the output of a randomizing device. Distinct possible *outcomes* of the same measurement will then correspond to the different patterns associated with distinct but parallel cross-sections. So there you have it: the outcome of carrying out a measurement of a compatible set of quantum-mechanical observables stands to the *state* of the measured system, at the time of measurement, as does the pattern manifested by a cross-section of a block of wood, the orientation of which can be deliberately chosen but the position of which depends on an uncontrollable random process. To get different finite probabilities for observing different patterns, we could imagine that the block of wood was comprised of parallel bands, of differing thickness, within which all the slices displayed the same pattern. (But although this can be coherently envisaged, for a real block of wood, with respect to some chosen orientation, it clearly cannot be coherently envisaged for all at once; here the analogy, useful though it is, begins to falter.)

I earlier stressed that, from an *external* perspective—the perspective of physics—there is an infinity of distinct compatible sets of observables, between which there is nothing to choose. In terms of our analogy, there is an infinity of different ways of 'carving up the wood'. Only one, however— so I am assuming at present—figures (at any given time, at least) in the *internal* view that is constitutive of consciousness. I earlier spoke of this compatible set of observables as being *subjectively* preferred. But let there be no misunderstanding: I take it to be a fully *objective* fact that it *is* subjectively preferred!

Crucially, I also assume that the compatible set of observables, corresponding eigenvalues of which jointly define a given state of consciousness, is invariably an *incomplete* set. A complete compatible set of observables is one that, when measured, yields *maximal information* concerning the measured system—information that cannot be improved on by adding further observables to the set. This relates directly to the grain problem. Only by allowing the operative compatible sets of observables to be *incomplete* can we ratchet down the degree of resolution and complexity of the corresponding conscious state to what one would intuitively judge to be the right level. The key point, however, is that the mathematically expressed structure to which I am appealing here is structure that physics itself posits: to the extent that reality mirrors physical theory, it is *there* in the world, just as tree rings are there in the wood. And given that, as I earlier emphasized, physics ultimately has nothing to say about intrinsic content, whether in the brain or elsewhere, we are free to picture some of this structure as being fleshed out with the contents of our own conscious states. But let me stress that I'm not offering a solution to the mind–body problem: that parts of this structure *are*, in this fashion, illumined by consciousness remains, in my account, an astonishing brute fact.[5]

6. Local Algebras and the Specious Present

Quite apart from its inability to explain what consciousness is, and why it should exist at all, the account given in the previous sections is inadequate as it stands, because it relies on what, for our purposes, is an unsatisfactory concept of a physical state. Elementary quantum mechanics, which has formed the setting for the discussion so far, follows classical physics in equating states of physical systems with time-slices. This is doubly problematic. In the first place, special relativity tells us that simultaneity is relative to

---

[5] Some readers may feel that, in the first instance, ontological priority should be given to *complete* compatible sets of observables, which should therefore serve as our starting point. On this conception, a state of consciousness, at a given time, t, is to be found, within the physical reality of the brain, at the centre of a set of Chinese boxes. We start with the brain, and then focus on a specific subsystem, the mind. Then we consider the quantum state, at t, of the mind. This state, in its turn, can be mathematically decomposed, relative to a particular compatible set of observables on the mind, as a weighted sum of terms, each of which corresponds to a different possible outcome of simultaneously measuring these observables. The spectra of these observables can serve as axes that jointly define an abstract space, S, points within which correspond to distinct possible outcomes of simultaneously measuring the observables in this complete compatible set. Embedded within this abstract space will be a phenomenal space, P. This can be defined by a set of axes, each of which corresponds to a subsegment of the spectrum of one of the observables that jointly define S. P is thus a subspace of S. Given a specific quantum state of the mind, there will, of course, be an infinity of different ways of carrying out the construction I have just described. But I take it that, at any given time, t, there will be just one subspace of S, capable of being constructed in the way I have just indicated, that is *subjectively* preferred at t. We thus end up, as before, associating states of consciousness with points in an abstract space defined by partial spectra of a substantially *less than complete* compatible set of observables on the mind.

one's choice of a frame of reference. Different choices of a reference frame will generate different so-called *simultaneity hyperplanes*, and hence issue in differently defined time-slices or instantaneous states. Secondly, it is in any case wholly implausible to regard conscious states as supervening on *instantaneous* physical states, such as figure in classical physics and elementary quantum mechanics. States of consciousness must surely, in reality, supervene on a portion of the *history* of the relevant subsystem of the brain, rather than on a time-slice, however defined. For the relevant neurophysiological observables must surely include *spatio-temporal integrals* of neuronal firing rates, such as have been discovered, for example, to underlie perceived colour. Moreover, it is a highly suggestive fact, here, that states of consciousness *seem* to possess temporal depth. E. R. Clay pointed this out, with his concept of the *specious present*. And the idea was enthusiastically taken up by William James (1907: 609), who famously declared:

In short, the practically cognized present is no knife-edge, but a saddle-back, with a certain breadth of its own on which we sit perched, and from which we look in two directions into time. The unit of composition of our perception of time is a *duration*, with a bow and a stern, as it were—a rearward-and a forward-looking end.

In this chapter I have been implicitly equating conscious states with what I have elsewhere called *maximal experiences*.[6] The idea is that certain items within consciousness are *co-presented*: that is to say, *experienced as a whole*. But as James makes clear, this is not the same as their being experienced as being *simultaneous*: if we pass on the street, and I say 'Hello', I take it that you will experience the two syllables of my utterance all in one go. When you hear the second syllable, you are not aware of consulting your *memory*, in order to determine what the first syllable was! Indeed, if the word is spoken at a normal pace, you will experience the first syllable *only as* the first syllable of 'Hello'. (Had I uttered only the first syllable, 'He . . .', this would have been associated with a different experience, which you didn't have in the actual situation, in which I said 'Hello'.) Nevertheless, you heard the second syllable *as* following the first. The immediacy of consciousness thus has an *internal* temporal extension which is distinct from the *external* temporal sequence that we impose on the stream of consciousness, on the basis of short- or long-term memory. Formally, a conscious state, or maximal experience, can be defined as a set of phenomenal items, any two of which will be pairwise co-presented, and which includes all items that are co-presented with every item in the set. This definition allows conscious states to overlap. That conscious states, thus understood, supervene on regions of space-time that possess an objective temporal depth, seems to me overwhelmingly

---

[6] See Lockwood (1989: 88–9).

plausible. But let me emphasize that there is no reason, in general, to suppose that the internal temporal extension that the mind attributes to a maximal experience is a good guide to the temporal spread of the brain activity on which this experience supervenes.

To find within physics a formalism that can naturally accommodate spatio-temporally spread out conscious states, understood as maximal experiences, we shall do best to turn to relativistic quantum field theory, which is one of the two fundamental mainstays of contemporary physics (the other being general relativity). The picture of reality associated with relativistic quantum field theory (hereafter RQFT) represents a striking departure from our common-sense way of looking at things. All that ultimately exists, according to RQFT, is relativistic space-time and a set of fields defined on space-time. (We can think of a field, by the way, as a physical system with an *infinite* number of degrees of freedom.) At each point in space-time, there will be a corresponding *value* of the field, though not, unless it is a so-called *scalar* field, a value that can be expressed by a single number. In general, the value of the field, at each space-time point, will be expressed by a *sequence* or *array* of numbers: technically, a vector or tensor. This appears, on the face of it, to be a totally inadequate basis for producing a world such as we find ourselves inhabiting. What about the *fundamental particles*—and in particular, those particles out of which atoms, then molecules, then material bodies are constructed? Well, strictly speaking, particles do not exist as the enduring, minuscule jots or scintillas of matter that, for non-physicists, naturally come to mind as the building blocks of what we see around us. The correct picture, in essence, runs as follows. The fields just referred to are *elastic*: they can vibrate. And for each field there is a set of vibratory motions that are known as *normal modes*. A normal mode is a form of vibration in which the *frequency* of vibration is everywhere the same, though with respect to any definition of simultaneity, the vibrations at different places will in general be out of phase with each other. Each of these normal modes can then be conceptualized as a harmonic oscillator, such as we discussed earlier by way of illustrating the concept of a physical system. Thus, the field as a whole can be pictured as a *set* of harmonic oscillators.

Now we have already seen that the energy of a harmonic oscillator is quantized, in the sense that a measurement of the energy can only yield one of a set of discrete values, or so-called *energy levels*. Any arbitrary instantan-eous state of the field as a whole can be expressed as a weighted sum of conjunctions of the respective energy levels of the component harmonic oscillators of the field. And hey presto! When we consider how such a field will be perceived as evolving over time, it turns out that this quantization of the energy automatically generates *particle-like* phenomena. Energy itself will be observed as propagating through the field in the form of discrete 'parcels'.

But what we have here are not at all the modern equivalents of the rigid, dense, sharply-defined grains of matter envisaged by Democritus. The so-called 'particles' of modern particle physics lack not only solidity and well-defined trajectories—they lack even a robust identity over time. It is meaningless, in general, to ask whether the electron you detect now is or is not the *same* electron that you detected a moment or so ago.

From these considerations it follows that the sort of localized persisting physical systems that we earlier discussed—whether a bob bouncing on a spring, a tuned circuit, a brain, or a subsystem thereof—are really *emergent* phenomena. Ultimately, they are ripples on the surface of reality. When viewed through the lens of fundamental physics, the ostensibly clear-cut boundaries of Austin's 'medium-sized dry goods' become a blur: the apparent tangibility and robust identity and individuality of ordinary macroscopic objects proves to be something of a sham. In short, enduring macroscopic objects are not the rocks on which metaphysicians respectful of science should be erecting their glass palaces. In the context of RQFT one *can*, however, regard finite regions of space-time as well-defined physical systems. And a very elegant formalism for RQFT has been developed, by Rudolf Haag (1992), in which this concept has pride of place. (The idea of applying this formalism to the mind is one that I owe to Matthew Donald.[7])

In line with our previous discussion, we now proceed on the assumption that any given conscious state (or maximal experience) supervenes, not on a time-slice of the mind, qua subsystem of the brain, but on a region of space-time, which I shall simply call a *local region*. A portion of the history of a person's stream of consciousness, uninterrupted by dreamless sleep, will then supervene on a continuous sequence of overlapping local regions, forming, in aggregate, a snake-like world-tube in space-time. The proposal now is that any given conscious state should be equated with the physical correlate of a point in an abstract space defined by the respective spectra of a compatible set of observables on the corresponding local region. The observables in question are no longer to be thought of as corresponding to measurements that are carried out *simultaneously* (for which, as we have seen, there is no relativistic-ally invariant criterion anyway); we're now talking merely of mutually compatible measurements that can in principle be made somewhere within the relevant local region. Let me stress, once again, that the measurements I am referring to are merely *hypothetical* ones, not measurements that are actually *performed*. Here, as elsewhere in this article, I appeal to observables only as capturing formal structure, present in the physics of the brain, that I take to be *manifested* in consciousness. And consciousness, as I conceive it, is just that: the activity of the internally *manifest* brain.

---

[7] See Donald (1990, 1992, 1995).

The set encompassing *all* observables on a local region is known as a *local Von Neumann algebra*, or *local algebra* for short. I should perhaps emphasize, here, that precisely *which* observable, within the algebra, is being measured by a given procedure, will in general be sensitive, amongst other things, to where and when, within the corresponding local region, the measurement takes place. For each element of the algebra, there will be a corresponding spectrum of possible outcomes of measuring this element. Each outcome, or eigen-value, will correspond to a number; and each will have a corresponding probability of being obtained, if the observable in question is measured. From these one can calculate the *expectation value* of the observable: this is the figure one gets, if one multiplies every eigenvalue by its probability of occurrence and adds up the results. (If there's a one-third probability of getting 6, and a two-thirds probability of getting 9, then the expectation value is 8.) A so-called *local state* of such a region can then be defined as a function from observables on this region (i.e. elements of the corresponding local algebra) to the corresponding expectation values. The local observables, and the probabilities of outcome of measuring these observables, thereby come to occupy centre-stage in this approach, with local *states* becoming a derived notion. This serves to enhance the Leibnizian flavour of the approach that I'm promoting here.

I assume that, over any period of continuous consciousness, the compatible sets of observables, associated with the states of consciousness that supervene on the overlapping local regions, change in a continuous fashion, as do the probabilities associated with the corresponding strings of eigenvalues. We could therefore think of these compatible sets as defining, in aggregate, an evolving 'window' on the mind–brain: a window through which different things are to be seen at different times. Moreover, we can think of some strings of eigenvalues associated with these observables as having *no* phenomenal correlates at all. This we need to do in order to accommodate periods of unconsciousness. If we picture such a compatible set of observables as consti-tuting a window on the world, we can think of periods of unconsciousness as ones in which *nothing* is to be seen through the window, since it looks out on to an unilluminated scene.

7. Branching Out

In attempting to convey an intuitive grasp of the place of states of conscious-ness in the overall edifice of physical reality, I have made repeated reference to the woodblock analogy. But anyone who reflects on this analogy will realize that it ostensibly commits one to *parallel* experiential realities within a single mind. How else, after all, can one interpret the fact that parallel cross-sections, situated at different places along the block's long axis, will in general, yield many distinct patterns? The reader may therefore protest that what has here been provided is an *embarras de richesse*. Corresponding to the state of a person's mind, at any given time, we are given a *multiplicity* of ways it is like to be that person, when we surely only wanted one!

If it were a matter of *measuring* the state that the block is supposed to represent, then one could conceivably avoid this multiplicity of distinct, simultaneously present perspectives. Taking the operation of slicing the wood as representing measurement, one could assign reality only to the pattern associated with the unique cross-section that is revealed by the cleaver. This could serve as a metaphor for the postulated process of *measurement-induced state vector reduction*, otherwise known as *collapse of the wave-function*. Indeed, the stream of consciousness itself could be thought of as being kept on a well-defined course, by a constant sequence of what amount to measurement interactions between the mind and its cerebral environment. Wigner (1962) famously (or notoriously) adopted a dualist version of this view, according to which it is the *self* that is responsible for continually collapsing the wave function of the brain, and thereby everything with which the brain itself is dynamically coupled. Such speculations, however, fit very uneasily within the mathematical framework of conventional quantum mechanics, the dynamics of which is governed by a differential equation—Schrödinger's equation or some suitable relativistic counterpart—that simply does not permit, as it stands, any such collapse. And the motive for introducing such a *deus ex machina* as wave-function collapse (calculated to preserve, at the macroscopic level, a passable simulacrum of a classical world) seems to me to be highly suspect anyway, grounded, as it is, in little more than a nostalgic attachment to the metaphysics of the nursery.

My own preference, therefore, is for the no-collapse interpretation put forward by Everett (1957). According to this interpretation, measurement interactions, as Schrödinger's equation stipulates, induce a systematic *pairing* between states of the measured system and (via the measuring apparatus) states of the observer. The observer thereby goes into a state which mirrors that of the measured system—a state that has the form of a weighted sum of terms, each of which corresponds to a recollection of having experienced a different measurement outcome. And the weights associated with these terms reflect the probabilities associated with these measurement outcomes. I should make it clear that, if the Everett interpretation is correct, it follows that we are all, in our waking lives, subject to a *constant* fissioning of our respective streams of consciousness, simply in consequence of the dependence of the macroscopic on the microscopic world. It doesn't require a deliberate measurement of a quantum system to produce such a state, nor a contrived set-up such as Schrödinger envisaged to produce his live-dead cat.

One normally thinks of a person's conscious states as forming a *one-dimensional* temporal array. For that is certainly the way it seems. In the context of the Everett interpretation, however, this one-dimensional array becomes a two-dimensional *experiential manifold* (as I have elsewhere called it).[8] The idea is that, in addition to the 'vertical' dimension, to which memory gives us access, there is a 'sideways' *superpositional* dimension. Along this dimension are to be found conscious states corresponding to all possible strings of eigenvalues of the relevant compatible set of observables. And the respective widths of the regions occupied by these states are proportional to the probabilities assigned to the associated strings. The subjective probability of finding oneself in a given such state at a given time is thus equal to the probability that a pin randomly stuck into the manifold, at a given height on the vertical (time) dimension, would land at a point within the region occupied by that state. But the idea is that, objectively speaking, one is in all these states at once. And the only reason that we are unaware of this is that there is no 'sideways' counterpart of memory.

The situation is, in fact, more complex than I have thus far made it seem. On the one hand, the observables associated with a given maximal experience, within a local region that encompasses the brain events on which this experience supervenes, will indeed be multivalued according to the Everett interpretation. On the quantum state of any given such space-time region, that is to say, there will simultaneously supervene *distinct* maximal experiences of the same individual, existing in parallel. But it goes further than this. For the very *position* of a person's brain will itself be multivalued. So the wormlike world-tubes, made up of these overlapping consciousness-supporting local regions, will repeatedly *branch*, as time passes. On the Everett view, a single such local region, at an earlier time, will have a multiplicity of spatially separated descendants at later times, on each of which multiple states of consciousness supervene. The result, for every conscious being, is therefore a tree-like spatio-temporal structure. And these structures will criss-cross each other in such a way that the experiences of distinct individuals will frequently supervene on respective brain events that occur, as parallel realities, in the same local regions.

All this may well strike the reader as highly fantastical; and it would take far more space than I have here even to give a fully rigorous exposition of it, let alone give an adequate explanation as to why anyone should think it worth taking seriously. (This is a task that I have undertaken elsewhere.[9]) Suffice it to say that a tremendous, and largely unappreciated, virtue of the Everett interpretation is that it is the only interpretation of quantum mechanics that avoids postulating *non-local*—that is to say faster-than-light—

---

[8] See Lockwood (1996).   [9] See ibid.

interactions between spatially separated physical systems. At the *theoretical* level, moreover, it is far more parsimonious than other interpretations. Everything proceeds smoothly, according to the dynamical laws, uninterrupted by 'collapses' or 'quantum jumps'. Moreover, there is no need to 'soup up' the ontology, by introducing extra properties, known as 'hidden variables'. And relativistic invariance is automatically preserved.

Having said that, however, I would not wish the reader to think that it is necessary to buy into the Everett interpretation, in order to accept the account I have been developing of how consciousness can be accommodated within the formal structure posited by quantum mechanics. No doubt many readers would prefer to cling to the common-sense assumption that, for anyone with an intact corpus callosum, there is at most *one* way, at any given time, that it is like to be that person. If so, fine. That would imply, in terms of my woodblock analogy, that with respect to the long axis of the block, the different patterns, associated with identically oriented but differently located cross-sections, somehow (to use a uniquely appropriate idiom!) get whittled down to just one. Fortunately, perhaps, to the extent that I wish to make converts of my readers, the main thesis of this chapter does not require the Everett interpretation to be correct. It depends only on there being, within a quantum-mechanical construal of the brain, mathematically expressible structure that lends itself to playing form to phenomenal content. That some physical systems do have states with this remarkable property of being, as it were, lit up from within, while others that are formally analogous do not, remains, as ever, utterly mystifying. But given that consciousness *does* exist, I can perhaps claim to have removed some of the obstacles to regarding consciousness itself as being as robustly material as anything in the quantum world can be said to be.

REFERENCES

DONALD, M. J. (1990), 'Quantum Theory and the Brain', *Proceedings of the Royal Society of London*, A427: 49–93.

—— (1992), 'A Priori Probability and Localized Observers', *Foundations of Physics*, 22: 1111–72.

—— (1995), 'A Mathematical Characterization of the Physical Structure of Observers', *Foundations of Physics*, 25: 529–71.

EVERETT, H. (1957), ' "Relative State" Formulation of Quantum Mechanics', *Reviews of Modern Physics*, 29: 454–62. Repr. in J. A. Wheeler and W. H. Zurek (eds.), *Quantum Theory and Measurement* (Princeton: Princeton University Press, 1987).

HAAG, R. (1992), *Local Quantum Physics* (Berlin: Springer-Verlag).

HAMEROFF, S. R., and PENROSE, R. (1996), 'Orchestrated Reduction of Quantum Coherence in Brain Microtubules—a Model for Consciousness', in

S. Hameroff, A. Kaszniak, and A. Scott (eds.), *Toward a Science of Consciousness: Contributions from the 1994 Tucson Conference* (Cambridge, Mass.: MIT Press), 508–40.

JAMES, W. (1907), *Principles of Psychology,* i (London: Macmillan; first published 1890).

LEIBNIZ, G. W. F. (1898), *Monadology* (written 1714), in Robert Latta (tr. and ed.), *Leibniz: Monadology and Other Philosophical Writings* (Oxford: Clarendon Press).

LOCKWOOD, M. (1981), 'What *was* Russell's Neutral Monism?', in Peter A. French, Theodore E. Uehling, Jr., and Howard K. Wettstein (eds.), *Midwest Studies in Philosophy,* vi. *The Foundations of Analytic Philosophy* (Minneapolis: University of Minnesota Press), 143–58.

—— (1989), *Mind, Brain and the Quantum* (Oxford: Blackwell).

—— (1996), ' "Many Minds" Interpretations of Quantum Mechanics', *British Journal for the Philosophy of Science,* 47: 445–61.

PENROSE, R. (1994), *Shadows of the Mind* (Oxford: Oxford University Press).

RUSSELL, B. (1927), *The Analysis of Matter* (London: Kegan Paul).

SAGAN, C. (1985), *Contact: A Novel* (New York: Simon & Schuster).

SELLARS, W. (1965), 'The Identity Approach to the Mind–Body Problem', *Journal of Metaphysics,* 18: 430–51.

WIGNER, E. P. (1962), 'Remarks on the Mind–Body Question', in I. J. Good (ed.), *The Scientist Speculates: An Anthology of Partly-Baked Ideas* (London: Heinemann), 284–302.

17. Mindless Sensationalism: A Quantum Framework for Consciousness

DON N. PAGE

I write as a physicist, with the knowledge that many physicists are studying the mathematical structure of our physical universe and hope to be able to find a 'theory of everything', or TOE, that will give a complete set of dynamical laws for this structure. This would essentially give the rules for how all the physical quantities in the universe evolve. Such a TOE would not by itself give the boundary conditions also necessary to determine the history of the universe, so it is a misnomer to say that it is a 'theory of everything', but it is convenient to retain the acronym TOE for this dynamical part of the laws of physics. Some physicists, such as Hartle and Hawking (1983), are also seeking to find rules specifying the boundary conditions (BC) of the universe. The combination of the TOE and the BC would then give a complete description of the mathematics of the state of the universe and its evolution. (This might be called a 'Theory Of More of Everything', or TOME.)

However, if one takes an even broader view, one realizes that even the TOME (the TOE and the BC) would not really comprise a theory of everything either, since they do not specify what conscious experiences occur within the universe. At least this seems to be the case if the TOME is assumed to be of the general mathematical types that are currently being sought, since such types do not seem by themselves to specify precisely what conscious experiences occur.

Nevertheless, there is the general consensus that there should be some sort of 'psychophysical parallelism' or connection between the mathematical structures described by current and sought-for theories of physics and the conscious experiences that each of us apparently has. Indeed, it can be argued

This work has been supported in part by the Natural Sciences and Engineering Council of Canada. Many of the people whom I have remembered as being influential in my formulation of my ideas are listed at the end of Page (1995), though of course none of them are ultimately responsible for it, and indeed most of them might well disagree with it.

that all we directly experience are these conscious experiences themselves, and our feelings that there is a mathematical structure for the physical world seem to be ultimately based upon the enormous success of our partial glimmerings of such a structure in explaining many aspects of our conscious experiences. In other words, we do not seem to experience directly the mathematical structure at all, but we seem to experience the feeling that our partial theories for such a structure help us understand our experiences better.

For example, as part of some of my conscious experiences while writing this, I have a feeling that I am looking at a computer screen that (except for the details of what is displayed upon it) is very similar to what I would consider to be the same computer screen that I think I remember viewing many times in the past. Furthermore, I have the feeling that my understanding of the feeling of the existence and persistence of certain properties of what I interpret to be the computer screen in front of me, is helped by my effective partial theory of the existence of this screen as a physical object and of its approximate 'object permanence' over the relevant timescales. (Incidentally, I do not believe that any ultimate theory of physics will have any precisely existing persons such as 'I', any precisely existing 'objects' such as computers screens, any absolute notions of 'personal identity' or 'object permanence', or even any absolute notion of time or of timescales, but to illustrate my ideas, I am merely using the crude notions from a rough instrumentalist theory to denote how 'I' feel 'I' 'believe' ideas about an 'external' 'physical' world seem to help explain my 'internal' 'mental' experiences.)

Therefore, very crudely, I think that I have the experience of remembering my computer screen as a persisting object because, according to my rough theory, there is such an object in the physical world.

Such a rough theory can be refined, and I might believe that a better theory claims that my conscious experience is more directly correlated with (or is 'caused by') certain physical processes within my brain. The point is that it certainly seems to have explanatory value to assume that in some sense there exists a physical world, and that our conscious experiences are either part of it or else are correlated with it.

Of course, it is logically possible that only the conscious experiences by themselves exist (or even just the one conscious experience that I am having 'now', to take an extreme solipsistic view that denies even the existence of my past experiences as anything other than the partial contents within the memory components of my present experience). However, the experienced correlation between the different components of the content of even my present experience would then seem to lack the explanation that appears possible from the assumed existence of an external physical world.

Therefore, I shall assume that an external physical world does exist in some sense and is helpful for explaining our conscious experiences. For it to be helpful, it must be connected or correlated with the internal conscious experiences in some way, and this connection is the 'psychophysical parallelism' or PPP that I shall assume exists.

Now the question arises as to what the form is of this assumed psychophysical parallelism. This form will of course be dependent upon the form of the two entities that are being connected, the internal conscious experiences and the external physical world. I am certainly no expert on the academic work that has been done on theories of the form of the internal conscious experiences, though I can claim to experience at least one of them directly myself. On the other hand, I have done academic work for many years on theories for the form of the external physical world, and so I have some idea of the constraints of current physical theories on that end of the psychophysical connection, even though we physicists certainly do not yet have the complete physical theory or TOME described above, and I would not be personally competent to assess it fully even if we physicists as a community did have such a theory.

An essential point here is that, so far as we know, and so far as current physics theories give any strong hint, the external physical world seems to be thoroughly quantum mechanical. Therefore, as Quentin Smith has emphasized in Ch. 15, a realistic theory of the psychophysical parallelism should include the quantum nature of the physical world in order to be consistent with the most basic feature of our current best theories of physics.

I should say that, unlike some, I do not believe that it is necessarily impossible for there to exist a (different) universe in which the physics is entirely classical and yet conscious experiences exist and are correlated with that external physical world. However, I am strongly convinced that such a classical universe is not ours, and so if we want a correct theory of the psychophysical connection for our universe, we must include the quantum nature of our universe (or possibly whatever it is that replaces the quantum if our current quantum theories are entirely superseded, though I think it highly unlikely that such a future theory would revert entirely to the completely classical picture held before quantum theory was discovered).

Of course, there are a multitude of ways in which one might postulate a connection between conscious experiences and a quantum physical world. Quentin Smith, Barry Loewer, and Michael Lockwood have discussed three within this volume. However, rather than reviewing the various possibilities that have been proposed, I shall summarize my own conjecture for the framework or basic form of the connection. When emphasizing the quantum side of the connection, I have called this Sensible Quantum Mechanics (SQM) (Page 1995*a*, *b*, 1996 *a–e*), but, for reasons that will become apparent, when emphasizing the conscious side of the connection, I might call it Mindless Sensationalism (MS).

Mindless Sensationalism is very similar in many ways to the many-minds theories developed by Lockwood (1989, 1992, 1996) and by David Albert (1992) and Loewer (Albert and Loewer 1988), except that the basic conscious entities, which Mindless Sensationalism asserts there are 'many' of, are conscious experiences rather than minds.

By a 'conscious experience', I mean all that one is consciously aware of or consciously experiencing at once. Lockwood has called this a 'phenomenal perspective', or 'maximal experience', or 'conscious state'. It could also be expressed as a total 'raw feel' that one has at once. In my papers on Sensible Quantum Mechanics (Page 1995a, b, 1996a–e), I have usually called it merely a 'perception', or sometimes an 'awareness' or 'sensation', but I do not wish to imply that I am using the same subtle meanings for those terms that others might. For example, I am not merely considering an individual sensory perception, or even just the set of simultaneous sensory perceptions of things external to the brain. Instead, what I mean by a conscious experience or perception is a total conscious awareness, a 'subjective', 'internal', 'first-person' experience by roughly what one crudely thinks of as one conscious 'being', at roughly the one 'time' that is then felt by the conscious 'being' to be 'now'. (However, I hasten to say that I doubt the absolute existence of any uniquely identifiable conscious 'beings' within our universe, and I also doubt the existence of any entity with the precise properties commonly ascribed to 'time', except possibly for the admitted existence of mental concepts within the contents of certain conscious experiences themselves. For me the conscious experiences themselves are the fundamental entities, and it is only in trying to illustrate, in commonly understood language, what I mean by them, that I am apparently forced to describe them in terms of what I regard as less fundamental concepts such as 'conscious beings' and 'at one time' or 'now'.)

A conscious experience can include components such as a visual sensation, an auditory sensation, a pain, a conscious memory, a conscious impression of a thought or belief, etc., that are all experienced together. However, it does not include a sequence of more than one immediate experience that in other proposals might be considered to be strung together to form a stream of consciousness of an individual mind.

Because I regard the basic conscious entities to be the conscious experiences themselves, which might crudely be called 'sensations' if one does not restrict the meaning of this word to be the conscious responses only to external stimuli, and because I doubt that these conscious experiences are arranged in any strictly defined sequences that one might define to be minds if they did exist, my framework has sensations without minds and hence may be labelled Mindless Sensationalism.

I should also emphasize that by a conscious experience, I mean the phenomenal, first-person, 'internal' subjective experience, and not the unconscious 'external' physical processes in the brain that accompany these subjective phenomena. Chalmers (1996) gives an excellent discussion of the distinction between the former, which he calls the phenomenal concept of mind, and the latter, which he calls the psychological concept of mind. In his language, what I mean by a conscious experience (and by other approximate synonyms that I might use, such as perception, sensation, or awareness) is the phenomenal concept, and not the psychological one.

Now that I have tried to illustrate what I mean by the conscious experiences that I take to be the basic entities that make up what might be called the 'internal' mental world (which I shall here call the 'conscious world'), let me turn to a quantum description of what might be called the 'external' physical world. (This world I shall here call the 'quantum world' to avoid offending the materialists who say that consciousness is part of the 'material world', whatever that is supposed to mean, and to avoid offending the physicists, myself included, who claim that consciousness is part of the 'physical world', whatever that is supposed to mean—as a physicist I shall take it to mean roughly whatever is studied by those who consider themselves doing physics. I'll nevertheless inevitably offend the smaller number of quantumists who consider consciousness to be a quantum phenomenon, but I want some short phrase to denote the non-conscious aspects of a physics description of our universe, without of course intending to deny that there is a relation between consciousness and the quantum world.)

For those who object that my terminology implies an unrealistic dualism between the internal mental world and the external physical world (between the 'conscious world' and the 'quantum world' as I am using these terms), I can say that I do not wish to imply that there is necessarily a fundamental distinction between these two 'worlds', but at the present level of description it seems to help to recognize the distinction between the two ways of describing aspects of our universe. Physicists often try to describe some aspects of our universe by using the mathematical language of current physics and ignoring consciousness, and it seems that others (idealists?) can consider conscious experiences separately from the aspects of our universe that physicists usually consider. There may be a deeper level of understanding at which the 'conscious world' and the 'quantum world' are unified, but to get to this level it does not seem to me to help to pretend that at our present level of understanding our descriptions do not usually make a distinction between what appears to be these two different aspects of reality.

Rather than restricting attention to particular theories or theoretical frameworks for the quantum world, such as non-relativistic quantum mechanics, relativistic quantum field theory, quantum gravity, or quantum string or M theory, I shall here focus on what I consider to be the basic elements of quantum theory as I presently understand it.

In the Feynman path-integral approach, the basic elements of quantum theory might be a set of 'paths' or fine-grained histories allowed for the universe, and a rule for assigning to each such history a complex number called an 'amplitude' (a number of the form of a real number plus i, the square root of -1, times another real number; the complex number is itself real if the real number multiplying i is 0). (The dynamical TOE would then be primarily concerned with specifying the rule for assigning the amplitudes, and the BC would essentially tell what paths are to be included.) That is not the whole story in this approach, however, as there seems to be a need to combine the individual paths into appropriate sets of paths and add up the amplitudes for all the paths in each set. Precisely how this is to be done is rather mysterious to me, and so I find it clearer to try to relate consciousness more directly to another approach to quantum theory, which might be called the operator approach. (There are crude rules for which amplitudes in the path-integral approach are to be added up in practical situations, but I'm not sure these rules are not implicitly invoking some assumptions about something like consciousness, whereas at the level of discussing only what I am calling the quantum world, I would like to start with a set of structures that do not depend in any way on consciousness.)

In the operator approach, the basic elements of quantum theory might be a set of 'operators' obeying some algebra (rules for adding and multiplying them), along with some 'quantum state' (or simply 'state') for the universe that determines a complex number called the 'expectation value' for each operator. I shall give some examples below, but for now one can think of the operators as some abstract mathematical entities that can be multiplied by complex numbers, added or subtracted, and multiplied together to give other operators. The expectation value of the operators, determined by the quantum state, is required to be linear in that the expectation value of a new operator that is a certain complex number times an old operator is simply that complex number times the expectation value of the old operator, and the expectation value of the sum of two operators is simply the sum of the expectation values of the two separate operators. (However, the expectation value of the product of two operators is not, in general, the product of the expectation values of the two separate operators.)

In the operator approach, the operators are somewhat analogous to the amplitudes for the paths in the path-integral approach and so would be the part primarily determined by the TOE. Similarly, the quantum state is somewhat analogous to the set of allowed paths in the path-integral approach and so would be primarily determined by the BC. Getting the expectation value for an operator would be analogous to adding up the amplitudes for a certain set of paths. (Actually, on this issue the operator approach seems a bit more complete, since to say what an operator means in the path-integral approach, one needs to say which set of paths contributes to each operator, usually with an additional complex weighting factor besides the amplitudes for the paths themselves.)

As an example of the operator approach, consider the example of a 'universe' consisting of a single non-relativistic particle moving in one spatial dimension, e.g. along the x-axis. In this simple case, the quantum states can be represented by 'wavefunctions' that are complex functions of x, say $\psi(x)$, and which are square-integrable, meaning in this case that the integral of $|\psi(x)|^2$ over all x is finite. (The absolute value squared of a complex number, such as $\psi = \psi_R + i\psi_I$ with ψ_R and ψ_I being the two real numbers that make it up, is $|\psi|^2 = \psi_R^2 + \psi_I^2$, a real non-negative quantity that is the square of the distance, from the origin, of the point representing ψ on the complex plane, which itself has a horizontal, or 'real', axis representing the real part, ψ_R, of the complex number ψ, and a vertical, or 'imaginary', axis representing the imaginary part, ψ_I, of the complex number ψ.)

In this one-dimensional quantum example, operators are mathematical entities that represent ways of changing one wavefunction to another in a linear way. For example, corresponding to the position x that the particle might be considered to have in a classical description, there is the quantum position operator, say X, that converts a wavefunction $\psi(x)$ to the wavefunction $x\psi(x)$. (Strictly speaking, X is not really a well-defined operator if the space of states is represented by all square-integrable wavefunctions, since there exist square-integrable wavefunctions $\psi(x)$, such as $\psi(x) = 1/\sqrt{\pi(1 + x^2)}$, for which $x\psi(x)$ is not square-integrable, but to get a simple example, I shall here ignore the mathematical technicalities that one can use to get a class of wavefunctions for which X is a good operator.) Similarly, corresponding to the momentum p that the particle might have in a classical description, there is the quantum momentum, say P, that converts a wavefunction $\psi(x)$ to the wavefunction $-id\psi(x)/dx$.

Operators change states in linear ways, so for complex numbers a and b, the operator $aX + bP$ converts a wavefunction $\psi(x)$ to the wavefunction $ax\psi(x) - ibd\psi(x)/dx$.

The product of two operators, such as PX, has the effect of performing the operation on the right first, followed by the operation to the left. Thus PX converts a wavefunction $\psi(x)$ to the wavefunction $-id(x\psi(x))/dx = -ixd\psi(x)/dx - i\psi(x)$. Note that, in general, the product of two operators depends on the order in which the are taken, so XP converts a wavefunction $\psi(x)$ to the wavefunction $-ixd\psi(x)/dx$, the same as $PX - iI$ does, where I is the identity operator that converts a wavefunction $\psi(x)$ to the same wavefunction $\psi(x)$. This example shows that, for any wavefunction, $XP = PX - iI$ or $PX - XP = iI$. (This is a so-called commutation relation, since $PX - XP$, which is mathematically denoted by $[P, X]$, is called the commutator of P and X. This commutation relation is what essentially gives the Heisenberg uncertainty relation for momentum and position, but it would take me too far afield to explain that here.)

Now that I have given an example of operators from one-dimensional non-relativistic quantum mechanics, let me illustrate how quantum states give expectation values to operators. In Dirac's 'bracket' notation, a 'pure' quantum state can written as the 'ket' $|\psi\rangle$, which in my example is represented by the wavefunction $\psi(x) = \psi_R + i\psi_I$, or alternatively, it can be written as the 'bra' $\langle\psi|$, which is represented by the complex conjugate wavefunction $\bar{\psi}(x) = \psi_R(x) - i\psi_I(x)$. A slightly better representation of the pure state is the combination $|\psi\rangle\langle\psi|$, which avoids the phase ambiguity in representing a pure state by either $|\psi\rangle$ or $\langle\psi|$ individually, since the state is physically the same if $|\psi\rangle$ is multiplied by the complex phase factor $e^{i\theta} = \cos\theta + i\sin\theta$ and $\langle\psi|$ is multiplied by the complex conjugate phase factor $e^{-i\theta} = \cos\theta - i\sin\theta$ for some real angle θ measured in radians (degrees divided by 180 and multiplied by π, so that a 180-degree rotation is represented by $\theta = \pi$, which gives $e^{i\theta} = e^{-i\theta} = -1$). The phase factor has no physical consequences, and indeed $|\psi\rangle\langle\psi|$ remains unchanged by it, since $e^{i\theta}e^{-i\theta} = 1$ so that $e^{i\theta}|\psi\rangle\langle\psi|e^{-i\theta} = |\psi\rangle\langle\psi|$.

The result of an operation, say X, on a quantum state denoted by $|\psi\rangle$ can be then denoted as $X|\psi\rangle$, say $|\phi\rangle$, and represented by the wavefunction $\phi(x)$ (which in this particular case is $x\psi(x)$). Then the expectation value of X, denoted by $\langle X\rangle$, is the 'inner product' of the bra $\langle\psi|$ with the ket $|\phi\rangle = X|\psi\rangle$, which is

$$\langle X\rangle = \langle\psi|X|\psi\rangle = \langle\psi|\phi\rangle = \int_{-\infty}^{\infty} dx\,\bar{\psi}(x)\phi(x) = \int_{-\infty}^{\infty} dx\,\bar{\psi}(x)x\psi(x). \quad (1)$$

One can readily see from this example that the expectation value is linear in the operators, e.g.

$$\langle aX + bP\rangle = a\langle X\rangle + b\langle P\rangle, \quad (2)$$

but in general,

$$\langle XP\rangle \neq \langle X\rangle\langle P\rangle. \quad (3)$$

Although for my purposes below it is generally sufficient to think of the universe as having a pure quantum state, for completeness I should say that besides the pure states best represented by the single term $|\psi\rangle\langle\psi|$, one can have 'mixed' or 'statistical' states represented by a sum of such terms,

$$\rho = \sum_{i,j} c_{ij}|\psi_j\rangle\langle\psi_i|, \tag{4}$$

with a set of different kets $|\psi_i\rangle$ and bras $\langle\psi_j|$, where the c_{ij}'s form what is known as the density matrix, which is Hermitian ($c_{ij} = \bar{c}_{ji}$), positive (eigenvalues non-negative), and normalized (eigenvalues summing to unity). For such a state, the expectation value of an operator such as X is

$$\langle X \rangle = tr(X\rho) = \sum_{i,j} c_{ij}\langle\psi_i|X|\psi_j\rangle. \tag{5}$$

For infinitely large systems, there are even more general states, known as C*-algebra states, which need not be represented by normalized density matrices. Instead, such states are represented by positive linear functionals of the operators. (A functional of a set of operators is something analogous to a formula that gives a number for each operator. A positive functional gives positive numbers for positive operators, which are operators that have positive eigenvalues. A linear functional gives a number for the sum of two operators that is the sum of the two numbers that it would give for each operator individually.) If such a state is written symbolically as σ, then one can write the expectation value of an operator like X as $\langle X \rangle = \sigma[X]$. The pure and mixed states described above are then special cases of these more general C*-algebra states, so for generality we can denote any quantum state by a positive linear functional σ.

So far I have not put time into the picture. I believe that time is not a basic fundamental part of physics, so in the ultimate description of the quantum world (at least if it continues to use what I am here regarding as the fundamental entities of quantum theory), there will be operators and a quantum state for the universe, but no time. However, in most of our approximate quantum theories for models of parts of the universe, time does enter. For example, in non-relativistic quantum theory, in the Heisenberg picture I shall use when speaking of time, the quantum state is considered to be independent of time, but the operators, like X and P, are defined to be functions of the time t, as $X(t)$ and $P(t)$. (The wavefunction that represents the time-independent quantum state $|\psi\rangle$ is then also a function of time, $\psi(x, t)$.) Then the quantum algebra relates the operators at different times. For example, for a free particle of unit mass, the relation takes the simple form

$$X(t) = X(0) + tP(0) \tag{6}$$

and

$$P(t) = P(0). \tag{7}$$

The form of the relation of these operators at different times, which I am considering to be part of the algebra of the operators, depends on the dynamics of the system, for example on the forces on the particle in this simple one-dimensional example. One might say that if time does not really exist, then there is no dynamics, which would trivialize the TOE, but I take the attitude that it is the algebra of the operators (the rules giving all their sums and products) that represents the dynamics, and this can persist even if time as we usually know it does not.

I might add that even if one has time within some model system, such as the one-dimensional non-relativistic quantum mechanical model described above, if this system is really a closed quantum system, what I believe is important about it is described by the quantum state and the quantum operators, but not the representation of the operators at various times. For example, in equation (6), even though $X(t)$ has a different representation from $X(0) + tP(0)$, I believe there is fundamentally no distinction between them, because they are equal operators. Therefore, even in models in which a time such at t exists, the operators cannot be uniquely identified with any single time, and so what I regard as the basic quantum entities are effectively timeless. Only if one augments the basic quantum theory of states and operators with distinctions between different forms of the same operators, such as the left and right hand sides of equation (6), does one get any real dependence upon the time parameter t. .

If the quantum world is described by operators and states (with our universe being described by one particular set of operators and by a particular state, the so-called 'quantum state of the universe'), then a goal of a theory of psycho-physical parallelism (PPP) would be to give the connection between the quantum state of the universe and the conscious experiences occurring within it. Eschewing the extreme solipsistic view that only my present conscious experience exists, I assume that many conscious experiences exist within the universe, so a PPP should give many conscious experiences for a single quantum state.

Suppose that one denotes an individual conscious experience by the letter p and defines the 'conscious world' M as the set of all possible conscious experiences in all universes with all possible quantum states (i.e. not just in our universe with its particular quantum state σ). One logically possible view would be that all possible conscious experiences exist equally, regardless of the quantum state. But this would make the quantum world completely irrelevant for the existing conscious experiences, and so the apparent order that I sense within my present experience would not at all be explained by any postulated quantum world. On the contrary, I feel that the order that I sense within my own experience is better explained by assuming that there is a quantum world and that the conscious experiences are in some sense correlated with it. Therefore, I shall make this assumption, that there is indeed a non-trivial psychophysical parallelism.

The next possibility one can consider is the assumption that the quantum state of the universe restricts the set of conscious experiences that actually exist to be a proper subset, say E, of the set M of all possible conscious experiences, but that each conscious experience within the existing set E is equally real. This would seem to be a reasonable assumption if the quantum world were actually classical, so that some physical possibilities definitely happen and others do not. Then it would be plausible that some conscious experiences definitely happen and that others do not.

For example, suppose that one takes a simplified non-relativistic classical model in which there are a certain set of pointlike elementary particles that move along definite trajectories through space as a function of time, so that at each time there is a definite configuration of the positions of these particles in space. The temporal sequence of these configurations could then be called the classical history of this universe. Certain sets of the configurations might be identified as conscious brain states, and for each of these one might identify a corresponding conscious experience p. Then one might propose that if a configuration corresponding to the conscious experience p occurs during the classical history of this universe, then this conscious experience exists, but if the configuration never occurs, the corresponding conscious experience does not exist either. If there is some correspondence between the orderliness of the physical brain configurations and the orderliness perceived within the conscious experience, then an orderly history could explain orderly conscious experiences.

A similar picture with a definite sequence of configurations occurs in the de Broglie and Bohm version of non-relativistic quantum theory (de Broglie 1928, 1953, 1956, 1970; Bohm 1952, 1953; Bohm and Hiley 1993; Holland 1993; Berndl et al. 1995; Cushing, Fine, and Goldstein 1996), in which to the normal operators and state there is added a definite trajectory whose evolution, but not whose initial configuration, is determined by the wavefunction, which acts as a 'pilot wave'. However, it seems to me unnecessary to add a trajectory to quantum theory, which for completeness would require a specification of its initial configuration as additional information. It also seems very ugly to try to do this for examples beyond non-relativistic quantum mechanics. For example, in relativistic quantum field theory, a trajectory of sequences of field configurations that obeyed Bohm's equation for the evolution of the configurations using the time corresponding to one observer would not obey that equation using instead the time corresponding to a moving observer, so that relativistic invariance would be broken by the trajectories.

However, in a quantum theory with operators and a state, unless one adds extra elements such as the definite trajectory of Bohm's version of quantum theory, it seems difficult or ugly to have the operators and state give a definite rule for saying that some possible conscious experiences definitely exist but that others do not. It is much easier to have a rule assigning different (non-negative real) weights or levels of reality to different conscious experiences, with the rule depending upon the quantum state of the universe. Then if all conscious experiences with positive weights w are said to exist, but if experiences with greater weights exist in some sense more, then one might expect that it is more likely that one's experience would be one that has greater weight. (One might like to propose that one simply takes all possible conscious experiences with positive weight as existing and all possible conscious experiences with zero weight as not existing, but for the simplest ways of assigning the weights from quantum theory, such as the one given below, almost all the possible conscious experiences would have weights at least a tiny bit positive, so this proposal would exclude as non-existing only an infinitesimally small fraction of the total set M of conscious experiences p. Therefore, I am not considering this particular proposal further.)

In other words, if the weight $w(p)$ gives the level of reality or existence of the conscious experience p, one can say that in the universe almost all possible conscious experiences exist in the sense of having at least some positive measure of reality, but some sets of experiences are much more real than others, existing to a much greater degree than other sets. One way to describe this is to imagine randomly selecting a conscious experience p out of all of the possible ones. For a random selection one always needs a weight, and if it is chosen to be the weight $w(p)$ that comes from the quantum state σ by some particular theory of psychophysical parallelism, then the probability that a particular conscious experience p will be chosen by the random selection will be proportional to its weight $w(p)$.

In this way one can say that the weight $w(p)$ is analogous to the probability for the conscious experience p, but it is not to be interpreted as the probability for the bare *existence* of p, since any conscious experience p exists (is actually experienced) if its weight is positive, $w(p) > 0$. Rather, $w(p)$ is to be interpreted as being proportional to the probability of *getting* this particular experience if a random selection is made.

A more picturesque way of viewing the weight, but one which has the danger of misinterpretation if all the elements used in the picture are assumed to have reality or are confused with similar elements that occur in our present approximate theories of the world, is by an analogy. Assume that God has His own time (not to be confused with the time that we use in our present approximate physical theories, but having some properties analogous to what we often assume, perhaps erroneously, that time does in our approximate physical theories), and that as He creates each conscious experience, He spends a time $w(p)$ giving existence to each. In other words, assume that each exists for an amount $w(p)$ of God's time. Then the conscious experiences with greater $w(p)$ will have a greater existence in the sense of their duration in God's time. The picture is then that the weight for conscious experiences may be viewed as somewhat analogous to the measure of physical time used for calculating time averages in dynamical systems, for example.

Because the specification of the conscious experience p completely determines its content and how it is experienced (how it feels), the weight $w(p)$ has absolutely no effect on that—there is absolutely no way within the experience to sense anything directly of what the weight is. A toothache within a particular conscious experience p is precisely as painful an experience no matter what $w(p)$ is. Furthermore, the experience p is whatever p is and has absolutely no memory of how long God may have had that experience existing within His time in the analogy. It is just that an experience with a greater $w(p)$ is more likely in the sense of being more probably chosen by a random selection using the weights $w(p)$. (Of course, the experience p might include a conscious awareness of belief in a theory that assigns a particular weight to that experience, but the awareness of that belief will be part of p itself and will not directly depend on whether the actual weight is what the believed theory assigns for it. In this way a conscious belief depends only on the conscious experience of which that belief is a part and not on the truth of the implications of that belief. It is only by faith in the orderliness of the universe that we can assume that our conscious orderly beliefs about it are true, and even that faith itself can be regarded to be just given as part of the corresponding conscious experience.)

If one takes the attitude that there is no reality to a divine temporal period $w(p)$ for the existence of the conscious experience p (in the analogy that admittedly is rather contrived), and that there is no reality to the random selection with weights proportional to $w(p)$, then one might think that the weights have no reality but are merely a meaningless arbitrary assignment. I do find it difficult to try to describe the weights in terms of anything more basic and of whose existence I am more confident, but I also believe that the weights really are fundamental elements of reality. In other words, I believe that some sets of conscious experiences really do have greater measures of reality than others, and this greater measure is the explanation of why my present experience has its experienced orderliness: such orderly experiences have greater weight than ones which are much more disorderly. Of course, I cannot prove this assumption, but it enables me to make progress towards finding an explanation of the orderliness that I experience, so I shall continue to make it here.

One technical point that it is now time to make is that to simplify the discussion above, I have often implicitly assumed that the set M of possible conscious experiences is a countable discrete set, so that, for example, one can imagine choosing an experience p at random with weight $w(p)$. In particular, if the total sum of the weights for all conscious experiences is finite and is normalized to be unity, then the weight $w(p)$ for each conscious experience is simply the probability for that experience to be chosen by the random selection. This is indeed the possibility that is the easiest to visualize, and it generally will not hurt to have it in mind for most of the discussion below, but in forming a fairly general framework for the connection between the quantum and mental worlds, I would not like to make unnecessary restrictions, and so I shall allow the possibility that the set of conscious experiences may be uncountable or continuous. (Is there a true continuum for the pain of a toothache, or is there only a countable set of discrete values for how painful it can feel? We don't know which it is, so I shall allow either possibility.)

If the set M of conscious experiences is a continuum, then a non-zero weight for a single conscious experience p (a point in this continuum) is rather meaningless, but in reasonable cases one can still have a weight for any set S of experiences, even if this weight is zero for any single individual experience. (For even this to be possible, the set M of all possible experiences must be a measurable set, which I shall continue to assume, since I personally don't know how to make much sense of a generalization in which that is not true.) To give the weight for a set of experiences a fancier name, let us henceforth call it the *measure* $\mu(S)$ of the subset S of the full set M of possible conscious experiences.

Then one can imagine that if exclusive subsets are being selected randomly with the measure μ, then the ratio of the probability of choosing S_1, say, to that of choosing S_2 would be $\mu(S_1)/\mu(S_2)$, so the measures for the sets would give their relative probabilities. If $\mu(M)$ is finite, then one can define a normalized weight $P(S) = \mu(S)/\mu(M)$ which would be the probability of choosing the subset S if one randomly selected, with the measure μ, among an exhaustive and exclusive set of subsets of M that includes the subset S. For example, if S_1 is the set of conscious experiences in which no toothache is felt and S_2 is the set of conscious experiences in which a toothache is felt, then these two subsets of M form an exhaustive and exclusive set of two subsets of M, since every conscious experience p in M is in S_1 or S_2 (exhaustive subsets), and no experience is in both (exclusive subsets). Therefore, $\mu(M) = \mu(S_1) + \mu(S_2)$, and $P(S_2) = \mu(S_2)/\mu(M)$ is the probability of randomly selecting a conscious experience with a toothache.

However, it might be that the total set M of conscious experiences is so large, and the measure $\mu(S)$ for its subsets S is so widely spread, that the total measure of M is divergent. (A simple example would be if M could be put into one-to-one correspondence with the real number line, $-\infty < x < \infty$, and if the measure for the set $S = \{x | x_1 < x < x_2\}$ were $\mu(S) = x_2 - x_1$, simply the length of the interval for x.) Then any subset with finite measure $\mu(S)$ would have zero absolute probability of being chosen if one divided by the infinite $\mu(M)$. Also, even if one chose subsets with infinite measure, dividing that infinity by the infinity of the total measure would generally give ambiguous results, and so absolute probabilities that are not zero would be ambiguous. This might make it hard to test such a theory. However, if one had two subsets with finite measure, say S_1 and S_2, then one would get a finite conditional probability to be in, say, S_1, given that one is in the union of the two sets, and so there still might be some tests of such a measure that one could make. Therefore, I am hesitant at this stage to demand that the total measure for the full set M of all possible conscious experiences be finite.

Now, having explained briefly what I take the basics of quantum theory to be and what it might mean to have a set of conscious experiences with a measure, it is time to write these as axioms and add my axiom for the basic structure of the psychophysical parallelism.

Mindless Sensationalism (MS) is given by three basic postulates or axioms (Page 1995):

Quantum World Axiom: The unconscious 'quantum world' Q is completely described by an appropriate algebra of operators and by a suitable state σ (a positive linear functional of the operators) giving the expectation value $\langle O \rangle \equiv \sigma[O]$ of each operator O.

Conscious World Axiom: The 'conscious world' M, the set of all conscious experiences or perceptions p, has a fundamental measure $\mu(S)$ for each subset S of M.

Psychophysical Parallelism Axiom: The measure $\mu(S)$ for each set S of conscious experiences is given by the expectation value of a corresponding 'awareness operator' $A(S)$, a positive-operator-valued (POV) measure, in the state σ of the quantum world:

$$\mu(S) = \langle A(S) \rangle \equiv \sigma[A(S)]. \tag{8}$$

For $A(S)$ to be a POV measure, it is necessary that $A(S)$ be zero when S is the empty set and otherwise be either zero or else a positive operator, which implies that $\sigma[A(S)] \geq 0$ for all positive linear functionals σ, and it is also necessary that if the set S is a countable union of disjoint sets s_i, $A(S)$ is the sum of the $A(s_i)$ when this sum 'converges in the weak operator topology' (E. B. Davies 1976).[1] Then $\mu(S)$ has the standard additivity property of a measure.

---

[1] I thank Shelley Goldstein (private communication) for suggesting the use of POV measures and directing me to this reference.

As essentially mentioned above in my description of what I consider to be the basics of quantum theory, the Quantum World Axiom is here deliberately vague as to the precise nature of the algebra of operators and of the state, because as the details of various quantum theories of the universe are being developed, I do not want the general framework of Sensible Quantum Mechanics at this time to be made too restrictive.

The PPP Axiom states my assumption of the structure of the 'psychophysical laws', the laws that presumably give the 'neural correlates of consciousness'. This axiom, when combined with the other two, gives what to me seems to be the simplest and most conservative framework for '*bridging* principles that link the physical facts with consciousness' and for stating 'the connection at the level of "Brain state X produces conscious state Y" for a vast collection of complex physical states and associated experiences' (Chalmers 1996) in language that is consistent with Sydney Coleman's description (Coleman 1993, 1995) of quantum theory as having 'N o special measurement process, N o reduction of the wavefunction, N o indeterminacy' (in particular, with a many-experiences variant of Everett's quantum theory (Everitt 1957; DeWitt and Graham 1973), in which measures for sets of conscious experiences are added to the bare unitary quantum theory that Coleman advocates).

The PPP Axiom is the simplest way I know of connecting the quantum world with the conscious world. One could easily imagine more complicated connections, such as having $\mu(S)$ be a sum or integral, over the conscious experiences p in the set of S, of some non-linear function of the expectation values, say $m(p)$, of positive 'experience operators' $E(p)$ depending in the ps (Page 1995). Instead, my PPP Axiom restricts the functions in the sum or integral to be linear in the expectation values. In short, I am proposing that the psychophysical parallelism is *linear.*

Of course, the PPP Axiom, like the Quantum World Axiom, is here also deliberately vague as to the form of the awareness operators $A(S)$, because I do not have a detailed theory of consciousness, but only a framework for fitting it with quantum theory. My suggestion is that a theory of consciousness that is not inconsistent with bare quantum theory should be formulated within this framework (unless a better framework can be found, of course). I am also suspicious of any present detailed theory that purports to say precisely under what conditions in the quantum world consciousness occurs, since it seems that we simply don't know yet. I feel that present detailed theories may be analogous to the cargo cults of the South Pacific after World War II, in which an incorrect theory was adopted, that aircraft with goods would land simply if airfields and towers were built.

Since all sets S of conscious experiences with $\mu(S) > 0$ really occur in the framework of Mindless Sensationalism, it is completely deterministic if the quantum state and the $A(S)$ are determined: there are no random or truly probabilistic elements in MS. Nevertheless, because the framework has measures for sets of conscious experiences, one can readily use them to calculate quantities that can be interpreted as conditional probabilities. One can consider sets of conscious experiences S_1, S_2, etc., defined in terms of properties of the conscious experiences. For example, S_1 might be the set of conscious experiences in which there is a conscious memory of having tossed a coin one hundred times, and S_2 might be the set of conscious experiences in which there is a conscious memory of getting more than seventy heads. Then one can interpret

$$P(S_2|S_1) \equiv \mu(S_1 \cap S_2)/\mu(S_1) \tag{9}$$

as the conditional probability that the conscious experience is in the set S_2, given that it is in the set S_1. In our example, this would be the conditional probability that a conscious experience included a conscious memory of getting more than seventy heads, given that it included a conscious memory of having tossed a coin one hundred times.

An analogue of this conditional 'probability' is the conditional probability that a person at the beginning of the twenty-first century is the Queen of England. If we consider a model of all the six billion people, including the Queen, that we agree to consider as living humans on Earth at the beginning of 2001, then at the basic level of this model the Queen certainly exists in it; there is nothing random or probabilistic about her *existence*. But if the model weights each of the six billion people equally, then one can in a manner of speaking say that the conditional probability that one of these persons is the Queen is somewhat less than 2×10^{-10}. That is, if one chooses at random one of the six billion people on Earth at the beginning of 2001, with each person being assigned an equal probability of being chosen, then the probability of *getting* the Queen by this random selection is, to one-digit accuracy, 2×10^{-10}. (One can see that this probability of getting the Queen would be much more if one instead weighted the probability for each person by the weight of his or her crown, which would be analogous to having a different quantum state giving a different $\mu(S) = \langle A(S) \rangle$.) I am proposing that it is in the same manner of speaking that one can assign conditional probabilities to sets of conscious experiences, even though there is nothing truly random about them at the basic level.

As it is defined by the three basic axioms above, Mindless Sensationalism is a framework and not a complete theory for the universe, since it would need to be completed by giving the detailed algebra of operators and state of the quantum world, the set of all possible conscious experiences of the conscious world, and the awareness operators $A(S)$ for the subsets of possible conscious experiences, whose quantum expectation values are the measures for these subsets.

Furthermore, even if such a complete theory were found, it would not necessarily be the final theory of the universe, since one would like to systematize the connection between the elements given above. As Chalmers (1996: 214–15) eloquently puts it,

An ultimate theory will not leave the connection at the level of 'Brain state X produces conscious state Y' for a vast collection of complex physical states and associated experiences. Instead, it will systematize this connection via an underlying explanatory framework, specifying simple underlying laws in virtue of which the connection holds. Physics does not content itself with being a mere mass of observations about the positions, velocities, and charges of various objects at various times; it systematizes these observations and shows how they are consequences of underlying laws, where the underlying laws are as simple and as powerful as possible. The same should hold of a theory of consciousness. We should seek to explain the supervenience of consciousness upon the physical in terms of the simplest possible set of laws.

Ultimately, we will wish for a set of *fundamental laws*. Physicists seek a set of basic laws simple enough that one might write them on the front of a T-shirt; in a theory of consciousness, we should expect the same thing. In both cases, we are questing for the basic structure of the universe, and we have good reason to believe that the basic structure has a remarkable simplicity. The discovery of fundamental laws may be a distant goal, however. . . .

When we finally have fundamental theories of physics and consciousness in hand, we may have what truly counts as a theory of everything. The fundamental physical laws will explain the character of physical processes; the psychophysical laws will explain the conscious experiences that are associated; and everything else will be a consequence.

Returning to the elements above of a postulated Mindless Sensationalism theory that is complete but not necessarily final, it is presently premature to try to give these elements precisely, particularly the awareness operators that have generally been left out of physics discussions. However, one might give a crude discussion of what they might be like in some highly approximate way.

One very strong assumption that might possibly be plausible for certain quantum theories, is what I have called the Orthogonal Projection Hypothesis (Page 1995). In the terms of this chapter, it implies that the awareness operators $A(S)$ are projection operators, say $\Pi(S)$ (operators that remain the same when multiplied by themselves: $\Pi\Pi = \Pi$, which implies that the eigenvalues of the operator are either zero or one), and that the awareness operators for two disjoint sets of conscious experiences, say S_1 and S_2, are orthogonal, so $A(S_1)A(S_2) = A(S_2)A(S_1) = 0$. (I should say that I see several reasons for doubting that this very strong Commuting Projection Hypothesis is really plausible as a precise condition on the awareness operators, so I am not advocating this assumption as the final word, but it might be approximately true at least for certain sets S of conscious experiences, and it does lead to various simple consequences.)

A projection operator corresponds to a corresponding property that a state may have with certainty (if it is an eigenstate of that operator with unit eigenvalue) or that a state may be certain not to have (if it is an eigenstate of that operator with zero eigenvalue). For a given projection operator, a generic state is not an eigenstate and so is not considered with certainty either to have the property or not to have it. This is an expression of what is often considered the uncertainty of quantum theory, though I would just regard it as a limitation on what properties a system has with 'certainty'.

In the Copenhagen version of quantum theory, to which I do not subscribe except in a very rough instrumentalist sense, a 'measurement' is assumed to cause a normalized quantum state to change or 'collapse' to another quantum state given by applying a projection operator to the original state and then renormalizing its magnitude. The expectation value of the projection operator, $P = \langle \Pi \rangle$ in the original state, is then interpreted as the probability that that state will thus collapse, effectively giving a 'yes' answer to the question posed by the measurement of whether the system being measured has the property corresponding to the projection operator Π. (Then $1 - P = \langle (I - \Pi) \rangle$ is the probability that the answer will be 'no,' so that the state will instead collapse to the other possibility, which is that given by applying the complementary projection operator $I - \Pi$ to the original state and renormalizing it—here I is the identity operator that leaves a state the same.) The fact that Π is a projection operator means that if the state collapsed to the 'yes' answer, a second measurement of precisely the same property would with certainty give the answer 'yes' again, so that after the state collapses the first time, to an eigenstate of the projection operator with unit eigenvalue, the property corresponding to the projection operator will with certainty be true.

To illustrate projection operators, return to the example of a single non-relativistic particle moving along the x axis, with its quantum state represented by a wavefunction $\psi(x)$ which is normalized so that the integral of $|\psi(x)|^2$ over all x is unity. In this case a simple example of a projection operator Π is one that determines whether the particle is in some range of x, say the range $x > 0$. The expectation value of this is then P, the integral of $|\psi(x)|^2$ over all positive x, and if the quantum state collapses to this possibility in the Copenhagen version of quantum theory, the wavefunction would change to $\psi(x)/\sqrt{P}$ for $x > 0$ and to 0 for $x < 0$, effectively giving a 'yes' answer to the measurement determination of whether the particle was to the right of the origin. On the other hand, if the answer is 'no', which would occur with a probability $1 - P$, the wavefunction would change to 0 for $x > 0$ and to

$\psi(x)\sqrt{1-P}$ for $x < 0$. This change is known as the 'collapse of the wave-function' or the 'reduction of the quantum state'.

In my Mindless Sensationalism, the quantum state of the universe never changes by any collapse or reduction mechanism. However, if the awareness operator $A(S)$ for a certain set of conscious experiences is a projection operator Π, and if the quantum state is normalized so that the expectation value of the unit operator I is unity, then $\mu(S) = \langle A(S) \rangle = \langle \Pi \rangle = P$, the same as the probability in the Copenhagen version of quantum theory that measuring the property corresponding to Π would give a 'yes' answer.

For example, it is tempting to suppose that if the set of conscious experiences is a set of very similar experiences (or perhaps just a single experience if the set of possible experiences is countably discrete) that would occur for a person having a particular brain configuration, then $A(S)$ is approximately a projection operator onto those brain configurations. In this case, the measure $\mu(S)$ for those experiences would then be the same as the probability for the corresponding brain configurations in Copenhagen quantum theory.

The Orthogonal Projection Hypothesis appears to be a specific mathematical realization of part of Lockwood's (1989: 215) proposal, that 'a phenomenal perspective [what I have here usually been calling a conscious experience p] may be equated with a shared eigenstate of some preferred (by consciousness) set of compatible brain observables'. Here I have expressed the 'equating' by my Quantum-Consciousness Connection Axiom, and presumably the 'shared eigenstate' can be expressed by a corresponding projection operator Π.

Or, as Lockwood has expressed it in the previous chapter, 'I am suggesting, in other words, that the contents of consciousness, at any given moment, correspond to a set of measurement outcomes that belong to the respective spectra of a compatible set of observables on the mind, construed as a subsystem of the brain.' If this suggestion is incorporated within my axioms, it effectively assumes that the awareness operators corresponding to sets of conscious experiences 'at any given moment' obey the Orthogonal Projection Hypothesis. However, in my axioms I do not need a definition of what 'at any given moment' might mean, and I do not need to be able to define the mind as a subsystem of the brain; for me the awareness operators $A(S)$ are basic. (I also do not need the Orthogonal Projection Hypothesis, though for now it is interesting to examine the consequences if it were true.)

I should also emphasize that if the same conscious experience is produced by several different orthogonal 'eigenstates of consciousness' (e.g. different states of a brain and surroundings that give rise to the same conscious experience p), then in the Orthogonal Projection Hypothesis the projection operator Π would be a sum of the corresponding rank-one projection operators and so would be a projection operator of rank higher than unity. This is what I would expect, since surely the surroundings could be different and yet the appropriate part of the brain, if unchanged, would lead to the same experience. As Lockwood (Chapter 16 above) has put it,

In particular, the contents of consciousness would seem to be highly *coarse-grained*, in relation to the immensely intricate physical processes on which they ostensibly supervene. A philosopher who took this difficulty for materialism very seriously was Wilfred Sellars (1965), who dubbed it the 'grain problem'.   (p. 453)

Crucially, I also assume that the compatible set of observables, corresponding eigenvalues of which jointly define a given state of consciousness, is invariably an *incomplete* set. A complete compatible set of observables is one that, when measured, yields *maximal information* concerning the measured system—information that cannot be improved on by adding further observables to the set. This relates directly to the grain problem. Only by allowing the operative compatible sets of observables to be *incomplete* can we ratchet down the degree of resolution and complexity of the corresponding conscious state to what one would intuitively judge to be the right level.   (pp. 458–9)

On the other hand, if $A(S)$ were a sum of non-commuting projection operators, or even a sum of commuting projection operators that are not orthogonal, or if it were a weighted sum of orthogonal projection operators with weights different from unity, then generically $A(S)$ would not be a projection operator Π as assumed in the Orthogonal Projection Hypothesis. Although it would mean that the situation would not be so simple as one (e.g. Lockwood, or I in an optimistic moment) might like to assume, I see no fundamental difficulty in having the awareness operators not be projection operators and not be orthogonal.

There are many other alternative technical assumptions that one might make about the awareness operators (Page 1995), but I shall not discuss them further here.

Another point I should emphasize is that in Mindless Sensationalism, there is no fundamental notion of a correlation between distinct conscious experiences. One can get the measure (and the normalized probability, if the total measure for the set M of all conscious experiences is finite) for any set S of experiences, but one does not get any non-trivial fundamental formula for the joint occurrence of distinct experiences. In particular, there does not seem to be any fundamental formula for the conditional probability of one set S of experiences given a second set S' that is exclusively distinct, having no elements in common with the first set S (other than the formula for the basic probability $P(S)$ of the first set, the trivial conditional probability). This essentially fits the crudely expressed fact that by the definition of a conscious experience p, a 'conscious being' can be directly aware of only 'one at a time'. From the memory components of a 'present' experience, one might postulate the existence of a 'past' experience in which what is now just remembered is at that 'past' 'time' then experienced as occurring simultaneously with the 'past' experience itself when that experience was being experienced. However, within one's present experience, one has no direct experience of the past experience itself. Correspondingly, within my framework of Mindless Sensationalism, there is no fundamental way to assign a probability of a 'past' experience given a particular present one. Instead, each experience (if countably discrete, or else each set of experiences if one must combine a continuum of them to get a non-zero measure $\mu(S)$) has its own measure, which is independent of the realization of any other experiences.

In the other direction of 'time', Mindless Sensationalism does not assign any fundamental conditional probabilities to any 'future' experiences given the existence of a particular present one. One might think that it should, since it is just common sense that probabilities for the future depend upon present conditions. For example, in Copenhagen quantum theory, if the quantum state of the universe collapses to, say, an eigenstate with unit eigenvalue of one of a particular $A(S)$ that is, say, a projection operator Π, then one expects that the probabilities of future conscious experiences will depend upon which $A(S)$ the quantum state collapsed to. If the quantum state collapses to an eigenstate of the assumed projection operator in which you are aware of winning a large lottery, one would expect that a month later, the probability that you would experience an awareness of having a lot of money would be greater than if the quantum state collapsed to an eigenstate in which you were not aware of winning any large lottery (assuming that you would not spend most of the money within the month).

However, in Mindless Sensationalism, the measure or probability of any 'future' conscious experience is completely determined by the (full) theory and is independent of the occurrence of any 'present' conscious experience. This sounds absurd. How can it be reconciled with our experience? I am aware of having a computer in front of me; isn't this correlated with my past awareness of buying a computer?

The answer is that this experience does not show any correlations between different experiences (e.g. between those at different 'times') but rather the correlations between the different components of a single present experience (e.g. of perceiving a visual image of a computer screen and of being consciously aware of a memory of buying the computer). These are the correlations to be explained by a full theory of Mindless Sensationalism. (I'm just giving the framework here; the full theory will involve an enormous amount of work, and I suspect that humans will never completely develop it, though I hope they will learn a lot more about it than the pittance we know now, and perhaps even develop an approximate outline of it.)

Similarly, a prediction of what might seem to be a correlation between a 'present' awareness of winning a large lottery and a 'future' awareness of having a lot of money is, I would claim, not that at all, but rather a prediction of a correlation between one's 'future' awareness of having a lot of money and, within the same conscious experience, a conscious awareness of a memory of having won a large lottery.

To give another example, I can predict that if you are consciously aware of reading this chapter today (i.e. if you are not reading it in a daze, with no conscious awareness of what you are doing, though I am not claiming that reading it unconsciously is impossible or even that this possible experience is uncorrelated with the content of this chapter), you will consciously remember my phrase 'Mindless Sensationalism' tomorrow if you think about my chapter then. Am I predicting something about your experience tomorrow that is conditional upon your experience today? No. I am just predicting that in your conscious experience of remembering reading this prediction of mine the day before, within the same conscious experience there will be a reasonably high probability that you will also be aware of my phrase 'Mindless Sensationalism'.

The fundamental timelessness of Mindless Sensationalism seems to fit very well with the viewpoint eloquently expressed by Julian Barbour (1999), that 'Heraclitan flux ... may well be nothing but a well-founded illusion.' (I might note that although I almost entirely agree with what Barbour writes, I am perhaps not quite such as extreme antitemporalist in that I suspect that the quantum state of the universe may be given by a path integral that has something analogous to histories in them, even though I agree with Barbour that the universe fundamentally does not have anything like a classical history or classical time. I think Barbour would also agree with me that there are no fundamental sequences of conscious experiences.)

In saying that Mindless Sensationalism posits no fundamental correlation between complete conscious experiences, I do not mean that it is impossible to define such correlations from the mathematics, but only that I do not see any fundamental physical meaning for such mathematically defined correlations. As an example of how such a correlation might be defined, consider that if an awareness operator $A(S)$ is a projection operator, and the quantum state of the universe is represented by the pure state $|\psi\rangle$, one can ascribe to the set of conscious experiences S the pure Everett 'relative state' (Everett 1957; DeWitt and Graham 1973).

$$|S\rangle = \frac{A(S)|\psi\rangle}{\|A(S)|\psi\rangle\|} = \frac{A(S)|\psi\rangle}{\langle\psi|A(S)A(S)|\psi\rangle^{1/2}}. \tag{10}$$

Alternatively, if the quantum state of the universe is represented by the density matrix ρ, one can associate the set of experiences S with a relative density matrix

$$\rho_s = \frac{A(S)\rho A(S)}{Tr[A(S)\rho A(S)]}. \tag{11}$$

Either of these formulas can be applied when the awareness operator $A(S)$ is not a projection operator, but then the meaning is not necessarily so clear.

Then if one is willing to say that $Tr[A(S)\rho]$ is the absolute probability for the set of experiences S (which might seem natural at least when $A(S)$ is a projection operator, though I am certainly not advocating this naïve interpretation, and in general it will not agree in absolute magnitude with $P(S) = \mu(S)/\mu(M)$), one might also naïvely interpret $Tr[A(S')\rho_s]$ as the conditional probability of the set of experiences S' given the set of experiences S.

Another thing one can do with two sets of experience S and S' is to calculate an 'overlap fraction' between them as

$$f(S, \ S') = \frac{\langle A(S)A(S')\rangle \langle A(S')A(S)\rangle}{\langle A(S)A(S)\rangle \langle A(S')A(S')\rangle}. \tag{12}$$

If the quantum state of the universe is pure, this is the same as the overlap probability between the two Everett relative states corresponding to the two sets of experiences: $f(S, S') = |\langle S|S'\rangle|^2$. Thus one might in some sense say that if $f(S, \ S')$ is near unity, the two sets of experiences are in nearly the same one of the Everett 'many worlds', but if $f(S, \ S')$ is near zero, the two conscious experiences are in nearly orthogonal different worlds. However, this is just a manner of speaking, since I do not wish to say that the quantum state of the universe is really divided up into many different worlds. In a slightly different way of putting it, one might also propose that $f(S, S')$, instead of $Tr[A(S')\rho s]$, be interpreted as the conditional probability of the set of experiences S' given the set of experiences S. Still, I do not see any evidence that $f(S, S')$ should be interpreted as a fundamental element of Mindless Sensationalism. In any case, one can be conscious only of a single conscious experience at once, so there is no way in principle that one can test any properties of joint sets of conscious experiences such as $f(S, S')$.

An amusing property of both of these ad hoc 'conditional probabilities' for one conscious experience given another is that they would both always be zero if the Orthogonal Projection Hypothesis were true. Even though the resulting theory would generally be a 'many-experiences' theory, it could be interpreted as being rather solipsistic in the sense that in the relative density matrix ρ_p corresponding to my present conscious experience p, no other disjoint set of conscious experiences would occur in it with non-zero measure! This has the appearance of being somewhat unpalatable, and might be taken to be an argument against adopting the Orthogonal Projection Hypothesis, but it is not clear to me that this is actually strong evidence against the Orthogonal Projection Hypothesis.

In addition to the fact that Mindless Sensationalism postulates no fundamental notion of any *correlation* between individual conscious experiences, it also postulates no fundamental *equivalence* relation on the set of conscious experiences. For example, the measure gives no way of classifying different conscious experiences as to whether they belong to the same conscious being (e.g. at different times) or to different conscious beings. The most reasonable such classification would seem to be by the content (including the *qualia*) of the conscious experiences themselves, which distinguish the conscious experiences, so that no two different conscious experiences, $p \neq p'$, have the same content. Based upon my own present conscious experience, I find it natural to suppose that conscious experiences that could be put into the classification of being alert human experiences have such enormous structure that they could easily distinguish between all the 10^{11} or so persons that are typically assigned to our history of the human race. In other words, in practice, different people can presumably be distinguished by their conscious experiences.

Another classification of conscious experiences might be given by classifying the awareness operators $A(S)$ rather than the content of the conscious experiences themselves. This would be more analogous to classifying people by the quantum nature of their bodies (in particular, presumably by the characteristics of the relevant parts of their brains). However, I doubt that in a fundamental sense there is any absolute classification that uniquely distinguishes each person in all circumstances. (Of course, one could presumably raise this criticism about the classification of any physical object, such as a 'chair' or even a 'proton': precisely what projection operators correspond to the existence of a 'chair' or of a 'proton'?) Therefore, in the present framework conscious experiences are fundamental, but persons (or individual minds), like other physical objects, are not, although they certainly do seem to be very good approximate entities (perhaps as good as chairs or even protons) that I do not wish to deny. Even if there is no absolute definition of persons in the framework of Mindless Sensationalism itself, the concept of persons and minds does occur in some sense as part of the *content* of my present conscious experience, just as the concepts of chairs and of protons do (in what are perhaps slightly different 'present conscious experiences', since I am not quite sure that I can be consciously aware of all three concepts at once, though I seem to be aware that I have been thinking of three concepts).

In this way the framework of Mindless Sensationalism proposed here is a particular manifestation of Hume's (1888: 207) ideas, that 'what we call a *mind*, is nothing but a heap or collection of different perceptions, united together by certain relations, and suppos'd, tho' falsely, to be endow'd with a perfect simplicity and identity', and that the self is 'nothing but a bundle or collection of different perceptions' (ibid. 252). As he explains in the Appendix (p. 634), 'When I turn my reflexion on *myself*, I never can perceive this *self* without some one or more perceptions; nor can I ever perceive any thing but the perceptions. 'Tis the composition of these, therefore, which forms the self.' (Here I should note that what Hume calls a perception may be only one *component* of the 'phenomenal perspective' or 'maximal experience' (Lockwood 1989) that I have been calling a perception or conscious experience p, so one of my ps can include 'one or more perceptions' in Hume's sense.)

Furthermore, each awareness operator $A(S)$ need not have any precise location in either space or time associated with it, so there need be no fundamental place or time connected with each conscious experience. Indeed, Mindless Sensationalism can easily survive a replacement of space-time with some other structure (e.g. superstrings) as more basic in the quantum world. Of course, the *contents* of a conscious experience can include a sense or impression of the time of the conscious experience, just as my present conscious experience when I perceive that I am writing this includes a feeling that it is now A D 2001, so the set of conscious experiences p must include conscious experiences with such beliefs, but there need not be any precise time in the physical world associated with a conscious experience. That is, conscious experiences are 'outside' physical space-time (even if space-time is a fundamental element of the physical world, which I doubt).

As a consequence of these considerations, there are no unique time-sequences of conscious experiences to form an individual mind or self in Mindless Sensationalism. In this way the present framework appears to differ from those proposed by Squires (1987, 1990, 1991, 1993), Albert (1996) and Loewer (Albert and Loewer 1988, 1991), and Stapp (1993, 1994*a*, *b*, 1995*a–e*, 1996*a–d*, 1998, 1999). (Stapp's also differs in having the wavefunction collapse at each 'Heisenberg actual event', whereas the other two agree with mine in having a fixed quantum state, in the Heisenberg picture, which never collapses.) Lockwood's (1989) proposal seems to be more similar to mine, though he also proposes (p. 232) 'a continuous infinity of parallel such streams' of consciousness, '*differentiating* over time', whereas Sensible Quantum Mechanics has no such stream as fundamental. On the other hand, later Lockwood (1992) does explicitly repudiate the Albert and Loewer many-minds interpretation, so there seems to me to be little disagreement between Lockwood's view and Mindless Sensationalism except for the detailed formalism and manner of presentation. Thus one might label Mindless Sensationalism as the Hume, Everett, Lockwood, and Page (HELP) interpretation, though I do not wish to imply that these other three scholars, on whose work my proposal is heavily based, would necessarily agree with my present formulation, which certainly is not contained in explicit detail in what they have written.

Of course, the conscious experiences themselves can include components that seem to be memories of past conscious experiences or events. In this way it can be a very good approximation to give an approximate order for conscious experiences whose contents include memories that are correlated with the contents of other conscious experiences. It might indeed be that the measure for conscious experiences including detailed memories is rather heavily peaked around approximate sequences constructed in this way. But I would doubt that the contents of the conscious experiences p, the awareness operators $A(S)$, or the measures $\mu(S)$ for the sets of conscious experiences S would give unique sequences of conscious experiences that one could rigorously identify with individual minds.

Because the physical state of our universe seems to obey the second law of thermodynamics, with growing correlations in some sense, I suspect that the measure may have rather a smeared peak (or better, ridge) along approximately tree-like structures of branching sequences of conscious experiences, with conscious experiences further out along the branches having contents that includes memories that are correlated with the present-sensation components of conscious experiences further back towards the trunks of the trees. This is different from what one might expect from a classical model with a discrete number of conscious beings, each of which might be expected to have a unique sharp sequence or non-branching trajectory of conscious experiences. In the quantum case, I would expect that what are crudely viewed as quantum choices would cause smeared-out trajectories to branch into larger numbers of smeared-out trajectories with the progression of what we call time. If each smeared-out trajectory is viewed as a different individual mind, we do get roughly a 'many-minds' picture that is analogous to the 'many-worlds' interpretation (Everett 1957; DeWitt and Graham 1973), but in my framework of Mindless Sensationalism, the 'many minds' are only approximate and are not fundamental as they are in the proposal of Albert and Loewer (1988, 1991). Instead, Mindless Sensationalism is a 'many-experiences' or 'many-sensations' interpretation.

Even in a classical model, if there is one conscious experience for each conscious being at each moment of time in which the being is conscious, the fact that there may be many conscious beings, and many conscious moments, can be said to lead to a 'many-experiences' interpretation. However, in Mindless Sensationalism, there may be vastly more conscious experiences, since they are not limited to a discrete set of one-parameter sharp sequences of conscious experiences, but occur for all sets of conscious experiences S for which $A(S)$ is positive. In this way a quantum model may be said to be even 'more sensible' (or is it 'more sensational'?) than a classical model. One might distinguish MS from a classical model with many conscious experiences by calling MS a 'very-many-experiences' framework, meaning that almost all sets of possible conscious experiences actually occur with non-zero measure. (Thus MS might, in a narrowly literal sense, almost be a version of panpsychism, but the enormous range possible for the logarithm of the measure means that it is really quite far from the usual connotations ascribed to panpsychism. This is perhaps comparable to noting that there may be a non-zero amplitude that almost any system, such as a star, has a personal computer in it, and then calling the resulting many-worlds theory 'pancomputerism'.)

One might fear that the present attack on the assumption of any definite notion of a precise identity for persons or minds as sequences of conscious experiences would threaten human dignity. Although I would not deny that I feel that it might, I can point out that on the other hand, the acceptance of the viewpoint of Mindless Sensationalism might increase one's sense of identity with all other humans and other conscious beings. Furthermore, it might tend to undercut the motivations towards selfishness that I perceive in myself if I could realize in a deeply psychological way that what I normally anticipate as my own future conscious experiences are in no fundamental way picked out from the set of all conscious experiences. (Of course, what I normally think of as my own future conscious experiences are presumably those that contain memory components that are correlated with the content of my present conscious experience, but I do not see logically why I should be much more concerned about trying to make such conscious experiences happy than about trying to make conscious experiences happy that do not have such memories: better to do unto others as I would wish they would do unto me.) One can find that Parfit (1971, 1984)[2] had earlier drawn similar, but much more sophisticated, conclusions from a view in which a unique personal identity is not fundamental.

The framework of Mindless Sensationalism can suggest various questions, methods of analysis, and speculations that might not occur to one using other frameworks. I have done an analysis (Page 1995) of the Einstein, Podolsky, and Rosen (EPR) 'paradox' (Einstein, Podolsky, and Rosen 1935) combined with that of Schrödinger's cat (1935), finding that if the components of one's awareness are correlated with different physical properties that are highly correlated (such as whether different parts of a cat are alive or dead), then one can indeed predict that one's conscious experience will have components that are highly correlated. For example, when one looks at the different parts of Schrödinger's cat, one will tend to have a strong agreement between the components of the awareness of the different parts of the cat's body as to whether the cat is dead or alive, if indeed the actual awareness operators cause

[2] I thank M. Lockwood (private communication) for drawing these references to my attention.

one to be aware of whether each part of the cat is dead or alive. (If instead one were aware of whether each part of the cat were in the symmetric or anti-symmetric linear superposition of being alive or dead, one would not have much agreement between the components of the awareness of the separate parts as to whether they were in the symmetric or antisymmetric states.)

However, it still leaves it mysterious as to why we seem to be aware of the properties that are highly correlated (such as whether the different parts of a cat are dead or alive), rather than of properties that are not highly correlated (such as whether the different parts of a cat are in the symmetric or antisym-metric superpositions of being dead or alive). In other words, it still is somewhat confusing to me why in idealized cases our conscious experiences actually seem to be rather unconfused. One might argue that if they were not unconfused, then we could not act coherently and so would not survive. This would seem to be a good argument only if our conscious experiences really do affect our actions in the quantum world and are not just epiphenomena that are determined by the quantum world without having any effect back on it. But on the other hand, it is not obvious how conscious experiences could affect the quantum world in a relatively simple way in detail (though it is easy to speculate on general ways in which there might be some effect; see Page (1995a, b, 1996a–e) and below). So although it appears to be unexplained, it conceivably could be that conscious experiences do not affect the quantum world but are determined by it in just such a way that in most cases they are not too confused. To mimic Einstein, I am tempted to say, 'The most confusing thing about conscious experiences is that they are generally uncon-fused.'

As an aside, I should say that although epiphenomenalism seems to leave it mysterious as to *why* typical conscious experiences are unconfused, I do not think it leaves it more mysterious than in other views *that* we have conscious experiences, despite a naïve expectation that the latter would be made more mysterious by epiphenomenalism. The naïve argument is that if the conscious world has no effect on the quantum world (usually called the physical world (Penrose 1994; Chalmers 1996), in contrast to my use of that term to include both the quantum world and the conscious world), and if the development of life in the quantum world occurs by natural selection, the development of consciousness would have no effect on this natural selection and so could not be explained by it.

Nevertheless, one can give an answer analogous to what I have heard was given by the late Fermilab Director Robert Wilson when he was asked by a Congressional committee what Fermilab contributed to the defence of the nation: 'Nothing. But it helps make the nation worth defending.' Similarly, if epiphenomenalism is correct, consciousness may contribute nothing to the survival of the species, but it may help make certain species worth surviving.

More accurately, it may not contribute to the evolution of complexity, but it may select us (probably not uniquely) as complex organisms that have typical conscious experiences. Then our consciousness would not be surprising, because we are selected simply as typical conscious beings.

This selection as typical conscious beings might also help explain why we can do highly abstract theoretical mathematics and physics that do not seem to help us much with our survival as a species. If we are selected by the measure of our consciousness, and if that is positively correlated with a certain kind of complexity that is itself correlated with the ability to do theoretical mathematics and physics, then it would not be surprising that we can do these better than the average hominid that survives as well as we do (say averaging over all the Everett many worlds).

Another question one might ask within the context of Mindless Sensationalism is whether and how the measures of the sets of conscious experiences associated with an individual brain depend on the brain characteristics. One might speculate that it might be greater for brains that are in some sense more intelligent, so that in a crude sense brighter brains have a bigger measure of conscious experiences. This could explain why you do not perceive yourself to be an insect, for example, even though there are far more insects than humans.

One might also be tempted to use this speculation to explain why you may consider yourself to be more intelligent than the average human (though another possible explanation is that it is likely that the average person considers himself brighter than average). However, in this case the statistical evidence, if present at all, is almost certainly much weaker than in the case of comparing ourselves with ants. Therefore, this speculation should not be used to justify any politically incorrect conclusions that one might be tempted to make from an assumption that he or she has a greater measure of consciousness than most other humans.

Also, one might conjecture that an appropriate measure on conscious experiences might give a possible explanation of why most of us perceive ourselves to be living on the same planet on which our species developed. This observation might seem surprising when one considers that we may be technologically near the point at which we could leave Earth and colonize large regions of the Galaxy (Dyson 1997), presumably greatly increasing the number of humans beyond the roughly 10^{11} that are believed to have lived on Earth. If so, why don't we have the conscious experiences of one of the vast numbers of humans that may be born away from Earth? One answer is that some sort of doom is likely to prevent this vast colonization of the Galaxy from happening (Carter 1983; Leslie 1989a, b, 1990a–c, 1992a–d, 1993a, b, 1994, 1996; Nielsen 1989; Gott 1993, 1994), though these arguments are not conclusive (Kopf 1994). Although I would not be surprised if such a doom were likely, I would naïvely expect it to be not so overwhelmingly probable that the probability of vast colonization would be so small as is the presumably very small ratio of the total number of humans who could ever live on Earth to those who could live throughout the Galaxy if the colonization occurs. Then, even though the colonization may be unlikely, I would expect that it should still produce a higher measure for conscious experiences of humans living off Earth than on it.

However, another possibility is that colonization of the Galaxy is not too improbable, but that it is mostly done by self-replicating computers or machines who do not tolerate many humans going along, so that the number of actual human colonizers is not nearly so large as the total number who *could* live throughout the Galaxy if the computers or machines did not dominate the colonization. If the number of these computers or machines dominate humans as 'intelligent' beings (in the sense of having certain information-processing capabilities), one might still have the question of why we perceive ourselves as being humans rather than as being one of the vastly greater numbers of such machines. But the explanation might simply be that the *measure* of conscious experiences is dominated by human conscious experiences, even if the *number* of intelligent beings is not. In other words, human brains may be much more efficient in producing conscious experiences than the kinds of self-replicating computers or machines that may be likely to dominate the colonization of the Galaxy. If such machines are more intelligent than humans in terms of information-processing capabilities and yet are less efficient in producing conscious experiences, our conscious experiences of being human would suggest that the measure of conscious experiences is not merely correlated with intelligence. (On the other hand, if the measure of conscious experiences is indeed strongly correlated with intelligence in the sense of information-processing capabilities, perhaps it might be the case that Galactic colonization is most efficiently done by self-replicating computers or machines that are not so intelligent as humans. After all, insects and even bacteria have been more efficient in colonizing a larger fraction of Earth than have humans.)

It might be tempting to take the observations that these speculations might explain (our conscious experiences of ourselves as human rather than as insect, and our experiences of ourselves as humans on our home planet) as evidence tending to support the speculations. One could summarize such reasoning as a generalization of the Weak Anthropic Principle (Dicke 1961, 1977; Carter 1974; Carr and Rees 1979; Rozental 1980; P. C. W. Davies 1982; Barrow and Tipler 1986; Leslie 1982, 1983a, b, 1986, 1987, 1988, 1989b, 1990c) that might be called the *Conditional Aesthemic Principle* (CAP, not entirely coincidentally the initials of my wife Cathy Anne): given that we are conscious beings, our conscious experiences are likely to be typical experiences in the conscious world with its measure.

Another use for the framework of Mindless Sensationalism would be to see how various general approaches to the problems of consciousness can be expressed in terms that are compatible (in the way I have suggested) with quantum theory. I have personally read so little of these approaches (fewer books than I have fingers) that I am not competent to try to see how to do that. However, I must admit that from what little I have read of, say functionalism, and from my mental attempts to translate what I have read into the language of my Mindless Sensationalism, I am confused as to precisely how functionalism would be expressed.

Functionalism is supposed to be 'the view that mental states are defined by their causes and effects' (Audi 1995). If a particular 'mental state' is to be identified with a particular conscious experience p, then I am not clear what its 'causes and effects' are supposed to be. Although I have no idea what the effects of p are supposed to be, I suppose that in one sense one could say that its causes are both the experience operator $E(p)$ (the p-dependent operator whose sum or integral over the ps in the set S gives the corresponding awareness operator $A(S)$) and the quantum state of the universe, σ, since both enter into the equation $m(p) = \sigma[E(p)]$ for the weight $m(p)$ that is summed or integrated over the conscious experiences in a set S to give the measure $\mu(S)$ for that set. If this interpretation of functionalism were correct, a consequence for the conjecture of functionalism would be that no two distinct conscious experiences, say p and p', have the same experience operators: If $p \neq p'$, then $E(p) \neq E(p')$. Equivalently, if $E(p) = E(p')$, then $p = p'$. This is certainly a plausible conjecture, but I see no way to justify it or test whether or not it is true, though I beleive that it is a conjecture with real content and logically could be either true or false.

Another interpretation might be to identify a mental state with a quantum state that gives rise to a particular conscious experience p. If any state σ that gives $m(p) = \sigma[E(p)] > 0$ is counted as a mental state that 'gives rise' to p, then all but a set of measure zero of possible quantum states σ could be said to give rise to p. This seems far too broad, so let us see whether we can get a narrower class of quantum states that give rise to p.

One way is to consider what different quantum states can be considered to contribute 'directly' to a conscious experience p. If, for a given conscious experience p, the corresponding experience operator $E(p)$ were decomposed into a weighted sum of orthogonal rank-one projection operators Π_i,

$$E(p) = \sum_i W_i \Pi_i \tag{13}$$

with positive weights W_i, then the eigenstate $|\psi_i\rangle$ with unit eigenvalue of each of these projection operators Π_i (the state which when written in the form

$|\psi_i\rangle\langle\psi_i|$ is identical to the rank-one projection operator Π_i) would give a contribution to the measure for the conscious experience p. In a sense one can say that it is each of these eigenstates (one for each rank-one projection operator that occurs in equation (13)) that *directly* gives rise to the conscious experience p. (Of course, any state σ that is not orthogonal to all of these eigenstates will give a positive weight for the conscious experience p,

$$m(p) = \langle E(p)\rangle = \sum_i W_i\sigma[\Pi_i] \tag{14}$$

the weighted sum of the overlaps of the state σ with the eigenstates $\Pi_i = |\psi_i\rangle\langle\psi_i|$. But it is the eigenstates themselves that can be considered to be most directly related to the conscious experience p.)

So if the mental states corresponding to the conscious experience p are defined to be the eigenstates Π_i that occur in the sum given by equation (13), the we can ask what the causes and effects of these are. If an answer to that could be found, perhaps the conjecture of functionalism might be that any two mental states Π_i corresponding to the same conscious experience p would have the same causes and effects. Or it might be the converse, that for any mental state Π_i that occurs in the sum given by equation (13), any other rank-one projection operator with the same causes and effects also occur in that sum. Either of these two conjectures seems to have non-trivial content, but precisely what that content would be depends upon what 'having the same causes and effects' is taken to mean. Without an understanding of that, my attempt to guess precisely what functionalism might mean remains stymied.

Therefore, it would be interesting indeed to see how functionalism might possibly be expressed in terms of the operators $E(p)$ and $A(S)$ that occur in Mindless Sensationalism.

I have used the example of functionalism not merely to express my own confusion (which might be merely due to my gross ignorance of the field), but also to illustrate that if one can translate conjectures from the philosophy of mind into the language of Mindless Sensationalism, one may be able to come up with some precise formulations for them that would be applicable to the real universe and not just to some imaginary universe that is modelled by, say, some classical Turing machine.

Similarly, it would also be an interesting challenge to interpret other approaches to the problems of consciousness within the framework of Mindless Sensationalism. If they cannot be interpreted within this framework, one would need to invent another framework in which they might be interpreted in order for them to be consistent with our quantum universe. This might impose a non-trivial constraint on approaches to the problems of consciousness.

In conclusion, I am proposing that Mindless Sensationalism is the best framework we have at the present level for understanding the connection between conscious experiences and quantum theory. Of course, the framework would only become a complete theory once one had the set M of all conscious experiences p, the awareness operators $A(S)$, and the quantum state σ of the universe.

Even such a complete theory of the quantum world and the conscious world affected by it need not be the ultimate simplest complete theory of the combined physical world. There might be a simpler set of unifying principles from which one could in principle deduce the conscious experiences, awareness operators, and quantum state, or perhaps some simpler entities that replaced them. For example, although in the present framework of Mindless Sensationalism, the quantum world (i.e. its state), along with the awareness operators, determines the measure for experiences in the conscious world, there might be a reverse effect of the conscious world affecting the quantum world to give a simpler explanation than we have at present of the coherence of our conscious experiences and of the correlation between will and action (why my desire to do something I feel am capable of doing is correlated with my conscious experience of actually doing it, i.e. why I 'do as I please'). If the quantum state is partially determined by an action functional, can desires in the conscious world affect that functional (say in a co-ordinate-invariant way that therefore does not violate energy-momentum conservation)? Such considerations may call for a more unified framework than Mindless Sensationalism (elsewhere called Sensible Quantum Mechanics), which one might call Sensational Quantum Mechanics (Page 1995*a*, *b*, 1996*a–e*). Such a more unified framework need not violate the limited assumptions of Mindless Sensationalism, though it might do that as well and perhaps reduce to Mindless Sensationalism only in a certain approximate sense.

To explain these frameworks in terms of an analogy, consider a classical model of spinless massive point charged particles and an electromagnetic field in Minkowski space-time. Let the charged particles be analogous to the quantum world (or the quantum state part of it), and the electromagnetic field be analogous to the conscious world (the set of conscious experiences with its measure $\mu(S)$). At the level of a simplistic materialist mind–body philosophy, one might merely say that the electromagnetic field is part of, or perhaps a property of, the material particles. At the level of Mindless Sensationalism, the charged particle worldlines are the analogue of the quantum state, the retarded electromagnetic field propagator (Coulomb's law in the non-relativistic approximation) is the analogue of the awareness operators, and the electromagnetic field determined by the worldlines of the charged particles and by the retarded propagator is the analogue of the conscious world. (Here one can see that this analogue of Mindless Sensationalism is valid only if there is no free incoming electromagnetic radiation.) At the level of Sensational Quantum Mechanics, at which the conscious world may affect the quantum world, the charged particle worldlines are partially determined by the electromagnetic field through the electromagnetic forces that it causes. (This more unified framework better explains the previous level but does not violate its description, which simply had the particle worldlines given.) At a yet higher level, there is the possibility of incoming free electromagnetic waves, which would violate the previous frameworks that assumed the electromagnetic field was uniquely determined by the charged particle worldlines. (An analogous suggestion for intrinsic degrees of freedom for consciousness has been made by the physicist Andrei Linde (1990).) Finally, at a still higher level, there might be an even more unifying framework in which both charged particles and the electromagnetic field are seen as modes of a single entity (e.g. to take a popular current speculation, a superstring, or perhaps some more basic entity in 'M theory').

Therefore, although it is doubtful that Mindless Sensationalism is the correct framework for the final unifying theory (if one does indeed exist), it seems to me to be a move in that direction that is consistent with what we presently know about the physical world and consciousness.

REFERENCES

ALBERT, D. Z. (1992), *Quantum Mechanics and Experience* (Cambridge, Mass.: Harvard University Press).

—— and LOEWER, B. (1988), *Synthese*, 77: 195.

—— (1991), *Synthese*, 86: 87.

AUDI, R. (ed.) (1995), *The Cambridge Dictionary of Philosophy* (Cambridge: Cambridge University Press), 288.

BARBOUR, J. (1999), *The End of Time: The Next Revolution in Our Understanding of the Universe* (London: Weidenfeld & Nicolson).

BARROW, J. D., and TIPLER, F. T. (1986), *The Anthropic Cosmological Principle* (Oxford: Clarendon Press).

BERNDL, K., DAUMER, M., DURR, D., GOLDSTEIN, S., and ZANGHI, N. (1995), *Nuovo Cimento*, B110: 737–50 ⟨http://arXiv.org/abs/quant-ph/9504010⟩.

BOHM, D. (1952), *Physical Review*, 85: 166–79, 180–93.

—— (1953), *Physical Review*, 89: 458–66.

—— and HILEY, B. J. (1993), *The Undivided Universe: An Ontological Interpretation of Quantum Theory* (London: Routledge & Kegan Paul).

CARR, B. J., and REES, M. J. (1979), *Nature*, 278: 605.

CARTER, B. (1974), in M. S. Longair (ed.), *Confrontation of Cosmological Theories with Observation* (Dordrecht: Reidel), 291.

—— (1983), *Philosophical Transactions of the Royal Society of London*, A310: 347.

CHALMERS, D. J. (1996), *The Conscious Mind: In Search of a Fundamental Theory* (New York: Oxford University Press).

COLEMAN, S. (1993), 'Quantum Mechanics with the Gloves Off', Dirac Memorial Lecture, St John's College, University of Cambridge, June 1993 (unpublished).

—— (1995), Physics Colloquium, University of Alberta, March 31, 1995 (unpublished).

CUSHING, J. T., FINE, A., and GOLDSTEIN, S. (eds.) (1996), *Bohmian Quantum Mechanics and Quantum Theory: An Appraisal* (Dordrecht: Kluwer).

DAVIES, E. B. (1976), *Quantum Theory of Open Systems* (London: Academic Press).

DAVIES, P. C. W. (1982), *The Accidental Universe* (Cambridge: Cambridge University Press).

DE BROGLIE, L. (1928), *Electrons et Photons: Rapports et Discussions du Cinquième Conseil de Physique tenu à Bruxelles du 24 au 29 Octobre 1927 sous les Auspices de l'Institut International de Physique Solvay* (Paris: Gauthier-Villars).

—— (1953), *Physicien et Penseur* (Paris: Gauthier-Villars), 465.

—— (1956), *Tentative d'interprétation causale et non-linéaire de la mécanique ondulatoire* (Paris: Gauthier-Villars).

—— (1970), *Foundations of Physics*, 1: 5.

DEWITT, B. S., and GRAHAM, N. (eds.) (1973), *The Many-Worlds Interpretation of Quantum Mechanics* (Princeton: Princeton University Press).

DICKE, R. H. (1961), *Nature* 192: 440.

—— (1977), *Reviews of Modern Physics*, 29: 355, 363.

DYSON, F. (1997), *Imagined Worlds* (Cambridge, Mass.: Harvard University Press).

EINSTEIN, A., PODOLSKY, B., and ROSEN, N. (1935), *Physical Review*, 47: 777, repr. in J. A. Wheeler and W. H. Zurek (eds.), *Quantum Theory and Measurement* (Princeton: Princeton University Press, 1983), 138.

EVERETT, H. III (1957), *Reviews of Modern Physics*, 29: 454–62.

GOTT, J. R. III (1993), *Nature*, 363: 315.

—— (1994), *Nature*, 368: 108.

HARTLE, J. B., and HAWKING, S. W. (1983), *Physical Review*, D28: 2960–75.

HOLLAND, P. R. (1993), *The Quantum Theory of Motion* (Cambridge: Cambridge University Press).

HUME, D. (1888), *A Treatise of Human Nature*, repr. from the original edn. in 3 vols., ed. L. A. Selby-Bigge (Oxford: Clarendon).

KOPF, T., KRTOUŠ, P., and PAGE, D. N. (1994), 'Too Soon for Doom Gloom?', University of Alberta report Alberta-Thy-17-94, ⟨http://arXiv.org/abs/gr-qc/9407002⟩.

LESLIE, J. (1982), *American Philosophical Quarterly* (April), 141.

—— (1983a), *Mind* (October 1983), 573.

—— (1983b), in N. Rescher (ed.), *Current Issues in Teleology* (Lanham and London: University Press of America), 111.

—— (1986), in *Proceedings of the Philosophy of Science Association 1986* (Ann Arbor: Edwards Bros.), i. 87.

LESLIE, J. (1987), in J. Demaret (ed.), *Origin and Early History of the Universe* (Liège: University of Liège), 439.

—— (1988), *Mind* (April 1988), 269.

—— (1989*a*), *Bulletin of the Canadian Nuclear Society*, 10: 10.

—— (1989*b*), *Universes* (London and New York: Routledge), 214.

—— (1990*a*), *Interchange*, 21: 49–58.

—— (1990*b*), *Philosophical Quarterly*, 40: 65.

—— (1990*c*), *Physical Cosmology and Philosophy* (New York: Macmillan).

—— (1992*a*), *Philosophical Quarterly*, 42: 85.

—— (1992*b*), *Mind*, 101: 521.

—— (1992*c*), *Mathematical Intelligencer*, 14: 48.

—— (1992*d*), *Interchange*, 23: 289.

—— (1993*a*), *Mind*, 102: 489.

—— (1993*b*), *Mathematical Intelligencer*, 15: 5.

—— (1994), *Journal of Applied Philosophy*, 11: 31.

—— (1996), *The End of the World: The Science and Ethics of Human Extinction* (London and New York: Routledge).

LINDE, A. (1990), *Particle Physics and Inflationary Cosmology* (Chur, Switzerland: Harwood Academic Publishers), 317.

LOCKWOOD, M. (1989), *Mind, Brain and the Quantum: The Compound 'I'* (Oxford: Basil Blackwell).

—— (1992), in M. Bitbol and O. Darrigol (eds.), *Erwin Schrödinger: Philosophy and the Birth of Quantum Mechanics* (Gif-sur-Yvette Cedex: Éditions Frontières), 363.

—— (1996), ' "Many Minds" Interpretations of Quantum Mechanics', *British Journal of the Philosophy of Science*, 47: 445–61.

NIELSEN, H. B. (1989), *Acta Physica Polonica*, B20: 427.

PAGE, D. N. (1995*a*), 'Sensible Quantum Mechanics: Are Only Perceptions Probabilistic?' University of Alberta report Alberta-Thy-05-95 ⟨http://arXiv.org/abs/quant-ph/9506010⟩.

—— (1995*b*), in S. A. Falling (ed.), *Heat Kernel Techniques and Quantum Gravity*, Discourses in Mathematics and Its Applications, No. 4, Texas A&M University Department of Mathematics, College Station, Texas, 461–71 ⟨http://arXiv.org/abs/hep-th/9411193⟩.

—— (1996*a*), in R. T. Jantzen and G. M. Keiser (eds.), *Proceedings of the 7th Marcel Grossmann Meeting on General Relativity* (World Scientific, Singapore), 983–1002 ⟨http://arXiv.org/abs/gr-qc/9411004⟩.

—— (1996*b*), in J. T. Cushing, A. Fine, and S. Goldstein (eds.), *Bohmian Quantum Mechanics and Quantum Theory: An Appraisal* (Dordrecht: Kluwer), 197–210 ⟨http://arXiv.org/abs/quant-ph/9507006⟩.

—— (1996*c*), *International Journal of Modern Physics*, D5: 583–96 ⟨http://arXiv.org/abs/gr-qc/9507024⟩.

—— (1996*d*), in N. Sanchez and A. Zichichi (eds.), *String Gravity and Physics at the Planck Energy Scale* (Dordrecht: Kluwer), 431–50 ⟨http://arXiv.org/abs/gr-qc/9507025⟩.

—— (1996e), in A. Macias, T. Matos, O. Obregon, and H. Quevedo (eds.), *Proceedings of the First Mexican School on Gravitation and Mathematical Physics, Guanajuato, Mexico, Dec. 12–16, 1994* (Singapore: World Scientific), 70–86 ⟨http://arXiv.org/abs/gr-qc/9507028⟩.

PARFIT, D. (1971), *Philosophical Review,* 80, repr. in J. Perry (ed.), *Personal Identity* (Berkeley: University of California Press, 1975), 199.

—— (1984), *Reasons and Persons* (Oxford: Clarendon Press).

PENROSE, R. (1994), *Shadows of the Mind: A Search for the Missing Science of Consciousness* (Oxford: Oxford University Press).

ROZENTAL, I. L. (1980), *Soviet Physics Uspekhi,* 23: 296.

SCHRÖDinger, E. (1935), *Naturwissenschaften,* 23: 807, Eng. tr. J. D. Trimmer, *Proceedings of the American Philosophical Society,* 124: 323; repr. in J. A. Wheeler and W. H. Zurek (eds.), *Quantum Theory and Measurement* (Princeton: Princeton University Press, 1983), 152.

SELLARS, W. (1965), *Journal of Metaphysics,* 18: 430–51.

SQUIRES, E. J. (1987), *Foundations of Physics Letters,* 1: 13.

—— (1990), *Conscious Mind in the Physical World* (Bristol and New York: Adam Hilger).

—— (1991), *Synthese,* 89: 283.

—— (1993), *Synthese,* 97: 109.

STAPP, H. P. (1993), *Mind, Matter, and Quantum Mechanics* (Berlin: Springer-Verlag).

—— (1994a), 'The Integration of Mind into Physics', Lawrence Berkeley Laboratory report LBL-35880, 13 July 1994.

—— (1994b), 'Is Mental Process Noncomputable?', Lawrence Berkeley Laboratory report LBL-36345, Dec. 1994 ⟨http://arXiv.org/abs/quant-ph/9502011⟩.

—— (1995a), 'Why Classical Mechanics Cannot Naturally Accommodate Consciousness But Quantum Mechanics Can', Lawrence Berkeley Laboratory report LBL-36574, 8 Feb. 1995 ⟨http://arXiv.org/abs/quant-ph/9502012⟩.

—— (1995b), 'Quantum Mechanical Coherence, Resonance, and Mind', Lawrence Berkeley Laboratory report LBL-36915, Nov. 1994 ⟨http://arXiv.org/abs/quant-ph/9504003⟩.

—— (1995c), 'The Hard Problem: A Quantum Approach', Lawrence Berkeley Laboratory report LBL-37163, May 1995 ⟨http://arXiv.org/abs/quant-ph/9505023⟩.

—— (1995d), 'Values and the Quantum Concept of Man', Lawrence Berkeley Laboratory report LBL-37315, June 1995 ⟨http://arXiv.org/abs/quant-ph/950603⟩.

—— (1995e), 'Chance, Choice, and Consciousness: The Role of Mind in the Quantum Brain', Lawrence Berkeley Laboratory report LBL-37944, Nov. 1995 ⟨http://arXiv.org/abs/quant-ph/9511029⟩.

—— (1996a), 'Science of Consciousness and the Hard Problem', Lawrence Berkeley Laboratory report LBL-38621, April 1996.

—— (1996b), 'Nonlocal Character of Quantum Theory', Lawrence Berkeley Laboratory report LBL-38803, May 1996.

—— (1996c), 'Review of Chalmers's Book', Lawrence Berkeley Laboratory report LBL-38890, May 1996.

STAPP, H. P. (1996d), 'The Evolution of Consciousness', Lawrence Berkeley Laboratory report LBL-39241, Aug. 1996.

—— (1998), 'Whiteheadian Process and Quantum Theory of Mind', Lawrence Berkeley Laboratory report LBL-42143, Aug. 1998.

—— (1999a), 'Quantum Ontologies and Mind-Matter Synthesis' ⟨http://arXiv.org/abs/quant-ph/9905053⟩.

—— (1999b), 'Attention, Intention, and Will in Quantum Physics', Lawrence Berkeley Laboratory report LBL-42650, May 1999 ⟨http://arXiv.org/abs/quant-ph/9905054⟩.

18. Consciousness and Quantum Theory: Strange Bedfellows

BARRY LOEWER

> When I look at the scale of the apparatus I know what it reads. Those absurdly delicate, hopelessly inaccessible, global correlations obviously vanish when they connect up with me. Whether this is because consciousness is beyond the range of phenomena that quantum mechanics is capable of dealing with, or because it has infinitely many degrees of freedom or special super selection rules of its own, I would not presume to guess. But this is a puzzle about consciousness that should not get mixed up with efforts to understand quantum mechanics as a theory of subsystem correlations in the nonconscious world.
>
> David Mermin (1998)

The nature of consciousness and the interpretation of quantum mechanics are two subjects that excite great interest. Even more exciting then is the idea percolating through certain quarters that there are deep and significant connections between the two. Among those who have advocated a quantum mechanics–consciousness connection are physicists Roger Penrose, Eugene Wigner, and Henry Stapp, philosophers David Chalmers, Michael Lockwood, and Quentin Smith and even a judge, David Hodgson, and an anaesthesiologist, Penrose's co-author Stuart Hameroff.[1] Why do these, and many of those who attend the huge consciousness conferences in Tucson, think that quantum theory has anything special to do with consciousness? There seem to be two kinds of reasons. One is that according to the standard way of thinking about quantum theory—also known as the Copenhagen Interpretation—measurement and observation play a central role in physical reality in ways that are utterly different from classical mechanics. The theory's founding fathers said and current orthodoxy concurs that quantum mechanics requires

---

[1] Lockwood (1989); Chalmers (1996); Penrose (1989, 1994); Stapp (1995); Smith (this vol.); Hogdson (1991); Hameroff and Penrose (1996).

for its *very formulation* reference to the measurement process; and while it might not be a majority view among physicists, it is often said that a measurement is not completed until it is registered in the mind of a conscious observer. Some physicists have taken this so far as to claim that reality is indeterminate until observed—or as it has been put 'the moon is not there until someone looks'. The other, complementary, reason is that the problem of understanding the relationship between consciousness and physical phenomena is so *hard*. Advocates of the quantum-consciousness connection think that it is so hard, in part, because the physical phenomena are understood in terms of classical physics. They suggest that progress can be made on this problem by recognizing that the physical basis of consciousness involves specifically quantum mechanical phenomena. Stapp, Penrose, and Smith, for example, claim that while classical mechanics is incapable of accounting for consciousness, quantum mechanics succeeds in providing explanations of how experience, unity of mind, free choice, and other features of mind emerge from physical states.[2] Quantum mechanics–consciousness enthusiasts see a mutual need: quantum mechanics needs consciousness for its formulation— consciousness needs quantum mechanics as its physics. Thus mutual necessity makes for *strange* bedfellows.

Here I will be mainly concerned with the idea that quantum mechanics implicates consciousness although I will also make a few remarks about whether philosophers have much reason to look to quantum mechanics to illuminate philosophical issues concerning consciousness. But first, since this book is primarily a collection of papers on philosophical problems of consciousness, I will provide a quick tour of some of the main features of quantum theory that explain why it is thought to involve consciousness in some way.

1. Quantum Mechanics

Quantum mechanics is the framework for fundamental theories of microscopic systems and phenomena. There are quantum theories of various kinds of elementary particles, of molecular bonding, of the interactions between electromagnetic radiation and atoms, and of the forces that bind nucleons. And while there is not yet a satisfactory quantum theory of gravity, it is thought by most physicists that a true theory that includes gravity (along with the other forces) will also be a quantum mechanical theory. Since macroscopic physical systems (gases, stars, measuring devices, living organisms, etc.) are composed of quantum mechanical systems these too will conform to the laws of quantum theory even if their complexity prevents

---

[2] Stapp (1996).

detailed application of quantum mechanics in explanations and predictions of their behaviours.

The main novel feature of quantum mechanics is its notion of *physical state*. In classical Newtonian mechanics the state of an (isolated) system of particles and fields at a time t is specified by specifying the positions and momenta at t of the particles and the values of the fields. The deterministic equations of motion describe how the state evolves. In quantum mechanics the state of a system is specified by a vector or *wavefunction* Ψ in a Hilbert space (appropriate to that system). Ψ contains all the information that can be objectively known about S. Physical quantities—so-called 'observables' such as position, momentum, energy, spin, field values, etc.—are identified with certain *operators* O on the Hilbert space. The wavefunction corresponding to an observable possessing a specific value b1 is expressed in vector notation as $|O = b1>$. The state represented by this wavefunction is said to be an 'eigenstate' of O with value b1.

Quantum mechanics contains a vast amount of information concerning the quantum mechanical states of various kinds of microsystems, how to prepare systems in various states, and how to measure various observables systems. It also includes some basic propositions concerning the nature of states: how states are connected with the values observables, how states evolve, and a rule for predicting the outcomes of measurements.[3] Among these are:

(1) The superposition principle: for any collection of states (of a given system) there are possible states that corresponds to vector sums (or 'superpositions') of the vectors corresponding to those states. For example, the state $c1|O = b1> + c2|O = b2>$ (where c1 and c2 are called the 'amplitudes' of the states in the superposition).

(2) A physical quantity O has the value b for a system S if and *only if* the wavefunction Ψ of S is an eigenvector of the operator associated with O. (This is called the 'eigenvector-eigenvalue link'.)

(3) The wavefunction Ψ of a (isolated) system S evolves in conformity with a linear deterministic law (e.g. Schrödinger's equation).

(4) If the state of S is $\Psi(S) = c1|O = b1> + c2|O = b2> + c3||O = b3> + \ldots$ and if an ideal measurement of O is made on S then the probability of obtaining result $O = bi$ is ci squared (Born's Rule).

Ever since its inception quantum mechanics has been a theory in search of an *interpretation*. By an 'interpretation' is meant an account of what a world

---

[3] There are many places that philosophers can go to for a quick course on quantum mechanics and its philosophical problems. The best in my view is David Albert's *Quantum Mechanics and Experience* (Albert 1992).

would be like in which the theory is true. For a theory such as quantum mechanics that aspires to be a theory of everything (or almost everything) physical that will involve an account reconciling quantum mechanics with our common-sense conception of the macroscopic phenomena including measurement. An interpretation of a theory might involve additions or modifications either to the theory or to our common-sense conceptions in order to achieve these goals. That quantum mechanics needs interpreting becomes obvious as soon as one notices that there are observables O1 and O2 such that no quantum state is an eigenstate of both. In this case O1 and O2 are then said to be 'complementary' (and their associated operators 'non-commuting'). Heisenberg's uncertainty principle—where the quantities are momentum and position—is an instance of complementarity. A state that is the superposition of eigenstates of O with different values is not an eigenstate of O but is an eigenstate of some other 'complementary' observable.[4] But what does it mean for a particle, e.g. an electron, to possess a position but no determinate momentum, or the other way round, or, as is the general case, neither a determinate position nor a determinate momentum?

Matters get even more puzzling when one considers so-called 'entangled states' such as the state of a pair of electrons 1 and 2:

$$\text{EPRB} \ \sqrt{1/2}(|up1>|down2>+|down1>|up2>)$$

'$|up1>$' refers to the state in which the x-spin of electron 1 has the value 'up' and so on. EPRB is not an eigenstate of the spins of the electrons in any direction but it is an eigenstate of the spins being correlated. Further, according to principle (3) the probability that a measurement of spin (in any direction) on particle 1 (or 2) will result in the value 'up' (or 'down') is $\frac{1}{2}$. This is very puzzling. What can it mean for particles to have correlated spins but no determinate spins? And what does it mean that an x-spin measurement on either particle has a $\frac{1}{2}$ probability of finding the electron with a determinate (either 'up' or 'down') spin? Einstein invoked a state similar to EPRB to argue that quantum theory is *incomplete*; that is there is more to physical reality than the quantum state. In a nutshell his argument was that if two particles in an EPRB state are far apart and the spin of one is measured and a result e.g. 'up' is obtained then since the spins are correlated the spin of the other particle can be known to be 'down'. The measurement on one particle would appear to change the physical facts pertaining to the other. But this would involve a 'spooky' non-local effect that seemed to Einstein to be incompatible with special relativity. To avoid this one apparently has

---

[4] Part of the rationale for the 'only if' part of principle (2) that is responsible for this consequence is that it has proved *experimentally* impossible to devise a way of simultaneously measuring both O1 and O2. But even when Ψ is not an eigenstate of O (4) tells us the probability of outcomes of measuring O.

to assume that both particles had determinate and correlated spins all along; in other words, that the quantum state isn't a complete specification of the electron's properties. Unfortunately, supplementing quantum mechanics with further, so-called 'hidden variables' is not an easy or straightforward matter. It can be shown that it is not possible for all observables to possess values that are disclosed by measurement and, as John Bell showed, the non-locality that bothered Einstein cannot be avoided.[5] Indeed it was and to an extent still is widely, although erroneously, believed that 'hidden variable' theories are impossible.[6] I will briefly discuss one kind of hidden variable theory later.

2. Quantum Theory Needs Consciousness

So what has all this to do with consciousness? To see why some physicists make a connection we need to discuss what quantum mechanics says happens when a measurement is made on a quantum system and when a human being observes that measurement outcome. Let O be an observable of a system S with two possible values b1 and b2 and M a measuring device with a macroscopic observable Q with three possible values: Ready, B1, and B2. A measurement of O recorded by Q is an interaction in which the measuring device starts off in state $|R>$ and if the state of S is $|O = b1>$ then at the conclusion of the measurement the state of M + S is $|P = B1> |O = b1>$ and if the state of S is $|O = b2>$ then the state of M + S at the conclusion of the measurement is $|P = B2>|O = b1>$. It follows from (2) that if S starts out in a superposition $|O = b1> +|O = b2>$ then at the conclusion of the measurement interaction the state of M + S is

MEAS $|P = B1>|O = b1 > + |P = B2>|O = b2 >$

MEAS is not an eigenstate of either O or P.[7] It follows from (1) that S does not possess a determinate value for O and also that M does not possess a determinate value for P! Schrödinger's famous thought experiment concerns a cat that acts as a measuring device of an observable O of a quantum mechanical system S. The cat's state of aliveness records the value of O. Schrödinger observed that it follows that if S's state is a superposition of values of O then at the conclusion of the measurement the cat + S will be in a

[5] The impossibility of supplementing the quantum mechanical state with hidden variables so that all observables possess values is shown by Kochen–Specker and the inevitability of non-locality is demonstrated by Bell. For discussion of these points see Bub (1999); Bell (1987).

[6] It is mildly ironic that Bell's theorem mentioned in n. 5 is often cited as showing the impossibility of hidden variable theories while Bell was a proponent and developer of Bohm's hidden variable theory.

[7] Although MEAS is an eigenstate of the values of O and B being correlated. That is why the interaction is a measurement.

state such as MEAS which is not an eigenstate of the Aliveness variable; i.e. the cat is not alive and is not dead but is in a superposition of the two conditions.[8] This consequence not only flies in the face of what we believe (that the cat will be determinately dead or determinately alive) but undercuts principle 3 that connects quantum mechanics with experiment. That principle says that the measurement in our example will result in one of the states $|B1 > |O = b1 >$ or $|P = B2 > |O = b2 >$ and not in the superposition MEAS.

To bring consciousness (finally) into the picture let's see what quantum mechanics says will happen if a human observer looks at a measuring device or cat in the state MEAS. I will suppose that there is a quantum state A1 (or collection of states) of an observer's brain corresponding to her experiencing seeing a live cat and an orthogonal state (or collection of states) corresponding to her experiencing seeing a dead cat. Then if the whole process is governed by Schrödinger's law the wavefunction of the system + cat + observer will evolve into the state:

$$\text{OBS:} \quad |M = M1 > |P = B1 > |O = b1 > + |M = m2 > |P = B2 > |O = b2 >$$

OBS is not an eigenstate of the observer consciously observing a live cat or of her consciously observing a dead cat. In OBS there is no determinate matter of fact concerning the observer's experience. It is important to keep in mind that a superposition of these two conscious states is not some other conscious state whose content is some vague amalgam of the two. It is a state with no determinate conscious content at all. One might think that states such as OBS seldom arise, but if the evolution of state is governed by Schrödinger's law, states such as MEAS and OBS—that is, states that are not eigenstates of familiar quantities—will be the rule rather than the exception. In fact, as the wavefunction evolves it is very unlikely that it will ever be an eigenstate of there being *any conscious observers at all*. Obviously, this result undercuts quantum mechanics since it entails that we don't exist and never have any evidence for the theory.

We can see how considerations involving consciousness can enter into interpreting quantum mechanics. As physics has developed it has undermined certain aspects of our common sense view of the world; what Sellars (1963) calls 'the manifest image'.[9] For example, it appears that the moon and

---

[8] If this is not problem enough what we have just described occurs in a measurement which conflicts with what principle (4) says. According to it if the state of S is $c1|O = b1 > +c2 |O = b2 >$ then the probability that a measurement of O will obtain result b1 is c1. But, as we have just seen, if the measurement interaction is governed by (3) the state at the conclusion of the measurement is not one in which O has any determinate value at all!

[9] See Maudlin (1994) for a very nice discussion of the problem of interpreting quantum mechanics in terms of Sellars's 'manifest' and 'scientific' images.

sun are approximately the same size, that earth stands still while the sun revolves about it; that ordinary objects (e.g. this table) are made of more or less homogeneous matter. But we know that these are just appearances and we have explanations based in physics (and psychology) of why things appear so but are actually quite different. If quantum mechanics understood realistically and including the universality of Schrödinger's law were true then almost no part of the manifest image would be correct; even that we have determinate appearances or even that we exist! Perhaps we can learn to live with the idea that elementary particles lack determinate position and even that cats lack determinate *aliveness*; but the thought that our mental states always lack determinateness is epistemologically self-defeating. We cannot explain that our mental states *merely appear* to be determinate since that assumes that the appearance is determinate. We feel certain that if we were to look at a cat in MEAS our experience would have a determinate content. We would experience the cat as dead or experience the cat as alive *even if the cat is in a superposition of being alive and being dead*. A *minimal* requirement on any adequate interpretation of quantum mechanics is that the actual quantum state supports the existence of conscious observers with sufficiently many determinate conscious states to provide an evidential basis for quantum theory. I will call the requirement that any adequate fundamental theory of the world satisfies this the 'determinate consciousness condition' (DCC). We also saw that there is a conflict between principles (1) and (2) on the one hand and (3) on the other. An adequate interpretation of quantum mechanics will have to reconcile this conflict as well as satisfying the DCC. There are basically two strategies for interpreting quantum mechanics that have a reasonable chance of succeeding at this.[10] One is to modify the dynamical law (Schrödinger's equation) either by restricting its application or replacing it. The other is to reject the eigenstate–eigenvalue link.

The so-called orthodox solution follows the first path. According to it the Schrödinger law is restricted to interactions that are *not* measurements.

---

[10] There are also various *inadequate* responses to the measurement problem. Chief among these are Denial and Instrumentalism. There is a tradition of denying that Schrödinger evolution results in states that are not eigenstates of observables that record measurement outcomes because 'there is no detectable difference' between a superposition of measurement effects such as MEAS and a probabilistic 'mixture' of outcomes when the measurement device interacts with the environment. But this is simply wrong. As long as the wavefunction evolves linearly interaction with the environment will never result in a state that is an eigenstate of measurement outcomes. There is another tradition that says that QM should be understood as a recipe for making predictions concerning the outcomes of experiments on microsystems and shouldn't be used at all to describe macroscopic interactions such as measurement. The trouble with this is that it is vague (what is 'microscopic'?), puzzling (how is it that QM describes microsystems but not macrosystems when the latter is composed of the former?), and unsatisfying (why does the QM recipe work?).

(2′) Except for *measurements* the wavefunction Ψ of a system S evolves in conformity with Schrödinger's law.

Measurement interactions satisfy the collapse postulate:

(4) The collapse postulate: In an interaction in which an observable O of S is being *measured* then the state does not evolve linearly (as in (2)) but rather 'collapses' so that at the conclusion of the measurement it is an eigenstate of O.

The collapse postulate says that the post-measurement state is not MEAS but one of the states |P = B1 > |O = b1 > or |P = B2 > |O = b2 > (with probabilities given by the squares of their amplitudes) which *are* eigenstates of O and P.

This 'solution' to the measurement problem raises the further problem of saying exactly which interactions count as measurements. Not every interaction in which one observable becomes correlated with another counts as a measurement since there are some such interactions (involving microscopic systems) which are known to evolve in accordance with (2) not (4). Some further condition must be placed on measurements. There are various proposals that have been made but the one that interests us gives a special role to consciousness.

A suggestion associated with von Neumann, Wigner, Wheeler, and Stapp is that 'measurements' occur only at the point at which a conscious observer interacts with the wavefunction.[11] I will call this 'the consciousness collapse proposal' or CCP. Although the proposal is vague its advocates seem to have something like this in mind: the quantum state evolves as described by Schrödinger's law until the systems it characterizes include a human being (or other system capable of consciousness) and can be represented as a superposition of eigenstates of states of consciousness. At that point the wavefunction collapses into one of the components of the superposition; i.e. into an eigenstate of consciousness. The probabilities of the various possible states are given by the collapse postulate.[12] So, for example, the state of the electron and measuring device evolves into MEAS and then when observed by a human being the state of the electron and measuring device and human being evolves into OBS which instantaneously collapses into one of its

---

[11] More exactly the proposal is that when the quantum state of a system containing a conscious observer evolves into a superposition of states some of which correspond to eigenstates of consciousness that wavefunction collapses to one of the states in the superposition with a probability given by Born's Rule.

[12] Proposals of this sort are usually vague concerning exactly which mental states initiate collapse. Perceptions in which a person is conscious of a determinate outcome is one kind of mental event that initiates a collapse. Some (e.g. Stapp, Kane) suggest that acts of will (consciously making a decision) initiate a collapse (selecting one component of a superposition of states corresponding to different plans of action).

components. The collapse, so to speak, propagates (instantaneously!) from the mind of the observer to the other systems with which it is entangled.

Henry Stapp (1995) characterizes the CCP this way:

The key point, in the context of the mind/brain problem, is that this most orthodox interpretation of quantum theory brings the experiences of the human observers into the basic physical theory on at least a co-equal basis with the 'physical' or 'matter-like' aspects of the description: the matter-like aspects give only half of the dynamical and ontological story.

The metaphysical view underlying the CCP is probably best understood as a kind of interactionist dualism. It is *dualist* in that it implies that the quantum mechanical description of the world is incomplete. A complete description would also specify which physical states are associated with consciousness. It is *interactionist* (as opposed to epiphenomenalist) in that consciousness has the causal power of initiating a collapse of the wave-function. It is also a species of *emergentism* in that conscious states emerge from certain complex physical states (e.g. brain states).

One can see why the CCP would appeal to those philosophers who are already antiphysicalists or think that fundamental physics *in so far as it makes no reference to consciousness* is incomplete.[13] But as attractive as it may be to such philosophers it fails to provide a viable interpretation of quantum theory. There are two main problems; the one remediable and the other fatal. The remediable one is that it is not explicit about exactly when collapses occur. Are cats sufficiently conscious to collapse wavefunctions? Does any conscious state collapse a wavefunction or only those in which the observer is attending to a measurement outcome?[14] Until a clear criterion emerges for which states are the conscious states that initiate collapses we don't have an explicit theory. The fatal objection is this: given what we know about the early universe its quantum state was not an eigenstate of consciousness; i.e. there were not conscious observers during the first three minutes! But if the state of that state of the early universe evolved by Schrödinger's law (as the CCP says it does) it would *never* result in a state that is an eigenstate associated with the existence of conscious observers. The problem is that the first collapse requires the existence of a conscious observer but the existence of a conscious observer requires prior collapses of states. The CCP can't get started.[15]

I can think of a modification of the CCP that might be thought to handle this problem. Suppose that whenever the state is a superposition of states that

---

[13] For example Henry Stapp and David Chalmers take the CCP seriously.

[14] If any brain state that supports a conscious state initiates a collapse irrespective of whether the state's content is about a measurement then a person will be constantly collapsing states.

[15] Frank Arntzenius reminded me of this point. The objection is also fatal to any version of the collapse postulate that says that collapses occur only when the wavefunction is an eigenstate of the existence of a complex phenomenon (e.g. measurement).

include states that support consciousness (i.e. states in which there are conscious subjects) that state collapses into one of its components. With this modification as soon as the state of the universe is such a superposition a collapse occurs and there is some chance that the collapse will produce a state in which there are conscious beings. The trouble with this suggestion is that it probably entails that collapses will occur too early in the history of the universe and too often. It is very likely that the state of the early universe was such a superposition.[16] If that is so then collapses would occur during the early universe at a rate contrary to what we know.[17]

The problem with the CCP is a problem for any version of the orthodox interpretation that identifies measurements with interactions involving systems of a certain degree of complexity. The problem is that it is unlikely that the initial state of the universe will evolve into an eigenstate of a complex measuring device. There is an ingenious collapse proposal that works quite differently due to Ghirardhi, Rimini, and Weber (GRW). Their proposal is, roughly, that the wavefunction of a system evolves in accordance with Schrödinger's law except that at any moment there is a chance that the wavefunction (as a function of particle position) is multiplied by a narrow Gaussian effectively collapsing it into a wavefunction almost all of whose amplitude is concentrated in a small region.[18] Such a wavefunction corresponds to a localized particle. If a system consists of many particles—say 10^{23}—then although the chance in a small interval of time of any one of them undergoing a collapse is tiny the chance that at least one will can be practically 1. If the wavefunction of the system is one like MEAS in which the positions of many particles are correlated with each other then a collapse centred on one particle will have the effect of localizing the positions of all particles. GRW provides the same probabilities for experimental outcomes as orthodox quantum mechanics, at least as far as any experiments that are feasible.

GRW is much more plausible than the standard collapse proposal and its CCP version.[19] The concept of *measurement* doesn't occur in its fundamental

---

[16] Recall that a state can be represented as a superposition in many (infinitely many) different basis vectors. Among these sets of basis vectors is a set of orthogonal vectors that are eigenstates of the physical quantities on which consciousness supervenes (i.e. these states specify what conscious beings exist, if any, and what conscious states they enjoy, if any). It is plausible that even the vacuum state (which, of course, is not an eigenstate of the quantities on which consciousness supervenes) is a superposition of such states some of which have positive amplitude for states that specify the existence of conscious beings.

[17] Collapses will be likely to localize particles and thus increase the velocity and temperatures of the system undergoing the collapse.

[18] See Ghirardhi et al. (1986); Bell (1987); Albert and Loewer (1997).

[19] The objection we made against the CCP that the collapses would never take place doesn't hold against GRW since the collapses (multiplication by a narrow Gaussian) occur randomly even in the early universe.

law. Rather, it is a consequence of that law that those interactions we consider measurements have determinate outcomes.[20] Whether or not GRW satisfies the DCC depends on exactly what the physical basis—assuming there is one—of consciousness is; i.e. on what it supervenes. If mental states and processes supervene on the approximate positions of many entangled elementary particles (and the approximate values of fundamental fields correlated with particles) then—as for example in the firing of many neurons—GRW will succeed in making mental states determinate.[21]

The second strategy for dealing with the measurement problem is to give up the eigenstate–eigenvalue link. This is the approach taken by hidden variable theories and by 'many worlds' interpretations. I will mainly discuss the latter since one of its versions involves conscious mental states in a fundamental way.

The many worlds interpretation was thought up by Hugh Everett in a Princeton dissertation he wrote under Wheeler the 1950s. For a few decades it was mostly ignored but now it seems to be replacing the Copenhagen account as the favourite interpretation among cosmologists and physicists who like to write about the interpretation of quantum theory. According to the many worlds interpretation a wavefunction such as MEAS characterizes two kinds of 'worlds' in which each of the outcomes of the measurement is obtained. More generally, the whole universe is said to have a quantum state or wavefunction (the universal wavefunction) which, as it evolves (in accordance with Schrödinger's law), describes a system of branching worlds. There is a problem of specifying exactly what worlds are described by the universal wavefunction. The problem is that a wavefunction can be represented in different basis sets. Exactly what worlds are described by a wavefunction depends on privileging a particular basis. If the basis is 'approximate position' then it can be shown that, given the kind of particles and fields that exist, the branching worlds will be fairly well behaved. When an observable in a microscopic system interacts with the environment—as occurs in a measurement—the wavefunction branches into parts that develop independently of each other. It is claimed that from the point of view of an observer on a branch it appears that the wavefunction has collapsed and the world develops macroscopically in a more or less classical way.

Some find the many worlds interpretation too ontologically extravagant to be acceptable. Given the difficult of coming up with any adequate interpret-

---

[20] The reason is that measurement interactions involve systems consisting of many particles whose quantum states are correlated with each other and with the system being measured. Because the system consists of many particles there is a very high chance that at least one particle in the system will undergo a collapse and because the particles' positions are correlated all the particles will end up in determinate positions.

[21] Not to say that GRW doesn't have its problems. For one, as I mentioned, the collapsed states are never exactly eigenstates of position. For another, it is not settled exactly how to extend the idea to take into account all kinds of fields.

ation I don't find this to be a serious worry. However, there are two more significant objections. One is that it might not satisfy the DCC. The other is that it provides no account of probability. Both of these worries have led some theorists to put consciousness into the foundations of the theory. One way to guarantee that many worlds satisfies the DCC is to select as the basis that determines the branching worlds whatever physical variables consciousness supervenes on. This is basically the idea of the so called 'many minds interpretation'.[22] The worry about probability is that Schrödinger evolution is deterministic so there seems to be no way to ground or explain quantum mechanical probabilities.

Here is how the many minds theory is supposed to work. First, it assumes that there exists for any isolated (or approximately isolated) system (including the entire universe) a collection of quantum states—called 'the mentality basis' for the system—each of which specifies exactly what minds would exist if that state were the quantum state of the system. If the state is a superposition of such quantum states then the minds associated with each element of the superposition all actually exist. So, for example, if we suppose that the states $|M = M1 > |P = B1 > |O = b1 >$ and $|M = m2 > |P = B2 > |O = b2 >$ belong to the mentality basis of observer + cat + quantum system and that the first is sufficient for the existence of a person seeing the cat alive and the second sufficient for the observer seeing a dead cat then there exists two minds associated with the observer; one seeing a live cat and the other seeing a dead cat.[23] On the many minds theory measurements have outcomes only in the minds. Thus the result of a measurement described by MEAS (where the measuring system does not involve a mind) is one in which neither outcome occurs (MEAS is a superposition of states corresponding to both outcomes) but once a sentient being becomes involved in the measurement and the resulting state is OBS mental states corresponding to seeing each outcome occur.

The worry concerning probabilities is that since the Schrödinger law is the sole dynamical law of the theory and is deterministic it is difficult to see how quantum mechanical probabilities can be accounted for by the interpretation. One idea is to suppose that associated with each branch in the consciousness basis are sets of minds and that quantum mechanical probabilities are values of a measure on these sets. Another suggestion is that the probabilities are

[22] The 'many minds interpretation' is the brainchild of Michael Lockwood (1989) and, simultaneously David Albert and myself (Albert and Loewer 1988). The former is an advocate of the view while the latter two authors' attitude is better described as finding the view intriguing. There is also an important difference between Lockwood's account and the Albert and Loewer account concerning how to accommodate probabilities.

[23] The supposition is only to give a rough idea of how 'many minds' works. The mentality basis is much more complicated and would determine a full set of mental states associated with a mind.

dynamical chances governing the evolution of minds. It has been argued that the first fails to supply genuine probabilities and that the latter involves a very hard-to-believe dualism since it requires continuant minds whose identities over time fail to supervene on physical facts. In any case, the problem of probabilities is a difficult one for many worlds/minds theories, and whether it can be solved is a highly controversial matter.[24]

The ontology of the many-minds theory is the quantum state (which can be thought of as a kind of field in configuration space) *and* minds with mental states. It is assumed that the quantum state determines what and how many minds there are but the minds are not themselves part of the physical—i.e. quantum mechanical—reality. Thus the theory is committed to mental/physical dualism. However, there is a way of looking at the ontology that is inspired by a metaphysical view of Russell's so that it appears to be a monist theory with the quantum state and the mental state being two aspects of a single underlying reality.[25] According to Russell, physics (and science more generally) reveals the causal and nomological structure of reality but is doesn't disclose its intrinsic nature. He went on to suggest that the intrinsic nature of reality is mental. Our knowledge of that intrinsic nature is restricted to the acquaintance that we have when we are conscious of our mental/brain states. However, the intrinsic natures of most properties are unknowable. The connection with quantum mechanics is the idea that the quantum state of a system characterizes its nomological/causal structure but that the intrinsic nature of the state corresponds to the conscious states associated with the quantum state. Of course, if by consciousness we mean the state of a human or humanlike conscious observer then there are quantum states of the universe (and plausibly the state of the early universe was like this) that are eigenstates of there being no human conscious observers at all. Some proponents of the Russellian view (Lockwood and Chalmers) seem to suggest that such physical states—even states of isolated elementary particles—possess an intrinsic mental aspect. I have no idea what can be meant by this. Is there *something it is like* to be a muon? And if the answer to this is positive it is still completely mysterious how these so called 'proto-mental' states can compose to result in human consciousness; e.g. an experience of vertigo.

If the many worlds or many minds interpretations were the only way of maintaining the Schrödinger law as the sole dynamical law then one might be willing to swallow their strange ontology of worlds and minds. But they are not. Another approach involves supplementing the state of a system with 'hidden variables'. This is the path taken by Bohmian

---

[24] For discussions see Lockwood (1989; Albert and Loewer (1988); Loewer (1996).
[25] Something along these lines is suggested by Lockwood (1989).

mechanics.[26] According to (non-relativistic) Bohmian mechanics the physical state of a system consisting of n-particles is specified by a wavefunction
and the positions of the particles. There are two dynamical laws; Schrödinger's law for the wavefunction and a deterministic law that specifies the
particles' velocities at t depending on the wavefunction at t. Probabilities
enter into the theory by way of a probability distribution over the initial
positions of the particles. Thus probabilities in Bohmian mechanics, as in
statistical mechanics, reflect ignorance of the exact physical state. The most
important features of Bohm's theory for the present discussion are (a) that
measurement, observation, and consciousness play *absolutely* no role in the
formulation of the fundamental laws of the theory, and (b) since positions
are always determinate all macroscopic entities and properties that supervene on position are determinate. For example, in MEAS the particle
positions will be associated with one or the other of its components and
so the measuring device (and Schrödinger's cat) will possess determinate
positions (be determinately alive or determinately dead). Since it is a
plausible assumption that our mental states supervene on positions of
particles in our brain (and the wavefunction) it is plausible that Bohmian
mechanics satisfies the DCC.

We have seen that quantum mechanics as embodied in principles (1)–(3)
while on the one hand providing recipes that accurately predict the results of
experiments involving elementary particles, atoms, molecules, and so forth,
on the other hand threatens to undermine our common-sense beliefs in the
existence of a determinate reality including our making determinate observations. It thus undermines itself. An interpretation of the theory must, at a
minimum, fix things so that at least some of our experiences (enough to
provide an evidential basis for the theory) are determinate. This is the DCC.
It is via the DCC that considerations involving consciousness are properly
brought into the interpretation of QM. But there are proposals that go much
further than satisfying DCC that make consciousness a more central player in
the interpretation itself. The two main ones are the CCP and the many minds
theory. We saw that the first suffers from vagueness and in the end fails at its
task. The second is far-fetched. If these kinds of approaches were the only ones
capable of grounding an interpretation that solves the measurement problem
and satisfies the DCC then perhaps it would be correct to say that quantum
theory has put consciousness in the centre of scientific ontology. But we saw
that they are not. There are interpretations of quantum mechanics in which
consciousness plays no special role and which plausibly succeed in resolving
the measurement problem. The chief candidates are GRW and Bohmian
mechanics. I do not mean to suggest that these accounts are free from puzzles

---

[26] For accounts of Bohm's theory see Bohm and Hiley (1993); Albert (1992).

and problems.[27] The interpretation of quantum mechanics, as with fundamental physics itself, is a far from finished matter.

3. Consciousness Needs Quantum Mechanics

I will conclude with a few reflections on the suggestion that consciousness needs quantum mechanics; that consciousness is a specifically quantum-mechanical phenomenon. Of course, if quantum mechanics is the fundamental physical theory then if consciousness is a physical phenomena it is a quantum-mechanical phenomena. But so are respiration, digestion, the weather, and every physical phenomenon. It is very likely that neurophysiological states and events constitute and realize mental phenomena and it is certain that neurophysiological states and events involve chemical and electrical phenomena whose correct description involves quantum theory. A complete understanding of neurochemistry will involve quantum theory. But advocates of a quantum mechanics–consciousness connection mean to assert more than this. They think that the problems that philosophers have wrestled with concerning how physical phenomena can give rise to consciousness are intractable as long as one sticks with classical physics but that quantum theory can solve or help solve these problems. Here are some illustrative remarks:

On the view that I am tentatively putting forward, consciousness would be some manifestation of this quantum entangled internal cytoskeletal state of its involvement in the interplay...between quantum and classical levels of activity.

(Penrose 1994: 376)

The unity of a single mind can arise, in such a description, only if there is some form of quantum coherence extending across at least an appreciable part of the entire brain.   (ibid. 372)

The quantum framework leads naturally to the normal 'folk' concept of free will and personal responsibility. The key point is the concept of 'I'. In classical mechanics the personally experienced 'I' is not entailed by the (dynamically complete) physical principles, and it thus lies impotently, and hence without responsibility, outside the causal chain of physical events. In the quantum picture the experienced quality of 'I-ness' is experienced, and is therefore [part] of the stream of conscious events: the experienced 'I-ness' belongs to the experience, not vice versa.   (Stapp 1995)

Penrose and Stapp think that when it comes to consciousness, functional, computational, and neurophysiological levels can be bypassed. We should go

[27] GRW has its 'tails problem' (see Albert and Loewer 1997) and problems reconciling it with special relativity and extending it to quantum field theory. Bohmian mechanics has problems concerning the interpretation of probability (see Loewer 2001) and extending it to field theory.

directly to physics—if that physics is quantum mechanics—for an account of the nature of consciousness. I am very sceptical of such claims. Nothing of this sort has ever been proposed for other biological phenomena even though these too are constituted by quantum mechanical processes. Perhaps consciousness possesses certain special features and these involve quantum mechanics in a more substantial way. Well, in the first place we should be clear that quantum mechanics is of no help with what has come to be called 'the hard problem' of consciousness. This is the problem of explaining how the qualitative nature of experience—the *what it's like* aspect of consciousness arises out of the physical (neurophysiological) brain. There are arguments that purport to show that a *physical* duplicate of a person (which would of course also be a neurophysiological duplicate) may lack conscious experience. This conclusion is sometimes put as the claim that *zombies* are metaphysically possible. It has been shown that these arguments are unsound.[28] But the important point for my purposes is that they in no way depend on the specific nature of what counts as physical as long as it is characterized in objective terms. However, the CCP does have consequences for physicalism and the 'hard problem'. If it were correct then a physical duplicate of the actual world that duplicated all its laws would also duplicate consciousness properties since consciousness is involved in the laws (the collapse law). So zombies (with respect to our world) would be impossible, but in a way quite different from what physicalists usually assume. Consciousness would be a fundamental causal feature of the world and not explicable in terms of objective physics (i.e. the wavefunction). The trouble with this is, as I have argued, the CCP and akin proposals fail to solve the very problem that occasioned them.

There are some other features of consciousness that quantum mechanics has been claimed to illuminate. For example, it has been claimed (as in the quote from Stapp) that the apparent *unity* of mind can be accounted for in terms of the phenomena of quantum coherence. A state exhibits 'quantum coherence' if it is a relatively stable state of a relatively isolated system consisting of many particles that is a superposition of particle positions. The idea is that the entangled positions of the particles involves a kind of orchestration or unity of their evolutions. While it may be (though I think the evidence for this is slight) that there are states of neurons or microtubules that are coherent superpositions, it is hard to see what this has to do with the unity of the mind. The unity of our mental lives involves our ability to integrate information from various sources, to store and retrieve memories, to form intentions, to conceive of ourselves as actors, and so on. As far as I can see the claim that quantum coherence accounts for the *unity* of mind is a wishful thinking founded on a pun.

[28] Balog (1999).

It has also been suggested that quantum mechanics can save free will from the shackles of Newtonian determinism. An idea pursued by a number of authors is that in the course of making decisions the brain's quantum state evolves into a superposition of various alternative decisions and that making a choice involves that state collapsing into one of the alternatives.[29] Whether or not freedom of the will is compatible with underlying deterministic or, for that matter, with indeterministic laws are big questions that I have discussed in some detail elsewhere.[30] Suffice it to say here that a quantum state collapsing into a particular choice rather than giving sense to the idea that the choice is made by the agent attributes it to an indeterministic process as much outside the agent's control as it would be if the laws were deterministic. I have little hope that philosophers will be liberated from the problem of free will by quantum theory.

While it is understandable why it has become fashionable to connect quantum mechanics and consciousness, news of their impending marriage is greatly exaggerated. Here I have mainly discussed the idea that quantum mechanics requires consciousness for its proper formulation. We saw that while there is a consideration—the DCC—that enters into evaluating the adequacy of interpretations of quantum mechanics, it is implausible that consciousness enters into physics in the ways suggested by quantum mechanics–consciousness enthusiasts. And while the nature of consciousness and its relation to neurophysiological and other physical phenomena are indeed hard problems there is little reason at present think that quantum mechanics will have much to say about them.

REFERENCES

ALBERT, DAVID (1992), *Quantum Mechanics and Experience* (Cambridge, Mass.: Harvard University Press).

ALBERT, DAVID, and LOEWER, BARRY (1988), 'Interpreting the Many Worlds Interpretation', *Synthese*, 77: 195–213.

——— (1997), 'Tails of Schrödinger's Cat', in R. Clifton (ed.), *Perspectives on Quantum Reality* (Dordrecht: Kluwer), 281–92.

BALOG, KATALIN (1999), 'Conceivability, Possibility, and the Mind–Body Problem', *The Philosophical Review*, 108/4:22–44.

BELL, JOHN (1987), *The Speakable and Unspeakable in Quantum Mechanics* (Cambridge: Cambridge University Press).

BOHM, DAVID, and HILEY, BASIL (1993), *The Undivided Universe* (London: Routledge & Kegan Paul).

[29] Nozick (1981); Kane (1996).
[30] Loewer (1998).

Bub, Jeffrey (1997), *Interpreting the Quantum World* (Cambridge: Cambridge University Press).

Chalmers, D. J. (1996), *The Conscious Mind: In Search of a Fundamental Theory* (New York: Oxford University Press).

Ghirardi, G. C., Rimini, A., and Weber, T. (1986), 'Unified Dynamics for Microscopic and Macroscopic Systems', *Physical Review*, D34: 470–91.

Hameroff, S., and Penrose, R. (1996), 'Orchestrated Reduction in Quantum Coherence in Brain Microtubules: A Model for Consciousness', in S. Hameroff, A. Kaszniak, and A. Scott (eds.), *Toward a Science of Consciousness I* (Cambridge, Mass.: MIT Press).

Hogdson, David (1991), *The Mind Matters* (Oxford: Clarendon Press).

Kane, Robert (1996), *The Significance of Free Will* (Oxford: Oxford University Press).

Lockwood, Michael (1989), *Mind, Brain, and Quantum* (Oxford: Blackwell).

Loewer, Barry (1996), 'Comments on Lockwood', *British Journal for the Philosophy of Science*, 47: 229–32.

——(1996), 'Freedom from Physics', *Philosophical Topics*, 24/2: 91–112.

——(2001), 'Determinism and Chance', *Studies in the History and Philosophy of Modern Physics*, 32/4: 609–20.

Maudlin, Tim (1994), *Quantum Non-locality and Relativity* (Cambridge: Blackwell).

Mermin, David (1998), 'What is Quantum Mechanics Trying to Tell Us', *American Journal of Physics*, 66: 753–67.

Nozick, Robert (1981), *Philosophical Explanations* (Cambridge, Mass.: Harvard University Press).

Penrose, Roger (1989), *The Emperor's New Mind* (New York: Penguin Books).

——(1994), *Shadows of the Mind* (Oxford: Oxford University Press).

Stapp, Henry (1995), 'Why Classical Mechanics Cannot Accommodate Consciousness But Quantum Mechanics Can', *Psyche*, 25.

——(1996), 'The Science of Consciousness and the Hard Problem', *Journal of Mind and Behavior*, 18: 171–93.

Wigner, Eugene (1961), 'Remarks on the Mind-Body Question', in I. J. Good (ed.), *The Scientist Speculates* (London: Heinemann), 284–302.

INDEX